The Complete Works of Plato

Volume I

By

Plato

Akasha Publishing

Akasha Classic Series

Akasha Classics is dedicated to the re-publication of cherished works of World Literature. Many of these writings play a special role in recording the history of human kind, who we are and where we have been. If you know of any out-of-print titles that you would like to see back in print, let us know.

Akasha Publishing, LLC
877-745-7317
AkashaPublishing.Com

The Complete Works of Plato, Volume I, by Plato

Library of Congress Control Number: 2009908389

ISBN-13: 978-1-60512-500-8 Hardcover
ISBN-13: 978-1-60512-522-0 Paperback

Works of Plato

Title	Hardcover ISBN	Paperback ISBN
Alcibiades I & II	978-1-60512-502-2	978-1-60512-524-4
Apology, Crito, Critias and ION Dialogues of Plato	978-1-60512-521-3	978-1-60512-543-5
Charmides	978-1-60512-503-9	978-1-60512-525-1
Cratylus	978-1-60512-504-6	978-1-60512-526-8
Euthydemus	978-1-60512-505-3	978-1-60512-527-5
Gorgias	978-1-60512-506-0	978-1-60512-528-2
Laws	978-1-60512-507-7	978-1-60512-529-9
Menexenus, Euthyphro, Laches and Lysis Dialogues of Plato	978-1-60512-520-6	978-1-60512-542-8
Meno	978-1-60512-508-4	978-1-60512-530-5
Parmenides	978-1-60512-509-1	978-1-60512-531-2
Phaedo	978-1-60512-510-7	978-1-60512-532-9
Phaedrus	978-1-60512-511-4	978-1-60512-533-6
Philebus	978-1-60512-512-1	978-1-60512-534-3
Protagoras	978-1-60512-513-8	978-1-60512-535-0
Sophist	978-1-60512-514-5	978-1-60512-536-7
Statesman	978-1-60512-515-2	978-1-60512-537-4
Symposium	978-1-60512-516-9	978-1-60512-538-1
The Complete Works of Plato, Vol I	978-1-60512-500-8	978-1-60512-522-0
The Complete Works of Plato, Vol II	978-1-60512-501-5	978-1-60512-523-7
The Republic	978-1-60512-517-6	978-1-60512-539-8
Theaetetus	978-1-60512-518-3	978-1-60512-540-4
Timaeus	978-1-60512-519-0	978-1-60512-541-1

Plato
(Born 428/427 BC – Died 348/347 BC)

Plato, was a Classical Greek philosopher, mathematician, writer of philosophical dialogues, and founder of the Academy in Athens, the first institution of higher learning in the Western world. Along with his mentor, Socrates, and his student, Aristotle, Plato helped to lay the foundations of natural philosophy, science, and Western philosophy. Plato was originally a student of Socrates, and was as much influenced by his thinking as by what he saw as his teacher's unjust death.

Plato's sophistication as a writer is evident in his Socratic dialogues; thirty-five dialogues and thirteen letters have traditionally been ascribed to him, although modern scholarship doubts the authenticity of at least some of these. Plato's writings have been published in several fashions; this has led to several conventions regarding the naming and referencing of Plato's texts.

Although there is little question that Plato lectured at the Academy that he founded, the pedagogical function of his dialogues, if any, is not known with certainty. The dialogues since Plato's time have been used to teach a range of subjects, mostly including philosophy, logic, rhetoric, mathematics, and other subjects about which he wrote.

Benjamin Jowett
(15 April 1817 – 1 October 1893)

Benjamin Jowett was an English scholar, classicist and theologian, and Master of Balliol College, Oxford.
Jowett (pronounced to rhyme with 'know it') was born in Camberwell, London. His father was from a Yorkshire family that, for three generations, had been supporters of the Evangelical movement in the Church of England. His mother was a Langhorne, related to the poet John Langhorne. At twelve, Jowett was placed on the foundation of St Paul's School (then in St Paul's Churchyard), and at age 18 he obtained an open scholarship to Balliol College, Oxford, where he remained for much of his life.
In 1838, Jowett gained a fellowship; he graduated with first-class honours in 1839. This was at the height of the Oxford Tractarian movement: through the friendship of W.G. Ward he was drawn for a time in the direction of High Anglicanism; but a stronger and more lasting influence was that of the Arnold school, represented by A.P. Stanley.
In connection with the Greek professorship, Jowett had undertaken a work on Plato which grew into a complete translation of the Dialogues with introductory essays. At this he laboured in vacation time for at least ten years.
Plato was published in 1871. It had a great and well-deserved success. While scholars criticized particular renderings (and there were many small errors to be removed in subsequent editions), it was generally agreed that he had succeeded in making Plato an English classic.

The Complete Works of Plato
Volume I

By Plato

Translated by Benjamin Jowett

ALCIBIADES I

by Plato

PERSONS OF THE DIALOGUE: Alcibiades, Socrates.

SOCRATES: I dare say that you may be surprised to find, O son of Cleinias, that I, who am your first lover, not having spoken to you for many years, when the rest of the world were wearying you with their attentions, am the last of your lovers who still speaks to you. The cause of my silence has been that I was hindered by a power more than human, of which I will some day explain to you the nature; this impediment has now been removed; I therefore here present myself before you, and I greatly hope that no similar hindrance will again occur. Meanwhile, I have observed that your pride has been too much for the pride of your admirers; they were numerous and high-spirited, but they have all run away, overpowered by your superior force of character; not one of them remains. And I want you to understand the reason why you have been too much for them. You think that you have no need of them or of any other man, for you have great possessions and lack nothing, beginning with the body, and ending with the soul. In the first place, you say to yourself that you are the fairest and tallest of the citizens, and this every one who has eyes may see to be true; in the second place, that you are among the noblest of them, highly connected both on the father's and the mother's side, and sprung from one of the most distinguished families in your own state, which is the greatest in Hellas, and having many friends and kinsmen of the best sort, who can assist you when in need; and there is one potent relative, who is more to you than all the rest, Pericles the son of Xanthippus, whom your father left guardian of you, and of your brother, and who can do as he pleases not only in this city, but in all Hellas, and among many and mighty barbarous nations. Moreover, you are rich; but I must say that you value yourself least of all upon your possessions. And all these things have lifted you up; you have overcome your lovers, and they have acknowledged that you were too much for them. Have you not remarked their absence? And now I know that you wonder why I, unlike the rest of them, have not gone away, and what can be my motive in remaining.

ALCIBIADES: Perhaps, Socrates, you are not aware that I was just going to ask you the very same question—What do you want? And what is your motive in annoying me, and always, wherever I am, making a point of coming? (Compare Symp.) I do really wonder what you mean, and should greatly like to know.

SOCRATES: Then if, as you say, you desire to know, I suppose that you will be willing to hear, and I may consider myself to be speaking to an auditor who will remain, and will not run away?

ALCIBIADES: Certainly, let me hear.

SOCRATES: You had better be careful, for I may very likely be as unwilling to end as I have hitherto been to begin.

ALCIBIADES: Proceed, my good man, and I will listen.

SOCRATES: I will proceed; and, although no lover likes to speak with one who has no feeling of love in him (compare Symp.), I will make an effort, and tell you what I meant: My love, Alcibiades, which I hardly like to confess, would long ago have passed away, as I flatter myself, if I saw you loving your good things, or thinking that you ought to pass life in the enjoyment of them. But I shall reveal other thoughts of yours, which you keep to yourself; whereby you will know that I have always had my eye on you. Suppose that at this moment some God came to you and said: Alcibiades, will you live as you are, or die in an instant if you are forbidden to make any further acquisition?—I verily believe that you would choose death. And I will tell you the hope in which you are at present living: Before many days have elapsed, you think that you will come before the Athenian assembly, and will prove to them that you are more worthy of honour than Pericles, or any other man that ever lived, and having proved this, you will have the greatest power in the state. When you have gained the greatest power among us, you will go on to other Hellenic states, and not only to Hellenes, but to all the barbarians who inhabit the same continent with us. And if the God were then to say to you again: Here in Europe is to be your seat of empire, and you must not cross over into Asia or meddle with Asiatic affairs, I do not believe that you would choose to live upon these terms; but the world, as I may say, must be filled with your power and name—no man less than Cyrus and Xerxes is of any account with you. Such I know to be your hopes—I am not guessing only—and very likely you, who know that I am speaking the truth, will reply, Well, Socrates, but what have my hopes to do with the explanation which you promised of your unwillingness to leave me? And that is what I am now going to tell you, sweet son of Cleinias and Dinomache. The explanation is, that all these designs of yours cannot be accomplished by you without my help; so great is the power which I believe myself to have over you and your concerns; and this I conceive to be the reason why the God has hitherto forbidden me to converse with you, and I have been long expecting his permission. For, as you hope to prove your own great value to the state, and having proved it, to attain at once to absolute power, so do I indulge a hope that I shall be the supreme power over you, if I am able to prove my own great value to you, and to show you that neither guardian, nor kinsman, nor any one is able to deliver into your hands the power which you desire, but I only, God being my helper. When you were young (compare Symp.) and your hopes were not yet matured, I should have wasted my time, and therefore, as I conceive, the God forbade me to converse with you; but now, having his permission, I will speak, for now you will listen to me.

ALCIBIADES: Your silence, Socrates, was always a surprise to me. I never could understand why you followed me about, and now that you have begun to speak again, I am still more amazed. Whether I think all this or not, is a matter about which you seem to have already made up your mind, and therefore my denial will have no effect upon you. But granting, if I must, that you have perfectly divined my purposes, why is your assistance necessary to the attainment of them? Can you tell me why?

SOCRATES: You want to know whether I can make a long speech, such as you are in the habit of hearing; but that is not my way. I think, however, that I can prove to you the truth of what I am saying, if you will grant me one little favour.

ALCIBIADES: Yes, if the favour which you mean be not a troublesome one.

SOCRATES: Will you be troubled at having questions to answer?

ALCIBIADES: Not at all.

SOCRATES: Then please to answer.

ALCIBIADES: Ask me.

SOCRATES: Have you not the intention which I attribute to you?

ALCIBIADES: I will grant anything you like, in the hope of hearing what more you have to say.

SOCRATES: You do, then, mean, as I was saying, to come forward in a little while in the character of an adviser of the Athenians? And suppose that when you are ascending the bema, I pull you by the sleeve and say, Alcibiades, you are getting up to advise the Athenians—do you know the matter about which they are going to deliberate, better than they?—How would you answer?

ALCIBIADES: I should reply, that I was going to advise them about a matter which I do know better than they.

SOCRATES: Then you are a good adviser about the things which you know?

ALCIBIADES: Certainly.

SOCRATES: And do you know anything but what you have learned of others, or found out yourself?

ALCIBIADES: That is all.

SOCRATES: And would you have ever learned or discovered anything, if you had not been willing either to learn of others or to examine yourself?

ALCIBIADES: I should not.

SOCRATES: And would you have been willing to learn or to examine what you supposed that you knew?

ALCIBIADES: Certainly not.

SOCRATES: Then there was a time when you thought that you did not know what you are now supposed to know?

ALCIBIADES: Certainly.

SOCRATES: I think that I know tolerably well the extent of your acquirements; and you must tell me if I forget any of them: according to my recollection, you learned the arts of writing, of playing on the lyre, and of wrestling; the flute you never would learn; this is the sum of your accomplishments, unless there were some which you acquired in secret; and I think that secrecy was hardly possible, as you could not have come out of your door, either by day or night, without my seeing you.

ALCIBIADES: Yes, that was the whole of my schooling.

SOCRATES: And are you going to get up in the Athenian assembly, and give them advice about writing?

ALCIBIADES: No, indeed.

SOCRATES: Or about the touch of the lyre?

ALCIBIADES: Certainly not.

SOCRATES: And they are not in the habit of deliberating about wrestling, in the assembly?

ALCIBIADES: Hardly.

SOCRATES: Then what are the deliberations in which you propose to advise them? Surely not about building?

ALCIBIADES: No.

SOCRATES: For the builder will advise better than you will about that?

ALCIBIADES: He will.

SOCRATES: Nor about divination?

ALCIBIADES: No.

SOCRATES: About that again the diviner will advise better than you will?

ALCIBIADES: True.

SOCRATES: Whether he be little or great, good or ill-looking, noble or ignoble—makes no difference.

ALCIBIADES: Certainly not.

SOCRATES: A man is a good adviser about anything, not because he has riches, but because he has knowledge?

ALCIBIADES: Assuredly.

SOCRATES: Whether their counsellor is rich or poor, is not a matter which will make any difference to the Athenians when they are deliberating about the health of the citizens; they only require that he should be a physician.

ALCIBIADES: Of course.

SOCRATES: Then what will be the subject of deliberation about which you will be justified in getting up and advising them?

ALCIBIADES: About their own concerns, Socrates.

SOCRATES: You mean about shipbuilding, for example, when the question is what sort of ships they ought to build?

ALCIBIADES: No, I should not advise them about that.

SOCRATES: I suppose, because you do not understand shipbuilding:—is that the reason?

ALCIBIADES: It is.

SOCRATES: Then about what concerns of theirs will you advise them?

ALCIBIADES: About war, Socrates, or about peace, or about any other concerns of the state.

SOCRATES: You mean, when they deliberate with whom they ought to make peace, and with whom they ought to go to war, and in what manner?

ALCIBIADES: Yes.

SOCRATES: And they ought to go to war with those against whom it is better to go to war?

ALCIBIADES: Yes.

SOCRATES: And when it is better?

ALCIBIADES: Certainly.

SOCRATES: And for as long a time as is better?

ALCIBIADES: Yes.

SOCRATES: But suppose the Athenians to deliberate with whom they ought to close in wrestling, and whom they should grasp by the hand, would you, or the master of gymnastics, be a better adviser of them?

ALCIBIADES: Clearly, the master of gymnastics.

SOCRATES: And can you tell me on what grounds the master of gymnastics would decide, with whom they ought or ought not to close, and when and how? To take an instance: Would he not say that they should wrestle with those against whom it is best to wrestle?

ALCIBIADES: Yes.

SOCRATES: And as much as is best?

ALCIBIADES: Certainly.

SOCRATES: And at such times as are best?

ALCIBIADES: Yes.

SOCRATES: Again; you sometimes accompany the lyre with the song and dance?

ALCIBIADES: Yes.

SOCRATES: When it is well to do so?

ALCIBIADES: Yes.

SOCRATES: And as much as is well?

ALCIBIADES: Just so.

SOCRATES: And as you speak of an excellence or art of the best in wrestling, and of an excellence in playing the lyre, I wish you would tell me what this latter is;—the excellence of wrestling I call gymnastic, and I want to know what you call the other.

ALCIBIADES: I do not understand you.

SOCRATES: Then try to do as I do; for the answer which I gave is universally right, and when I say right, I mean according to rule.

ALCIBIADES: Yes.

SOCRATES: And was not the art of which I spoke gymnastic?

ALCIBIADES: Certainly.

SOCRATES: And I called the excellence in wrestling gymnastic?

ALCIBIADES: You did.

SOCRATES: And I was right?

ALCIBIADES: I think that you were.

SOCRATES: Well, now,—for you should learn to argue prettily—let me ask you in return to tell me, first, what is that art of which playing and singing, and stepping properly in the dance, are parts,—what is the name of the whole? I think that by this time you must be able to tell.

ALCIBIADES: Indeed I cannot.

SOCRATES: Then let me put the matter in another way: what do you call the Goddesses who are the patronesses of art?

ALCIBIADES: The Muses do you mean, Socrates?

SOCRATES: Yes, I do; and what is the name of the art which is called after them?

ALCIBIADES: I suppose that you mean music.

SOCRATES: Yes, that is my meaning; and what is the excellence of the art of music, as I told you truly that the excellence of wrestling was gymnastic—what is the excellence of music—to be what?

ALCIBIADES: To be musical, I suppose.

SOCRATES: Very good; and now please to tell me what is the excellence of war and peace; as the more musical was the more excellent, or the more gymnastical was the more excellent, tell me, what name do you give to the more excellent in war and peace?

ALCIBIADES: But I really cannot tell you.

SOCRATES: But if you were offering advice to another and said to him—This food is better than that, at this time and in this quantity, and he said to you—What do you mean, Alcibiades, by the word 'better'? you would have no difficulty in replying that you meant 'more wholesome,' although you do not profess to be a physician: and when the subject is one of which you profess to have knowledge, and about which you are ready to get up and advise as if you knew, are you not ashamed, when you are asked, not to be able to answer the question? Is it not disgraceful?

ALCIBIADES: Very.

SOCRATES: Well, then, consider and try to explain what is the meaning of 'better,' in the matter of making peace and going to war with those against whom you ought to go to war? To what does the word refer?

ALCIBIADES: I am thinking, and I cannot tell.

SOCRATES: But you surely know what are the charges which we bring against one another, when we arrive at the point of making war, and what name we give them?

ALCIBIADES: Yes, certainly; we say that deceit or violence has been employed, or that we have been defrauded.

SOCRATES: And how does this happen? Will you tell me how? For there may be a difference in the manner.

ALCIBIADES: Do you mean by 'how,' Socrates, whether we suffered these things justly or unjustly?

SOCRATES: Exactly.

ALCIBIADES: There can be no greater difference than between just and unjust.

SOCRATES: And would you advise the Athenians to go to war with the just or with the unjust?

ALCIBIADES: That is an awkward question; for certainly, even if a person did intend to go to war with the just, he would not admit that they were just.

SOCRATES: He would not go to war, because it would be unlawful?

ALCIBIADES: Neither lawful nor honourable.

SOCRATES: Then you, too, would address them on principles of justice?

ALCIBIADES: Certainly.

SOCRATES: What, then, is justice but that better, of which I spoke, in going to war or not going to war with those against whom we ought or ought not, and when we ought or ought not to go to war?

ALCIBIADES: Clearly.

SOCRATES: But how is this, friend Alcibiades? Have you forgotten that you do not know this, or have you been to the schoolmaster without my knowledge, and has he taught you to discern the just from the unjust? Who is he? I wish you would tell me, that I may go and learn of him—you shall introduce me.

ALCIBIADES: You are mocking, Socrates.

SOCRATES: No, indeed; I most solemnly declare to you by Zeus, who is the God of our common friendship, and whom I never will forswear, that I am not; tell me, then, who this instructor is, if he exists.

ALCIBIADES: But, perhaps, he does not exist; may I not have acquired the knowledge of just and unjust in some other way?

SOCRATES: Yes; if you have discovered them.

ALCIBIADES: But do you not think that I could discover them?

SOCRATES: I am sure that you might, if you enquired about them.

ALCIBIADES: And do you not think that I would enquire?

SOCRATES: Yes; if you thought that you did not know them.

ALCIBIADES: And was there not a time when I did so think?

SOCRATES: Very good; and can you tell me how long it is since you thought that you did not know the nature of the just and the unjust? What do you say to a year ago? Were you then in a state of conscious ignorance and enquiry? Or did you think that you knew? And please to answer truly, that our discussion may not be in vain.

ALCIBIADES: Well, I thought that I knew.

SOCRATES: And two years ago, and three years ago, and four years ago, you knew all the same?

ALCIBIADES: I did.

SOCRATES: And more than four years ago you were a child—were you not?

ALCIBIADES: Yes.

SOCRATES: And then I am quite sure that you thought you knew.

ALCIBIADES: Why are you so sure?

SOCRATES: Because I often heard you when a child, in your teacher's house, or elsewhere, playing at dice or some other game with the boys, not hesitating at all about the nature of the just and unjust; but very confident—crying and shouting that one of the boys was a rogue and a cheat, and had been cheating. Is it not true?

ALCIBIADES: But what was I to do, Socrates, when anybody cheated me?

SOCRATES: And how can you say, 'What was I to do'? if at the time you did not know whether you were wronged or not?

ALCIBIADES: To be sure I knew; I was quite aware that I was being cheated.

SOCRATES: Then you suppose yourself even when a child to have known the nature of just and unjust?

ALCIBIADES: Certainly; and I did know then.

SOCRATES: And when did you discover them—not, surely, at the time when you thought that you knew them?

ALCIBIADES: Certainly not.

SOCRATES: And when did you think that you were ignorant—if you consider, you will find that there never was such a time?

ALCIBIADES: Really, Socrates, I cannot say.

SOCRATES: Then you did not learn them by discovering them?

ALCIBIADES: Clearly not.

SOCRATES: But just before you said that you did not know them by learning; now, if you have neither discovered nor learned them, how and whence do you come to know them?

ALCIBIADES: I suppose that I was mistaken in saying that I knew them through my own discovery of them; whereas, in truth, I learned them in the same way that other people learn.

SOCRATES: So you said before, and I must again ask, of whom? Do tell me.

ALCIBIADES: Of the many.

SOCRATES: Do you take refuge in them? I cannot say much for your teachers.

ALCIBIADES: Why, are they not able to teach?

SOCRATES: They could not teach you how to play at draughts, which you would acknowledge (would you not) to be a much smaller matter than justice?

ALCIBIADES: Yes.

SOCRATES: And can they teach the better who are unable to teach the worse?

ALCIBIADES: I think that they can; at any rate, they can teach many far better things than to play at draughts.

SOCRATES: What things?

ALCIBIADES: Why, for example, I learned to speak Greek of them, and I cannot say who was my teacher, or to whom I am to attribute my knowledge of Greek, if not to those good-for-nothing teachers, as you call them.

SOCRATES: Why, yes, my friend; and the many are good enough teachers of Greek, and some of their instructions in that line may be justly praised.

ALCIBIADES: Why is that?

SOCRATES: Why, because they have the qualities which good teachers ought to have.

ALCIBIADES: What qualities?

SOCRATES: Why, you know that knowledge is the first qualification of any teacher?

ALCIBIADES: Certainly.

SOCRATES: And if they know, they must agree together and not differ?

ALCIBIADES: Yes.

SOCRATES: And would you say that they knew the things about which they differ?

ALCIBIADES: No.

SOCRATES: Then how can they teach them?

ALCIBIADES: They cannot.

SOCRATES: Well, but do you imagine that the many would differ about the nature of wood and stone? are they not agreed if you ask them what they are? and do they not run to fetch the same thing, when they want a piece of wood or a stone? And so in similar cases, which I suspect to be pretty nearly all that you mean by speaking Greek.

ALCIBIADES: True.

SOCRATES: These, as we were saying, are matters about which they are agreed with one another and with themselves; both individuals and states use the same words about them; they do not use some one word and some another.

ALCIBIADES: They do not.

SOCRATES: Then they may be expected to be good teachers of these things?

ALCIBIADES: Yes.

SOCRATES: And if we want to instruct any one in them, we shall be right in sending him to be taught by our friends the many?

ALCIBIADES: Very true.

SOCRATES: But if we wanted further to know not only which are men and which are horses, but which men or horses have powers of running, would the many still be able to inform us?

ALCIBIADES: Certainly not.

SOCRATES: And you have a sufficient proof that they do not know these things and are not the best teachers of them, inasmuch as they are never agreed about them?

ALCIBIADES: Yes.

SOCRATES: And suppose that we wanted to know not only what men are like, but what healthy or diseased men are like—would the many be able to teach us?

ALCIBIADES: They would not.

SOCRATES: And you would have a proof that they were bad teachers of these matters, if you saw them at variance?

ALCIBIADES: I should.

SOCRATES: Well, but are the many agreed with themselves, or with one another, about the justice or injustice of men and things?

ALCIBIADES: Assuredly not, Socrates.

SOCRATES: There is no subject about which they are more at variance?

ALCIBIADES: None.

SOCRATES: I do not suppose that you ever saw or heard of men quarrelling over the principles of health and disease to such an extent as to go to war and kill one another for the sake of them?

ALCIBIADES: No indeed.

SOCRATES: But of the quarrels about justice and injustice, even if you have never seen them, you have certainly heard from many people, including Homer; for you have heard of the Iliad and Odyssey?

ALCIBIADES: To be sure, Socrates.

SOCRATES: A difference of just and unjust is the argument of those poems?

ALCIBIADES: True.

SOCRATES: Which difference caused all the wars and deaths of Trojans and Achaeans, and the deaths of the suitors of Penelope in their quarrel with Odysseus.

ALCIBIADES: Very true.

SOCRATES: And when the Athenians and Lacedaemonians and Boeotians fell at Tanagra, and afterwards in the battle of Coronea, at which your father Cleinias met his end, the question was one of justice—this was the sole cause of the battles, and of their deaths.

ALCIBIADES: Very true.

SOCRATES: But can they be said to understand that about which they are quarrelling to the death?

ALCIBIADES: Clearly not.

SOCRATES: And yet those whom you thus allow to be ignorant are the teachers to whom you are appealing.

ALCIBIADES: Very true.

SOCRATES: But how are you ever likely to know the nature of justice and injustice, about which you are so perplexed, if you have neither learned them of others nor discovered them yourself?

ALCIBIADES: From what you say, I suppose not.

SOCRATES: See, again, how inaccurately you speak, Alcibiades!

ALCIBIADES: In what respect?

SOCRATES: In saying that I say so.

ALCIBIADES: Why, did you not say that I know nothing of the just and unjust?

SOCRATES: No; I did not.

ALCIBIADES: Did I, then?

SOCRATES: Yes.

ALCIBIADES: How was that?

SOCRATES: Let me explain. Suppose I were to ask you which is the greater number, two or one; you would reply 'two'?

ALCIBIADES: I should.

SOCRATES: And by how much greater?

ALCIBIADES: By one.

SOCRATES: Which of us now says that two is more than one?

ALCIBIADES: I do.

SOCRATES: Did not I ask, and you answer the question?

ALCIBIADES: Yes.

SOCRATES: Then who is speaking? I who put the question, or you who answer me?

ALCIBIADES: I am.

SOCRATES: Or suppose that I ask and you tell me the letters which make up the name Socrates, which of us is the speaker?

ALCIBIADES: I am.

SOCRATES: Now let us put the case generally: whenever there is a question and answer, who is the speaker,—the questioner or the answerer?

ALCIBIADES: I should say, Socrates, that the answerer was the speaker.

SOCRATES: And have I not been the questioner all through?

ALCIBIADES: Yes.

SOCRATES: And you the answerer?

ALCIBIADES: Just so.

SOCRATES: Which of us, then, was the speaker?

ALCIBIADES: The inference is, Socrates, that I was the speaker.

SOCRATES: Did not some one say that Alcibiades, the fair son of Cleinias, not understanding about just and unjust, but thinking that he did understand, was going to the assembly to advise the Athenians about what he did not know? Was not that said?

ALCIBIADES: Very true.

SOCRATES: Then, Alcibiades, the result may be expressed in the language of Euripides. I think that you have heard all this 'from yourself, and not from me'; nor did I say this, which you erroneously attribute to me, but you yourself, and what you said was very true. For indeed, my dear fellow, the design which you meditate of teaching what you do not know, and have not taken any pains to learn, is downright insanity.

ALCIBIADES: But, Socrates, I think that the Athenians and the rest of the Hellenes do not often advise as to the more just or unjust; for they see no difficulty in them, and therefore they leave them, and consider which course of action will be most expedient; for there is a difference between justice and expediency. Many persons have done great wrong and profited by their injustice; others have done rightly and come to no good.

SOCRATES: Well, but granting that the just and the expedient are ever so much opposed, you surely do not imagine that you know what is expedient for mankind, or why a thing is expedient?

ALCIBIADES: Why not, Socrates?—But I am not going to be asked again from whom I learned, or when I made the discovery.

SOCRATES: What a way you have! When you make a mistake which might be refuted by a previous argument, you insist on having a new and different refutation; the old argument is a worn-our garment which you will no longer put on, but some one must produce another which is clean and new. Now I shall disregard this move of yours, and shall ask over again,—Where did you learn and how do you know the nature of the expedient, and who is your teacher? All this I comprehend in a single question, and now you will manifestly be in the old difficulty, and will not be able to show that you know the expedient, either because you learned or because you discovered it yourself. But, as I perceive that you are dainty, and dislike the taste of a stale argument, I will enquire no further into your knowledge of what is expedient or what is not expedient for the Athenian people, and simply request you to say why you do not explain whether justice and expediency are the same or different? And if you like you may examine me as I have examined you, or, if you would rather, you may carry on the discussion by yourself.

ALCIBIADES: But I am not certain, Socrates, whether I shall be able to discuss the matter with you.

SOCRATES: Then imagine, my dear fellow, that I am the demus and the ecclesia; for in the ecclesia, too, you will have to persuade men individually.

ALCIBIADES: Yes.

SOCRATES: And is not the same person able to persuade one individual singly and many individuals of the things which he knows? The grammarian, for example, can persuade one and he can persuade many about letters.

ALCIBIADES: True.

SOCRATES: And about number, will not the same person persuade one and persuade many?

ALCIBIADES: Yes.

SOCRATES: And this will be he who knows number, or the arithmetician?

ALCIBIADES: Quite true.

SOCRATES: And cannot you persuade one man about that of which you can persuade many?

ALCIBIADES: I suppose so.

SOCRATES: And that of which you can persuade either is clearly what you know?

ALCIBIADES: Yes.

SOCRATES: And the only difference between one who argues as we are doing, and the orator who is addressing an assembly, is that the one seeks to persuade a number, and the other an individual, of the same things.

ALCIBIADES: I suppose so.

SOCRATES: Well, then, since the same person who can persuade a multitude can persuade individuals, try conclusions upon me, and prove to me that the just is not always expedient.

ALCIBIADES: You take liberties, Socrates.

SOCRATES: I shall take the liberty of proving to you the opposite of that which you will not prove to me.

ALCIBIADES: Proceed.

SOCRATES: Answer my questions—that is all.

ALCIBIADES: Nay, I should like you to be the speaker.

SOCRATES: What, do you not wish to be persuaded?

ALCIBIADES: Certainly I do.

SOCRATES: And can you be persuaded better than out of your own mouth?

ALCIBIADES: I think not.

SOCRATES: Then you shall answer; and if you do not hear the words, that the just is the expedient, coming from your own lips, never believe another man again.

ALCIBIADES: I won't; but answer I will, for I do not see how I can come to any harm.

SOCRATES: A true prophecy! Let me begin then by enquiring of you whether you allow that the just is sometimes expedient and sometimes not?

ALCIBIADES: Yes.

SOCRATES: And sometimes honourable and sometimes not?

ALCIBIADES: What do you mean?

SOCRATES: I am asking if you ever knew any one who did what was dishonourable and yet just?

ALCIBIADES: Never.

SOCRATES: All just things are honourable?

ALCIBIADES: Yes.

SOCRATES: And are honourable things sometimes good and sometimes not good, or are they always good?

ALCIBIADES: I rather think, Socrates, that some honourable things are evil.

SOCRATES: And are some dishonourable things good?

ALCIBIADES: Yes.

SOCRATES: You mean in such a case as the following:—In time of war, men have been wounded or have died in rescuing a companion or kinsman, when others who have neglected the duty of rescuing them have escaped in safety?

ALCIBIADES: True.

SOCRATES: And to rescue another under such circumstances is honourable, in respect of the attempt to save those whom we ought to save; and this is courage?

ALCIBIADES: True.

SOCRATES: But evil in respect of death and wounds?

ALCIBIADES: Yes.

SOCRATES: And the courage which is shown in the rescue is one thing, and the death another?

ALCIBIADES: Certainly.

SOCRATES: Then the rescue of one's friends is honourable in one point of view, but evil in another?

ALCIBIADES: True.

SOCRATES: And if honourable, then also good: Will you consider now whether I may not be right, for you were acknowledging that the courage which is shown in the rescue is honourable? Now is this courage good or evil? Look at the matter thus: which would you rather choose, good or evil?

ALCIBIADES: Good.

SOCRATES: And the greatest goods you would be most ready to choose, and would least like to be deprived of them?

ALCIBIADES: Certainly.

SOCRATES: What would you say of courage? At what price would you be willing to be deprived of courage?

ALCIBIADES: I would rather die than be a coward.

SOCRATES: Then you think that cowardice is the worst of evils?

ALCIBIADES: I do.

SOCRATES: As bad as death, I suppose?

ALCIBIADES: Yes.

SOCRATES: And life and courage are the extreme opposites of death and cowardice?

ALCIBIADES: Yes.

SOCRATES: And they are what you would most desire to have, and their opposites you would least desire?

ALCIBIADES: Yes.

SOCRATES: Is this because you think life and courage the best, and death and cowardice the worst?

ALCIBIADES: Yes.

SOCRATES: And you would term the rescue of a friend in battle honourable, in as much as courage does a good work?

ALCIBIADES: I should.

SOCRATES: But evil because of the death which ensues?

ALCIBIADES: Yes.

SOCRATES: Might we not describe their different effects as follows:—You may call either of them evil in respect of the evil which is the result, and good in respect of the good which is the result of either of them?

ALCIBIADES: Yes.

SOCRATES: And they are honourable in so far as they are good, and dishonourable in so far as they are evil?

ALCIBIADES: True.

SOCRATES: Then when you say that the rescue of a friend in battle is honourable and yet evil, that is equivalent to saying that the rescue is good and yet evil?

ALCIBIADES: I believe that you are right, Socrates.

SOCRATES: Nothing honourable, regarded as honourable, is evil; nor anything base, regarded as base, good.

ALCIBIADES: Clearly not.

SOCRATES: Look at the matter yet once more in a further light: he who acts honourably acts well?

ALCIBIADES: Yes.

SOCRATES: And he who acts well is happy?

ALCIBIADES: Of course.

SOCRATES: And the happy are those who obtain good?

ALCIBIADES: True.

SOCRATES: And they obtain good by acting well and honourably?

ALCIBIADES: Yes.

SOCRATES: Then acting well is a good?

ALCIBIADES: Certainly.

SOCRATES: And happiness is a good?

ALCIBIADES: Yes.

SOCRATES: Then the good and the honourable are again identified.

ALCIBIADES: Manifestly.

SOCRATES: Then, if the argument holds, what we find to be honourable we shall also find to be good?

ALCIBIADES: Certainly.

SOCRATES: And is the good expedient or not?

ALCIBIADES: Expedient.

SOCRATES: Do you remember our admissions about the just?

ALCIBIADES: Yes; if I am not mistaken, we said that those who acted justly must also act honourably.

SOCRATES: And the honourable is the good?

ALCIBIADES: Yes.

SOCRATES: And the good is expedient?

ALCIBIADES: Yes.

SOCRATES: Then, Alcibiades, the just is expedient?

ALCIBIADES: I should infer so.

SOCRATES: And all this I prove out of your own mouth, for I ask and you answer?

ALCIBIADES: I must acknowledge it to be true.

SOCRATES: And having acknowledged that the just is the same as the expedient, are you not (let me ask) prepared to ridicule any one who, pretending to understand the principles of justice and injustice, gets up to advise the noble Athenians or the ignoble Peparethians, that the just may be the evil?

ALCIBIADES: I solemnly declare, Socrates, that I do not know what I am saying. Verily, I am in a strange state, for when you put questions to me I am of different minds in successive instants.

SOCRATES: And are you not aware of the nature of this perplexity, my friend?

ALCIBIADES: Indeed I am not.

SOCRATES: Do you suppose that if some one were to ask you whether you have two eyes or three, or two hands or four, or anything of that sort, you would then be of different minds in successive instants?

ALCIBIADES: I begin to distrust myself, but still I do not suppose that I should.

SOCRATES: You would feel no doubt; and for this reason—because you would know?

ALCIBIADES: I suppose so.

SOCRATES: And the reason why you involuntarily contradict yourself is clearly that you are ignorant?

ALCIBIADES: Very likely.

SOCRATES: And if you are perplexed in answering about just and unjust, honourable and dishonourable, good and evil, expedient and inexpedient, the reason is that you are ignorant of them, and therefore in perplexity. Is not that clear?

ALCIBIADES: I agree.

SOCRATES: But is this always the case, and is a man necessarily perplexed about that of which he has no knowledge?

ALCIBIADES: Certainly he is.

SOCRATES: And do you know how to ascend into heaven?

ALCIBIADES: Certainly not.

SOCRATES: And in this case, too, is your judgment perplexed?

ALCIBIADES: No.

SOCRATES: Do you see the reason why, or shall I tell you?

ALCIBIADES: Tell me.

SOCRATES: The reason is, that you not only do not know, my friend, but you do not think that you know.

ALCIBIADES: There again; what do you mean?

SOCRATES: Ask yourself; are you in any perplexity about things of which you are ignorant? You know, for example, that you know nothing about the preparation of food.

ALCIBIADES: Very true.

SOCRATES: And do you think and perplex yourself about the preparation of food: or do you leave that to some one who understands the art?

ALCIBIADES: The latter.

SOCRATES: Or if you were on a voyage, would you bewilder yourself by considering whether the rudder is to be drawn inwards or outwards, or do you leave that to the pilot, and do nothing?

ALCIBIADES: It would be the concern of the pilot.

SOCRATES: Then you are not perplexed about what you do not know, if you know that you do not know it?

ALCIBIADES: I imagine not.

SOCRATES: Do you not see, then, that mistakes in life and practice are likewise to be attributed to the ignorance which has conceit of knowledge?

ALCIBIADES: Once more, what do you mean?

SOCRATES: I suppose that we begin to act when we think that we know what we are doing?

ALCIBIADES: Yes.

SOCRATES: But when people think that they do not know, they entrust their business to others?

ALCIBIADES: Yes.

SOCRATES: And so there is a class of ignorant persons who do not make mistakes in life, because they trust others about things of which they are ignorant?

ALCIBIADES: True.

SOCRATES: Who, then, are the persons who make mistakes? They cannot, of course, be those who know?

ALCIBIADES: Certainly not.

SOCRATES: But if neither those who know, nor those who know that they do not know, make mistakes, there remain those only who do not know and think that they know.

ALCIBIADES: Yes, only those.

SOCRATES: Then this is ignorance of the disgraceful sort which is mischievous?

ALCIBIADES: Yes.

SOCRATES: And most mischievous and most disgraceful when having to do with the greatest matters?

ALCIBIADES: By far.

SOCRATES: And can there be any matters greater than the just, the honourable, the good, and the expedient?

ALCIBIADES: There cannot be.

SOCRATES: And these, as you were saying, are what perplex you?

ALCIBIADES: Yes.

SOCRATES: But if you are perplexed, then, as the previous argument has shown, you are not only ignorant of the greatest matters, but being ignorant you fancy that you know them?

ALCIBIADES: I fear that you are right.

SOCRATES: And now see what has happened to you, Alcibiades! I hardly like to speak of your evil case, but as we are alone I will: My good friend, you are wedded to ignorance of the most disgraceful kind, and of this you are convicted, not by me, but out of your own mouth and by your own argument; wherefore also you rush into politics before you are educated. Neither is your case to be deemed singular. For I might say the same of almost all our statesmen, with the exception, perhaps of your guardian, Pericles.

ALCIBIADES: Yes, Socrates; and Pericles is said not to have got his wisdom by the light of nature, but to have associated with several of the philosophers; with Pythocleides, for example, and with Anaxagoras, and now in advanced life with Damon, in the hope of gaining wisdom.

SOCRATES: Very good; but did you ever know a man wise in anything who was unable to impart his particular wisdom? For example, he who taught you letters was not only wise, but he made you and any others whom he liked wise.

ALCIBIADES: Yes.

SOCRATES: And you, whom he taught, can do the same?

ALCIBIADES: True.

SOCRATES: And in like manner the harper and gymnastic-master?

ALCIBIADES: Certainly.

SOCRATES: When a person is enabled to impart knowledge to another, he thereby gives an excellent proof of his own understanding of any matter.

ALCIBIADES: I agree.

SOCRATES: Well, and did Pericles make any one wise; did he begin by making his sons wise?

ALCIBIADES: But, Socrates, if the two sons of Pericles were simpletons, what has that to do with the matter?

SOCRATES: Well, but did he make your brother, Cleinias, wise?

ALCIBIADES: Cleinias is a madman; there is no use in talking of him.

SOCRATES: But if Cleinias is a madman and the two sons of Pericles were simpletons, what reason can be given why he neglects you, and lets you be as you are?

ALCIBIADES: I believe that I am to blame for not listening to him.

SOCRATES: But did you ever hear of any other Athenian or foreigner, bond or free, who was deemed to have grown wiser in the society of Pericles,—as I might cite Pythodorus, the son of Isolochus, and Callias, the son of Calliades, who have grown wiser in the society of Zeno, for which privilege they have each of them paid him the sum of a hundred minae (about 406 pounds sterling) to the increase of their wisdom and fame.

ALCIBIADES: I certainly never did hear of any one.

SOCRATES: Well, and in reference to your own case, do you mean to remain as you are, or will you take some pains about yourself?

ALCIBIADES: With your aid, Socrates, I will. And indeed, when I hear you speak, the truth of what you are saying strikes home to me, and I agree with you, for our statesmen, all but a few, do appear to be quite uneducated.

SOCRATES: What is the inference?

ALCIBIADES: Why, that if they were educated they would be trained athletes, and he who means to rival them ought to have knowledge and experience when he attacks them; but now, as they have become politicians without any special training, why should I have the trouble of learning and practising? For I know well that by the light of nature I shall get the better of them.

SOCRATES: My dear friend, what a sentiment! And how unworthy of your noble form and your high estate!

ALCIBIADES: What do you mean, Socrates; why do you say so?

SOCRATES: I am grieved when I think of our mutual love.

ALCIBIADES: At what?

SOCRATES: At your fancying that the contest on which you are entering is with people here.

ALCIBIADES: Why, what others are there?

SOCRATES: Is that a question which a magnanimous soul should ask?

ALCIBIADES: Do you mean to say that the contest is not with these?

SOCRATES: And suppose that you were going to steer a ship into action, would you only aim at being the best pilot on board? Would you not, while acknowledging that you must possess this degree of excellence, rather look to your antagonists, and not, as you are now doing, to your fellow combatants? You ought to be so far above these latter, that they will not even dare to be your rivals; and, being regarded by you as inferiors, will do battle for you against the enemy; this is the kind of superiority which you must establish over them, if you mean to accomplish any noble action really worthy of yourself and of the state.

ALCIBIADES: That would certainly be my aim.

SOCRATES: Verily, then, you have good reason to be satisfied, if you are better than the soldiers; and you need not, when you are their superior and have your thoughts and actions fixed upon them, look away to the generals of the enemy.

ALCIBIADES: Of whom are you speaking, Socrates?

SOCRATES: Why, you surely know that our city goes to war now and then with the Lacedaemonians and with the great king?

ALCIBIADES: True enough.

SOCRATES: And if you meant to be the ruler of this city, would you not be right in considering that the Lacedaemonian and Persian king were your true rivals?

ALCIBIADES: I believe that you are right.

SOCRATES: Oh no, my friend, I am quite wrong, and I think that you ought rather to turn your attention to Midias the quail-breeder and others like him, who manage our politics; in whom, as the women would remark, you may still see the slaves' cut of hair, cropping out in their minds as well as on their pates; and they come with their barbarous lingo to flatter us and not to rule us. To these, I say, you should look, and then you need not trouble yourself about your own fitness to contend in such a noble arena: there is no reason why you should either learn what has to be learned, or practise what has to be practised, and only when thoroughly prepared enter on a political career.

ALCIBIADES: There, I think, Socrates, that you are right; I do not suppose, however, that the Spartan generals or the great king are really different from anybody else.

SOCRATES: But, my dear friend, do consider what you are saying.

ALCIBIADES: What am I to consider?

SOCRATES: In the first place, will you be more likely to take care of yourself, if you are in a wholesome fear and dread of them, or if you are not?

ALCIBIADES: Clearly, if I have such a fear of them.

SOCRATES: And do you think that you will sustain any injury if you take care of yourself?

ALCIBIADES: No, I shall be greatly benefited.

SOCRATES: And this is one very important respect in which that notion of yours is bad.

ALCIBIADES: True.

SOCRATES: In the next place, consider that what you say is probably false.

ALCIBIADES: How so?

SOCRATES: Let me ask you whether better natures are likely to be found in noble races or not in noble races?

ALCIBIADES: Clearly in noble races.

SOCRATES: Are not those who are well born and well bred most likely to be perfect in virtue?

ALCIBIADES: Certainly.

SOCRATES: Then let us compare our antecedents with those of the Lacedaemonian and Persian kings; are they inferior to us in descent? Have we not heard that the former are sprung from Heracles, and the latter from Achaemenes, and that the race of Heracles and the race of Achaemenes go back to Perseus, son of Zeus?

ALCIBIADES: Why, so does mine go back to Eurysaces, and he to Zeus!

SOCRATES: And mine, noble Alcibiades, to Daedalus, and he to Hephaestus, son of Zeus. But, for all that, we are far inferior to them. For they are descended 'from Zeus,' through a line of kings—either kings of Argos and Lacedaemon, or kings of Persia, a country which the descendants of Achaemenes have always possessed, besides being at various times sovereigns of Asia, as they now are; whereas, we and our fathers were but private persons. How ridiculous would you be thought if you were to make a display of your ancestors and of Salamis the island of Eurysaces, or of Aegina, the habitation of the still more ancient Aeacus, before Artaxerxes, son of Xerxes. You should consider how inferior we are to them both in the derivation of our birth and in other particulars. Did you never observe how great is the property of the Spartan kings? And their wives are under the guardianship of the Ephori, who are public officers and watch over them, in order to preserve as far as possible the purity of the Heracleid blood. Still greater is the difference among the Persians; for no one entertains a suspicion that the father of a prince of Persia can be any one but the king. Such is the awe which invests the person of the queen, that any other guard is needless. And when the heir of the kingdom is born, all the subjects of the king feast; and the day of his birth is for ever afterwards kept as a holiday and time of sacrifice by all Asia; whereas, when you and I were born, Alcibiades, as the comic poet says, the neighbours hardly knew of the important event. After the birth of the royal child, he is tended, not by a good-for-nothing woman-nurse, but by the best of the royal eunuchs, who are charged with the care of him, and especially with the fashioning and right formation of his limbs, in order that he may be as shapely as possible; which being their calling, they are held in great honour. And when the young prince is seven years old he is put upon a horse and taken to the riding-masters, and begins to go out hunting. And at fourteen years of age he is handed over to the royal schoolmasters, as they are termed: these are four chosen men, reputed to be the best among the Persians of a certain age; and one of them is the wisest, another the justest, a third the most temperate, and a fourth the most valiant. The first instructs him in the magianism of Zoroaster, the son of Oromasus, which is the worship of the Gods, and teaches him also the duties of his royal office; the second, who is the justest, teaches him always to speak the truth; the third, or most temperate, forbids him to allow any pleasure to be lord over him, that he may be accustomed to be a freeman and king indeed,—lord of himself first, and not a slave; the most valiant trains him to be bold and fearless, telling him that if he fears he is to deem himself a slave; whereas Pericles gave you, Alcibiades, for a tutor Zopyrus the Thracian, a slave of his who was past all other work. I might enlarge on the nurture and education of your rivals, but that would be tedious; and what I have said is a sufficient sample of what remains to be said. I have only to remark, by way of contrast, that no one cares about your birth or nurture or education, or, I may say, about that of any other Athenian, unless he has a lover who looks after him. And if you cast an eye on the wealth, the luxury, the garments with their flowing trains, the anointings with myrrh, the multitudes of attendants, and all the other bravery of the Persians, you will be ashamed when you discern your own inferiority; or if you look at the temperance and orderliness and ease and grace and magnanimity and courage and endurance and love of toil and desire of glory and ambition of the Lacedaemonians—in all these respects you will see that you are but a child in comparison of them. Even in the matter of wealth, if you value yourself upon that, I must reveal to you how you stand; for if you form an estimate of the wealth of the Lacedaemonians, you will see that our possessions fall far short of theirs. For no one here can compete with them either in the extent and fertility of their own and the Messenian territory, or in the number of their slaves, and especially of the Helots, or of their horses, or of the animals which feed on the Messenian pastures. But I have said enough of this: and as to gold and silver, there is more of them in Lacedaemon than in all the rest of Hellas, for during many generations gold has been always flowing in to them from the whole Hellenic world, and often from the barbarian also, and never going out, as in the fable of Aesop the fox said to the lion, 'The prints of the feet of those going in are distinct enough;' but who ever saw the trace of money going out of Lacedaemon? And therefore you may safely infer that the inhabitants are the richest of the Hellenes in gold and silver, and that their kings are the richest of them, for they have a larger share of these things, and they have also a tribute paid to them which is very considerable. Yet the Spartan wealth, though great in comparison of the wealth of the other Hellenes, is as nothing in comparison of that of the Persians and their kings. Why, I have been informed by a credible person who went up to the king (at Susa), that he passed through a large tract of excellent land, extending for nearly a day's journey, which the people of the country called the queen's girdle, and another, which they called her veil; and several other fair and fertile districts, which were reserved for the adornment of the queen, and are named after her several habiliments. Now, I cannot help thinking to myself, What if some one were to go to Amestris, the wife of Xerxes and mother of Artaxerxes, and say to her, There is a certain Dinomache, whose whole wardrobe is not worth fifty minae—and that will be more than the value—and she has a son who is possessed of a three-hundred acre patch at Erchiae, and he has a mind to go to war with your son—would she not wonder to what this Alcibiades trusts for success in the conflict? 'He must rely,' she would say to herself, 'upon his training and wisdom—these are the things which Hellenes value.' And if she heard that this Alcibiades who is making the attempt is not as yet twenty years old, and is wholly uneducated, and when his lover tells him that he ought to get education and training first, and then go and fight the king, he refuses, and says that he is well enough as he is, would she not be amazed, and ask 'On what, then, does the youth rely?' And if we replied: He relies on his beauty, and stature, and birth, and mental endowments, she would think that we were mad, Alcibiades, when she compared the advantages which you possess with those of her own people. And I believe that even Lampido, the daughter of Leotychides, the wife of Archidamus and mother of Agis, all of whom were kings, would have the same feeling; if, in your present uneducated state, you were to turn your thoughts against her son, she too would be equally astonished. But how disgraceful, that we should not have as high a notion of what is required in us as our enemies' wives and mothers have of the qualities which are required in their assailants! O my friend, be persuaded by me, and hear the Delphian inscription, 'Know thyself'—not the men whom you think, but these kings are our rivals, and we can only overcome them by pains and skill. And if you fail in the required qualities, you will fail also in becoming renowned among Hellenes and Barbarians, which you seem to desire more than any other man ever desired anything.

ALCIBIADES: I entirely believe you; but what are the sort of pains which are required, Socrates,—can you tell me?

SOCRATES: Yes, I can; but we must take counsel together concerning the manner in which both of us may be most improved. For what I am telling you of the necessity of education applies to myself as well as to you; and there is only one point in which I have an advantage over you.

ALCIBIADES: What is that?

SOCRATES: I have a guardian who is better and wiser than your guardian, Pericles.

ALCIBIADES: Who is he, Socrates?

SOCRATES: God, Alcibiades, who up to this day has not allowed me to converse with you; and he inspires in me the faith that I am especially designed to bring you to honour.

ALCIBIADES: You are jesting, Socrates.

SOCRATES: Perhaps, at any rate, I am right in saying that all men greatly need pains and care, and you and I above all men.

ALCIBIADES: You are not far wrong about me.

SOCRATES: And certainly not about myself.

ALCIBIADES: But what can we do?

SOCRATES: There must be no hesitation or cowardice, my friend.

ALCIBIADES: That would not become us, Socrates.

SOCRATES: No, indeed, and we ought to take counsel together: for do we not wish to be as good as possible?

ALCIBIADES: We do.

SOCRATES: In what sort of virtue?

ALCIBIADES: Plainly, in the virtue of good men.

SOCRATES: Who are good in what?

ALCIBIADES: Those, clearly, who are good in the management of affairs.

SOCRATES: What sort of affairs? Equestrian affairs?

ALCIBIADES: Certainly not.

SOCRATES: You mean that about them we should have recourse to horsemen?

ALCIBIADES: Yes.

SOCRATES: Well, naval affairs?

ALCIBIADES: No.

SOCRATES: You mean that we should have recourse to sailors about them?

ALCIBIADES: Yes.

SOCRATES: Then what affairs? And who do them?

ALCIBIADES: The affairs which occupy Athenian gentlemen.

SOCRATES: And when you speak of gentlemen, do you mean the wise or the unwise?

ALCIBIADES: The wise.

SOCRATES: And a man is good in respect of that in which he is wise?

ALCIBIADES: Yes.

SOCRATES: And evil in respect of that in which he is unwise?

ALCIBIADES: Certainly.

SOCRATES: The shoemaker, for example, is wise in respect of the making of shoes?

ALCIBIADES: Yes.

SOCRATES: Then he is good in that?

ALCIBIADES: He is.

SOCRATES: But in respect of the making of garments he is unwise?

ALCIBIADES: Yes.

SOCRATES: Then in that he is bad?

ALCIBIADES: Yes.

SOCRATES: Then upon this view of the matter the same man is good and also bad?

ALCIBIADES: True.

SOCRATES: But would you say that the good are the same as the bad?

ALCIBIADES: Certainly not.

SOCRATES: Then whom do you call the good?

ALCIBIADES: I mean by the good those who are able to rule in the city.

SOCRATES: Not, surely, over horses?

ALCIBIADES: Certainly not.

SOCRATES: But over men?

ALCIBIADES: Yes.

SOCRATES: When they are sick?

ALCIBIADES: No.

SOCRATES: Or on a voyage?

ALCIBIADES: No.

SOCRATES: Or reaping the harvest?

ALCIBIADES: No.

SOCRATES: When they are doing something or nothing?

ALCIBIADES: When they are doing something, I should say.

SOCRATES: I wish that you would explain to me what this something is.

ALCIBIADES: When they are having dealings with one another, and using one another's services, as we citizens do in our daily life.

SOCRATES: Those of whom you speak are ruling over men who are using the services of other men?

ALCIBIADES: Yes.

SOCRATES: Are they ruling over the signal-men who give the time to the rowers?

ALCIBIADES: No; they are not.

SOCRATES: That would be the office of the pilot?

ALCIBIADES: Yes.

SOCRATES: But, perhaps you mean that they rule over flute-players, who lead the singers and use the services of the dancers?

ALCIBIADES: Certainly not.

SOCRATES: That would be the business of the teacher of the chorus?

ALCIBIADES: Yes.

SOCRATES: Then what is the meaning of being able to rule over men who use other men?

ALCIBIADES: I mean that they rule over men who have common rights of citizenship, and dealings with one another.

SOCRATES: And what sort of an art is this? Suppose that I ask you again, as I did just now, What art makes men know how to rule over their fellow-sailors,—how would you answer?

ALCIBIADES: The art of the pilot.

SOCRATES: And, if I may recur to another old instance, what art enables them to rule over their fellow-singers?

ALCIBIADES: The art of the teacher of the chorus, which you were just now mentioning.

SOCRATES: And what do you call the art of fellow-citizens?

ALCIBIADES: I should say, good counsel, Socrates.

SOCRATES: And is the art of the pilot evil counsel?

ALCIBIADES: No.

SOCRATES: But good counsel?

ALCIBIADES: Yes, that is what I should say,—good counsel, of which the aim is the preservation of the voyagers.

SOCRATES: True. And what is the aim of that other good counsel of which you speak?

ALCIBIADES: The aim is the better order and preservation of the city.

SOCRATES: And what is that of which the absence or presence improves and preserves the order of the city? Suppose you were to ask me, what is that of which the presence or absence improves or preserves the order of the body? I should reply, the presence of health and the absence of disease. You would say the same?

ALCIBIADES: Yes.

SOCRATES: And if you were to ask me the same question about the eyes, I should reply in the same way, 'the presence of sight and the absence of blindness;' or about the ears, I should reply, that they were improved and were in better case, when deafness was absent, and hearing was present in them.

ALCIBIADES: True.

SOCRATES: And what would you say of a state? What is that by the presence or absence of which the state is improved and better managed and ordered?

ALCIBIADES: I should say, Socrates:—the presence of friendship and the absence of hatred and division.

SOCRATES: And do you mean by friendship agreement or disagreement?

ALCIBIADES: Agreement.

SOCRATES: What art makes cities agree about numbers?

ALCIBIADES: Arithmetic.

SOCRATES: And private individuals?

ALCIBIADES: The same.

SOCRATES: And what art makes each individual agree with himself?

ALCIBIADES: The same.

SOCRATES: And what art makes each of us agree with himself about the comparative length of the span and of the cubit? Does not the art of measure?

ALCIBIADES: Yes.

SOCRATES: Individuals are agreed with one another about this; and states, equally?

ALCIBIADES: Yes.

SOCRATES: And the same holds of the balance?

ALCIBIADES: True.

SOCRATES: But what is the other agreement of which you speak, and about what? what art can give that agreement? And does that which gives it to the state give it also to the individual, so as to make him consistent with himself and with another?

ALCIBIADES: I should suppose so.

SOCRATES: But what is the nature of the agreement?—answer, and faint not.

ALCIBIADES: I mean to say that there should be such friendship and agreement as exists between an affectionate father and mother and their son, or between brothers, or between husband and wife.

SOCRATES: But can a man, Alcibiades, agree with a woman about the spinning of wool, which she understands and he does not?

ALCIBIADES: No, truly.

SOCRATES: Nor has he any need, for spinning is a female accomplishment.

ALCIBIADES: Yes.

SOCRATES: And would a woman agree with a man about the science of arms, which she has never learned?

ALCIBIADES: Certainly not.

SOCRATES: I suppose that the use of arms would be regarded by you as a male accomplishment?

ALCIBIADES: It would.

SOCRATES: Then, upon your view, women and men have two sorts of knowledge?

ALCIBIADES: Certainly.

SOCRATES: Then in their knowledge there is no agreement of women and men?

ALCIBIADES: There is not.

SOCRATES: Nor can there be friendship, if friendship is agreement?

ALCIBIADES: Plainly not.

SOCRATES: Then women are not loved by men when they do their own work?

ALCIBIADES: I suppose not.

SOCRATES: Nor men by women when they do their own work?

ALCIBIADES: No.

SOCRATES: Nor are states well administered, when individuals do their own work?

ALCIBIADES: I should rather think, Socrates, that the reverse is the truth. (Compare Republic.)

SOCRATES: What! do you mean to say that states are well administered when friendship is absent, the presence of which, as we were saying, alone secures their good order?

ALCIBIADES: But I should say that there is friendship among them, for this very reason, that the two parties respectively do their own work.

SOCRATES: That was not what you were saying before; and what do you mean now by affirming that friendship exists when there is no agreement? How can there be agreement about matters which the one party knows, and of which the other is in ignorance?

ALCIBIADES: Impossible.

SOCRATES: And when individuals are doing their own work, are they doing what is just or unjust?

ALCIBIADES: What is just, certainly.

SOCRATES: And when individuals do what is just in the state, is there no friendship among them?

ALCIBIADES: I suppose that there must be, Socrates.

SOCRATES: Then what do you mean by this friendship or agreement about which we must be wise and discreet in order that we may be good men? I cannot make out where it exists or among whom; according to you, the same persons may sometimes have it, and sometimes not.

ALCIBIADES: But, indeed, Socrates, I do not know what I am saying; and I have long been, unconsciously to myself, in a most disgraceful state.

SOCRATES: Nevertheless, cheer up; at fifty, if you had discovered your deficiency, you would have been too old, and the time for taking care of yourself would have passed away, but yours is just the age at which the discovery should be made.

ALCIBIADES: And what should he do, Socrates, who would make the discovery?

SOCRATES: Answer questions, Alcibiades; and that is a process which, by the grace of God, if I may put any faith in my oracle, will be very improving to both of us.

ALCIBIADES: If I can be improved by answering, I will answer.

SOCRATES: And first of all, that we may not peradventure be deceived by appearances, fancying, perhaps, that we are taking care of ourselves when we are not, what is the meaning of a man taking care of himself? and when does he take care? Does he take care of himself when he takes care of what belongs to him?

ALCIBIADES: I should think so.

SOCRATES: When does a man take care of his feet? Does he not take care of them when he takes care of that which belongs to his feet?

ALCIBIADES: I do not understand.

SOCRATES: Let me take the hand as an illustration; does not a ring belong to the finger, and to the finger only?

ALCIBIADES: Yes.

SOCRATES: And the shoe in like manner to the foot?

ALCIBIADES: Yes.

SOCRATES: And when we take care of our shoes, do we not take care of our feet?

ALCIBIADES: I do not comprehend, Socrates.

SOCRATES: But you would admit, Alcibiades, that to take proper care of a thing is a correct expression?

ALCIBIADES: Yes.

SOCRATES: And taking proper care means improving?

ALCIBIADES: Yes.

SOCRATES: And what is the art which improves our shoes?

ALCIBIADES: Shoemaking.

SOCRATES: Then by shoemaking we take care of our shoes?

ALCIBIADES: Yes.

SOCRATES: And do we by shoemaking take care of our feet, or by some other art which improves the feet?

ALCIBIADES: By some other art.

SOCRATES: And the same art improves the feet which improves the rest of the body?

ALCIBIADES: Very true.

SOCRATES: Which is gymnastic?

ALCIBIADES: Certainly.

SOCRATES: Then by gymnastic we take care of our feet, and by shoemaking of that which belongs to our feet?

ALCIBIADES: Very true.

SOCRATES: And by gymnastic we take care of our hands, and by the art of graving rings of that which belongs to our hands?

ALCIBIADES: Yes.

SOCRATES: And by gymnastic we take care of the body, and by the art of weaving and the other arts we take care of the things of the body?

ALCIBIADES: Clearly.

SOCRATES: Then the art which takes care of each thing is different from that which takes care of the belongings of each thing?

ALCIBIADES: True.

SOCRATES: Then in taking care of what belongs to you, you do not take care of yourself?

ALCIBIADES: Certainly not.

SOCRATES: For the art which takes care of our belongings appears not to be the same as that which takes care of ourselves?

ALCIBIADES: Clearly not.

SOCRATES: And now let me ask you what is the art with which we take care of ourselves?

ALCIBIADES: I cannot say.

SOCRATES: At any rate, thus much has been admitted, that the art is not one which makes any of our possessions, but which makes ourselves better?

ALCIBIADES: True.

SOCRATES: But should we ever have known what art makes a shoe better, if we did not know a shoe?

ALCIBIADES: Impossible.

SOCRATES: Nor should we know what art makes a ring better, if we did not know a ring?

ALCIBIADES: That is true.

SOCRATES: And can we ever know what art makes a man better, if we do not know what we are ourselves?

ALCIBIADES: Impossible.

SOCRATES: And is self-knowledge such an easy thing, and was he to be lightly esteemed who inscribed the text on the temple at Delphi? Or is self-knowledge a difficult thing, which few are able to attain?

ALCIBIADES: At times I fancy, Socrates, that anybody can know himself; at other times the task appears to be very difficult.

SOCRATES: But whether easy or difficult, Alcibiades, still there is no other way; knowing what we are, we shall know how to take care of ourselves, and if we are ignorant we shall not know.

ALCIBIADES: That is true.

SOCRATES: Well, then, let us see in what way the self-existent can be discovered by us; that will give us a chance of discovering our own existence, which otherwise we can never know.

ALCIBIADES: You say truly.

SOCRATES: Come, now, I beseech you, tell me with whom you are conversing?—with whom but with me?

ALCIBIADES: Yes.

SOCRATES: As I am, with you?

ALCIBIADES: Yes.

SOCRATES: That is to say, I, Socrates, am talking?

ALCIBIADES: Yes.

SOCRATES: And Alcibiades is my hearer?

ALCIBIADES: Yes.

SOCRATES: And I in talking use words?

ALCIBIADES: Certainly.

SOCRATES: And talking and using words have, I suppose, the same meaning?

ALCIBIADES: To be sure.

SOCRATES: And the user is not the same as the thing which he uses?

ALCIBIADES: What do you mean?

SOCRATES: I will explain; the shoemaker, for example, uses a square tool, and a circular tool, and other tools for cutting?

ALCIBIADES: Yes.

SOCRATES: But the tool is not the same as the cutter and user of the tool?

ALCIBIADES: Of course not.

SOCRATES: And in the same way the instrument of the harper is to be distinguished from the harper himself?

ALCIBIADES: It is.

SOCRATES: Now the question which I asked was whether you conceive the user to be always different from that which he uses?

ALCIBIADES: I do.

SOCRATES: Then what shall we say of the shoemaker? Does he cut with his tools only or with his hands?

ALCIBIADES: With his hands as well.

SOCRATES: He uses his hands too?

ALCIBIADES: Yes.

SOCRATES: And does he use his eyes in cutting leather?

ALCIBIADES: He does.

SOCRATES: And we admit that the user is not the same with the things which he uses?

ALCIBIADES: Yes.

SOCRATES: Then the shoemaker and the harper are to be distinguished from the hands and feet which they use?

ALCIBIADES: Clearly.

SOCRATES: And does not a man use the whole body?

ALCIBIADES: Certainly.

SOCRATES: And that which uses is different from that which is used?

ALCIBIADES: True.

SOCRATES: Then a man is not the same as his own body?

ALCIBIADES: That is the inference.

SOCRATES: What is he, then?

ALCIBIADES: I cannot say.

SOCRATES: Nay, you can say that he is the user of the body.

ALCIBIADES: Yes.

SOCRATES: And the user of the body is the soul?

ALCIBIADES: Yes, the soul.

SOCRATES: And the soul rules?

ALCIBIADES: Yes.

SOCRATES: Let me make an assertion which will, I think, be universally admitted.

ALCIBIADES: What is it?

SOCRATES: That man is one of three things.

ALCIBIADES: What are they?

SOCRATES: Soul, body, or both together forming a whole.

ALCIBIADES: Certainly.

SOCRATES: But did we not say that the actual ruling principle of the body is man?

ALCIBIADES: Yes, we did.

SOCRATES: And does the body rule over itself?

ALCIBIADES: Certainly not.

SOCRATES: It is subject, as we were saying?

ALCIBIADES: Yes.

SOCRATES: Then that is not the principle which we are seeking?

ALCIBIADES: It would seem not.

SOCRATES: But may we say that the union of the two rules over the body, and consequently that this is man?

ALCIBIADES: Very likely.

SOCRATES: The most unlikely of all things; for if one of the members is subject, the two united cannot possibly rule.

ALCIBIADES: True.

SOCRATES: But since neither the body, nor the union of the two, is man, either man has no real existence, or the soul is man?

ALCIBIADES: Just so.

SOCRATES: Is anything more required to prove that the soul is man?

ALCIBIADES: Certainly not; the proof is, I think, quite sufficient.

SOCRATES: And if the proof, although not perfect, be sufficient, we shall be satisfied;—more precise proof will be supplied when we have discovered that which we were led to omit, from a fear that the enquiry would be too much protracted.

ALCIBIADES: What was that?

SOCRATES: What I meant, when I said that absolute existence must be first considered; but now, instead of absolute existence, we have been considering the nature of individual existence, and this may, perhaps, be sufficient; for surely there is nothing which may be called more properly ourselves than the soul?

ALCIBIADES: There is nothing.

SOCRATES: Then we may truly conceive that you and I are conversing with one another, soul to soul?

ALCIBIADES: Very true.

SOCRATES: And that is just what I was saying before—that I, Socrates, am not arguing or talking with the face of Alcibiades, but with the real Alcibiades; or in other words, with his soul.

ALCIBIADES: True.

SOCRATES: Then he who bids a man know himself, would have him know his soul?

ALCIBIADES: That appears to be true.

SOCRATES: He whose knowledge only extends to the body, knows the things of a man, and not the man himself?

ALCIBIADES: That is true.

SOCRATES: Then neither the physician regarded as a physician, nor the trainer regarded as a trainer, knows himself?

ALCIBIADES: He does not.

SOCRATES: The husbandmen and the other craftsmen are very far from knowing themselves, for they would seem not even to know their own belongings? When regarded in relation to the arts which they practise they are even further removed from self-knowledge, for they only know the belongings of the body, which minister to the body.

ALCIBIADES: That is true.

SOCRATES: Then if temperance is the knowledge of self, in respect of his art none of them is temperate?

ALCIBIADES: I agree.

SOCRATES: And this is the reason why their arts are accounted vulgar, and are not such as a good man would practise?

ALCIBIADES: Quite true.

SOCRATES: Again, he who cherishes his body cherishes not himself, but what belongs to him?

ALCIBIADES: That is true.

SOCRATES: But he who cherishes his money, cherishes neither himself nor his belongings, but is in a stage yet further removed from himself?

ALCIBIADES: I agree.

SOCRATES: Then the money-maker has really ceased to be occupied with his own concerns?

ALCIBIADES: True.

SOCRATES: And if any one has fallen in love with the person of Alcibiades, he loves not Alcibiades, but the belongings of Alcibiades?

ALCIBIADES: True.

SOCRATES: But he who loves your soul is the true lover?

ALCIBIADES: That is the necessary inference.

SOCRATES: The lover of the body goes away when the flower of youth fades?

ALCIBIADES: True.

SOCRATES: But he who loves the soul goes not away, as long as the soul follows after virtue?

ALCIBIADES: Yes.

SOCRATES: And I am the lover who goes not away, but remains with you, when you are no longer young and the rest are gone?

ALCIBIADES: Yes, Socrates; and therein you do well, and I hope that you will remain.

SOCRATES: Then you must try to look your best.

ALCIBIADES: I will.

SOCRATES: The fact is, that there is only one lover of Alcibiades the son of Cleinias; there neither is nor ever has been seemingly any other; and he is his darling,—Socrates, the son of Sophroniscus and Phaenarete.

ALCIBIADES: True.

SOCRATES: And did you not say, that if I had not spoken first, you were on the point of coming to me, and enquiring why I only remained?

ALCIBIADES: That is true.

SOCRATES: The reason was that I loved you for your own sake, whereas other men love what belongs to you; and your beauty, which is not you, is fading away, just as your true self is beginning to bloom. And I will never desert you, if you are not spoiled and deformed by the Athenian people; for the danger which I most fear is that you will become a lover of the people and will be spoiled by them. Many a noble Athenian has been ruined in this way. For the demus of the great-hearted Erechteus is of a fair countenance, but you should see him naked; wherefore observe the caution which I give you.

ALCIBIADES: What caution?

SOCRATES: Practise yourself, sweet friend, in learning what you ought to know, before you enter on politics; and then you will have an antidote which will keep you out of harm's way.

ALCIBIADES: Good advice, Socrates, but I wish that you would explain to me in what way I am to take care of myself.

SOCRATES: Have we not made an advance? for we are at any rate tolerably well agreed as to what we are, and there is no longer any danger, as we once feared, that we might be taking care not of ourselves, but of something which is not ourselves.

ALCIBIADES: That is true.

SOCRATES: And the next step will be to take care of the soul, and look to that?

ALCIBIADES: Certainly.

SOCRATES: Leaving the care of our bodies and of our properties to others?

ALCIBIADES: Very good.

SOCRATES: But how can we have a perfect knowledge of the things of the soul?—For if we know them, then I suppose we shall know ourselves. Can we really be ignorant of the excellent meaning of the Delphian inscription, of which we were just now speaking?

ALCIBIADES: What have you in your thoughts, Socrates?

SOCRATES: I will tell you what I suspect to be the meaning and lesson of that inscription. Let me take an illustration from sight, which I imagine to be the only one suitable to my purpose.

ALCIBIADES: What do you mean?

SOCRATES: Consider; if some one were to say to the eye, 'See thyself,' as you might say to a man, 'Know thyself,' what is the nature and meaning of this precept? Would not his meaning be:—That the eye should look at that in which it would see itself?

ALCIBIADES: Clearly.

SOCRATES: And what are the objects in looking at which we see ourselves?

ALCIBIADES: Clearly, Socrates, in looking at mirrors and the like.

SOCRATES: Very true; and is there not something of the nature of a mirror in our own eyes?

ALCIBIADES: Certainly.

SOCRATES: Did you ever observe that the face of the person looking into the eye of another is reflected as in a mirror; and in the visual organ which is over against him, and which is called the pupil, there is a sort of image of the person looking?

ALCIBIADES: That is quite true.

SOCRATES: Then the eye, looking at another eye, and at that in the eye which is most perfect, and which is the instrument of vision, will there see itself?

ALCIBIADES: That is evident.

SOCRATES: But looking at anything else either in man or in the world, and not to what resembles this, it will not see itself?

ALCIBIADES: Very true.

SOCRATES: Then if the eye is to see itself, it must look at the eye, and at that part of the eye where sight which is the virtue of the eye resides?

ALCIBIADES: True.

SOCRATES: And if the soul, my dear Alcibiades, is ever to know herself, must she not look at the soul; and especially at that part of the soul in which her virtue resides, and to any other which is like this?

ALCIBIADES: I agree, Socrates.

SOCRATES: And do we know of any part of our souls more divine than that which has to do with wisdom and knowledge?

ALCIBIADES: There is none.

SOCRATES: Then this is that part of the soul which resembles the divine; and he who looks at this and at the whole class of things divine, will be most likely to know himself?

ALCIBIADES: Clearly.

SOCRATES: And self-knowledge we agree to be wisdom?

ALCIBIADES: True.

SOCRATES: But if we have no self-knowledge and no wisdom, can we ever know our own good and evil?

ALCIBIADES: How can we, Socrates?

SOCRATES: You mean, that if you did not know Alcibiades, there would be no possibility of your knowing that what belonged to Alcibiades was really his?

ALCIBIADES: It would be quite impossible.

SOCRATES: Nor should we know that we were the persons to whom anything belonged, if we did not know ourselves?

ALCIBIADES: How could we?

SOCRATES: And if we did not know our own belongings, neither should we know the belongings of our belongings?

ALCIBIADES: Clearly not.

SOCRATES: Then we were not altogether right in acknowledging just now that a man may know what belongs to him and yet not know himself; nay, rather he cannot even know the belongings of his belongings; for the discernment of the things of self, and of the things which belong to the things of self, appear all to be the business of the same man, and of the same art.

ALCIBIADES: So much may be supposed.

SOCRATES: And he who knows not the things which belong to himself, will in like manner be ignorant of the things which belong to others?

ALCIBIADES: Very true.

SOCRATES: And if he knows not the affairs of others, he will not know the affairs of states?

ALCIBIADES: Certainly not.

SOCRATES: Then such a man can never be a statesman?

ALCIBIADES: He cannot.

SOCRATES: Nor an economist?

ALCIBIADES: He cannot.

SOCRATES: He will not know what he is doing?

ALCIBIADES: He will not.

SOCRATES: And will not he who is ignorant fall into error?

ALCIBIADES: Assuredly.

SOCRATES: And if he falls into error will he not fail both in his public and private capacity?

ALCIBIADES: Yes, indeed.

SOCRATES: And failing, will he not be miserable?

ALCIBIADES: Very.

SOCRATES: And what will become of those for whom he is acting?

ALCIBIADES: They will be miserable also.

SOCRATES: Then he who is not wise and good cannot be happy?

ALCIBIADES: He cannot.

SOCRATES: The bad, then, are miserable?

ALCIBIADES: Yes, very.

SOCRATES: And if so, not he who has riches, but he who has wisdom, is delivered from his misery?

ALCIBIADES: Clearly.

SOCRATES: Cities, then, if they are to be happy, do not want walls, or triremes, or docks, or numbers, or size, Alcibiades, without virtue? (Compare Arist. Pol.)

ALCIBIADES: Indeed they do not.

SOCRATES: And you must give the citizens virtue, if you mean to administer their affairs rightly or nobly?

ALCIBIADES: Certainly.

SOCRATES: But can a man give that which he has not?

ALCIBIADES: Impossible.

SOCRATES: Then you or any one who means to govern and superintend, not only himself and the things of himself, but the state and the things of the state, must in the first place acquire virtue.

ALCIBIADES: That is true.

SOCRATES: You have not therefore to obtain power or authority, in order to enable you to do what you wish for yourself and the state, but justice and wisdom.

ALCIBIADES: Clearly.

SOCRATES: You and the state, if you act wisely and justly, will act according to the will of God?

ALCIBIADES: Certainly.

SOCRATES: As I was saying before, you will look only at what is bright and divine, and act with a view to them?

ALCIBIADES: Yes.

SOCRATES: In that mirror you will see and know yourselves and your own good?

ALCIBIADES: Yes.

SOCRATES: And so you will act rightly and well?

ALCIBIADES: Yes.

SOCRATES: In which case, I will be security for your happiness.

ALCIBIADES: I accept the security.

SOCRATES: But if you act unrighteously, your eye will turn to the dark and godless, and being in darkness and ignorance of yourselves, you will probably do deeds of darkness.

ALCIBIADES: Very possibly.

SOCRATES: For if a man, my dear Alcibiades, has the power to do what he likes, but has no understanding, what is likely to be the result, either to him as an individual or to the state—for example, if he be sick and is able to do what he likes, not having the mind of a physician—having moreover tyrannical power, and no one daring to reprove him, what will happen to him? Will he not be likely to have his constitution ruined?

ALCIBIADES: That is true.

SOCRATES: Or again, in a ship, if a man having the power to do what he likes, has no intelligence or skill in navigation, do you see what will happen to him and to his fellow-sailors?

ALCIBIADES: Yes; I see that they will all perish.

SOCRATES: And in like manner, in a state, and where there is any power and authority which is wanting in virtue, will not misfortune, in like manner, ensue?

ALCIBIADES: Certainly.

SOCRATES: Not tyrannical power, then, my good Alcibiades, should be the aim either of individuals or states, if they would be happy, but virtue.

ALCIBIADES: That is true.

SOCRATES: And before they have virtue, to be commanded by a superior is better for men as well as for children? (Compare Arist. Pol.)

ALCIBIADES: That is evident.

SOCRATES: And that which is better is also nobler?

ALCIBIADES: True.

SOCRATES: And what is nobler is more becoming?

ALCIBIADES: Certainly.

SOCRATES: Then to the bad man slavery is more becoming, because better?

ALCIBIADES: True.

SOCRATES: Then vice is only suited to a slave?

ALCIBIADES: Yes.

SOCRATES: And virtue to a freeman?

ALCIBIADES: Yes.

SOCRATES: And, O my friend, is not the condition of a slave to be avoided?

ALCIBIADES: Certainly, Socrates.

SOCRATES: And are you now conscious of your own state? And do you know whether you are a freeman or not?

ALCIBIADES: I think that I am very conscious indeed of my own state.

SOCRATES: And do you know how to escape out of a state which I do not even like to name to my beauty?

ALCIBIADES: Yes, I do.

SOCRATES: How?

ALCIBIADES: By your help, Socrates.

SOCRATES: That is not well said, Alcibiades.

ALCIBIADES: What ought I to have said?

SOCRATES: By the help of God.

ALCIBIADES: I agree; and I further say, that our relations are likely to be reversed. From this day forward, I must and will follow you as you have followed me; I will be the disciple, and you shall be my master.

SOCRATES: O that is rare! My love breeds another love: and so like the stork I shall be cherished by the bird whom I have hatched.

ALCIBIADES: Strange, but true; and henceforward I shall begin to think about justice.

SOCRATES: And I hope that you will persist; although I have fears, not because I doubt you; but I see the power of the state, which may be too much for both of us.

ALCIBIADES II

by An Imitator of Plato

PERSONS OF THE DIALOGUE: Socrates and Alcibiades.

SOCRATES: Are you going, Alcibiades, to offer prayer to Zeus?

ALCIBIADES: Yes, Socrates, I am.

SOCRATES: you seem to be troubled and to cast your eyes on the ground, as though you were thinking about something.

ALCIBIADES: Of what do you suppose that I am thinking?

SOCRATES: Of the greatest of all things, as I believe. Tell me, do you not suppose that the Gods sometimes partly grant and partly reject the requests which we make in public and private, and favour some persons and not others?

ALCIBIADES: Certainly.

SOCRATES: Do you not imagine, then, that a man ought to be very careful, lest perchance without knowing it he implore great evils for himself, deeming that he is asking for good, especially if the Gods are in the mood to grant whatever he may request? There is the story of Oedipus, for instance, who prayed that his children might divide their inheritance between them by the sword: he did not, as he might have done, beg that his present evils might be averted, but called down new ones. And was not his prayer accomplished, and did not many and terrible evils thence arise, upon which I need not dilate?

ALCIBIADES: Yes, Socrates, but you are speaking of a madman: surely you do not think that any one in his senses would venture to make such a prayer?

SOCRATES: Madness, then, you consider to be the opposite of discretion?

ALCIBIADES: Of course.

SOCRATES: And some men seem to you to be discreet, and others the contrary?

ALCIBIADES: They do.

SOCRATES: Well, then, let us discuss who these are. We acknowledge that some are discreet, some foolish, and that some are mad?

ALCIBIADES: Yes.

SOCRATES: And again, there are some who are in health?

ALCIBIADES: There are.

SOCRATES: While others are ailing?

ALCIBIADES: Yes.

SOCRATES: And they are not the same?

ALCIBIADES: Certainly not.

SOCRATES: Nor are there any who are in neither state?

ALCIBIADES: No.

SOCRATES: A man must either be sick or be well?

ALCIBIADES: That is my opinion.

SOCRATES: Very good: and do you think the same about discretion and want of discretion?

ALCIBIADES: How do you mean?

SOCRATES: Do you believe that a man must be either in or out of his senses; or is there some third or intermediate condition, in which he is neither one nor the other?

ALCIBIADES: Decidedly not.

SOCRATES: He must be either sane or insane?

ALCIBIADES: So I suppose.

SOCRATES: Did you not acknowledge that madness was the opposite of discretion?

ALCIBIADES: Yes.

SOCRATES: And that there is no third or middle term between discretion and indiscretion?

ALCIBIADES: True.

SOCRATES: And there cannot be two opposites to one thing?

ALCIBIADES: There cannot.

SOCRATES: Then madness and want of sense are the same?

ALCIBIADES: That appears to be the case.

SOCRATES: We shall be in the right, therefore, Alcibiades, if we say that all who are senseless are mad. For example, if among persons of your own age or older than yourself there are some who are senseless,—as there certainly are,—they are mad. For tell me, by heaven, do you not think that in the city the wise are few, while the foolish, whom you call mad, are many?

ALCIBIADES: I do.

SOCRATES: But how could we live in safety with so many crazy people? Should we not long since have paid the penalty at their hands, and have been struck and beaten and endured every other form of ill-usage which madmen are wont to inflict? Consider, my dear friend: may it not be quite otherwise?

ALCIBIADES: Why, Socrates, how is that possible? I must have been mistaken.

SOCRATES: So it seems to me. But perhaps we may consider the matter thus:—

ALCIBIADES: How?

SOCRATES: I will tell you. We think that some are sick; do we not?

ALCIBIADES: Yes.

SOCRATES: And must every sick person either have the gout, or be in a fever, or suffer from ophthalmia? Or do you believe that a man may labour under some other disease, even although he has none of these complaints? Surely, they are not the only maladies which exist?

ALCIBIADES: Certainly not.

SOCRATES: And is every kind of ophthalmia a disease?

ALCIBIADES: Yes.

SOCRATES: And every disease ophthalmia?

ALCIBIADES: Surely not. But I scarcely understand what I mean myself.

SOCRATES: Perhaps, if you give me your best attention, 'two of us' looking together, we may find what we seek.

ALCIBIADES: I am attending, Socrates, to the best of my power.

SOCRATES: We are agreed, then, that every form of ophthalmia is a disease, but not every disease ophthalmia?

ALCIBIADES: We are.

SOCRATES: And so far we seem to be right. For every one who suffers from a fever is sick; but the sick, I conceive, do not all have fever or gout or ophthalmia, although each of these is a disease, which, according to those whom we call physicians, may require a different treatment. They are not all alike, nor do they produce the same result, but each has its own effect, and yet they are all diseases. May we not take an illustration from the artizans?

ALCIBIADES: Certainly.

SOCRATES: There are cobblers and carpenters and sculptors and others of all sorts and kinds, whom we need not stop to enumerate. All have their distinct employments and all are workmen, although they are not all of them cobblers or carpenters or sculptors.

ALCIBIADES: No, indeed.

SOCRATES: And in like manner men differ in regard to want of sense. Those who are most out of their wits we call 'madmen,' while we term those who are less far gone 'stupid' or 'idiotic,' or, if we prefer gentler language, describe them as 'romantic' or 'simple-minded,' or, again, as 'innocent' or 'inexperienced' or 'foolish.' You may even find other names, if you seek for them; but by all of them lack of sense is intended.

They only differ as one art appeared to us to differ from another or one disease from another. Or what is your opinion?

ALCIBIADES: I agree with you.

SOCRATES: Then let us return to the point at which we digressed. We said at first that we should have to consider who were the wise and who the foolish. For we acknowledged that there are these two classes? Did we not?

ALCIBIADES: To be sure.

SOCRATES: And you regard those as sensible who know what ought to be done or said?

ALCIBIADES: Yes.

SOCRATES: The senseless are those who do not know this?

ALCIBIADES: True.

SOCRATES: The latter will say or do what they ought not without their own knowledge?

ALCIBIADES: Exactly.

SOCRATES: Oedipus, as I was saying, Alcibiades, was a person of this sort. And even now-a-days you will find many who (have offered inauspicious prayers), although, unlike him, they were not in anger nor thought that they were asking evil. He neither sought, nor supposed that he sought for good, but others have had quite the contrary notion. I believe that if the God whom you are about to consult should appear to you, and, in anticipation of your request, enquired whether you would be contented to become tyrant of Athens, and if this seemed in your eyes a small and mean thing, should add to it the dominion of all Hellas; and seeing that even then you would not be satisfied unless you were ruler of the whole of Europe, should promise, not only that, but, if you so desired, should proclaim to all mankind in one and the same day that Alcibiades, son of Cleinias, was tyrant:—in such a case, I imagine, you would depart full of joy, as one who had obtained the greatest of goods.

ALCIBIADES: And not only I, Socrates, but any one else who should meet with such luck.

SOCRATES: Yet you would not accept the dominion and lordship of all the Hellenes and all the barbarians in exchange for your life?

ALCIBIADES: Certainly not: for then what use could I make of them?

SOCRATES: And would you accept them if you were likely to use them to a bad and mischievous end?

ALCIBIADES: I would not.

SOCRATES: You see that it is not safe for a man either rashly to accept whatever is offered him, or himself to request a thing, if he is likely to suffer thereby or immediately to lose his life. And yet we could tell of many who, having long desired and diligently laboured to obtain a tyranny, thinking that thus they would procure an advantage, have nevertheless fallen victims to designing enemies. You must have heard of what happened only the other day, how Archelaus of Macedonia was slain by his beloved (compare Aristotle, Pol.), whose love for the tyranny was not less than that of Archelaus for him. The tyrannicide expected by his crime to become tyrant and afterwards to have a happy life; but when he had held the tyranny three or four days, he was in his turn conspired against and slain. Or look at certain of our own citizens,—and of their actions we have been not hearers, but eyewitnesses,—who have desired to obtain military command: of those who have gained their object, some are even to this day exiles from the city, while others have lost their lives. And even they who seem to have fared best, have not only gone through many perils and terrors during their office, but after their return home they have been beset by informers worse than they once were by their foes, insomuch that several of them have wished that they had remained in a private station rather than have had the glories of command. If, indeed, such perils and terrors were of profit to the commonwealth, there would be reason in undergoing them; but the very contrary is the case. Again, you will find persons who have prayed for offspring, and when their prayers were heard, have fallen into the greatest pains and sufferings. For some have begotten children who were utterly bad, and have therefore passed all their days in misery, while the parents of good children have undergone the misfortune of losing them, and have been so little happier than the others that they would have preferred never to have had children rather than to have had them and lost them. And yet, although these and the like examples are manifest and known of all, it is rare to find any one who has refused what has been offered him, or, if he were likely to gain aught by prayer, has refrained from making his petition. The mass of mankind would not decline to accept a tyranny, or the command of an army, or any of the numerous things which cause more harm than good: but rather, if they had them not, would have prayed to obtain them. And often in a short space of time they change their tone, and wish their old prayers unsaid. Wherefore also I suspect that men are entirely wrong when they blame the gods as the authors of the ills which befall them (compare Republic): 'their own presumption,' or folly (whichever is the right word)—

'Has brought these unmeasured woes upon them.' (Homer. Odyss.)

He must have been a wise poet, Alcibiades, who, seeing as I believe, his friends foolishly praying for and doing things which would not really profit them, offered up a common prayer in behalf of them all:—

'King Zeus, grant us good whether prayed for or unsought by us; But that which we ask amiss, do thou avert.' (The author of these lines, which are probably of Pythagorean origin, is unknown. They are found also in the Anthology (Anth. Pal.).)

In my opinion, I say, the poet spoke both well and prudently; but if you have anything to say in answer to him, speak out.

ALCIBIADES: It is difficult, Socrates, to oppose what has been well said. And I perceive how many are the ills of which ignorance is the cause, since, as would appear, through ignorance we not only do, but what is worse, pray for the greatest evils. No man would imagine that he would do so; he would rather suppose that he was quite capable of praying for what was best: to call down evils seems more like a curse than a prayer.

SOCRATES: But perhaps, my good friend, some one who is wiser than either you or I will say that we have no right to blame ignorance thus rashly, unless we can add what ignorance we mean and of what, and also to whom and how it is respectively a good or an evil?

ALCIBIADES: How do you mean? Can ignorance possibly be better than knowledge for any person in any conceivable case?

SOCRATES: So I believe:—you do not think so?

ALCIBIADES: Certainly not.

SOCRATES: And yet surely I may not suppose that you would ever wish to act towards your mother as they say that Orestes and Alcmeon and others have done towards their parent.

ALCIBIADES: Good words, Socrates, prithee.

SOCRATES: You ought not to bid him use auspicious words, who says that you would not be willing to commit so horrible a deed, but rather him who affirms the contrary, if the act appear to you unfit even to be mentioned. Or do you think that Orestes, had he been in his senses and knew what was best for him to do, would ever have dared to venture on such a crime?

ALCIBIADES: Certainly not.

SOCRATES: Nor would any one else, I fancy?

ALCIBIADES: No.

SOCRATES: That ignorance is bad then, it would appear, which is of the best and does not know what is best?

ALCIBIADES: So I think, at least.

SOCRATES: And both to the person who is ignorant and everybody else?

ALCIBIADES: Yes.

SOCRATES: Let us take another case. Suppose that you were suddenly to get into your head that it would be a good thing to kill Pericles, your kinsman and guardian, and were to seize a sword and, going to the doors of his house, were to enquire if he were at home, meaning to slay only him and no one else:—the servants reply, 'Yes': (Mind, I do not mean that you would really do such a thing; but there is nothing, you think, to prevent a man who is ignorant of the best, having occasionally the whim that what is worst is best?

ALCIBIADES: No.)

SOCRATES:—If, then, you went indoors, and seeing him, did not know him, but thought that he was some one else, would you venture to slay him?

ALCIBIADES: Most decidedly not (it seems to me). (These words are omitted in several MSS.)

SOCRATES: For you designed to kill, not the first who offered, but Pericles himself?

ALCIBIADES: Certainly.

SOCRATES: And if you made many attempts, and each time failed to recognize Pericles, you would never attack him?

ALCIBIADES: Never.

SOCRATES: Well, but if Orestes in like manner had not known his mother, do you think that he would ever have laid hands upon her?

ALCIBIADES: No.

SOCRATES: He did not intend to slay the first woman he came across, nor any one else's mother, but only his own?

ALCIBIADES: True.

SOCRATES: Ignorance, then, is better for those who are in such a frame of mind, and have such ideas?

ALCIBIADES: Obviously.

SOCRATES: You acknowledge that for some persons in certain cases the ignorance of some things is a good and not an evil, as you formerly supposed?

ALCIBIADES: I do.

SOCRATES: And there is still another case which will also perhaps appear strange to you, if you will consider it? (The reading is here uncertain.)

ALCIBIADES: What is that, Socrates?

SOCRATES: It may be, in short, that the possession of all the sciences, if unaccompanied by the knowledge of the best, will more often than not injure the possessor. Consider the matter thus:—Must we not, when we intend either to do or say anything, suppose that we know or ought to know that which we propose so confidently to do or say?

ALCIBIADES: Yes, in my opinion.

SOCRATES: We may take the orators for an example, who from time to time advise us about war and peace, or the building of walls and the construction of harbours, whether they understand the business in hand, or only think that they do. Whatever the city, in a word, does to another city, or in the management of her own affairs, all happens by the counsel of the orators.

ALCIBIADES: True.

SOCRATES: But now see what follows, if I can (make it clear to you). (Some words appear to have dropped out here.) You would distinguish the wise from the foolish?

ALCIBIADES: Yes.

SOCRATES: The many are foolish, the few wise?

ALCIBIADES: Certainly.

SOCRATES: And you use both the terms, 'wise' and 'foolish,' in reference to something?

ALCIBIADES: I do.

SOCRATES: Would you call a person wise who can give advice, but does not know whether or when it is better to carry out the advice?

ALCIBIADES: Decidedly not.

SOCRATES: Nor again, I suppose, a person who knows the art of war, but does not know whether it is better to go to war or for how long?

ALCIBIADES: No.

SOCRATES: Nor, once more, a person who knows how to kill another or to take away his property or to drive him from his native land, but not when it is better to do so or for whom it is better?

ALCIBIADES: Certainly not.

SOCRATES: But he who understands anything of the kind and has at the same time the knowledge of the best course of action:—and the best and the useful are surely the same?—

ALCIBIADES: Yes.

SOCRATES:—Such an one, I say, we should call wise and a useful adviser both of himself and of the city. What do you think?

ALCIBIADES: I agree.

SOCRATES: And if any one knows how to ride or to shoot with the bow or to box or to wrestle, or to engage in any other sort of contest or to do anything whatever which is in the nature of an art,—what do you call him who knows what is best according to that art? Do you not speak of one who knows what is best in riding as a good rider?

ALCIBIADES: Yes.

SOCRATES: And in a similar way you speak of a good boxer or a good flute-player or a good performer in any other art?

ALCIBIADES: True.

SOCRATES: But is it necessary that the man who is clever in any of these arts should be wise also in general? Or is there a difference between the clever artist and the wise man?

ALCIBIADES: All the difference in the world.

SOCRATES: And what sort of a state do you think that would be which was composed of good archers and flute-players and athletes and masters in other arts, and besides them of those others about whom we spoke, who knew how to go to war and how to kill, as well as of orators puffed up with political pride, but in which not one of them all had this knowledge of the best, and there was no one who could tell when it was better to apply any of these arts or in regard to whom?

ALCIBIADES: I should call such a state bad, Socrates.

SOCRATES: You certainly would when you saw each of them rivalling the other and esteeming that of the greatest importance in the state,

'Wherein he himself most excelled.' (Euripides, Antiope.) —I mean that which was best in any art, while he was entirely ignorant of what was best for himself and for the state, because, as I think, he trusts to opinion which is devoid of intelligence. In such a case should we not be right if we said that the state would be full of anarchy and lawlessness?

ALCIBIADES: Decidedly.

SOCRATES: But ought we not then, think you, either to fancy that we know or really to know, what we confidently propose to do or say?

ALCIBIADES: Yes.

SOCRATES: And if a person does that which he knows or supposes that he knows, and the result is beneficial, he will act advantageously both for himself and for the state?

ALCIBIADES: True.

SOCRATES: And if he do the contrary, both he and the state will suffer?

ALCIBIADES: Yes.

SOCRATES: Well, and are you of the same mind, as before?

ALCIBIADES: I am.

SOCRATES: But were you not saying that you would call the many unwise and the few wise?

ALCIBIADES: I was.

SOCRATES: And have we not come back to our old assertion that the many fail to obtain the best because they trust to opinion which is devoid of intelligence?

ALCIBIADES: That is the case.

SOCRATES: It is good, then, for the many, if they particularly desire to do that which they know or suppose that they know, neither to know nor to suppose that they know, in cases where if they carry out their ideas in action they will be losers rather than gainers?

ALCIBIADES: What you say is very true.

SOCRATES: Do you not see that I was really speaking the truth when I affirmed that the possession of any other kind of knowledge was more likely to injure than to benefit the possessor, unless he had also the knowledge of the best?

ALCIBIADES: I do now, if I did not before, Socrates.

SOCRATES: The state or the soul, therefore, which wishes to have a right existence must hold firmly to this knowledge, just as the sick man clings to the physician, or the passenger depends for safety on the pilot. And if the soul does not set sail until she have obtained this she will be all the safer in the voyage through life. But when she rushes in pursuit of wealth or bodily strength or anything else, not having the knowledge of the best, so much the more is she likely to meet with misfortune. And he who has the love of learning (Or, reading polumatheian, 'abundant learning.'), and is skilful in many arts, and does not possess the knowledge of the best, but is under some other guidance, will make, as he deserves, a sorry voyage:—he will, I believe, hurry through the brief space of human life, pilotless in mid-ocean, and the words will apply to him in which the poet blamed his enemy:—

'...Full many a thing he knew; But knew them all badly.' (A fragment from the pseudo-Homeric poem, 'Margites.')

ALCIBIADES: How in the world, Socrates, do the words of the poet apply to him? They seem to me to have no bearing on the point whatever.

SOCRATES: Quite the contrary, my sweet friend: only the poet is talking in riddles after the fashion of his tribe. For all poetry has by nature an enigmatical character, and it is by no means everybody who can interpret it. And if, moreover, the spirit of poetry happen to seize on a man who is of a begrudging temper and does not care to manifest his wisdom but keeps it to himself as far as he can, it does indeed require an almost superhuman wisdom to discover what the poet would be at. You surely do not suppose that Homer, the wisest and most divine of poets, was unaware of the impossibility of knowing a thing badly: for it was no less a person than he who said of Margites that 'he knew many things, but knew them all badly.' The solution of the riddle is this, I imagine:—By 'badly' Homer meant 'bad' and 'knew' stands for 'to know.' Put the words together;—the metre will suffer, but the poet's meaning is clear;—'Margites knew all these things, but it was bad for him to know them.' And, obviously, if it was bad for him to know so many things, he must have been a good-for-nothing, unless the argument has played us false.

ALCIBIADES: But I do not think that it has, Socrates: at least, if the argument is fallacious, it would be difficult for me to find another which I could trust.

SOCRATES: And you are right in thinking so.

ALCIBIADES: Well, that is my opinion.

SOCRATES: But tell me, by Heaven:—you must see now the nature and greatness of the difficulty in which you, like others, have your part. For you change about in all directions, and never come to rest anywhere: what you once most strongly inclined to suppose, you put aside again and quite alter your mind. If the God to whose shrine you are going should appear at this moment, and ask before you made your prayer, 'Whether you would desire to have one of the things which we mentioned at first, or whether he should leave you to make your own request:'—what in either case, think you, would be the best way to take advantage of the opportunity?

ALCIBIADES: Indeed, Socrates, I could not answer you without consideration. It seems to me to be a wild thing (The Homeric word margos is said to be here employed in allusion to the quotation from the 'Margites' which Socrates has just made; but it is not used in the sense which it has in Homer.) to make such a request; a man must be very careful lest he pray for evil under the idea that he is asking for good, when shortly after he may have to recall his prayer, and, as you were saying, demand the opposite of what he at first requested.

SOCRATES: And was not the poet whose words I originally quoted wiser than we are, when he bade us (pray God) to defend us from evil even though we asked for it?

ALCIBIADES: I believe that you are right.

SOCRATES: The Lacedaemonians, too, whether from admiration of the poet or because they have discovered the idea for themselves, are wont to offer the prayer alike in public and private, that the Gods will give unto them the beautiful as well as the good:—no one is likely to hear them make any further petition. And yet up to the present time they have not been less fortunate than other men; or if they have sometimes met with misfortune, the fault has not been due to their prayer. For surely, as I conceive, the Gods have power either to grant our requests, or to send us the contrary of what we ask.

And now I will relate to you a story which I have heard from certain of our elders. It chanced that when the Athenians and Lacedaemonians were at war, our city lost every battle by land and sea and never gained a victory. The Athenians being annoyed and perplexed how to find a remedy for their troubles, decided to send and enquire at the shrine of Ammon. Their envoys were also to ask, 'Why the Gods always granted the victory to the Lacedaemonians?' 'We,' (they were to say,) 'offer them more and finer sacrifices than any other Hellenic state, and adorn their temples with gifts, as nobody else does; moreover, we make the most solemn and costly processions to them every year, and spend more money in their service than all the rest of the Hellenes put together. But the Lacedaemonians take no thought of such matters, and pay so little respect to the Gods that they have a habit of sacrificing blemished animals to them, and in various ways are less zealous than we are, although their wealth is quite equal to ours.' When they had thus spoken, and had made their request to know what remedy they could find against the evils which troubled them, the prophet made no direct answer,—clearly because he was not allowed by the God to do so;—but he summoned them to him and said: 'Thus saith Ammon to the Athenians: "The silent worship of the Lacedaemonians pleaseth me better than all the offerings of the other Hellenes."' Such were the words of the God, and nothing more. He seems to have meant by 'silent worship' the prayer of the Lacedaemonians, which is indeed widely different from the usual requests of the Hellenes. For they either bring to the altar bulls with gilded horns or make offerings to the Gods, and beg at random for what they need, good or bad. When, therefore, the Gods hear them using words of ill omen they reject these costly processions and sacrifices of theirs. And we ought, I think, to be very careful and consider well what we should say and what leave unsaid. Homer, too, will furnish us with similar stories. For he tells us how the Trojans in making their encampment,

'Offered up whole hecatombs to the immortals,'

and how the 'sweet savour' was borne 'to the heavens by the winds;

'But the blessed Gods were averse and received it not.

For exceedingly did they hate the holy Ilium,

Both Priam and the people of the spear-skilled king.'

So that it was in vain for them to sacrifice and offer gifts, seeing that they were hateful to the Gods, who are not, like vile usurers, to be gained over by bribes. And it is foolish for us to boast that we are superior to the Lacedaemonians by reason of our much worship. The idea is inconceivable that the Gods have regard, not to the justice and purity of our souls, but to costly processions and sacrifices, which men may celebrate year after year, although they have committed innumerable crimes against the Gods or against their fellow-men or the state. For the Gods, as Ammon and his prophet declare, are no receivers of gifts, and they scorn such unworthy service. Wherefore also it would seem that wisdom and justice are especially honoured both by the Gods and by men of sense; and they are the wisest and most just who know how to speak and act towards Gods and men. But I should like to hear what your opinion is about these matters.

ALCIBIADES: I agree, Socrates, with you and with the God, whom, indeed, it would be unbecoming for me to oppose.

SOCRATES: Do you not remember saying that you were in great perplexity, lest perchance you should ask for evil, supposing that you were asking for good?

ALCIBIADES: I do.

SOCRATES: You see, then, that there is a risk in your approaching the God in prayer, lest haply he should refuse your sacrifice when he hears the blasphemy which you utter, and make you partake of other evils as well. The wisest plan, therefore, seems to me that you should keep silence; for your 'highmindedness'—to use the mildest term which men apply to folly—will most likely prevent you from using the prayer of the Lacedaemonians. You had better wait until we find out how we should behave towards the Gods and towards men.

ALCIBIADES: And how long must I wait, Socrates, and who will be my teacher? I should be very glad to see the man.

SOCRATES: It is he who takes an especial interest in you. But first of all, I think, the darkness must be taken away in which your soul is now enveloped, just as Athene in Homer removes the mist from the eyes of Diomede that

'He may distinguish between God and mortal man.'

Afterwards the means may be given to you whereby you may distinguish between good and evil. At present, I fear, this is beyond your power.

ALCIBIADES: Only let my instructor take away the impediment, whether it pleases him to call it mist or anything else! I care not who he is; but I am resolved to disobey none of his commands, if I am likely to be the better for them.

SOCRATES: And surely he has a wondrous care for you.

ALCIBIADES: It seems to be altogether advisable to put off the sacrifice until he is found.

SOCRATES: You are right: that will be safer than running such a tremendous risk.

ALCIBIADES: But how shall we manage, Socrates?—At any rate I will set this crown of mine upon your head, as you have given me such excellent advice, and to the Gods we will offer crowns and perform the other customary rites when I see that day approaching: nor will it be long hence, if they so will.

SOCRATES: I accept your gift, and shall be ready and willing to receive whatever else you may proffer. Euripides makes Creon say in the play, when he beholds Teiresias with his crown and hears that he has gained it by his skill as the first-fruits of the spoil:—

'An auspicious omen I deem thy victor's wreath: For well thou knowest that wave and storm oppress us.'

And so I count your gift to be a token of good-fortune; for I am in no less stress than Creon, and would fain carry off the victory over your lovers.

APOLOGY

By Plato

APOLOGY

How you, O Athenians, have been affected by my accusers, I cannot tell; but I know that they almost made me forget who I was—so persuasively did they speak; and yet they have hardly uttered a word of truth. But of the many falsehoods told by them, there was one which quite amazed me;—I mean when they said that you should be upon your guard and not allow yourselves to be deceived by the force of my eloquence. To say this, when they were certain to be detected as soon as I opened my lips and proved myself to be anything but a great speaker, did indeed appear to me most shameless—unless by the force of eloquence they mean the force of truth; for is such is their meaning, I admit that I am eloquent. But in how different a way from theirs! Well, as I was saying, they have scarcely spoken the truth at all; but from me you shall hear the whole truth: not, however, delivered after their manner in a set oration duly ornamented with words and phrases. No, by heaven! but I shall use the words and arguments which occur to me at the moment; for I am confident in the justice of my cause (Or, I am certain that I am right in taking this course.): at my time of life I ought not to be appearing before you, O men of Athens, in the character of a juvenile orator—let no one expect it of me. And I must beg of you to grant me a favour:—If I defend myself in my accustomed manner, and you hear me using the words which I have been in the habit of using in the agora, at the tables of the money-changers, or anywhere else, I would ask you not to be surprised, and not to interrupt me on this account. For I am more than seventy years of age, and appearing now for the first time in a court of law, I am quite a stranger to the language of the place; and therefore I would have you regard me as if I were really a stranger, whom you would excuse if he spoke in his native tongue, and after the fashion of his country:—Am I making an unfair request of you? Never mind the manner, which may or may not be good; but think only of the truth of my words, and give heed to that: let the speaker speak truly and the judge decide justly.

And first, I have to reply to the older charges and to my first accusers, and then I will go on to the later ones. For of old I have had many accusers, who have accused me falsely to you during many years; and I am more afraid of them than of Anytus and his associates, who are dangerous, too, in their own way. But far more dangerous are the others, who began when you were children, and took possession of your minds with their falsehoods, telling of one Socrates, a wise man, who speculated about the heaven above, and searched into the earth beneath, and made the worse appear the better cause. The disseminators of this tale are the accusers whom I dread; for their hearers are apt to fancy that such enquirers do not believe in the existence of the gods. And they are many, and their charges against me are of ancient date, and they were made by them in the days when you were more impressible than you are now—in childhood, or it may have been in youth—and the cause when heard went by default, for there was none to answer. And hardest of all, I do not know and cannot tell the names of my accusers; unless in the chance case of a Comic poet. All who from envy and malice have persuaded you—some of them having first convinced themselves—all this class of men are most difficult to deal with; for I cannot have them up here, and cross-examine them, and therefore I must simply fight with shadows in my own defence, and argue when there is no one who answers. I will ask you then to assume with me, as I was saying, that my opponents are of two kinds; one recent, the other ancient: and I hope that you will see the propriety of my answering the latter first, for these accusations you heard long before the others, and much oftener.

Well, then, I must make my defence, and endeavour to clear away in a short time, a slander which has lasted a long time. May I succeed, if to succeed be for my good and yours, or likely to avail me in my cause! The task is not an easy one; I quite understand the nature of it. And so leaving the event with God, in obedience to the law I will now make my defence.

I will begin at the beginning, and ask what is the accusation which has given rise to the slander of me, and in fact has encouraged Meletus to proof this charge against me. Well, what do the slanderers say? They shall be my prosecutors, and I will sum up their words in an affidavit: 'Socrates is an evil-doer, and a curious person, who searches into things under the earth and in heaven, and he makes the worse appear the better cause; and he teaches the aforesaid doctrines to others.' Such is the nature of the accusation: it is just what you have yourselves seen in the comedy of Aristophanes (Aristoph., Clouds.), who has introduced a man whom he calls Socrates, going about and saying that he walks in air, and talking a deal of nonsense concerning matters of which I do not pretend to know either much or little—not that I mean to speak disparagingly of any one who is a student of natural philosophy. I should be very sorry if Meletus could bring so grave a charge against me. But the simple truth is, O Athenians, that I have nothing to do with physical speculations. Very many of those here present are witnesses to the truth of this, and to them I appeal. Speak then, you who have heard me, and tell your neighbours whether any of you have ever known me hold forth in few words or in many upon such matters...You hear their answer. And from what they say of this part of the charge you will be able to judge of the truth of the rest.

As little foundation is there for the report that I am a teacher, and take money; this accusation has no more truth in it than the other. Although, if a man were really able to instruct mankind, to receive money for giving instruction would, in my opinion, be an honour to him. There is Gorgias of Leontium, and Prodicus of Ceos, and Hippias of Elis, who go the round of the cities, and are able to persuade the young men to leave their own citizens by whom they might be taught for nothing, and come to them whom they not only pay, but are thankful if they may be allowed to pay them. There is at this time a Parian philosopher residing in Athens, of whom I have heard; and I came to hear of him in this way:—I came across a man who has spent a world of money on the Sophists, Callias, the son of Hipponicus, and knowing that he had sons, I asked him: 'Callias,' I said, 'if your two sons were foals or calves, there would be no difficulty in finding some one to put over them; we should hire a trainer of horses, or a farmer probably, who would improve and perfect them in their own proper virtue and excellence; but as they are human beings, whom are you thinking of placing over them? Is there any one who understands human and political virtue? You must have thought about the matter, for you have sons; is there any one?' 'There is,' he said. 'Who is he?' said I; 'and of what country? and what does he charge?' 'Evenus the Parian,' he replied; 'he is the man, and his charge is five minae.' Happy is Evenus, I said to myself, if he really has this wisdom, and teaches at such a moderate charge. Had I the same, I should have been very proud and conceited; but the truth is that I have no knowledge of the kind.

I dare say, Athenians, that some one among you will reply, 'Yes, Socrates, but what is the origin of these accusations which are brought against you; there must have been something strange which you have been doing? All these rumours and this talk about you would never have arisen if you had been like other men: tell us, then, what is the cause of them, for we should be sorry to judge hastily of you.' Now I regard this as a fair challenge, and I will endeavour to explain to you the reason why I am called wise and have such an evil fame. Please to attend then. And although some of you may think that I am joking, I declare that I will tell you the entire truth. Men of Athens, this reputation of mine has come of a certain sort of wisdom which I possess. If you ask me what kind of wisdom, I reply, wisdom such as may perhaps be attained by man, for to that extent I am inclined to believe that I am wise; whereas the persons of whom I was speaking have a superhuman wisdom which I may fail to describe, because I have it not myself; and he who says that I have, speaks falsely, and is taking away my character. And here, O men of Athens, I must beg you not to interrupt me, even if I seem to say something extravagant. For the word which I will speak is not mine. I will refer you to a witness who is worthy of credit; that witness shall be the God of Delphi—he will tell you about my wisdom, if I have any, and of what sort it is. You must have known Chaerephon; he was early a friend of mine, and also a friend of yours, for he shared in the recent exile of the people, and returned with you. Well, Chaerephon, as you know, was very impetuous in all his doings, and he went to Delphi and boldly asked the oracle to tell him whether—as I was saying, I must beg you not to interrupt—he asked the oracle to tell him whether anyone was wiser than I was, and the Pythian prophetess answered, that there was no man wiser. Chaerephon is dead himself; but his brother, who is in court, will confirm the truth of what I am saying.

Why do I mention this? Because I am going to explain to you why I have such an evil name. When I heard the answer, I said to myself, What can the god mean? and what is the interpretation of his riddle? for I know that I have no wisdom, small or great. What then can he mean when he says that I am the wisest of men? And yet he is a god, and cannot lie; that would be against his nature. After long consideration, I thought of a method of trying the question. I reflected that if I could only find a man wiser than myself, then I might go to the god with a refutation in my hand. I should say to him, 'Here is a man who is wiser than I am; but you said that I was the wisest.' Accordingly I went to one who had the reputation of wisdom, and observed him—his name I need not mention; he was a politician whom I selected for examination—and the result was as follows: When I began to talk with him, I could not help thinking that he was not really wise, although he was thought wise by many, and still wiser by himself; and thereupon I tried to explain to him that he thought himself wise, but was not really wise; and the consequence was that he hated me, and his enmity was shared by several who were present and heard me. So I left him, saying to myself, as I went away: Well, although I do not suppose that either of us knows anything really beautiful and good, I am better off than he is,—for he knows nothing, and thinks that he knows; I neither know nor think that I know. In this latter particular, then, I seem to have slightly the advantage of him. Then I went to another who had still higher pretensions to wisdom, and my conclusion was exactly the same. Whereupon I made another enemy of him, and of many others besides him.

Then I went to one man after another, being not unconscious of the enmity which I provoked, and I lamented and feared this: but necessity was laid upon me,—the word of God, I thought, ought to be considered first. And I said to myself, Go I must to all who appear to know, and find out the meaning of the oracle. And I swear to you, Athenians, by the dog I swear!—for I must tell you the truth—the result of my mission was just this: I found that the men most in repute were all but the most foolish; and that others less esteemed were really wiser and better. I will tell you the tale of my wanderings and of the 'Herculean' labours, as I may call them, which I endured only to find at last the oracle irrefutable. After the politicians, I went to the poets; tragic, dithyrambic, and all sorts. And there, I said to myself, you will be instantly detected; now you will find out that you are more ignorant than they are. Accordingly, I took them some of the most elaborate passages in their own writings, and asked what was the meaning of them—thinking that they would teach me something. Will you believe me? I am almost ashamed to confess the truth, but I must say that there is hardly a person present who would not have talked better about their poetry than they did themselves. Then I knew that not by wisdom do poets write poetry, but by a sort of genius and inspiration; they are like diviners or soothsayers who also say many fine things, but do not understand the meaning of them. The poets appeared to me to be much in the same case; and I further observed that upon the strength of their poetry they believed themselves to be the wisest of men in other things in which they were not wise. So I departed, conceiving myself to be superior to them for the same reason that I was superior to the politicians.

At last I went to the artisans. I was conscious that I knew nothing at all, as I may say, and I was sure that they knew many fine things; and here I was not mistaken, for they did know many things of which I was ignorant, and in this they certainly were wiser than I was. But I observed that even the good artisans fell into the same error as the poets;—because they were good workmen they thought that they also knew all sorts of high matters, and this defect in them overshadowed their wisdom; and therefore I asked myself on behalf of the oracle, whether I would like to be as I was, neither having their knowledge nor their ignorance, or like them in both; and I made answer to myself and to the oracle that I was better off as I was.

This inquisition has led to my having many enemies of the worst and most dangerous kind, and has given occasion also to many calumnies. And I am called wise, for my hearers always imagine that I myself possess the wisdom which I find wanting in others: but the truth is, O men of Athens, that God only is wise; and by his answer he intends to show that the wisdom of men is worth little or nothing; he is not speaking of Socrates, he is only using my name by way of illustration, as if he said, He, O men, is the wisest, who, like Socrates, knows that his wisdom is in truth worth nothing. And so I go about the world, obedient to the god, and search and make enquiry into the wisdom of any one, whether citizen or stranger, who appears to be wise; and if he is not wise, then in vindication of the oracle I show him that he is not wise; and my occupation quite absorbs me, and I have no time to give either to any public matter of interest or to any concern of my own, but I am in utter poverty by reason of my devotion to the god.

There is another thing:—young men of the richer classes, who have not much to do, come about me of their own accord; they like to hear the pretenders examined, and they often imitate me, and proceed to examine others; there are plenty of persons, as they quickly discover, who think that they know something, but really know little or nothing; and then those who are examined by them instead of being angry with themselves are angry with me: This confounded Socrates, they say; this villainous misleader of youth!—and then if somebody asks them, Why, what evil does he practise or teach? they do not know, and cannot tell; but in order that they may not appear to be at a loss, they repeat the ready-made charges which are used against all philosophers about teaching things up in the clouds and under the earth, and having no gods, and making the worse appear the better cause; for they do not like to confess that their pretence of knowledge has been detected—which is the truth; and as they are numerous and ambitious and energetic, and are drawn up in battle array and have persuasive tongues, they have filled your ears with their loud and inveterate calumnies. And this is the reason why my three accusers, Meletus and Anytus and Lycon, have set upon me; Meletus, who has a quarrel with me on behalf of the poets; Anytus, on behalf of the craftsmen and politicians; Lycon, on behalf of the rhetoricians: and as I said at the beginning, I cannot expect to get rid of such a mass of calumny all in a moment. And this, O men of Athens, is the truth and the whole truth; I have concealed nothing, I have dissembled nothing. And yet, I know that my plainness of speech makes them hate me, and what is their hatred but a proof that I am speaking the truth?—Hence has arisen the prejudice against me; and this is the reason of it, as you will find out either in this or in any future enquiry.

I have said enough in my defence against the first class of my accusers; I turn to the second class. They are headed by Meletus, that good man and true lover of his country, as he calls himself. Against these, too, I must try to make a defence:—Let their affidavit be read: it contains something of this kind: It says that Socrates is a doer of evil, who corrupts the youth; and who does not believe in the gods of the state, but has other new divinities of his own. Such is the charge; and now let us examine the particular counts. He says that I am a doer of evil, and corrupt the youth; but I say, O men of Athens, that Meletus is a doer of evil, in that he pretends to be in earnest when he is only in jest, and is so eager to bring men to trial from a pretended zeal and interest about matters in which he really never had the smallest interest. And the truth of this I will endeavour to prove to you.

Come hither, Meletus, and let me ask a question of you. You think a great deal about the improvement of youth?

Yes, I do.

Tell the judges, then, who is their improver; for you must know, as you have taken the pains to discover their corrupter, and are citing and accusing me before them. Speak, then, and tell the judges who their improver is.—Observe, Meletus, that you are silent, and have nothing to say. But is not this rather disgraceful, and a very considerable proof of what I was saying, that you have no interest in the matter? Speak up, friend, and tell us who their improver is.

The laws.

But that, my good sir, is not my meaning. I want to know who the person is, who, in the first place, knows the laws.

The judges, Socrates, who are present in court.

What, do you mean to say, Meletus, that they are able to instruct and improve youth?

Certainly they are.

What, all of them, or some only and not others?

All of them.

By the goddess Here, that is good news! There are plenty of improvers, then. And what do you say of the audience,—do they improve them?

Yes, they do.

And the senators?

Yes, the senators improve them.

But perhaps the members of the assembly corrupt them?—or do they too improve them?

They improve them.

Then every Athenian improves and elevates them; all with the exception of myself; and I alone am their corrupter? Is that what you affirm?

That is what I stoutly affirm.

I am very unfortunate if you are right. But suppose I ask you a question: How about horses? Does one man do them harm and all the world good? Is not the exact opposite the truth? One man is able to do them good, or at least not many;—the trainer of horses, that is to say, does them good, and others who have to do with them rather injure them? Is not that true, Meletus, of horses, or of any other animals? Most assuredly it is; whether you and Anytus say yes or no. Happy indeed would be the condition of youth if they had one corrupter only, and all the rest of the world were their improvers. But you, Meletus, have sufficiently shown that you never had a thought about the young: your carelessness is seen in your not caring about the very things which you bring against me.

And now, Meletus, I will ask you another question—by Zeus I will: Which is better, to live among bad citizens, or among good ones? Answer, friend, I say; the question is one which may be easily answered. Do not the good do their neighbours good, and the bad do them evil?

Certainly.

And is there anyone who would rather be injured than benefited by those who live with him? Answer, my good friend, the law requires you to answer—does any one like to be injured?

Certainly not.

And when you accuse me of corrupting and deteriorating the youth, do you allege that I corrupt them intentionally or unintentionally?

Intentionally, I say.

But you have just admitted that the good do their neighbours good, and the evil do them evil. Now, is that a truth which your superior wisdom has recognized thus early in life, and am I, at my age, in such darkness and ignorance as not to know that if a man with whom I have to live is corrupted by me, I am very likely to be harmed by him; and yet I corrupt him, and intentionally, too—so you say, although neither I nor any other human being is ever likely to be convinced by you. But either I do not corrupt them, or I corrupt them unintentionally; and on either view of the case you lie. If my offence is unintentional, the law has no cognizance of unintentional offences: you ought to have taken me privately, and warned and admonished me; for if I had been better advised, I should have left off doing what I only did unintentionally—no doubt I should; but you would have nothing to say to me and refused to teach me. And now you bring me up in this court, which is a place not of instruction, but of punishment.

It will be very clear to you, Athenians, as I was saying, that Meletus has no care at all, great or small, about the matter. But still I should like to know, Meletus, in what I am affirmed to corrupt the young. I suppose you mean, as I infer from your indictment, that I teach them not to acknowledge the gods which the state acknowledges, but some other new divinities or spiritual agencies in their stead. These are the lessons by which I corrupt the youth, as you say.

Yes, that I say emphatically.

Then, by the gods, Meletus, of whom we are speaking, tell me and the court, in somewhat plainer terms, what you mean! for I do not as yet understand whether you affirm that I teach other men to acknowledge some gods, and therefore that I do believe in gods, and am not an entire atheist—this you do not lay to my charge,—but only you say that they are not the same gods which the city recognizes—the charge is that they are different gods. Or, do you mean that I am an atheist simply, and a teacher of atheism?

I mean the latter—that you are a complete atheist.

What an extraordinary statement! Why do you think so, Meletus? Do you mean that I do not believe in the godhead of the sun or moon, like other men?

I assure you, judges, that he does not: for he says that the sun is stone, and the moon earth.

Friend Meletus, you think that you are accusing Anaxagoras: and you have but a bad opinion of the judges, if you fancy them illiterate to such a degree as not to know that these doctrines are found in the books of Anaxagoras the Clazomenian, which are full of them. And so, forsooth, the youth are said to be taught them by Socrates, when there are not unfrequently exhibitions of them at the theatre (Probably in allusion to Aristophanes who caricatured, and to Euripides who borrowed the notions of Anaxagoras, as well as to other dramatic poets.) (price of admission one drachma at the most); and they might pay their money, and laugh at Socrates if he pretends to father these extraordinary views. And so, Meletus, you really think that I do not believe in any god?

I swear by Zeus that you believe absolutely in none at all.

Nobody will believe you, Meletus, and I am pretty sure that you do not believe yourself. I cannot help thinking, men of Athens, that Meletus is reckless and impudent, and that he has written this indictment in a spirit of mere wantonness and youthful bravado. Has he not compounded a riddle, thinking to try me? He said to himself:—I shall see whether the wise Socrates will discover my facetious contradiction, or whether I shall be able to deceive him and the rest of them. For he certainly does appear to me to contradict himself in the indictment as much as if he said that Socrates is guilty of not believing in the gods, and yet of believing in them—but this is not like a person who is in earnest.

I should like you, O men of Athens, to join me in examining what I conceive to be his inconsistency; and do you, Meletus, answer. And I must remind the audience of my request that they would not make a disturbance if I speak in my accustomed manner:

Did ever man, Meletus, believe in the existence of human things, and not of human beings?...I wish, men of Athens, that he would answer, and not be always trying to get up an interruption. Did ever any man believe in horsemanship, and not in horses? or in flute-playing, and not in flute-players? No, my friend; I will answer to you and to the court, as you refuse to answer for yourself. There is no man who ever did. But now please to answer the next question: Can a man believe in spiritual and divine agencies, and not in spirits or demigods?

He cannot.

How lucky I am to have extracted that answer, by the assistance of the court! But then you swear in the indictment that I teach and believe in divine or spiritual agencies (new or old, no matter for that); at any rate, I believe in spiritual agencies,—so you say and swear in the affidavit; and yet if I believe in divine beings, how can I help believing in spirits or demigods;—must I not? To be sure I must; and therefore I may assume that your silence gives consent. Now what are spirits or demigods? Are they not either gods or the sons of gods?

Certainly they are.

But this is what I call the facetious riddle invented by you: the demigods or spirits are gods, and you say first that I do not believe in gods, and then again that I do believe in gods; that is, if I believe in demigods. For if the demigods are the illegitimate sons of gods, whether by the nymphs or by any other mothers, of whom they are said to be the sons—what human being will ever believe that there are no gods if they are the sons of gods? You might as well affirm the existence of mules, and deny that of horses and asses. Such nonsense, Meletus, could only have been intended by you to make trial of me. You have put this into the indictment because you had nothing real of which to accuse me. But no one who has a particle of understanding will ever be convinced by you that the same men can believe in divine and superhuman things, and yet not believe that there are gods and demigods and heroes.

I have said enough in answer to the charge of Meletus: any elaborate defence is unnecessary, but I know only too well how many are the enmities which I have incurred, and this is what will be my destruction if I am destroyed;—not Meletus, nor yet Anytus, but the envy and detraction of the world, which has been the death of many good men, and will probably be the death of many more; there is no danger of my being the last of them.

Some one will say: And are you not ashamed, Socrates, of a course of life which is likely to bring you to an untimely end? To him I may fairly answer: There you are mistaken: a man who is good for anything ought not to calculate the chance of living or dying; he ought only to consider whether in doing anything he is doing right or wrong—acting the part of a good man or of a bad. Whereas, upon your view, the heroes who fell at Troy were not good for much, and the son of Thetis above all, who altogether despised danger in comparison with disgrace; and when he was so eager to slay Hector, his goddess mother said to him, that if he avenged his companion

Patroclus, and slew Hector, he would die himself—'Fate,' she said, in these or the like words, 'waits for you next after Hector;' he, receiving this warning, utterly despised danger and death, and instead of fearing them, feared rather to live in dishonour, and not to avenge his friend. 'Let me die forthwith,' he replies, 'and be avenged of my enemy, rather than abide here by the beaked ships, a laughing-stock and a burden of the earth.' Had Achilles any thought of death and danger? For wherever a man's place is, whether the place which he has chosen or that in which he has been placed by a commander, there he ought to remain in the hour of danger; he should not think of death or of anything but of disgrace. And this, O men of Athens, is a true saying.

Strange, indeed, would be my conduct, O men of Athens, if I who, when I was ordered by the generals whom you chose to command me at Potidaea and Amphipolis and Delium, remained where they placed me, like any other man, facing death—if now, when, as I conceive and imagine, God orders me to fulfil the philosopher's mission of searching into myself and other men, I were to desert my post through fear of death, or any other fear; that would indeed be strange, and I might justly be arraigned in court for denying the existence of the gods, if I disobeyed the oracle because I was afraid of death, fancying that I was wise when I was not wise. For the fear of death is indeed the pretence of wisdom, and not real wisdom, being a pretence of knowing the unknown; and no one knows whether death, which men in their fear apprehend to be the greatest evil, may not be the greatest good. Is not this ignorance of a disgraceful sort, the ignorance which is the conceit that a man knows what he does not know? And in this respect only I believe myself to differ from men in general, and may perhaps claim to be wiser than they are:—that whereas I know but little of the world below, I do not suppose that I know: but I do know that injustice and disobedience to a better, whether God or man, is evil and dishonourable, and I will never fear or avoid a possible good rather than a certain evil. And therefore if you let me go now, and are not convinced by Anytus, who said that since I had been prosecuted I must be put to death; (or if not that I ought never to have been prosecuted at all); and that if I escape now, your sons will all be utterly ruined by listening to my words—if you say to me, Socrates, this time we will not mind Anytus, and you shall be let off, but upon one condition, that you are not to enquire and speculate in this way any more, and that if you are caught doing so again you shall die;—if this was the condition on which you let me go, I should reply: Men of Athens, I honour and love you; but I shall obey God rather than you, and while I have life and strength I shall never cease from the practice and teaching of philosophy, exhorting any one whom I meet and saying to him after my manner: You, my friend,—a citizen of the great and mighty and wise city of Athens,—are you not ashamed of heaping up the greatest amount of money and honour and reputation, and caring so little about wisdom and truth and the greatest improvement of the soul, which you never regard or heed at all? And if the person with whom I am arguing, says: Yes, but I do care; then I do not leave him or let him go at once; but I proceed to interrogate and examine and cross-examine him, and if I think that he has no virtue in him, but only says that he has, I reproach him with undervaluing the greater, and overvaluing the less. And I shall repeat the same words to every one whom I meet, young and old, citizen and alien, but especially to the citizens, inasmuch as they are my brethren. For know that this is the command of God; and I believe that no greater good has ever happened in the state than my service to the God. For I do nothing but go about persuading you all, old and young alike, not to take thought for your persons or your properties, but first and chiefly to care about the greatest improvement of the soul. I tell you that virtue is not given by money, but that from virtue comes money and every other good of man, public as well as private. This is my teaching, and if this is the doctrine which corrupts the youth, I am a mischievous person. But if any one says that this is not my teaching, he is speaking an untruth. Wherefore, O men of Athens, I say to you, do as Anytus bids or not as Anytus bids, and either acquit me or not; but whichever you do, understand that I shall never alter my ways, not even if I have to die many times.

Men of Athens, do not interrupt, but hear me; there was an understanding between us that you should hear me to the end: I have something more to say, at which you may be inclined to cry out; but I believe that to hear me will be good for you, and therefore I beg that you will not cry out. I would have you know, that if you kill such an one as I am, you will injure yourselves more than you will injure me. Nothing will injure me, not Meletus nor yet Anytus—they cannot, for a bad man is not permitted to injure a better than himself. I do not deny that Anytus may, perhaps, kill him, or drive him into exile, or deprive him of civil rights; and he may imagine, and others may imagine, that he is inflicting a great injury upon him: but there I do not agree. For the evil of doing as he is doing—the evil of unjustly taking away the life of another—is greater far.

And now, Athenians, I am not going to argue for my own sake, as you may think, but for yours, that you may not sin against the God by condemning me, who am his gift to you. For if you kill me you will not easily find a successor to me, who, if I may use such a ludicrous figure of speech, am a sort of gadfly, given to the state by God; and the state is a great and noble steed who is tardy in his motions owing to his very size, and requires to be stirred into life. I am that gadfly which God has attached to the state, and all day long and in all places am always fastening upon you, arousing and persuading and reproaching you. You will not easily find another like me, and therefore I would advise you to spare me. I dare say that you may feel out of temper (like a person who is suddenly awakened from sleep), and you think that you might easily strike me dead as Anytus advises, and then you would sleep on for the remainder of your lives, unless God in his care of you sent you another gadfly. When I say that I am given to you by God, the proof of my mission is this:—if I had been like other men, I should not have neglected all my own concerns or patiently seen the neglect of them during all these years, and have been doing yours, coming to you individually like a father or elder brother, exhorting you to regard virtue; such conduct, I say, would be unlike human nature. If I had gained anything, or if my exhortations had been paid, there would have been some sense in my doing so; but now, as you will perceive, not even the impudence of my accusers dares to say that I have ever exacted or sought pay of any one; of that they have no witness. And I have a sufficient witness to the truth of what I say—my poverty.

Some one may wonder why I go about in private giving advice and busying myself with the concerns of others, but do not venture to come forward in public and advise the state. I will tell you why. You have heard me speak at sundry times and in divers places of an oracle or sign which comes to me, and is the divinity which Meletus ridicules in the indictment. This sign, which is a kind of voice, first began to come to me when I was a child; it always forbids but never commands me to do anything which I am going to do. This is what deters me from being a politician. And rightly, as I think. For I am certain, O men of Athens, that if I had engaged in politics, I should have perished long ago, and done no good either to you or to myself. And do not be offended at my telling you the truth: for the truth is, that no man who goes to war with you or any other multitude, honestly striving against the many lawless and unrighteous deeds which are done in a state, will save his life; he who will fight for the right, if he would live even for a brief space, must have a private station and not a public one.

I can give you convincing evidence of what I say, not words only, but what you value far more—actions. Let me relate to you a passage of my own life which will prove to you that I should never have yielded to injustice from any fear of death, and that 'as I should have refused to yield' I must have died at once. I will tell you a tale of the courts, not very interesting perhaps, but nevertheless true. The only office of state which I ever held, O men of Athens, was that of senator: the tribe Antiochis, which is my tribe, had the presidency at the trial of the generals who had not taken up the bodies of the slain after the battle of Arginusae; and you proposed to try them in a body, contrary to law, as you all thought afterwards; but at the time I was the only one of the Prytanes who was opposed to the illegality, and I gave my vote against you; and when the orators threatened to impeach and arrest me, and you called and shouted, I made up my mind that I would run the risk, having law and justice with me, rather than take part in your injustice because I feared imprisonment and death. This happened in the days of the democracy. But when the oligarchy of the Thirty was in power, they sent for me and four others into the rotunda, and bade us bring Leon the Salaminian from Salamis, as they wanted to put him to death. This was a specimen of the sort of commands which they were always giving with the view of implicating as many as possible in their crimes; and then I showed, not in word only but in deed, that, if I may be allowed to use such an expression, I cared not a straw for death, and that my great and only care was lest I should do an unrighteous or unholy thing. For the strong arm of that oppressive power did not frighten me into doing wrong; and when we came out of the rotunda the other four went to Salamis and fetched Leon, but I went quietly home. For which I might have lost my life, had not the power of the Thirty shortly afterwards come to an end. And many will witness to my words.

Now do you really imagine that I could have survived all these years, if I had led a public life, supposing that like a good man I had always maintained the right and had made justice, as I ought, the first thing? No indeed, men of Athens, neither I nor any other man. But I have been always the same in all my actions, public as well as private, and never have I yielded any base compliance to those who are slanderously termed my disciples, or to any other. Not that I have any regular disciples. But if any one likes to come and hear me while I am pursuing my mission, whether he be young or old, he is not excluded. Nor do I converse only with those who pay; but any one, whether he be rich or poor, may ask and answer me and listen to my words; and whether he turns out to be a bad man or a good one, neither result can be justly imputed to me; for I never taught or professed to teach him anything. And if any one says that he has ever learned or heard anything from me in private which all the world has not heard, let me tell you that he is lying.

But I shall be asked, Why do people delight in continually conversing with you? I have told you already, Athenians, the whole truth about this matter: they like to hear the cross-examination of the pretenders to wisdom; there is amusement in it. Now this duty of cross-examining other men has been imposed upon me by God; and has been signified to me by oracles, visions, and in every way in which the will of divine power was ever intimated to any one. This is true, O Athenians, or, if not true, would be soon refuted. If I am or have been corrupting the youth, those of them who are now grown up and have become sensible that I gave them bad advice in the days of their youth should come forward as accusers, and take their revenge; or if they do not like to come themselves, some of their relatives, fathers, brothers, or other kinsmen, should say what evil their families have suffered at my hands. Now is their time. Many of them I see in the court. There is Crito, who is of the same age and of the same deme with myself, and there is Critobulus his son, whom I also see. Then again there is Lysanias of Sphettus, who is the father of Aeschines—he is present; and also there is Antiphon of Cephisus, who is the father of Epigenes; and there are the brothers of several who have associated with me. There is Nicostratus the son of Theosdotides, and the brother of Theodotus (now Theodotus himself is dead, and therefore he, at any rate, will not seek to stop him); and there is Paralus the son of Demodocus, who had a brother Theages; and Adeimantus the son of Ariston, whose brother Plato is present; and Aeantodorus, who is the brother of Apollodorus, whom I also see. I might mention a great many others, some of whom Meletus should have produced as witnesses in the course of his speech; and let him still produce them, if he has forgotten—I will make way for him. And let him say, if he has any testimony of the sort which he can produce. Nay, Athenians, the very opposite is the truth. For all these are ready to witness on behalf of the corrupter, of the injurer of their kindred, as Meletus and Anytus call me; not the corrupted youth only—there might have been a motive for that—but their uncorrupted elder relatives. Why should they too support me with their testimony? Why, indeed, except for the sake of truth and justice, and because they know that I am speaking the truth, and that Meletus is a liar.

Well, Athenians, this and the like of this is all the defence which I have to offer. Yet a word more. Perhaps there may be some one who is offended at me, when he calls to mind how he himself on a similar, or even a less serious occasion, prayed and entreated the judges with many tears, and how he produced his children in court, which was a moving spectacle, together with a host of relations and friends; whereas I, who am probably in danger of my life, will do none of these things. The contrast may occur to his mind, and he may be set against me, and vote in anger because he is displeased at me on this account. Now if there be such a person among you,—mind, I do not say that there is,—to him I may fairly reply: My friend, I am a man, and like other men, a creature of flesh and blood, and not 'of wood or stone,' as Homer says; and I have a family, yes, and sons, O Athenians, three in number, one almost a man, and two others who are still young; and yet I will not bring any of them hither in order to petition you for an acquittal. And why not? Not from any self-assertion or want of respect for you. Whether I am or am not afraid of death is another question, of which I will not now speak. But, having regard to public opinion, I feel that such conduct would be discreditable to myself, and to you, and to the whole state. One who has reached my years, and who has a name for wisdom, ought not to demean himself. Whether this opinion of me be deserved or not, at any rate the world has decided that Socrates is in some way superior to other men. And if those among you who are said to be superior in wisdom and courage, and any other virtue, demean themselves in this way, how shameful is their conduct! I have seen men of reputation, when they have been condemned, behaving in the strangest manner: they seemed to fancy that they were going to suffer something dreadful if they died, and that they could be immortal if you only allowed them to live; and I think that such are a dishonour to the state, and that any stranger coming in would have said of them that the most eminent men of Athens, to whom the Athenians themselves give honour and command, are no better than women. And I say that these things ought not to be done by those of us who have a reputation; and if they are done, you ought not to permit them; you ought rather to show that you are far more disposed to condemn the man who gets up a doleful scene and makes the city ridiculous, than him who holds his peace.

But, setting aside the question of public opinion, there seems to be something wrong in asking a favour of a judge, and thus procuring an acquittal, instead of informing and convincing him. For his duty is, not to make a present of justice, but to give judgment; and he has sworn that he will judge according to the laws, and not according to his own good pleasure; and we ought not to encourage you, nor should you allow yourselves to be encouraged, in this habit of perjury—there can be no piety in that. Do not then require me to do what I consider dishonourable and impious and wrong, especially now, when I am being tried for impiety on the indictment of Meletus. For if, O men of Athens, by force of persuasion and entreaty I could overpower your oaths, then I should be teaching you to believe that there are no gods, and in defending should simply convict myself of the charge of not believing in them. But that is not so—far otherwise. For I do believe that there are gods, and in a sense higher than that in which any of my accusers believe in them. And to you and to God I commit my cause, to be determined by you as is best for you and me.

There are many reasons why I am not grieved, O men of Athens, at the vote of condemnation. I expected it, and am only surprised that the votes are so nearly equal; for I had thought that the majority against me would have been far larger; but now, had thirty votes gone over to the other side, I should have been acquitted. And I may say, I think, that I have escaped Meletus. I may say more; for without the assistance of Anytus and Lycon, any one may see that he would not have had a fifth part of the votes, as the law requires, in which case he would have incurred a fine of a thousand drachmae.

And so he proposes death as the penalty. And what shall I propose on my part, O men of Athens? Clearly that which is my due. And what is my due? What return shall be made to the man who has never had the wit to be idle during his whole life; but has been careless of what the many care for—wealth, and family interests, and military offices, and speaking in the assembly, and magistracies, and plots, and parties. Reflecting that I was really too honest a man to be a politician and live, I did not go where I could do no good to you or to myself; but where I could do the greatest good privately to every one of you, thither I went, and sought to persuade every man among you that he must look to himself, and seek virtue and wisdom before he looks to his private interests, and look to the state before he looks to the interests of the state; and that this should be the order which he observes in all his actions. What shall be done to such an one? Doubtless some good thing, O men of Athens, if he has his reward; and the good should be of a kind suitable to him. What would be a reward suitable to a poor man who is your benefactor, and who desires leisure that he may instruct you? There can be no reward so fitting as maintenance in the Prytaneum, O men of Athens, a reward which he deserves far more than the citizen who has won the prize at Olympia in the horse or chariot race, whether the chariots were drawn by two horses or by many. For I am in want, and he has enough; and he only gives you the appearance of happiness, and I give you the reality. And if I am to estimate the penalty fairly, I should say that maintenance in the Prytaneum is the just return.

Perhaps you think that I am braving you in what I am saying now, as in what I said before about the tears and prayers. But this is not so. I speak rather because I am convinced that I never intentionally wronged any one, although I cannot convince you—the time has been too short; if there were a law at Athens, as there is in other cities, that a capital cause should not be decided in one day, then I believe that I should have convinced you. But I cannot in a moment refute great slanders; and, as I am convinced that I never wronged another, I will assuredly not wrong myself. I will not say of myself that I deserve any evil, or propose any penalty. Why should I? because I am afraid of the penalty of death which Meletus proposes? When I do not know whether death is a good or an evil, why should I propose a penalty which would certainly be an evil? Shall I say imprisonment? And why should I live in prison, and be the slave of the magistrates of the year—of the Eleven? Or shall the penalty be a fine, and imprisonment until the fine is paid? There is the same objection. I should have to lie in prison, for money I have none, and cannot pay. And if I say exile (and this may possibly be the penalty which you will affix), I must indeed be blinded by the love of life, if I am so irrational as to expect that when you, who are my own citizens, cannot endure my discourses and words, and have found them so grievous and odious that you will have no more of them, others are likely to endure me. No indeed, men of Athens, that is not very likely. And what a life should I lead, at my age, wandering from city to city, ever changing my place of exile, and always being driven out! For I am quite sure that wherever I go, there, as here, the young men will flock to me; and if I drive them away, their elders will drive me out at their request; and if I let them come, their fathers and friends will drive me out for their sakes.

Some one will say: Yes, Socrates, but cannot you hold your tongue, and then you may go into a foreign city, and no one will interfere with you? Now I have great difficulty in making you understand my answer to this. For if I tell you that to do as you say would be a disobedience to the God, and therefore that I cannot hold my tongue, you will not believe that I am serious; and if I say again that daily to discourse about virtue, and of those other things about which you hear me examining myself and others, is the greatest good of man, and that the unexamined life is not worth living, you are still less likely to believe me. Yet I say what is true, although a thing of which it is hard for me to persuade you. Also, I have never been accustomed to think that I deserve to suffer any harm. Had I money I might have estimated the offence at what I was able to pay, and not have been much the worse. But I have none, and therefore I must ask you to proportion the fine to my means. Well, perhaps I could afford a mina, and therefore I propose that penalty: Plato, Crito, Critobulus, and Apollodorus, my friends here, bid me say thirty minae, and they will be the sureties. Let thirty minae be the penalty; for which sum they will be ample security to you.

Not much time will be gained, O Athenians, in return for the evil name which you will get from the detractors of the city, who will say that you killed Socrates, a wise man; for they will call me wise, even although I am not wise, when they want to reproach you. If you had waited a little while, your desire would have been fulfilled in the course of nature. For I am far advanced in years, as you may perceive, and not far from death. I am speaking now not to all of you, but only to those who have condemned me to death. And I have another thing to say to them: you think that I was convicted because I had no words of the sort which would have procured my acquittal—I mean, if I had thought fit to leave nothing undone or unsaid. Not so; the deficiency which led to my conviction was not of words—certainly not. But I had not the boldness or impudence or inclination to address you as you would have liked me to do, weeping and wailing and lamenting, and saying and doing many things which you have been accustomed to hear from others, and which, as I maintain, are unworthy of me. I thought at the time that I ought not to do anything common or mean when in danger: nor do I now repent of the style of my defence; I would rather die having spoken after my manner, than speak in your manner and live. For neither in war nor yet at law ought I or any man to use every way of escaping death. Often in battle there can be no doubt that if a man will throw away his arms, and fall on his knees before his pursuers, he may escape death; and in other dangers there are other ways of escaping death, if a man is willing to say and do anything. The difficulty, my friends, is not to avoid death, but to avoid unrighteousness; for that runs faster than death. I am old and move slowly, and the slower runner has overtaken me, and my accusers are keen and quick, and the faster runner, who is unrighteousness, has overtaken them. And now I depart hence condemned by you to suffer the penalty of death,—they too go their ways condemned by the truth to suffer the penalty of villainy and wrong; and I must abide by my award—let them abide by theirs. I suppose that these things may be regarded as fated,—and I think that they are well.

And now, O men who have condemned me, I would fain prophesy to you; for I am about to die, and in the hour of death men are gifted with prophetic power. And I prophesy to you who are my murderers, that immediately after my departure punishment far heavier than you have inflicted on me will surely await you. Me you have killed because you wanted to escape the accuser, and not to give an account of your lives. But that will not be as you suppose: far otherwise. For I say that there will be more accusers of you than there are now; accusers whom hitherto I have restrained: and as they are younger they will be more inconsiderate with you, and you will be more offended at them. If you think that by killing men you can prevent some one from censuring your evil lives, you are mistaken; that is not a way of escape which is either possible or honourable; the easiest and the noblest way is not to be disabling others, but to be improving yourselves. This is the prophecy which I utter before my departure to the judges who have condemned me.

Friends, who would have acquitted me, I would like also to talk with you about the thing which has come to pass, while the magistrates are busy, and before I go to the place at which I must die. Stay then a little, for we may as well talk with one another while there is time. You are my friends, and I should like to show you the meaning of this event which has happened to me. O my judges—for you I may truly call judges—I should like to tell you of a wonderful circumstance. Hitherto the divine faculty of which the internal oracle is the source has constantly been in the habit of opposing me even about trifles, if I was going to make a slip or error in any matter; and now as you see there has come upon me that which may be thought, and is generally believed to be, the last and worst evil. But the oracle made no sign of opposition, either when I was leaving my house in the morning, or when I was on my way to the court, or while I was speaking, at anything which I was going to say; and yet I have often been stopped in the middle of a speech, but now in nothing I either said or did touching the matter in hand has the oracle opposed me. What do I take to be the explanation of this silence? I will tell you. It is an intimation that what has happened to me is a good, and that those of us who think that death is an evil are in error. For the customary sign would surely have opposed me had I been going to evil and not to good.

Let us reflect in another way, and we shall see that there is great reason to hope that death is a good; for one of two things—either death is a state of nothingness and utter unconsciousness, or, as men say, there is a change and migration of the soul from this world to another. Now if you suppose that there is no consciousness, but a sleep like the sleep of him who is undisturbed even by dreams, death will be an unspeakable gain. For if a person were to select the night in which his sleep was undisturbed even by dreams, and were to compare with this the other days and nights of his life, and then were to tell us how many days and nights he had passed in the course of his life better and more pleasantly than this one, I think that any man, I will not say a private man, but even the great king will not find many such days or nights, when compared with the others. Now if death be of such a nature, I say that to die is gain; for eternity is then only a single night. But if death is the journey to another place, and there, as men say, all the dead abide, what good, O my friends and judges, can be greater than this? If indeed when the pilgrim arrives in the world below, he is delivered from the professors of justice in this world, and finds the true judges who are said to give judgment there, Minos and Rhadamanthus and Aeacus and Triptolemus, and other sons of God who were righteous in their own life, that pilgrimage will be worth making. What would not a man give if he might converse with Orpheus and Musaeus and Hesiod and Homer? Nay, if this be true, let me die again and again. I myself, too, shall have a wonderful interest in there meeting and conversing with Palamedes, and Ajax the son of Telamon, and any other ancient hero who has suffered death through an unjust judgment; and there will be no small pleasure, as I think, in comparing my own sufferings with theirs. Above all, I shall then be able to continue my search into true and false knowledge; as in this world, so also in the next; and I shall find out who is wise, and who pretends to be wise, and is not. What would not a man give, O judges, to be able to examine the leader of the great Trojan expedition; or Odysseus or Sisyphus, or numberless others, men and women too! What infinite delight would there be in conversing with them and asking them questions! In another world they do not put a man to death for asking questions: assuredly not. For besides being happier than we are, they will be immortal, if what is said is true.

Wherefore, O judges, be of good cheer about death, and know of a certainty, that no evil can happen to a good man, either in life or after death. He and his are not neglected by the gods; nor has my own approaching end happened by mere chance. But I see clearly that the time had arrived when it was better for me to die and be released from trouble; wherefore the oracle gave no sign. For which reason, also, I am not angry with my condemners, or with my accusers; they have done me no harm, although they did not mean to do me any good; and for this I may gently blame them.

Still I have a favour to ask of them. When my sons are grown up, I would ask you, O my friends, to punish them; and I would have you trouble them, as I have troubled you, if they seem to care about riches, or anything, more than about virtue; or if they pretend to be something when they are really nothing,—then reprove them, as I have reproved you, for not caring about that for which they ought to care, and thinking that they are something when they are really nothing. And if you do this, both I and my sons will have received justice at your hands.

The hour of departure has arrived, and we go our ways—I to die, and you to live. Which is better God only knows.

CHARMIDES

By Plato

CHARMIDES,

OR TEMPERANCE

PERSONS OF THE DIALOGUE: Socrates, who is the narrator, Charmides, Chaerephon, Critias.

SCENE: The Palaestra of Taureas, which is near the Porch of the King Archon.

Yesterday evening I returned from the army at Potidaea, and having been a good while away, I thought that I should like to go and look at my old haunts. So I went into the palaestra of Taureas, which is over against the temple adjoining the porch of the King Archon, and there I found a number of persons, most of whom I knew, but not all. My visit was unexpected, and no sooner did they see me entering than they saluted me from afar on all sides; and Chaerephon, who is a kind of madman, started up and ran to me, seizing my hand, and saying, How did you escape, Socrates?—(I should explain that an engagement had taken place at Potidaea not long before we came away, of which the news had only just reached Athens.)

You see, I replied, that here I am.

There was a report, he said, that the engagement was very severe, and that many of our acquaintance had fallen.

That, I replied, was not far from the truth.

I suppose, he said, that you were present.

I was.

Then sit down, and tell us the whole story, which as yet we have only heard imperfectly.

I took the place which he assigned to me, by the side of Critias the son of Callaeschrus, and when I had saluted him and the rest of the company, I told them the news from the army, and answered their several enquiries.

Then, when there had been enough of this, I, in my turn, began to make enquiries about matters at home—about the present state of philosophy, and about the youth. I asked whether any of them were remarkable for wisdom or beauty, or both. Critias, glancing at the door, invited my attention to some youths who were coming in, and talking noisily to one another, followed by a crowd. Of the beauties, Socrates, he said, I fancy that you will soon be able to form a judgment. For those who are just entering are the advanced guard of the great beauty, as he is thought to be, of the day, and he is likely to be not far off himself.

Who is he, I said; and who is his father?

Charmides, he replied, is his name; he is my cousin, and the son of my uncle Glaucon: I rather think that you know him too, although he was not grown up at the time of your departure.

Certainly, I know him, I said, for he was remarkable even then when he was still a child, and I should imagine that by this time he must be almost a young man.

You will see, he said, in a moment what progress he has made and what he is like. He had scarcely said the word, when Charmides entered.

Now you know, my friend, that I cannot measure anything, and of the beautiful, I am simply such a measure as a white line is of chalk; for almost all young persons appear to be beautiful in my eyes. But at that moment, when I saw him coming in, I confess that I was quite astonished at his beauty and stature; all the world seemed to be enamoured of him; amazement and confusion reigned when he entered; and a troop of lovers followed him. That grown-up men like ourselves should have been affected in this way was not surprising, but I observed that there was the same feeling among the boys; all of them, down to the very least child, turned and looked at him, as if he had been a statue.

Chaerephon called me and said: What do you think of him, Socrates? Has he not a beautiful face?

Most beautiful, I said.

But you would think nothing of his face, he replied, if you could see his naked form: he is absolutely perfect.

And to this they all agreed.

By Heracles, I said, there never was such a paragon, if he has only one other slight addition.

What is that? said Critias.

If he has a noble soul; and being of your house, Critias, he may be expected to have this.

He is as fair and good within, as he is without, replied Critias.

Then, before we see his body, should we not ask him to show us his soul, naked and undisguised? he is just of an age at which he will like to talk.

That he will, said Critias, and I can tell you that he is a philosopher already, and also a considerable poet, not in his own opinion only, but in that of others.

That, my dear Critias, I replied, is a distinction which has long been in your family, and is inherited by you from Solon. But why do you not call him, and show him to us? for even if he were younger than he is, there could be no impropriety in his talking to us in the presence of you, who are his guardian and cousin.

Very well, he said; then I will call him; and turning to the attendant, he said, Call Charmides, and tell him that I want him to come and see a physician about the illness of which he spoke to me the day before yesterday. Then again addressing me, he added: He has been complaining lately of having a headache when he rises in the morning: now why should you not make him believe that you know a cure for the headache?

Why not, I said; but will he come?

He will be sure to come, he replied.

He came as he was bidden, and sat down between Critias and me. Great amusement was occasioned by every one pushing with might and main at his neighbour in order to make a place for him next to themselves, until at the two ends of the row one had to get up and the other was rolled over sideways. Now I, my friend, was beginning to feel awkward; my former bold belief in my powers of conversing with him had vanished. And when Critias told him that I was the person who had the cure, he looked at me in such an indescribable manner, and was just going to ask a question. And at that moment all the people in the palaestra crowded about us, and, O rare! I caught a sight of the inwards of his garment, and took the flame. Then I could no longer contain myself. I thought how well Cydias understood the nature of love, when, in speaking of a fair youth, he warns some one 'not to bring the fawn in the sight of the lion to be devoured by him,' for I felt that I had been overcome by a sort of wild-beast appetite. But I controlled myself, and when he asked me if I knew the cure of the headache, I answered, but with an effort, that I did know.

And what is it? he said.

I replied that it was a kind of leaf, which required to be accompanied by a charm, and if a person would repeat the charm at the same time that he used the cure, he would be made whole; but that without the charm the leaf would be of no avail.

Then I will write out the charm from your dictation, he said.

With my consent? I said, or without my consent?

With your consent, Socrates, he said, laughing.

Very good, I said; and are you quite sure that you know my name?

I ought to know you, he replied, for there is a great deal said about you among my companions; and I remember when I was a child seeing you in company with my cousin Critias.

I am glad to find that you remember me, I said; for I shall now be more at home with you and shall be better able to explain the nature of the charm, about which I felt a difficulty before. For the charm will do more, Charmides, than only cure the headache. I dare say that you have heard eminent physicians say to a patient who comes to them with bad eyes, that they cannot cure his eyes by themselves, but that if his eyes are to be cured, his head must be treated; and then again they say that to think of curing the head alone, and not the rest of the body also, is the height of folly. And arguing in this way they apply their methods to the whole body, and try to treat and heal the whole and the part together. Did you ever observe that this is what they say?

Yes, he said.

And they are right, and you would agree with them?

Yes, he said, certainly I should.

His approving answers reassured me, and I began by degrees to regain confidence, and the vital heat returned. Such, Charmides, I said, is the nature of the charm, which I learned when serving with the army from one of the physicians of the Thracian king Zamolxis, who are said to be so skilful that they can even give immortality. This Thracian told me that in these notions of theirs, which I was just now mentioning, the Greek physicians are quite right as far as they go; but Zamolxis, he added, our king, who is also a god, says further, 'that as you ought not to attempt to cure the eyes without the head, or the head without the body, so neither ought you to attempt to cure the body without the soul; and this,' he said, 'is the reason why the cure of many diseases is unknown to the physicians of Hellas, because they are ignorant of the whole, which ought to be studied also; for the part can never be well unless the whole is well.' For all good and evil, whether in the body or in human nature, originates, as he declared, in the soul, and overflows from thence, as if from the head into the eyes. And therefore if the head and body are to be well, you must begin by curing the soul; that is the first thing. And the cure, my dear youth, has to be effected by the use of certain charms, and these charms are fair words; and by them temperance is implanted in the soul, and where temperance is, there health is speedily imparted, not only to the head, but to the whole body. And he who taught me the cure and the charm at the same time added a special direction: 'Let no one,' he said, 'persuade you to cure the head, until he has first given you his soul to be cured by the charm. For this,' he said, 'is the great error of our day in the treatment of the human body, that physicians separate the soul from the body.' And he added with emphasis, at the same time making me swear to his words, 'Let no one, however rich, or noble, or fair, persuade you to give him the cure, without the charm.' Now I have sworn, and I must keep my oath, and therefore if you will allow me to apply the Thracian charm first to your soul, as the stranger directed, I will afterwards proceed to apply the cure to your head. But if not, I do not know what I am to do with you, my dear Charmides.

Critias, when he heard this, said: The headache will be an unexpected gain to my young relation, if the pain in his head compels him to improve his mind: and I can tell you, Socrates, that Charmides is not only pre-eminent in beauty among his equals, but also in that quality which is given by the charm; and this, as you say, is temperance?

Yes, I said.

Then let me tell you that he is the most temperate of human beings, and for his age inferior to none in any quality.

Yes, I said, Charmides; and indeed I think that you ought to excel others in all good qualities; for if I am not mistaken there is no one present who could easily point out two Athenian houses, whose union would be likely to produce a better or nobler scion than the two from which you are sprung. There is your father's house, which is descended from Critias the son of Dropidas, whose family has been commemorated in the panegyrical verses of Anacreon, Solon, and many other poets, as famous for beauty and virtue and all other high fortune: and your mother's house is equally distinguished; for your maternal uncle, Pyrilampes, is reputed never to have found his equal, in Persia at the court of the great king, or on the continent of Asia, in all the places to which he went as ambassador, for stature and beauty; that whole family is not a whit inferior to the other. Having such ancestors you ought to be first in all things, and, sweet son of Glaucon, your outward form is no dishonour to any of them. If to beauty you add temperance, and if in other respects you are what Critias declares you to be, then, dear Charmides, blessed art thou, in being the son of thy mother. And here lies the point; for if, as he declares, you have this gift of temperance already, and are temperate enough, in that case you have no need of any charms, whether of Zamolxis or of Abaris the Hyperborean, and I may as well let you have the cure of the head at once; but if you have not yet acquired this quality, I must use the charm before I give you the medicine. Please, therefore, to inform me whether you admit the truth of what Critias has been saying;—have you or have you not this quality of temperance?

Charmides blushed, and the blush heightened his beauty, for modesty is becoming in youth; he then said very ingenuously, that he really could not at once answer, either yes, or no, to the question which I had asked: For, said he, if I affirm that I am not temperate, that would be a strange thing for me to say of myself, and also I should give the lie to Critias, and many others who think as he tells you, that I am temperate: but, on the other hand, if I say that I am, I shall have to praise myself, which would be ill manners; and therefore I do not know how to answer you.

I said to him: That is a natural reply, Charmides, and I think that you and I ought together to enquire whether you have this quality about which I am asking or not; and then you will not be compelled to say what you do not like; neither shall I be a rash practitioner of medicine: therefore, if you please, I will share the enquiry with you, but I will not press you if you would rather not.

There is nothing which I should like better, he said; and as far as I am concerned you may proceed in the way which you think best.

I think, I said, that I had better begin by asking you a question; for if temperance abides in you, you must have an opinion about her; she must give some intimation of her nature and qualities, which may enable you to form a notion of her. Is not that true?

Yes, he said, that I think is true.

You know your native language, I said, and therefore you must be able to tell what you feel about this.

Certainly, he said.

In order, then, that I may form a conjecture whether you have temperance abiding in you or not, tell me, I said, what, in your opinion, is Temperance?

At first he hesitated, and was very unwilling to answer: then he said that he thought temperance was doing things orderly and quietly, such things for example as walking in the streets, and talking, or anything else of that nature. In a word, he said, I should answer that, in my opinion, temperance is quietness.

Are you right, Charmides? I said. No doubt some would affirm that the quiet are the temperate; but let us see whether these words have any meaning; and first tell me whether you would not acknowledge temperance to be of the class of the noble and good?

Yes.

But which is best when you are at the writing-master's, to write the same letters quickly or quietly?

Quickly.

And to read quickly or slowly?

Quickly again.

And in playing the lyre, or wrestling, quickness or sharpness are far better than quietness and slowness?

Yes.

And the same holds in boxing and in the pancratium?

Certainly.

And in leaping and running and in bodily exercises generally, quickness and agility are good; slowness, and inactivity, and quietness, are bad?

That is evident.

Then, I said, in all bodily actions, not quietness, but the greatest agility and quickness, is noblest and best?

Yes, certainly.

And is temperance a good?

Yes.

Then, in reference to the body, not quietness, but quickness will be the higher degree of temperance, if temperance is a good?

True, he said.

And which, I said, is better—facility in learning, or difficulty in learning?

Facility.

Yes, I said; and facility in learning is learning quickly, and difficulty in learning is learning quietly and slowly?

True.

And is it not better to teach another quickly and energetically, rather than quietly and slowly?

Yes.

And which is better, to call to mind, and to remember, quickly and readily, or quietly and slowly?

The former.

And is not shrewdness a quickness or cleverness of the soul, and not a quietness?

True.

And is it not best to understand what is said, whether at the writing-master's or the music-master's, or anywhere else, not as quietly as possible, but as quickly as possible?

Yes.

And in the searchings or deliberations of the soul, not the quietest, as I imagine, and he who with difficulty deliberates and discovers, is thought worthy of praise, but he who does so most easily and quickly?

Quite true, he said.

And in all that concerns either body or soul, swiftness and activity are clearly better than slowness and quietness?

Clearly they are.

Then temperance is not quietness, nor is the temperate life quiet,—certainly not upon this view; for the life which is temperate is supposed to be the good. And of two things, one is true,—either never, or very seldom, do the quiet actions in life appear to be better than the quick and energetic ones; or supposing that of the nobler actions, there are as many quiet, as quick and vehement: still, even if we grant this, temperance will not be acting quietly any more than acting quickly and energetically, either in walking or talking or in anything else; nor will the quiet life be more temperate than the unquiet, seeing that temperance is admitted by us to be a good and noble thing, and the quick have been shown to be as good as the quiet.

I think, he said, Socrates, that you are right.

Then once more, Charmides, I said, fix your attention, and look within; consider the effect which temperance has upon yourself, and the nature of that which has the effect. Think over all this, and, like a brave youth, tell me—What is temperance?

After a moment's pause, in which he made a real manly effort to think, he said: My opinion is, Socrates, that temperance makes a man ashamed or modest, and that temperance is the same as modesty.

Very good, I said; and did you not admit, just now, that temperance is noble?

Yes, certainly, he said.

And the temperate are also good?

Yes.

And can that be good which does not make men good?

Certainly not.

And you would infer that temperance is not only noble, but also good?

That is my opinion.

Well, I said; but surely you would agree with Homer when he says,

'Modesty is not good for a needy man'?

Yes, he said; I agree.

Then I suppose that modesty is and is not good?

Clearly.

But temperance, whose presence makes men only good, and not bad, is always good?

That appears to me to be as you say.

And the inference is that temperance cannot be modesty—if temperance is a good, and if modesty is as much an evil as a good?

All that, Socrates, appears to me to be true; but I should like to know what you think about another definition of temperance, which I just now remember to have heard from some one, who said, 'That temperance is doing our own business.' Was he right who affirmed that?

You monster! I said; this is what Critias, or some philosopher has told you.

Some one else, then, said Critias; for certainly I have not.

But what matter, said Charmides, from whom I heard this?

No matter at all, I replied; for the point is not who said the words, but whether they are true or not.

There you are in the right, Socrates, he replied.

To be sure, I said; yet I doubt whether we shall ever be able to discover their truth or falsehood; for they are a kind of riddle.

What makes you think so? he said.

Because, I said, he who uttered them seems to me to have meant one thing, and said another. Is the scribe, for example, to be regarded as doing nothing when he reads or writes?

I should rather think that he was doing something.

And does the scribe write or read, or teach you boys to write or read, your own names only, or did you write your enemies' names as well as your own and your friends'?

As much one as the other.

And was there anything meddling or intemperate in this?

Certainly not.

And yet if reading and writing are the same as doing, you were doing what was not your own business?

But they are the same as doing.

And the healing art, my friend, and building, and weaving, and doing anything whatever which is done by art,—these all clearly come under the head of doing?

Certainly.

And do you think that a state would be well ordered by a law which compelled every man to weave and wash his own coat, and make his own shoes, and his own flask and strigil, and other implements, on this principle of every one doing and performing his own, and abstaining from what is not his own?

I think not, he said.

But, I said, a temperate state will be a well-ordered state.

Of course, he replied.

Then temperance, I said, will not be doing one's own business; not at least in this way, or doing things of this sort?

Clearly not.

Then, as I was just now saying, he who declared that temperance is a man doing his own business had another and a hidden meaning; for I do not think that he could have been such a fool as to mean this. Was he a fool who told you, Charmides?

Nay, he replied, I certainly thought him a very wise man.

Then I am quite certain that he put forth his definition as a riddle, thinking that no one would know the meaning of the words 'doing his own business.'

I dare say, he replied.

And what is the meaning of a man doing his own business? Can you tell me?

Indeed, I cannot; and I should not wonder if the man himself who used this phrase did not understand what he was saying. Whereupon he laughed slyly, and looked at Critias.

Critias had long been showing uneasiness, for he felt that he had a reputation to maintain with Charmides and the rest of the company. He had, however, hitherto managed to restrain himself; but now he could no longer forbear, and I am convinced of the truth of the suspicion which I entertained at the time, that Charmides had heard this answer about temperance from Critias. And Charmides, who did not want to answer himself, but to make Critias answer, tried to stir him up. He went on pointing out that he had been refuted, at which Critias grew angry, and appeared, as I thought, inclined to quarrel with him; just as a poet might quarrel with an actor who spoiled his poems in repeating them; so he looked hard at him and said—

Do you imagine, Charmides, that the author of this definition of temperance did not understand the meaning of his own words, because you do not understand them?

Why, at his age, I said, most excellent Critias, he can hardly be expected to understand; but you, who are older, and have studied, may well be assumed to know the meaning of them; and therefore, if you agree with him, and accept his definition of temperance, I would much rather argue with you than with him about the truth or falsehood of the definition.

I entirely agree, said Critias, and accept the definition.

Very good, I said; and now let me repeat my question—Do you admit, as I was just now saying, that all craftsmen make or do something?

I do.

And do they make or do their own business only, or that of others also?

They make or do that of others also.

And are they temperate, seeing that they make not for themselves or their own business only?

Why not? he said.

No objection on my part, I said, but there may be a difficulty on his who proposes as a definition of temperance, 'doing one's own business,' and then says that there is no reason why those who do the business of others should not be temperate.

Nay (The English reader has to observe that the word 'make' (Greek), in Greek, has also the sense of 'do' (Greek).), said he; did I ever acknowledge that those who do the business of others are temperate? I said, those who make, not those who do.

What! I asked; do you mean to say that doing and making are not the same?

No more, he replied, than making or working are the same; thus much I have learned from Hesiod, who says that 'work is no disgrace.' Now do you imagine that if he had meant by working and doing such things as you were describing, he would have said that there was no disgrace in them—for example, in the manufacture of shoes, or in selling pickles, or sitting for hire in a house of ill-fame? That, Socrates, is not to be supposed: but I conceive him to have distinguished making from doing and work; and, while admitting that the making anything might sometimes become a disgrace, when the employment was not honourable, to have thought that work was never any disgrace at all. For things nobly and usefully made he called works; and such makings he called workings, and doings; and he must be supposed to have called such things only man's proper business, and what is hurtful, not his business: and in that sense Hesiod, and any other wise man, may be reasonably supposed to call him wise who does his own work.

O Critias, I said, no sooner had you opened your mouth, than I pretty well knew that you would call that which is proper to a man, and that which is his own, good; and that the makings (Greek) of the good you would call doings (Greek), for I am no stranger to the endless distinctions which Prodicus draws about names. Now I have no objection to your giving names any signification which you please, if you will only tell me what you mean by them. Please then to begin again, and be a little plainer. Do you mean that this doing or making, or whatever is the word which you would use, of good actions, is temperance?

I do, he said.

Then not he who does evil, but he who does good, is temperate?

Yes, he said; and you, friend, would agree.

No matter whether I should or not; just now, not what I think, but what you are saying, is the point at issue.

Well, he answered; I mean to say, that he who does evil, and not good, is not temperate; and that he is temperate who does good, and not evil: for temperance I define in plain words to be the doing of good actions.

And you may be very likely right in what you are saying; but I am curious to know whether you imagine that temperate men are ignorant of their own temperance?

I do not think so, he said.

And yet were you not saying, just now, that craftsmen might be temperate in doing another's work, as well as in doing their own?

I was, he replied; but what is your drift?

I have no particular drift, but I wish that you would tell me whether a physician who cures a patient may do good to himself and good to another also?

I think that he may.

And he who does so does his duty?

Yes.

And does not he who does his duty act temperately or wisely?

Yes, he acts wisely.

But must the physician necessarily know when his treatment is likely to prove beneficial, and when not? or must the craftsman necessarily know when he is likely to be benefited, and when not to be benefited, by the work which he is doing?

I suppose not.

Then, I said, he may sometimes do good or harm, and not know what he is himself doing, and yet, in doing good, as you say, he has done temperately or wisely. Was not that your statement?

Yes.

Then, as would seem, in doing good, he may act wisely or temperately, and be wise or temperate, but not know his own wisdom or temperance?

But that, Socrates, he said, is impossible; and therefore if this is, as you imply, the necessary consequence of any of my previous admissions, I will withdraw them, rather than admit that a man can be temperate or wise who does not know himself; and I am not ashamed to confess that I was in error. For self-knowledge would certainly be maintained by me to be the very essence of knowledge, and in this I agree with him who dedicated the inscription, 'Know thyself!' at Delphi. That word, if I am not mistaken, is put there as a sort of salutation which the god addresses to those who enter the temple; as much as to say that the ordinary salutation of 'Hail!' is not right, and that the exhortation 'Be temperate!' would be a far better way of saluting one another. The notion of him who dedicated the inscription was, as I believe, that the god speaks to those who enter his temple, not as men speak; but, when a worshipper enters, the first word which he hears is 'Be temperate!' This, however, like a prophet he expresses in a sort of riddle, for 'Know thyself!' and 'Be temperate!' are the same, as I maintain, and as the letters imply (Greek), and yet they may be easily misunderstood; and succeeding sages who added 'Never too much,' or, 'Give a pledge, and evil is nigh at hand,' would appear to have so misunderstood them; for they imagined that 'Know thyself!' was a piece of advice which the god gave, and not his salutation of the worshippers at their first coming in; and they dedicated their own inscription under the idea that they too would give equally useful pieces of advice. Shall I tell you, Socrates, why I say all this? My object is to leave the previous discussion (in which I know not whether you or I are more right, but, at any rate, no clear result was attained), and to raise a new one in which I will attempt to prove, if you deny, that temperance is self-knowledge.

Yes, I said, Critias; but you come to me as though I professed to know about the questions which I ask, and as though I could, if I only would, agree with you. Whereas the fact is that I enquire with you into the truth of that which is advanced from time to time, just because I do not know; and when I have enquired, I will say whether I agree with you or not. Please then to allow me time to reflect.

Reflect, he said.

I am reflecting, I replied, and discover that temperance, or wisdom, if implying a knowledge of anything, must be a science, and a science of something.

Yes, he said; the science of itself.

Is not medicine, I said, the science of health?

True.

And suppose, I said, that I were asked by you what is the use or effect of medicine, which is this science of health, I should answer that medicine is of very great use in producing health, which, as you will admit, is an excellent effect.

Granted.

And if you were to ask me, what is the result or effect of architecture, which is the science of building, I should say houses, and so of other arts, which all have their different results. Now I want you, Critias, to answer a similar question about temperance, or wisdom, which, according to you, is the science of itself. Admitting this view, I ask of you, what good work, worthy of the name wise, does temperance or wisdom, which is the science of itself, effect? Answer me.

That is not the true way of pursuing the enquiry, Socrates, he said; for wisdom is not like the other sciences, any more than they are like one another: but you proceed as if they were alike. For tell me, he said, what result is there of computation or geometry, in the same sense as a house is the result of building, or a garment of weaving, or any other work of any other art? Can you show me any such result of them? You cannot.

That is true, I said; but still each of these sciences has a subject which is different from the science. I can show you that the art of computation has to do with odd and even numbers in their numerical relations to themselves and to each other. Is not that true?

Yes, he said.

And the odd and even numbers are not the same with the art of computation?

They are not.

The art of weighing, again, has to do with lighter and heavier; but the art of weighing is one thing, and the heavy and the light another. Do you admit that?

Yes.

Now, I want to know, what is that which is not wisdom, and of which wisdom is the science?

You are just falling into the old error, Socrates, he said. You come asking in what wisdom or temperance differs from the other sciences, and then you try to discover some respect in which they are alike; but they are not, for all the other sciences are of something else, and not of themselves; wisdom alone is a science of other sciences, and of itself. And of this, as I believe, you are very well aware: and that you are only doing what you denied that you were doing just now, trying to refute me, instead of pursuing the argument.

And what if I am? How can you think that I have any other motive in refuting you but what I should have in examining into myself? which motive would be just a fear of my unconsciously fancying that I knew something of which I was ignorant. And at this moment I pursue the argument chiefly for my own sake, and perhaps in some degree also for the sake of my other friends. For is not the discovery of things as they truly are, a good common to all mankind?

Yes, certainly, Socrates, he said.

Then, I said, be cheerful, sweet sir, and give your opinion in answer to the question which I asked, never minding whether Critias or Socrates is the person refuted; attend only to the argument, and see what will come of the refutation.

I think that you are right, he replied; and I will do as you say.

Tell me, then, I said, what you mean to affirm about wisdom.

I mean to say that wisdom is the only science which is the science of itself as well as of the other sciences.

But the science of science, I said, will also be the science of the absence of science.

Very true, he said.

Then the wise or temperate man, and he only, will know himself, and be able to examine what he knows or does not know, and to see what others know and think that they know and do really know; and what they do not know, and fancy that they know, when they do not. No other person will be able to do this. And this is wisdom and temperance and self-knowledge—for a man to know what he knows, and what he does not know. That is your meaning?

Yes, he said.

Now then, I said, making an offering of the third or last argument to Zeus the Saviour, let us begin again, and ask, in the first place, whether it is or is not possible for a person to know that he knows and does not know what he knows and does not know; and in the second place, whether, if perfectly possible, such knowledge is of any use.

That is what we have to consider, he said.

And here, Critias, I said, I hope that you will find a way out of a difficulty into which I have got myself. Shall I tell you the nature of the difficulty?

By all means, he replied.

Does not what you have been saying, if true, amount to this: that there must be a single science which is wholly a science of itself and of other sciences, and that the same is also the science of the absence of science?

Yes.

But consider how monstrous this proposition is, my friend: in any parallel case, the impossibility will be transparent to you.

How is that? and in what cases do you mean?

In such cases as this: Suppose that there is a kind of vision which is not like ordinary vision, but a vision of itself and of other sorts of vision, and of the defect of them, which in seeing sees no colour, but only itself and other sorts of vision: Do you think that there is such a kind of vision?

Certainly not.

Or is there a kind of hearing which hears no sound at all, but only itself and other sorts of hearing, or the defects of them?

There is not.

Or take all the senses: can you imagine that there is any sense of itself and of other senses, but which is incapable of perceiving the objects of the senses?

I think not.

Could there be any desire which is not the desire of any pleasure, but of itself, and of all other desires?

Certainly not.

Or can you imagine a wish which wishes for no good, but only for itself and all other wishes?

I should answer, No.

Or would you say that there is a love which is not the love of beauty, but of itself and of other loves?

I should not.

Or did you ever know of a fear which fears itself or other fears, but has no object of fear?

I never did, he said.

Or of an opinion which is an opinion of itself and of other opinions, and which has no opinion on the subjects of opinion in general?

Certainly not.

But surely we are assuming a science of this kind, which, having no subject-matter, is a science of itself and of the other sciences?

Yes, that is what is affirmed.

But how strange is this, if it be indeed true: we must not however as yet absolutely deny the possibility of such a science; let us rather consider the matter.

You are quite right.

Well then, this science of which we are speaking is a science of something, and is of a nature to be a science of something?

Yes.

Just as that which is greater is of a nature to be greater than something else? (Socrates is intending to show that science differs from the object of science, as any other relative differs from the object of relation. But where there is comparison—greater, less, heavier, lighter, and the like—a relation to self as well as to other things involves an absolute contradiction; and in other cases, as in the case of the senses, is hardly conceivable. The use of the genitive after the comparative in Greek, (Greek), creates an unavoidable obscurity in the translation.)

Yes.

Which is less, if the other is conceived to be greater?

To be sure.

And if we could find something which is at once greater than itself, and greater than other great things, but not greater than those things in comparison of which the others are greater, then that thing would have the property of being greater and also less than itself?

That, Socrates, he said, is the inevitable inference.

Or if there be a double which is double of itself and of other doubles, these will be halves; for the double is relative to the half?

That is true.

And that which is greater than itself will also be less, and that which is heavier will also be lighter, and that which is older will also be younger: and the same of other things; that which has a nature relative to self will retain also the nature of its object: I mean to say, for example, that hearing is, as we say, of sound or voice. Is that true?

Yes.

Then if hearing hears itself, it must hear a voice; for there is no other way of hearing.

Certainly.

And sight also, my excellent friend, if it sees itself must see a colour, for sight cannot see that which has no colour.

No.

Do you remark, Critias, that in several of the examples which have been recited the notion of a relation to self is altogether inadmissible, and in other cases hardly credible—inadmissible, for example, in the case of magnitudes, numbers, and the like?

Very true.

But in the case of hearing and sight, or in the power of self-motion, and the power of heat to burn, this relation to self will be regarded as incredible by some, but perhaps not by others. And some great man, my friend, is wanted, who will satisfactorily determine for us, whether there is nothing which has an inherent property of relation to self, or some things only and not others; and whether in this class of self-related things, if there be such a class, that science which is called wisdom or temperance is included. I altogether distrust my own power of determining these matters: I am not certain whether there is such a science of science at all; and even if there be, I should not acknowledge this to be wisdom or temperance, until I can also see whether such a science would or would not do us any good; for I have an impression that temperance is a benefit and a good. And therefore, O son of Callaeschrus, as you maintain that temperance or wisdom is a science of science, and also of the absence of science, I will request you to show in the first place, as I was saying before, the possibility, and in the second place, the advantage, of such a science; and then perhaps you may satisfy me that you are right in your view of temperance.

Critias heard me say this, and saw that I was in a difficulty; and as one person when another yawns in his presence catches the infection of yawning from him, so did he seem to be driven into a difficulty by my difficulty. But as he had a reputation to maintain, he was ashamed to admit before the company that he could not answer my challenge or determine the question at issue; and he made an unintelligible attempt to hide his perplexity. In order that the argument might proceed, I said to him, Well then Critias, if you like, let us assume that there is this science of science; whether the assumption is right or wrong may hereafter be investigated. Admitting the existence of it, will you tell me how such a science enables us to distinguish what we know or do not know, which, as we were saying, is self-knowledge or wisdom: so we were saying?

Yes, Socrates, he said; and that I think is certainly true: for he who has this science or knowledge which knows itself will become like the knowledge which he has, in the same way that he who has swiftness will be swift, and he who has beauty will be beautiful, and he who has knowledge will know. In the same way he who has that knowledge which is self-knowing, will know himself.

I do not doubt, I said, that a man will know himself, when he possesses that which has self-knowledge: but what necessity is there that, having this, he should know what he knows and what he does not know?

Because, Socrates, they are the same.

Very likely, I said; but I remain as stupid as ever; for still I fail to comprehend how this knowing what you know and do not know is the same as the knowledge of self.

What do you mean? he said.

This is what I mean, I replied: I will admit that there is a science of science;—can this do more than determine that of two things one is and the other is not science or knowledge?

No, just that.

But is knowledge or want of knowledge of health the same as knowledge or want of knowledge of justice?

Certainly not.

The one is medicine, and the other is politics; whereas that of which we are speaking is knowledge pure and simple.

Very true.

And if a man knows only, and has only knowledge of knowledge, and has no further knowledge of health and justice, the probability is that he will only know that he knows something, and has a certain knowledge, whether concerning himself or other men.

True.

Then how will this knowledge or science teach him to know what he knows? Say that he knows health;—not wisdom or temperance, but the art of medicine has taught it to him;—and he has learned harmony from the art of music, and building from the art of building,—neither, from wisdom or temperance: and the same of other things.

That is evident.

How will wisdom, regarded only as a knowledge of knowledge or science of science, ever teach him that he knows health, or that he knows building?

It is impossible.

Then he who is ignorant of these things will only know that he knows, but not what he knows?

True.

Then wisdom or being wise appears to be not the knowledge of the things which we do or do not know, but only the knowledge that we know or do not know?

That is the inference.

Then he who has this knowledge will not be able to examine whether a pretender knows or does not know that which he says that he knows: he will only know that he has a knowledge of some kind; but wisdom will not show him of what the knowledge is?

Plainly not.

Neither will he be able to distinguish the pretender in medicine from the true physician, nor between any other true and false professor of knowledge. Let us consider the matter in this way: If the wise man or any other man wants to distinguish the true physician from the false, how will he proceed? He will not talk to him about medicine; and that, as we were saying, is the only thing which the physician understands.

True.

And, on the other hand, the physician knows nothing of science, for this has been assumed to be the province of wisdom.

True.

And further, since medicine is science, we must infer that he does not know anything of medicine.

Exactly.

Then the wise man may indeed know that the physician has some kind of science or knowledge; but when he wants to discover the nature of this he will ask, What is the subject-matter? For the several sciences are distinguished not by the mere fact that they are sciences, but by the nature of their subjects. Is not that true?

Quite true.

And medicine is distinguished from other sciences as having the subject-matter of health and disease?

Yes.

And he who would enquire into the nature of medicine must pursue the enquiry into health and disease, and not into what is extraneous?

True.

And he who judges rightly will judge of the physician as a physician in what relates to these?

He will.

He will consider whether what he says is true, and whether what he does is right, in relation to health and disease?

He will.

But can any one attain the knowledge of either unless he have a knowledge of medicine?

He cannot.

No one at all, it would seem, except the physician can have this knowledge; and therefore not the wise man; he would have to be a physician as well as a wise man.

Very true.

Then, assuredly, wisdom or temperance, if only a science of science, and of the absence of science or knowledge, will not be able to distinguish the physician who knows from one who does not know but pretends or thinks that he knows, or any other professor of anything at all; like any other artist, he will only know his fellow in art or wisdom, and no one else.

That is evident, he said.

But then what profit, Critias, I said, is there any longer in wisdom or temperance which yet remains, if this is wisdom? If, indeed, as we were supposing at first, the wise man had been able to distinguish what he knew and did not know, and that he knew the one and did not know the other, and to recognize a similar faculty of discernment in others, there would certainly have been a great advantage in being wise; for then we should never have made a mistake, but have passed through life the unerring guides of ourselves and of those who are under us; and we should not have attempted to do what we did not know, but we should have found out those who knew, and have handed the business over to them and trusted in them; nor should we have allowed those who were under us to do anything which they were not likely to do well; and they would be likely to do well just that of which they had knowledge; and the house or state which was ordered or administered under the guidance of wisdom, and everything else of which wisdom was the lord, would have been well ordered; for truth guiding, and error having been eliminated, in all their doings, men would have done well, and would have been happy. Was not this, Critias, what we spoke of as the great advantage of wisdom—to know what is known and what is unknown to us?

Very true, he said.

And now you perceive, I said, that no such science is to be found anywhere.

I perceive, he said.

May we assume then, I said, that wisdom, viewed in this new light merely as a knowledge of knowledge and ignorance, has this advantage:—that he who possesses such knowledge will more easily learn anything which he learns; and that everything will be clearer to him, because, in addition to the knowledge of individuals, he sees the science, and this also will better enable him to test the knowledge which others have of what he knows himself; whereas the enquirer who is without this knowledge may be supposed to have a feebler and weaker insight? Are not these, my friend, the real advantages which are to be gained from wisdom? And are not we looking and seeking after something more than is to be found in her?

That is very likely, he said.

That is very likely, I said; and very likely, too, we have been enquiring to no purpose; as I am led to infer, because I observe that if this is wisdom, some strange consequences would follow. Let us, if you please, assume the possibility of this science of sciences, and further admit and allow, as was originally suggested, that wisdom is the knowledge of what we know and do not know. Assuming all this, still, upon further consideration, I am doubtful, Critias, whether wisdom, such as this, would do us much good. For we were wrong, I think, in supposing, as we were saying just now, that such wisdom ordering the government of house or state would be a great benefit.

How so? he said.

Why, I said, we were far too ready to admit the great benefits which mankind would obtain from their severally doing the things which they knew, and committing the things of which they are ignorant to those who were better acquainted with them.

Were we not right in making that admission?

I think not.

How very strange, Socrates!

By the dog of Egypt, I said, there I agree with you; and I was thinking as much just now when I said that strange consequences would follow, and that I was afraid we were on the wrong track; for however ready we may be to admit that this is wisdom, I certainly cannot make out what good this sort of thing does to us.

What do you mean? he said; I wish that you could make me understand what you mean.

I dare say that what I am saying is nonsense, I replied; and yet if a man has any feeling of what is due to himself, he cannot let the thought which comes into his mind pass away unheeded and unexamined.

I like that, he said.

Hear, then, I said, my own dream; whether coming through the horn or the ivory gate, I cannot tell. The dream is this: Let us suppose that wisdom is such as we are now defining, and that she has absolute sway over us; then each action will be done according to the arts or sciences, and no one professing to be a pilot when he is not, or any physician or general, or any one else pretending to know matters of which he is ignorant, will deceive or elude us; our health will be improved; our safety at sea, and also in battle, will be assured; our coats and shoes, and all other instruments and implements will be skilfully made, because the workmen will be good and true. Aye, and if you please, you may suppose that prophecy, which is the knowledge of the future, will be under the control of wisdom, and that she will deter deceivers and set up the true prophets in their place as the revealers of the future. Now I quite agree that mankind, thus provided, would live and act according to knowledge, for wisdom would watch and prevent ignorance from intruding on us. But whether by acting according to knowledge we shall act well and be happy, my dear Critias,—this is a point which we have not yet been able to determine.

Yet I think, he replied, that if you discard knowledge, you will hardly find the crown of happiness in anything else.

But of what is this knowledge? I said. Just answer me that small question. Do you mean a knowledge of shoemaking?

God forbid.

Or of working in brass?

Certainly not.

Or in wool, or wood, or anything of that sort?

No, I do not.

Then, I said, we are giving up the doctrine that he who lives according to knowledge is happy, for these live according to knowledge, and yet they are not allowed by you to be happy; but I think that you mean to confine happiness to particular individuals who live according to knowledge, such for example as the prophet, who, as I was saying, knows the future. Is it of him you are speaking or of some one else?

Yes, I mean him, but there are others as well.

Yes, I said, some one who knows the past and present as well as the future, and is ignorant of nothing. Let us suppose that there is such a person, and if there is, you will allow that he is the most knowing of all living men.

Certainly he is.

Yet I should like to know one thing more: which of the different kinds of knowledge makes him happy? or do all equally make him happy?

Not all equally, he replied.

But which most tends to make him happy? the knowledge of what past, present, or future thing? May I infer this to be the knowledge of the game of draughts?

Nonsense about the game of draughts.

Or of computation?

No.

Or of health?

That is nearer the truth, he said.

And that knowledge which is nearest of all, I said, is the knowledge of what?

The knowledge with which he discerns good and evil.

Monster! I said; you have been carrying me round in a circle, and all this time hiding from me the fact that the life according to knowledge is not that which makes men act rightly and be happy, not even if knowledge include all the sciences, but one science only, that of good and evil. For, let me ask you, Critias, whether, if you take away this, medicine will not equally give health, and shoemaking equally produce shoes, and the art of the weaver clothes?—whether the art of the pilot will not equally save our lives at sea, and the art of the general in war?

Quite so.

And yet, my dear Critias, none of these things will be well or beneficially done, if the science of the good be wanting.

True.

But that science is not wisdom or temperance, but a science of human advantage; not a science of other sciences, or of ignorance, but of good and evil: and if this be of use, then wisdom or temperance will not be of use.

And why, he replied, will not wisdom be of use? For, however much we assume that wisdom is a science of sciences, and has a sway over other sciences, surely she will have this particular science of the good under her control, and in this way will benefit us.

And will wisdom give health? I said; is not this rather the effect of medicine? Or does wisdom do the work of any of the other arts,—do they not each of them do their own work? Have we not long ago asseverated that wisdom is only the knowledge of knowledge and of ignorance, and of nothing else?

That is obvious.

Then wisdom will not be the producer of health.

Certainly not.

The art of health is different.

Yes, different.

Nor does wisdom give advantage, my good friend; for that again we have just now been attributing to another art.

Very true.

How then can wisdom be advantageous, when giving no advantage?

That, Socrates, is certainly inconceivable.

You see then, Critias, that I was not far wrong in fearing that I could have no sound notion about wisdom; I was quite right in depreciating myself; for that which is admitted to be the best of all things would never have seemed to us useless, if I had been good for anything at an enquiry. But now I have been utterly defeated, and have failed to discover what that is to which the imposer of names gave this name of temperance or wisdom. And yet many more admissions were made by us than could be fairly granted; for we admitted that there was a science of science, although the argument said No, and protested against us; and we admitted further, that this science knew the works of the other sciences (although this too was denied by the argument), because we wanted to show that the wise man had knowledge of what he knew and did not know; also we nobly disregarded, and never even considered, the impossibility of a man knowing in a sort of way that which he does not know at all; for our assumption was, that he knows that which he does not know; than which nothing, as I think, can be more irrational. And yet, after finding us so easy and good-natured, the enquiry is still unable to discover the truth; but mocks us to a degree, and has gone out of its way to prove the inutility of that which we admitted only by a sort of supposition and fiction to be the true definition of temperance or wisdom: which result, as far as I am concerned, is not so much to be lamented, I said. But for your sake, Charmides, I am very sorry—that you, having such beauty and such wisdom and temperance of soul, should have no profit or good in life from your wisdom and temperance. And still more am I grieved about the charm which I learned with so much pain, and to so little profit, from the Thracian, for the sake of a thing which is nothing worth. I think indeed that there is a mistake, and that I must be a bad enquirer, for wisdom or temperance I believe to be really a great good; and happy are you, Charmides, if you certainly possess it. Wherefore examine yourself, and see whether you have this gift and can do without the charm; for if you can, I would rather advise you to regard me simply as a fool who is never able to reason out anything; and to rest assured that the more wise and temperate you are, the happier you will be.

Charmides said: I am sure that I do not know, Socrates, whether I have or have not this gift of wisdom and temperance; for how can I know whether I have a thing, of which even you and Critias are, as you say, unable to discover the nature?—(not that I believe you.) And further, I am sure, Socrates, that I do need the charm, and as far as I am concerned, I shall be willing to be charmed by you daily, until you say that I have had enough.

Very good, Charmides, said Critias; if you do this I shall have a proof of your temperance, that is, if you allow yourself to be charmed by Socrates, and never desert him at all.

You may depend on my following and not deserting him, said Charmides: if you who are my guardian command me, I should be very wrong not to obey you.

And I do command you, he said.

Then I will do as you say, and begin this very day.

You sirs, I said, what are you conspiring about?

We are not conspiring, said Charmides, we have conspired already.

And are you about to use violence, without even going through the forms of justice?

Yes, I shall use violence, he replied, since he orders me; and therefore you had better consider well.

But the time for consideration has passed, I said, when violence is employed; and you, when you are determined on anything, and in the mood of violence, are irresistible.

Do not you resist me then, he said.

I will not resist you, I replied.

CRATYLUS

By Plato

Translated by Benjamin Jowett

PERSONS OF THE DIALOGUE: Socrates, Hermogenes, Cratylus.

HERMOGENES: Suppose that we make Socrates a party to the argument?

CRATYLUS: If you please.

HERMOGENES: I should explain to you, Socrates, that our friend Cratylus has been arguing about names; he says that they are natural and not conventional; not a portion of the human voice which men agree to use; but that there is a truth or correctness in them, which is the same for Hellenes as for barbarians. Whereupon I ask him, whether his own name of Cratylus is a true name or not, and he answers 'Yes.' And Socrates? 'Yes.' Then every man's name, as I tell him, is that which he is called. To this he replies—'If all the world were to call you Hermogenes, that would not be your name.' And when I am anxious to have a further explanation he is ironical and mysterious, and seems to imply that he has a notion of his own about the matter, if he would only tell, and could entirely convince me, if he chose to be intelligible. Tell me, Socrates, what this oracle means; or rather tell me, if you will be so good, what is your own view of the truth or correctness of names, which I would far sooner hear.

SOCRATES: Son of Hipponicus, there is an ancient saying, that 'hard is the knowledge of the good.' And the knowledge of names is a great part of knowledge. If I had not been poor, I might have heard the fifty-drachma course of the great Prodicus, which is a complete education in grammar and language—these are his own words—and then I should have been at once able to answer your question about the correctness of names. But, indeed, I have only heard the single-drachma course, and therefore, I do not know the truth about such matters; I will, however, gladly assist you and Cratylus in the investigation of them. When he declares that your name is not really Hermogenes, I suspect that he is only making fun of you;—he means to say that you are no true son of Hermes, because you are always looking after a fortune and never in luck. But, as I was saying, there is a good deal of difficulty in this sort of knowledge, and therefore we had better leave the question open until we have heard both sides.

HERMOGENES: I have often talked over this matter, both with Cratylus and others, and cannot convince myself that there is any principle of correctness in names other than convention and agreement; any name which you give, in my opinion, is the right one, and if you change that and give another, the new name is as correct as the old—we frequently change the names of our slaves, and the newly-imposed name is as good as the old: for there is no name given to anything by nature; all is convention and habit of the users;—such is my view. But if I am mistaken I shall be happy to hear and learn of Cratylus, or of any one else.

SOCRATES: I dare say that you may be right, Hermogenes: let us see;—Your meaning is, that the name of each thing is only that which anybody agrees to call it?

HERMOGENES: That is my notion.

SOCRATES: Whether the giver of the name be an individual or a city?

HERMOGENES: Yes.

SOCRATES: Well, now, let me take an instance;—suppose that I call a man a horse or a horse a man, you mean to say that a man will be rightly called a horse by me individually, and rightly called a man by the rest of the world; and a horse again would be rightly called a man by me and a horse by the world:—that is your meaning?

HERMOGENES: He would, according to my view.

SOCRATES: But how about truth, then? you would acknowledge that there is in words a true and a false?

HERMOGENES: Certainly.

SOCRATES: And there are true and false propositions?

HERMOGENES: To be sure.

SOCRATES: And a true proposition says that which is, and a false proposition says that which is not?

HERMOGENES: Yes; what other answer is possible?

SOCRATES: Then in a proposition there is a true and false?

HERMOGENES: Certainly.

SOCRATES: But is a proposition true as a whole only, and are the parts untrue?

HERMOGENES: No; the parts are true as well as the whole.

SOCRATES: Would you say the large parts and not the smaller ones, or every part?

HERMOGENES: I should say that every part is true.

SOCRATES: Is a proposition resolvable into any part smaller than a name?

HERMOGENES: No; that is the smallest.

SOCRATES: Then the name is a part of the true proposition?

HERMOGENES: Yes.

SOCRATES: Yes, and a true part, as you say.

HERMOGENES: Yes.

SOCRATES: And is not the part of a falsehood also a falsehood?

HERMOGENES: Yes.

SOCRATES: Then, if propositions may be true and false, names may be true and false?

HERMOGENES: So we must infer.

SOCRATES: And the name of anything is that which any one affirms to be the name?

HERMOGENES: Yes.

SOCRATES: And will there be so many names of each thing as everybody says that there are? and will they be true names at the time of uttering them?

HERMOGENES: Yes, Socrates, I can conceive no correctness of names other than this; you give one name, and I another; and in different cities and countries there are different names for the same things; Hellenes differ from barbarians in their use of names, and the several Hellenic tribes from one another.

SOCRATES: But would you say, Hermogenes, that the things differ as the names differ? and are they relative to individuals, as Protagoras tells us? For he says that man is the measure of all things, and that things are to me as they appear to me, and that they are to you as they appear to you. Do you agree with him, or would you say that things have a permanent essence of their own?

HERMOGENES: There have been times, Socrates, when I have been driven in my perplexity to take refuge with Protagoras; not that I agree with him at all.

SOCRATES: What! have you ever been driven to admit that there was no such thing as a bad man?

HERMOGENES: No, indeed; but I have often had reason to think that there are very bad men, and a good many of them.

SOCRATES: Well, and have you ever found any very good ones?

HERMOGENES: Not many.

SOCRATES: Still you have found them?

HERMOGENES: Yes.

SOCRATES: And would you hold that the very good were the very wise, and the very evil very foolish? Would that be your view?

HERMOGENES: It would.

SOCRATES: But if Protagoras is right, and the truth is that things are as they appear to any one, how can some of us be wise and some of us foolish?

HERMOGENES: Impossible.

SOCRATES: And if, on the other hand, wisdom and folly are really distinguishable, you will allow, I think, that the assertion of Protagoras can hardly be correct. For if what appears to each man is true to him, one man cannot in reality be wiser than another.

HERMOGENES: He cannot.

SOCRATES: Nor will you be disposed to say with Euthydemus, that all things equally belong to all men at the same moment and always; for neither on his view can there be some good and others bad, if virtue and vice are always equally to be attributed to all.

HERMOGENES: There cannot.

SOCRATES: But if neither is right, and things are not relative to individuals, and all things do not equally belong to all at the same moment and always, they must be supposed to have their own proper and permanent essence: they are not in relation to us, or influenced by us, fluctuating according to our fancy, but they are independent, and maintain to their own essence the relation prescribed by nature.

HERMOGENES: I think, Socrates, that you have said the truth.

SOCRATES: Does what I am saying apply only to the things themselves, or equally to the actions which proceed from them? Are not actions also a class of being?

HERMOGENES: Yes, the actions are real as well as the things.

SOCRATES: Then the actions also are done according to their proper nature, and not according to our opinion of them? In cutting, for example, we do not cut as we please, and with any chance instrument; but we cut with the proper instrument only, and according to the natural process of cutting; and the natural process is right and will succeed, but any other will fail and be of no use at all.

HERMOGENES: I should say that the natural way is the right way.

SOCRATES: Again, in burning, not every way is the right way; but the right way is the natural way, and the right instrument the natural instrument.

HERMOGENES: True.

SOCRATES: And this holds good of all actions?

HERMOGENES: Yes.

SOCRATES: And speech is a kind of action?

HERMOGENES: True.

SOCRATES: And will a man speak correctly who speaks as he pleases? Will not the successful speaker rather be he who speaks in the natural way of speaking, and as things ought to be spoken, and with the natural instrument? Any other mode of speaking will result in error and failure.

HERMOGENES: I quite agree with you.

SOCRATES: And is not naming a part of speaking? for in giving names men speak.

HERMOGENES: That is true.

SOCRATES: And if speaking is a sort of action and has a relation to acts, is not naming also a sort of action?

HERMOGENES: True.

SOCRATES: And we saw that actions were not relative to ourselves, but had a special nature of their own?

HERMOGENES: Precisely.

SOCRATES: Then the argument would lead us to infer that names ought to be given according to a natural process, and with a proper instrument, and not at our pleasure: in this and no other way shall we name with success.

HERMOGENES: I agree.

SOCRATES: But again, that which has to be cut has to be cut with something?

HERMOGENES: Yes.

SOCRATES: And that which has to be woven or pierced has to be woven or pierced with something?

HERMOGENES: Certainly.

SOCRATES: And that which has to be named has to be named with something?

HERMOGENES: True.

SOCRATES: What is that with which we pierce?

HERMOGENES: An awl.

SOCRATES: And with which we weave?

HERMOGENES: A shuttle.

SOCRATES: And with which we name?

HERMOGENES: A name.

SOCRATES: Very good: then a name is an instrument?

HERMOGENES: Certainly.

SOCRATES: Suppose that I ask, 'What sort of instrument is a shuttle?' And you answer, 'A weaving instrument.'

HERMOGENES: Well.

SOCRATES: And I ask again, 'What do we do when we weave?'—The answer is, that we separate or disengage the warp from the woof.

HERMOGENES: Very true.

SOCRATES: And may not a similar description be given of an awl, and of instruments in general?

HERMOGENES: To be sure.

SOCRATES: And now suppose that I ask a similar question about names: will you answer me? Regarding the name as an instrument, what do we do when we name?

HERMOGENES: I cannot say.

SOCRATES: Do we not give information to one another, and distinguish things according to their natures?

HERMOGENES: Certainly we do.

SOCRATES: Then a name is an instrument of teaching and of distinguishing natures, as the shuttle is of distinguishing the threads of the web.

HERMOGENES: Yes.

SOCRATES: And the shuttle is the instrument of the weaver?

HERMOGENES: Assuredly.

SOCRATES: Then the weaver will use the shuttle well—and well means like a weaver? and the teacher will use the name well—and well means like a teacher?

HERMOGENES: Yes.

SOCRATES: And when the weaver uses the shuttle, whose work will he be using well?

HERMOGENES: That of the carpenter.

SOCRATES: And is every man a carpenter, or the skilled only?

HERMOGENES: Only the skilled.

SOCRATES: And when the piercer uses the awl, whose work will he be using well?

HERMOGENES: That of the smith.

SOCRATES: And is every man a smith, or only the skilled?

HERMOGENES: The skilled only.

SOCRATES: And when the teacher uses the name, whose work will he be using?

HERMOGENES: There again I am puzzled.

SOCRATES: Cannot you at least say who gives us the names which we use?

HERMOGENES: Indeed I cannot.

SOCRATES: Does not the law seem to you to give us them?

HERMOGENES: Yes, I suppose so.

SOCRATES: Then the teacher, when he gives us a name, uses the work of the legislator?

HERMOGENES: I agree.

SOCRATES: And is every man a legislator, or the skilled only?

HERMOGENES: The skilled only.

SOCRATES: Then, Hermogenes, not every man is able to give a name, but only a maker of names; and this is the legislator, who of all skilled artisans in the world is the rarest.

HERMOGENES: True.

SOCRATES: And how does the legislator make names? and to what does he look? Consider this in the light of the previous instances: to what does the carpenter look in making the shuttle? Does he not look to that which is naturally fitted to act as a shuttle?

HERMOGENES: Certainly.

SOCRATES: And suppose the shuttle to be broken in making, will he make another, looking to the broken one? or will he look to the form according to which he made the other?

HERMOGENES: To the latter, I should imagine.

SOCRATES: Might not that be justly called the true or ideal shuttle?

HERMOGENES: I think so.

SOCRATES: And whatever shuttles are wanted, for the manufacture of garments, thin or thick, of flaxen, woollen, or other material, ought all of them to have the true form of the shuttle; and whatever is the shuttle best adapted to each kind of work, that ought to be the form which the maker produces in each case.

HERMOGENES: Yes.

SOCRATES: And the same holds of other instruments: when a man has discovered the instrument which is naturally adapted to each work, he must express this natural form, and not others which he fancies, in the material, whatever it may be, which he employs; for example, he ought to know how to put into iron the forms of awls adapted by nature to their several uses?

HERMOGENES: Certainly.

SOCRATES: And how to put into wood forms of shuttles adapted by nature to their uses?

HERMOGENES: True.

SOCRATES: For the several forms of shuttles naturally answer to the several kinds of webs; and this is true of instruments in general.

HERMOGENES: Yes.

SOCRATES: Then, as to names: ought not our legislator also to know how to put the true natural name of each thing into sounds and syllables, and to make and give all names with a view to the ideal name, if he is to be a namer in any true sense? And we must remember that different legislators will not use the same syllables. For neither does every smith, although he may be making the same instrument for the same purpose, make them all of the same iron. The form must be the same, but the material may vary, and still the instrument may be equally good of whatever iron made, whether in Hellas or in a foreign country;—there is no difference.

HERMOGENES: Very true.

SOCRATES: And the legislator, whether he be Hellene or barbarian, is not therefore to be deemed by you a worse legislator, provided he gives the true and proper form of the name in whatever syllables; this or that country makes no matter.

HERMOGENES: Quite true.

SOCRATES: But who then is to determine whether the proper form is given to the shuttle, whatever sort of wood may be used? the carpenter who makes, or the weaver who is to use them?

HERMOGENES: I should say, he who is to use them, Socrates.

SOCRATES: And who uses the work of the lyre-maker? Will not he be the man who knows how to direct what is being done, and who will know also whether the work is being well done or not?

HERMOGENES: Certainly.

SOCRATES: And who is he?

HERMOGENES: The player of the lyre.

SOCRATES: And who will direct the shipwright?

HERMOGENES: The pilot.

SOCRATES: And who will be best able to direct the legislator in his work, and will know whether the work is well done, in this or any other country? Will not the user be the man?

HERMOGENES: Yes.

SOCRATES: And this is he who knows how to ask questions?

HERMOGENES: Yes.

SOCRATES: And how to answer them?

HERMOGENES: Yes.

SOCRATES: And him who knows how to ask and answer you would call a dialectician?

HERMOGENES: Yes; that would be his name.

SOCRATES: Then the work of the carpenter is to make a rudder, and the pilot has to direct him, if the rudder is to be well made.

HERMOGENES: True.

SOCRATES: And the work of the legislator is to give names, and the dialectician must be his director if the names are to be rightly given?

HERMOGENES: That is true.

SOCRATES: Then, Hermogenes, I should say that this giving of names can be no such light matter as you fancy, or the work of light or chance persons; and Cratylus is right in saying that things have names by nature, and that not every man is an artificer of names, but he only who looks to the name which each thing by nature has, and is able to express the true forms of things in letters and syllables.

HERMOGENES: I cannot answer you, Socrates; but I find a difficulty in changing my opinion all in a moment, and I think that I should be more readily persuaded, if you would show me what this is which you term the natural fitness of names.

SOCRATES: My good Hermogenes, I have none to show. Was I not telling you just now (but you have forgotten), that I knew nothing, and proposing to share the enquiry with you? But now that you and I have talked over the matter, a step has been gained; for we have discovered that names have by nature a truth, and that not every man knows how to give a thing a name.

HERMOGENES: Very good.

SOCRATES: And what is the nature of this truth or correctness of names? That, if you care to know, is the next question.

HERMOGENES: Certainly, I care to know.

SOCRATES: Then reflect.

HERMOGENES: How shall I reflect?

SOCRATES: The true way is to have the assistance of those who know, and you must pay them well both in money and in thanks; these are the Sophists, of whom your brother, Callias, has—rather dearly—bought the reputation of wisdom. But you have not yet come into your inheritance, and therefore you had better go to him, and beg and entreat him to tell you what he has learnt from Protagoras about the fitness of names.

HERMOGENES: But how inconsistent should I be, if, whilst repudiating Protagoras and his truth ('Truth' was the title of the book of Protagoras; compare Theaet.), I were to attach any value to what he and his book affirm!

SOCRATES: Then if you despise him, you must learn of Homer and the poets.

HERMOGENES: And where does Homer say anything about names, and what does he say?

SOCRATES: He often speaks of them; notably and nobly in the places where he distinguishes the different names which Gods and men give to the same things. Does he not in these passages make a remarkable statement about the correctness of names? For the Gods must clearly be supposed to call things by their right and natural names; do you not think so?

HERMOGENES: Why, of course they call them rightly, if they call them at all. But to what are you referring?

SOCRATES: Do you not know what he says about the river in Troy who had a single combat with Hephaestus?

'Whom,' as he says, 'the Gods call Xanthus, and men call Scamander.'

HERMOGENES: I remember.

SOCRATES: Well, and about this river—to know that he ought to be called Xanthus and not Scamander—is not that a solemn lesson? Or about the bird which, as he says,

'The Gods call Chalcis, and men Cymindis:'

to be taught how much more correct the name Chalcis is than the name Cymindis—do you deem that a light matter? Or about Batieia and Myrina? (Compare Il. 'The hill which men call Batieia and the immortals the tomb of the sportive Myrina.') And there are many other observations of the same kind in Homer and other poets. Now, I think that this is beyond the understanding of you and me; but the names of Scamandrius and Astyanax, which he affirms to have been the names of Hector's son, are more within the range of human faculties, as I am disposed to think; and what the poet means by correctness may be more readily apprehended in that instance: you will remember I dare say the lines to which I refer? (Il.)

HERMOGENES: I do.

SOCRATES: Let me ask you, then, which did Homer think the more correct of the names given to Hector's son—Astyanax or Scamandrius?

HERMOGENES: I do not know.

SOCRATES: How would you answer, if you were asked whether the wise or the unwise are more likely to give correct names?

HERMOGENES: I should say the wise, of course.

SOCRATES: And are the men or the women of a city, taken as a class, the wiser?

HERMOGENES: I should say, the men.

SOCRATES: And Homer, as you know, says that the Trojan men called him Astyanax (king of the city); but if the men called him Astyanax, the other name of Scamandrius could only have been given to him by the women.

HERMOGENES: That may be inferred.

SOCRATES: And must not Homer have imagined the Trojans to be wiser than their wives?

HERMOGENES: To be sure.

SOCRATES: Then he must have thought Astyanax to be a more correct name for the boy than Scamandrius?

HERMOGENES: Clearly.

SOCRATES: And what is the reason of this? Let us consider:—does he not himself suggest a very good reason, when he says,

'For he alone defended their city and long walls'?

This appears to be a good reason for calling the son of the saviour king of the city which his father was saving, as Homer observes.

HERMOGENES: I see.

SOCRATES: Why, Hermogenes, I do not as yet see myself; and do you?

HERMOGENES: No, indeed; not I.

SOCRATES: But tell me, friend, did not Homer himself also give Hector his name?

HERMOGENES: What of that?

SOCRATES: The name appears to me to be very nearly the same as the name of Astyanax—both are Hellenic; and a king (anax) and a holder (ektor) have nearly the same meaning, and are both descriptive of a king; for a man is clearly the holder of that of which he is king; he rules, and owns, and holds it. But, perhaps, you may think that I am talking nonsense; and indeed I believe that I myself did not know what I meant when I imagined that I had found some indication of the opinion of Homer about the correctness of names.

HERMOGENES: I assure you that I think otherwise, and I believe you to be on the right track.

SOCRATES: There is reason, I think, in calling the lion's whelp a lion, and the foal of a horse a horse; I am speaking only of the ordinary course of nature, when an animal produces after his kind, and not of extraordinary births;—if contrary to nature a horse have a calf, then I should not call that a foal but a calf; nor do I call any inhuman birth a man, but only a natural birth. And the same may be said of trees and other things. Do you agree with me?

HERMOGENES: Yes, I agree.

SOCRATES: Very good. But you had better watch me and see that I do not play tricks with you. For on the same principle the son of a king is to be called a king. And whether the syllables of the name are the same or not the same, makes no difference, provided the meaning is retained; nor does the addition or subtraction of a letter make any difference so long as the essence of the thing remains in possession of the name and appears in it.

HERMOGENES: What do you mean?

SOCRATES: A very simple matter. I may illustrate my meaning by the names of letters, which you know are not the same as the letters themselves with the exception of the four epsilon, upsilon, omicron, omega; the names of the rest, whether vowels or consonants, are made up of other letters which we add to them; but so long as we introduce the meaning, and there can be no mistake, the name of the letter is quite correct. Take, for example, the letter beta—the addition of eta, tau, alpha, gives no offence, and does not prevent the whole name from having the value which the legislator intended—so well did he know how to give the letters names.

HERMOGENES: I believe you are right.

SOCRATES: And may not the same be said of a king? a king will often be the son of a king, the good son or the noble son of a good or noble sire; and similarly the offspring of every kind, in the regular course of nature, is like the parent, and therefore has the same name. Yet the syllables may be disguised until they appear different to the ignorant person, and he may not recognize them, although they are the same, just as any one of us would not recognize the same drugs under different disguises of colour and smell, although to the physician, who regards the power of them, they are the same, and he is not put out by the addition; and in like manner the etymologist is not put out by the addition or transposition or subtraction of a letter or two, or indeed by the change of all the letters, for this need not interfere with the meaning. As was just now said, the names of Hector and Astyanax have only one letter alike, which is tau, and yet they have the same meaning. And how little in common with the letters of their names has Archepolis (ruler of the city)—and yet the meaning is the same. And there are many other names which just mean 'king.' Again, there are several names for a general, as, for example, Agis (leader) and Polemarchus (chief in war) and Eupolemus (good warrior); and others which denote a physician, as Iatrocles (famous healer) and Acesimbrotus (curer of mortals); and there are many others which might be cited, differing in their syllables and letters, but having the same meaning. Would you not say so?

HERMOGENES: Yes.

SOCRATES: The same names, then, ought to be assigned to those who follow in the course of nature?

HERMOGENES: Yes.

SOCRATES: And what of those who follow out of the course of nature, and are prodigies? for example, when a good and religious man has an irreligious son, he ought to bear the name not of his father, but of the class to which he belongs, just as in the case which was before supposed of a horse foaling a calf.

HERMOGENES: Quite true.

SOCRATES: Then the irreligious son of a religious father should be called irreligious?

HERMOGENES: Certainly.

SOCRATES: He should not be called Theophilus (beloved of God) or Mnesitheus (mindful of God), or any of these names: if names are correctly given, his should have an opposite meaning.

HERMOGENES: Certainly, Socrates.

SOCRATES: Again, Hermogenes, there is Orestes (the man of the mountains) who appears to be rightly called; whether chance gave the name, or perhaps some poet who meant to express the brutality and fierceness and mountain wildness of his hero's nature.

HERMOGENES: That is very likely, Socrates.

SOCRATES: And his father's name is also according to nature.

HERMOGENES: Clearly.

SOCRATES: Yes, for as his name, so also is his nature; Agamemnon (admirable for remaining) is one who is patient and persevering in the accomplishment of his resolves, and by his virtue crowns them; and his continuance at Troy with all the vast army is a proof of that admirable endurance in him which is signified by the name Agamemnon. I also think that Atreus is rightly called; for his murder of Chrysippus and his exceeding cruelty to Thyestes are damaging and destructive to his reputation—the name is a little altered and disguised so as not to be intelligible to every one, but to the etymologist there is no difficulty in seeing the meaning, for whether you think of him as ateires the stubborn, or as atrestos the fearless, or as ateros the destructive one, the name is perfectly correct in every point of view. And I think that Pelops is also named appropriately; for, as the name implies, he is rightly called Pelops who sees what is near only (o ta pelas oron).

HERMOGENES: How so?

SOCRATES: Because, according to the tradition, he had no forethought or foresight of all the evil which the murder of Myrtilus would entail upon his whole race in remote ages; he saw only what was at hand and immediate,—or in other words, pelas (near), in his eagerness to win Hippodamia by all means for his bride. Every one would agree that the name of Tantalus is rightly given and in accordance with nature, if the traditions about him are true.

HERMOGENES: And what are the traditions?

SOCRATES: Many terrible misfortunes are said to have happened to him in his life—last of all, came the utter ruin of his country; and after his death he had the stone suspended (talanteia) over his head in the world below—all this agrees wonderfully well with his name. You might imagine that some person who wanted to call him Talantatos (the most weighted down by misfortune), disguised the name by altering it into Tantalus; and into this form, by some accident of tradition, it has actually been transmuted. The name of Zeus, who is his alleged father, has also an excellent meaning, although hard to be understood, because really like a sentence, which is divided into two parts, for some call him Zena, and use the one half, and others who use the other half call him Dia; the two together signify the nature of the God, and the business of a name, as we were saying, is to express the nature. For there is none who is more the author of life to us and to all, than the lord and king of all. Wherefore we are right in calling him Zena and Dia, which are one name, although divided, meaning the God through whom all creatures always have life (di on zen aei pasi tois zosin uparchei). There is an irreverence, at first sight, in calling him son of Cronos (who is a proverb for stupidity), and we might rather expect Zeus to be the child of a mighty intellect. Which is the fact; for this is the meaning of his father's name: Kronos quasi Koros (Choreo, to sweep), not in the sense of a youth, but signifying to chatharon chai acheraton tou nou, the pure and garnished mind (sc. apo tou chorein). He, as we are informed by tradition, was begotten of Uranus, rightly so called (apo tou oran ta ano) from looking upwards; which, as philosophers tell us, is the way to have a pure mind, and the name Uranus is therefore correct. If I could remember the genealogy of Hesiod, I would have gone on and tried more conclusions of the same sort on the remoter ancestors of the Gods,—then I might have seen whether this wisdom, which has come to me all in an instant, I know not whence, will or will not hold good to the end.

HERMOGENES: You seem to me, Socrates, to be quite like a prophet newly inspired, and to be uttering oracles.

SOCRATES: Yes, Hermogenes, and I believe that I caught the inspiration from the great Euthyphro of the Prospaltian deme, who gave me a long lecture which commenced at dawn: he talked and I listened, and his wisdom and enchanting ravishment has not only filled my ears but taken possession of my soul, and to-day I shall let his superhuman power work and finish the investigation of names—that will be the way; but to-morrow, if you are so disposed, we will conjure him away, and make a purgation of him, if we can only find some priest or sophist who is skilled in purifications of this sort.

HERMOGENES: With all my heart; for am very curious to hear the rest of the enquiry about names.

SOCRATES: Then let us proceed; and where would you have us begin, now that we have got a sort of outline of the enquiry? Are there any names which witness of themselves that they are not given arbitrarily, but have a natural fitness? The names of heroes and of men in general are apt to be deceptive because they are often called after ancestors with whose names, as we were saying, they may have no business; or they are the expression of a wish like Eutychides (the son of good fortune), or Sosias (the Saviour), or Theophilus (the beloved of God), and others. But I think that we had better leave these, for there will be more chance of finding correctness in the names of immutable essences;—there ought to have been more care taken about them when they were named, and perhaps there may have been some more than human power at work occasionally in giving them names.

HERMOGENES: I think so, Socrates.

SOCRATES: Ought we not to begin with the consideration of the Gods, and show that they are rightly named Gods?

HERMOGENES: Yes, that will be well.

SOCRATES: My notion would be something of this sort:—I suspect that the sun, moon, earth, stars, and heaven, which are still the Gods of many barbarians, were the only Gods known to the aboriginal Hellenes. Seeing that they were always moving and running, from their running nature they were called Gods or runners (Theous, Theontas); and when men became acquainted with the other Gods, they proceeded to apply the same name to them all. Do you think that likely?

HERMOGENES: I think it very likely indeed.

SOCRATES: What shall follow the Gods?

HERMOGENES: Must not demons and heroes and men come next?

SOCRATES: Demons! And what do you consider to be the meaning of this word? Tell me if my view is right.

HERMOGENES: Let me hear.

SOCRATES: You know how Hesiod uses the word?

HERMOGENES: I do not.

SOCRATES: Do you not remember that he speaks of a golden race of men who came first?

HERMOGENES: Yes, I do.

SOCRATES: He says of them—

'But now that fate has closed over this race They are holy demons upon the earth, Beneficent, averters of ills, guardians of mortal men.' (Hesiod, Works and Days.)

HERMOGENES: What is the inference?

SOCRATES: What is the inference! Why, I suppose that he means by the golden men, not men literally made of gold, but good and noble; and I am convinced of this, because he further says that we are the iron race.

HERMOGENES: That is true.

SOCRATES: And do you not suppose that good men of our own day would by him be said to be of golden race?

HERMOGENES: Very likely.

SOCRATES: And are not the good wise?

HERMOGENES: Yes, they are wise.

SOCRATES: And therefore I have the most entire conviction that he called them demons, because they were daemones (knowing or wise), and in our older Attic dialect the word itself occurs. Now he and other poets say truly, that when a good man dies he has honour and a mighty portion among the dead, and becomes a demon; which is a name given to him signifying wisdom. And I say too, that every wise man who happens to be a good man is more than human (daimonion) both in life and death, and is rightly called a demon.

HERMOGENES: Then I rather think that I am of one mind with you; but what is the meaning of the word 'hero'? (Eros with an eta, in the old writing eros with an epsilon.)

SOCRATES: I think that there is no difficulty in explaining, for the name is not much altered, and signifies that they were born of love.

HERMOGENES: What do you mean?

SOCRATES: Do you not know that the heroes are demigods?

HERMOGENES: What then?

SOCRATES: All of them sprang either from the love of a God for a mortal woman, or of a mortal man for a Goddess; think of the word in the old Attic, and you will see better that the name heros is only a slight alteration of Eros, from whom the heroes sprang: either this is the meaning, or, if not this, then they must have been skilful as rhetoricians and dialecticians, and able to put the question (erotan), for eirein is equivalent to legein. And therefore, as I was saying, in the Attic dialect the heroes turn out to be rhetoricians and questioners. All this is easy enough; the noble breed of heroes are a tribe of sophists and rhetors. But can you tell me why men are called anthropoi?—that is more difficult.

HERMOGENES: No, I cannot; and I would not try even if I could, because I think that you are the more likely to succeed.

SOCRATES: That is to say, you trust to the inspiration of Euthyphro.

HERMOGENES: Of course.

SOCRATES: Your faith is not vain; for at this very moment a new and ingenious thought strikes me, and, if I am not careful, before to-morrow's dawn I shall be wiser than I ought to be. Now, attend to me; and first, remember that we often put in and pull out letters in words, and give names as we please and change the accents. Take, for example, the word Dii Philos; in order to convert this from a sentence into a noun, we omit one of the iotas and sound the middle syllable grave instead of acute; as, on the other hand, letters are sometimes inserted in words instead of being omitted, and the acute takes the place of the grave.

HERMOGENES: That is true.

SOCRATES: The name anthropos, which was once a sentence, and is now a noun, appears to be a case just of this sort, for one letter, which is the alpha, has been omitted, and the acute on the last syllable has been changed to a grave.

HERMOGENES: What do you mean?

SOCRATES: I mean to say that the word 'man' implies that other animals never examine, or consider, or look up at what they see, but that man not only sees (opope) but considers and looks up at that which he sees, and hence he alone of all animals is rightly anthropos, meaning anathron a opopen.

HERMOGENES: May I ask you to examine another word about which I am curious?

SOCRATES: Certainly.

HERMOGENES: I will take that which appears to me to follow next in order. You know the distinction of soul and body?

SOCRATES: Of course.

HERMOGENES: Let us endeavour to analyze them like the previous words.

SOCRATES: You want me first of all to examine the natural fitness of the word psuche (soul), and then of the word soma (body)?

HERMOGENES: Yes.

SOCRATES: If I am to say what occurs to me at the moment, I should imagine that those who first used the name psuche meant to express that the soul when in the body is the source of life, and gives the power of breath and revival (anapsuchon), and when this reviving power fails then the body perishes and dies, and this, if I am not mistaken, they called psyche. But please stay a moment; I fancy that I can discover something which will be more acceptable to the disciples of Euthyphro, for I am afraid that they will scorn this explanation. What do you say to another?

HERMOGENES: Let me hear.

SOCRATES: What is that which holds and carries and gives life and motion to the entire nature of the body? What else but the soul?

HERMOGENES: Just that.

SOCRATES: And do you not believe with Anaxagoras, that mind or soul is the ordering and containing principle of all things?

HERMOGENES: Yes; I do.

SOCRATES: Then you may well call that power phuseche which carries and holds nature (e phusin okei, kai ekei), and this may be refined away into psuche.

HERMOGENES: Certainly; and this derivation is, I think, more scientific than the other.

SOCRATES: It is so; but I cannot help laughing, if I am to suppose that this was the true meaning of the name.

HERMOGENES: But what shall we say of the next word?

SOCRATES: You mean soma (the body).

HERMOGENES: Yes.

SOCRATES: That may be variously interpreted; and yet more variously if a little permutation is allowed. For some say that the body is the grave (sema) of the soul which may be thought to be buried in our present life; or again the index of the soul, because the soul gives indications to (semainei) the body; probably the Orphic poets were the inventors of the name, and they were under the impression that the soul is suffering the punishment of sin, and that the body is an enclosure or prison in which the soul is incarcerated, kept safe (soma, sozetai), as the name soma implies, until the penalty is paid; according to this view, not even a letter of the word need be changed.

HERMOGENES: I think, Socrates, that we have said enough of this class of words. But have we any more explanations of the names of the Gods, like that which you were giving of Zeus? I should like to know whether any similar principle of correctness is to be applied to them.

SOCRATES: Yes, indeed, Hermogenes; and there is one excellent principle which, as men of sense, we must acknowledge,—that of the Gods we know nothing, either of their natures or of the names which they give themselves; but we are sure that the names by which they call themselves, whatever they may be, are true. And this is the best of all principles; and the next best is to say, as in prayers, that we will call them by any sort or kind of names or patronymics which they like, because we do not know of any other. That also, I think, is a very good custom, and one which I should much wish to observe. Let us, then, if you please, in the first place announce to them that we are not enquiring about them; we do not presume that we are able to do so; but we are enquiring about the meaning of men in giving them these names,—in this there can be small blame.

HERMOGENES: I think, Socrates, that you are quite right, and I would like to do as you say.

SOCRATES: Shall we begin, then, with Hestia, according to custom?

HERMOGENES: Yes, that will be very proper.

SOCRATES: What may we suppose him to have meant who gave the name Hestia?

HERMOGENES: That is another and certainly a most difficult question.

SOCRATES: My dear Hermogenes, the first imposers of names must surely have been considerable persons; they were philosophers, and had a good deal to say.

HERMOGENES: Well, and what of them?

SOCRATES: They are the men to whom I should attribute the imposition of names. Even in foreign names, if you analyze them, a meaning is still discernible. For example, that which we term ousia is by some called esia, and by others again osia. Now that the essence of things should be called estia, which is akin to the first of these (esia = estia), is rational enough. And there is reason in the Athenians calling that estia which participates in ousia. For in ancient times we too seem to have said esia for ousia, and this you may note to have been the idea of those who appointed that sacrifices should be first offered to estia, which was natural enough if they meant that estia was the essence of things. Those again who read osia seem to have inclined to the opinion of Heracleitus, that all things flow and nothing stands; with them the pushing principle (othoun) is the cause and ruling power of all things, and is therefore rightly called osia. Enough of this, which is all that we who know nothing can affirm. Next in order after Hestia we ought to consider Rhea and Cronos, although the name of Cronos has been already discussed. But I dare say that I am talking great nonsense.

HERMOGENES: Why, Socrates?

SOCRATES: My good friend, I have discovered a hive of wisdom.

HERMOGENES: Of what nature?

SOCRATES: Well, rather ridiculous, and yet plausible.

HERMOGENES: How plausible?

SOCRATES: I fancy to myself Heracleitus repeating wise traditions of antiquity as old as the days of Cronos and Rhea, and of which Homer also spoke.

HERMOGENES: How do you mean?

SOCRATES: Heracleitus is supposed to say that all things are in motion and nothing at rest; he compares them to the stream of a river, and says that you cannot go into the same water twice.

HERMOGENES: That is true.

SOCRATES: Well, then, how can we avoid inferring that he who gave the names of Cronos and Rhea to the ancestors of the Gods, agreed pretty much in the doctrine of Heracleitus? Is the giving of the names of streams to both of them purely accidental? Compare the line in which Homer, and, as I believe, Hesiod also, tells of

'Ocean, the origin of Gods, and mother Tethys (Il.—the line is not found in the extant works of Hesiod.).'

And again, Orpheus says, that

'The fair river of Ocean was the first to marry, and he espoused his sister Tethys, who was his mother's daughter.'

You see that this is a remarkable coincidence, and all in the direction of Heracleitus.

HERMOGENES: I think that there is something in what you say, Socrates; but I do not understand the meaning of the name Tethys.

SOCRATES: Well, that is almost self-explained, being only the name of a spring, a little disguised; for that which is strained and filtered (diattomenon, ethoumenon) may be likened to a spring, and the name Tethys is made up of these two words.

HERMOGENES: The idea is ingenious, Socrates.

SOCRATES: To be sure. But what comes next?—of Zeus we have spoken.

HERMOGENES: Yes.

SOCRATES: Then let us next take his two brothers, Poseidon and Pluto, whether the latter is called by that or by his other name.

HERMOGENES: By all means.

SOCRATES: Poseidon is Posidesmos, the chain of the feet; the original inventor of the name had been stopped by the watery element in his walks, and not allowed to go on, and therefore he called the ruler of this element Poseidon; the epsilon was probably inserted as an ornament. Yet, perhaps, not so; but the name may have been originally written with a double lamda and not with a sigma, meaning that the God knew many things (Polla eidos). And perhaps also he being the shaker of the earth, has been named from shaking (seiein), and then pi and delta have been added. Pluto gives wealth (Ploutos), and his name means the giver of wealth, which comes out of the earth beneath. People in general appear to imagine that the term Hades is connected with the invisible (aeides) and so they are led by their fears to call the God Pluto instead.

HERMOGENES: And what is the true derivation?

SOCRATES: In spite of the mistakes which are made about the power of this deity, and the foolish fears which people have of him, such as the fear of always being with him after death, and of the soul denuded of the body going to him (compare Rep.), my belief is that all is quite consistent, and that the office and name of the God really correspond.

HERMOGENES: Why, how is that?

SOCRATES: I will tell you my own opinion; but first, I should like to ask you which chain does any animal feel to be the stronger? and which confines him more to the same spot,—desire or necessity?

HERMOGENES: Desire, Socrates, is stronger far.

SOCRATES: And do you not think that many a one would escape from Hades, if he did not bind those who depart to him by the strongest of chains?

HERMOGENES: Assuredly they would.

SOCRATES: And if by the greatest of chains, then by some desire, as I should certainly infer, and not by necessity?

HERMOGENES: That is clear.

SOCRATES: And there are many desires?

HERMOGENES: Yes.

SOCRATES: And therefore by the greatest desire, if the chain is to be the greatest?

HERMOGENES: Yes.

SOCRATES: And is any desire stronger than the thought that you will be made better by associating with another?

HERMOGENES: Certainly not.

SOCRATES: And is not that the reason, Hermogenes, why no one, who has been to him, is willing to come back to us? Even the Sirens, like all the rest of the world, have been laid under his spells. Such a charm, as I imagine, is the God able to infuse into his words. And, according to this view, he is the perfect and accomplished Sophist, and the great benefactor of the inhabitants of the other world; and even to us who are upon earth he sends from below exceeding blessings. For he has much more than he wants down there; wherefore he is called Pluto (or the rich). Note also, that he will have nothing to do with men while they are in the body, but only when the soul is liberated from the desires and evils of the body. Now there is a great deal of philosophy and reflection in that; for in their liberated state he can bind them with the desire of virtue, but while they are flustered and maddened by the body, not even father Cronos himself would suffice to keep them with him in his own far-famed chains.

HERMOGENES: There is a deal of truth in what you say.

SOCRATES: Yes, Hermogenes, and the legislator called him Hades, not from the unseen (aeides)—far otherwise, but from his knowledge (eidenai) of all noble things.

HERMOGENES: Very good; and what do we say of Demeter, and Here, and Apollo, and Athene, and Hephaestus, and Ares, and the other deities?

SOCRATES: Demeter is e didousa meter, who gives food like a mother; Here is the lovely one (erate)—for Zeus, according to tradition, loved and married her; possibly also the name may have been given when the legislator was thinking of the heavens, and may be only a disguise of the air (aer), putting the end in the place of the beginning. You will recognize the truth of this if you repeat the letters of Here several times over. People dread the name of Pherephatta as they dread the name of Apollo,—and with as little reason; the fear, if I am not mistaken, only arises from their ignorance of the nature of names. But they go changing the name into Phersephone, and they are terrified at this; whereas the new name means only that the Goddess is wise (sophe); for seeing that all things in the world are in motion (pheromenon), that principle which embraces and touches and is able to follow them, is wisdom. And therefore the Goddess may be truly called Pherepaphe (Pherepapha), or some name like it, because she touches that which is in motion (tou pheromenon ephaptomene), herein showing her wisdom. And Hades, who is wise, consorts with her, because she is wise. They alter her name into Pherephatta now-a-days, because the present generation care for euphony more than truth. There is the other name, Apollo, which, as I was saying, is generally supposed to have some terrible signification. Have you remarked this fact?

HERMOGENES: To be sure I have, and what you say is true.

SOCRATES: But the name, in my opinion, is really most expressive of the power of the God.

HERMOGENES: How so?

SOCRATES: I will endeavour to explain, for I do not believe that any single name could have been better adapted to express the attributes of the God, embracing and in a manner signifying all four of them,—music, and prophecy, and medicine, and archery.

HERMOGENES: That must be a strange name, and I should like to hear the explanation.

SOCRATES: Say rather an harmonious name, as beseems the God of Harmony. In the first place, the purgations and purifications which doctors and diviners use, and their fumigations with drugs magical or medicinal, as well as their washings and lustral sprinklings, have all one and the same object, which is to make a man pure both in body and soul.

HERMOGENES: Very true.

SOCRATES: And is not Apollo the purifier, and the washer, and the absolver from all impurities?

HERMOGENES: Very true.

SOCRATES: Then in reference to his ablutions and absolutions, as being the physician who orders them, he may be rightly called Apolouon (purifier); or in respect of his powers of divination, and his truth and sincerity, which is the same as truth, he may be most fitly called Aplos, from aplous (sincere), as in the Thessalian dialect, for all the Thessalians call him Aplos; also he is aei Ballon (always shooting), because he is a master archer who never misses; or again, the name may refer to his musical attributes, and then, as in akolouthos, and akoitis, and in many other words the alpha is supposed to mean 'together,' so the meaning of the name Apollo will be 'moving together,' whether in the poles of heaven as they are called, or in the harmony of song, which is termed concord, because he moves all together by an harmonious power, as astronomers and musicians ingeniously declare. And he is the God who presides over harmony, and makes all things move together, both among Gods and among men. And as in the words akolouthos and akoitis the alpha is substituted for an omicron, so the name Apollon is equivalent to omopolon; only the second lambda is added in order to avoid the ill-omened sound of destruction (apolon). Now the suspicion of this destructive power still haunts the minds of some who do not consider the true value of the name, which, as I was saying just now, has reference to all the powers of the God, who is the single one, the everdarting, the purifier, the mover together (aplous, aei Ballon, apolouon, omopolon). The name of the Muses and of music would seem to be derived from their making philosophical enquiries (mosthai); and Leto is called by this name, because she is such a gentle Goddess, and so willing (ethelemon) to grant our requests; or her name may be Letho, as she is often called by strangers—they seem to imply by it her amiability, and her smooth and easy-going way of behaving. Artemis is named from her healthy (artemes), well-ordered nature, and because of her love of virginity, perhaps because she is a proficient in virtue (arete), and perhaps also as hating intercourse of the sexes (ton aroton misesasa). He who gave the Goddess her name may have had any or all of these reasons.

HERMOGENES: What is the meaning of Dionysus and Aphrodite?

SOCRATES: Son of Hipponicus, you ask a solemn question; there is a serious and also a facetious explanation of both these names; the serious explanation is not to be had from me, but there is no objection to your hearing the facetious one; for the Gods too love a joke. Dionusos is simply didous oinon (giver of wine), Didoinusos, as he might be called in fun,—and oinos is properly oionous, because wine makes those who drink, think (oiesthai) that they have a mind (noun) when they have none. The derivation of Aphrodite, born of the foam (aphros), may be fairly accepted on the authority of Hesiod.

HERMOGENES: Still there remains Athene, whom you, Socrates, as an Athenian, will surely not forget; there are also Hephaestus and Ares.

SOCRATES: I am not likely to forget them.

HERMOGENES: No, indeed.

SOCRATES: There is no difficulty in explaining the other appellation of Athene.

HERMOGENES: What other appellation?

SOCRATES: We call her Pallas.

HERMOGENES: To be sure.

SOCRATES: And we cannot be wrong in supposing that this is derived from armed dances. For the elevation of oneself or anything else above the earth, or by the use of the hands, we call shaking (pallein), or dancing.

HERMOGENES: That is quite true.

SOCRATES: Then that is the explanation of the name Pallas?

HERMOGENES: Yes; but what do you say of the other name?

SOCRATES: Athene?

HERMOGENES: Yes.

SOCRATES: That is a graver matter, and there, my friend, the modern interpreters of Homer may, I think, assist in explaining the view of the ancients. For most of these in their explanations of the poet, assert that he meant by Athene 'mind' (nous) and 'intelligence' (dianoia), and the maker of names appears to have had a singular notion about her; and indeed calls her by a still higher title, 'divine intelligence' (Thou noesis), as though he would say: This is she who has the mind of God (Theonoa);—using alpha as a dialectical variety for eta, and taking away iota and sigma (There seems to be some error in the MSS. The meaning is that the word theonoa = theounoa is a curtailed form of theou noesis, but the omitted letters do not agree.). Perhaps, however, the name Theonoe may mean 'she who knows divine things' (Theia noousa) better than others. Nor shall we be far wrong in supposing that the author of it wished to identify this Goddess with moral intelligence (en ethei noesin), and therefore gave her the name ethonoe; which, however, either he or his successors have altered into what they thought a nicer form, and called her Athene.

HERMOGENES: But what do you say of Hephaestus?

SOCRATES: Speak you of the princely lord of light (Phaeos istora)?

HERMOGENES: Surely.

SOCRATES: Ephaistos is Phaistos, and has added the eta by attraction; that is obvious to anybody.

HERMOGENES: That is very probable, until some more probable notion gets into your head.

SOCRATES: To prevent that, you had better ask what is the derivation of Ares.

HERMOGENES: What is Ares?

SOCRATES: Ares may be called, if you will, from his manhood (arren) and manliness, or if you please, from his hard and unchangeable nature, which is the meaning of arratos: the latter is a derivation in every way appropriate to the God of war.

HERMOGENES: Very true.

SOCRATES: And now, by the Gods, let us have no more of the Gods, for I am afraid of them; ask about anything but them, and thou shalt see how the steeds of Euthyphro can prance.

HERMOGENES: Only one more God! I should like to know about Hermes, of whom I am said not to be a true son. Let us make him out, and then I shall know whether there is any meaning in what Cratylus says.

SOCRATES: I should imagine that the name Hermes has to do with speech, and signifies that he is the interpreter (ermeneus), or messenger, or thief, or liar, or bargainer; all that sort of thing has a great deal to do with language; as I was telling you, the word eirein is expressive of the use of speech, and there is an often-recurring Homeric word emesato, which means 'he contrived'—out of these two words, eirein and mesasthai, the legislator formed the name of the God who invented language and speech; and we may imagine him dictating to us the use of this name: 'O my friends,' says he to us, 'seeing that he is the contriver of tales or speeches, you may rightly call him Eirhemes.' And this has been improved by us, as we think, into Hermes. Iris also appears to have been called from the verb 'to tell' (eirein), because she was a messenger.

HERMOGENES: Then I am very sure that Cratylus was quite right in saying that I was no true son of Hermes (Ermogenes), for I am not a good hand at speeches.

SOCRATES: There is also reason, my friend, in Pan being the double-formed son of Hermes.

HERMOGENES: How do you make that out?

SOCRATES: You are aware that speech signifies all things (pan), and is always turning them round and round, and has two forms, true and false?

HERMOGENES: Certainly.

SOCRATES: Is not the truth that is in him the smooth or sacred form which dwells above among the Gods, whereas falsehood dwells among men below, and is rough like the goat of tragedy; for tales and falsehoods have generally to do with the tragic or goatish life, and tragedy is the place of them?

HERMOGENES: Very true.

SOCRATES: Then surely Pan, who is the declarer of all things (pan) and the perpetual mover (aei polon) of all things, is rightly called aipolos (goat-herd), he being the two-formed son of Hermes, smooth in his upper part, and rough and goatlike in his lower regions. And, as the son of Hermes, he is speech or the brother of speech, and that brother should be like brother is no marvel. But, as I was saying, my dear Hermogenes, let us get away from the Gods.

HERMOGENES: From these sort of Gods, by all means, Socrates. But why should we not discuss another kind of Gods—the sun, moon, stars, earth, aether, air, fire, water, the seasons, and the year?

SOCRATES: You impose a great many tasks upon me. Still, if you wish, I will not refuse.

HERMOGENES: You will oblige me.

SOCRATES: How would you have me begin? Shall I take first of all him whom you mentioned first—the sun?

HERMOGENES: Very good.

SOCRATES: The origin of the sun will probably be clearer in the Doric form, for the Dorians call him alios, and this name is given to him because when he rises he gathers (alizoi) men together or because he is always rolling in his course (aei eilein ion) about the earth; or from aiolein, of which the meaning is the same as poikillein (to variegate), because he variegates the productions of the earth.

HERMOGENES: But what is selene (the moon)?

SOCRATES: That name is rather unfortunate for Anaxagoras.

HERMOGENES: How so?

SOCRATES: The word seems to forestall his recent discovery, that the moon receives her light from the sun.

HERMOGENES: Why do you say so?

SOCRATES: The two words selas (brightness) and phos (light) have much the same meaning?

HERMOGENES: Yes.

SOCRATES: This light about the moon is always new (neon) and always old (enon), if the disciples of Anaxagoras say truly. For the sun in his revolution always adds new light, and there is the old light of the previous month.

HERMOGENES: Very true.

SOCRATES: The moon is not unfrequently called selanaia.

HERMOGENES: True.

SOCRATES: And as she has a light which is always old and always new (enon neon aei) she may very properly have the name selaenoneoaeia; and this when hammered into shape becomes selanaia.

HERMOGENES: A real dithyrambic sort of name that, Socrates. But what do you say of the month and the stars?

SOCRATES: Meis (month) is called from meiousthai (to lessen), because suffering diminution; the name of astra (stars) seems to be derived from astrape, which is an improvement on anastrope, signifying the upsetting of the eyes (anastrephein opa).

HERMOGENES: What do you say of pur (fire) and udor (water)?

SOCRATES: I am at a loss how to explain pur; either the muse of Euthyphro has deserted me, or there is some very great difficulty in the word. Please, however, to note the contrivance which I adopt whenever I am in a difficulty of this sort.

HERMOGENES: What is it?

SOCRATES: I will tell you; but I should like to know first whether you can tell me what is the meaning of the pur?

HERMOGENES: Indeed I cannot.

SOCRATES: Shall I tell you what I suspect to be the true explanation of this and several other words?—My belief is that they are of foreign origin. For the Hellenes, especially those who were under the dominion of the barbarians, often borrowed from them.

HERMOGENES: What is the inference?

SOCRATES: Why, you know that any one who seeks to demonstrate the fitness of these names according to the Hellenic language, and not according to the language from which the words are derived, is rather likely to be at fault.

HERMOGENES: Yes, certainly.

SOCRATES: Well then, consider whether this pur is not foreign; for the word is not easily brought into relation with the Hellenic tongue, and the Phrygians may be observed to have the same word slightly changed, just as they have udor (water) and kunes (dogs), and many other words.

HERMOGENES: That is true.

SOCRATES: Any violent interpretations of the words should be avoided; for something to say about them may easily be found. And thus I get rid of pur and udor. Aer (air), Hermogenes, may be explained as the element which raises (airei) things from the earth, or as ever flowing (aei rei), or because the flux of the air is wind, and the poets call the winds 'air-blasts,' (aetai); he who uses the term may mean, so to speak, air-flux (aetorroun), in the sense of wind-flux (pneumatorroun); and because this moving wind may be expressed by either term he employs the word air (aer = aetes rheo). Aither (aether) I should interpret as aeitheer; this may be correctly said, because this element is always running in a flux about the air (aei thei peri tou aera reon). The meaning of the word ge (earth) comes out better when in the form of gaia, for the earth may be truly called 'mother' (gaia, genneteira), as in the language of Homer (Od.) gegaasi means gegennesthai.

HERMOGENES: Good.

SOCRATES: What shall we take next?

HERMOGENES: There are orai (the seasons), and the two names of the year, eniautos and etos.

SOCRATES: The orai should be spelt in the old Attic way, if you desire to know the probable truth about them; they are rightly called the orai because they divide (orizousin) the summers and winters and winds and the fruits of the earth. The words eniautos and etos appear to be the same,—'that which brings to light the plants and growths of the earth in their turn, and passes them in review within itself (en eauto exetazei)': this is broken up into two words, eniautos from en eauto, and etos from etazei, just as the original name of Zeus was divided into Zena and Dia; and the whole proposition means that his power of reviewing from within is one, but has two names, two words etos and eniautos being thus formed out of a single proposition.

HERMOGENES: Indeed, Socrates, you make surprising progress.

SOCRATES: I am run away with.

HERMOGENES: Very true.

SOCRATES: But am not yet at my utmost speed.

HERMOGENES: I should like very much to know, in the next place, how you would explain the virtues. What principle of correctness is there in those charming words—wisdom, understanding, justice, and the rest of them?

SOCRATES: That is a tremendous class of names which you are disinterring; still, as I have put on the lion's skin, I must not be faint of heart; and I suppose that I must consider the meaning of wisdom (phronesis) and understanding (sunesis), and judgment (gnome), and knowledge (episteme), and all those other charming words, as you call them?

HERMOGENES: Surely, we must not leave off until we find out their meaning.

SOCRATES: By the dog of Egypt I have a not bad notion which came into my head only this moment: I believe that the primeval givers of names were undoubtedly like too many of our modern philosophers, who, in their search after the nature of things, are always getting dizzy from constantly going round and round, and then they imagine that the world is going round and round and moving in all directions; and this appearance, which arises out of their own internal condition, they suppose to be a reality of nature; they think that there is nothing stable or permanent, but only flux and motion, and that the world is always full of every sort of motion and change. The consideration of the names which I mentioned has led me into making this reflection.

HERMOGENES: How is that, Socrates?

SOCRATES: Perhaps you did not observe that in the names which have been just cited, the motion or flux or generation of things is most surely indicated.

HERMOGENES: No, indeed, I never thought of it.

SOCRATES: Take the first of those which you mentioned; clearly that is a name indicative of motion.

HERMOGENES: What was the name?

SOCRATES: Phronesis (wisdom), which may signify phoras kai rhou noesis (perception of motion and flux), or perhaps phoras onesis (the blessing of motion), but is at any rate connected with pheresthai (motion); gnome (judgment), again, certainly implies the ponderation or consideration (nomesis) of generation, for to ponder is the same as to consider; or, if you would rather, here is noesis, the very word just now mentioned, which is neou esis (the desire of the new); the word neos implies that the world is always in process of creation. The giver of the name wanted to express this longing of the soul, for the original name was neoesis, and not noesis; but eta took the place of a double epsilon. The word sophrosune is the salvation (soteria) of that wisdom (phronesis) which we were just now considering. Epioteme (knowledge) is akin to this, and indicates that the soul which is good for anything follows (epetai) the motion of things, neither anticipating them nor falling behind them; wherefore the word should rather be read as epistemene, inserting epsilon nu. Sunesis (understanding) may be regarded in like manner as a kind of conclusion; the word is derived from sunienai (to go along with), and, like epistasthai (to know), implies the progression of the soul in company with the nature of things. Sophia (wisdom) is very dark, and appears not to be of native growth; the meaning is, touching the motion or stream of things. You must remember that the poets, when they speak of the commencement of any rapid motion, often use the word esuthe (he rushed); and there was a famous Lacedaemonian who was named Sous (Rush), for by this word the Lacedaemonians signify rapid motion, and the touching (epaphe) of motion is expressed by sophia, for all things are supposed to be in motion. Good (agathon) is the name which is given to the admirable (agasto) in nature; for, although all things move, still there are degrees of motion; some are swifter, some slower; but there are some things which are admirable for their swiftness, and this admirable part of nature is called agathon. Dikaiosune (justice) is clearly dikaiou sunesis (understanding of the just); but the actual word dikaion is more difficult: men are only agreed to a certain extent about justice, and then they begin to disagree. For those who suppose all things to be in motion conceive the greater part of nature to be a mere receptacle; and they say that there is a penetrating power which passes through all this, and is the instrument of creation in all, and is the subtlest and swiftest element; for if it were not the subtlest, and a power which none can keep out, and also the swiftest, passing by other things as if they were standing still, it could not penetrate through the moving universe. And this element, which superintends all things and pierces (diaion) all, is rightly called dikaion; the letter k is only added for the sake of euphony. Thus far, as I was saying, there is a general agreement about the nature of justice; but I, Hermogenes, being an enthusiastic disciple, have been told in a mystery that the justice of which I am speaking is also the cause of the world: now a cause is that because of which anything is created; and some one comes and whispers in my ear that justice is rightly so called because partaking of the nature of the cause, and I begin, after hearing what he has said, to interrogate him gently: 'Well, my excellent friend,' say I, 'but if all this be true, I still want to know what is justice.' Thereupon they think that I ask tiresome questions, and am leaping over the barriers, and have been already sufficiently answered, and they try to satisfy me with one derivation after another, and at length they quarrel. For one of them says that justice is the sun, and that he only is the piercing (diaionta) and burning (kaonta) element which is the guardian of nature. And when I joyfully repeat this beautiful notion, I am answered by the satirical remark, 'What, is there no justice in the world when the sun is down?' And when I earnestly beg my questioner to tell me his own honest opinion, he says, 'Fire in the abstract'; but this is not very intelligible. Another says, 'No, not fire in the abstract, but the abstraction of heat in the fire.' Another man professes to laugh at all this, and says, as Anaxagoras says, that justice is mind, for mind, as they say, has absolute power, and mixes with nothing, and orders all things, and passes through all things. At last, my friend, I find myself in far greater perplexity about the nature of justice than I was before I began to learn. But still I am of opinion that the name, which has led me into this digression, was given to justice for the reasons which I have mentioned.

HERMOGENES: I think, Socrates, that you are not improvising now; you must have heard this from some one else.

SOCRATES: And not the rest?

HERMOGENES: Hardly.

SOCRATES: Well, then, let me go on in the hope of making you believe in the originality of the rest. What remains after justice? I do not think that we have as yet discussed courage (andreia),—injustice (adikia), which is obviously nothing more than a hindrance to the penetrating principle (diaiontos), need not be considered. Well, then, the name of andreia seems to imply a battle;—this battle is in the world of existence, and according to the doctrine of flux is only the counterflux (enantia rhon): if you extract the delta from andreia, the name at once signifies the thing, and you may clearly understand that andreia is not the stream opposed to every stream, but only to that which is contrary to justice, for otherwise courage would not have been praised. The words arren (male) and aner (man) also contain a similar allusion to the same principle of the upward flux (te ano rhon). Gune (woman) I suspect to be the same word as goun (birth): thelu (female) appears to be partly derived from thele (the teat), because the teat is like rain, and makes things flourish (tethelenai).

HERMOGENES: That is surely probable.

SOCRATES: Yes; and the very word thallein (to flourish) seems to figure the growth of youth, which is swift and sudden ever. And this is expressed by the legislator in the name, which is a compound of thein (running), and allesthai (leaping). Pray observe how I gallop away when I get on smooth ground. There are a good many names generally thought to be of importance, which have still to be explained.

HERMOGENES: True.

SOCRATES: There is the meaning of the word techne (art), for example.

HERMOGENES: Very true.

SOCRATES: That may be identified with echonoe, and expresses the possession of mind: you have only to take away the tau and insert two omichrons, one between the chi and nu, and another between the nu and eta.

HERMOGENES: That is a very shabby etymology.

SOCRATES: Yes, my dear friend; but then you know that the original names have been long ago buried and disguised by people sticking on and stripping off letters for the sake of euphony, and twisting and bedizening them in all sorts of ways: and time too may have had a share in the change. Take, for example, the word katoptron; why is the letter rho inserted? This must surely be the addition of some one who cares nothing about the truth, but thinks only of putting the mouth into shape. And the additions are often such that at last no human being can possibly make out the original meaning of the word. Another example is the word sphigx, sphiggos, which ought properly to be phigx, phiggos, and there are other examples.

HERMOGENES: That is quite true, Socrates.

SOCRATES: And yet, if you are permitted to put in and pull out any letters which you please, names will be too easily made, and any name may be adapted to any object.

HERMOGENES: True.

SOCRATES: Yes, that is true. And therefore a wise dictator, like yourself, should observe the laws of moderation and probability.

HERMOGENES: Such is my desire.

SOCRATES: And mine, too, Hermogenes. But do not be too much of a precisian, or 'you will unnerve me of my strength (Iliad.).' When you have allowed me to add mechane (contrivance) to techne (art) I shall be at the top of my bent, for I conceive mechane to be a sign of great accomplishment—anein; for mekos has the meaning of greatness, and these two, mekos and anein, make up the word mechane. But, as I was saying, being now at the top of my bent, I should like to consider the meaning of the two words arete (virtue) and kakia (vice); arete I do not as yet understand, but kakia is transparent, and agrees with the principles which preceded, for all things being in a flux (ionton), kakia is kakos ion (going badly); and this evil motion when existing in the soul has the general name of kakia, or vice, specially appropriated to it. The meaning of kakos ienai may be further illustrated by the use of deilia (cowardice), which ought to have come after andreia, but was forgotten, and, as I fear, is not the only word which has been passed over. Deilia signifies that the soul is bound with a strong chain (desmos), for lian means strength, and therefore deilia expresses the greatest and strongest bond of the soul; and aporia (difficulty) is an evil of the same nature (from a (alpha) not, and poreuesthai to go), like anything else which is an impediment to motion and movement. Then the word kakia appears to mean kakos ienai, or going badly, or limping and halting; of which the consequence is, that the soul becomes filled with vice. And if kakia is the name of this sort of thing, arete will be the opposite of it, signifying in the first place ease of motion, then that the stream of the good soul is unimpeded, and has therefore the attribute of ever flowing without let or hindrance, and is therefore called arete, or, more correctly, aeireite (ever-flowing), and may perhaps have had another form, airete (eligible), indicating that nothing is more eligible than virtue, and this has been hammered into arete. I daresay that you will deem this to be another invention of mine, but I think that if the previous word kakia was right, then arete is also right.

HERMOGENES: But what is the meaning of kakon, which has played so great a part in your previous discourse?

SOCRATES: That is a very singular word about which I can hardly form an opinion, and therefore I must have recourse to my ingenious device.

HERMOGENES: What device?

SOCRATES: The device of a foreign origin, which I shall give to this word also.

HERMOGENES: Very likely you are right; but suppose that we leave these words and endeavour to see the rationale of kalon and aischron.

SOCRATES: The meaning of aischron is evident, being only aei ischon roes (always preventing from flowing), and this is in accordance with our former derivations. For the name-giver was a great enemy to stagnation of all sorts, and hence he gave the name aeischoroun to that which hindered the flux (aei ischon roun), and that is now beaten together into aischron.

HERMOGENES: But what do you say of kalon?

SOCRATES: That is more obscure; yet the form is only due to the quantity, and has been changed by altering omicron upsilon into omicron.

HERMOGENES: What do you mean?

SOCRATES: This name appears to denote mind.

HERMOGENES: How so?

SOCRATES: Let me ask you what is the cause why anything has a name; is not the principle which imposes the name the cause?

HERMOGENES: Certainly.

SOCRATES: And must not this be the mind of Gods, or of men, or of both?

HERMOGENES: Yes.

SOCRATES: Is not mind that which called (kalesan) things by their names, and is not mind the beautiful (kalon)?

HERMOGENES: That is evident.

SOCRATES: And are not the works of intelligence and mind worthy of praise, and are not other works worthy of blame?

HERMOGENES: Certainly.

SOCRATES: Physic does the work of a physician, and carpentering does the works of a carpenter?

HERMOGENES: Exactly.

SOCRATES: And the principle of beauty does the works of beauty?

HERMOGENES: Of course.

SOCRATES: And that principle we affirm to be mind?

HERMOGENES: Very true.

SOCRATES: Then mind is rightly called beauty because she does the works which we recognize and speak of as the beautiful?

HERMOGENES: That is evident.

SOCRATES: What more names remain to us?

HERMOGENES: There are the words which are connected with agathon and kalon, such as sumpheron and lusiteloun, ophelimon, kerdaleon, and their opposites.

SOCRATES: The meaning of sumpheron (expedient) I think that you may discover for yourself by the light of the previous examples,—for it is a sister word to episteme, meaning just the motion (pora) of the soul accompanying the world, and things which are done upon this principle are called sumphora or sumpheronta, because they are carried round with the world.

HERMOGENES: That is probable.

SOCRATES: Again, cherdaleon (gainful) is called from cherdos (gain), but you must alter the delta into nu if you want to get at the meaning; for this word also signifies good, but in another way; he who gave the name intended to express the power of admixture (kerannumenon) and universal penetration in the good; in forming the word, however, he inserted a delta instead of a nu, and so made kerdos.

HERMOGENES: Well, but what is lusiteloun (profitable)?

SOCRATES: I suppose, Hermogenes, that people do not mean by the profitable the gainful or that which pays (luei) the retailer, but they use the word in the sense of swift. You regard the profitable (lusiteloun), as that which being the swiftest thing in existence, allows of no stay in things and no pause or end of motion, but always, if there begins to be any end, lets things go again (luei), and makes motion immortal and unceasing: and in this point of view, as appears to me, the good is happily denominated lusiteloun—being that which looses (luon) the end (telos) of motion. Ophelimon (the advantageous) is derived from ophellein, meaning that which creates and increases; this latter is a common Homeric word, and has a foreign character.

HERMOGENES: And what do you say of their opposites?

SOCRATES: Of such as are mere negatives I hardly think that I need speak.

HERMOGENES: Which are they?

SOCRATES: The words axumphoron (inexpedient), anopheles (unprofitable), alusiteles (unadvantageous), akerdes (ungainful).

HERMOGENES: True.

SOCRATES: I would rather take the words blaberon (harmful), zemiodes (hurtful).

HERMOGENES: Good.

SOCRATES: The word blaberon is that which is said to hinder or harm (blaptein) the stream (roun); blapton is boulomenon aptein (seeking to hold or bind); for aptein is the same as dein, and dein is always a term of censure; boulomenon aptein roun (wanting to bind the stream) would properly be boulapteroun, and this, as I imagine, is improved into blaberon.

HERMOGENES: You bring out curious results, Socrates, in the use of names; and when I hear the word boulapteroun I cannot help imagining that you are making your mouth into a flute, and puffing away at some prelude to Athene.

SOCRATES: That is the fault of the makers of the name, Hermogenes; not mine.

HERMOGENES: Very true; but what is the derivation of zemiodes?

SOCRATES: What is the meaning of zemiodes?—let me remark, Hermogenes, how right I was in saying that great changes are made in the meaning of words by putting in and pulling out letters; even a very slight permutation will sometimes give an entirely opposite sense; I may instance the word deon, which occurs to me at the moment, and reminds me of what I was going to say to you, that the fine fashionable language of modern times has twisted and disguised and entirely altered the original meaning both of deon, and also of zemiodes, which in the old language is clearly indicated.

HERMOGENES: What do you mean?

SOCRATES: I will try to explain. You are aware that our forefathers loved the sounds iota and delta, especially the women, who are most conservative of the ancient language, but now they change iota into eta or epsilon, and delta into zeta; this is supposed to increase the grandeur of the sound.

HERMOGENES: How do you mean?

SOCRATES: For example, in very ancient times they called the day either imera or emera (short e), which is called by us emera (long e).

HERMOGENES: That is true.

SOCRATES: Do you observe that only the ancient form shows the intention of the giver of the name? of which the reason is, that men long for (imeirousi) and love the light which comes after the darkness, and is therefore called imera, from imeros, desire.

HERMOGENES: Clearly.

SOCRATES: But now the name is so travestied that you cannot tell the meaning, although there are some who imagine the day to be called emera because it makes things gentle (emera different accents).

HERMOGENES: Such is my view.

SOCRATES: And do you know that the ancients said duogon and not zugon?

HERMOGENES: They did so.

SOCRATES: And zugon (yoke) has no meaning,—it ought to be duogon, which word expresses the binding of two together (duein agoge) for the purpose of drawing;—this has been changed into zugon, and there are many other examples of similar changes.

HERMOGENES: There are.

SOCRATES: Proceeding in the same train of thought I may remark that the word deon (obligation) has a meaning which is the opposite of all the other appellations of good; for deon is here a species of good, and is, nevertheless, the chain (desmos) or hinderer of motion, and therefore own brother of blaberon.

HERMOGENES: Yes, Socrates; that is quite plain.

SOCRATES: Not if you restore the ancient form, which is more likely to be the correct one, and read dion instead of deon; if you convert the epsilon into an iota after the old fashion, this word will then agree with other words meaning good; for dion, not deon, signifies the good, and is a term of praise; and the author of names has not contradicted himself, but in all these various appellations, deon (obligatory), ophelimon (advantageous), lusiteloun (profitable), kerdaleon (gainful), agathon (good), sumpheron (expedient), euporon (plenteous), the same conception is implied of the ordering or all-pervading principle which is praised, and the restraining and binding principle which is censured. And this is further illustrated by the word zemiodes (hurtful), which if the zeta is only changed into delta as in the ancient language, becomes demiodes; and this name, as you will perceive, is given to that which binds motion (dounti ion).

HERMOGENES: What do you say of edone (pleasure), lupe (pain), epithumia (desire), and the like, Socrates?

SOCRATES: I do not think, Hermogenes, that there is any great difficulty about them—edone is e (eta) onesis, the action which tends to advantage; and the original form may be supposed to have been eone, but this has been altered by the insertion of the delta. Lupe appears to be derived from the relaxation (luein) which the body feels when in sorrow; ania (trouble) is the hindrance of motion (alpha and ienai); algedon (distress), if I am not mistaken, is a foreign word, which is derived from aleinos (grievous); odune (grief) is called from the putting on (endusis) sorrow; in achthedon (vexation) 'the word too labours,' as any one may see; chara (joy) is the very expression of the fluency and diffusion of the soul (cheo); terpsis (delight) is so called from the pleasure creeping (erpon) through the soul, which may be likened to a breath (pnoe) and is properly erpnoun, but has been altered by time into terpnon; eupherosune (cheerfulness) and epithumia explain themselves; the former, which ought to be eupherosune and has been changed euphrosune, is named, as every one may see, from the soul moving (pheresthai) in harmony with nature; epithumia is really e epi ton thumon iousa dunamis, the power which enters into the soul; thumos (passion) is called from the rushing (thuseos) and boiling of the soul; imeros (desire) denotes the stream (rous) which most draws the soul dia ten esin tes roes—because flowing with desire (iemenos), and expresses a longing after things and violent attraction of the soul to them, and is termed imeros from possessing this power; pothos (longing) is expressive of the desire of that which is not present but absent, and in another place (pou); this is the reason why the name pothos is applied to things absent, as imeros is to things present; eros (love) is so called because flowing in (esron) from without; the stream is not inherent, but is an influence introduced through the eyes, and from flowing in was called esros (influx) in the old time when they used omicron for omega, and is called eros, now that omega is substituted for omicron. But why do you not give me another word?

HERMOGENES: What do you think of doxa (opinion), and that class of words?

SOCRATES: Doxa is either derived from dioxis (pursuit), and expresses the march of the soul in the pursuit of knowledge, or from the shooting of a bow (toxon); the latter is more likely, and is confirmed by oiesis (thinking), which is only oisis (moving), and implies the movement of the soul to the essential nature of each thing—just as boule (counsel) has to do with shooting (bole); and boulesthai (to wish) combines the notion of aiming and deliberating—all these words seem to follow doxa, and all involve the idea of shooting, just as aboulia, absence of counsel, on the other hand, is a mishap, or missing, or mistaking of the mark, or aim, or proposal, or object.

HERMOGENES: You are quickening your pace now, Socrates.

SOCRATES: Why yes, the end I now dedicate to God, not, however, until I have explained anagke (necessity), which ought to come next, and ekousion (the voluntary). Ekousion is certainly the yielding (eikon) and unresisting—the notion implied is yielding and not opposing, yielding, as I was just now saying, to that motion which is in accordance with our will; but the necessary and resistant being contrary to our will, implies error and ignorance; the idea is taken from walking through a ravine which is impassable, and rugged, and overgrown, and impedes motion—and this is the derivation of the word anagkaion (necessary) an agke ion, going through a ravine. But while my strength lasts let us persevere, and I hope that you will persevere with your questions.

HERMOGENES: Well, then, let me ask about the greatest and noblest, such as aletheia (truth) and pseudos (falsehood) and on (being), not forgetting to enquire why the word onoma (name), which is the theme of our discussion, has this name of onoma.

SOCRATES: You know the word maiesthai (to seek)?

HERMOGENES: Yes;—meaning the same as zetein (to enquire).

SOCRATES: The word onoma seems to be a compressed sentence, signifying on ou zetema (being for which there is a search); as is still more obvious in onomaston (notable), which states in so many words that real existence is that for which there is a seeking (on ou masma); aletheia is also an agglomeration of theia ale (divine wandering), implying the divine motion of existence; pseudos (falsehood) is the opposite of motion; here is another ill name given by the legislator to stagnation and forced inaction, which he compares to sleep (eudein); but the original meaning of the word is disguised by the addition of psi; on and ousia are ion with an iota broken off; this agrees with the true principle, for being (on) is also moving (ion), and the same may be said of not being, which is likewise called not going (oukion or ouki on = ouk ion).

HERMOGENES: You have hammered away at them manfully; but suppose that some one were to say to you, what is the word ion, and what are reon and doun?—show me their fitness.

SOCRATES: You mean to say, how should I answer him?

HERMOGENES: Yes.

SOCRATES: One way of giving the appearance of an answer has been already suggested.

HERMOGENES: What way?

SOCRATES: To say that names which we do not understand are of foreign origin; and this is very likely the right answer, and something of this kind may be true of them; but also the original forms of words may have been lost in the lapse of ages; names have been so twisted in all manner of ways, that I should not be surprised if the old language when compared with that now in use would appear to us to be a barbarous tongue.

HERMOGENES: Very likely.

SOCRATES: Yes, very likely. But still the enquiry demands our earnest attention and we must not flinch. For we should remember, that if a person go on analysing names into words, and enquiring also into the elements out of which the words are formed, and keeps on always repeating this process, he who has to answer him must at last give up the enquiry in despair.

HERMOGENES: Very true.

SOCRATES: And at what point ought he to lose heart and give up the enquiry? Must he not stop when he comes to the names which are the elements of all other names and sentences; for these cannot be supposed to be made up of other names? The word agathon (good), for example, is, as we were saying, a compound of agastos (admirable) and thoos (swift). And probably thoos is made up of other elements, and these again of others. But if we take a word which is incapable of further resolution, then we shall be right in saying that we have at last reached a primary element, which need not be resolved any further.

HERMOGENES: I believe you to be in the right.

SOCRATES: And suppose the names about which you are now asking should turn out to be primary elements, must not their truth or law be examined according to some new method?

HERMOGENES: Very likely.

SOCRATES: Quite so, Hermogenes; all that has preceded would lead to this conclusion. And if, as I think, the conclusion is true, then I shall again say to you, come and help me, that I may not fall into some absurdity in stating the principle of primary names.

HERMOGENES: Let me hear, and I will do my best to assist you.

SOCRATES: I think that you will acknowledge with me, that one principle is applicable to all names, primary as well as secondary—when they are regarded simply as names, there is no difference in them.

HERMOGENES: Certainly not.

SOCRATES: All the names that we have been explaining were intended to indicate the nature of things.

HERMOGENES: Of course.

SOCRATES: And that this is true of the primary quite as much as of the secondary names, is implied in their being names.

HERMOGENES: Surely.

SOCRATES: But the secondary, as I conceive, derive their significance from the primary.

HERMOGENES: That is evident.

SOCRATES: Very good; but then how do the primary names which precede analysis show the natures of things, as far as they can be shown; which they must do, if they are to be real names? And here I will ask you a question: Suppose that we had no voice or tongue, and wanted to communicate with one another, should we not, like the deaf and dumb, make signs with the hands and head and the rest of the body?

HERMOGENES: There would be no choice, Socrates.

SOCRATES: We should imitate the nature of the thing; the elevation of our hands to heaven would mean lightness and upwardness; heaviness and downwardness would be expressed by letting them drop to the ground; if we were describing the running of a horse, or any other animal, we should make our bodies and their gestures as like as we could to them.

HERMOGENES: I do not see that we could do anything else.

SOCRATES: We could not; for by bodily imitation only can the body ever express anything.

HERMOGENES: Very true.

SOCRATES: And when we want to express ourselves, either with the voice, or tongue, or mouth, the expression is simply their imitation of that which we want to express.

HERMOGENES: It must be so, I think.

SOCRATES: Then a name is a vocal imitation of that which the vocal imitator names or imitates?

HERMOGENES: I think so.

SOCRATES: Nay, my friend, I am disposed to think that we have not reached the truth as yet.

HERMOGENES: Why not?

SOCRATES: Because if we have we shall be obliged to admit that the people who imitate sheep, or cocks, or other animals, name that which they imitate.

HERMOGENES: Quite true.

SOCRATES: Then could I have been right in what I was saying?

HERMOGENES: In my opinion, no. But I wish that you would tell me, Socrates, what sort of an imitation is a name?

SOCRATES: In the first place, I should reply, not a musical imitation, although that is also vocal; nor, again, an imitation of what music imitates; these, in my judgment, would not be naming. Let me put the matter as follows: All objects have sound and figure, and many have colour?

HERMOGENES: Certainly.

SOCRATES: But the art of naming appears not to be concerned with imitations of this kind; the arts which have to do with them are music and drawing?

HERMOGENES: True.

SOCRATES: Again, is there not an essence of each thing, just as there is a colour, or sound? And is there not an essence of colour and sound as well as of anything else which may be said to have an essence?

HERMOGENES: I should think so.

SOCRATES: Well, and if any one could express the essence of each thing in letters and syllables, would he not express the nature of each thing?

HERMOGENES: Quite so.

SOCRATES: The musician and the painter were the two names which you gave to the two other imitators. What will this imitator be called?

HERMOGENES: I imagine, Socrates, that he must be the namer, or name-giver, of whom we are in search.

SOCRATES: If this is true, then I think that we are in a condition to consider the names ron (stream), ienai (to go), schesis (retention), about which you were asking; and we may see whether the namer has grasped the nature of them in letters and syllables in such a manner as to imitate the essence or not.

HERMOGENES: Very good.

SOCRATES: But are these the only primary names, or are there others?

HERMOGENES: There must be others.

SOCRATES: So I should expect. But how shall we further analyse them, and where does the imitator begin? Imitation of the essence is made by syllables and letters; ought we not, therefore, first to separate the letters, just as those who are beginning rhythm first distinguish the powers of elementary, and then of compound sounds, and when they have done so, but not before, they proceed to the consideration of rhythms?

HERMOGENES: Yes.

SOCRATES: Must we not begin in the same way with letters; first separating the vowels, and then the consonants and mutes (letters which are neither vowels nor semivowels), into classes, according to the received distinctions of the learned; also the semivowels, which are neither vowels, nor yet mutes; and distinguishing into classes the vowels themselves? And when we have perfected the classification of things, we shall give them names, and see whether, as in the case of letters, there are any classes to which they may be all referred (cf. Phaedrus); and hence we shall see their natures, and see, too, whether they have in them classes as there are in the letters; and when we have well considered all this, we shall know how to apply them to what they resemble—whether one letter is used to denote one thing, or whether there is to be an admixture of several of them; just, as in painting, the painter who wants to depict anything sometimes uses purple only, or any other colour, and sometimes mixes up several colours, as his method is when he has to paint flesh colour or anything of that kind—he uses his colours as his figures appear to require them; and so, too, we shall apply letters to the expression of objects, either single letters when required, or several letters; and so we shall form syllables, as they are called, and from syllables make nouns and verbs; and thus, at last, from the combinations of nouns and verbs arrive at language, large and fair and whole; and as the painter made a figure, even so shall we make speech by the art of the namer or the rhetorician, or by some other art. Not that I am literally speaking of ourselves, but I was carried away—meaning to say that this was the way in which (not we but) the ancients formed language, and what they put together we must take to pieces in like manner, if we are to attain a scientific view of the whole subject, and we must see whether the primary, and also whether the secondary elements are rightly given or not, for if they are not, the composition of them, my dear Hermogenes, will be a sorry piece of work, and in the wrong direction.

HERMOGENES: That, Socrates, I can quite believe.

SOCRATES: Well, but do you suppose that you will be able to analyse them in this way? for I am certain that I should not.

HERMOGENES: Much less am I likely to be able.

SOCRATES: Shall we leave them, then? or shall we seek to discover, if we can, something about them, according to the measure of our ability, saying by way of preface, as I said before of the Gods, that of the truth about them we know nothing, and do but entertain human notions of them. And in this present enquiry, let us say to ourselves, before we proceed, that the higher method is the one which we or others who would analyse language to any good purpose must follow; but under the circumstances, as men say, we must do as well as we can. What do you think?

HERMOGENES: I very much approve.

SOCRATES: That objects should be imitated in letters and syllables, and so find expression, may appear ridiculous, Hermogenes, but it cannot be avoided—there is no better principle to which we can look for the truth of first names. Deprived of this, we must have recourse to divine help, like the tragic poets, who in any perplexity have their gods waiting in the air; and must get out of our difficulty in like fashion, by saying that 'the Gods gave the first names, and therefore they are right.' This will be the best contrivance, or perhaps that other notion may be even better still, of deriving them from some barbarous people, for the barbarians are older than we are; or we may say that antiquity has cast a veil over them, which is the same sort of excuse as the last; for all these are not reasons but only ingenious excuses for having no reasons concerning the truth of words. And yet any sort of ignorance of first or primitive names involves an ignorance of secondary words; for they can only be explained by the primary. Clearly then the professor of languages should be able to give a very lucid explanation of first names, or let him be assured he will only talk nonsense about the rest. Do you not suppose this to be true?

HERMOGENES: Certainly, Socrates.

SOCRATES: My first notions of original names are truly wild and ridiculous, though I have no objection to impart them to you if you desire, and I hope that you will communicate to me in return anything better which you may have.

HERMOGENES: Fear not; I will do my best.

SOCRATES: In the first place, the letter rho appears to me to be the general instrument expressing all motion (kinesis). But I have not yet explained the meaning of this latter word, which is just iesis (going); for the letter eta was not in use among the ancients, who only employed epsilon; and the root is kiein, which is a foreign form, the same as ienai. And the old word kinesis will be correctly given as iesis in corresponding modern letters. Assuming this foreign root kiein, and allowing for the change of the eta and the insertion of the nu, we have kinesis, which should have been kieinsis or eisis; and stasis is the negative of ienai (or eisis), and has been improved into stasis. Now the letter rho, as I was saying, appeared to the imposer of names an excellent instrument for the expression of motion; and he frequently uses the letter for this purpose: for example, in the actual words rein and roe he represents motion by rho; also in the words tromos (trembling), trachus (rugged); and again, in words such as krouein (strike), thrauein (crush), ereikein (bruise), thruptein (break), kermatixein (crumble), rumbein (whirl): of all these sorts of movements he generally finds an expression in the letter R, because, as I imagine, he had observed that the tongue was most agitated and least at rest in the pronunciation of this letter, which he therefore used in order to express motion, just as by the letter iota he expresses the subtle elements which pass through all things. This is why he uses the letter iota as imitative of motion, ienai, iesthai. And there is another class of letters, phi, psi, sigma, and xi, of which the pronunciation is accompanied by great expenditure of breath; these are used in the imitation of such notions as psuchron (shivering), xeon (seething), seiesthai, (to be shaken), seismos (shock), and are always introduced by the giver of names when he wants to imitate what is phusodes (windy). He seems to have thought that the closing and pressure of the tongue in the utterance of delta and tau was expressive of binding and rest in a place: he further observed the liquid movement of lambda, in the pronunciation of which the tongue slips, and in this he found the expression of smoothness, as in leios (level), and in the word oliothanein (to slip) itself, liparon (sleek), in the word kollodes (gluey), and the like: the heavier sound of gamma detained the slipping tongue, and the union of the two gave the notion of a glutinous clammy nature, as in glischros, glukus, gloiodes. The nu he observed to be sounded from within, and therefore to have a notion of inwardness; hence he introduced the sound in endos and entos: alpha he assigned to the expression of size, and nu of length, because they are great letters: omicron was the sign of roundness, and therefore there is plenty of omicron mixed up in the word goggulon (round). Thus did the legislator, reducing all things into letters and syllables, and impressing on them names and signs, and out of them by imitation compounding other signs. That is my view, Hermogenes, of the truth of names; but I should like to hear what Cratylus has more to say.

HERMOGENES: But, Socrates, as I was telling you before, Cratylus mystifies me; he says that there is a fitness of names, but he never explains what is this fitness, so that I cannot tell whether his obscurity is intended or not. Tell me now, Cratylus, here in the presence of Socrates, do you agree in what Socrates has been saying about names, or have you something better of your own? and if you have, tell me what your view is, and then you will either learn of Socrates, or Socrates and I will learn of you.

CRATYLUS: Well, but surely, Hermogenes, you do not suppose that you can learn, or I explain, any subject of importance all in a moment; at any rate, not such a subject as language, which is, perhaps, the very greatest of all.

HERMOGENES: No, indeed; but, as Hesiod says, and I agree with him, 'to add little to little' is worth while. And, therefore, if you think that you can add anything at all, however small, to our knowledge, take a little trouble and oblige Socrates, and me too, who certainly have a claim upon you.

SOCRATES: I am by no means positive, Cratylus, in the view which Hermogenes and myself have worked out; and therefore do not hesitate to say what you think, which if it be better than my own view I shall gladly accept. And I should not be at all surprized to find that you have found some better notion. For you have evidently reflected on these matters and have had teachers, and if you have really a better theory of the truth of names, you may count me in the number of your disciples.

CRATYLUS: You are right, Socrates, in saying that I have made a study of these matters, and I might possibly convert you into a disciple. But I fear that the opposite is more probable, and I already find myself moved to say to you what Achilles in the 'Prayers' says to Ajax,—

'Illustrious Ajax, son of Telamon, lord of the people, You appear to have spoken in all things much to my mind.'

And you, Socrates, appear to me to be an oracle, and to give answers much to my mind, whether you are inspired by Euthyphro, or whether some Muse may have long been an inhabitant of your breast, unconsciously to yourself.

SOCRATES: Excellent Cratylus, I have long been wondering at my own wisdom; I cannot trust myself. And I think that I ought to stop and ask myself What am I saying? for there is nothing worse than self-deception—when the deceiver is always at home and always with you—it is quite terrible, and therefore I ought often to retrace my steps and endeavour to 'look fore and aft,' in the words of the aforesaid Homer. And now let me see; where are we? Have we not been saying that the correct name indicates the nature of the thing:—has this proposition been sufficiently proven?

CRATYLUS: Yes, Socrates, what you say, as I am disposed to think, is quite true.

SOCRATES: Names, then, are given in order to instruct?

CRATYLUS: Certainly.

SOCRATES: And naming is an art, and has artificers?

CRATYLUS: Yes.

SOCRATES: And who are they?

CRATYLUS: The legislators, of whom you spoke at first.

SOCRATES: And does this art grow up among men like other arts? Let me explain what I mean: of painters, some are better and some worse?

CRATYLUS: Yes.

SOCRATES: The better painters execute their works, I mean their figures, better, and the worse execute them worse; and of builders also, the better sort build fairer houses, and the worse build them worse.

CRATYLUS: True.

SOCRATES: And among legislators, there are some who do their work better and some worse?

CRATYLUS: No; there I do not agree with you.

SOCRATES: Then you do not think that some laws are better and others worse?

CRATYLUS: No, indeed.

SOCRATES: Or that one name is better than another?

CRATYLUS: Certainly not.

SOCRATES: Then all names are rightly imposed?

CRATYLUS: Yes, if they are names at all.

SOCRATES: Well, what do you say to the name of our friend Hermogenes, which was mentioned before:—assuming that he has nothing of the nature of Hermes in him, shall we say that this is a wrong name, or not his name at all?

CRATYLUS: I should reply that Hermogenes is not his name at all, but only appears to be his, and is really the name of somebody else, who has the nature which corresponds to it.

SOCRATES: And if a man were to call him Hermogenes, would he not be even speaking falsely? For there may be a doubt whether you can call him Hermogenes, if he is not.

CRATYLUS: What do you mean?

SOCRATES: Are you maintaining that falsehood is impossible? For if this is your meaning I should answer, that there have been plenty of liars in all ages.

CRATYLUS: Why, Socrates, how can a man say that which is not?—say something and yet say nothing? For is not falsehood saying the thing which is not?

SOCRATES: Your argument, friend, is too subtle for a man of my age. But I should like to know whether you are one of those philosophers who think that falsehood may be spoken but not said?

CRATYLUS: Neither spoken nor said.

SOCRATES: Nor uttered nor addressed? For example: If a person, saluting you in a foreign country, were to take your hand and say: 'Hail, Athenian stranger, Hermogenes, son of Smicrion'—these words, whether spoken, said, uttered, or addressed, would have no application to you but only to our friend Hermogenes, or perhaps to nobody at all?

CRATYLUS: In my opinion, Socrates, the speaker would only be talking nonsense.

SOCRATES: Well, but that will be quite enough for me, if you will tell me whether the nonsense would be true or false, or partly true and partly false:—which is all that I want to know.

CRATYLUS: I should say that he would be putting himself in motion to no purpose; and that his words would be an unmeaning sound like the noise of hammering at a brazen pot.

SOCRATES: But let us see, Cratylus, whether we cannot find a meeting-point, for you would admit that the name is not the same with the thing named?

CRATYLUS: I should.

SOCRATES: And would you further acknowledge that the name is an imitation of the thing?

CRATYLUS: Certainly.

SOCRATES: And you would say that pictures are also imitations of things, but in another way?

CRATYLUS: Yes.

SOCRATES: I believe you may be right, but I do not rightly understand you. Please to say, then, whether both sorts of imitation (I mean both pictures or words) are not equally attributable and applicable to the things of which they are the imitation.

CRATYLUS: They are.

SOCRATES: First look at the matter thus: you may attribute the likeness of the man to the man, and of the woman to the woman; and so on?

CRATYLUS: Certainly.

SOCRATES: And conversely you may attribute the likeness of the man to the woman, and of the woman to the man?

CRATYLUS: Very true.

SOCRATES: And are both modes of assigning them right, or only the first?

CRATYLUS: Only the first.

SOCRATES: That is to say, the mode of assignment which attributes to each that which belongs to them and is like them?

CRATYLUS: That is my view.

SOCRATES: Now then, as I am desirous that we being friends should have a good understanding about the argument, let me state my view to you: the first mode of assignment, whether applied to figures or to names, I call right, and when applied to names only, true as well as right; and the other mode of giving and assigning the name which is unlike, I call wrong, and in the case of names, false as well as wrong.

CRATYLUS: That may be true, Socrates, in the case of pictures; they may be wrongly assigned; but not in the case of names—they must be always right.

SOCRATES: Why, what is the difference? May I not go to a man and say to him, 'This is your picture,' showing him his own likeness, or perhaps the likeness of a woman; and when I say 'show,' I mean bring before the sense of sight.

CRATYLUS: Certainly.

SOCRATES: And may I not go to him again, and say, 'This is your name'?—for the name, like the picture, is an imitation. May I not say to him—'This is your name'? and may I not then bring to his sense of hearing the imitation of himself, when I say, 'This is a man'; or of a female of the human species, when I say, 'This is a woman,' as the case may be? Is not all that quite possible?

CRATYLUS: I would fain agree with you, Socrates; and therefore I say, Granted.

SOCRATES: That is very good of you, if I am right, which need hardly be disputed at present. But if I can assign names as well as pictures to objects, the right assignment of them we may call truth, and the wrong assignment of them falsehood. Now if there be such a wrong assignment of names, there may also be a wrong or inappropriate assignment of verbs; and if of names and verbs then of the sentences, which are made up of them. What do you say, Cratylus?

CRATYLUS: I agree; and think that what you say is very true.

SOCRATES: And further, primitive nouns may be compared to pictures, and in pictures you may either give all the appropriate colours and figures, or you may not give them all—some may be wanting; or there may be too many or too much of them—may there not?

CRATYLUS: Very true.

SOCRATES: And he who gives all gives a perfect picture or figure; and he who takes away or adds also gives a picture or figure, but not a good one.

CRATYLUS: Yes.

SOCRATES: In like manner, he who by syllables and letters imitates the nature of things, if he gives all that is appropriate will produce a good image, or in other words a name; but if he subtracts or perhaps adds a little, he will make an image but not a good one; whence I infer that some names are well and others ill made.

CRATYLUS: That is true.

SOCRATES: Then the artist of names may be sometimes good, or he may be bad?

CRATYLUS: Yes.

SOCRATES: And this artist of names is called the legislator?

CRATYLUS: Yes.

SOCRATES: Then like other artists the legislator may be good or he may be bad; it must surely be so if our former admissions hold good?

CRATYLUS: Very true, Socrates; but the case of language, you see, is different; for when by the help of grammar we assign the letters alpha or beta, or any other letters to a certain name, then, if we add, or subtract, or misplace a letter, the name which is written is not only written wrongly, but not written at all; and in any of these cases becomes other than a name.

SOCRATES: But I doubt whether your view is altogether correct, Cratylus.

CRATYLUS: How so?

SOCRATES: I believe that what you say may be true about numbers, which must be just what they are, or not be at all; for example, the number ten at once becomes other than ten if a unit be added or subtracted, and so of any other number: but this does not apply to that which is qualitative or to anything which is represented under an image. I should say rather that the image, if expressing in every point the entire reality, would no longer be an image. Let us suppose the existence of two objects: one of them shall be Cratylus, and the other the image of Cratylus; and we will suppose, further, that some God makes not only a representation such as a painter would make of your outward form and colour, but also creates an inward organization like yours, having the same warmth and softness; and into this infuses motion, and soul, and mind, such as you have, and in a word copies all your qualities, and places them by you in another form; would you say that this was Cratylus and the image of Cratylus, or that there were two Cratyluses?

CRATYLUS: I should say that there were two Cratyluses.

SOCRATES: Then you see, my friend, that we must find some other principle of truth in images, and also in names; and not insist that an image is no longer an image when something is added or subtracted. Do you not perceive that images are very far from having qualities which are the exact counterpart of the realities which they represent?

CRATYLUS: Yes, I see.

SOCRATES: But then how ridiculous would be the effect of names on things, if they were exactly the same with them! For they would be the doubles of them, and no one would be able to determine which were the names and which were the realities.

CRATYLUS: Quite true.

SOCRATES: Then fear not, but have the courage to admit that one name may be correctly and another incorrectly given; and do not insist that the name shall be exactly the same with the thing; but allow the occasional substitution of a wrong letter, and if of a letter also of a noun in a sentence, and if of a noun in a sentence also of a sentence which is not appropriate to the matter, and acknowledge that the thing may be named, and described, so long as the general character of the thing which you are describing is retained; and this, as you will remember, was remarked by Hermogenes and myself in the particular instance of the names of the letters.

CRATYLUS: Yes, I remember.

SOCRATES: Good; and when the general character is preserved, even if some of the proper letters are wanting, still the thing is signified;—well, if all the letters are given; not well, when only a few of them are given. I think that we had better admit this, lest we be punished like travellers in Aegina who wander about the street late at night: and be likewise told by truth herself that we have arrived too late; or if not, you must find out some new notion of correctness of names, and no longer maintain that a name is the expression of a thing in letters or syllables; for if you say both, you will be inconsistent with yourself.

CRATYLUS: I quite acknowledge, Socrates, what you say to be very reasonable.

SOCRATES: Then as we are agreed thus far, let us ask ourselves whether a name rightly imposed ought not to have the proper letters.

CRATYLUS: Yes.

SOCRATES: And the proper letters are those which are like the things?

CRATYLUS: Yes.

SOCRATES: Enough then of names which are rightly given. And in names which are incorrectly given, the greater part may be supposed to be made up of proper and similar letters, or there would be no likeness; but there will be likewise a part which is improper and spoils the beauty and formation of the word: you would admit that?

CRATYLUS: There would be no use, Socrates, in my quarrelling with you, since I cannot be satisfied that a name which is incorrectly given is a name at all.

SOCRATES: Do you admit a name to be the representation of a thing?

CRATYLUS: Yes, I do.

SOCRATES: But do you not allow that some nouns are primitive, and some derived?

CRATYLUS: Yes, I do.

SOCRATES: Then if you admit that primitive or first nouns are representations of things, is there any better way of framing representations than by assimilating them to the objects as much as you can; or do you prefer the notion of Hermogenes and of many others, who say that names are conventional, and have a meaning to those who have agreed about them, and who have previous knowledge of the things intended by them, and that convention is the only principle; and whether you abide by our present convention, or make a new and opposite one, according to which you call small great and great small—that, they would say, makes no difference, if you are only agreed. Which of these two notions do you prefer?

CRATYLUS: Representation by likeness, Socrates, is infinitely better than representation by any chance sign.

SOCRATES: Very good: but if the name is to be like the thing, the letters out of which the first names are composed must also be like things. Returning to the image of the picture, I would ask, How could any one ever compose a picture which would be like anything at all, if there were not pigments in nature which resembled the things imitated, and out of which the picture is composed?

CRATYLUS: Impossible.

SOCRATES: No more could names ever resemble any actually existing thing, unless the original elements of which they are compounded bore some degree of resemblance to the objects of which the names are the imitation: And the original elements are letters?

CRATYLUS: Yes.

SOCRATES: Let me now invite you to consider what Hermogenes and I were saying about sounds. Do you agree with me that the letter rho is expressive of rapidity, motion, and hardness? Were we right or wrong in saying so?

CRATYLUS: I should say that you were right.

SOCRATES: And that lamda was expressive of smoothness, and softness, and the like?

CRATYLUS: There again you were right.

SOCRATES: And yet, as you are aware, that which is called by us sklerotes, is by the Eretrians called skleroter.

CRATYLUS: Very true.

SOCRATES: But are the letters rho and sigma equivalents; and is there the same significance to them in the termination rho, which there is to us in sigma, or is there no significance to one of us?

CRATYLUS: Nay, surely there is a significance to both of us.

SOCRATES: In as far as they are like, or in as far as they are unlike?

CRATYLUS: In as far as they are like.

SOCRATES: Are they altogether alike?

CRATYLUS: Yes; for the purpose of expressing motion.

SOCRATES: And what do you say of the insertion of the lamda? for that is expressive not of hardness but of softness.

CRATYLUS: Why, perhaps the letter lamda is wrongly inserted, Socrates, and should be altered into rho, as you were saying to Hermogenes and in my opinion rightly, when you spoke of adding and subtracting letters upon occasion.

SOCRATES: Good. But still the word is intelligible to both of us; when I say skleros (hard), you know what I mean.

CRATYLUS: Yes, my dear friend, and the explanation of that is custom.

SOCRATES: And what is custom but convention? I utter a sound which I understand, and you know that I understand the meaning of the sound: this is what you are saying?

CRATYLUS: Yes.

SOCRATES: And if when I speak you know my meaning, there is an indication given by me to you?

CRATYLUS: Yes.

SOCRATES: This indication of my meaning may proceed from unlike as well as from like, for example in the lamda of sklerotes. But if this is true, then you have made a convention with yourself, and the correctness of a name turns out to be convention, since letters which are unlike are indicative equally with those which are like, if they are sanctioned by custom and convention. And even supposing that you distinguish custom from convention ever so much, still you must say that the signification of words is given by custom and not by likeness, for custom may indicate by the unlike as well as by the like. But as we are agreed thus far, Cratylus (for I shall assume that your silence gives consent), then custom and convention must be supposed to contribute to the indication of our thoughts; for suppose we take the instance of number, how can you ever imagine, my good friend, that you will find names resembling every individual number, unless you allow that which you term convention and agreement to have authority in determining the correctness of names? I quite agree with you that words should as far as possible resemble things; but I fear that this dragging in of resemblance, as Hermogenes says, is a shabby thing, which has to be supplemented by the mechanical aid of convention with a view to correctness; for I believe that if we could always, or almost always, use likenesses, which are perfectly appropriate, this would be the most perfect state of language; as the opposite is the most imperfect. But let me ask you, what is the force of names, and what is the use of them?

CRATYLUS: The use of names, Socrates, as I should imagine, is to inform: the simple truth is, that he who knows names knows also the things which are expressed by them.

SOCRATES: I suppose you mean to say, Cratylus, that as the name is, so also is the thing; and that he who knows the one will also know the other, because they are similars, and all similars fall under the same art or science; and therefore you would say that he who knows names will also know things.

CRATYLUS: That is precisely what I mean.

SOCRATES: But let us consider what is the nature of this information about things which, according to you, is given us by names. Is it the best sort of information? or is there any other? What do you say?

CRATYLUS: I believe that to be both the only and the best sort of information about them; there can be no other.

SOCRATES: But do you believe that in the discovery of them, he who discovers the names discovers also the things; or is this only the method of instruction, and is there some other method of enquiry and discovery.

CRATYLUS: I certainly believe that the methods of enquiry and discovery are of the same nature as instruction.

SOCRATES: Well, but do you not see, Cratylus, that he who follows names in the search after things, and analyses their meaning, is in great danger of being deceived?

CRATYLUS: How so?

SOCRATES: Why clearly he who first gave names gave them according to his conception of the things which they signified—did he not?

CRATYLUS: True.

SOCRATES: And if his conception was erroneous, and he gave names according to his conception, in what position shall we who are his followers find ourselves? Shall we not be deceived by him?

CRATYLUS: But, Socrates, am I not right in thinking that he must surely have known; or else, as I was saying, his names would not be names at all? And you have a clear proof that he has not missed the truth, and the proof is—that he is perfectly consistent. Did you ever observe in speaking that all the words which you utter have a common character and purpose?

SOCRATES: But that, friend Cratylus, is no answer. For if he did begin in error, he may have forced the remainder into agreement with the original error and with himself; there would be nothing strange in this, any more than in geometrical diagrams, which have often a slight and invisible flaw in the first part of the process, and are consistently mistaken in the long deductions which follow. And this is the reason why every man should expend his chief thought and attention on the consideration of his first principles:—are they or are they not rightly laid down? and when he has duly sifted them, all the rest will follow. Now I should be astonished to find that names are really consistent. And here let us revert to our former discussion: Were we not saying that all things are in motion and progress and flux, and that this idea of motion is expressed by names? Do you not conceive that to be the meaning of them?

CRATYLUS: Yes; that is assuredly their meaning, and the true meaning.

SOCRATES: Let us revert to episteme (knowledge) and observe how ambiguous this word is, seeming rather to signify stopping the soul at things than going round with them; and therefore we should leave the beginning as at present, and not reject the epsilon, but make an insertion of an iota instead of an epsilon (not pioteme, but epiisteme). Take another example: bebaion (sure) is clearly the expression of station and position, and not of motion. Again, the word istoria (enquiry) bears upon the face of it the stopping (istanai) of the stream; and the word piston (faithful) certainly indicates cessation of motion; then, again, mneme (memory), as any one may see, expresses rest in the soul, and not motion. Moreover, words such as amartia and sumphora, which have a bad sense, viewed in the light of their etymologies will be the same as sunesis and episteme and other words which have a good sense (compare omartein, sunienai, epesthai, sumpheresthai); and much the same may be said of amathia and akolasia, for amathia may be explained as e ama theo iontos poreia, and akolasia as e akolouthia tois pragmasin. Thus the names which in these instances we find to have the worst sense, will turn out to be framed on the same principle as those which have the best. And any one I believe who would take the trouble might find many other examples in which the giver of names indicates, not that things are in motion or progress, but that they are at rest; which is the opposite of motion.

CRATYLUS: Yes, Socrates, but observe; the greater number express motion.

SOCRATES: What of that, Cratylus? Are we to count them like votes? and is correctness of names the voice of the majority? Are we to say of whichever sort there are most, those are the true ones?

CRATYLUS: No; that is not reasonable.

SOCRATES: Certainly not. But let us have done with this question and proceed to another, about which I should like to know whether you think with me. Were we not lately acknowledging that the first givers of names in states, both Hellenic and barbarous, were the legislators, and that the art which gave names was the art of the legislator?

CRATYLUS: Quite true.

SOCRATES: Tell me, then, did the first legislators, who were the givers of the first names, know or not know the things which they named?

CRATYLUS: They must have known, Socrates.

SOCRATES: Why, yes, friend Cratylus, they could hardly have been ignorant.

CRATYLUS: I should say not.

SOCRATES: Let us return to the point from which we digressed. You were saying, if you remember, that he who gave names must have known the things which he named; are you still of that opinion?

CRATYLUS: I am.

SOCRATES: And would you say that the giver of the first names had also a knowledge of the things which he named?

CRATYLUS: I should.

SOCRATES: But how could he have learned or discovered things from names if the primitive names were not yet given? For, if we are correct in our view, the only way of learning and discovering things, is either to discover names for ourselves or to learn them from others.

CRATYLUS: I think that there is a good deal in what you say, Socrates.

SOCRATES: But if things are only to be known through names, how can we suppose that the givers of names had knowledge, or were legislators before there were names at all, and therefore before they could have known them?

CRATYLUS: I believe, Socrates, the true account of the matter to be, that a power more than human gave things their first names, and that the names which are thus given are necessarily their true names.

SOCRATES: Then how came the giver of the names, if he was an inspired being or God, to contradict himself? For were we not saying just now that he made some names expressive of rest and others of motion? Were we mistaken?

CRATYLUS: But I suppose one of the two not to be names at all.

SOCRATES: And which, then, did he make, my good friend; those which are expressive of rest, or those which are expressive of motion? This is a point which, as I said before, cannot be determined by counting them.

CRATYLUS: No; not in that way, Socrates.

SOCRATES: But if this is a battle of names, some of them asserting that they are like the truth, others contending that THEY are, how or by what criterion are we to decide between them? For there are no other names to which appeal can be made, but obviously recourse must be had to another standard which, without employing names, will make clear which of the two are right; and this must be a standard which shows the truth of things.

CRATYLUS: I agree.

SOCRATES: But if that is true, Cratylus, then I suppose that things may be known without names?

CRATYLUS: Clearly.

SOCRATES: But how would you expect to know them? What other way can there be of knowing them, except the true and natural way, through their affinities, when they are akin to each other, and through themselves? For that which is other and different from them must signify something other and different from them.

CRATYLUS: What you are saying is, I think, true.

SOCRATES: Well, but reflect; have we not several times acknowledged that names rightly given are the likenesses and images of the things which they name?

CRATYLUS: Yes.

SOCRATES: Let us suppose that to any extent you please you can learn things through the medium of names, and suppose also that you can learn them from the things themselves—which is likely to be the nobler and clearer way; to learn of the image, whether the image and the truth of which the image is the expression have been rightly conceived, or to learn of the truth whether the truth and the image of it have been duly executed?

CRATYLUS: I should say that we must learn of the truth.

SOCRATES: How real existence is to be studied or discovered is, I suspect, beyond you and me. But we may admit so much, that the knowledge of things is not to be derived from names. No; they must be studied and investigated in themselves.

CRATYLUS: Clearly, Socrates.

SOCRATES: There is another point. I should not like us to be imposed upon by the appearance of such a multitude of names, all tending in the same direction. I myself do not deny that the givers of names did really give them under the idea that all things were in motion and flux; which was their sincere but, I think, mistaken opinion. And having fallen into a kind of whirlpool themselves, they are carried round, and want to drag us in after them. There is a matter, master Cratylus, about which I often dream, and should like to ask your opinion: Tell me, whether there is or is not any absolute beauty or good, or any other absolute existence?

CRATYLUS: Certainly, Socrates, I think so.

SOCRATES: Then let us seek the true beauty: not asking whether a face is fair, or anything of that sort, for all such things appear to be in a flux; but let us ask whether the true beauty is not always beautiful.

CRATYLUS: Certainly.

SOCRATES: And can we rightly speak of a beauty which is always passing away, and is first this and then that; must not the same thing be born and retire and vanish while the word is in our mouths?

CRATYLUS: Undoubtedly.

SOCRATES: Then how can that be a real thing which is never in the same state? for obviously things which are the same cannot change while they remain the same; and if they are always the same and in the same state, and never depart from their original form, they can never change or be moved.

CRATYLUS: Certainly they cannot.

SOCRATES: Nor yet can they be known by any one; for at the moment that the observer approaches, then they become other and of another nature, so that you cannot get any further in knowing their nature or state, for you cannot know that which has no state.

CRATYLUS: True.

SOCRATES: Nor can we reasonably say, Cratylus, that there is knowledge at all, if everything is in a state of transition and there is nothing abiding; for knowledge too cannot continue to be knowledge unless continuing always to abide and exist. But if the very nature of knowledge changes, at the time when the change occurs there will be no knowledge; and if the transition is always going on, there will always be no knowledge, and, according to this view, there will be no one to know and nothing to be known: but if that which knows and that which is known exists ever, and the beautiful and the good and every other thing also exist, then I do not think that they can resemble a process or flux, as we were just now supposing. Whether there is this eternal nature in things, or whether the truth is what Heracleitus and his followers and many others say, is a question hard to determine; and no man of sense will like to put himself or the education of his mind in the power of names: neither will he so far trust names or the givers of names as to be confident in any knowledge which condemns himself and other existences to an unhealthy state of unreality; he will not believe that all things leak like a pot, or imagine that the world is a man who has a running at the nose. This may be true, Cratylus, but is also very likely to be untrue; and therefore I would not have you be too easily persuaded of it. Reflect well and like a man, and do not easily accept such a doctrine; for you are young and of an age to learn. And when you have found the truth, come and tell me.

CRATYLUS: I will do as you say, though I can assure you, Socrates, that I have been considering the matter already, and the result of a great deal of trouble and consideration is that I incline to Heracleitus.

SOCRATES: Then, another day, my friend, when you come back, you shall give me a lesson; but at present, go into the country, as you are intending, and Hermogenes shall set you on your way.

CRATYLUS: Very good, Socrates; I hope, however, that you will continue to think about these things yourself.

CRITIAS

by Plato

Translated by Benjamin Jowett

PERSONS OF THE DIALOGUE: Critias, Hermocrates, Timaeus, Socrates.

TIMAEUS: How thankful I am, Socrates, that I have arrived at last, and, like a weary traveller after a long journey, may be at rest! And I pray the being who always was of old, and has now been by me revealed, to grant that my words may endure in so far as they have been spoken truly and acceptably to him; but if unintentionally I have said anything wrong, I pray that he will impose upon me a just retribution, and the just retribution of him who errs is that he should be set right. Wishing, then, to speak truly in future concerning the generation of the gods, I pray him to give me knowledge, which of all medicines is the most perfect and best. And now having offered my prayer I deliver up the argument to Critias, who is to speak next according to our agreement. (Tim.)

CRITIAS: And I, Timaeus, accept the trust, and as you at first said that you were going to speak of high matters, and begged that some forbearance might be shown to you, I too ask the same or greater forbearance for what I am about to say. And although I very well know that my request may appear to be somewhat ambitious and discourteous, I must make it nevertheless. For will any man of sense deny that you have spoken well? I can only attempt to show that I ought to have more indulgence than you, because my theme is more difficult; and I shall argue that to seem to speak well of the gods to men is far easier than to speak well of men to men: for the inexperience and utter ignorance of his hearers about any subject is a great assistance to him who has to speak of it, and we know how ignorant we are concerning the gods. But I should like to make my meaning clearer, if you will follow me. All that is said by any of us can only be imitation and representation. For if we consider the likenesses which painters make of bodies divine and heavenly, and the different degrees of gratification with which the eye of the spectator receives them, we shall see that we are satisfied with the artist who is able in any degree to imitate the earth and its mountains, and the rivers, and the woods, and the universe, and the things that are and move therein, and further, that knowing nothing precise about such matters, we do not examine or analyze the painting; all that is required is a sort of indistinct and deceptive mode of shadowing them forth. But when a person endeavours to paint the human form we are quick at finding out defects, and our familiar knowledge makes us severe judges of any one who does not render every point of similarity. And we may observe the same thing to happen in discourse; we are satisfied with a picture of divine and heavenly things which has very little likeness to them; but we are more precise in our criticism of mortal and human things. Wherefore if at the moment of speaking I cannot suitably express my meaning, you must excuse me, considering that to form approved likenesses of human things is the reverse of easy. This is what I want to suggest to you, and at the same time to beg, Socrates, that I may have not less, but more indulgence conceded to me in what I am about to say. Which favour, if I am right in asking, I hope that you will be ready to grant.

SOCRATES: Certainly, Critias, we will grant your request, and we will grant the same by anticipation to Hermocrates, as well as to you and Timaeus; for I have no doubt that when his turn comes a little while hence, he will make the same request which you have made. In order, then, that he may provide himself with a fresh beginning, and not be compelled to say the same things over again, let him understand that the indulgence is already extended by anticipation to him. And now, friend Critias, I will announce to you the judgment of the theatre. They are of opinion that the last performer was wonderfully successful, and that you will need a great deal of indulgence before you will be able to take his place.

HERMOCRATES: The warning, Socrates, which you have addressed to him, I must also take to myself. But remember, Critias, that faint heart never yet raised a trophy; and therefore you must go and attack the argument like a man. First invoke Apollo and the Muses, and then let us hear you sound the praises and show forth the virtues of your ancient citizens.

CRITIAS: Friend Hermocrates, you, who are stationed last and have another in front of you, have not lost heart as yet; the gravity of the situation will soon be revealed to you; meanwhile I accept your exhortations and encouragements. But besides the gods and goddesses whom you have mentioned, I would specially invoke Mnemosyne; for all the important part of my discourse is dependent on her favour, and if I can recollect and recite enough of what was said by the priests and brought hither by Solon, I doubt not that I shall satisfy the requirements of this theatre. And now, making no more excuses, I will proceed.

Let me begin by observing first of all, that nine thousand was the sum of years which had elapsed since the war which was said to have taken place between those who dwelt outside the pillars of Heracles and all who dwelt within them; this war I am going to describe. Of the combatants on the one side, the city of Athens was reported to have been the leader and to have fought out the war; the combatants on the other side were commanded by the kings of Atlantis, which, as I was saying, was an island greater in extent than Libya and Asia, and when afterwards sunk by an earthquake, became an impassable barrier of mud to voyagers sailing from hence to any part of the ocean. The progress of the history will unfold the various nations of barbarians and families of Hellenes which then existed, as they successively appear on the scene; but I must describe first of all the Athenians of that day, and their enemies who fought with them, and then the respective powers and governments of the two kingdoms. Let us give the precedence to Athens.

In the days of old, the gods had the whole earth distributed among them by allotment (Cp. Polit.) There was no quarrelling; for you cannot rightly suppose that the gods did not know what was proper for each of them to have, or, knowing this, that they would seek to procure for themselves by contention that which more properly belonged to others. They all of them by just apportionment obtained what they wanted, and peopled their own districts; and when they had peopled them they tended us, their nurselings and possessions, as shepherds tend their flocks, excepting only that they did not use blows or bodily force, as shepherds do, but governed us like pilots from the stern of the vessel, which is an easy way of guiding animals, holding our souls by the rudder of persuasion according to their own pleasure;—thus did they guide all mortal creatures. Now different gods had their allotments in different places which they set in order. Hephaestus and Athene, who were brother and sister, and sprang from the same father, having a common nature, and being united also in the love of philosophy and art, both obtained as their common portion this land, which was naturally adapted for wisdom and virtue; and there they implanted brave children of the soil, and put into their minds the order of government; their names are preserved, but their actions have disappeared by reason of the destruction of those who received the tradition, and the lapse of ages. For when there were any survivors, as I have already said, they were men who dwelt in the mountains; and they were ignorant of the art of writing, and had heard only the names of the chiefs of the land, but very little about their actions. The names they were willing enough to give to their children; but the virtues and the laws of their predecessors, they knew only by obscure traditions; and as they themselves and their children lacked for many generations the necessaries of life, they directed their attention to the supply of their wants, and of them they conversed, to the neglect of events that had happened in times long past; for mythology and the enquiry into antiquity are first introduced into cities when they begin to have leisure (Cp. Arist. Metaphys.), and when they see that the necessaries of life have already been provided, but not before. And this is the reason why the names of the ancients have been preserved to us and not their actions. This I infer because Solon said that the priests in their narrative of that war mentioned most of the names which are recorded prior to the time of Theseus, such as Cecrops, and Erechtheus, and Erichthonius, and Erysichthon, and the names of the women in like manner. Moreover, since military pursuits were then common to men and women, the men of those days in accordance with the custom of the time set up a figure and image of the goddess in full armour, to be a testimony that all animals which associate together, male as well as female, may, if they please, practise in common the virtue which belongs to them without distinction of sex.

Now the country was inhabited in those days by various classes of citizens;—there were artisans, and there were husbandmen, and there was also a warrior class originally set apart by divine men. The latter dwelt by themselves, and had all things suitable for nurture and education; neither had any of them anything of their own, but they regarded all that they had as common property; nor did they claim to receive of the other citizens anything more than their necessary food. And they practised all the pursuits which we yesterday described as those of our imaginary guardians. Concerning the country the Egyptian priests said what is not only probable but manifestly true, that the boundaries were in those days fixed by the Isthmus, and that in the direction of the continent they extended as far as the heights of Cithaeron and Parnes; the boundary line came down in the direction of the sea, having the district of Oropus on the right, and with the river Asopus as the limit on the left. The land was the best in the world, and was therefore able in those days to support a vast army, raised from the surrounding people. Even the remnant of Attica which now exists may compare with any region in the world for the variety and excellence of its fruits and the suitableness of its pastures to every sort of animal, which proves what I am saying; but in those days the country was fair as now and yielded far more abundant produce. How shall I establish my words? and what part of it can be truly called a remnant of the land that then was? The whole country is only a long promontory extending far into the sea away from the rest of the continent, while the surrounding basin of the sea is everywhere deep in the neighbourhood of the shore. Many great deluges have taken place during the nine thousand years, for that is the number of years which have elapsed since the time of which I am speaking; and during all this time and through so many changes, there has never been any considerable accumulation of the soil coming down from the mountains, as in other places, but the earth has fallen away all round and sunk out of sight. The consequence is, that in comparison of what then was, there are remaining only the bones of the wasted body, as they may be called, as in the case of small islands, all the richer and softer parts of the soil having fallen away, and the mere skeleton of the land being left. But in the primitive state of the country, its mountains were high hills covered with soil, and the plains, as they are termed by us, of Phelleus were full of rich earth, and there was abundance of wood in the mountains. Of this last the traces still remain, for although some of the mountains now only afford sustenance to bees, not so very long ago there were still to be seen roofs of timber cut from trees growing there, which were of a size sufficient to cover the largest houses; and there were many other high trees, cultivated by man and bearing abundance of food for cattle. Moreover, the land reaped the benefit of the annual rainfall, not as now losing the water which flows off the bare earth into the sea, but, having an abundant supply in all places, and receiving it into herself and treasuring it up in the close clay soil, it let off into the hollows the streams which it absorbed from the heights, providing everywhere abundant fountains and rivers, of which there may still be observed sacred memorials in places where fountains once existed; and this proves the truth of what I am saying.

Such was the natural state of the country, which was cultivated, as we may well believe, by true husbandmen, who made husbandry their business, and were lovers of honour, and of a noble nature, and had a soil the best in the world, and abundance of water, and in the heaven above an excellently attempered climate. Now the city in those days was arranged on this wise. In the first place the Acropolis was not as now. For the fact is that a single night of excessive rain washed away the earth and laid bare the rock; at the same time there were earthquakes, and then occurred the extraordinary inundation, which was the third before the great destruction of Deucalion. But in primitive times the hill of the Acropolis extended to the Eridanus and Ilissus, and included the Pnyx on one side, and the Lycabettus as a boundary on the opposite side to the Pnyx, and was all well covered with soil, and level at the top, except in one or two places. Outside the Acropolis and under the sides of the hill there dwelt artisans, and such of the husbandmen as were tilling the ground near; the warrior class dwelt by themselves around the temples of Athene and Hephaestus at the summit, which moreover they had enclosed with a single fence like the garden of a single house. On the north side they had dwellings in common and had erected halls for dining in winter, and had all the buildings which they needed for their common life, besides temples, but there was no adorning of them with gold and silver, for they made no use of these for any purpose; they took a middle course between meanness and ostentation, and built modest houses in which they and their children's children grew old, and they handed them down to others who were like themselves, always the same. But in summer-time they left their gardens and gymnasia and dining halls, and then the southern side of the hill was made use of by them for the same purpose. Where the Acropolis now is there was a fountain, which was choked by the earthquake, and has left only the few small streams which still exist in the vicinity, but in those days the fountain gave an abundant supply of water for all and of suitable temperature in summer and in winter. This is how they dwelt, being the guardians of their own citizens and the leaders of the Hellenes, who were their willing followers. And they took care to preserve the same number of men and women through all time, being so many as were required for warlike purposes, then as now—that is to say, about twenty thousand. Such were the ancient Athenians, and after this manner they righteously administered their own land and the rest of Hellas; they were renowned all over Europe and Asia for the beauty of their persons and for the many virtues of their souls, and of all men who lived in those days they were the most illustrious. And next, if I have not forgotten what I heard when I was a child, I will impart to you the character and origin of their adversaries. For friends should not keep their stories to themselves, but have them in common.

Yet, before proceeding further in the narrative, I ought to warn you, that you must not be surprised if you should perhaps hear Hellenic names given to foreigners. I will tell you the reason of this: Solon, who was intending to use the tale for his poem, enquired into the meaning of the names, and found that the early Egyptians in writing them down had translated them into their own language, and he recovered the meaning of the several names and when copying them out again translated them into our language. My great-grandfather, Dropides, had the original writing, which is still in my possession, and was carefully studied by me when I was a child. Therefore if you hear names such as are used in this country, you must not be surprised, for I have told how they came to be introduced. The tale, which was of great length, began as follows:—

I have before remarked in speaking of the allotments of the gods, that they distributed the whole earth into portions differing in extent, and made for themselves temples and instituted sacrifices. And Poseidon, receiving for his lot the island of Atlantis, begat children by a mortal woman, and settled them in a part of the island, which I will describe. Looking towards the sea, but in the centre of the whole island, there was a plain which is said to have been the fairest of all plains and very fertile. Near the plain again, and also in the centre of the island at a distance of about fifty stadia, there was a mountain not very high on any side. In this mountain there dwelt one of the earth-born primeval men of that country, whose name was Evenor, and he had a wife named Leucippe, and they had an only daughter who was called Cleito. The maiden had already reached womanhood, when her father and mother died; Poseidon fell in love with her and had intercourse with her, and breaking the ground, inclosed the hill in which she dwelt all round, making alternate zones of sea and land larger and smaller, encircling one another; there were two of land and three of water, which he turned as with a lathe, each having its circumference equidistant every way from the centre, so that no man could get to the island, for ships and voyages were not as yet. He himself, being a god, found no difficulty in making special arrangements for the centre island, bringing up two springs of water from beneath the earth, one of warm water and the other of cold, and making every variety of food to spring up abundantly from the soil. He also begat and brought up five pairs of twin male children; and dividing the island of Atlantis into ten portions, he gave to the first-born of the eldest pair his mother's dwelling and the surrounding allotment, which was the largest and best, and made him king over the rest; the others he made princes, and gave them rule over many men, and a large territory. And he named them all; the eldest, who was the first king, he named Atlas, and after him the whole island and the ocean were called Atlantic. To his twin brother, who was born after him, and obtained as his lot the extremity of the island towards the pillars of Heracles, facing the country which is now called the region of Gades in that part of the world, he gave the name which in the Hellenic language is Eumelus, in the language of the country which is named after him, Gadeirus. Of the second pair of twins he called one Ampheres, and the other Evaemon. To the elder of the third pair of twins he gave the name Mneseus, and

Autochthon to the one who followed him. Of the fourth pair of twins he called the elder Elasippus, and the younger Mestor. And of the fifth pair he gave to the elder the name of Azaes, and to the younger that of Diaprepes. All these and their descendants for many generations were the inhabitants and rulers of divers islands in the open sea; and also, as has been already said, they held sway in our direction over the country within the pillars as far as Egypt and Tyrrhenia. Now Atlas had a numerous and honourable family, and they retained the kingdom, the eldest son handing it on to his eldest for many generations; and they had such an amount of wealth as was never before possessed by kings and potentates, and is not likely ever to be again, and they were furnished with everything which they needed, both in the city and country. For because of the greatness of their empire many things were brought to them from foreign countries, and the island itself provided most of what was required by them for the uses of life. In the first place, they dug out of the earth whatever was to be found there, solid as well as fusile, and that which is now only a name and was then something more than a name, orichalcum, was dug out of the earth in many parts of the island, being more precious in those days than anything except gold. There was an abundance of wood for carpenter's work, and sufficient maintenance for tame and wild animals. Moreover, there were a great number of elephants in the island; for as there was provision for all other sorts of animals, both for those which live in lakes and marshes and rivers, and also for those which live in mountains and on plains, so there was for the animal which is the largest and most voracious of all. Also whatever fragrant things there now are in the earth, whether roots, or herbage, or woods, or essences which distil from fruit and flower, grew and thrived in that land; also the fruit which admits of cultivation, both the dry sort, which is given us for nourishment and any other which we use for food—we call them all by the common name of pulse, and the fruits having a hard rind, affording drinks and meats and ointments, and good store of chestnuts and the like, which furnish pleasure and amusement, and are fruits which spoil with keeping, and the pleasant kinds of dessert, with which we console ourselves after dinner, when we are tired of eating—all these that sacred island which then beheld the light of the sun, brought forth fair and wondrous and in infinite abundance. With such blessings the earth freely furnished them; meanwhile they went on constructing their temples and palaces and harbours and docks. And they arranged the whole country in the following manner:—

First of all they bridged over the zones of sea which surrounded the ancient metropolis, making a road to and from the royal palace. And at the very beginning they built the palace in the habitation of the god and of their ancestors, which they continued to ornament in successive generations, every king surpassing the one who went before him to the utmost of his power, until they made the building a marvel to behold for size and for beauty. And beginning from the sea they bored a canal of three hundred feet in width and one hundred feet in depth and fifty stadia in length, which they carried through to the outermost zone, making a passage from the sea up to this, which became a harbour, and leaving an opening sufficient to enable the largest vessels to find ingress. Moreover, they divided at the bridges the zones of land which parted the zones of sea, leaving room for a single trireme to pass out of one zone into another, and they covered over the channels so as to leave a way underneath for the ships; for the banks were raised considerably above the water. Now the largest of the zones into which a passage was cut from the sea was three stadia in breadth, and the zone of land which came next of equal breadth; but the next two zones, the one of water, the other of land, were two stadia, and the one which surrounded the central island was a stadium only in width. The island in which the palace was situated had a diameter of five stadia. All this including the zones and the bridge, which was the sixth part of a stadium in width, they surrounded by a stone wall on every side, placing towers and gates on the bridges where the sea passed in. The stone which was used in the work they quarried from underneath the centre island, and from underneath the zones, on the outer as well as the inner side. One kind was white, another black, and a third red, and as they quarried, they at the same time hollowed out double docks, having roofs formed out of the native rock. Some of their buildings were simple, but in others they put together different stones, varying the colour to please the eye, and to be a natural source of delight. The entire circuit of the wall, which went round the outermost zone, they covered with a coating of brass, and the circuit of the next wall they coated with tin, and the third, which encompassed the citadel, flashed with the red light of orichalcum. The palaces in the interior of the citadel were constructed on this wise:—In the centre was a holy temple dedicated to Cleito and Poseidon, which remained inaccessible, and was surrounded by an enclosure of gold; this was the spot where the family of the ten princes first saw the light, and thither the people annually brought the fruits of the earth in their season from all the ten portions, to be an offering to each of the ten. Here was Poseidon's own temple which was a stadium in length, and half a stadium in width, and of a proportionate height, having a strange barbaric appearance. All the outside of the temple, with the exception of the pinnacles, they covered with silver, and the pinnacles with gold. In the interior of the temple the roof was of ivory, curiously wrought everywhere with gold and silver and orichalcum; and all the other parts, the walls and pillars and floor, they coated with orichalcum. In the temple they placed statues of gold: there was the god himself standing in a chariot—the charioteer of six winged horses—and of such a size that he touched the roof of the building with his head; around him there were a hundred Nereids riding on dolphins, for such was thought to be the number of them by the men of those days. There were also in the interior of the temple other images which had been dedicated by private persons. And around the temple on the outside were placed statues of gold of all the descendants of the ten kings and of their wives, and there were many other great offerings of kings and of private persons, coming both from the city itself and from the foreign cities over which they held sway. There was an altar too, which in size and workmanship corresponded to this magnificence, and the palaces, in like manner, answered to the greatness of the kingdom and the glory of the temple.

In the next place, they had fountains, one of cold and another of hot water, in gracious plenty flowing; and they were wonderfully adapted for use by reason of the pleasantness and excellence of their waters. They constructed buildings about them and planted suitable trees, also they made cisterns, some open to the heaven, others roofed over, to be used in winter as warm baths; there were the kings' baths, and the baths of private persons, which were kept apart; and there were separate baths for women, and for horses and cattle, and to each of them they gave as much adornment as was suitable. Of the water which ran off they carried some to the grove of Poseidon, where were growing all manner of trees of wonderful height and beauty, owing to the excellence of the soil, while the remainder was conveyed by aqueducts along the bridges to the outer circles; and there were many temples built and dedicated to many gods; also gardens and places of exercise, some for men, and others for horses in both of the two islands formed by the zones; and in the centre of the larger of the two there was set apart a race-course of a stadium in width, and in length allowed to extend all round the island, for horses to race in. Also there were guard-houses at intervals for the guards, the more trusted of whom were appointed to keep watch in the lesser zone, which was nearer the Acropolis; while the most trusted of all had houses given them within the citadel, near the persons of the kings. The docks were full of triremes and naval stores, and all things were quite ready for use. Enough of the plan of the royal palace.

Leaving the palace and passing out across the three harbours, you came to a wall which began at the sea and went all round: this was everywhere distant fifty stadia from the largest zone or harbour, and enclosed the whole, the ends meeting at the mouth of the channel which led to the sea. The entire area was densely crowded with habitations; and the canal and the largest of the harbours were full of vessels and merchants coming from all parts, who, from their numbers, kept up a multitudinous sound of human voices, and din and clatter of all sorts night and day.

I have described the city and the environs of the ancient palace nearly in the words of Solon, and now I must endeavour to represent to you the nature and arrangement of the rest of the land. The whole country was said by him to be very lofty and precipitous on the side of the sea, but the country immediately about and surrounding the city was a level plain, itself surrounded by mountains which descended towards the sea; it was smooth and even, and of an oblong shape, extending in one direction three thousand stadia, but across the centre inland it was two thousand stadia. This part of the island looked towards the south, and was sheltered from the north. The surrounding mountains were celebrated for their number and size and beauty, far beyond any which still exist, having in them also many wealthy villages of country folk, and rivers, and lakes, and meadows supplying food enough for every animal, wild or tame, and much wood of various sorts, abundant for each and every kind of work.

I will now describe the plain, as it was fashioned by nature and by the labours of many generations of kings through long ages. It was for the most part rectangular and oblong, and where falling out of the straight line followed the circular ditch. The depth, and width, and length of this ditch were incredible, and gave the impression that a work of such extent, in addition to so many others, could never have been artificial. Nevertheless I must say what I was told. It was excavated to the depth of a hundred feet, and its breadth was a stadium everywhere; it was carried round the whole of the plain, and was ten thousand stadia in length. It received the streams which came down from the mountains, and winding round the plain and meeting at the city, was there let off into the sea. Further inland, likewise, straight canals of a hundred feet in width were cut from it through the plain, and again let off into the ditch leading to the sea: these canals were at intervals of a hundred stadia, and by them they brought down the wood from the mountains to the city, and conveyed the fruits of the earth in ships, cutting transverse passages from one canal into another, and to the city. Twice in the year they gathered the fruits of the earth—in winter having the benefit of the rains of heaven, and in summer the water which the land supplied by introducing streams from the canals.

As to the population, each of the lots in the plain had to find a leader for the men who were fit for military service, and the size of a lot was a square of ten stadia each way, and the total number of all the lots was sixty thousand. And of the inhabitants of the mountains and of the rest of the country there was also a vast multitude, which was distributed among the lots and had leaders assigned to them according to their districts and villages. The leader was required to furnish for the war the sixth portion of a war-chariot, so as to make up a total of ten thousand chariots; also two horses and riders for them, and a pair of chariot-horses without a seat, accompanied by a horseman who could fight on foot carrying a small shield, and having a charioteer who stood behind the man-at-arms to guide the two horses; also, he was bound to furnish two heavy-armed soldiers, two archers, two slingers, three stone-shooters and three javelin-men, who were light-armed, and four sailors to make up the complement of twelve hundred ships. Such was the military order of the royal city—the order of the other nine governments varied, and it would be wearisome to recount their several differences.

As to offices and honours, the following was the arrangement from the first. Each of the ten kings in his own division and in his own city had the absolute control of the citizens, and, in most cases, of the laws, punishing and slaying whomsoever he would. Now the order of precedence among them and their mutual relations were regulated by the commands of Poseidon which the law had handed down. These were inscribed by the first kings on a pillar of orichalcum, which was situated in the middle of the island, at the temple of Poseidon, whither the kings were gathered together every fifth and every sixth year alternately, thus giving equal honour to the odd and to the even number. And when they were gathered together they consulted about their common interests, and enquired if any one had transgressed in anything, and passed judgment, and before they passed judgment they gave their pledges to one another on this wise:—There were bulls who had the range of the temple of Poseidon; and the ten kings, being left alone in the temple, after they had offered prayers to the god that they might capture the victim which was acceptable to him, hunted the bulls, without weapons, but with staves and nooses; and the bull which they caught they led up to the pillar and cut its throat over the top of it so that the blood fell upon the sacred inscription. Now on the pillar, besides the laws, there was inscribed an oath invoking mighty curses on the disobedient. When therefore, after slaying the bull in the accustomed manner, they had burnt its limbs, they filled a bowl of wine and cast in a clot of blood for each of them; the rest of the victim they put in the fire, after having purified the column all round. Then they drew from the bowl in golden cups, and pouring a libation on the fire, they swore that they would judge according to the laws on the pillar, and would punish him who in any point had already transgressed them, and that for the future they would not, if they could help, offend against the writing on the pillar, and would neither command others, nor obey any ruler who commanded them, to act otherwise than according to the laws of their father Poseidon. This was the prayer which each of them offered up for himself and for his descendants, at the same time drinking and dedicating the cup out of which he drank in the temple of the god; and after they had supped and satisfied their needs, when darkness came on, and the fire about the sacrifice was cool, all of them put on most beautiful azure robes, and, sitting on the ground, at night, over the embers of the sacrifices by which they had sworn, and extinguishing all the fire about the temple, they received and gave judgment, if any of them had an accusation to bring against any one; and when they had given judgment, at daybreak they wrote down their sentences on a golden tablet, and dedicated it together with their robes to be a memorial.

There were many special laws affecting the several kings inscribed about the temples, but the most important was the following: They were not to take up arms against one another, and they were all to come to the rescue if any one in any of their cities attempted to overthrow the royal house; like their ancestors, they were to deliberate in common about war and other matters, giving the supremacy to the descendants of Atlas. And the king was not to have the power of life and death over any of his kinsmen unless he had the assent of the majority of the ten.

Such was the vast power which the god settled in the lost island of Atlantis; and this he afterwards directed against our land for the following reasons, as tradition tells: For many generations, as long as the divine nature lasted in them, they were obedient to the laws, and well-affectioned towards the god, whose seed they were; for they possessed true and in every way great spirits, uniting gentleness with wisdom in the various chances of life, and in their intercourse with one another. They despised everything but virtue, caring little for their present state of life, and thinking lightly of the possession of gold and other property, which seemed only a burden to them; neither were they intoxicated by luxury; nor did wealth deprive them of their self-control; but they were sober, and saw clearly that all these goods are increased by virtue and friendship with one another, whereas by too great regard and respect for them, they are lost and friendship with them. By such reflections and by the continuance in them of a divine nature, the qualities which we have described grew and increased among them; but when the divine portion began to fade away, and became diluted too often and too much with the mortal admixture, and the human nature got the upper hand, they then, being unable to bear their fortune, behaved unseemly, and to him who had an eye to see grew visibly debased, for they were losing the fairest of their precious gifts; but to those who had no eye to see the true happiness, they appeared glorious and blessed at the very time when they were full of avarice and unrighteous power. Zeus, the god of gods, who rules according to law, and is able to see into such things, perceiving that an honourable race was in a woeful plight, and wanting to inflict punishment on them, that they might be chastened and improve, collected all the gods into their most holy habitation, which, being placed in the centre of the world, beholds all created things. And when he had called them together, he spake as follows—[*]

* *The rest of the Dialogue of Critias has been lost.*

CRITO

BY PLATO

TRANSLATED BY BENJAMIN JOWETT

PERSONS OF THE DIALOGUE:
Socrates, Crito.

SCENE: The Prison of Socrates.

SOCRATES: Why have you come at this hour, Crito? it must be quite early?

CRITO: Yes, certainly.

SOCRATES: What is the exact time?

CRITO: The dawn is breaking.

SOCRATES: I wonder that the keeper of the prison would let you in.

CRITO: He knows me, because I often come, Socrates; moreover, I have done him a kindness.

SOCRATES: And are you only just arrived?

CRITO: No, I came some time ago.

SOCRATES: Then why did you sit and say nothing, instead of at once awakening me?

CRITO: I should not have liked myself, Socrates, to be in such great trouble and unrest as you are—indeed I should not: I have been watching with amazement your peaceful slumbers; and for that reason I did not awake you, because I wished to minimize the pain. I have always thought you to be of a happy disposition; but never did I see anything like the easy, tranquil manner in which you bear this calamity.

SOCRATES: Why, Crito, when a man has reached my age he ought not to be repining at the approach of death.

CRITO: And yet other old men find themselves in similar misfortunes, and age does not prevent them from repining.

SOCRATES: That is true. But you have not told me why you come at this early hour.

CRITO: I come to bring you a message which is sad and painful; not, as I believe, to yourself, but to all of us who are your friends, and saddest of all to me.

SOCRATES: What? Has the ship come from Delos, on the arrival of which I am to die?

CRITO: No, the ship has not actually arrived, but she will probably be here to-day, as persons who have come from Sunium tell me that they have left her there; and therefore to-morrow, Socrates, will be the last day of your life.

SOCRATES: Very well, Crito; if such is the will of God, I am willing; but my belief is that there will be a delay of a day.

CRITO: Why do you think so?

SOCRATES: I will tell you. I am to die on the day after the arrival of the ship?

CRITO: Yes; that is what the authorities say.

SOCRATES: But I do not think that the ship will be here until to-morrow; this I infer from a vision which I had last night, or rather only just now, when you fortunately allowed me to sleep.

CRITO: And what was the nature of the vision?

SOCRATES: There appeared to me the likeness of a woman, fair and comely, clothed in bright raiment, who called to me and said: O Socrates,

'The third day hence to fertile Phthia shalt thou go.'

CRITO: What a singular dream, Socrates!

SOCRATES: There can be no doubt about the meaning, Crito, I think.

CRITO: Yes; the meaning is only too clear. But, oh! my beloved Socrates, let me entreat you once more to take my advice and escape. For if you die I shall not only lose a friend who can never be replaced, but there is another evil: people who do not know you and me will believe that I might have saved you if I had been willing to give money, but that I did not care. Now, can there be a worse disgrace than this—that I should be thought to value money more than the life of a friend? For the many will not be persuaded that I wanted you to escape, and that you refused.

SOCRATES: But why, my dear Crito, should we care about the opinion of the many? Good men, and they are the only persons who are worth considering, will think of these things truly as they occurred.

CRITO: But you see, Socrates, that the opinion of the many must be regarded, for what is now happening shows that they can do the greatest evil to anyone who has lost their good opinion.

SOCRATES: I only wish it were so, Crito; and that the many could do the greatest evil; for then they would also be able to do the greatest good—and what a fine thing this would be! But in reality they can do neither; for they cannot make a man either wise or foolish; and whatever they do is the result of chance.

CRITO: Well, I will not dispute with you; but please to tell me, Socrates, whether you are not acting out of regard to me and your other friends: are you not afraid that if you escape from prison we may get into trouble with the informers for having stolen you away, and lose either the whole or a great part of our property; or that even a worse evil may happen to us? Now, if you fear on our account, be at ease; for in order to save you, we ought surely to run this, or even a greater risk; be persuaded, then, and do as I say.

SOCRATES: Yes, Crito, that is one fear which you mention, but by no means the only one.

CRITO: Fear not—there are persons who are willing to get you out of prison at no great cost; and as for the informers, they are far from being exorbitant in their demands—a little money will satisfy them. My means, which are certainly ample, are at your service, and if you have a scruple about spending all mine, here are strangers who will give you the use of theirs; and one of them, Simmias the Theban, has brought a large sum of money for this very purpose; and Cebes and many others are prepared to spend their money in helping you to escape. I say, therefore, do not hesitate on our account, and do not say, as you did in the court that you will have a difficulty in knowing what to do with yourself anywhere else. For men will love you in other places to which you may go, and not in Athens only; there are friends of mine in Thessaly, if you like to go to them, who will value and protect you, and no Thessalian will give you any trouble. Nor can I think that you are at all justified, Socrates, in betraying your own life when you might be saved; in acting thus you are playing into the hands of your enemies, who are hurrying on your destruction. And further I should say that you are deserting your own children; for you might bring them up and educate them; instead of which you go away and leave them, and they will have to take their chance; and if they do not meet with the usual fate of orphans, there will be small thanks to you. No man should bring children into the world who is unwilling to persevere to the end in their nurture and education. But you appear to be choosing the easier part, not the better and manlier, which would have been more becoming in one who professes to care for virtue in all his actions, like yourself. And indeed, I am ashamed not only of you, but of us who are your friends, when I reflect that the whole business will be attributed entirely to our want of courage. The trial need never have come on, or might have been managed differently; and this last act, or crowning folly, will seem to have occurred through our negligence and cowardice, who might have saved you, if we had been good for anything; and you might have saved yourself, for there was no difficulty at all. See now, Socrates, how sad and discreditable are the consequences, both to us and you. Make up your mind then, or rather have your mind already made up, for the time of deliberation is over, and there is only one thing to be done, which must be done this very night, and, if we delay at all, will be no longer practicable or possible; I beseech you therefore, Socrates, be persuaded by me, and do as I say.

SOCRATES: Dear Crito, your zeal is invaluable, if a right one; but if wrong, the greater the zeal the greater the danger; and therefore we ought to consider whether I shall or shall not do as you say. For I am and always have been one of those natures who must be guided by reason, whatever the reason may be which upon reflection appears to me to be the best; and now that this chance has befallen me, I cannot repudiate my own words: the principles which I have hitherto honoured and revered I still honour, and unless we can at once find other and better principles, I am certain not to agree with you; no, not even if the power of the multitude could inflict many more imprisonments, confiscations, deaths, frightening us like children with hobgoblin terrors. What will be the fairest way of considering the question? Shall I return to your old argument about the opinions of men?—we were saying that some of them are to be regarded, and others not. Now were we right in maintaining this before I was condemned? And has the argument which was once good now proved to be talk for the sake of talking—mere childish nonsense? That is what I want to consider with your help, Crito:—whether, under my present circumstances, the argument appears to be in any way different or not; and is to be allowed by me or disallowed. That argument, which, as I believe, is maintained by many persons of authority, was to the effect, as I was saying, that the opinions of some men are to be regarded, and of other men not to be regarded. Now you, Crito, are not going to die to-morrow—at least, there is no human probability of this—and therefore you are disinterested and not liable to be deceived by the circumstances in which you are placed. Tell me then, whether I am right in saying that some opinions, and the opinions of some men only, are to be valued, and that other opinions, and the opinions of other men, are not to be valued. I ask you whether I was right in maintaining this?

CRITO: Certainly.

SOCRATES: The good are to be regarded, and not the bad?

CRITO: Yes.

SOCRATES: And the opinions of the wise are good, and the opinions of the unwise are evil?

CRITO: Certainly.

SOCRATES: And what was said about another matter? Is the pupil who devotes himself to the practice of gymnastics supposed to attend to the praise and blame and opinion of every man, or of one man only—his physician or trainer, whoever he may be?

CRITO: Of one man only.

SOCRATES: And he ought to fear the censure and welcome the praise of that one only, and not of the many?

CRITO: Clearly so.

SOCRATES: And he ought to act and train, and eat and drink in the way which seems good to his single master who has understanding, rather than according to the opinion of all other men put together?

CRITO: True.

SOCRATES: And if he disobeys and disregards the opinion and approval of the one, and regards the opinion of the many who have no understanding, will he not suffer evil?

CRITO: Certainly he will.

SOCRATES: And what will the evil be, whither tending and what affecting, in the disobedient person?

CRITO: Clearly, affecting the body; that is what is destroyed by the evil.

SOCRATES: Very good; and is not this true, Crito, of other things which we need not separately enumerate? In questions of just and unjust, fair and foul, good and evil, which are the subjects of our present consultation, ought we to follow the opinion of the many and to fear them; or the opinion of the one man who has understanding? ought we not to fear and reverence him more than all the rest of the world: and if we desert him shall we not destroy and injure that principle in us which may be assumed to be improved by justice and deteriorated by injustice—there is such a principle?

CRITO: Certainly there is, Socrates.

SOCRATES: Take a parallel instance:—if, acting under the advice of those who have no understanding, we destroy that which is improved by health and is deteriorated by disease, would life be worth having? And that which has been destroyed is—the body?

CRITO: Yes.

SOCRATES: Could we live, having an evil and corrupted body?

CRITO: Certainly not.

SOCRATES: And will life be worth having, if that higher part of man be destroyed, which is improved by justice and depraved by injustice? Do we suppose that principle, whatever it may be in man, which has to do with justice and injustice, to be inferior to the body?

CRITO: Certainly not.

SOCRATES: More honourable than the body?

CRITO: Far more.

SOCRATES: Then, my friend, we must not regard what the many say of us; but what he, the one man who has understanding of just and unjust, will say, and what the truth will say. And therefore you begin in error when you advise that we should regard the opinion of the many about just and unjust, good and evil, honourable and dishonourable.—'Well,' someone will say, 'but the many can kill us.'

CRITO: Yes, Socrates; that will clearly be the answer.

SOCRATES: And it is true; but still I find with surprise that the old argument is unshaken as ever. And I should like to know whether I may say the same of another proposition—that not life, but a good life, is to be chiefly valued?

CRITO: Yes, that also remains unshaken.

SOCRATES: And a good life is equivalent to a just and honourable one—that holds also?

CRITO: Yes, it does.

SOCRATES: From these premises I proceed to argue the question whether I ought or ought not to try and escape without the consent of the Athenians: and if I am clearly right in escaping, then I will make the attempt; but if not, I will abstain. The other considerations which you mention, of money and loss of character and the duty of educating one's children, are, I fear, only the doctrines of the multitude, who would be as ready to restore people to life, if they were able, as they are to put them to death—and with as little reason. But now, since the argument has thus far prevailed, the only question which remains to be considered is whether we shall do rightly either in escaping or in suffering others to aid in our escape and paying them in money and thanks, or whether in reality we shall not do rightly; and if the latter, then death or any other calamity which may ensue on my remaining here must not be allowed to enter into the calculation.

CRITO: I think that you are right, Socrates; how then shall we proceed?

SOCRATES: Let us consider the matter together, and do you either refute me if you can, and I will be convinced; or else cease, my dear friend, from repeating to me that I ought to escape against the wishes of the Athenians: for I highly value your attempts to persuade me to do so, but I may not be persuaded against my own better judgment. And now please to consider my first position, and try how you can best answer me.

CRITO: I will.

SOCRATES: Are we to say that we are never intentionally to do wrong, or that in one way we ought and in another way we ought not to do wrong, or is doing wrong always evil and dishonourable, as I was just now saying, and as has been already acknowledged by us? Are all our former admissions which were made within a few days to be thrown away? And have we, at our age, been earnestly discoursing with one another all our life long only to discover that we are no better than children? Or, in spite of the opinion of the many, and in spite of consequences whether better or worse, shall we insist on the truth of what was then said, that injustice is always an evil and dishonour to him who acts unjustly? Shall we say so or not?

CRITO: Yes.

SOCRATES: Then we must do no wrong?

CRITO: Certainly not.

SOCRATES: Nor, when injured, injure in return, as the many imagine; for we must injure no one at all?

CRITO: Clearly not.

SOCRATES: Again, Crito, may we do evil?

CRITO: Surely not, Socrates.

SOCRATES: And what of doing evil in return for evil, which is the morality of the many—is that just or not?

CRITO: Not just.

SOCRATES: For doing evil to another is the same as injuring him?

CRITO: Very true.

SOCRATES: Then we ought not to retaliate or render evil for evil to anyone, whatever evil we may have suffered from him. But I would have you consider, Crito, whether you really mean what you are saying. For this opinion has never been held, and never will be held, by any considerable number of persons; and those who are agreed and those who are not agreed upon this point have no common ground, and can only despise one another when they see how widely they differ. Tell me, then, whether you agree with and assent to my first principle, that neither injury nor retaliation nor warding off evil by evil is ever right. And shall that be the premise of our argument? Or do you decline and dissent from this? For so I have ever thought, and continue to think; but, if you are of another opinion, let me hear what you have to say. If, however, you remain of the same mind as formerly, I will proceed to the next step.

CRITO: You may proceed, for I have not changed my mind.

SOCRATES: Then I will go on to the next point, which may be put in the form of a question:—Ought a man to do what he admits to be right, or ought he to betray the right?

CRITO: He ought to do what he thinks right.

SOCRATES: But if this is true, what is the application? In leaving the prison against the will of the Athenians, do I wrong any? or rather do I not wrong those whom I ought least to wrong? Do I not desert the principles which were acknowledged by us to be just—what do you say?

CRITO: I cannot tell, Socrates; for I do not know.

SOCRATES: Then consider the matter in this way:—Imagine that I am about to play truant (you may call the proceeding by any name which you like), and the laws and the government come and interrogate me: 'Tell us, Socrates,' they say; 'what are you about? are you not going by an act of yours to overturn us—the laws, and the whole state, as far as in you lies? Do you imagine that a state can subsist and not be overthrown, in which the decisions of law have no power, but are set aside and trampled upon by individuals?' What will be our answer, Crito, to these and the like words? Anyone, and especially a rhetorician, will have a good deal to say on behalf of the law which requires a sentence to be carried out. He will argue that this law should not be set aside; and shall we reply, 'Yes; but the state has injured us and given an unjust sentence.' Suppose I say that?

CRITO: Very good, Socrates.

SOCRATES: 'And was that our agreement with you?' the law would answer; 'or were you to abide by the sentence of the state?' And if I were to express my astonishment at their words, the law would probably add: 'Answer, Socrates, instead of opening your eyes—you are in the habit of asking and answering questions. Tell us,—What complaint have you to make against us which justifies you in attempting to destroy us and the state? In the first place did we not bring you into existence? Your father married your mother by our aid and begat you. Say whether you have any objection to urge against those of us who regulate marriage?' None, I should reply. 'Or against those of us who after birth regulate the nurture and education of children, in which you also were trained? Were not the laws, which have the charge of education, right in commanding your father to train you in music and gymnastic?' Right, I should reply. 'Well then, since you were brought into the world and nurtured and educated by us, can you deny in the first place that you are our child and slave, as your fathers were before you? And if this is true you are not on equal terms with us; nor can you think that you have a right to do to us what we are doing to you. Would you have any right to strike or revile or do any other evil to your father or your master, if you had one, because you have been struck or reviled by him, or received some other evil at his hands? You would not say this. And because we think right to destroy you, do you think that you have any right to destroy us in return, and your country as far as in you lies? Will you, O professor of true virtue, pretend that you are justified in this? Has a philosopher like you failed to discover that our country is more to be valued and higher and holier far than mother or father or any ancestor, and more to be regarded in the eyes of the gods and of men of understanding? also to be soothed, and gently and reverently entreated when angry, even more than a father, and either to be persuaded, or if not persuaded, to be obeyed? And when we are punished by her, whether with imprisonment or stripes, the punishment is to be endured in silence; and if she lead us to wounds or death in battle, thither we follow as is right; neither may anyone yield or retreat or leave his rank, but whether in battle or in a court of law, or in any other place, he must do what his city and his country order him; or he must change their view of what is just: and if he may do no violence to his father or mother, much less may he do violence to his country.' What answer shall we make to this, Crito? Do the laws speak truly, or do they not?

CRITO: I think that they do.

SOCRATES: Then the laws will say: 'Consider, Socrates, if we are speaking truly that in your present attempt you are going to do us an injury. For, having brought you into the world, and nurtured and educated you, and given you and every other citizen a share in every good which we had to give, we further proclaim to any Athenian by the liberty which we allow him, that if he does not like us when he has become of age and has seen the ways of the city, and made our acquaintance, he may go where he pleases and take his goods with him. None of us laws will forbid him or interfere with him. Anyone who does not like us and the city, and who wants to emigrate to a colony or to any other city, may go where he likes, retaining his property. But he who has experience of the manner in which we order justice and administer the state, and still remains, has entered into an implied contract that he will do as we command him. And he who disobeys us is, as we maintain, thrice wrong; first, because in disobeying us he is disobeying his parents; secondly, because we are the authors of his education; thirdly, because he has made an agreement with us that he will duly obey our commands; and he neither obeys them nor convinces us that our commands are unjust; and we do not rudely impose them, but give him the alternative of obeying or convincing us;—that is what we offer, and he does neither. These are the sort of accusations to which, as we were saying, you, Socrates, will be exposed if you accomplish your intentions; you, above all other Athenians.'

Suppose now I ask, why I rather than anybody else? they will justly retort upon me that I above all other men have acknowledged the agreement. 'There is clear proof,' they will say, 'Socrates, that we and the city were not displeasing to you. Of all Athenians you have been the most constant resident in the city, which, as you never leave, you may be supposed to love. For you never went out of the city either to see the games, except once when you went to the Isthmus, or to any other place unless when you were on military service; nor did you travel as other men do. Nor had you any curiosity to know other states or their laws: your affections did not go beyond us and our state; we were your especial favourites, and you acquiesced in our government of you; and here in this city you begat your children, which is a proof of your satisfaction. Moreover, you might in the course of the trial, if you had liked, have fixed the penalty at banishment; the state which refuses to let you go now would have let you go then. But you pretended that you preferred death to exile, and that you were not unwilling to die. And now you have forgotten these fine sentiments, and pay no respect to us the laws, of whom you are the destroyer; and are doing what only a miserable slave would do, running away and turning your back upon the compacts and agreements which you made as a citizen. And first of all answer this very question: Are we right in saying that you agreed to be governed according to us in deed, and not in word only? Is that true or not?' How shall we answer, Crito? Must we not assent?

CRITO: We cannot help it, Socrates.

SOCRATES: Then will they not say: 'You, Socrates, are breaking the covenants and agreements which you made with us at your leisure, not in any haste or under any compulsion or deception, but after you have had seventy years to think of them, during which time you were at liberty to leave the city, if we were not to your mind, or if our covenants appeared to you to be unfair. You had your choice, and might have gone either to Lacedaemon or Crete, both which states are often praised by you for their good government, or to some other Hellenic or foreign state. Whereas you, above all other Athenians, seemed to be so fond of the state, or, in other words, of us, her laws (and who would care about a state which has no laws?), that you never stirred out of her; the halt, the blind, the maimed were not more stationary in her than you were. And now you run away and forsake your agreements. Not so, Socrates, if you will take our advice; do not make yourself ridiculous by escaping out of the city.

'For just consider, if you transgress and err in this sort of way, what good will you do either to yourself or to your friends? That your friends will be driven into exile and deprived of citizenship, or will lose their property, is tolerably certain; and you yourself, if you fly to one of the neighbouring cities, as, for example, Thebes or Megara, both of which are well governed, will come to them as an enemy, Socrates, and their government will be against you, and all patriotic citizens will cast an evil eye upon you as a subverter of the laws, and you will confirm in the minds of the judges the justice of their own condemnation of you. For he who is a corrupter of the laws is more than likely to be a corrupter of the young and foolish portion of mankind. Will you then flee from well-ordered cities and virtuous men? and is existence worth having on these terms? Or will you go to them without shame, and talk to them, Socrates? And what will you say to them? What you say here about virtue and justice and institutions and laws being the best things among men? Would that be decent of you? Surely not. But if you go away from well-governed states to Crito's friends in Thessaly, where there is great disorder and licence, they will be charmed to hear the tale of your escape from prison, set off with ludicrous particulars of the manner in which you were wrapped in a goatskin or some other disguise, and metamorphosed as the manner is of runaways; but will there be no one to remind you that in your old age you were not ashamed to violate the most sacred laws from a miserable desire of a little more life? Perhaps not, if you keep them in a good temper; but if they are out of temper you will hear many degrading things; you will live, but how?—as the flatterer of all men, and the servant of all men; and doing what?—eating and drinking in Thessaly, having gone abroad in order that you may get a dinner. And where will be your fine sentiments about justice and virtue? Say that you wish to live for the sake of your children—you want to bring them up and educate them—will you take them into Thessaly and deprive them of Athenian citizenship? Is this the benefit which you will confer upon them? Or are you under the impression that they will be better cared for and educated here if you are still alive, although absent from them; for your friends will take care of them? Do you fancy that if you are an inhabitant of Thessaly they will take care of them, and if you are an inhabitant of the other world that they will not take care of them? Nay; but if they who call themselves friends are good for anything, they will—to be sure they will.

'Listen, then, Socrates, to us who have brought you up. Think not of life and children first, and of justice afterwards, but of justice first, that you may be justified before the princes of the world below. For neither will you nor any that belong to you be happier or holier or juster in this life, or happier in another, if you do as Crito bids. Now you depart in innocence, a sufferer and not a doer of evil; a victim, not of the laws, but of men. But if you go forth, returning evil for evil, and injury for injury, breaking the covenants and agreements which you have made with us, and wronging those whom you ought least of all to wrong, that is to say, yourself, your friends, your country, and us, we shall be angry with you while you live, and our brethren, the laws in the world below, will receive you as an enemy; for they will know that you have done your best to destroy us. Listen, then, to us and not to Crito.'

This, dear Crito, is the voice which I seem to hear murmuring in my ears, like the sound of the flute in the ears of the mystic; that voice, I say, is humming in my ears, and prevents me from hearing any other. And I know that anything more which you may say will be vain. Yet speak, if you have anything to say.

CRITO: I have nothing to say, Socrates.

SOCRATES: Leave me then, Crito, to fulfil the will of God, and to follow whither he leads.

EUTHYDEMUS

by Plato

Translated by Benjamin Jowett

PERSONS OF THE DIALOGUE: Socrates, who is the narrator of the Dialogue. Crito, Cleinias, Euthydemus, Dionysodorus, Ctesippus.

SCENE: The Lyceum.

CRITO: Who was the person, Socrates, with whom you were talking yesterday at the Lyceum? There was such a crowd around you that I could not get within hearing, but I caught a sight of him over their heads, and I made out, as I thought, that he was a stranger with whom you were talking: who was he?

SOCRATES: There were two, Crito; which of them do you mean?

CRITO: The one whom I mean was seated second from you on the right-hand side. In the middle was Cleinias the young son of Axiochus, who has wonderfully grown; he is only about the age of my own Critobulus, but he is much forwarder and very good-looking: the other is thin and looks younger than he is.

SOCRATES: He whom you mean, Crito, is Euthydemus; and on my left hand there was his brother Dionysodorus, who also took part in the conversation.

CRITO: Neither of them are known to me, Socrates; they are a new importation of Sophists, as I should imagine. Of what country are they, and what is their line of wisdom?

SOCRATES: As to their origin, I believe that they are natives of this part of the world, and have migrated from Chios to Thurii; they were driven out of Thurii, and have been living for many years past in these regions. As to their wisdom, about which you ask, Crito, they are wonderful—consummate! I never knew what the true pancratiast was before; they are simply made up of fighting, not like the two Acarnanian brothers who fight with their bodies only, but this pair of heroes, besides being perfect in the use of their bodies, are invincible in every sort of warfare; for they are capital at fighting in armour, and will teach the art to any one who pays them; and also they are most skilful in legal warfare; they will plead themselves and teach others to speak and to compose speeches which will have an effect upon the courts. And this was only the beginning of their wisdom, but they have at last carried out the pancratiastic art to the very end, and have mastered the only mode of fighting which had been hitherto neglected by them; and now no one dares even to stand up against them: such is their skill in the war of words, that they can refute any proposition whether true or false. Now I am thinking, Crito, of placing myself in their hands; for they say that in a short time they can impart their skill to any one.

CRITO: But, Socrates, are you not too old? there may be reason to fear that.

SOCRATES: Certainly not, Crito; as I will prove to you, for I have the consolation of knowing that they began this art of disputation which I covet, quite, as I may say, in old age; last year, or the year before, they had none of their new wisdom. I am only apprehensive that I may bring the two strangers into disrepute, as I have done Connus the son of Metrobius, the harp-player, who is still my music-master; for when the boys who go to him see me going with them, they laugh at me and call him grandpapa's master. Now I should not like the strangers to experience similar treatment; the fear of ridicule may make them unwilling to receive me; and therefore, Crito, I shall try and persuade some old men to accompany me to them, as I persuaded them to go with me to Connus, and I hope that you will make one: and perhaps we had better take your sons as a bait; they will want to have them as pupils, and for the sake of them willing to receive us.

CRITO: I see no objection, Socrates, if you like; but first I wish that you would give me a description of their wisdom, that I may know beforehand what we are going to learn.

SOCRATES: In less than no time you shall hear; for I cannot say that I did not attend—I paid great attention to them, and I remember and will endeavour to repeat the whole story. Providentially I was sitting alone in the dressing-room of the Lyceum where you saw me, and was about to depart; when I was getting up I recognized the familiar divine sign: so I sat down again, and in a little while the two brothers Euthydemus and Dionysodorus came in, and several others with them, whom I believe to be their disciples, and they walked about in the covered court; they had not taken more than two or three turns when Cleinias entered, who, as you truly say, is very much improved: he was followed by a host of lovers, one of whom was Ctesippus the Paeanian, a well-bred youth, but also having the wildness of youth. Cleinias saw me from the entrance as I was sitting alone, and at once came and sat down on the right hand of me, as you describe; and Dionysodorus and Euthydemus, when they saw him, at first stopped and talked with one another, now and then glancing at us, for I particularly watched them; and then Euthydemus came and sat down by the youth, and the other by me on the left hand; the rest anywhere. I saluted the brothers, whom I had not seen for a long time; and then I said to Cleinias: Here are two wise men, Euthydemus and Dionysodorus, Cleinias, wise not in a small but in a large way of wisdom, for they know all about war,—all that a good general ought to know about the array and command of an army, and the whole art of fighting in armour: and they know about law too, and can teach a man how to use the weapons of the courts when he is injured.

They heard me say this, but only despised me. I observed that they looked at one another, and both of them laughed; and then Euthydemus said: Those, Socrates, are matters which we no longer pursue seriously; to us they are secondary occupations.

Indeed, I said, if such occupations are regarded by you as secondary, what must the principal one be; tell me, I beseech you, what that noble study is?

The teaching of virtue, Socrates, he replied, is our principal occupation; and we believe that we can impart it better and quicker than any man.

My God! I said, and where did you learn that? I always thought, as I was saying just now, that your chief accomplishment was the art of fighting in armour; and I used to say as much of you, for I remember that you professed this when you were here before. But now if you really have the other knowledge, O forgive me: I address you as I would superior beings, and ask you to pardon the impiety of my former expressions. But are you quite sure about this, Dionysodorus and Euthydemus? the promise is so vast, that a feeling of incredulity steals over me.

You may take our word, Socrates, for the fact.

Then I think you happier in having such a treasure than the great king is in the possession of his kingdom. And please to tell me whether you intend to exhibit your wisdom; or what will you do?

That is why we have come hither, Socrates; and our purpose is not only to exhibit, but also to teach any one who likes to learn.

But I can promise you, I said, that every unvirtuous person will want to learn. I shall be the first; and there is the youth Cleinias, and Ctesippus: and here are several others, I said, pointing to the lovers of Cleinias, who were beginning to gather round us. Now Ctesippus was sitting at some distance from Cleinias; and when Euthydemus leaned forward in talking with me, he was prevented from seeing Cleinias, who was between us; and so, partly because he wanted to look at his love, and also because he was interested, he jumped up and stood opposite to us: and all the other admirers of Cleinias, as well as the disciples of Euthydemus and Dionysodorus, followed his example. And these were the persons whom I showed to Euthydemus, telling him that they were all eager to learn: to which Ctesippus and all of them with one voice vehemently assented, and bid him exhibit the power of his wisdom. Then I said: O Euthydemus and Dionysodorus, I earnestly request you to do myself and the company the favour to exhibit. There may be some trouble in giving the whole exhibition; but tell me one thing,—can you make a good man of him only who is already convinced that he ought to learn of you, or of him also who is not convinced, either because he imagines that virtue is a thing which cannot be taught at all, or that you are not the teachers of it? Has your art power to persuade him, who is of the latter temper of mind, that virtue can be taught; and that you are the men from whom he will best learn it?

Certainly, Socrates, said Dionysodorus; our art will do both.

And you and your brother, Dionysodorus, I said, of all men who are now living are the most likely to stimulate him to philosophy and to the study of virtue?

Yes, Socrates, I rather think that we are.

Then I wish that you would be so good as to defer the other part of the exhibition, and only try to persuade the youth whom you see here that he ought to be a philosopher and study virtue. Exhibit that, and you will confer a great favour on me and on every one present; for the fact is I and all of us are extremely anxious that he should become truly good. His name is Cleinias, and he is the son of Axiochus, and grandson of the old Alcibiades, cousin of the Alcibiades that now is. He is quite young, and we are naturally afraid that some one may get the start of us, and turn his mind in a wrong direction, and he may be ruined. Your visit, therefore, is most happily timed; and I hope that you will make a trial of the young man, and converse with him in our presence, if you have no objection.

These were pretty nearly the expressions which I used; and Euthydemus, in a manly and at the same time encouraging tone, replied: There can be no objection, Socrates, if the young man is only willing to answer questions.

He is quite accustomed to do so, I replied; for his friends often come and ask him questions and argue with him; and therefore he is quite at home in answering.

What followed, Crito, how can I rightly narrate? For not slight is the task of rehearsing infinite wisdom, and therefore, like the poets, I ought to commence my relation with an invocation to Memory and the Muses. Now Euthydemus, if I remember rightly, began nearly as follows: O Cleinias, are those who learn the wise or the ignorant?

The youth, overpowered by the question blushed, and in his perplexity looked at me for help; and I, knowing that he was disconcerted, said: Take courage, Cleinias, and answer like a man whichever you think; for my belief is that you will derive the greatest benefit from their questions.

Whichever he answers, said Dionysodorus, leaning forward so as to catch my ear, his face beaming with laughter, I prophesy that he will be refuted, Socrates.

While he was speaking to me, Cleinias gave his answer: and therefore I had no time to warn him of the predicament in which he was placed, and he answered that those who learned were the wise.

Euthydemus proceeded: There are some whom you would call teachers, are there not?

The boy assented.

And they are the teachers of those who learn—the grammar-master and the lyre-master used to teach you and other boys; and you were the learners?

Yes.

And when you were learners you did not as yet know the things which you were learning?

No, he said.

And were you wise then?

No, indeed, he said.

But if you were not wise you were unlearned?

Certainly.

You then, learning what you did not know, were unlearned when you were learning?

The youth nodded assent.

Then the unlearned learn, and not the wise, Cleinias, as you imagine.

At these words the followers of Euthydemus, of whom I spoke, like a chorus at the bidding of their director, laughed and cheered. Then, before the youth had time to recover his breath, Dionysodorus cleverly took him in hand, and said: Yes, Cleinias;

and when the grammar-master dictated anything to you, were they the wise boys or the unlearned who learned the dictation?

The wise, replied Cleinias.

Then after all the wise are the learners and not the unlearned; and your last answer to Euthydemus was wrong.

Then once more the admirers of the two heroes, in an ecstasy at their wisdom, gave vent to another peal of laughter, while the rest of us were silent and amazed. Euthydemus, observing this, determined to persevere with the youth; and in order to heighten the effect went on asking another similar question, which might be compared to the double turn of an expert dancer. Do those, said he, who learn, learn what they know, or what they do not know?

Again Dionysodorus whispered to me: That, Socrates, is just another of the same sort.

Good heavens, I said; and your last question was so good!

Like all our other questions, Socrates, he replied—inevitable.

I see the reason, I said, why you are in such reputation among your disciples.

Meanwhile Cleinias had answered Euthydemus that those who learned learn what they do not know; and he put him through a series of questions the same as before.

Do you not know letters?

He assented.

All letters?

Yes.

But when the teacher dictates to you, does he not dictate letters?

To this also he assented.

Then if you know all letters, he dictates that which you know?

This again was admitted by him.

Then, said the other, you do not learn that which he dictates; but he only who does not know letters learns?

Nay, said Cleinias; but I do learn.

Then, said he, you learn what you know, if you know all the letters?

He admitted that.

Then, he said, you were wrong in your answer.

The word was hardly out of his mouth when Dionysodorus took up the argument, like a ball which he caught, and had another throw at the youth. Cleinias, he said, Euthydemus is deceiving you. For tell me now, is not learning acquiring knowledge of that which one learns?

Cleinias assented.

And knowing is having knowledge at the time?

He agreed.

And not knowing is not having knowledge at the time?

He admitted that.

And are those who acquire those who have or have not a thing?

Those who have not.

And have you not admitted that those who do not know are of the number of those who have not?

He nodded assent.

Then those who learn are of the class of those who acquire, and not of those who have?

He agreed.

Then, Cleinias, he said, those who do not know learn, and not those who know.

Euthydemus was proceeding to give the youth a third fall; but I knew that he was in deep water, and therefore, as I wanted to give him a respite lest he should be disheartened, I said to him consolingly: You must not be surprised, Cleinias, at the singularity of their mode of speech: this I say because you may not understand what the two strangers are doing with you; they are only initiating you after the manner of the Corybantes in the mysteries; and this answers to the enthronement, which, if you have ever been initiated, is, as you will know, accompanied by dancing and sport; and now they are just prancing and dancing about you, and will next proceed to initiate you; imagine then that you have gone through the first part of the sophistical ritual, which, as Prodicus says, begins with initiation into the correct use of terms. The two foreign gentlemen, perceiving that you did not know, wanted to explain to you that the word 'to learn' has two meanings, and is used, first, in the sense of acquiring knowledge of some matter of which you previously have no knowledge, and also, when you have the knowledge, in the sense of reviewing this matter, whether something done or spoken by the light of this newly-acquired knowledge; the latter is generally called 'knowing' rather than 'learning,' but the word 'learning' is also used; and you did not see, as they explained to you, that the term is employed of two opposite sorts of men, of those who know, and of those who do not know. There was a similar trick in the second question, when they asked you whether men learn what they know or what they do not know. These parts of learning are not serious, and therefore I say that the gentlemen are not serious, but are only playing with you. For if a man had all that sort of knowledge that ever was, he would not be at all the wiser; he would only be able to play with men, tripping them up and oversetting them with distinctions of words. He would be like a person who pulls away a stool from some one when he is about to sit down, and then laughs and makes merry at the sight of his friend overturned and laid on his back. And you must regard all that has hitherto passed between you and them as merely play. But in what is to follow I am certain that they will exhibit to you their serious purpose, and keep their promise (I will show them how); for they promised to give me a sample of the hortatory philosophy, but I suppose that they wanted to have a game with you first. And now, Euthydemus and Dionysodorus, I think that we have had enough of this. Will you let me see you explaining to the young man how he is to apply himself to the study of virtue and wisdom? And I will first show you what I conceive to be the nature of the task, and what sort of a discourse I desire to hear; and if I do this in a very inartistic and ridiculous manner, do not laugh at me, for I only venture to improvise before you because I am eager to hear your wisdom: and I must therefore ask you and your disciples to refrain from laughing. And now, O son of Axiochus, let me put a question to you: Do not all men desire happiness? And yet, perhaps, this is one of those ridiculous questions which I am afraid to ask, and which ought not to be asked by a sensible man: for what human being is there who does not desire happiness?

There is no one, said Cleinias, who does not.

Well, then, I said, since we all of us desire happiness, how can we be happy?—that is the next question. Shall we not be happy if we have many good things? And this, perhaps, is even a more simple question than the first, for there can be no doubt of the answer.

He assented.

And what things do we esteem good? No solemn sage is required to tell us this, which may be easily answered; for every one will say that wealth is a good.

Certainly, he said.

And are not health and beauty goods, and other personal gifts?

He agreed.

Can there be any doubt that good birth, and power, and honours in one's own land, are goods?

He assented.

And what other goods are there? I said. What do you say of temperance, justice, courage: do you not verily and indeed think, Cleinias, that we shall be more right in ranking them as goods than in not ranking them as goods? For a dispute might possibly arise about this. What then do you say?

They are goods, said Cleinias.

Very well, I said; and where in the company shall we find a place for wisdom—among the goods or not?

Among the goods.

And now, I said, think whether we have left out any considerable goods.

I do not think that we have, said Cleinias.

Upon recollection, I said, indeed I am afraid that we have left out the greatest of them all.

What is that? he asked.

Fortune, Cleinias, I replied; which all, even the most foolish, admit to be the greatest of goods.

True, he said.

On second thoughts, I added, how narrowly, O son of Axiochus, have you and I escaped making a laughing-stock of ourselves to the strangers.

Why do you say so?

Why, because we have already spoken of good-fortune, and are but repeating ourselves.

What do you mean?

I mean that there is something ridiculous in again putting forward good-fortune, which has a place in the list already, and saying the same thing twice over.

He asked what was the meaning of this, and I replied: Surely wisdom is good-fortune; even a child may know that.

The simple-minded youth was amazed; and, observing his surprise, I said to him: Do you not know, Cleinias, that flute-players are most fortunate and successful in performing on the flute?

He assented.

And are not the scribes most fortunate in writing and reading letters?

Certainly.

Amid the dangers of the sea, again, are any more fortunate on the whole than wise pilots?

None, certainly.

And if you were engaged in war, in whose company would you rather take the risk—in company with a wise general, or with a foolish one?

With a wise one.

And if you were ill, whom would you rather have as a companion in a dangerous illness—a wise physician, or an ignorant one?

A wise one.

You think, I said, that to act with a wise man is more fortunate than to act with an ignorant one?

He assented.

Then wisdom always makes men fortunate: for by wisdom no man would ever err, and therefore he must act rightly and succeed, or his wisdom would be wisdom no longer.

We contrived at last, somehow or other, to agree in a general conclusion, that he who had wisdom had no need of fortune. I then recalled to his mind the previous state of the question. You remember, I said, our making the admission that we should be happy and fortunate if many good things were present with us?

He assented.

And should we be happy by reason of the presence of good things, if they profited us not, or if they profited us?

If they profited us, he said.

And would they profit us, if we only had them and did not use them? For example, if we had a great deal of food and did not eat, or a great deal of drink and did not drink, should we be profited?

Certainly not, he said.

Or would an artisan, who had all the implements necessary for his work, and did not use them, be any the better for the possession of them? For example, would a carpenter be any the better for having all his tools and plenty of wood, if he never worked?

Certainly not, he said.

And if a person had wealth and all the goods of which we were just now speaking, and did not use them, would he be happy because he possessed them?

No indeed, Socrates.

Then, I said, a man who would be happy must not only have the good things, but he must also use them; there is no advantage in merely having them?

True.

Well, Cleinias, but if you have the use as well as the possession of good things, is that sufficient to confer happiness?

Yes, in my opinion.

And may a person use them either rightly or wrongly?

He must use them rightly.

That is quite true, I said. And the wrong use of a thing is far worse than the non-use; for the one is an evil, and the other is neither a good nor an evil. You admit that?

He assented.

Now in the working and use of wood, is not that which gives the right use simply the knowledge of the carpenter?

Nothing else, he said.

And surely, in the manufacture of vessels, knowledge is that which gives the right way of making them?

He agreed.

And in the use of the goods of which we spoke at first—wealth and health and beauty, is not knowledge that which directs us to the right use of them, and regulates our practice about them?

He assented.

Then in every possession and every use of a thing, knowledge is that which gives a man not only good-fortune but success?

He again assented.

And tell me, I said, O tell me, what do possessions profit a man, if he have neither good sense nor wisdom? Would a man be better off, having and doing many things without wisdom, or a few things with wisdom? Look at the matter thus: If he did fewer things would he not make fewer mistakes? if he made fewer mistakes would he not have fewer misfortunes? and if he had fewer misfortunes would he not be less miserable?

Certainly, he said.

And who would do least—a poor man or a rich man?

A poor man.

A weak man or a strong man?

A weak man.

A noble man or a mean man?

A mean man.

And a coward would do less than a courageous and temperate man?

Yes.

And an indolent man less than an active man?

He assented.

And a slow man less than a quick; and one who had dull perceptions of seeing and hearing less than one who had keen ones?

All this was mutually allowed by us.

Then, I said, Cleinias, the sum of the matter appears to be that the goods of which we spoke before are not to be regarded as goods in themselves, but the degree of good and evil in them depends on whether they are or are not under the guidance of knowledge: under the guidance of ignorance, they are greater evils than their opposites, inasmuch as they are more able to minister to the evil principle which rules them; and when under the guidance of wisdom and prudence, they are greater goods: but in themselves they are nothing?

That, he replied, is obvious.

What then is the result of what has been said? Is not this the result—that other things are indifferent, and that wisdom is the only good, and ignorance the only evil?

He assented.

Let us consider a further point, I said: Seeing that all men desire happiness, and happiness, as has been shown, is gained by a use, and a right use, of the things of life, and the right use of them, and good-fortune in the use of them, is given by knowledge,—the inference is that everybody ought by all means to try and make himself as wise as he can?

Yes, he said.

And when a man thinks that he ought to obtain this treasure, far more than money, from a father or a guardian or a friend or a suitor, whether citizen or stranger—the eager desire and prayer to them that they would impart wisdom to you, is not at all dishonourable, Cleinias; nor is any one to be blamed for doing any honourable service or ministration to any man, whether a lover or not, if his aim is to get wisdom. Do you agree? I said.

Yes, he said, I quite agree, and think that you are right.

Yes, I said, Cleinias, if only wisdom can be taught, and does not come to man spontaneously; for this is a point which has still to be considered, and is not yet agreed upon by you and me—

But I think, Socrates, that wisdom can be taught, he said.

Best of men, I said, I am delighted to hear you say so; and I am also grateful to you for having saved me from a long and tiresome investigation as to whether wisdom can be taught or not. But now, as you think that wisdom can be taught, and that wisdom only can make a man happy and fortunate, will you not acknowledge that all of us ought to love wisdom, and you individually will try to love her?

Certainly, Socrates, he said; I will do my best.

I was pleased at hearing this; and I turned to Dionysodorus and Euthydemus and said: That is an example, clumsy and tedious I admit, of the sort of exhortations which I would have you give; and I hope that one of you will set forth what I have been saying in a more artistic style: or at least take up the enquiry where I left off, and proceed to show the youth whether he should have all knowledge; or whether there is one sort of knowledge only which will make him good and happy, and what that is. For, as I was saying at first, the improvement of this young man in virtue and wisdom is a matter which we have very much at heart.

Thus I spoke, Crito, and was all attention to what was coming. I wanted to see how they would approach the question, and where they would start in their exhortation to the young man that he should practise wisdom and virtue. Dionysodorus, who was the elder, spoke first. Everybody's eyes were directed towards him, perceiving that something wonderful might shortly be expected. And certainly they were not far wrong; for the man, Crito, began a remarkable discourse well worth hearing, and wonderfully persuasive regarded as an exhortation to virtue.

Tell me, he said, Socrates and the rest of you who say that you want this young man to become wise, are you in jest or in real earnest?

I was led by this to imagine that they fancied us to have been jesting when we asked them to converse with the youth, and that this made them jest and play, and being under this impression, I was the more decided in saying that we were in profound earnest. Dionysodorus said:

Reflect, Socrates; you may have to deny your words.

I have reflected, I said; and I shall never deny my words.

Well, said he, and so you say that you wish Cleinias to become wise?

Undoubtedly.

And he is not wise as yet?

At least his modesty will not allow him to say that he is.

You wish him, he said, to become wise and not, to be ignorant?

That we do.

You wish him to be what he is not, and no longer to be what he is?

I was thrown into consternation at this.

Taking advantage of my consternation he added: You wish him no longer to be what he is, which can only mean that you wish him to perish. Pretty lovers and friends they must be who want their favourite not to be, or to perish!

When Ctesippus heard this he got very angry (as a lover well might) and said: Stranger of Thurii—if politeness would allow me I should say, A plague upon you! What can make you tell such a lie about me and the others, which I hardly like to repeat, as that I wish Cleinias to perish?

Euthydemus replied: And do you think, Ctesippus, that it is possible to tell a lie?

Yes, said Ctesippus; I should be mad to say anything else.

And in telling a lie, do you tell the thing of which you speak or not?

You tell the thing of which you speak.

And he who tells, tells that thing which he tells, and no other?

Yes, said Ctesippus.

And that is a distinct thing apart from other things?

Certainly.

And he who says that thing says that which is?

Yes.

And he who says that which is, says the truth. And therefore Dionysodorus, if he says that which is, says the truth of you and no lie.

Yes, Euthydemus, said Ctesippus; but in saying this, he says what is not.

Euthydemus answered: And that which is not is not?

True.

And that which is not is nowhere?

Nowhere.

And can any one do anything about that which has no existence, or do to Cleinias that which is not and is nowhere?

I think not, said Ctesippus.

Well, but do rhetoricians, when they speak in the assembly, do nothing?

Nay, he said, they do something.

And doing is making?

Yes.

And speaking is doing and making?

He agreed.

Then no one says that which is not, for in saying what is not he would be doing something; and you have already acknowledged that no one can do what is not. And therefore, upon your own showing, no one says what is false; but if Dionysodorus says anything, he says what is true and what is.

Yes, Euthydemus, said Ctesippus; but he speaks of things in a certain way and manner, and not as they really are.

Why, Ctesippus, said Dionysodorus, do you mean to say that any one speaks of things as they are?

Yes, he said—all gentlemen and truth-speaking persons.

And are not good things good, and evil things evil?

He assented.

And you say that gentlemen speak of things as they are?

Yes.

Then the good speak evil of evil things, if they speak of them as they are?

Yes, indeed, he said; and they speak evil of evil men. And if I may give you a piece of advice, you had better take care that they do not speak evil of you, since I can tell you that the good speak evil of the evil.

And do they speak great things of the great, rejoined Euthydemus, and warm things of the warm?

To be sure they do, said Ctesippus; and they speak coldly of the insipid and cold dialectician.

You are abusive, Ctesippus, said Dionysodorus, you are abusive!

Indeed, I am not, Dionysodorus, he replied; for I love you and am giving you friendly advice, and, if I could, would persuade you not like a boor to say in my presence that I desire my beloved, whom I value above all men, to perish.

I saw that they were getting exasperated with one another, so I made a joke with him and said: O Ctesippus, I think that we must allow the strangers to use language in their own way, and not quarrel with them about words, but be thankful for what they give us. If they know how to destroy men in such a way as to make good and sensible men out of bad and foolish ones—whether this is a discovery of their own, or whether they have learned from some one else this new sort of death and destruction which enables them to get rid of a bad man and turn him into a good one—if they know this (and they do know this—at any rate they said just now that this was the secret of their newly-discovered art)—let them, in their phraseology, destroy the youth and make him wise, and all of us with him. But if you young men do not like to trust yourselves with them, then fiat experimentum in corpore senis; I will be the Carian on whom they shall operate. And here I offer my old person to Dionysodorus; he may put me into the pot, like Medea the Colchian, kill me, boil me, if he will only make me good.

Ctesippus said: And I, Socrates, am ready to commit myself to the strangers; they may skin me alive, if they please (and I am pretty well skinned by them already), if only my skin is made at last, not like that of Marsyas, into a leathern bottle, but into a piece of virtue. And here is Dionysodorus fancying that I am angry with him, when really I am not angry at all; I do but contradict him when I think that he is speaking improperly to me: and you must not confound abuse and contradiction, O illustrious Dionysodorus; for they are quite different things.

Contradiction! said Dionysodorus; why, there never was such a thing.

Certainly there is, he replied; there can be no question of that. Do you, Dionysodorus, maintain that there is not?

You will never prove to me, he said, that you have heard any one contradicting any one else.

Indeed, said Ctesippus; then now you may hear me contradicting Dionysodorus.

Are you prepared to make that good?

Certainly, he said.

Well, have not all things words expressive of them?

Yes.

Of their existence or of their non-existence?

Of their existence.

Yes, Ctesippus, and we just now proved, as you may remember, that no man could affirm a negative; for no one could affirm that which is not.

And what does that signify? said Ctesippus; you and I may contradict all the same for that.

But can we contradict one another, said Dionysodorus, when both of us are describing the same thing? Then we must surely be speaking the same thing?

He assented.

Or when neither of us is speaking of the same thing? For then neither of us says a word about the thing at all?

He granted that proposition also.

But when I describe something and you describe another thing, or I say something and you say nothing—is there any contradiction? How can he who speaks contradict him who speaks not?

Here Ctesippus was silent; and I in my astonishment said: What do you mean, Dionysodorus? I have often heard, and have been amazed to hear, this thesis of yours, which is maintained and employed by the disciples of Protagoras, and others before them, and which to me appears to be quite wonderful, and suicidal as well as destructive, and I think that I am most likely to hear the truth about it from you. The dictum is that there is no such thing as falsehood; a man must either say what is true or say nothing. Is not that your position?

He assented.

But if he cannot speak falsely, may he not think falsely?

No, he cannot, he said.

Then there is no such thing as false opinion?

No, he said.

Then there is no such thing as ignorance, or men who are ignorant; for is not ignorance, if there be such a thing, a mistake of fact?

Certainly, he said.

And that is impossible?

Impossible, he replied.

Are you saying this as a paradox, Dionysodorus; or do you seriously maintain no man to be ignorant?

Refute me, he said.

But how can I refute you, if, as you say, to tell a falsehood is impossible?

Very true, said Euthydemus.

Neither did I tell you just now to refute me, said Dionysodorus; for how can I tell you to do that which is not?

O Euthydemus, I said, I have but a dull conception of these subtleties and excellent devices of wisdom; I am afraid that I hardly understand them, and you must forgive me therefore if I ask a very stupid question: if there be no falsehood or false opinion or ignorance, there can be no such thing as erroneous action, for a man cannot fail of acting as he is acting—that is what you mean?

Yes, he replied.

And now, I said, I will ask my stupid question: If there is no such thing as error in deed, word, or thought, then what, in the name of goodness, do you come hither to teach? And were you not just now saying that you could teach virtue best of all men, to any one who was willing to learn?

And are you such an old fool, Socrates, rejoined Dionysodorus, that you bring up now what I said at first—and if I had said anything last year, I suppose that you would bring that up too—but are non-plussed at the words which I have just uttered?

Why, I said, they are not easy to answer; for they are the words of wise men: and indeed I know not what to make of this word 'nonplussed,' which you used last: what do you mean by it, Dionysodorus? You must mean that I cannot refute your argument. Tell me if the words have any other sense.

No, he replied, they mean what you say. And now answer.

What, before you, Dionysodorus? I said.

Answer, said he.

And is that fair?

Yes, quite fair, he said.

Upon what principle? I said. I can only suppose that you are a very wise man who comes to us in the character of a great logician, and who knows when to answer and when not to answer—and now you will not open your mouth at all, because you know that you ought not.

You prate, he said, instead of answering. But if, my good sir, you admit that I am wise, answer as I tell you.

I suppose that I must obey, for you are master. Put the question.

Are the things which have sense alive or lifeless?

They are alive.

And do you know of any word which is alive?

I cannot say that I do.

Then why did you ask me what sense my words had?

Why, because I was stupid and made a mistake. And yet, perhaps, I was right after all in saying that words have a sense;—what do you say, wise man? If I was not in error, even you will not refute me, and all your wisdom will be non-plussed; but if I did fall into error, then again you are wrong in saying that there is no error,—and this remark was made by you not quite a year ago. I am inclined to think, however, Dionysodorus and Euthydemus, that this argument lies where it was and is not very likely to advance: even your skill in the subtleties of logic, which is really amazing, has not found out the way of throwing another and not falling yourself, now any more than of old.

Ctesippus said: Men of Chios, Thurii, or however and whatever you call yourselves, I wonder at you, for you seem to have no objection to talking nonsense.

Fearing that there would be high words, I again endeavoured to soothe Ctesippus, and said to him: To you, Ctesippus, I must repeat what I said before to Cleinias—that you do not understand the ways of these philosophers from abroad. They are not serious, but, like the Egyptian wizard, Proteus, they take different forms and deceive us by their enchantments: and let us, like Menelaus, refuse to let them go until they show themselves to us in earnest. When they begin to be in earnest their full beauty will appear: let us then beg and entreat and beseech them to shine forth. And I think that I had better once more exhibit the form in which I pray to behold them; it might be a guide to them. I will go on therefore where I left off, as well as I can, in the hope that I may touch their hearts and move them to pity, and that when they see me deeply serious and interested, they also may be serious. You, Cleinias, I said, shall remind me at what point we left off. Did we not agree that philosophy should be studied? and was not that our conclusion?

Yes, he replied.

And philosophy is the acquisition of knowledge?

Yes, he said.

And what knowledge ought we to acquire? May we not answer with absolute truth—A knowledge which will do us good?

Certainly, he said.

And should we be any the better if we went about having a knowledge of the places where most gold was hidden in the earth?

Perhaps we should, he said.

But have we not already proved, I said, that we should be none the better off, even if without trouble and digging all the gold which there is in the earth were ours? And if we knew how to convert stones into gold, the knowledge would be of no value to us, unless we also knew how to use the gold? Do you not remember? I said.

I quite remember, he said.

Nor would any other knowledge, whether of money-making, or of medicine, or of any other art which knows only how to make a thing, and not to use it when made, be of any good to us. Am I not right?

He agreed.

And if there were a knowledge which was able to make men immortal, without giving them the knowledge of the way to use the immortality, neither would there be any use in that, if we may argue from the analogy of the previous instances?

To all this he agreed.

Then, my dear boy, I said, the knowledge which we want is one that uses as well as makes?

True, he said.

And our desire is not to be skilful lyre-makers, or artists of that sort—far otherwise; for with them the art which makes is one, and the art which uses is another. Although they have to do with the same, they are divided: for the art which makes and the art which plays on the lyre differ widely from one another. Am I not right?

He agreed.

And clearly we do not want the art of the flute-maker; this is only another of the same sort?

He assented.

But suppose, I said, that we were to learn the art of making speeches—would that be the art which would make us happy?

I should say, no, rejoined Cleinias.

And why should you say so? I asked.

I see, he replied, that there are some composers of speeches who do not know how to use the speeches which they make, just as the makers of lyres do not know how to use the lyres; and also some who are of themselves unable to compose speeches, but are able to use the speeches which the others make for them; and this proves that the art of making speeches is not the same as the art of using them.

Yes, I said; and I take your words to be a sufficient proof that the art of making speeches is not one which will make a man happy. And yet I did think that the art which we have so long been seeking might be discovered in that direction; for the composers of speeches, whenever I meet them, always appear to me to be very extraordinary men, Cleinias, and their art is lofty and divine, and no wonder. For their art is a part of the great art of enchantment, and hardly, if at all, inferior to it: and whereas the art of the enchanter is a mode of charming snakes and spiders and scorpions, and other monsters and pests, this art of their's acts upon dicasts and ecclesiasts and bodies of men, for the charming and pacifying of them. Do you agree with me?

Yes, he said, I think that you are quite right.

Whither then shall we go, I said, and to what art shall we have recourse?

I do not see my way, he said.

But I think that I do, I replied.

And what is your notion? asked Cleinias.

I think that the art of the general is above all others the one of which the possession is most likely to make a man happy.

I do not think so, he said.

Why not? I said.

The art of the general is surely an art of hunting mankind.

What of that? I said.

Why, he said, no art of hunting extends beyond hunting and capturing; and when the prey is taken the huntsman or fisherman cannot use it; but they hand it over to the cook, and the geometricians and astronomers and calculators (who all belong to the hunting class, for they do not make their diagrams, but only find out that which was previously contained in them)—they, I say, not being able to use but only to catch their prey, hand over their inventions to the dialectician to be applied by him, if they have any sense in them.

Good, I said, fairest and wisest Cleinias. And is this true?

Certainly, he said; just as a general when he takes a city or a camp hands over his new acquisition to the statesman, for he does not know how to use them himself; or as the quail-taker transfers the quails to the keeper of them. If we are looking for the art which is to make us blessed, and which is able to use that which it makes or takes, the art of the general is not the one, and some other must be found.

CRITO: And do you mean, Socrates, that the youngster said all this?

SOCRATES: Are you incredulous, Crito?

CRITO: Indeed, I am; for if he did say so, then in my opinion he needs neither Euthydemus nor any one else to be his instructor.

SOCRATES: Perhaps I may have forgotten, and Ctesippus was the real answerer.

CRITO: Ctesippus! nonsense.

SOCRATES: All I know is that I heard these words, and that they were not spoken either by Euthydemus or Dionysodorus. I dare say, my good Crito, that they may have been spoken by some superior person: that I heard them I am certain.

CRITO: Yes, indeed, Socrates, by some one a good deal superior, as I should be disposed to think. But did you carry the search any further, and did you find the art which you were seeking?

SOCRATES: Find! my dear sir, no indeed. And we cut a poor figure; we were like children after larks, always on the point of catching the art, which was always getting away from us. But why should I repeat the whole story? At last we came to the kingly art, and enquired whether that gave and caused happiness, and then we got into a labyrinth, and when we thought we were at the end, came out again at the beginning, having still to seek as much as ever.

CRITO: How did that happen, Socrates?

SOCRATES: I will tell you; the kingly art was identified by us with the political.

CRITO: Well, and what came of that?

SOCRATES: To this royal or political art all the arts, including the art of the general, seemed to render up the supremacy, that being the only one which knew how to use what they produce. Here obviously was the very art which we were seeking—the art which is the source of good government, and which may be described, in the language of Aeschylus, as alone sitting at the helm of the vessel of state, piloting and governing all things, and utilizing them.

CRITO: And were you not right, Socrates?

SOCRATES: You shall judge, Crito, if you are willing to hear what followed; for we resumed the enquiry, and a question of this sort was asked: Does the kingly art, having this supreme authority, do anything for us? To be sure, was the answer. And would not you, Crito, say the same?

CRITO: Yes, I should.

SOCRATES: And what would you say that the kingly art does? If medicine were supposed to have supreme authority over the subordinate arts, and I were to ask you a similar question about that, you would say—it produces health?

CRITO: I should.

SOCRATES: And what of your own art of husbandry, supposing that to have supreme authority over the subject arts—what does that do? Does it not supply us with the fruits of the earth?

CRITO: Yes.

SOCRATES: And what does the kingly art do when invested with supreme power? Perhaps you may not be ready with an answer?

CRITO: Indeed I am not, Socrates.

SOCRATES: No more were we, Crito. But at any rate you know that if this is the art which we were seeking, it ought to be useful.

CRITO: Certainly.

SOCRATES: And surely it ought to do us some good?

CRITO: Certainly, Socrates.

SOCRATES: And Cleinias and I had arrived at the conclusion that knowledge of some kind is the only good.

CRITO: Yes, that was what you were saying.

SOCRATES: All the other results of politics, and they are many, as for example, wealth, freedom, tranquillity, were neither good nor evil in themselves; but the political science ought to make us wise, and impart knowledge to us, if that is the science which is likely to do us good, and make us happy.

CRITO: Yes; that was the conclusion at which you had arrived, according to your report of the conversation.

SOCRATES: And does the kingly art make men wise and good?

CRITO: Why not, Socrates?

SOCRATES: What, all men, and in every respect? and teach them all the arts,—carpentering, and cobbling, and the rest of them?

CRITO: I think not, Socrates.

SOCRATES: But then what is this knowledge, and what are we to do with it? For it is not the source of any works which are neither good nor evil, and gives no knowledge, but the knowledge of itself; what then can it be, and what are we to do with it? Shall we say, Crito, that it is the knowledge by which we are to make other men good?

CRITO: By all means.

SOCRATES: And in what will they be good and useful? Shall we repeat that they will make others good, and that these others will make others again, without ever determining in what they are to be good; for we have put aside the results of politics, as they are called. This is the old, old song over again; and we are just as far as ever, if not farther, from the knowledge of the art or science of happiness.

CRITO: Indeed, Socrates, you do appear to have got into a great perplexity.

SOCRATES: Thereupon, Crito, seeing that I was on the point of shipwreck, I lifted up my voice, and earnestly entreated and called upon the strangers to save me and the youth from the whirlpool of the argument; they were our Castor and Pollux, I said, and they should be serious, and show us in sober earnest what that knowledge was which would enable us to pass the rest of our lives in happiness.

CRITO: And did Euthydemus show you this knowledge?

SOCRATES: Yes, indeed; he proceeded in a lofty strain to the following effect: Would you rather, Socrates, said he, that I should show you this knowledge about which you have been doubting, or shall I prove that you already have it?

What, I said, are you blessed with such a power as this?

Indeed I am.

Then I would much rather that you should prove me to have such a knowledge; at my time of life that will be more agreeable than having to learn.

Then tell me, he said, do you know anything?

Yes, I said, I know many things, but not anything of much importance.

That will do, he said: And would you admit that anything is what it is, and at the same time is not what it is?

Certainly not.

And did you not say that you knew something?

I did.

If you know, you are knowing.

Certainly, of the knowledge which I have.

That makes no difference;—and must you not, if you are knowing, know all things?

Certainly not, I said, for there are many other things which I do not know.

And if you do not know, you are not knowing.

Yes, friend, of that which I do not know.

Still you are not knowing, and you said just now that you were knowing; and therefore you are and are not at the same time, and in reference to the same things.

A pretty clatter, as men say, Euthydemus, this of yours! and will you explain how I possess that knowledge for which we were seeking? Do you mean to say that the same thing cannot be and also not be; and therefore, since I know one thing, that I know all, for I cannot be knowing and not knowing at the same time, and if I know all things, then I must have the knowledge for which we are seeking—May I assume this to be your ingenious notion?

Out of your own mouth, Socrates, you are convicted, he said.

Well, but, Euthydemus, I said, has that never happened to you? for if I am only in the same case with you and our beloved Dionysodorus, I cannot complain. Tell me, then, you two, do you not know some things, and not know others?

Certainly not, Socrates, said Dionysodorus.

What do you mean, I said; do you know nothing?

Nay, he replied, we do know something.

Then, I said, you know all things, if you know anything?

Yes, all things, he said; and that is as true of you as of us.

O, indeed, I said, what a wonderful thing, and what a great blessing! And do all other men know all things or nothing?

Certainly, he replied; they cannot know some things, and not know others, and be at the same time knowing and not knowing.

Then what is the inference? I said.

They all know all things, he replied, if they know one thing.

O heavens, Dionysodorus, I said, I see now that you are in earnest; hardly have I got you to that point. And do you really and truly know all things, including carpentering and leather-cutting?

Certainly, he said.

And do you know stitching?

Yes, by the gods, we do, and cobbling, too.

And do you know things such as the numbers of the stars and of the sand?

Certainly; did you think we should say No to that?

By Zeus, said Ctesippus, interrupting, I only wish that you would give me some proof which would enable me to know whether you speak truly.

What proof shall I give you? he said.

Will you tell me how many teeth Euthydemus has? and Euthydemus shall tell how many teeth you have.

Will you not take our word that we know all things?

Certainly not, said Ctesippus: you must further tell us this one thing, and then we shall know that you are speak the truth; if you tell us the number, and we count them, and you are found to be right, we will believe the rest. They fancied that Ctesippus was making game of them, and they refused, and they would only say in answer to each of his questions, that they knew all things. For at last Ctesippus began to throw off all restraint; no question in fact was too bad for him; he would ask them if they knew the foulest things, and they, like wild boars, came rushing on his blows, and fearlessly replied that they did. At last, Crito, I too was carried away by my incredulity, and asked Euthydemus whether Dionysodorus could dance.

Certainly, he replied.

And can he vault among swords, and turn upon a wheel, at his age? has he got to such a height of skill as that?

He can do anything, he said.

And did you always know this?

Always, he said.

When you were children, and at your birth?

They both said that they did.

This we could not believe. And Euthydemus said: You are incredulous, Socrates.

Yes, I said, and I might well be incredulous, if I did not know you to be wise men.

But if you will answer, he said, I will make you confess to similar marvels.

Well, I said, there is nothing that I should like better than to be self-convicted of this, for if I am really a wise man, which I never knew before, and you will prove to me that I know and have always known all things, nothing in life would be a greater gain to me.

Answer then, he said.

Ask, I said, and I will answer.

Do you know something, Socrates, or nothing?

Something, I said.

And do you know with what you know, or with something else?

With what I know; and I suppose that you mean with my soul?

Are you not ashamed, Socrates, of asking a question when you are asked one?

Well, I said; but then what am I to do? for I will do whatever you bid; when I do not know what you are asking, you tell me to answer nevertheless, and not to ask again.

Why, you surely have some notion of my meaning, he said.

Yes, I replied.

Well, then, answer according to your notion of my meaning.

Yes, I said; but if the question which you ask in one sense is understood and answered by me in another, will that please you—if I answer what is not to the point?

That will please me very well; but will not please you equally well, as I imagine.

I certainly will not answer unless I understand you, I said.

You will not answer, he said, according to your view of the meaning, because you will be prating, and are an ancient.

Now I saw that he was getting angry with me for drawing distinctions, when he wanted to catch me in his springes of words. And I remembered that Connus was always angry with me when I opposed him, and then he neglected me, because he thought that I was stupid; and as I was intending to go to Euthydemus as a pupil, I reflected that I had better let him have his way, as he might think me a blockhead, and refuse to take me. So I said: You are a far better dialectician than myself, Euthydemus, for I have never made a profession of the art, and therefore do as you say; ask your questions once more, and I will answer.

Answer then, he said, again, whether you know what you know with something, or with nothing.

Yes, I said; I know with my soul.

The man will answer more than the question; for I did not ask you, he said, with what you know, but whether you know with something.

Again I replied, Through ignorance I have answered too much, but I hope that you will forgive me. And now I will answer simply that I always know what I know with something.

And is that something, he rejoined, always the same, or sometimes one thing, and sometimes another thing?

Always, I replied, when I know, I know with this.

Will you not cease adding to your answers?

My fear is that this word 'always' may get us into trouble.

You, perhaps, but certainly not us. And now answer: Do you always know with this?

Always; since I am required to withdraw the words 'when I know.'

You always know with this, or, always knowing, do you know some things with this, and some things with something else, or do you know all things with this?

All that I know, I replied, I know with this.

There again, Socrates, he said, the addition is superfluous.

Well, then, I said, I will take away the words 'that I know.'

Nay, take nothing away; I desire no favours of you; but let me ask: Would you be able to know all things, if you did not know all things?

Quite impossible.

And now, he said, you may add on whatever you like, for you confess that you know all things.

I suppose that is true, I said, if my qualification implied in the words 'that I know' is not allowed to stand; and so I do know all things.

And have you not admitted that you always know all things with that which you know, whether you make the addition of 'when you know them' or not? for you have acknowledged that you have always and at once known all things, that is to say, when you were a child, and at your birth, and when you were growing up, and before you were born, and before the heaven and earth existed, you knew all things, if you always know them; and I swear that you shall always continue to know all things, if I am of the mind to make you.

But I hope that you will be of that mind, reverend Euthydemus, I said, if you are really speaking the truth, and yet I a little doubt your power to make good your words unless you have the help of your brother Dionysodorus; then you may do it. Tell me now, both of you, for although in the main I cannot doubt that I really do know all things, when I am told so by men of your prodigious wisdom—how can I say that I know such things, Euthydemus, as that the good are unjust; come, do I know that or not?

Certainly, you know that.

What do I know?

That the good are not unjust.

Quite true, I said; and that I have always known; but the question is, where did I learn that the good are unjust?

Nowhere, said Dionysodorus.

Then, I said, I do not know this.

You are ruining the argument, said Euthydemus to Dionysodorus; he will be proved not to know, and then after all he will be knowing and not knowing at the same time.

Dionysodorus blushed.

I turned to the other, and said, What do you think, Euthydemus? Does not your omniscient brother appear to you to have made a mistake?

What, replied Dionysodorus in a moment; am I the brother of Euthydemus?

Thereupon I said, Please not to interrupt, my good friend, or prevent Euthydemus from proving to me that I know the good to be unjust; such a lesson you might at least allow me to learn.

You are running away, Socrates, said Dionysodorus, and refusing to answer.

No wonder, I said, for I am not a match for one of you, and a fortiori I must run away from two. I am no Heracles; and even Heracles could not fight against the Hydra, who was a she-Sophist, and had the wit to shoot up many new heads when one of them was cut off; especially when he saw a second monster of a sea-crab, who was also a Sophist, and appeared to have newly arrived from a sea-voyage, bearing down upon him from the left, opening his mouth and biting. When the monster was growing troublesome he called Iolaus, his nephew, to his help, who ably succoured him; but if my Iolaus, who is my brother Patrocles (the statuary), were to come, he would only make a bad business worse.

And now that you have delivered yourself of this strain, said Dionysodorus, will you inform me whether Iolaus was the nephew of Heracles any more than he is yours?

I suppose that I had best answer you, Dionysodorus, I said, for you will insist on asking—that I pretty well know—out of envy, in order to prevent me from learning the wisdom of Euthydemus.

Then answer me, he said.

Well then, I said, I can only reply that Iolaus was not my nephew at all, but the nephew of Heracles; and his father was not my brother Patrocles, but Iphicles, who has a name rather like his, and was the brother of Heracles.

And is Patrocles, he said, your brother?

Yes, I said, he is my half-brother, the son of my mother, but not of my father.

Then he is and is not your brother.

Not by the same father, my good man, I said, for Chaeredemus was his father, and mine was Sophroniscus.

And was Sophroniscus a father, and Chaeredemus also?

Yes, I said; the former was my father, and the latter his.

Then, he said, Chaeredemus is not a father.

He is not my father, I said.

But can a father be other than a father? or are you the same as a stone?

I certainly do not think that I am a stone, I said, though I am afraid that you may prove me to be one.

Are you not other than a stone?

I am.

And being other than a stone, you are not a stone; and being other than gold, you are not gold?

Very true.

And so Chaeredemus, he said, being other than a father, is not a father?

I suppose that he is not a father, I replied.

For if, said Euthydemus, taking up the argument, Chaeredemus is a father, then Sophroniscus, being other than a father, is not a father; and you, Socrates, are without a father.

Ctesippus, here taking up the argument, said: And is not your father in the same case, for he is other than my father?

Assuredly not, said Euthydemus.

Then he is the same?

He is the same.

I cannot say that I like the connection; but is he only my father, Euthydemus, or is he the father of all other men?

Of all other men, he replied. Do you suppose the same person to be a father and not a father?

Certainly, I did so imagine, said Ctesippus.

And do you suppose that gold is not gold, or that a man is not a man?

They are not 'in pari materia,' Euthydemus, said Ctesippus, and you had better take care, for it is monstrous to suppose that your father is the father of all.

But he is, he replied.

What, of men only, said Ctesippus, or of horses and of all other animals?

Of all, he said.

And your mother, too, is the mother of all?

Yes, our mother too.

Yes; and your mother has a progeny of sea-urchins then?

Yes; and yours, he said.

And gudgeons and puppies and pigs are your brothers?

And yours too.

And your papa is a dog?

And so is yours, he said.

If you will answer my questions, said Dionysodorus, I will soon extract the same admissions from you, Ctesippus. You say that you have a dog.

Yes, a villain of a one, said Ctesippus.

And he has puppies?

Yes, and they are very like himself.

And the dog is the father of them?

Yes, he said, I certainly saw him and the mother of the puppies come together.

And is he not yours?

To be sure he is.

Then he is a father, and he is yours; ergo, he is your father, and the puppies are your brothers.

Let me ask you one little question more, said Dionysodorus, quickly interposing, in order that Ctesippus might not get in his word: You beat this dog?

Ctesippus said, laughing, Indeed I do; and I only wish that I could beat you instead of him.

Then you beat your father, he said.

I should have far more reason to beat yours, said Ctesippus; what could he have been thinking of when he begat such wise sons? much good has this father of you and your brethren the puppies got out of this wisdom of yours.

But neither he nor you, Ctesippus, have any need of much good.

And have you no need, Euthydemus? he said.

Neither I nor any other man; for tell me now, Ctesippus, if you think it good or evil for a man who is sick to drink medicine when he wants it; or to go to war armed rather than unarmed.

Good, I say. And yet I know that I am going to be caught in one of your charming puzzles.

That, he replied, you will discover, if you answer; since you admit medicine to be good for a man to drink, when wanted, must it not be good for him to drink as much as possible; when he takes his medicine, a cartload of hellebore will not be too much for him?

Ctesippus said: Quite so, Euthydemus, that is to say, if he who drinks is as big as the statue of Delphi.

And seeing that in war to have arms is a good thing, he ought to have as many spears and shields as possible?

Very true, said Ctesippus; and do you think, Euthydemus, that he ought to have one shield only, and one spear?

I do.

And would you arm Geryon and Briareus in that way? Considering that you and your companion fight in armour, I thought that you would have known better...Here Euthydemus held his peace, but Dionysodorus returned to the previous answer of Ctesippus and said:—

Do you not think that the possession of gold is a good thing?

Yes, said Ctesippus, and the more the better.

And to have money everywhere and always is a good?

Certainly, a great good, he said.

And you admit gold to be a good?

Certainly, he replied.

And ought not a man then to have gold everywhere and always, and as much as possible in himself, and may he not be deemed the happiest of men who has three talents of gold in his belly, and a talent in his pate, and a stater of gold in either eye?

Yes, Euthydemus, said Ctesippus; and the Scythians reckon those who have gold in their own skulls to be the happiest and bravest of men (that is only another instance of your manner of speaking about the dog and father), and what is still more extraordinary, they drink out of their own skulls gilt, and see the inside of them, and hold their own head in their hands.

And do the Scythians and others see that which has the quality of vision, or that which has not? said Euthydemus.

That which has the quality of vision clearly.

And you also see that which has the quality of vision? he said. [Note: the ambiguity of (Greek), 'things visible and able to see,' (Greek), 'the speaking of the silent,' the silent denoting either the speaker or the subject of the speech, cannot be perfectly rendered in English.] Compare Aristot. Soph. Elenchi (Poste's translation):—

'Of ambiguous propositions the following are instances:—

'I hope that you the enemy may slay.

'Whom one knows, he knows. Either the person knowing or the person known is here affirmed to know.

'What one sees, that one sees: one sees a pillar: ergo, that one pillar sees.

'What you ARE holding, that you are: you are holding a stone: ergo, a stone you are.

'Is a speaking of the silent possible? "The silent" denotes either the speaker are the subject of speech.

'There are three kinds of ambiguity of term or proposition. The first is when there is an equal linguistic propriety in several interpretations; the second when one is improper but customary; the third when the ambiguity arises in the combination of elements that are in themselves unambiguous, as in "knowing letters." "Knowing" and "letters" are perhaps separately unambiguous, but in combination may imply either that the letters are known, or that they themselves have knowledge. Such are the modes in which propositions and terms may be ambiguous.'

Yes, I do.

Then do you see our garments?

Yes.

Then our garments have the quality of vision.

They can see to any extent, said Ctesippus.

What can they see?

Nothing; but you, my sweet man, may perhaps imagine that they do not see; and certainly, Euthydemus, you do seem to me to have been caught napping when you were not asleep, and that if it be possible to speak and say nothing—you are doing so.

And may there not be a silence of the speaker? said Dionysodorus.

Impossible, said Ctesippus.

Or a speaking of the silent?

That is still more impossible, he said.

But when you speak of stones, wood, iron bars, do you not speak of the silent?

Not when I pass a smithy; for then the iron bars make a tremendous noise and outcry if they are touched: so that here your wisdom is strangely mistaken; please, however, to tell me how you can be silent when speaking (I thought that Ctesippus was put upon his mettle because Cleinias was present).

When you are silent, said Euthydemus, is there not a silence of all things?

Yes, he said.

But if speaking things are included in all things, then the speaking are silent.

What, said Ctesippus; then all things are not silent?

Certainly not, said Euthydemus.

Then, my good friend, do they all speak?

Yes; those which speak.

Nay, said Ctesippus, but the question which I ask is whether all things are silent or speak?

Neither and both, said Dionysodorus, quickly interposing; I am sure that you will be 'non-plussed' at that answer.

Here Ctesippus, as his manner was, burst into a roar of laughter; he said, That brother of yours, Euthydemus, has got into a dilemma; all is over with him. This delighted Cleinias, whose laughter made Ctesippus ten times as uproarious; but I cannot help thinking that the rogue must have picked up this answer from them; for there has been no wisdom like theirs in our time. Why do you laugh, Cleinias, I said, at such solemn and beautiful things?

Why, Socrates, said Dionysodorus, did you ever see a beautiful thing?

Yes, Dionysodorus, I replied, I have seen many.

Were they other than the beautiful, or the same as the beautiful?

Now I was in a great quandary at having to answer this question, and I thought that I was rightly served for having opened my mouth at all: I said however, They are not the same as absolute beauty, but they have beauty present with each of them.

And are you an ox because an ox is present with you, or are you Dionysodorus, because Dionysodorus is present with you?

God forbid, I replied.

But how, he said, by reason of one thing being present with another, will one thing be another?

Is that your difficulty? I said. For I was beginning to imitate their skill, on which my heart was set.

Of course, he replied, I and all the world are in a difficulty about the non-existent.

What do you mean, Dionysodorus? I said. Is not the honourable honourable and the base base?

That, he said, is as I please.

And do you please?

Yes, he said.

And you will admit that the same is the same, and the other other; for surely the other is not the same; I should imagine that even a child will hardly deny the other to be other. But I think, Dionysodorus, that you must have intentionally missed the last question; for in general you and your brother seem to me to be good workmen in your own department, and to do the dialectician's business excellently well.

What, said he, is the business of a good workman? tell me, in the first place, whose business is hammering?

The smith's.

And whose the making of pots?

The potter's.

And who has to kill and skin and mince and boil and roast?

The cook, I said.

And if a man does his business he does rightly?

Certainly.

And the business of the cook is to cut up and skin; you have admitted that?

Yes, I have admitted that, but you must not be too hard upon me.

Then if some one were to kill, mince, boil, roast the cook, he would do his business, and if he were to hammer the smith, and make a pot of the potter, he would do their business.

Poseidon, I said, this is the crown of wisdom; can I ever hope to have such wisdom of my own?

And would you be able, Socrates, to recognize this wisdom when it has become your own?

Certainly, I said, if you will allow me.

What, he said, do you think that you know what is your own?

Yes, I do, subject to your correction; for you are the bottom, and Euthydemus is the top, of all my wisdom.

Is not that which you would deem your own, he said, that which you have in your own power, and which you are able to use as you would desire, for example, an ox or a sheep—would you not think that which you could sell and give and sacrifice to any god whom you pleased, to be your own, and that which you could not give or sell or sacrifice you would think not to be in your own power?

Yes, I said (for I was certain that something good would come out of the questions, which I was impatient to hear); yes, such things, and such things only are mine.

Yes, he said, and you would mean by animals living beings?

Yes, I said.

You agree then, that those animals only are yours with which you have the power to do all these things which I was just naming?

I agree.

Then, after a pause, in which he seemed to be lost in the contemplation of something great, he said: Tell me, Socrates, have you an ancestral Zeus? Here, anticipating the final move, like a person caught in a net, who gives a desperate twist that he may get away, I said: No, Dionysodorus, I have not.

What a miserable man you must be then, he said; you are not an Athenian at all if you have no ancestral gods or temples, or any other mark of gentility.

Nay, Dionysodorus, I said, do not be rough; good words, if you please; in the way of religion I have altars and temples, domestic and ancestral, and all that other Athenians have.

And have not other Athenians, he said, an ancestral Zeus?

That name, I said, is not to be found among the Ionians, whether colonists or citizens of Athens; an ancestral Apollo there is, who is the father of Ion, and a family Zeus, and a Zeus guardian of the phratry, and an Athene guardian of the phratry. But the name of ancestral Zeus is unknown to us.

No matter, said Dionysodorus, for you admit that you have Apollo, Zeus, and Athene.

Certainly, I said.

And they are your gods, he said.

Yes, I said, my lords and ancestors.

At any rate they are yours, he said, did you not admit that?

I did, I said; what is going to happen to me?

And are not these gods animals? for you admit that all things which have life are animals; and have not these gods life?

They have life, I said.

Then are they not animals?

They are animals, I said.

And you admitted that of animals those are yours which you could give away or sell or offer in sacrifice, as you pleased?

I did admit that, Euthydemus, and I have no way of escape.

Well then, said he, if you admit that Zeus and the other gods are yours, can you sell them or give them away or do what you will with them, as you would with other animals?

At this I was quite struck dumb, Crito, and lay prostrate. Ctesippus came to the rescue.

Bravo, Heracles, brave words, said he.

Bravo Heracles, or is Heracles a Bravo? said Dionysodorus.

Poseidon, said Ctesippus, what awful distinctions. I will have no more of them; the pair are invincible.

Then, my dear Crito, there was universal applause of the speakers and their words, and what with laughing and clapping of hands and rejoicings the two men were quite overpowered; for hitherto their partisans only had cheered at each successive hit, but now the whole company shouted with delight until the columns of the Lyceum returned the sound, seeming to sympathize in their joy. To such a pitch was I affected myself, that I made a speech, in which I acknowledged that I had never seen the like of their wisdom; I was their devoted servant, and fell to praising and admiring of them. What marvellous dexterity of wit, I said, enabled you to acquire this great perfection in such a short time? There is much, indeed, to admire in your words, Euthydemus and Dionysodorus, but there is nothing that I admire more than your magnanimous disregard of any opinion—whether of the many, or of the grave and reverend seigniors—you regard only those who are like yourselves. And I do verily believe that there are few who are like you, and who would approve of such arguments; the majority of mankind are so ignorant of their value, that they would be more ashamed of employing them in the refutation of others than of being refuted by them. I must further express my approval of your kind and public-spirited denial of all differences, whether of good and evil, white or black, or any other; the result of which is that, as you say, every mouth is sewn up, not excepting your own, which graciously follows the example of others; and thus all ground of offence is taken away. But what appears to me to be more than all is, that this art and invention of yours has been so admirably contrived by you, that in a very short time it can be imparted to any one. I observed that Ctesippus learned to imitate you in no time. Now this quickness of attainment is an excellent thing; but at the same time I would advise you not to have any more public entertainments; there is a danger that men may undervalue an art which they have so easy an opportunity of acquiring; the exhibition would be best of all, if the discussion were confined to your two selves; but if there must be an audience, let him only be present who is willing to pay a handsome fee;—you should be careful of this;—and if you are wise, you will also bid your disciples discourse with no man but you and themselves. For only what is rare is valuable; and 'water,' which, as Pindar says, is the 'best of all things,' is also the cheapest. And now I have only to request that you will receive Cleinias and me among your pupils.

Such was the discussion, Crito; and after a few more words had passed between us we went away. I hope that you will come to them with me, since they say that they are able to teach any one who will give them money; no age or want of capacity is an impediment. And I must repeat one thing which they said, for your especial benefit,—that the learning of their art did not at all interfere with the business of money-making.

CRITO: Truly, Socrates, though I am curious and ready to learn, yet I fear that I am not like-minded with Euthydemus, but one of the other sort, who, as you were saying, would rather be refuted by such arguments than use them in refutation of others. And though I may appear ridiculous in venturing to advise you, I think that you may as well hear what was said to me by a man of very considerable pretensions—he was a professor of legal oratory—who came away from you while I was walking up and down. 'Crito,' said he to me, 'are you giving no attention to these wise men?' 'No, indeed,' I said to him; 'I could not get within hearing of them—there was such a crowd.' 'You would have heard something worth hearing if you had.' 'What was that?' I said. 'You would have heard the greatest masters of the art of rhetoric discoursing.' 'And what did you think of them?' I said. 'What did I think of them?' he said:—'theirs was the sort of discourse which anybody might hear from men who were playing the fool, and making much ado about nothing.' That was the expression which he used.

'Surely,' I said, 'philosophy is a charming thing.' 'Charming!' he said; 'what simplicity! philosophy is nought; and I think that if you had been present you would have been ashamed of your friend—his conduct was so very strange in placing himself at the mercy of men who care not what they say, and fasten upon every word. And these, as I was telling you, are supposed to be the most eminent professors of their time. But the truth is, Crito, that the study itself and the men themselves are utterly mean and ridiculous.' Now censure of the pursuit, Socrates, whether coming from him or from others, appears to me to be undeserved; but as to the impropriety of holding a public discussion with such men, there, I confess that, in my opinion, he was in the right.

SOCRATES: O Crito, they are marvellous men; but what was I going to say? First of all let me know;—What manner of man was he who came up to you and censured philosophy; was he an orator who himself practises in the courts, or an instructor of orators, who makes the speeches with which they do battle?

CRITO: He was certainly not an orator, and I doubt whether he had ever been into court; but they say that he knows the business, and is a clever man, and composes wonderful speeches.

SOCRATES: Now I understand, Crito; he is one of an amphibious class, whom I was on the point of mentioning—one of those whom Prodicus describes as on the border-ground between philosophers and statesmen—they think that they are the wisest of all men, and that they are generally esteemed the wisest; nothing but the rivalry of the philosophers stands in their way; and they are of the opinion that if they can prove the philosophers to be good for nothing, no one will dispute their title to the palm of wisdom, for that they are themselves really the wisest, although they are apt to be mauled by Euthydemus and his friends, when they get hold of them in conversation. This opinion which they entertain of their own wisdom is very natural; for they have a certain amount of philosophy, and a certain amount of political wisdom; there is reason in what they say, for they argue that they have just enough of both, and so they keep out of the way of all risks and conflicts and reap the fruits of their wisdom.

CRITO: What do you say of them, Socrates? There is certainly something specious in that notion of theirs.

SOCRATES: Yes, Crito, there is more speciousness than truth; they cannot be made to understand the nature of intermediates. For all persons or things, which are intermediate between two other things, and participate in both of them—if one of these two things is good and the other evil, are better than the one and worse than the other; but if they are in a mean between two good things which do not tend to the same end, they fall short of either of their component elements in the attainment of their ends. Only in the case when the two component elements which do not tend to the same end are evil is the participant better than either. Now, if philosophy and political action are both good, but tend to different ends, and they participate in both, and are in a mean between them, then they are talking nonsense, for they are worse than either; or, if the one be good and the other evil, they are better than the one and worse than the other; only on the supposition that they are both evil could there be any truth in what they say. I do not think that they will admit that their two pursuits are either wholly or partly evil; but the truth is, that these philosopher-politicians who aim at both fall short of both in the attainment of their respective ends, and are really third, although they would like to stand first. There is no need, however, to be angry at this ambition of theirs—which may be forgiven; for every man ought to be loved who says and manfully pursues and works out anything which is at all like wisdom: at the same time we shall do well to see them as they really are.

CRITO: I have often told you, Socrates, that I am in a constant difficulty about my two sons. What am I to do with them? There is no hurry about the younger one, who is only a child; but the other, Critobulus, is getting on, and needs some one who will improve him. I cannot help thinking, when I hear you talk, that there is a sort of madness in many of our anxieties about our children:—in the first place, about marrying a wife of good family to be the mother of them, and then about heaping up money for them—and yet taking no care about their education. But then again, when I contemplate any of those who pretend to educate others, I am amazed. To me, if I am to confess the truth, they all seem to be such outrageous beings: so that I do not know how I can advise the youth to study philosophy.

SOCRATES: Dear Crito, do you not know that in every profession the inferior sort are numerous and good for nothing, and the good are few and beyond all price: for example, are not gymnastic and rhetoric and money-making and the art of the general, noble arts?

CRITO: Certainly they are, in my judgment.

SOCRATES: Well, and do you not see that in each of these arts the many are ridiculous performers?

CRITO: Yes, indeed, that is very true.

SOCRATES: And will you on this account shun all these pursuits yourself and refuse to allow them to your son?

CRITO: That would not be reasonable, Socrates.

SOCRATES: Do you then be reasonable, Crito, and do not mind whether the teachers of philosophy are good or bad, but think only of philosophy herself. Try and examine her well and truly, and if she be evil seek to turn away all men from her, and not your sons only; but if she be what I believe that she is, then follow her and serve her, you and your house, as the saying is, and be of good cheer.

EUTHYPHRO

By Plato

Translated by Benjamin Jowett

PERSONS OF THE DIALOGUE: Socrates, Euthyphro.

SCENE: The Porch of the King Archon.

EUTHYPHRO: Why have you left the Lyceum, Socrates? and what are you doing in the Porch of the King Archon? Surely you cannot be concerned in a suit before the King, like myself?

SOCRATES: Not in a suit, Euthyphro; impeachment is the word which the Athenians use.

EUTHYPHRO: What! I suppose that some one has been prosecuting you, for I cannot believe that you are the prosecutor of another.

SOCRATES: Certainly not.

EUTHYPHRO: Then some one else has been prosecuting you?

SOCRATES: Yes.

EUTHYPHRO: And who is he?

SOCRATES: A young man who is little known, Euthyphro; and I hardly know him: his name is Meletus, and he is of the deme of Pitthis. Perhaps you may remember his appearance; he has a beak, and long straight hair, and a beard which is ill grown.

EUTHYPHRO: No, I do not remember him, Socrates. But what is the charge which he brings against you?

SOCRATES: What is the charge? Well, a very serious charge, which shows a good deal of character in the young man, and for which he is certainly not to be despised. He says he knows how the youth are corrupted and who are their corruptors. I fancy that he must be a wise man, and seeing that I am the reverse of a wise man, he has found me out, and is going to accuse me of corrupting his young friends. And of this our mother the state is to be the judge. Of all our political men he is the only one who seems to me to begin in the right way, with the cultivation of virtue in youth; like a good husbandman, he makes the young shoots his first care, and clears away us who are the destroyers of them. This is only the first step; he will afterwards attend to the elder branches; and if he goes on as he has begun, he will be a very great public benefactor.

EUTHYPHRO: I hope that he may; but I rather fear, Socrates, that the opposite will turn out to be the truth. My opinion is that in attacking you he is simply aiming a blow at the foundation of the state. But in what way does he say that you corrupt the young?

SOCRATES: He brings a wonderful accusation against me, which at first hearing excites surprise: he says that I am a poet or maker of gods, and that I invent new gods and deny the existence of old ones; this is the ground of his indictment.

EUTHYPHRO: I understand, Socrates; he means to attack you about the familiar sign which occasionally, as you say, comes to you. He thinks that you are a neologian, and he is going to have you up before the court for this. He knows that such a charge is readily received by the world, as I myself know too well; for when I speak in the assembly about divine things, and foretell the future to them, they laugh at me and think me a madman. Yet every word that I say is true. But they are jealous of us all; and we must be brave and go at them.

SOCRATES: Their laughter, friend Euthyphro, is not a matter of much consequence. For a man may be thought wise; but the Athenians, I suspect, do not much trouble themselves about him until he begins to impart his wisdom to others, and then for some reason or other, perhaps, as you say, from jealousy, they are angry.

EUTHYPHRO: I am never likely to try their temper in this way.

SOCRATES: I dare say not, for you are reserved in your behaviour, and seldom impart your wisdom. But I have a benevolent habit of pouring out myself to everybody, and would even pay for a listener, and I am afraid that the Athenians may think me too talkative. Now if, as I was saying, they would only laugh at me, as you say that they laugh at you, the time might pass gaily enough in the court; but perhaps they may be in earnest, and then what the end will be you soothsayers only can predict.

EUTHYPHRO: I dare say that the affair will end in nothing, Socrates, and that you will win your cause; and I think that I shall win my own.

SOCRATES: And what is your suit, Euthyphro? are you the pursuer or the defendant?

EUTHYPHRO: I am the pursuer.

SOCRATES: Of whom?

EUTHYPHRO: You will think me mad when I tell you.

SOCRATES: Why, has the fugitive wings?

EUTHYPHRO: Nay, he is not very volatile at his time of life.

SOCRATES: Who is he?

EUTHYPHRO: My father.

SOCRATES: Your father! my good man?

EUTHYPHRO: Yes.

SOCRATES: And of what is he accused?

EUTHYPHRO: Of murder, Socrates.

SOCRATES: By the powers, Euthyphro! how little does the common herd know of the nature of right and truth. A man must be an extraordinary man, and have made great strides in wisdom, before he could have seen his way to bring such an action.

EUTHYPHRO: Indeed, Socrates, he must.

SOCRATES: I suppose that the man whom your father murdered was one of your relatives—clearly he was; for if he had been a stranger you would never have thought of prosecuting him.

EUTHYPHRO: I am amused, Socrates, at your making a distinction between one who is a relation and one who is not a relation; for surely the pollution is the same in either case, if you knowingly associate with the murderer when you ought to clear yourself and him by proceeding against him. The real question is whether the murdered man has been justly slain. If justly, then your duty is to let the matter alone; but if unjustly, then even if the murderer lives under the same roof with you and eats at the same table, proceed against him. Now the man who is dead was a poor dependant of mine who worked for us as a field labourer on our farm in Naxos, and one day in a fit of drunken passion he got into a quarrel with one of our domestic servants and slew him. My father bound him hand and foot and threw him into a ditch, and then sent to Athens to ask of a diviner what he should do with him. Meanwhile he never attended to him and took no care about him, for he regarded him as a murderer; and thought that no great harm would be done even if he did die. Now this was just what happened. For such was the effect of cold and hunger and chains upon him, that before the messenger returned from the diviner, he was dead. And my father and family are angry with me for taking the part of the murderer and prosecuting my father. They say that he did not kill him, and that if he did, the dead man was but a murderer, and I ought not to take any notice, for that a son is impious who prosecutes a father. Which shows, Socrates, how little they know what the gods think about piety and impiety.

SOCRATES: Good heavens, Euthyphro! and is your knowledge of religion and of things pious and impious so very exact, that, supposing the circumstances to be as you state them, you are not afraid lest you too may be doing an impious thing in bringing an action against your father?

EUTHYPHRO: The best of Euthyphro, and that which distinguishes him, Socrates, from other men, is his exact knowledge of all such matters. What should I be good for without it?

SOCRATES: Rare friend! I think that I cannot do better than be your disciple. Then before the trial with Meletus comes on I shall challenge him, and say that I have always had a great interest in religious questions, and now, as he charges me with rash imaginations and innovations in religion, I have become your disciple. You, Meletus, as I shall say to him, acknowledge Euthyphro to be a great theologian, and sound in his opinions; and if you approve of him you ought to approve of me, and not have me into court; but if you disapprove, you should begin by indicting him who is my teacher, and who will be the ruin, not of the young, but of the old; that is to say, of myself whom he instructs, and of his old father whom he admonishes and chastises. And if Meletus refuses to listen to me, but will go on, and will not shift the indictment from me to you, I cannot do better than repeat this challenge in the court.

EUTHYPHRO: Yes, indeed, Socrates; and if he attempts to indict me I am mistaken if I do not find a flaw in him; the court shall have a great deal more to say to him than to me.

SOCRATES: And I, my dear friend, knowing this, am desirous of becoming your disciple. For I observe that no one appears to notice you—not even this Meletus; but his sharp eyes have found me out at once, and he has indicted me for impiety. And therefore, I adjure you to tell me the nature of piety and impiety, which you said that you knew so well, and of murder, and of other offences against the gods. What are they? Is not piety in every action always the same? and impiety, again—is it not always the opposite of piety, and also the same with itself, having, as impiety, one notion which includes whatever is impious?

EUTHYPHRO: To be sure, Socrates.

SOCRATES: And what is piety, and what is impiety?

EUTHYPHRO: Piety is doing as I am doing; that is to say, prosecuting any one who is guilty of murder, sacrilege, or of any similar crime—whether he be your father or mother, or whoever he may be—that makes no difference; and not to prosecute them is impiety. And please to consider, Socrates, what a notable proof I will give you of the truth of my words, a proof which I have already given to others:—of the principle, I mean, that the impious, whoever he may be, ought not to go unpunished. For do not men regard Zeus as the best and most righteous of the gods?—and yet they admit that he bound his father (Cronos) because he wickedly devoured his sons, and that he too had punished his own father (Uranus) for a similar reason, in a nameless manner. And yet when I proceed against my father, they are angry with me. So inconsistent are they in their way of talking when the gods are concerned, and when I am concerned.

SOCRATES: May not this be the reason, Euthyphro, why I am charged with impiety—that I cannot away with these stories about the gods? and therefore I suppose that people think me wrong. But, as you who are well informed about them approve of them, I cannot do better than assent to your superior wisdom. What else can I say, confessing as I do, that I know nothing about them? Tell me, for the love of Zeus, whether you really believe that they are true.

EUTHYPHRO: Yes, Socrates; and things more wonderful still, of which the world is in ignorance.

SOCRATES: And do you really believe that the gods fought with one another, and had dire quarrels, battles, and the like, as the poets say, and as you may see represented in the works of great artists? The temples are full of them; and notably the robe of Athene, which is carried up to the Acropolis at the great Panathenaea, is embroidered with them. Are all these tales of the gods true, Euthyphro?

EUTHYPHRO: Yes, Socrates; and, as I was saying, I can tell you, if you would like to hear them, many other things about the gods which would quite amaze you.

SOCRATES: I dare say; and you shall tell me them at some other time when I have leisure. But just at present I would rather hear from you a more precise answer, which you have not as yet given, my friend, to the question, What is 'piety'? When asked, you only replied, Doing as you do, charging your father with murder.

EUTHYPHRO: And what I said was true, Socrates.

SOCRATES: No doubt, Euthyphro; but you would admit that there are many other pious acts?

EUTHYPHRO: There are.

SOCRATES: Remember that I did not ask you to give me two or three examples of piety, but to explain the general idea which makes all pious things to be pious. Do you not recollect that there was one idea which made the impious impious, and the pious pious?

EUTHYPHRO: I remember.

SOCRATES: Tell me what is the nature of this idea, and then I shall have a standard to which I may look, and by which I may measure actions, whether yours or those of any one else, and then I shall be able to say that such and such an action is pious, such another impious.

EUTHYPHRO: I will tell you, if you like.

SOCRATES: I should very much like.

EUTHYPHRO: Piety, then, is that which is dear to the gods, and impiety is that which is not dear to them.

SOCRATES: Very good, Euthyphro; you have now given me the sort of answer which I wanted. But whether what you say is true or not I cannot as yet tell, although I make no doubt that you will prove the truth of your words.

EUTHYPHRO: Of course.

SOCRATES: Come, then, and let us examine what we are saying. That thing or person which is dear to the gods is pious, and that thing or person which is hateful to the gods is impious, these two being the extreme opposites of one another. Was not that said?

EUTHYPHRO: It was.

SOCRATES: And well said?

EUTHYPHRO: Yes, Socrates, I thought so; it was certainly said.

SOCRATES: And further, Euthyphro, the gods were admitted to have enmities and hatreds and differences?

EUTHYPHRO: Yes, that was also said.

SOCRATES: And what sort of difference creates enmity and anger? Suppose for example that you and I, my good friend, differ about a number; do differences of this sort make us enemies and set us at variance with one another? Do we not go at once to arithmetic, and put an end to them by a sum?

EUTHYPHRO: True.

SOCRATES: Or suppose that we differ about magnitudes, do we not quickly end the differences by measuring?

EUTHYPHRO: Very true.

SOCRATES: And we end a controversy about heavy and light by resorting to a weighing machine?

EUTHYPHRO: To be sure.

SOCRATES: But what differences are there which cannot be thus decided, and which therefore make us angry and set us at enmity with one another? I dare say the answer does not occur to you at the moment, and therefore I will suggest that these enmities arise when the matters of difference are the just and unjust, good and evil, honourable and dishonourable. Are not these the points about which men differ, and about which when we are unable satisfactorily to decide our differences, you and I and all of us quarrel, when we do quarrel? (Compare Alcib.)

EUTHYPHRO: Yes, Socrates, the nature of the differences about which we quarrel is such as you describe.

SOCRATES: And the quarrels of the gods, noble Euthyphro, when they occur, are of a like nature?

EUTHYPHRO: Certainly they are.

SOCRATES: They have differences of opinion, as you say, about good and evil, just and unjust, honourable and dishonourable: there would have been no quarrels among them, if there had been no such differences—would there now?

EUTHYPHRO: You are quite right.

SOCRATES: Does not every man love that which he deems noble and just and good, and hate the opposite of them?

EUTHYPHRO: Very true.

SOCRATES: But, as you say, people regard the same things, some as just and others as unjust,—about these they dispute; and so there arise wars and fightings among them.

EUTHYPHRO: Very true.

SOCRATES: Then the same things are hated by the gods and loved by the gods, and are both hateful and dear to them?

EUTHYPHRO: True.

SOCRATES: And upon this view the same things, Euthyphro, will be pious and also impious?

EUTHYPHRO: So I should suppose.

SOCRATES: Then, my friend, I remark with surprise that you have not answered the question which I asked. For I certainly did not ask you to tell me what action is both pious and impious: but now it would seem that what is loved by the gods is also hated by them. And therefore, Euthyphro, in thus chastising your father you may very likely be doing what is agreeable to Zeus but disagreeable to Cronos or Uranus, and what is acceptable to Hephaestus but unacceptable to Here, and there may be other gods who have similar differences of opinion.

EUTHYPHRO: But I believe, Socrates, that all the gods would be agreed as to the propriety of punishing a murderer: there would be no difference of opinion about that.

SOCRATES: Well, but speaking of men, Euthyphro, did you ever hear any one arguing that a murderer or any sort of evil-doer ought to be let off?

EUTHYPHRO: I should rather say that these are the questions which they are always arguing, especially in courts of law: they commit all sorts of crimes, and there is nothing which they will not do or say in their own defence.

SOCRATES: But do they admit their guilt, Euthyphro, and yet say that they ought not to be punished?

EUTHYPHRO: No; they do not.

SOCRATES: Then there are some things which they do not venture to say and do: for they do not venture to argue that the guilty are to be unpunished, but they deny their guilt, do they not?

EUTHYPHRO: Yes.

SOCRATES: Then they do not argue that the evil-doer should not be punished, but they argue about the fact of who the evil-doer is, and what he did and when?

EUTHYPHRO: True.

SOCRATES: And the gods are in the same case, if as you assert they quarrel about just and unjust, and some of them say while others deny that injustice is done among them. For surely neither God nor man will ever venture to say that the doer of injustice is not to be punished?

EUTHYPHRO: That is true, Socrates, in the main.

SOCRATES: But they join issue about the particulars—gods and men alike; and, if they dispute at all, they dispute about some act which is called in question, and which by some is affirmed to be just, by others to be unjust. Is not that true?

EUTHYPHRO: Quite true.

SOCRATES: Well then, my dear friend Euthyphro, do tell me, for my better instruction and information, what proof have you that in the opinion of all the gods a servant who is guilty of murder, and is put in chains by the master of the dead man, and dies because he is put in chains before he who bound him can learn from the interpreters of the gods what he ought to do with him, dies unjustly; and that on behalf of such an one a son ought to proceed against his father and accuse him of murder. How would you show that all the gods absolutely agree in approving of his act? Prove to me that they do, and I will applaud your wisdom as long as I live.

EUTHYPHRO: It will be a difficult task; but I could make the matter very clear indeed to you.

SOCRATES: I understand; you mean to say that I am not so quick of apprehension as the judges: for to them you will be sure to prove that the act is unjust, and hateful to the gods.

EUTHYPHRO: Yes indeed, Socrates; at least if they will listen to me.

SOCRATES: But they will be sure to listen if they find that you are a good speaker. There was a notion that came into my mind while you were speaking; I said to myself: 'Well, and what if Euthyphro does prove to me that all the gods regarded the death of the serf as unjust, how do I know anything more of the nature of piety and impiety? for granting that this action may be hateful to the gods, still piety and impiety are not adequately defined by these distinctions, for that which is hateful to the gods has been shown to be also pleasing and dear to them.' And therefore,

Euthyphro, I do not ask you to prove this; I will suppose, if you like, that all the gods condemn and abominate such an action. But I will amend the definition so far as to say that what all the gods hate is impious, and what they love pious or holy; and what some of them love and others hate is both or neither. Shall this be our definition of piety and impiety?

EUTHYPHRO: Why not, Socrates?

SOCRATES: Why not! certainly, as far as I am concerned, Euthyphro, there is no reason why not. But whether this admission will greatly assist you in the task of instructing me as you promised, is a matter for you to consider.

EUTHYPHRO: Yes, I should say that what all the gods love is pious and holy, and the opposite which they all hate, impious.

SOCRATES: Ought we to enquire into the truth of this, Euthyphro, or simply to accept the mere statement on our own authority and that of others? What do you say?

EUTHYPHRO: We should enquire; and I believe that the statement will stand the test of enquiry.

SOCRATES: We shall know better, my good friend, in a little while. The point which I should first wish to understand is whether the pious or holy is beloved by the gods because it is holy, or holy because it is beloved of the gods.

EUTHYPHRO: I do not understand your meaning, Socrates.

SOCRATES: I will endeavour to explain: we, speak of carrying and we speak of being carried, of leading and being led, seeing and being seen. You know that in all such cases there is a difference, and you know also in what the difference lies?

EUTHYPHRO: I think that I understand.

SOCRATES: And is not that which is beloved distinct from that which loves?

EUTHYPHRO: Certainly.

SOCRATES: Well; and now tell me, is that which is carried in this state of carrying because it is carried, or for some other reason?

EUTHYPHRO: No; that is the reason.

SOCRATES: And the same is true of what is led and of what is seen?

EUTHYPHRO: True.

SOCRATES: And a thing is not seen because it is visible, but conversely, visible because it is seen; nor is a thing led because it is in the state of being led, or carried because it is in the state of being carried, but the converse of this. And now I think, Euthyphro, that my meaning will be intelligible; and my meaning is, that any state of action or passion implies previous action or passion. It does not become because it is becoming, but it is in a state of becoming because it becomes; neither does it suffer because it is in a state of suffering, but it is in a state of suffering because it suffers. Do you not agree?

EUTHYPHRO: Yes.

SOCRATES: Is not that which is loved in some state either of becoming or suffering?

EUTHYPHRO: Yes.

SOCRATES: And the same holds as in the previous instances; the state of being loved follows the act of being loved, and not the act the state.

EUTHYPHRO: Certainly.

SOCRATES: And what do you say of piety, Euthyphro: is not piety, according to your definition, loved by all the gods?

EUTHYPHRO: Yes.

SOCRATES: Because it is pious or holy, or for some other reason?

EUTHYPHRO: No, that is the reason.

SOCRATES: It is loved because it is holy, not holy because it is loved?

EUTHYPHRO: Yes.

SOCRATES: And that which is dear to the gods is loved by them, and is in a state to be loved of them because it is loved of them?

EUTHYPHRO: Certainly.

SOCRATES: Then that which is dear to the gods, Euthyphro, is not holy, nor is that which is holy loved of God, as you affirm; but they are two different things.

EUTHYPHRO: How do you mean, Socrates?

SOCRATES: I mean to say that the holy has been acknowledged by us to be loved of God because it is holy, not to be holy because it is loved.

EUTHYPHRO: Yes.

SOCRATES: But that which is dear to the gods is dear to them because it is loved by them, not loved by them because it is dear to them.

EUTHYPHRO: True.

SOCRATES: But, friend Euthyphro, if that which is holy is the same with that which is dear to God, and is loved because it is holy, then that which is dear to God would have been loved as being dear to God; but if that which is dear to God is dear to him because loved by him, then that which is holy would have been holy because loved by him. But now you see that the reverse is the case, and that they are quite different from one another. For one (theophiles) is of a kind to be loved cause it is loved, and the other (osion) is loved because it is of a kind to be loved. Thus you appear to me, Euthyphro, when I ask you what is the essence of holiness, to offer an attribute only, and not the essence—the attribute of being loved by all the gods. But you still refuse to explain to me the nature of holiness. And therefore, if you please, I will ask you not to hide your treasure, but to tell me once more what holiness or piety really is, whether dear to the gods or not (for that is a matter about which we will not quarrel); and what is impiety?

EUTHYPHRO: I really do not know, Socrates, how to express what I mean. For somehow or other our arguments, on whatever ground we rest them, seem to turn round and walk away from us.

SOCRATES: Your words, Euthyphro, are like the handiwork of my ancestor Daedalus; and if I were the sayer or propounder of them, you might say that my arguments walk away and will not remain fixed where they are placed because I am a descendant of his. But now, since these notions are your own, you must find some other gibe, for they certainly, as you yourself allow, show an inclination to be on the move.

EUTHYPHRO: Nay, Socrates, I shall still say that you are the Daedalus who sets arguments in motion; not I, certainly, but you make them move or go round, for they would never have stirred, as far as I am concerned.

SOCRATES: Then I must be a greater than Daedalus: for whereas he only made his own inventions to move, I move those of other people as well. And the beauty of it is, that I would rather not. For I would give the wisdom of Daedalus, and the wealth of Tantalus, to be able to detain them and keep them fixed. But enough of this. As I perceive that you are lazy, I will myself endeavour to show you how you might instruct me in the nature of piety; and I hope that you will not grudge your labour. Tell me, then—Is not that which is pious necessarily just?

EUTHYPHRO: Yes.

SOCRATES: And is, then, all which is just pious? or, is that which is pious all just, but that which is just, only in part and not all, pious?

EUTHYPHRO: I do not understand you, Socrates.

SOCRATES: And yet I know that you are as much wiser than I am, as you are younger. But, as I was saying, revered friend, the abundance of your wisdom makes you lazy. Please to exert yourself, for there is no real difficulty in understanding me. What I mean I may explain by an illustration of what I do not mean. The poet (Stasinus) sings—

'Of Zeus, the author and creator of all these things, You will not tell: for where there is fear there is also reverence.'

Now I disagree with this poet. Shall I tell you in what respect?

EUTHYPHRO: By all means.

SOCRATES: I should not say that where there is fear there is also reverence; for I am sure that many persons fear poverty and disease, and the like evils, but I do not perceive that they reverence the objects of their fear.

EUTHYPHRO: Very true.

SOCRATES: But where reverence is, there is fear; for he who has a feeling of reverence and shame about the commission of any action, fears and is afraid of an ill reputation.

EUTHYPHRO: No doubt.

SOCRATES: Then we are wrong in saying that where there is fear there is also reverence; and we should say, where there is reverence there is also fear. But there is not always reverence where there is fear; for fear is a more extended notion, and reverence is a part of fear, just as the odd is a part of number, and number is a more extended notion than the odd. I suppose that you follow me now?

EUTHYPHRO: Quite well.

SOCRATES: That was the sort of question which I meant to raise when I asked whether the just is always the pious, or the pious always the just; and whether there may not be justice where there is not piety; for justice is the more extended notion of which piety is only a part. Do you dissent?

EUTHYPHRO: No, I think that you are quite right.

SOCRATES: Then, if piety is a part of justice, I suppose that we should enquire what part? If you had pursued the enquiry in the previous cases; for instance, if you had asked me what is an even number, and what part of number the even is, I should have had no difficulty in replying, a number which represents a figure having two equal sides. Do you not agree?

EUTHYPHRO: Yes, I quite agree.

SOCRATES: In like manner, I want you to tell me what part of justice is piety or holiness, that I may be able to tell Meletus not to do me injustice, or indict me for impiety, as I am now adequately instructed by you in the nature of piety or holiness, and their opposites.

EUTHYPHRO: Piety or holiness, Socrates, appears to me to be that part of justice which attends to the gods, as there is the other part of justice which attends to men.

SOCRATES: That is good, Euthyphro; yet still there is a little point about which I should like to have further information, What is the meaning of 'attention'? For attention can hardly be used in the same sense when applied to the gods as when applied to other things. For instance, horses are said to require attention, and not every person is able to attend to them, but only a person skilled in horsemanship. Is it not so?

EUTHYPHRO: Certainly.

SOCRATES: I should suppose that the art of horsemanship is the art of attending to horses?

EUTHYPHRO: Yes.

SOCRATES: Nor is every one qualified to attend to dogs, but only the huntsman?

EUTHYPHRO: True.

SOCRATES: And I should also conceive that the art of the huntsman is the art of attending to dogs?

EUTHYPHRO: Yes.

SOCRATES: As the art of the oxherd is the art of attending to oxen?

EUTHYPHRO: Very true.

SOCRATES: In like manner holiness or piety is the art of attending to the gods?—that would be your meaning, Euthyphro?

EUTHYPHRO: Yes.

SOCRATES: And is not attention always designed for the good or benefit of that to which the attention is given? As in the case of horses, you may observe that when attended to by the horseman's art they are benefited and improved, are they not?

EUTHYPHRO: True.

SOCRATES: As the dogs are benefited by the huntsman's art, and the oxen by the art of the oxherd, and all other things are tended or attended for their good and not for their hurt?

EUTHYPHRO: Certainly, not for their hurt.

SOCRATES: But for their good?

EUTHYPHRO: Of course.

SOCRATES: And does piety or holiness, which has been defined to be the art of attending to the gods, benefit or improve them? Would you say that when you do a holy act you make any of the gods better?

EUTHYPHRO: No, no; that was certainly not what I meant.

SOCRATES: And I, Euthyphro, never supposed that you did. I asked you the question about the nature of the attention, because I thought that you did not.

EUTHYPHRO: You do me justice, Socrates; that is not the sort of attention which I mean.

SOCRATES: Good: but I must still ask what is this attention to the gods which is called piety?

EUTHYPHRO: It is such, Socrates, as servants show to their masters.

SOCRATES: I understand—a sort of ministration to the gods.

EUTHYPHRO: Exactly.

SOCRATES: Medicine is also a sort of ministration or service, having in view the attainment of some object—would you not say of health?

EUTHYPHRO: I should.

SOCRATES: Again, there is an art which ministers to the ship-builder with a view to the attainment of some result?

EUTHYPHRO: Yes, Socrates, with a view to the building of a ship.

SOCRATES: As there is an art which ministers to the house-builder with a view to the building of a house?

EUTHYPHRO: Yes.

SOCRATES: And now tell me, my good friend, about the art which ministers to the gods: what work does that help to accomplish? For you must surely know if, as you say, you are of all men living the one who is best instructed in religion.

EUTHYPHRO: And I speak the truth, Socrates.

SOCRATES: Tell me then, oh tell me—what is that fair work which the gods do by the help of our ministrations?

EUTHYPHRO: Many and fair, Socrates, are the works which they do.

SOCRATES: Why, my friend, and so are those of a general. But the chief of them is easily told. Would you not say that victory in war is the chief of them?

EUTHYPHRO: Certainly.

SOCRATES: Many and fair, too, are the works of the husbandman, if I am not mistaken; but his chief work is the production of food from the earth?

EUTHYPHRO: Exactly.

SOCRATES: And of the many and fair things done by the gods, which is the chief or principal one?

EUTHYPHRO: I have told you already, Socrates, that to learn all these things accurately will be very tiresome. Let me simply say that piety or holiness is learning how to please the gods in word and deed, by prayers and sacrifices. Such piety is the salvation of families and states, just as the impious, which is unpleasing to the gods, is their ruin and destruction.

SOCRATES: I think that you could have answered in much fewer words the chief question which I asked, Euthyphro, if you had chosen. But I see plainly that you are not disposed to instruct me—clearly not: else why, when we reached the point, did you turn aside? Had you only answered me I should have truly learned of you by this time the nature of piety. Now, as the asker of a question is necessarily dependent on the answerer, whither he leads I must follow; and can only ask again, what is the pious, and what is piety? Do you mean that they are a sort of science of praying and sacrificing?

EUTHYPHRO: Yes, I do.

SOCRATES: And sacrificing is giving to the gods, and prayer is asking of the gods?

EUTHYPHRO: Yes, Socrates.

SOCRATES: Upon this view, then, piety is a science of asking and giving?

EUTHYPHRO: You understand me capitally, Socrates.

SOCRATES: Yes, my friend; the reason is that I am a votary of your science, and give my mind to it, and therefore nothing which you say will be thrown away upon me. Please then to tell me, what is the nature of this service to the gods? Do you mean that we prefer requests and give gifts to them?

EUTHYPHRO: Yes, I do.

SOCRATES: Is not the right way of asking to ask of them what we want?

EUTHYPHRO: Certainly.

SOCRATES: And the right way of giving is to give to them in return what they want of us. There would be no meaning in an art which gives to any one that which he does not want.

EUTHYPHRO: Very true, Socrates.

SOCRATES: Then piety, Euthyphro, is an art which gods and men have of doing business with one another?

EUTHYPHRO: That is an expression which you may use, if you like.

SOCRATES: But I have no particular liking for anything but the truth. I wish, however, that you would tell me what benefit accrues to the gods from our gifts.

There is no doubt about what they give to us; for there is no good thing which they do not give; but how we can give any good thing to them in return is far from being equally clear. If they give everything and we give nothing, that must be an affair of business in which we have very greatly the advantage of them.

EUTHYPHRO: And do you imagine, Socrates, that any benefit accrues to the gods from our gifts?

SOCRATES: But if not, Euthyphro, what is the meaning of gifts which are conferred by us upon the gods?

EUTHYPHRO: What else, but tributes of honour; and, as I was just now saying, what pleases them?

SOCRATES: Piety, then, is pleasing to the gods, but not beneficial or dear to them?

EUTHYPHRO: I should say that nothing could be dearer.

SOCRATES: Then once more the assertion is repeated that piety is dear to the gods?

EUTHYPHRO: Certainly.

SOCRATES: And when you say this, can you wonder at your words not standing firm, but walking away? Will you accuse me of being the Daedalus who makes them walk away, not perceiving that there is another and far greater artist than Daedalus who makes them go round in a circle, and he is yourself; for the argument, as you will perceive, comes round to the same point. Were we not saying that the holy or pious was not the same with that which is loved of the gods? Have you forgotten?

EUTHYPHRO: I quite remember.

SOCRATES: And are you not saying that what is loved of the gods is holy; and is not this the same as what is dear to them—do you see?

EUTHYPHRO: True.

SOCRATES: Then either we were wrong in our former assertion; or, if we were right then, we are wrong now.

EUTHYPHRO: One of the two must be true.

SOCRATES: Then we must begin again and ask, What is piety? That is an enquiry which I shall never be weary of pursuing as far as in me lies; and I entreat you not to scorn me, but to apply your mind to the utmost, and tell me the truth. For, if any man knows, you are he; and therefore I must detain you, like Proteus, until you tell. If you had not certainly known the nature of piety and impiety, I am confident that you would never, on behalf of a serf, have charged your aged father with murder. You would not have run such a risk of doing wrong in the sight of the gods, and you would have had too much respect for the opinions of men. I am sure, therefore, that you know the nature of piety and impiety. Speak out then, my dear Euthyphro, and do not hide your knowledge.

EUTHYPHRO: Another time, Socrates; for I am in a hurry, and must go now.

SOCRATES: Alas! my companion, and will you leave me in despair? I was hoping that you would instruct me in the nature of piety and impiety; and then I might have cleared myself of Meletus and his indictment. I would have told him that I had been enlightened by Euthyphro, and had given up rash innovations and speculations, in which I indulged only through ignorance, and that now I am about to lead a better life.

GORGIAS

By Plato

Translated by Benjamin Jowett

PERSONS OF THE DIALOGUE: Callicles, Socrates, Chaerephon, Gorgias, Polus.

SCENE: The house of Callicles.

CALLICLES: The wise man, as the proverb says, is late for a fray, but not for a feast.

SOCRATES: And are we late for a feast?

CALLICLES: Yes, and a delightful feast; for Gorgias has just been exhibiting to us many fine things.

SOCRATES: It is not my fault, Callicles; our friend Chaerephon is to blame; for he would keep us loitering in the Agora.

CHAEREPHON: Never mind, Socrates; the misfortune of which I have been the cause I will also repair; for Gorgias is a friend of mine, and I will make him give the exhibition again either now, or, if you prefer, at some other time.

CALLICLES: What is the matter, Chaerephon—does Socrates want to hear Gorgias?

CHAEREPHON: Yes, that was our intention in coming.

CALLICLES: Come into my house, then; for Gorgias is staying with me, and he shall exhibit to you.

SOCRATES: Very good, Callicles; but will he answer our questions? for I want to hear from him what is the nature of his art, and what it is which he professes and teaches; he may, as you (Chaerephon) suggest, defer the exhibition to some other time.

CALLICLES: There is nothing like asking him, Socrates; and indeed to answer questions is a part of his exhibition, for he was saying only just now, that any one in my house might put any question to him, and that he would answer.

SOCRATES: How fortunate! will you ask him, Chaerephon—?

CHAEREPHON: What shall I ask him?

SOCRATES: Ask him who he is.

CHAEREPHON: What do you mean?

SOCRATES: I mean such a question as would elicit from him, if he had been a maker of shoes, the answer that he is a cobbler. Do you understand?

CHAEREPHON: I understand, and will ask him: Tell me, Gorgias, is our friend Callicles right in saying that you undertake to answer any questions which you are asked?

GORGIAS: Quite right, Chaerephon: I was saying as much only just now; and I may add, that many years have elapsed since any one has asked me a new one.

CHAEREPHON: Then you must be very ready, Gorgias.

GORGIAS: Of that, Chaerephon, you can make trial.

POLUS: Yes, indeed, and if you like, Chaerephon, you may make trial of me too, for I think that Gorgias, who has been talking a long time, is tired.

CHAEREPHON: And do you, Polus, think that you can answer better than Gorgias?

POLUS: What does that matter if I answer well enough for you?

CHAEREPHON: Not at all:—and you shall answer if you like.

POLUS: Ask:—

CHAEREPHON: My question is this: If Gorgias had the skill of his brother Herodicus, what ought we to call him? Ought he not to have the name which is given to his brother?

POLUS: Certainly.

CHAEREPHON: Then we should be right in calling him a physician?

POLUS: Yes.

CHAEREPHON: And if he had the skill of Aristophon the son of Aglaophon, or of his brother Polygnotus, what ought we to call him?

POLUS: Clearly, a painter.

CHAEREPHON: But now what shall we call him—what is the art in which he is skilled.

POLUS: O Chaerephon, there are many arts among mankind which are experimental, and have their origin in experience, for experience makes the days of men to proceed according to art, and inexperience according to chance, and different persons in different ways are proficient in different arts, and the best persons in the best arts. And our friend Gorgias is one of the best, and the art in which he is a proficient is the noblest.

SOCRATES: Polus has been taught how to make a capital speech, Gorgias; but he is not fulfilling the promise which he made to Chaerephon.

GORGIAS: What do you mean, Socrates?

SOCRATES: I mean that he has not exactly answered the question which he was asked.

GORGIAS: Then why not ask him yourself?

SOCRATES: But I would much rather ask you, if you are disposed to answer: for I see, from the few words which Polus has uttered, that he has attended more to the art which is called rhetoric than to dialectic.

POLUS: What makes you say so, Socrates?

SOCRATES: Because, Polus, when Chaerephon asked you what was the art which Gorgias knows, you praised it as if you were answering some one who found fault with it, but you never said what the art was.

POLUS: Why, did I not say that it was the noblest of arts?

SOCRATES: Yes, indeed, but that was no answer to the question: nobody asked what was the quality, but what was the nature, of the art, and by what name we were to describe Gorgias. And I would still beg you briefly and clearly, as you answered Chaerephon when he asked you at first, to say what this art is, and what we ought to call Gorgias: Or rather, Gorgias, let me turn to you, and ask the same question,—what are we to call you, and what is the art which you profess?

GORGIAS: Rhetoric, Socrates, is my art.

SOCRATES: Then I am to call you a rhetorician?

GORGIAS: Yes, Socrates, and a good one too, if you would call me that which, in Homeric language, 'I boast myself to be.'

SOCRATES: I should wish to do so.

GORGIAS: Then pray do.

SOCRATES: And are we to say that you are able to make other men rhetoricians?

GORGIAS: Yes, that is exactly what I profess to make them, not only at Athens, but in all places.

SOCRATES: And will you continue to ask and answer questions, Gorgias, as we are at present doing, and reserve for another occasion the longer mode of speech which Polus was attempting? Will you keep your promise, and answer shortly the questions which are asked of you?

GORGIAS: Some answers, Socrates, are of necessity longer; but I will do my best to make them as short as possible; for a part of my profession is that I can be as short as any one.

SOCRATES: That is what is wanted, Gorgias; exhibit the shorter method now, and the longer one at some other time.

GORGIAS: Well, I will; and you will certainly say, that you never heard a man use fewer words.

SOCRATES: Very good then; as you profess to be a rhetorician, and a maker of rhetoricians, let me ask you, with what is rhetoric concerned: I might ask with what is weaving concerned, and you would reply (would you not?), with the making of garments?

GORGIAS: Yes.

SOCRATES: And music is concerned with the composition of melodies?

GORGIAS: It is.

SOCRATES: By Here, Gorgias, I admire the surpassing brevity of your answers.

GORGIAS: Yes, Socrates, I do think myself good at that.

SOCRATES: I am glad to hear it; answer me in like manner about rhetoric: with what is rhetoric concerned?

GORGIAS: With discourse.

SOCRATES: What sort of discourse, Gorgias?—such discourse as would teach the sick under what treatment they might get well?

GORGIAS: No.

SOCRATES: Then rhetoric does not treat of all kinds of discourse?

GORGIAS: Certainly not.

SOCRATES: And yet rhetoric makes men able to speak?

GORGIAS: Yes.

SOCRATES: And to understand that about which they speak?

GORGIAS: Of course.

SOCRATES: But does not the art of medicine, which we were just now mentioning, also make men able to understand and speak about the sick?

GORGIAS: Certainly.

SOCRATES: Then medicine also treats of discourse?

GORGIAS: Yes.

SOCRATES: Of discourse concerning diseases?

GORGIAS: Just so.

SOCRATES: And does not gymnastic also treat of discourse concerning the good or evil condition of the body?

GORGIAS: Very true.

SOCRATES: And the same, Gorgias, is true of the other arts:—all of them treat of discourse concerning the subjects with which they severally have to do.

GORGIAS: Clearly.

SOCRATES: Then why, if you call rhetoric the art which treats of discourse, and all the other arts treat of discourse, do you not call them arts of rhetoric?

GORGIAS: Because, Socrates, the knowledge of the other arts has only to do with some sort of external action, as of the hand; but there is no such action of the hand in rhetoric which works and takes effect only through the medium of discourse. And therefore I am justified in saying that rhetoric treats of discourse.

SOCRATES: I am not sure whether I entirely understand you, but I dare say I shall soon know better; please to answer me a question:—you would allow that there are arts?

GORGIAS: Yes.

SOCRATES: As to the arts generally, they are for the most part concerned with doing, and require little or no speaking; in painting, and statuary, and many other arts, the work may proceed in silence; and of such arts I suppose you would say that they do not come within the province of rhetoric.

GORGIAS: You perfectly conceive my meaning, Socrates.

SOCRATES: But there are other arts which work wholly through the medium of language, and require either no action or very little, as, for example, the arts of arithmetic, of calculation, of geometry, and of playing draughts; in some of these speech is pretty nearly co-extensive with action, but in most of them the verbal element is greater—they depend wholly on words for their efficacy and power: and I take your meaning to be that rhetoric is an art of this latter sort?

GORGIAS: Exactly.

SOCRATES: And yet I do not believe that you really mean to call any of these arts rhetoric; although the precise expression which you used was, that rhetoric is an art which works and takes effect only through the medium of discourse; and an adversary who wished to be captious might say, 'And so, Gorgias, you call arithmetic rhetoric.' But I do not think that you really call arithmetic rhetoric any more than geometry would be so called by you.

GORGIAS: You are quite right, Socrates, in your apprehension of my meaning.

SOCRATES: Well, then, let me now have the rest of my answer:—seeing that rhetoric is one of those arts which works mainly by the use of words, and there are other arts which also use words, tell me what is that quality in words with which rhetoric is concerned:—Suppose that a person asks me about some of the arts which I was mentioning just now; he might say, 'Socrates, what is arithmetic?' and I should reply to him, as you replied to me, that arithmetic is one of those arts which take effect through words. And then he would proceed to ask: 'Words about what?' and I should reply, Words about odd and even numbers, and how many there are of each. And if he asked again: 'What is the art of calculation?' I should say, That also is one of the arts which is concerned wholly with words. And if he further said, 'Concerned with what?' I should say, like the clerks in the assembly, 'as aforesaid' of arithmetic, but with a difference, the difference being that the art of calculation considers not only the quantities of odd and even numbers, but also their numerical relations to themselves and to one another. And suppose, again, I were to say that astronomy is only words—he would ask, 'Words about what, Socrates?' and I should answer, that astronomy tells us about the motions of the stars and sun and moon, and their relative swiftness.

GORGIAS: You would be quite right, Socrates.

SOCRATES: And now let us have from you, Gorgias, the truth about rhetoric: which you would admit (would you not?) to be one of those arts which act always and fulfil all their ends through the medium of words?

GORGIAS: True.

SOCRATES: Words which do what? I should ask. To what class of things do the words which rhetoric uses relate?

GORGIAS: To the greatest, Socrates, and the best of human things.

SOCRATES: That again, Gorgias is ambiguous; I am still in the dark: for which are the greatest and best of human things? I dare say that you have heard men singing at feasts the old drinking song, in which the singers enumerate the goods of life, first health, beauty next, thirdly, as the writer of the song says, wealth honestly obtained.

GORGIAS: Yes, I know the song; but what is your drift?

SOCRATES: I mean to say, that the producers of those things which the author of the song praises, that is to say, the physician, the trainer, the money-maker, will at once come to you, and first the physician will say: 'O Socrates, Gorgias is deceiving you, for my art is concerned with the greatest good of men and not his.' And when I ask, Who are you? he will reply, 'I am a physician.' What do you mean? I shall say. Do you mean that your art produces the greatest good? 'Certainly,' he will answer, 'for is not health the greatest good? What greater good can men have, Socrates?' And after him the trainer will come and say, 'I too, Socrates, shall be greatly surprised if Gorgias can show more good of his art than I can show of mine.' To him again I shall say, Who are you, honest friend, and what is your business? 'I am a trainer,' he will reply, 'and my business is to make men beautiful and strong in body.' When I have done with the trainer, there arrives the money-maker, and he, as I expect, will utterly despise them all. 'Consider Socrates,' he will say, 'whether Gorgias or any one else can produce any greater good than wealth.' Well, you and I say to him, and are you a creator of wealth? 'Yes,' he replies. And who are you? 'A money-maker.' And do you consider wealth to be the greatest good of man? 'Of course,' will be his reply. And we shall rejoin: Yes; but our friend Gorgias contends that his art produces a greater good than yours. And then he will be sure to go on and ask, 'What good? Let Gorgias answer.' Now I want you, Gorgias, to imagine that this question is asked of you by them and by me; What is that which, as you say, is the greatest good of man, and of which you are the creator? Answer us.

GORGIAS: That good, Socrates, which is truly the greatest, being that which gives to men freedom in their own persons, and to individuals the power of ruling over others in their several states.

SOCRATES: And what would you consider this to be?

GORGIAS: What is there greater than the word which persuades the judges in the courts, or the senators in the council, or the citizens in the assembly, or at any other political meeting?—if you have the power of uttering this word, you will have the physician your slave, and the trainer your slave, and the money-maker of whom you talk will be found to gather treasures, not for himself, but for you who are able to speak and to persuade the multitude.

SOCRATES: Now I think, Gorgias, that you have very accurately explained what you conceive to be the art of rhetoric; and you mean to say, if I am not mistaken, that rhetoric is the artificer of persuasion, having this and no other business, and that this is her crown and end. Do you know any other effect of rhetoric over and above that of producing persuasion?

GORGIAS: No: the definition seems to me very fair, Socrates; for persuasion is the chief end of rhetoric.

SOCRATES: Then hear me, Gorgias, for I am quite sure that if there ever was a man who entered on the discussion of a matter from a pure love of knowing the truth, I am such a one, and I should say the same of you.

GORGIAS: What is coming, Socrates?

SOCRATES: I will tell you: I am very well aware that I do not know what, according to you, is the exact nature, or what are the topics of that persuasion of which you speak, and which is given by rhetoric; although I have a suspicion about both the one and the other. And I am going to ask—what is this power of persuasion which is given by rhetoric, and about what? But why, if I have a suspicion, do I ask instead of telling you? Not for your sake, but in order that the argument may proceed in such a manner as is most likely to set forth the truth. And I would have you observe, that I am right in asking this further question: If I asked, 'What sort of a painter is Zeuxis?' and you said, 'The painter of figures,' should I not be right in asking, 'What kind of figures, and where do you find them?'

GORGIAS: Certainly.

SOCRATES: And the reason for asking this second question would be, that there are other painters besides, who paint many other figures?

GORGIAS: True.

SOCRATES: But if there had been no one but Zeuxis who painted them, then you would have answered very well?

GORGIAS: Quite so.

SOCRATES: Now I want to know about rhetoric in the same way;—is rhetoric the only art which brings persuasion, or do other arts have the same effect? I mean to say—Does he who teaches anything persuade men of that which he teaches or not?

GORGIAS: He persuades, Socrates,—there can be no mistake about that.

SOCRATES: Again, if we take the arts of which we were just now speaking:—do not arithmetic and the arithmeticians teach us the properties of number?

GORGIAS: Certainly.

SOCRATES: And therefore persuade us of them?

GORGIAS: Yes.

SOCRATES: Then arithmetic as well as rhetoric is an artificer of persuasion?

GORGIAS: Clearly.

SOCRATES: And if any one asks us what sort of persuasion, and about what,—we shall answer, persuasion which teaches the quantity of odd and even; and we shall be able to show that all the other arts of which we were just now speaking are artificers of persuasion, and of what sort, and about what.

GORGIAS: Very true.

SOCRATES: Then rhetoric is not the only artificer of persuasion?

GORGIAS: True.

SOCRATES: Seeing, then, that not only rhetoric works by persuasion, but that other arts do the same, as in the case of the painter, a question has arisen which is a very fair one: Of what persuasion is rhetoric the artificer, and about what?—is not that a fair way of putting the question?

GORGIAS: I think so.

SOCRATES: Then, if you approve the question, Gorgias, what is the answer?

GORGIAS: I answer, Socrates, that rhetoric is the art of persuasion in courts of law and other assemblies, as I was just now saying, and about the just and unjust.

SOCRATES: And that, Gorgias, was what I was suspecting to be your notion; yet I would not have you wonder if by-and-by I am found repeating a seemingly plain question; for I ask not in order to confute you, but as I was saying that the argument may proceed consecutively, and that we may not get the habit of anticipating and suspecting the meaning of one another's words; I would have you develope your own views in your own way, whatever may be your hypothesis.

GORGIAS: I think that you are quite right, Socrates.

SOCRATES: Then let me raise another question; there is such a thing as 'having learned'?

GORGIAS: Yes.

SOCRATES: And there is also 'having believed'?

GORGIAS: Yes.

SOCRATES: And is the 'having learned' the same as 'having believed,' and are learning and belief the same things?

GORGIAS: In my judgment, Socrates, they are not the same.

SOCRATES: And your judgment is right, as you may ascertain in this way:—If a person were to say to you, 'Is there, Gorgias, a false belief as well as a true?'—you would reply, if I am not mistaken, that there is.

GORGIAS: Yes.

SOCRATES: Well, but is there a false knowledge as well as a true?

GORGIAS: No.

SOCRATES: No, indeed; and this again proves that knowledge and belief differ.

GORGIAS: Very true.

SOCRATES: And yet those who have learned as well as those who have believed are persuaded?

GORGIAS: Just so.

SOCRATES: Shall we then assume two sorts of persuasion,—one which is the source of belief without knowledge, as the other is of knowledge?

GORGIAS: By all means.

SOCRATES: And which sort of persuasion does rhetoric create in courts of law and other assemblies about the just and unjust, the sort of persuasion which gives belief without knowledge, or that which gives knowledge?

GORGIAS: Clearly, Socrates, that which only gives belief.

SOCRATES: Then rhetoric, as would appear, is the artificer of a persuasion which creates belief about the just and unjust, but gives no instruction about them?

GORGIAS: True.

SOCRATES: And the rhetorician does not instruct the courts of law or other assemblies about things just and unjust, but he creates belief about them; for no one can be supposed to instruct such a vast multitude about such high matters in a short time?

GORGIAS: Certainly not.

SOCRATES: Come, then, and let us see what we really mean about rhetoric; for I do not know what my own meaning is as yet. When the assembly meets to elect a physician or a shipwright or any other craftsman, will the rhetorician be taken into counsel? Surely not. For at every election he ought to be chosen who is most skilled; and, again, when walls have to be built or harbours or docks to be constructed, not the rhetorician but the master workman will advise; or when generals have to be chosen and an order of battle arranged, or a position taken, then the military will advise and not the rhetoricians: what do you say, Gorgias? Since you profess to be a rhetorician and a maker of rhetoricians, I cannot do better than learn the nature of your art from you. And here let me assure you that I have your interest in view as well as my own. For likely enough some one or other of the young men present might desire to become your pupil, and in fact I see some, and a good many too, who have this wish, but they would be too modest to question you. And therefore when you are interrogated by me, I would have you imagine that you are interrogated by them. 'What is the use of coming to you, Gorgias?' they will say—'about what will you teach us to advise the state?—about the just and unjust only, or about those other things also which Socrates has just mentioned?' How will you answer them?

GORGIAS: I like your way of leading us on, Socrates, and I will endeavour to reveal to you the whole nature of rhetoric. You must have heard, I think, that the docks and the walls of the Athenians and the plan of the harbour were devised in accordance with the counsels, partly of Themistocles, and partly of Pericles, and not at the suggestion of the builders.

SOCRATES: Such is the tradition, Gorgias, about Themistocles; and I myself heard the speech of Pericles when he advised us about the middle wall.

GORGIAS: And you will observe, Socrates, that when a decision has to be given in such matters the rhetoricians are the advisers; they are the men who win their point.

SOCRATES: I had that in my admiring mind, Gorgias, when I asked what is the nature of rhetoric, which always appears to me, when I look at the matter in this way, to be a marvel of greatness.

GORGIAS: A marvel, indeed, Socrates, if you only knew how rhetoric comprehends and holds under her sway all the inferior arts. Let me offer you a striking example of this. On several occasions I have been with my brother Herodicus or some other physician to see one of his patients, who would not allow the physician to give him medicine, or apply the knife or hot iron to him; and I have persuaded him to do for me what he would not do for the physician just by the use of rhetoric. And I say that if a rhetorician and a physician were to go to any city, and had there to argue in the Ecclesia or any other assembly as to which of them should be elected state-physician, the physician would have no chance; but he who could speak would be chosen if he wished; and in a contest with a man of any other profession the rhetorician more than any one would have the power of getting himself chosen, for he can speak more persuasively to the multitude than any of them, and on any subject. Such is the nature and power of the art of rhetoric! And yet, Socrates, rhetoric should be used like any other competitive art, not against everybody,—the rhetorician ought not to abuse his strength any more than a pugilist or pancratiast or other master of fence;—because he has powers which are more than a match either for friend or enemy, he ought not therefore to strike, stab, or slay his friends. Suppose a man to have been trained in the palestra and to be a skilful boxer,—he in the fulness of his strength goes and strikes his father or mother or one of his familiars or friends; but that is no reason why the trainers or fencing-masters should be held in detestation or banished from the city;—surely not. For they taught their art for a good purpose, to be used against enemies and evil-doers, in self-defence not in aggression, and others have perverted their instructions, and turned to a bad use their own strength and skill. But not on this account are the teachers bad, neither is the art in fault, or bad in itself; I should rather say that those who make a bad use of the art are to blame. And the same argument holds good of rhetoric; for the rhetorician can speak against all men and upon any subject,—in short, he can persuade the multitude better than any other man of anything which he pleases, but he should not therefore seek to defraud the physician or any other artist of his reputation merely because he has the power; he ought to use rhetoric fairly, as he would also use his athletic powers. And if after having become a rhetorician he makes a bad use of his strength and skill, his instructor surely ought not on that account to be held in detestation or banished. For he was intended by his teacher to make a good use of his instructions, but he abuses them. And therefore he is the person who ought to be held in detestation, banished, and put to death, and not his instructor.

SOCRATES: You, Gorgias, like myself, have had great experience of disputations, and you must have observed, I think, that they do not always terminate in mutual edification, or in the definition by either party of the subjects which they are discussing; but disagreements are apt to arise—somebody says that another has not spoken truly or clearly; and then they get into a passion and begin to quarrel, both parties conceiving that their opponents are arguing from personal feeling only and jealousy of themselves, not from any interest in the question at issue. And sometimes they will go on abusing one another until the company at last are quite vexed at themselves for ever listening to such fellows. Why do I say this? Why, because I cannot help feeling that you are now saying what is not quite consistent or accordant with what you were saying at first about rhetoric. And I am afraid to point this out to you, lest you should think that I have some animosity against you, and that I speak, not for the sake of discovering the truth, but from jealousy of you. Now if you are one of my sort, I should like to cross-examine you, but if not I will let you alone. And what is my sort? you will ask. I am one of those who are very willing to be refuted if I say anything which is not true, and very willing to refute any one else who says what is not true, and quite as ready to be refuted as to refute; for I hold that this is the greater gain of the two, just as the gain is greater of being cured of a very great evil than of curing another. For I imagine that there is no evil which a man can endure so great as an erroneous opinion about the matters of which we are speaking; and if you claim to be one of my sort, let us have the discussion out, but if you would rather have done, no matter;—let us make an end of it.

GORGIAS: I should say, Socrates, that I am quite the man whom you indicate; but, perhaps, we ought to consider the audience, for, before you came, I had already given a long exhibition, and if we proceed the argument may run on to a great length. And therefore I think that we should consider whether we may not be detaining some part of the company when they are wanting to do something else.

CHAEREPHON: You hear the audience cheering, Gorgias and Socrates, which shows their desire to listen to you; and for myself, Heaven forbid that I should have any business on hand which would take me away from a discussion so interesting and so ably maintained.

CALLICLES: By the gods, Chaerephon, although I have been present at many discussions, I doubt whether I was ever so much delighted before, and therefore if you go on discoursing all day I shall be the better pleased.

SOCRATES: I may truly say, Callicles, that I am willing, if Gorgias is.

GORGIAS: After all this, Socrates, I should be disgraced if I refused, especially as I have promised to answer all comers; in accordance with the wishes of the company, then, do you begin, and ask of me any question which you like.

SOCRATES: Let me tell you then, Gorgias, what surprises me in your words; though I dare say that you may be right, and I may have misunderstood your meaning. You say that you can make any man, who will learn of you, a rhetorician?

GORGIAS: Yes.

SOCRATES: Do you mean that you will teach him to gain the ears of the multitude on any subject, and this not by instruction but by persuasion?

GORGIAS: Quite so.

SOCRATES: You were saying, in fact, that the rhetorician will have greater powers of persuasion than the physician even in a matter of health?

GORGIAS: Yes, with the multitude,—that is.

SOCRATES: You mean to say, with the ignorant; for with those who know he cannot be supposed to have greater powers of persuasion.

GORGIAS: Very true.

SOCRATES: But if he is to have more power of persuasion than the physician, he will have greater power than he who knows?

GORGIAS: Certainly.

SOCRATES: Although he is not a physician:—is he?

GORGIAS: No.

SOCRATES: And he who is not a physician must, obviously, be ignorant of what the physician knows.

GORGIAS: Clearly.

SOCRATES: Then, when the rhetorician is more persuasive than the physician, the ignorant is more persuasive with the ignorant than he who has knowledge?—is not that the inference?

GORGIAS: In the case supposed:—yes.

SOCRATES: And the same holds of the relation of rhetoric to all the other arts; the rhetorician need not know the truth about things; he has only to discover some way of persuading the ignorant that he has more knowledge than those who know?

GORGIAS: Yes, Socrates, and is not this a great comfort?—not to have learned the other arts, but the art of rhetoric only, and yet to be in no way inferior to the professors of them?

SOCRATES: Whether the rhetorician is or not inferior on this account is a question which we will hereafter examine if the enquiry is likely to be of any service to us; but I would rather begin by asking, whether he is or is not as ignorant of the just and unjust, base and honourable, good and evil, as he is of medicine and the other arts; I mean to say, does he really know anything of what is good and evil, base or honourable, just or unjust in them; or has he only a way with the ignorant of persuading them that he not knowing is to be esteemed to know more about these things than some one else who knows? Or must the pupil know these things and come to you knowing them before he can acquire the art of rhetoric? If he is ignorant, you who are the teacher of rhetoric will not teach him—it is not your business; but you will make him seem to the multitude to know them, when he does not know them; and seem to be a good man, when he is not. Or will you be unable to teach him rhetoric at all, unless he knows the truth of these things first? What is to be said about all this? By heavens, Gorgias, I wish that you would reveal to me the power of rhetoric, as you were saying that you would.

GORGIAS: Well, Socrates, I suppose that if the pupil does chance not to know them, he will have to learn of me these things as well.

SOCRATES: Say no more, for there you are right; and so he whom you make a rhetorician must either know the nature of the just and unjust already, or he must be taught by you.

GORGIAS: Certainly.

SOCRATES: Well, and is not he who has learned carpentering a carpenter?

GORGIAS: Yes.

SOCRATES: And he who has learned music a musician?

GORGIAS: Yes.

SOCRATES: And he who has learned medicine is a physician, in like manner? He who has learned anything whatever is that which his knowledge makes him.

GORGIAS: Certainly.

SOCRATES: And in the same way, he who has learned what is just is just?

GORGIAS: To be sure.

SOCRATES: And he who is just may be supposed to do what is just?

GORGIAS: Yes.

SOCRATES: And must not the just man always desire to do what is just?

GORGIAS: That is clearly the inference.

SOCRATES: Surely, then, the just man will never consent to do injustice?

GORGIAS: Certainly not.

SOCRATES: And according to the argument the rhetorician must be a just man?

GORGIAS: Yes.

SOCRATES: And will therefore never be willing to do injustice?

GORGIAS: Clearly not.

SOCRATES: But do you remember saying just now that the trainer is not to be accused or banished if the pugilist makes a wrong use of his pugilistic art; and in like manner, if the rhetorician makes a bad and unjust use of his rhetoric, that is not to be laid to the charge of his teacher, who is not to be banished, but the wrong-doer himself who made a bad use of his rhetoric—he is to be banished—was not that said?

GORGIAS: Yes, it was.

SOCRATES: But now we are affirming that the aforesaid rhetorician will never have done injustice at all?

GORGIAS: True.

SOCRATES: And at the very outset, Gorgias, it was said that rhetoric treated of discourse, not (like arithmetic) about odd and even, but about just and unjust? Was not this said?

GORGIAS: Yes.

SOCRATES: I was thinking at the time, when I heard you saying so, that rhetoric, which is always discoursing about justice, could not possibly be an unjust thing. But when you added, shortly afterwards, that the rhetorician might make a bad use of rhetoric I noted with surprise the inconsistency into which you had fallen; and I said, that if you thought, as I did, that there was a gain in being refuted, there would be an advantage in going on with the question, but if not, I would leave off. And in the course of our investigations, as you will see yourself, the rhetorician has been acknowledged to be incapable of making an unjust use of rhetoric, or of willingness to do injustice. By the dog, Gorgias, there will be a great deal of discussion, before we get at the truth of all this.

POLUS: And do even you, Socrates, seriously believe what you are now saying about rhetoric? What! because Gorgias was ashamed to deny that the rhetorician knew the just and the honourable and the good, and admitted that to any one who came to him ignorant of them he could teach them, and then out of this admission there arose a contradiction—the thing which you dearly love, and to which not he, but you, brought the argument by your captious questions—(do you seriously believe that there is any truth in all this?) For will any one ever acknowledge that he does not know, or cannot teach, the nature of justice? The truth is, that there is great want of manners in bringing the argument to such a pass.

SOCRATES: Illustrious Polus, the reason why we provide ourselves with friends and children is, that when we get old and stumble, a younger generation may be at hand to set us on our legs again in our words and in our actions: and now, if I and Gorgias are stumbling, here are you who should raise us up; and I for my part engage to retract any error into which you may think that I have fallen-upon one condition:

POLUS: What condition?

SOCRATES: That you contract, Polus, the prolixity of speech in which you indulged at first.

POLUS: What! do you mean that I may not use as many words as I please?

SOCRATES: Only to think, my friend, that having come on a visit to Athens, which is the most free-spoken state in Hellas, you when you got there, and you alone, should be deprived of the power of speech—that would be hard indeed. But then consider my case:—shall not I be very hardly used, if, when you are making a long oration, and refusing to answer what you are asked, I am compelled to stay and listen to you, and may not go away? I say rather, if you have a real interest in the argument, or, to repeat my former expression, have any desire to set it on its legs, take back any statement which you please; and in your turn ask and answer, like myself and Gorgias—refute and be refuted: for I suppose that you would claim to know what Gorgias knows—would you not?

POLUS: Yes.

SOCRATES: And you, like him, invite any one to ask you about anything which he pleases, and you will know how to answer him?

POLUS: To be sure.

SOCRATES: And now, which will you do, ask or answer?

POLUS: I will ask; and do you answer me, Socrates, the same question which Gorgias, as you suppose, is unable to answer: What is rhetoric?

SOCRATES: Do you mean what sort of an art?

POLUS: Yes.

SOCRATES: To say the truth, Polus, it is not an art at all, in my opinion.

POLUS: Then what, in your opinion, is rhetoric?

SOCRATES: A thing which, as I was lately reading in a book of yours, you say that you have made an art.

POLUS: What thing?

SOCRATES: I should say a sort of experience.

POLUS: Does rhetoric seem to you to be an experience?

SOCRATES: That is my view, but you may be of another mind.

POLUS: An experience in what?

SOCRATES: An experience in producing a sort of delight and gratification.

POLUS: And if able to gratify others, must not rhetoric be a fine thing?

SOCRATES: What are you saying, Polus? Why do you ask me whether rhetoric is a fine thing or not, when I have not as yet told you what rhetoric is?

POLUS: Did I not hear you say that rhetoric was a sort of experience?

SOCRATES: Will you, who are so desirous to gratify others, afford a slight gratification to me?

POLUS: I will.

SOCRATES: Will you ask me, what sort of an art is cookery?

POLUS: What sort of an art is cookery?

SOCRATES: Not an art at all, Polus.

POLUS: What then?

SOCRATES: I should say an experience.

POLUS: In what? I wish that you would explain to me.

SOCRATES: An experience in producing a sort of delight and gratification, Polus.

POLUS: Then are cookery and rhetoric the same?

SOCRATES: No, they are only different parts of the same profession.

POLUS: Of what profession?

SOCRATES: I am afraid that the truth may seem discourteous; and I hesitate to answer, lest Gorgias should imagine that I am making fun of his own profession. For whether or no this is that art of rhetoric which Gorgias practises I really cannot tell:—from what he was just now saying, nothing appeared of what he thought of his art, but the rhetoric which I mean is a part of a not very creditable whole.

GORGIAS: A part of what, Socrates? Say what you mean, and never mind me.

SOCRATES: In my opinion then, Gorgias, the whole of which rhetoric is a part is not an art at all, but the habit of a bold and ready wit, which knows how to manage mankind: this habit I sum up under the word 'flattery'; and it appears to me to have many other parts, one of which is cookery, which may seem to be an art, but, as I maintain, is only an experience or routine and not an art:—another part is rhetoric, and the art of attiring and sophistry are two others: thus there are four branches, and four different things answering to them. And Polus may ask, if he likes, for he has not as yet been informed, what part of flattery is rhetoric: he did not see that I had not yet answered him when he proceeded to ask a further question: Whether I do not think rhetoric a fine thing? But I shall not tell him whether rhetoric is a fine thing or not, until I have first answered, 'What is rhetoric?' For that would not be right, Polus; but I shall be happy to answer, if you will ask me, What part of flattery is rhetoric?

POLUS: I will ask and do you answer? What part of flattery is rhetoric?

SOCRATES: Will you understand my answer? Rhetoric, according to my view, is the ghost or counterfeit of a part of politics.

POLUS: And noble or ignoble?

SOCRATES: Ignoble, I should say, if I am compelled to answer, for I call what is bad ignoble: though I doubt whether you understand what I was saying before.

GORGIAS: Indeed, Socrates, I cannot say that I understand myself.

SOCRATES: I do not wonder, Gorgias; for I have not as yet explained myself, and our friend Polus, colt by name and colt by nature, is apt to run away. (This is an untranslatable play on the name 'Polus,' which means 'a colt.')

GORGIAS: Never mind him, but explain to me what you mean by saying that rhetoric is the counterfeit of a part of politics.

SOCRATES: I will try, then, to explain my notion of rhetoric, and if I am mistaken, my friend Polus shall refute me. We may assume the existence of bodies and of souls?

GORGIAS: Of course.

SOCRATES: You would further admit that there is a good condition of either of them?

GORGIAS: Yes.

SOCRATES: Which condition may not be really good, but good only in appearance? I mean to say, that there are many persons who appear to be in good health, and whom only a physician or trainer will discern at first sight not to be in good health.

GORGIAS: True.

SOCRATES: And this applies not only to the body, but also to the soul: in either there may be that which gives the appearance of health and not the reality?

GORGIAS: Yes, certainly.

SOCRATES: And now I will endeavour to explain to you more clearly what I mean: The soul and body being two, have two arts corresponding to them: there is the art of politics attending on the soul; and another art attending on the body, of which I know no single name, but which may be described as having two divisions, one of them gymnastic, and the other medicine. And in politics there is a legislative part, which answers to gymnastic, as justice does to medicine; and the two parts run into one another, justice having to do with the same subject as legislation, and medicine with the same subject as gymnastic, but with a difference. Now, seeing that there are these four arts, two attending on the body and two on the soul for their highest good; flattery knowing, or rather guessing their natures, has distributed herself into four shams or simulations of them; she puts on the likeness of some one or other of them, and pretends to be that which she simulates, and having no regard for men's highest interests, is ever making pleasure the bait of the unwary, and deceiving them into the belief that she is of the highest value to them. Cookery simulates the disguise of medicine, and pretends to know what food is the best for the body; and if the physician and the cook had to enter into a competition in which children were the judges, or men who had no more sense than children, as to which of them best understands the goodness or badness of food, the physician would be starved to death. A flattery I deem this to be and of an ignoble sort, Polus, for to you I am now addressing myself, because it aims at pleasure without any thought of the best. An art I do not call it, but only an experience, because it is unable to explain or to give a reason of the nature of its own applications. And I do not call any irrational thing an art; but if you dispute my words, I am prepared to argue in defence of them.

Cookery, then, I maintain to be a flattery which takes the form of medicine; and tiring, in like manner, is a flattery which takes the form of gymnastic, and is knavish, false, ignoble, illiberal, working deceitfully by the help of lines, and colours, and enamels, and garments, and making men affect a spurious beauty to the neglect of the true beauty which is given by gymnastic.

I would rather not be tedious, and therefore I will only say, after the manner of the geometricians (for I think that by this time you will be able to follow)

as tiring: gymnastic:: cookery: medicine;

or rather,

as tiring: gymnastic:: sophistry: legislation;

and

as cookery: medicine:: rhetoric: justice.

And this, I say, is the natural difference between the rhetorician and the sophist, but by reason of their near connection, they are apt to be jumbled up together; neither do they know what to make of themselves, nor do other men know what to make of them. For if the body presided over itself, and were not under the guidance of the soul, and the soul did not discern and discriminate between cookery and medicine, but the body was made the judge of them, and the rule of judgment was the bodily delight which was given by them, then the word of Anaxagoras, that word with which you, friend Polus, are so well acquainted, would prevail far and wide: 'Chaos' would come again, and cookery, health, and medicine would mingle in an indiscriminate mass. And now I have told you my notion of rhetoric, which is, in relation to the soul, what cookery is to the body. I may have been inconsistent in making a long speech, when I would not allow you to discourse at length. But I think that I may be excused, because you did not understand me, and could make no use of my answer when I spoke shortly, and therefore I had to enter into an explanation. And if I show an equal inability to make use of yours, I hope that you will speak at equal length; but if I am able to understand you, let me have the benefit of your brevity, as is only fair: And now you may do what you please with my answer.

POLUS: What do you mean? do you think that rhetoric is flattery?

SOCRATES: Nay, I said a part of flattery; if at your age, Polus, you cannot remember, what will you do by-and-by, when you get older?

POLUS: And are the good rhetoricians meanly regarded in states, under the idea that they are flatterers?

SOCRATES: Is that a question or the beginning of a speech?

POLUS: I am asking a question.

SOCRATES: Then my answer is, that they are not regarded at all.

POLUS: How not regarded? Have they not very great power in states?

SOCRATES: Not if you mean to say that power is a good to the possessor.

POLUS: And that is what I do mean to say.

SOCRATES: Then, if so, I think that they have the least power of all the citizens.

POLUS: What! are they not like tyrants? They kill and despoil and exile any one whom they please.

SOCRATES: By the dog, Polus, I cannot make out at each deliverance of yours, whether you are giving an opinion of your own, or asking a question of me.

POLUS: I am asking a question of you.

SOCRATES: Yes, my friend, but you ask two questions at once.

POLUS: How two questions?

SOCRATES: Why, did you not say just now that the rhetoricians are like tyrants, and that they kill and despoil or exile any one whom they please?

POLUS: I did.

SOCRATES: Well then, I say to you that here are two questions in one, and I will answer both of them. And I tell you, Polus, that rhetoricians and tyrants have the least possible power in states, as I was just now saying; for they do literally nothing which they will, but only what they think best.

POLUS: And is not that a great power?

SOCRATES: Polus has already said the reverse.

POLUS: Said the reverse! nay, that is what I assert.

SOCRATES: No, by the great—what do you call him?—not you, for you say that power is a good to him who has the power.

POLUS: I do.

SOCRATES: And would you maintain that if a fool does what he thinks best, this is a good, and would you call this great power?

POLUS: I should not.

SOCRATES: Then you must prove that the rhetorician is not a fool, and that rhetoric is an art and not a flattery—and so you will have refuted me; but if you leave me unrefuted, why, the rhetoricians who do what they think best in states, and the tyrants, will have nothing upon which to congratulate themselves, if as you say, power be indeed a good, admitting at the same time that what is done without sense is an evil.

POLUS: Yes; I admit that.

SOCRATES: How then can the rhetoricians or the tyrants have great power in states, unless Polus can refute Socrates, and prove to him that they do as they will?

POLUS: This fellow—

SOCRATES: I say that they do not do as they will;—now refute me.

POLUS: Why, have you not already said that they do as they think best?

SOCRATES: And I say so still.

POLUS: Then surely they do as they will?

SOCRATES: I deny it.

POLUS: But they do what they think best?

SOCRATES: Aye.

POLUS: That, Socrates, is monstrous and absurd.

SOCRATES: Good words, good Polus, as I may say in your own peculiar style; but if you have any questions to ask of me, either prove that I am in error or give the answer yourself.

POLUS: Very well, I am willing to answer that I may know what you mean.

SOCRATES: Do men appear to you to will that which they do, or to will that further end for the sake of which they do a thing? when they take medicine, for example, at the bidding of a physician, do they will the drinking of the medicine which is painful, or the health for the sake of which they drink?

POLUS: Clearly, the health.

SOCRATES: And when men go on a voyage or engage in business, they do not will that which they are doing at the time; for who would desire to take the risk of a voyage or the trouble of business?—But they will, to have the wealth for the sake of which they go on a voyage.

POLUS: Certainly.

SOCRATES: And is not this universally true? If a man does something for the sake of something else, he wills not that which he does, but that for the sake of which he does it.

POLUS: Yes.

SOCRATES: And are not all things either good or evil, or intermediate and indifferent?

POLUS: To be sure, Socrates.

SOCRATES: Wisdom and health and wealth and the like you would call goods, and their opposites evils?

POLUS: I should.

SOCRATES: And the things which are neither good nor evil, and which partake sometimes of the nature of good and at other times of evil, or of neither, are such as sitting, walking, running, sailing; or, again, wood, stones, and the like:—these are the things which you call neither good nor evil?

POLUS: Exactly so.

SOCRATES: Are these indifferent things done for the sake of the good, or the good for the sake of the indifferent?

POLUS: Clearly, the indifferent for the sake of the good.

SOCRATES: When we walk we walk for the sake of the good, and under the idea that it is better to walk, and when we stand we stand equally for the sake of the good?

POLUS: Yes.

SOCRATES: And when we kill a man we kill him or exile him or despoil him of his goods, because, as we think, it will conduce to our good?

POLUS: Certainly.

SOCRATES: Men who do any of these things do them for the sake of the good?

POLUS: Yes.

SOCRATES: And did we not admit that in doing something for the sake of something else, we do not will those things which we do, but that other thing for the sake of which we do them?

POLUS: Most true.

SOCRATES: Then we do not will simply to kill a man or to exile him or to despoil him of his goods, but we will to do that which conduces to our good, and if the act is not conducive to our good we do not will it; for we will, as you say, that which is our good, but that which is neither good nor evil, or simply evil, we do not will. Why are you silent, Polus? Am I not right?

POLUS: You are right.

SOCRATES: Hence we may infer, that if any one, whether he be a tyrant or a rhetorician, kills another or exiles another or deprives him of his property, under the idea that the act is for his own interests when really not for his own interests, he may be said to do what seems best to him?

POLUS: Yes.

SOCRATES: But does he do what he wills if he does what is evil? Why do you not answer?

POLUS: Well, I suppose not.

SOCRATES: Then if great power is a good as you allow, will such a one have great power in a state?

POLUS: He will not.

SOCRATES: Then I was right in saying that a man may do what seems good to him in a state, and not have great power, and not do what he wills?

POLUS: As though you, Socrates, would not like to have the power of doing what seemed good to you in the state, rather than not; you would not be jealous when you saw any one killing or despoiling or imprisoning whom he pleased, Oh, no!

SOCRATES: Justly or unjustly, do you mean?

POLUS: In either case is he not equally to be envied?

SOCRATES: Forbear, Polus!

POLUS: Why 'forbear'?

SOCRATES: Because you ought not to envy wretches who are not to be envied, but only to pity them.

POLUS: And are those of whom I spoke wretches?

SOCRATES: Yes, certainly they are.

POLUS: And so you think that he who slays any one whom he pleases, and justly slays him, is pitiable and wretched?

SOCRATES: No, I do not say that of him: but neither do I think that he is to be envied.

POLUS: Were you not saying just now that he is wretched?

SOCRATES: Yes, my friend, if he killed another unjustly, in which case he is also to be pitied; and he is not to be envied if he killed him justly.

POLUS: At any rate you will allow that he who is unjustly put to death is wretched, and to be pitied?

SOCRATES: Not so much, Polus, as he who kills him, and not so much as he who is justly killed.

POLUS: How can that be, Socrates?

SOCRATES: That may very well be, inasmuch as doing injustice is the greatest of evils.

POLUS: But is it the greatest? Is not suffering injustice a greater evil?

SOCRATES: Certainly not.

POLUS: Then would you rather suffer than do injustice?

SOCRATES: I should not like either, but if I must choose between them, I would rather suffer than do.

POLUS: Then you would not wish to be a tyrant?

SOCRATES: Not if you mean by tyranny what I mean.

POLUS: I mean, as I said before, the power of doing whatever seems good to you in a state, killing, banishing, doing in all things as you like.

SOCRATES: Well then, illustrious friend, when I have said my say, do you reply to me. Suppose that I go into a crowded Agora, and take a dagger under my arm. Polus, I say to you, I have just acquired rare power, and become a tyrant; for if I think that any of these men whom you see ought to be put to death, the man whom I have a mind to kill is as good as dead; and if I am disposed to break his head or tear his garment, he will have his head broken or his garment torn in an instant. Such is my great power in this city. And if you do not believe me, and I show you the dagger, you would probably reply: Socrates, in that sort of way any one may have great power—he may burn any house which he pleases, and the docks and triremes of the Athenians, and all their other vessels, whether public or private—but can you believe that this mere doing as you think best is great power?

POLUS: Certainly not such doing as this.

SOCRATES: But can you tell me why you disapprove of such a power?

POLUS: I can.

SOCRATES: Why then?

POLUS: Why, because he who did as you say would be certain to be punished.

SOCRATES: And punishment is an evil?

POLUS: Certainly.

SOCRATES: And you would admit once more, my good sir, that great power is a benefit to a man if his actions turn out to his advantage, and that this is the meaning of great power; and if not, then his power is an evil and is no power. But let us look at the matter in another way:—do we not acknowledge that the things of which we were speaking, the infliction of death, and exile, and the deprivation of property are sometimes a good and sometimes not a good?

POLUS: Certainly.

SOCRATES: About that you and I may be supposed to agree?

POLUS: Yes.

SOCRATES: Tell me, then, when do you say that they are good and when that they are evil—what principle do you lay down?

POLUS: I would rather, Socrates, that you should answer as well as ask that question.

SOCRATES: Well, Polus, since you would rather have the answer from me, I say that they are good when they are just, and evil when they are unjust.

POLUS: You are hard of refutation, Socrates, but might not a child refute that statement?

SOCRATES: Then I shall be very grateful to the child, and equally grateful to you if you will refute me and deliver me from my foolishness. And I hope that refute me you will, and not weary of doing good to a friend.

POLUS: Yes, Socrates, and I need not go far or appeal to antiquity; events which happened only a few days ago are enough to refute you, and to prove that many men who do wrong are happy.

SOCRATES: What events?

POLUS: You see, I presume, that Archelaus the son of Perdiccas is now the ruler of Macedonia?

SOCRATES: At any rate I hear that he is.

POLUS: And do you think that he is happy or miserable?

SOCRATES: I cannot say, Polus, for I have never had any acquaintance with him.

POLUS: And cannot you tell at once, and without having an acquaintance with him, whether a man is happy?

SOCRATES: Most certainly not.

POLUS: Then clearly, Socrates, you would say that you did not even know whether the great king was a happy man?

SOCRATES: And I should speak the truth; for I do not know how he stands in the matter of education and justice.

POLUS: What! and does all happiness consist in this?

SOCRATES: Yes, indeed, Polus, that is my doctrine; the men and women who are gentle and good are also happy, as I maintain, and the unjust and evil are miserable.

POLUS: Then, according to your doctrine, the said Archelaus is miserable?

SOCRATES: Yes, my friend, if he is wicked.

POLUS: That he is wicked I cannot deny; for he had no title at all to the throne which he now occupies, he being only the son of a woman who was the slave of Alcetas the brother of Perdiccas; he himself therefore in strict right was the slave of Alcetas; and if he had meant to do rightly he would have remained his slave, and then, according to your doctrine, he would have been happy. But now he is unspeakably miserable, for he has been guilty of the greatest crimes: in the first place he invited his uncle and master, Alcetas, to come to him, under the pretence that he would restore to him the throne which Perdiccas has usurped, and after entertaining him and his son Alexander, who was his own cousin, and nearly of an age with him, and making them drunk, he threw them into a waggon and carried them off by night, and slew them, and got both of them out of the way; and when he had done all this wickedness he never discovered that he was the most miserable of all men, and was very far from repenting: shall I tell you how he showed his remorse? he had a younger brother, a child of seven years old, who was the legitimate son of Perdiccas, and to him of right the kingdom belonged; Archelaus, however, had no mind to bring him up as he ought and restore the kingdom to him; that was not his notion of happiness; but not long afterwards he threw him into a well and drowned him, and declared to his mother Cleopatra that he had fallen in while running after a goose, and had been killed. And now as he is the greatest criminal of all the Macedonians, he may be supposed to be the most miserable and not the happiest of them, and I dare say that there are many Athenians, and you would be at the head of them, who would rather be any other Macedonian than Archelaus!

SOCRATES: I praised you at first, Polus, for being a rhetorician rather than a reasoner. And this, as I suppose, is the sort of argument with which you fancy that a child might refute me, and by which I stand refuted when I say that the unjust man is not happy. But, my good friend, where is the refutation? I cannot admit a word which you have been saying.

POLUS: That is because you will not; for you surely must think as I do.

SOCRATES: Not so, my simple friend, but because you will refute me after the manner which rhetoricians practise in courts of law. For there the one party think that they refute the other when they bring forward a number of witnesses of good repute in proof of their allegations, and their adversary has only a single one or none at all. But this kind of proof is of no value where truth is the aim; a man may often be sworn down by a multitude of false witnesses who have a great air of respectability. And in this argument nearly every one, Athenian and stranger alike, would be on your side, if you should bring witnesses in disproof of my statement;—you may, if you will, summon Nicias the son of Niceratus, and let his brothers, who gave the row of tripods which stand in the precincts of Dionysus, come with him; or you may summon Aristocrates, the son of Scellius, who is the giver of that famous offering which is at Delphi; summon, if you will, the whole house of Pericles, or any other great Athenian family whom you choose;—they will all agree with you: I only am left alone and cannot agree, for you do not convince me; although you produce many false witnesses against me, in the hope of depriving me of my inheritance, which is the truth. But I consider that nothing worth speaking of will have been effected by me unless I make you the one witness of my words; nor by you, unless you make me the one witness of yours; no matter about the rest of the world. For there are two ways of refutation, one which is yours and that of the world in general; but mine is of another sort—let us compare them, and see in what they differ. For, indeed, we are at issue about matters which to know is honourable and not to know disgraceful; to know or not to know happiness and misery—that is the chief of them. And what knowledge can be nobler? or what ignorance more disgraceful than this? And therefore I will begin by asking you whether you do not think that a man who is unjust and doing injustice can be happy, seeing that you think Archelaus unjust, and yet happy? May I assume this to be your opinion?

POLUS: Certainly.

SOCRATES: But I say that this is an impossibility—here is one point about which we are at issue:—very good. And do you mean to say also that if he meets with retribution and punishment he will still be happy?

POLUS: Certainly not; in that case he will be most miserable.

SOCRATES: On the other hand, if the unjust be not punished, then, according to you, he will be happy?

POLUS: Yes.

SOCRATES: But in my opinion, Polus, the unjust or doer of unjust actions is miserable in any case,—more miserable, however, if he be not punished and does not meet with retribution, and less miserable if he be punished and meets with retribution at the hands of gods and men.

POLUS: You are maintaining a strange doctrine, Socrates.

SOCRATES: I shall try to make you agree with me, O my friend, for as a friend I regard you. Then these are the points at issue between us—are they not? I was saying that to do is worse than to suffer injustice?

POLUS: Exactly so.

SOCRATES: And you said the opposite?

POLUS: Yes.

SOCRATES: I said also that the wicked are miserable, and you refuted me?

POLUS: By Zeus, I did.

SOCRATES: In your own opinion, Polus.

POLUS: Yes, and I rather suspect that I was in the right.

SOCRATES: You further said that the wrong-doer is happy if he be unpunished?

POLUS: Certainly.

SOCRATES: And I affirm that he is most miserable, and that those who are punished are less miserable—are you going to refute this proposition also?

POLUS: A proposition which is harder of refutation than the other, Socrates.

SOCRATES: Say rather, Polus, impossible; for who can refute the truth?

POLUS: What do you mean? If a man is detected in an unjust attempt to make himself a tyrant, and when detected is racked, mutilated, has his eyes burned out, and after having had all sorts of great injuries inflicted on him, and having seen his wife and children suffer the like, is at last impaled or tarred and burned alive, will he be happier than if he escape and become a tyrant, and continue all through life doing what he likes and holding the reins of government, the envy and admiration both of citizens and strangers? Is that the paradox which, as you say, cannot be refuted?

SOCRATES: There again, noble Polus, you are raising hobgoblins instead of refuting me; just now you were calling witnesses against me. But please to refresh my memory a little; did you say—'in an unjust attempt to make himself a tyrant'?

POLUS: Yes, I did.

SOCRATES: Then I say that neither of them will be happier than the other,—neither he who unjustly acquires a tyranny, nor he who suffers in the attempt, for of two miserables one cannot be the happier, but that he who escapes and becomes a tyrant is the more miserable of the two. Do you laugh, Polus? Well, this is a new kind of refutation,—when any one says anything, instead of refuting him to laugh at him.

POLUS: But do you not think, Socrates, that you have been sufficiently refuted, when you say that which no human being will allow? Ask the company.

SOCRATES: O Polus, I am not a public man, and only last year, when my tribe were serving as Prytanes, and it became my duty as their president to take the votes, there was a laugh at me, because I was unable to take them. And as I failed then, you must not ask me to count the suffrages of the company now; but if, as I was saying, you have no better argument than numbers, let me have a turn, and do you make trial of the sort of proof which, as I think, is required; for I shall produce one witness only of the truth of my words, and he is the person with whom I am arguing; his suffrage I know how to take; but with the many I have nothing to do, and do not even address myself to them. May I ask then whether you will answer in turn and have your words put to the proof? For I certainly think that I and you and every man do really believe, that to do is a greater evil than to suffer injustice: and not to be punished than to be punished.

POLUS: And I should say neither I, nor any man: would you yourself, for example, suffer rather than do injustice?

SOCRATES: Yes, and you, too; I or any man would.

POLUS: Quite the reverse; neither you, nor I, nor any man.

SOCRATES: But will you answer?

POLUS: To be sure, I will; for I am curious to hear what you can have to say.

SOCRATES: Tell me, then, and you will know, and let us suppose that I am beginning at the beginning: which of the two, Polus, in your opinion, is the worst?—to do injustice or to suffer?

POLUS: I should say that suffering was worst.

SOCRATES: And which is the greater disgrace?—Answer.

POLUS: To do.

SOCRATES: And the greater disgrace is the greater evil?

POLUS: Certainly not.

SOCRATES: I understand you to say, if I am not mistaken, that the honourable is not the same as the good, or the disgraceful as the evil?

POLUS: Certainly not.

SOCRATES: Let me ask a question of you: When you speak of beautiful things, such as bodies, colours, figures, sounds, institutions, do you not call them beautiful in reference to some standard: bodies, for example, are beautiful in proportion as they are useful, or as the sight of them gives pleasure to the spectators; can you give any other account of personal beauty?

POLUS: I cannot.

SOCRATES: And you would say of figures or colours generally that they were beautiful, either by reason of the pleasure which they give, or of their use, or of both?

POLUS: Yes, I should.

SOCRATES: And you would call sounds and music beautiful for the same reason?

POLUS: I should.

SOCRATES: Laws and institutions also have no beauty in them except in so far as they are useful or pleasant or both?

POLUS: I think not.

SOCRATES: And may not the same be said of the beauty of knowledge?

POLUS: To be sure, Socrates; and I very much approve of your measuring beauty by the standard of pleasure and utility.

SOCRATES: And deformity or disgrace may be equally measured by the opposite standard of pain and evil?

POLUS: Certainly.

SOCRATES: Then when of two beautiful things one exceeds in beauty, the measure of the excess is to be taken in one or both of these; that is to say, in pleasure or utility or both?

POLUS: Very true.

SOCRATES: And of two deformed things, that which exceeds in deformity or disgrace, exceeds either in pain or evil—must it not be so?

POLUS: Yes.

SOCRATES: But then again, what was the observation which you just now made, about doing and suffering wrong? Did you not say, that suffering wrong was more evil, and doing wrong more disgraceful?

POLUS: I did.

SOCRATES: Then, if doing wrong is more disgraceful than suffering, the more disgraceful must be more painful and must exceed in pain or in evil or both: does not that also follow?

POLUS: Of course.

SOCRATES: First, then, let us consider whether the doing of injustice exceeds the suffering in the consequent pain: Do the injurers suffer more than the injured?

POLUS: No, Socrates; certainly not.

SOCRATES: Then they do not exceed in pain?

POLUS: No.

SOCRATES: But if not in pain, then not in both?

POLUS: Certainly not.

SOCRATES: Then they can only exceed in the other?

POLUS: Yes.

SOCRATES: That is to say, in evil?

POLUS: True.

SOCRATES: Then doing injustice will have an excess of evil, and will therefore be a greater evil than suffering injustice?

POLUS: Clearly.

SOCRATES: But have not you and the world already agreed that to do injustice is more disgraceful than to suffer?

POLUS: Yes.

SOCRATES: And that is now discovered to be more evil?

POLUS: True.

SOCRATES: And would you prefer a greater evil or a greater dishonour to a less one? Answer, Polus, and fear not; for you will come to no harm if you nobly resign yourself into the healing hand of the argument as to a physician without shrinking, and either say 'Yes' or 'No' to me.

POLUS: I should say 'No.'

SOCRATES: Would any other man prefer a greater to a less evil?

POLUS: No, not according to this way of putting the case, Socrates.

SOCRATES: Then I said truly, Polus, that neither you, nor I, nor any man, would rather do than suffer injustice; for to do injustice is the greater evil of the two.

POLUS: That is the conclusion.

SOCRATES: You see, Polus, when you compare the two kinds of refutations, how unlike they are. All men, with the exception of myself, are of your way of thinking; but your single assent and witness are enough for me,—I have no need of any other, I take your suffrage, and am regardless of the rest. Enough of this, and now let us proceed to the next question; which is, Whether the greatest of evils to a guilty man is to suffer punishment, as you supposed, or whether to escape punishment is not a greater evil, as I supposed. Consider:—You would say that to suffer punishment is another name for being justly corrected when you do wrong?

POLUS: I should.

SOCRATES: And would you not allow that all just things are honourable in so far as they are just? Please to reflect, and tell me your opinion.

POLUS: Yes, Socrates, I think that they are.

SOCRATES: Consider again:—Where there is an agent, must there not also be a patient?

POLUS: I should say so.

SOCRATES: And will not the patient suffer that which the agent does, and will not the suffering have the quality of the action? I mean, for example, that if a man strikes, there must be something which is stricken?

POLUS: Yes.

SOCRATES: And if the striker strikes violently or quickly, that which is struck will be struck violently or quickly?

POLUS: True.

SOCRATES: And the suffering to him who is stricken is of the same nature as the act of him who strikes?

POLUS: Yes.

SOCRATES: And if a man burns, there is something which is burned?

POLUS: Certainly.

SOCRATES: And if he burns in excess or so as to cause pain, the thing burned will be burned in the same way?

POLUS: Truly.

SOCRATES: And if he cuts, the same argument holds—there will be something cut?

POLUS: Yes.

SOCRATES: And if the cutting be great or deep or such as will cause pain, the cut will be of the same nature?

POLUS: That is evident.

SOCRATES: Then you would agree generally to the universal proposition which I was just now asserting: that the affection of the patient answers to the affection of the agent?

POLUS: I agree.

SOCRATES: Then, as this is admitted, let me ask whether being punished is suffering or acting?

POLUS: Suffering, Socrates; there can be no doubt of that.

SOCRATES: And suffering implies an agent?

POLUS: Certainly, Socrates; and he is the punisher.

SOCRATES: And he who punishes rightly, punishes justly?

POLUS: Yes.

SOCRATES: And therefore he acts justly?

POLUS: Justly.

SOCRATES: Then he who is punished and suffers retribution, suffers justly?

POLUS: That is evident.

SOCRATES: And that which is just has been admitted to be honourable?

POLUS: Certainly.

SOCRATES: Then the punisher does what is honourable, and the punished suffers what is honourable?

POLUS: True.

SOCRATES: And if what is honourable, then what is good, for the honourable is either pleasant or useful?

POLUS: Certainly.

SOCRATES: Then he who is punished suffers what is good?

POLUS: That is true.

SOCRATES: Then he is benefited?

POLUS: Yes.

SOCRATES: Do I understand you to mean what I mean by the term 'benefited'? I mean, that if he be justly punished his soul is improved.

POLUS: Surely.

SOCRATES: Then he who is punished is delivered from the evil of his soul?

POLUS: Yes.

SOCRATES: And is he not then delivered from the greatest evil? Look at the matter in this way:—In respect of a man's estate, do you see any greater evil than poverty?

POLUS: There is no greater evil.

SOCRATES: Again, in a man's bodily frame, you would say that the evil is weakness and disease and deformity?

POLUS: I should.

SOCRATES: And do you not imagine that the soul likewise has some evil of her own?

POLUS: Of course.

SOCRATES: And this you would call injustice and ignorance and cowardice, and the like?

POLUS: Certainly.

SOCRATES: So then, in mind, body, and estate, which are three, you have pointed out three corresponding evils—injustice, disease, poverty?

POLUS: True.

SOCRATES: And which of the evils is the most disgraceful?—Is not the most disgraceful of them injustice, and in general the evil of the soul?

POLUS: By far the most.

SOCRATES: And if the most disgraceful, then also the worst?

POLUS: What do you mean, Socrates?

SOCRATES: I mean to say, that is most disgraceful has been already admitted to be most painful or hurtful, or both.

POLUS: Certainly.

SOCRATES: And now injustice and all evil in the soul has been admitted by us to be most disgraceful?

POLUS: It has been admitted.

SOCRATES: And most disgraceful either because most painful and causing excessive pain, or most hurtful, or both?

POLUS: Certainly.

SOCRATES: And therefore to be unjust and intemperate, and cowardly and ignorant, is more painful than to be poor and sick?

POLUS: Nay, Socrates; the painfulness does not appear to me to follow from your premises.

SOCRATES: Then, if, as you would argue, not more painful, the evil of the soul is of all evils the most disgraceful; and the excess of disgrace must be caused by some preternatural greatness, or extraordinary hurtfulness of the evil.

POLUS: Clearly.

SOCRATES: And that which exceeds most in hurtfulness will be the greatest of evils?

POLUS: Yes.

SOCRATES: Then injustice and intemperance, and in general the depravity of the soul, are the greatest of evils?

POLUS: That is evident.

SOCRATES: Now, what art is there which delivers us from poverty? Does not the art of making money?

POLUS: Yes.

SOCRATES: And what art frees us from disease? Does not the art of medicine?

POLUS: Very true.

SOCRATES: And what from vice and injustice? If you are not able to answer at once, ask yourself whither we go with the sick, and to whom we take them.

POLUS: To the physicians, Socrates.

SOCRATES: And to whom do we go with the unjust and intemperate?

POLUS: To the judges, you mean.

SOCRATES: —Who are to punish them?

POLUS: Yes.

SOCRATES: And do not those who rightly punish others, punish them in accordance with a certain rule of justice?

POLUS: Clearly.

SOCRATES: Then the art of money-making frees a man from poverty; medicine from disease; and justice from intemperance and injustice?

POLUS: That is evident.

SOCRATES: Which, then, is the best of these three?

POLUS: Will you enumerate them?

SOCRATES: Money-making, medicine, and justice.

POLUS: Justice, Socrates, far excels the two others.

SOCRATES: And justice, if the best, gives the greatest pleasure or advantage or both?

POLUS: Yes.

SOCRATES: But is the being healed a pleasant thing, and are those who are being healed pleased?

POLUS: I think not.

SOCRATES: A useful thing, then?

POLUS: Yes.

SOCRATES: Yes, because the patient is delivered from a great evil; and this is the advantage of enduring the pain—that you get well?

POLUS: Certainly.

SOCRATES: And would he be the happier man in his bodily condition, who is healed, or who never was out of health?

POLUS: Clearly he who was never out of health.

SOCRATES: Yes; for happiness surely does not consist in being delivered from evils, but in never having had them.

POLUS: True.

SOCRATES: And suppose the case of two persons who have some evil in their bodies, and that one of them is healed and delivered from evil, and another is not healed, but retains the evil—which of them is the most miserable?

POLUS: Clearly he who is not healed.

SOCRATES: And was not punishment said by us to be a deliverance from the greatest of evils, which is vice?

POLUS: True.

SOCRATES: And justice punishes us, and makes us more just, and is the medicine of our vice?

POLUS: True.

SOCRATES: He, then, has the first place in the scale of happiness who has never had vice in his soul; for this has been shown to be the greatest of evils.

POLUS: Clearly.

SOCRATES: And he has the second place, who is delivered from vice?

POLUS: True.

SOCRATES: That is to say, he who receives admonition and rebuke and punishment?

POLUS: Yes.

SOCRATES: Then he lives worst, who, having been unjust, has no deliverance from injustice?

POLUS: Certainly.

SOCRATES: That is, he lives worst who commits the greatest crimes, and who, being the most unjust of men, succeeds in escaping rebuke or correction or punishment; and this, as you say, has been accomplished by Archelaus and other tyrants and rhetoricians and potentates? (Compare Republic.)

POLUS: True.

SOCRATES: May not their way of proceeding, my friend, be compared to the conduct of a person who is afflicted with the worst of diseases and yet contrives not to pay the penalty to the physician for his sins against his constitution, and will not be cured, because, like a child, he is afraid of the pain of being burned or cut:—Is not that a parallel case?

POLUS: Yes, truly.

SOCRATES: He would seem as if he did not know the nature of health and bodily vigour; and if we are right, Polus, in our previous conclusions, they are in a like case who strive to evade justice, which they see to be painful, but are blind to the advantage which ensues from it, not knowing how far more miserable a companion a diseased soul is than a diseased body; a soul, I say, which is corrupt and unrighteous and unholy. And hence they do all that they can to avoid punishment and to avoid being released from the greatest of evils; they provide themselves with money and friends, and cultivate to the utmost their powers of persuasion. But if we, Polus, are right, do you see what follows, or shall we draw out the consequences in form?

POLUS: If you please.

SOCRATES: Is it not a fact that injustice, and the doing of injustice, is the greatest of evils?

POLUS: That is quite clear.

SOCRATES: And further, that to suffer punishment is the way to be released from this evil?

POLUS: True.

SOCRATES: And not to suffer, is to perpetuate the evil?

POLUS: Yes.

SOCRATES: To do wrong, then, is second only in the scale of evils; but to do wrong and not to be punished, is first and greatest of all?

POLUS: That is true.

SOCRATES: Well, and was not this the point in dispute, my friend? You deemed Archelaus happy, because he was a very great criminal and unpunished: I, on the other hand, maintained that he or any other who like him has done wrong and has not been punished, is, and ought to be, the most miserable of all men; and that the doer of injustice is more miserable than the sufferer; and he who escapes punishment, more miserable than he who suffers.—Was not that what I said?

POLUS: Yes.

SOCRATES: And it has been proved to be true?

POLUS: Certainly.

SOCRATES: Well, Polus, but if this is true, where is the great use of rhetoric? If we admit what has been just now said, every man ought in every way to guard himself against doing wrong, for he will thereby suffer great evil?

POLUS: True.

SOCRATES: And if he, or any one about whom he cares, does wrong, he ought of his own accord to go where he will be immediately punished; he will run to the judge, as he would to the physician, in order that the disease of injustice may not be rendered chronic and become the incurable cancer of the soul; must we not allow this consequence, Polus, if our former admissions are to stand:—is any other inference consistent with them?

POLUS: To that, Socrates, there can be but one answer.

SOCRATES: Then rhetoric is of no use to us, Polus, in helping a man to excuse his own injustice, that of his parents or friends, or children or country; but may be of use to any one who holds that instead of excusing he ought to accuse—himself above all, and in the next degree his family or any of his friends who may be doing wrong; he should bring to light the iniquity and not conceal it, that so the wrong-doer may suffer and be made whole; and he should even force himself and others not to shrink, but with closed eyes like brave men to let the physician operate with knife or searing iron, not regarding the pain, in the hope of attaining the good and the honourable; let him who has done things worthy of stripes, allow himself to be scourged, if of bonds, to be bound, if of a fine, to be fined, if of exile, to be exiled, if of death, to die, himself being the first to accuse himself and his own relations, and using rhetoric to this end, that his and their unjust actions may be made manifest, and that they themselves may be delivered from injustice, which is the greatest evil. Then, Polus, rhetoric would indeed be useful. Do you say 'Yes' or 'No' to that?

POLUS: To me, Socrates, what you are saying appears very strange, though probably in agreement with your premises.

SOCRATES: Is not this the conclusion, if the premises are not disproven?

POLUS: Yes; it certainly is.

SOCRATES: And from the opposite point of view, if indeed it be our duty to harm another, whether an enemy or not—I except the case of self-defence—then I have to be upon my guard—but if my enemy injures a third person, then in every sort of way, by word as well as deed, I should try to prevent his being punished, or appearing before the judge; and if he appears, I should contrive that he should escape, and not suffer punishment: if he has stolen a sum of money, let him keep what he has stolen and spend it on him and his, regardless of religion and justice; and if he have done things worthy of death, let him not die, but rather be immortal in his wickedness; or, if this is not possible, let him at any rate be allowed to live as long as he can. For such purposes, Polus, rhetoric may be useful, but is of small if of any use to him who is not intending to commit injustice; at least, there was no such use discovered by us in the previous discussion.

CALLICLES: Tell me, Chaerephon, is Socrates in earnest, or is he joking?

CHAEREPHON: I should say, Callicles, that he is in most profound earnest; but you may well ask him.

CALLICLES: By the gods, and I will. Tell me, Socrates, are you in earnest, or only in jest? For if you are in earnest, and what you say is true, is not the whole of human life turned upside down; and are we not doing, as would appear, in everything the opposite of what we ought to be doing?

SOCRATES: O Callicles, if there were not some community of feelings among mankind, however varying in different persons—I mean to say, if every man's feelings were peculiar to himself and were not shared by the rest of his species—I do not see how we could ever communicate our impressions to one another. I make this remark because I perceive that you and I have a common feeling. For we are lovers both, and both of us have two loves apiece:—I am the lover of Alcibiades, the son of Cleinias, and of philosophy; and you of the Athenian Demus, and of Demus the son of Pyrilampes. Now, I observe that you, with all your cleverness, do not venture to contradict your favourite in any word or opinion of his; but as he changes you change, backwards and forwards. When the Athenian Demus denies anything that you are saying in the assembly, you go over to his opinion; and you do the same with Demus, the fair young son of Pyrilampes. For you have not the power to resist the words and ideas of your loves; and if a person were to express surprise at the strangeness of what you say from time to time when under their influence, you would probably reply to him, if you were honest, that you cannot help saying what your loves say unless they are prevented; and that you can only be silent when they are. Now you must understand that my words are an echo too, and therefore you need not wonder at me; but if you want to silence me, silence philosophy, who is my love, for she is always telling me what I am now telling you, my friend; neither is she capricious like my other love, for the son of Cleinias says one thing to-day and another thing to-morrow, but philosophy is always true. She is the teacher at whose words you are now wondering, and you have heard her yourself. Her you must refute, and either show, as I was saying, that to do injustice and to escape punishment is not the worst of all evils; or, if you leave her word unrefuted, by the dog the god of Egypt, I declare, O Callicles, that Callicles will never be at one with himself, but that his whole life will be a discord. And yet, my friend, I would rather that my lyre should be inharmonious, and that there should be no music in the chorus which I provided; aye, or that the whole world should be at odds with me, and oppose me, rather than that I myself should be at odds with myself, and contradict myself.

CALLICLES: O Socrates, you are a regular declaimer, and seem to be running riot in the argument. And now you are declaiming in this way because Polus has fallen into the same error himself of which he accused Gorgias:—for he said that when Gorgias was asked by you, whether, if some one came to him who wanted to learn rhetoric, and did not know justice, he would teach him justice, Gorgias in his modesty replied that he would, because he thought that mankind in general would be displeased if he answered 'No'; and then in consequence of this admission, Gorgias was compelled to contradict himself, that being just the sort of thing in which you delight. Whereupon Polus laughed at you deservedly, as I think; but now he has himself fallen into the same trap. I cannot say very much for his wit when he conceded to you that to do is more dishonourable than to suffer injustice, for this was the admission which led to his being entangled by you; and because he was too modest to say what he thought, he had his mouth stopped. For the truth is, Socrates, that you, who pretend to be engaged in the pursuit of truth, are appealing now to the popular and vulgar notions of right, which are not natural, but only conventional. Convention and nature are generally at variance with one another: and hence, if a person is too modest to say what he thinks, he is compelled to contradict himself; and you, in your ingenuity perceiving the advantage to be thereby gained, slyly ask of him who is arguing conventionally a question which is to be determined by the rule of nature; and if he is talking of the rule of nature, you slip away to custom: as, for instance, you did in this very discussion about doing and suffering injustice. When Polus was speaking of the conventionally dishonourable, you assailed him from the point of view of nature; for by the rule of nature, to suffer injustice is the greater disgrace because the greater evil; but conventionally, to do evil is the more disgraceful. For the suffering of injustice is not the part of a man, but of a slave, who indeed had better die than live; since when he is wronged and trampled upon, he is unable to help himself, or any other about whom he cares. The reason, as I conceive, is that the makers of laws are the majority who are weak; and they make laws and distribute praises and censures with a view to themselves and to their own interests; and they terrify the stronger sort of men, and those who are able to get the better of them, in order that they may not get the better of them; and they say, that dishonesty is shameful and unjust; meaning, by the word injustice, the desire of a man to have more than his neighbours; for knowing their own inferiority, I suspect that they are too glad of equality. And therefore the endeavour to have more than the many, is conventionally said to be shameful and unjust, and is called injustice (compare Republic), whereas nature herself intimates that it is just for the better to have more than the worse, the more powerful than the weaker; and in many ways she shows, among men as well as among animals, and indeed among whole cities and races, that justice consists in the superior ruling over and having more than the inferior. For on what principle of justice did Xerxes invade Hellas, or his father the Scythians? (not to speak of numberless other examples). Nay, but these are the men who act according to nature; yes, by Heaven, and according to the law of nature: not, perhaps, according to that artificial law, which we invent and impose upon our fellows, of whom we take the best and strongest from their youth upwards, and tame them like young lions,—charming them with the sound of the voice, and saying to them, that with equality they must be content, and that the equal is the honourable and the just. But if there were a man who had sufficient force, he would shake off and break through, and escape from all this; he would trample under foot all our formulas and spells and charms, and all our laws which are against nature: the slave would rise in rebellion and be lord over us, and the light of natural justice would shine forth. And this I take to be the sentiment of Pindar, when he says in his poem, that

'Law is the king of all, of mortals as well as of immortals;'

this, as he says,

'Makes might to be right, doing violence with highest hand; as I infer from the deeds of Heracles, for without buying them—' (Fragm. Incert. 151 (Bockh).) —I do not remember the exact words, but the meaning is, that without buying them, and without their being given to him, he carried off the oxen of Geryon, according to the law of natural right, and that the oxen and other possessions of the weaker and inferior properly belong to the stronger and superior. And this is true, as you may ascertain, if you will leave philosophy and go on to higher things: for philosophy, Socrates, if pursued in moderation and at the proper age, is an elegant accomplishment, but too much philosophy is the ruin of human life. Even if a man has good parts, still, if he carries philosophy into later life, he is necessarily ignorant of all those things which a gentleman and a person of honour ought to know; he is inexperienced in the laws of the State, and in the language which ought to be used in the dealings of man with man, whether private or public, and utterly ignorant of the pleasures and desires of mankind and of human character in general. And people of this sort, when they betake themselves to politics or business, are as ridiculous as I imagine the politicians to be, when they make their appearance in the arena of philosophy. For, as Euripides says,

'Every man shines in that and pursues that, and devotes the greatest portion of the day to that in which he most excels,' (Antiope, fragm. 20 (Dindorf).)

but anything in which he is inferior, he avoids and depreciates, and praises the opposite from partiality to himself, and because he thinks that he will thus praise himself. The true principle is to unite them. Philosophy, as a part of education, is an excellent thing, and there is no disgrace to a man while he is young in pursuing such a study; but when he is more advanced in years, the thing becomes ridiculous, and I feel towards philosophers as I do towards those who lisp and imitate children. For I love to see a little child, who is not of an age to speak plainly, lisping at his play; there is an appearance of grace and freedom in his utterance, which is natural to his childish years. But when I hear some small creature carefully articulating its words, I am offended; the sound is disagreeable, and has to my ears the twang of slavery. So when I hear a man lisping, or see him playing like a child, his behaviour appears to me ridiculous and unmanly and worthy of stripes. And I have the same feeling about students of philosophy; when I see a youth thus engaged,—the study appears to me to be in character, and becoming a man of liberal education, and him who neglects philosophy I regard as an inferior man, who will never aspire to anything great or noble. But if I see him continuing the study in later life, and not leaving off, I should like to beat him, Socrates; for, as I was saying, such a one, even though he have good natural parts, becomes effeminate. He flies from the busy centre and the market-place, in which, as the poet says, men become distinguished; he creeps into a corner for the rest of his life, and talks in a whisper with three or four admiring youths, but never speaks out like a freeman in a satisfactory manner. Now I, Socrates, am very well inclined towards you, and my feeling may be compared with that of Zethus towards Amphion, in the play of Euripides, whom I was mentioning just now: for I am disposed to say to you much what Zethus said to his brother, that you, Socrates, are careless about the things of which you ought to be careful; and that you

'Who have a soul so noble, are remarkable for a puerile exterior; Neither in a court of justice could you state a case, or give any reason or proof, Or offer valiant counsel on another's behalf.'

And you must not be offended, my dear Socrates, for I am speaking out of good-will towards you, if I ask whether you are not ashamed of being thus defenceless; which I affirm to be the condition not of you only but of all those who will carry the study of philosophy too far. For suppose that some one were to take you, or any one of your sort, off to prison, declaring that you had done wrong when you had done no wrong, you must allow that you would not know what to do:—there you would stand giddy and gaping, and not having a word to say; and when you went up before the Court, even if the accuser were a poor creature and not good for much, you would die if he were disposed to claim the penalty of death. And yet, Socrates, what is the value of

'An art which converts a man of sense into a fool,'

who is helpless, and has no power to save either himself or others, when he is in the greatest danger and is going to be despoiled by his enemies of all his goods, and has to live, simply deprived of his rights of citizenship?—he being a man who, if I may use the expression, may be boxed on the ears with impunity. Then, my good friend, take my advice, and refute no more:

'Learn the philosophy of business, and acquire the reputation of wisdom. But leave to others these niceties,'

whether they are to be described as follies or absurdities:

'For they will only Give you poverty for the inmate of your dwelling.'

Cease, then, emulating these paltry splitters of words, and emulate only the man of substance and honour, who is well to do.

SOCRATES: If my soul, Callicles, were made of gold, should I not rejoice to discover one of those stones with which they test gold, and the very best possible one to which I might bring my soul; and if the stone and I agreed in approving of her training, then I should know that I was in a satisfactory state, and that no other test was needed by me.

CALLICLES: What is your meaning, Socrates?

SOCRATES: I will tell you; I think that I have found in you the desired touchstone.

CALLICLES: Why?

SOCRATES: Because I am sure that if you agree with me in any of the opinions which my soul forms, I have at last found the truth indeed. For I consider that if a man is to make a complete trial of the good or evil of the soul, he ought to have three qualities—knowledge, good-will, outspokenness, which are all possessed by you. Many whom I meet are unable to make trial of me, because they are not wise as you are; others are wise, but they will not tell me the truth, because they have not the same interest in me which you have; and these two strangers, Gorgias and Polus, are undoubtedly wise men and my very good friends, but they are not outspoken enough, and they are too modest. Why, their modesty is so great that they are driven to contradict themselves, first one and then the other of them, in the face of a large company, on matters of the highest moment. But you have all the qualities in which these others are deficient, having received an excellent education; to this many

Athenians can testify. And you are my friend. Shall I tell you why I think so? I know that you, Callicles, and Tisander of Aphidnae, and Andron the son of Androtion, and Nausicydes of the deme of Cholarges, studied together: there were four of you, and I once heard you advising with one another as to the extent to which the pursuit of philosophy should be carried, and, as I know, you came to the conclusion that the study should not be pushed too much into detail. You were cautioning one another not to be overwise; you were afraid that too much wisdom might unconsciously to yourselves be the ruin of you. And now when I hear you giving the same advice to me which you then gave to your most intimate friends, I have a sufficient evidence of your real good-will to me. And of the frankness of your nature and freedom from modesty I am assured by yourself, and the assurance is confirmed by your last speech. Well then, the inference in the present case clearly is, that if you agree with me in an argument about any point, that point will have been sufficiently tested by us, and will not require to be submitted to any further test. For you could not have agreed with me, either from lack of knowledge or from superfluity of modesty, nor yet from a desire to deceive me, for you are my friend, as you tell me yourself. And therefore when you and I are agreed, the result will be the attainment of perfect truth. Now there is no nobler enquiry, Callicles, than that which you censure me for making,—What ought the character of a man to be, and what his pursuits, and how far is he to go, both in maturer years and in youth? For be assured that if I err in my own conduct I do not err intentionally, but from ignorance. Do not then desist from advising me, now that you have begun, until I have learned clearly what this is which I am to practise, and how I may acquire it. And if you find me assenting to your words, and hereafter not doing that to which I assented, call me 'dolt,' and deem me unworthy of receiving further instruction. Once more, then, tell me what you and Pindar mean by natural justice: Do you not mean that the superior should take the property of the inferior by force; that the better should rule the worse, the noble have more than the mean? Am I not right in my recollection?

CALLICLES: Yes; that is what I was saying, and so I still aver.

SOCRATES: And do you mean by the better the same as the superior? for I could not make out what you were saying at the time—whether you meant by the superior the stronger, and that the weaker must obey the stronger, as you seemed to imply when you said that great cities attack small ones in accordance with natural right, because they are superior and stronger, as though the superior and stronger and better were the same; or whether the better may be also the inferior and weaker, and the superior the worse, or whether better is to be defined in the same way as superior:—this is the point which I want to have cleared up. Are the superior and better and stronger the same or different?

CALLICLES: I say unequivocally that they are the same.

SOCRATES: Then the many are by nature superior to the one, against whom, as you were saying, they make the laws?

CALLICLES: Certainly.

SOCRATES: Then the laws of the many are the laws of the superior?

CALLICLES: Very true.

SOCRATES: Then they are the laws of the better; for the superior class are far better, as you were saying?

CALLICLES: Yes.

SOCRATES: And since they are superior, the laws which are made by them are by nature good?

CALLICLES: Yes.

SOCRATES: And are not the many of opinion, as you were lately saying, that justice is equality, and that to do is more disgraceful than to suffer injustice?—is that so or not? Answer, Callicles, and let no modesty be found to come in the way; do the many think, or do they not think thus?—I must beg of you to answer, in order that if you agree with me I may fortify myself by the assent of so competent an authority.

CALLICLES: Yes; the opinion of the many is what you say.

SOCRATES: Then not only custom but nature also affirms that to do is more disgraceful than to suffer injustice, and that justice is equality; so that you seem to have been wrong in your former assertion, when accusing me you said that nature and custom are opposed, and that I, knowing this, was dishonestly playing between them, appealing to custom when the argument is about nature, and to nature when the argument is about custom?

CALLICLES: This man will never cease talking nonsense. At your age, Socrates, are you not ashamed to be catching at words and chuckling over some verbal slip? do you not see—have I not told you already, that by superior I mean better: do you imagine me to say, that if a rabble of slaves and nondescripts, who are of no use except perhaps for their physical strength, get together, their ipsissima verba are laws?

SOCRATES: Ho! my philosopher, is that your line?

CALLICLES: Certainly.

SOCRATES: I was thinking, Callicles, that something of the kind must have been in your mind, and that is why I repeated the question,—What is the superior? I wanted to know clearly what you meant; for you surely do not think that two men are better than one, or that your slaves are better than you because they are stronger? Then please to begin again, and tell me who the better are, if they are not the stronger; and I will ask you, great Sir, to be a little milder in your instructions, or I shall have to run away from you.

CALLICLES: You are ironical.

SOCRATES: No, by the hero Zethus, Callicles, by whose aid you were just now saying many ironical things against me, I am not:—tell me, then, whom you mean, by the better?

CALLICLES: I mean the more excellent.

SOCRATES: Do you not see that you are yourself using words which have no meaning and that you are explaining nothing?—will you tell me whether you mean by the better and superior the wiser, or if not, whom?

CALLICLES: Most assuredly, I do mean the wiser.

SOCRATES: Then according to you, one wise man may often be superior to ten thousand fools, and he ought to rule them, and they ought to be his subjects, and he ought to have more than they should. This is what I believe that you mean (and you must not suppose that I am word-catching), if you allow that the one is superior to the ten thousand?

CALLICLES: Yes; that is what I mean, and that is what I conceive to be natural justice—that the better and wiser should rule and have more than the inferior.

SOCRATES: Stop there, and let me ask you what you would say in this case: Let us suppose that we are all together as we are now; there are several of us, and we have a large common store of meats and drinks, and there are all sorts of persons in our company having various degrees of strength and weakness, and one of us, being a physician, is wiser in the matter of food than all the rest, and he is probably stronger than some and not so strong as others of us—will he not, being wiser, be also better than we are, and our superior in this matter of food?

CALLICLES: Certainly.

SOCRATES: Either, then, he will have a larger share of the meats and drinks, because he is better, or he will have the distribution of all of them by reason of his authority, but he will not expend or make use of a larger share of them on his own person, or if he does, he will be punished;—his share will exceed that of some, and be less than that of others, and if he be the weakest of all, he being the best of all will have the smallest share of all, Callicles:—am I not right, my friend?

CALLICLES: You talk about meats and drinks and physicians and other nonsense; I am not speaking of them.

SOCRATES: Well, but do you admit that the wiser is the better? Answer 'Yes' or 'No.'

CALLICLES: Yes.

SOCRATES: And ought not the better to have a larger share?

CALLICLES: Not of meats and drinks.

SOCRATES: I understand: then, perhaps, of coats—the skilfullest weaver ought to have the largest coat, and the greatest number of them, and go about clothed in the best and finest of them?

CALLICLES: Fudge about coats!

SOCRATES: Then the skilfullest and best in making shoes ought to have the advantage in shoes; the shoemaker, clearly, should walk about in the largest shoes, and have the greatest number of them?

CALLICLES: Fudge about shoes! What nonsense are you talking?

SOCRATES: Or, if this is not your meaning, perhaps you would say that the wise and good and true husbandman should actually have a larger share of seeds, and have as much seed as possible for his own land?

CALLICLES: How you go on, always talking in the same way, Socrates!

SOCRATES: Yes, Callicles, and also about the same things.

CALLICLES: Yes, by the Gods, you are literally always talking of cobblers and fullers and cooks and doctors, as if this had to do with our argument.

SOCRATES: But why will you not tell me in what a man must be superior and wiser in order to claim a larger share; will you neither accept a suggestion, nor offer one?

CALLICLES: I have already told you. In the first place, I mean by superiors not cobblers or cooks, but wise politicians who understand the administration of a state, and who are not only wise, but also valiant and able to carry out their designs, and not the men to faint from want of soul.

SOCRATES: See now, most excellent Callicles, how different my charge against you is from that which you bring against me, for you reproach me with always saying the same; but I reproach you with never saying the same about the same things, for at one time you were defining the better and the superior to be the stronger, then again as the wiser, and now you bring forward a new notion; the superior and the better are now declared by you to be the more courageous: I wish, my good friend, that you would tell me, once for all, whom you affirm to be the better and superior, and in what they are better?

CALLICLES: I have already told you that I mean those who are wise and courageous in the administration of a state—they ought to be the rulers of their states, and justice consists in their having more than their subjects.

SOCRATES: But whether rulers or subjects will they or will they not have more than themselves, my friend?

CALLICLES: What do you mean?

SOCRATES: I mean that every man is his own ruler; but perhaps you think that there is no necessity for him to rule himself; he is only required to rule others?

CALLICLES: What do you mean by his 'ruling over himself'?

SOCRATES: A simple thing enough; just what is commonly said, that a man should be temperate and master of himself, and ruler of his own pleasures and passions.

CALLICLES: What innocence! you mean those fools,—the temperate?

SOCRATES: Certainly:—any one may know that to be my meaning.

CALLICLES: Quite so, Socrates; and they are really fools, for how can a man be happy who is the servant of anything? On the contrary, I plainly assert, that he who would truly live ought to allow his desires to wax to the uttermost, and not to chastise them; but when they have grown to their greatest he should have courage and intelligence to minister to them and to satisfy all his longings. And this I affirm to be natural justice and nobility. To this however the many cannot attain; and they blame the strong man because they are ashamed of their own weakness, which they desire to conceal, and hence they say that intemperance is base. As I have remarked already, they enslave the nobler natures, and being unable to satisfy their pleasures, they praise temperance and justice out of their own cowardice. For if a man had been originally the son of a king, or had a nature capable of acquiring an empire or a tyranny or sovereignty, what could be more truly base or evil than temperance—to a man like him, I say, who might freely be enjoying every good, and has no one to stand in his way, and yet has admitted custom and reason and the opinion of other men to be lords over him?—must not he be in a miserable plight whom the reputation of justice and temperance hinders from giving more to his friends than to his enemies, even though he be a ruler in his city? Nay, Socrates, for you profess to be a votary of the truth, and the truth is this:—that luxury and intemperance and licence, if they be provided with means, are virtue and happiness—all the rest is a mere bauble, agreements contrary to nature, foolish talk of men, nothing worth. (Compare Republic.)

SOCRATES: There is a noble freedom, Callicles, in your way of approaching the argument; for what you say is what the rest of the world think, but do not like to say. And I must beg of you to persevere, that the true rule of human life may become manifest. Tell me, then:—you say, do you not, that in the rightly-developed man the passions ought not to be controlled, but that we should let them grow to the utmost and somehow or other satisfy them, and that this is virtue?

CALLICLES: Yes; I do.

SOCRATES: Then those who want nothing are not truly said to be happy?

CALLICLES: No indeed, for then stones and dead men would be the happiest of all.

SOCRATES: But surely life according to your view is an awful thing; and indeed I think that Euripides may have been right in saying,

'Who knows if life be not death and death life;'

and that we are very likely dead; I have heard a philosopher say that at this moment we are actually dead, and that the body (soma) is our tomb (sema (compare Phaedr.)), and that the part of the soul which is the seat of the desires is liable to be tossed about by words and blown up and down; and some ingenious person, probably a Sicilian or an Italian, playing with the word, invented a tale in which he called the soul—because of its believing and make-believe nature—a vessel (An untranslatable pun,—dia to pithanon te kai pistikon onomase pithon.), and the ignorant he called the uninitiated or leaky, and the place in the souls of the uninitiated in which the desires are seated, being the intemperate and incontinent part, he compared to a vessel full of holes, because it can never be satisfied. He is not of your way of thinking, Callicles, for he declares, that of all the souls in Hades, meaning the invisible world (aeides), these uninitiated or leaky persons are the most miserable, and that they pour water into a vessel which is full of holes out of a colander which is similarly perforated. The colander, as my informer assures me, is the soul, and the soul which he compares to a colander is the soul of the ignorant, which is likewise full of holes, and therefore incontinent, owing to a bad memory and want of faith. These notions are strange enough, but they show the principle which, if I can, I would fain prove to you; that you should change your mind, and, instead of the intemperate and insatiate life, choose that which is orderly and sufficient and has a due provision for daily needs. Do I make any impression on you, and are you coming over to the opinion that the orderly are happier than the intemperate? Or do I fail to persuade you, and, however many tales I rehearse to you, do you continue of the same opinion still?

CALLICLES: The latter, Socrates, is more like the truth.

SOCRATES: Well, I will tell you another image, which comes out of the same school:—Let me request you to consider how far you would accept this as an account of the two lives of the temperate and intemperate in a figure:—There are two men, both of whom have a number of casks; the one man has his casks sound and full, one of wine, another of honey, and a third of milk, besides others filled with other liquids, and the streams which fill them are few and scanty, and he can only obtain them with a great deal of toil and difficulty; but when his casks are once filled he has no need to feed them any more, and has no further trouble with them or care about them. The other, in like manner, can procure streams, though not without difficulty; but his vessels are leaky and unsound, and night and day he is compelled to be filling them, and if he pauses for a moment, he is in an agony of pain. Such are their respective lives:—And now would you say that the life of the intemperate is happier than that of the temperate? Do I not convince you that the opposite is the truth?

CALLICLES: You do not convince me, Socrates, for the one who has filled himself has no longer any pleasure left; and this, as I was just now saying, is the life of a stone: he has neither joy nor sorrow after he is once filled; but the pleasure depends on the superabundance of the influx.

SOCRATES: But the more you pour in, the greater the waste; and the holes must be large for the liquid to escape.

CALLICLES: Certainly.

SOCRATES: The life which you are now depicting is not that of a dead man, or of a stone, but of a cormorant; you mean that he is to be hungering and eating?

CALLICLES: Yes.

SOCRATES: And he is to be thirsting and drinking?

CALLICLES: Yes, that is what I mean; he is to have all his desires about him, and to be able to live happily in the gratification of them.

SOCRATES: Capital, excellent; go on as you have begun, and have no shame; I, too, must disencumber myself of shame: and first, will you tell me whether you include itching and scratching, provided you have enough of them and pass your life in scratching, in your notion of happiness?

CALLICLES: What a strange being you are, Socrates! a regular mob-orator.

SOCRATES: That was the reason, Callicles, why I scared Polus and Gorgias, until they were too modest to say what they thought; but you will not be too modest and will not be scared, for you are a brave man. And now, answer my question.

CALLICLES: I answer, that even the scratcher would live pleasantly.

SOCRATES: And if pleasantly, then also happily?

CALLICLES: To be sure.

SOCRATES: But what if the itching is not confined to the head? Shall I pursue the question? And here, Callicles, I would have you consider how you would reply if consequences are pressed upon you, especially if in the last resort you are asked, whether the life of a catamite is not terrible, foul, miserable? Or would you venture to say, that they too are happy, if they only get enough of what they want?

CALLICLES: Are you not ashamed, Socrates, of introducing such topics into the argument?

SOCRATES: Well, my fine friend, but am I the introducer of these topics, or he who says without any qualification that all who feel pleasure in whatever manner are happy, and who admits of no distinction between good and bad pleasures? And I would still ask, whether you say that pleasure and good are the same, or whether there is some pleasure which is not a good?

CALLICLES: Well, then, for the sake of consistency, I will say that they are the same.

SOCRATES: You are breaking the original agreement, Callicles, and will no longer be a satisfactory companion in the search after truth, if you say what is contrary to your real opinion.

CALLICLES: Why, that is what you are doing too, Socrates.

SOCRATES: Then we are both doing wrong. Still, my dear friend, I would ask you to consider whether pleasure, from whatever source derived, is the good; for, if this be true, then the disagreeable consequences which have been darkly intimated must follow, and many others.

CALLICLES: That, Socrates, is only your opinion.

SOCRATES: And do you, Callicles, seriously maintain what you are saying?

CALLICLES: Indeed I do.

SOCRATES: Then, as you are in earnest, shall we proceed with the argument?

CALLICLES: By all means. (Or, 'I am in profound earnest.')

SOCRATES: Well, if you are willing to proceed, determine this question for me:—There is something, I presume, which you would call knowledge?

CALLICLES: There is.

SOCRATES: And were you not saying just now, that some courage implied knowledge?

CALLICLES: I was.

SOCRATES: And you were speaking of courage and knowledge as two things different from one another?

CALLICLES: Certainly I was.

SOCRATES: And would you say that pleasure and knowledge are the same, or not the same?

CALLICLES: Not the same, O man of wisdom.

SOCRATES: And would you say that courage differed from pleasure?

CALLICLES: Certainly.

SOCRATES: Well, then, let us remember that Callicles, the Acharnian, says that pleasure and good are the same; but that knowledge and courage are not the same, either with one another, or with the good.

CALLICLES: And what does our friend Socrates, of Foxton, say—does he assent to this, or not?

SOCRATES: He does not assent; neither will Callicles, when he sees himself truly. You will admit, I suppose, that good and evil fortune are opposed to each other?

CALLICLES: Yes.

SOCRATES: And if they are opposed to each other, then, like health and disease, they exclude one another; a man cannot have them both, or be without them both, at the same time?

CALLICLES: What do you mean?

SOCRATES: Take the case of any bodily affection:—a man may have the complaint in his eyes which is called ophthalmia?

CALLICLES: To be sure.

SOCRATES: But he surely cannot have the same eyes well and sound at the same time?

CALLICLES: Certainly not.

SOCRATES: And when he has got rid of his ophthalmia, has he got rid of the health of his eyes too? Is the final result, that he gets rid of them both together?

CALLICLES: Certainly not.

SOCRATES: That would surely be marvellous and absurd?

CALLICLES: Very.

SOCRATES: I suppose that he is affected by them, and gets rid of them in turns?

CALLICLES: Yes.

SOCRATES: And he may have strength and weakness in the same way, by fits?

CALLICLES: Yes.

SOCRATES: Or swiftness and slowness?

CALLICLES: Certainly.

SOCRATES: And does he have and not have good and happiness, and their opposites, evil and misery, in a similar alternation? (Compare Republic.)

CALLICLES: Certainly he has.

SOCRATES: If then there be anything which a man has and has not at the same time, clearly that cannot be good and evil—do we agree? Please not to answer without consideration.

CALLICLES: I entirely agree.

SOCRATES: Go back now to our former admissions.—Did you say that to hunger, I mean the mere state of hunger, was pleasant or painful?

CALLICLES: I said painful, but that to eat when you are hungry is pleasant.

SOCRATES: I know; but still the actual hunger is painful: am I not right?

CALLICLES: Yes.

SOCRATES: And thirst, too, is painful?

CALLICLES: Yes, very.

SOCRATES: Need I adduce any more instances, or would you agree that all wants or desires are painful?

CALLICLES: I agree, and therefore you need not adduce any more instances.

SOCRATES: Very good. And you would admit that to drink, when you are thirsty, is pleasant?

CALLICLES: Yes.

SOCRATES: And in the sentence which you have just uttered, the word 'thirsty' implies pain?

CALLICLES: Yes.

SOCRATES: And the word 'drinking' is expressive of pleasure, and of the satisfaction of the want?

CALLICLES: Yes.

SOCRATES: There is pleasure in drinking?

CALLICLES: Certainly.

SOCRATES: When you are thirsty?

SOCRATES: And in pain?

CALLICLES: Yes.

SOCRATES: Do you see the inference:—that pleasure and pain are simultaneous, when you say that being thirsty, you drink? For are they not simultaneous, and do they not affect at the same time the same part, whether of the soul or the body?—which of them is affected cannot be supposed to be of any consequence: Is not this true?

CALLICLES: It is.

SOCRATES: You said also, that no man could have good and evil fortune at the same time?

CALLICLES: Yes, I did.

SOCRATES: But you admitted, that when in pain a man might also have pleasure?

CALLICLES: Clearly.

SOCRATES: Then pleasure is not the same as good fortune, or pain the same as evil fortune, and therefore the good is not the same as the pleasant?

CALLICLES: I wish I knew, Socrates, what your quibbling means.

SOCRATES: You know, Callicles, but you affect not to know.

CALLICLES: Well, get on, and don't keep fooling: then you will know what a wiseacre you are in your admonition of me.

SOCRATES: Does not a man cease from his thirst and from his pleasure in drinking at the same time?

CALLICLES: I do not understand what you are saying.

GORGIAS: Nay, Callicles, answer, if only for our sakes;—we should like to hear the argument out.

CALLICLES: Yes, Gorgias, but I must complain of the habitual trifling of Socrates; he is always arguing about little and unworthy questions.

GORGIAS: What matter? Your reputation, Callicles, is not at stake. Let Socrates argue in his own fashion.

CALLICLES: Well, then, Socrates, you shall ask these little peddling questions, since Gorgias wishes to have them.

SOCRATES: I envy you, Callicles, for having been initiated into the great mysteries before you were initiated into the lesser. I thought that this was not allowable. But to return to our argument:—Does not a man cease from thirsting and from the pleasure of drinking at the same moment?

CALLICLES: True.

SOCRATES: And if he is hungry, or has any other desire, does he not cease from the desire and the pleasure at the same moment?

CALLICLES: Very true.

SOCRATES: Then he ceases from pain and pleasure at the same moment?

CALLICLES: Yes.

SOCRATES: But he does not cease from good and evil at the same moment, as you have admitted: do you still adhere to what you said?

CALLICLES: Yes, I do; but what is the inference?

SOCRATES: Why, my friend, the inference is that the good is not the same as the pleasant, or the evil the same as the painful; there is a cessation of pleasure and pain at the same moment; but not of good and evil, for they are different. How then can pleasure be the same as good, or pain as evil? And I would have you look at the matter in another light, which could hardly, I think, have been considered by you when you identified them: Are not the good good because they have good present with them, as the beautiful are those who have beauty present with them?

CALLICLES: Yes.

SOCRATES: And do you call the fools and cowards good men? For you were saying just now that the courageous and the wise are the good—would you not say so?

CALLICLES: Certainly.

SOCRATES: And did you never see a foolish child rejoicing?

CALLICLES: Yes, I have.

SOCRATES: And a foolish man too?

CALLICLES: Yes, certainly; but what is your drift?

SOCRATES: Nothing particular, if you will only answer.

CALLICLES: Yes, I have.

SOCRATES: And did you ever see a sensible man rejoicing or sorrowing?

CALLICLES: Yes.

SOCRATES: Which rejoice and sorrow most—the wise or the foolish?

CALLICLES: They are much upon a par, I think, in that respect.

SOCRATES: Enough: And did you ever see a coward in battle?

CALLICLES: To be sure.

SOCRATES: And which rejoiced most at the departure of the enemy, the coward or the brave?

CALLICLES: I should say 'most' of both; or at any rate, they rejoiced about equally.

SOCRATES: No matter; then the cowards, and not only the brave, rejoice?

CALLICLES: Greatly.

SOCRATES: And the foolish; so it would seem?

CALLICLES: Yes.

SOCRATES: And are only the cowards pained at the approach of their enemies, or are the brave also pained?

CALLICLES: Both are pained.

SOCRATES: And are they equally pained?

CALLICLES: I should imagine that the cowards are more pained.

SOCRATES: And are they not better pleased at the enemy's departure?

CALLICLES: I dare say.

SOCRATES: Then are the foolish and the wise and the cowards and the brave all pleased and pained, as you were saying, in nearly equal degree; but are the cowards more pleased and pained than the brave?

CALLICLES: Yes.

SOCRATES: But surely the wise and brave are the good, and the foolish and the cowardly are the bad?

CALLICLES: Yes.

SOCRATES: Then the good and the bad are pleased and pained in a nearly equal degree?

CALLICLES: Yes.

SOCRATES: Then are the good and bad good and bad in a nearly equal degree, or have the bad the advantage both in good and evil? (i.e. in having more pleasure and more pain.)

CALLICLES: I really do not know what you mean.

SOCRATES: Why, do you not remember saying that the good were good because good was present with them, and the evil because evil; and that pleasures were goods and pains evils?

CALLICLES: Yes, I remember.

SOCRATES: And are not these pleasures or goods present to those who rejoice—if they do rejoice?

CALLICLES: Certainly.

SOCRATES: Then those who rejoice are good when goods are present with them?

CALLICLES: Yes.

SOCRATES: And those who are in pain have evil or sorrow present with them?

CALLICLES: Yes.

SOCRATES: And would you still say that the evil are evil by reason of the presence of evil?

CALLICLES: I should.

SOCRATES: Then those who rejoice are good, and those who are in pain evil?

CALLICLES: Yes.

SOCRATES: The degrees of good and evil vary with the degrees of pleasure and of pain?

CALLICLES: Yes.

SOCRATES: Have the wise man and the fool, the brave and the coward, joy and pain in nearly equal degrees? or would you say that the coward has more?

CALLICLES: I should say that he has.

SOCRATES: Help me then to draw out the conclusion which follows from our admissions; for it is good to repeat and review what is good twice and thrice over, as they say. Both the wise man and the brave man we allow to be good?

CALLICLES: Yes.

SOCRATES: And the foolish man and the coward to be evil?

CALLICLES: Certainly.

SOCRATES: And he who has joy is good?

CALLICLES: Yes.

SOCRATES: And he who is in pain is evil?

CALLICLES: Certainly.

SOCRATES: The good and evil both have joy and pain, but, perhaps, the evil has more of them?

CALLICLES: Yes.

SOCRATES: Then must we not infer, that the bad man is as good and bad as the good, or, perhaps, even better?—is not this a further inference which follows equally with the preceding from the assertion that the good and the pleasant are the same:—can this be denied, Callicles?

CALLICLES: I have been listening and making admissions to you, Socrates; and I remark that if a person grants you anything in play, you, like a child, want to keep hold and will not give it back. But do you really suppose that I or any other human being denies that some pleasures are good and others bad?

SOCRATES: Alas, Callicles, how unfair you are! you certainly treat me as if I were a child, sometimes saying one thing, and then another, as if you were meaning to deceive me. And yet I thought at first that you were my friend, and would not have deceived me if you could have helped. But I see that I was mistaken; and now I suppose that I must make the best of a bad business, as they said of old, and take what I can get out of you.—Well, then, as I understand you to say, I may assume that some pleasures are good and others evil?

CALLICLES: Yes.

SOCRATES: The beneficial are good, and the hurtful are evil?

CALLICLES: To be sure.

SOCRATES: And the beneficial are those which do some good, and the hurtful are those which do some evil?

CALLICLES: Yes.

SOCRATES: Take, for example, the bodily pleasures of eating and drinking, which we were just now mentioning—you mean to say that those which promote health, or any other bodily excellence, are good, and their opposites evil?

CALLICLES: Certainly.

SOCRATES: And in the same way there are good pains and there are evil pains?

CALLICLES: To be sure.

SOCRATES: And ought we not to choose and use the good pleasures and pains?

CALLICLES: Certainly.

SOCRATES: But not the evil?

CALLICLES: Clearly.

SOCRATES: Because, if you remember, Polus and I have agreed that all our actions are to be done for the sake of the good;—and will you agree with us in saying, that the good is the end of all our actions, and that all our actions are to be done for the sake of the good, and not the good for the sake of them?—will you add a third vote to our two?

CALLICLES: I will.

SOCRATES: Then pleasure, like everything else, is to be sought for the sake of that which is good, and not that which is good for the sake of pleasure?

CALLICLES: To be sure.

SOCRATES: But can every man choose what pleasures are good and what are evil, or must he have art or knowledge of them in detail?

CALLICLES: He must have art.

SOCRATES: Let me now remind you of what I was saying to Gorgias and Polus; I was saying, as you will not have forgotten, that there were some processes which aim only at pleasure, and know nothing of a better and worse, and there are other processes which know good and evil. And I considered that cookery, which I do not call an art, but only an experience, was of the former class, which is concerned with pleasure, and that the art of medicine was of the class which is concerned with the good. And now, by the god of friendship, I must beg you, Callicles, not to jest, or to imagine that I am jesting with you; do not answer at random and contrary to your real opinion—for you will observe that we are arguing about the way of human life; and to a man who has any sense at all, what question can be more serious than this?—whether he should follow after that way of life to which you exhort me, and act what you call the manly part of speaking in the assembly, and cultivating rhetoric, and engaging in public affairs, according to the principles now in vogue; or whether he should pursue the life of philosophy;—and in what the latter way differs from the former. But perhaps we had better first try to distinguish them, as I did before, and when we have come to an agreement that they are distinct, we may proceed to consider in what they differ from one another, and which of them we should choose. Perhaps, however, you do not even now understand what I mean?

CALLICLES: No, I do not.

SOCRATES: Then I will explain myself more clearly: seeing that you and I have agreed that there is such a thing as good, and that there is such a thing as pleasure, and that pleasure is not the same as good, and that the pursuit and process of acquisition of the one, that is pleasure, is different from the pursuit and process of acquisition of the other, which is good—I wish that you would tell me whether you agree with me thus far or not—do you agree?

CALLICLES: I do.

SOCRATES: Then I will proceed, and ask whether you also agree with me, and whether you think that I spoke the truth when I further said to Gorgias and Polus that cookery in my opinion is only an experience, and not an art at all; and that whereas medicine is an art, and attends to the nature and constitution of the patient, and has principles of action and reason in each case, cookery in attending upon pleasure never regards either the nature or reason of that pleasure to which she devotes herself, but goes straight to her end, nor ever considers or calculates anything, but works by experience and routine, and just preserves the recollection of what she has usually done when producing pleasure. And first, I would have you consider whether I have proved what I was saying, and then whether there are not other similar processes which have to do with the soul—some of them processes of art, making a provision for the soul's highest interest—others despising the interest, and, as in the previous case, considering only the pleasure of the soul, and how this may be acquired, but not considering what pleasures are good or bad, and having no other aim but to afford gratification, whether good or bad. In my opinion, Callicles, there are such processes, and this is the sort of thing which I term flattery, whether concerned with the body or the soul, or whenever employed with a view to pleasure and without any consideration of good and evil. And now I wish that you would tell me whether you agree with us in this notion, or whether you differ.

CALLICLES: I do not differ; on the contrary, I agree; for in that way I shall soonest bring the argument to an end, and shall oblige my friend Gorgias.

SOCRATES: And is this notion true of one soul, or of two or more?

CALLICLES: Equally true of two or more.

SOCRATES: Then a man may delight a whole assembly, and yet have no regard for their true interests?

CALLICLES: Yes.

SOCRATES: Can you tell me the pursuits which delight mankind—or rather, if you would prefer, let me ask, and do you answer, which of them belong to the pleasurable class, and which of them not? In the first place, what say you of flute-playing? Does not that appear to be an art which seeks only pleasure, Callicles, and thinks of nothing else?

CALLICLES: I assent.

SOCRATES: And is not the same true of all similar arts, as, for example, the art of playing the lyre at festivals?

CALLICLES: Yes.

SOCRATES: And what do you say of the choral art and of dithyrambic poetry?—are not they of the same nature? Do you imagine that Cinesias the son of Meles cares about what will tend to the moral improvement of his hearers, or about what will give pleasure to the multitude?

CALLICLES: There can be no mistake about Cinesias, Socrates.

SOCRATES: And what do you say of his father, Meles the harp-player? Did he perform with any view to the good of his hearers? Could he be said to regard even their pleasure? For his singing was an infliction to his audience. And of harp-playing and dithyrambic poetry in general, what would you say? Have they not been invented wholly for the sake of pleasure?

CALLICLES: That is my notion of them.

SOCRATES: And as for the Muse of Tragedy, that solemn and august personage—what are her aspirations? Is all her aim and desire only to give pleasure to the spectators, or does she fight against them and refuse to speak of their pleasant vices, and willingly proclaim in word and song truths welcome and unwelcome?—which in your judgment is her character?

CALLICLES: There can be no doubt, Socrates, that Tragedy has her face turned towards pleasure and the gratification of the audience.

SOCRATES: And is not that the sort of thing, Callicles, which we were just now describing as flattery?

CALLICLES: Quite true.

SOCRATES: Well now, suppose that we strip all poetry of song and rhythm and metre, there will remain speech? (Compare Republic.)

CALLICLES: To be sure.

SOCRATES: And this speech is addressed to a crowd of people?

CALLICLES: Yes.

SOCRATES: Then poetry is a sort of rhetoric?

CALLICLES: True.

SOCRATES: And do not the poets in the theatres seem to you to be rhetoricians?

CALLICLES: Yes.

SOCRATES: Then now we have discovered a sort of rhetoric which is addressed to a crowd of men, women, and children, freemen and slaves. And this is not much to our taste, for we have described it as having the nature of flattery.

CALLICLES: Quite true.

SOCRATES: Very good. And what do you say of that other rhetoric which addresses the Athenian assembly and the assemblies of freemen in other states? Do the rhetoricians appear to you always to aim at what is best, and do they seek to improve the citizens by their speeches, or are they too, like the rest of mankind, bent upon giving them pleasure, forgetting the public good in the thought of their own interest, playing with the people as with children, and trying to amuse them, but never considering whether they are better or worse for this?

CALLICLES: I must distinguish. There are some who have a real care of the public in what they say, while others are such as you describe.

SOCRATES: I am contented with the admission that rhetoric is of two sorts; one, which is mere flattery and disgraceful declamation; the other, which is noble and aims at the training and improvement of the souls of the citizens, and strives to say what is best, whether welcome or unwelcome, to the audience; but have you ever known such a rhetoric; or if you have, and can point out any rhetorician who is of this stamp, who is he?

CALLICLES: But, indeed, I am afraid that I cannot tell you of any such among the orators who are at present living.

SOCRATES: Well, then, can you mention any one of a former generation, who may be said to have improved the Athenians, who found them worse and made them better, from the day that he began to make speeches? for, indeed, I do not know of such a man.

CALLICLES: What! did you never hear that Themistocles was a good man, and Cimon and Miltiades and Pericles, who is just lately dead, and whom you heard yourself?

SOCRATES: Yes, Callicles, they were good men, if, as you said at first, true virtue consists only in the satisfaction of our own desires and those of others; but if not, and if, as we were afterwards compelled to acknowledge, the satisfaction of some desires makes us better, and of others, worse, and we ought to gratify the one and not the other, and there is an art in distinguishing them,—can you tell me of any of these statesmen who did distinguish them?

CALLICLES: No, indeed, I cannot.

SOCRATES: Yet, surely, Callicles, if you look you will find such a one. Suppose that we just calmly consider whether any of these was such as I have described. Will not the good man, who says whatever he says with a view to the best, speak with a reference to some standard and not at random; just as all other artists, whether the painter, the builder, the shipwright, or any other look all of them to their own work, and do not select and apply at random what they apply, but strive to give a definite form to it? The artist disposes all things in order, and compels the one part to harmonize and accord with the other part, until he has constructed a regular and systematic whole; and this is true of all artists, and in the same way the trainers and physicians, of whom we spoke before, give order and regularity to the body: do you deny this?

CALLICLES: No; I am ready to admit it.

SOCRATES: Then the house in which order and regularity prevail is good; that in which there is disorder, evil?

CALLICLES: Yes.

SOCRATES: And the same is true of a ship?

CALLICLES: Yes.

SOCRATES: And the same may be said of the human body?

CALLICLES: Yes.

SOCRATES: And what would you say of the soul? Will the good soul be that in which disorder is prevalent, or that in which there is harmony and order?

CALLICLES: The latter follows from our previous admissions.

SOCRATES: What is the name which is given to the effect of harmony and order in the body?

CALLICLES: I suppose that you mean health and strength?

SOCRATES: Yes, I do; and what is the name which you would give to the effect of harmony and order in the soul? Try and discover a name for this as well as for the other.

CALLICLES: Why not give the name yourself, Socrates?

SOCRATES: Well, if you had rather that I should, I will; and you shall say whether you agree with me, and if not, you shall refute and answer me. 'Healthy,' as I conceive, is the name which is given to the regular order of the body, whence comes health and every other bodily excellence: is that true or not?

CALLICLES: True.

SOCRATES: And 'lawful' and 'law' are the names which are given to the regular order and action of the soul, and these make men lawful and orderly:—and so we have temperance and justice: have we not?

CALLICLES: Granted.

SOCRATES: And will not the true rhetorician who is honest and understands his art have his eye fixed upon these, in all the words which he addresses to the souls of men, and in all his actions, both in what he gives and in what he takes away? Will not his aim be to implant justice in the souls of his citizens and take away injustice, to implant temperance and take away intemperance, to implant every virtue and take away every vice? Do you not agree?

CALLICLES: I agree.

SOCRATES: For what use is there, Callicles, in giving to the body of a sick man who is in a bad state of health a quantity of the most delightful food or drink or any other pleasant thing, which may be really as bad for him as if you gave him nothing, or even worse if rightly estimated. Is not that true?

CALLICLES: I will not say No to it.

SOCRATES: For in my opinion there is no profit in a man's life if his body is in an evil plight—in that case his life also is evil: am I not right?

CALLICLES: Yes.

SOCRATES: When a man is in health the physicians will generally allow him to eat when he is hungry and drink when he is thirsty, and to satisfy his desires as he likes, but when he is sick they hardly suffer him to satisfy his desires at all: even you will admit that?

CALLICLES: Yes.

SOCRATES: And does not the same argument hold of the soul, my good sir? While she is in a bad state and is senseless and intemperate and unjust and unholy, her desires ought to be controlled, and she ought to be prevented from doing anything which does not tend to her own improvement.

CALLICLES: Yes.

SOCRATES: Such treatment will be better for the soul herself?

CALLICLES: To be sure.

SOCRATES: And to restrain her from her appetites is to chastise her?

CALLICLES: Yes.

SOCRATES: Then restraint or chastisement is better for the soul than intemperance or the absence of control, which you were just now preferring?

CALLICLES: I do not understand you, Socrates, and I wish that you would ask some one who does.

SOCRATES: Here is a gentleman who cannot endure to be improved or to subject himself to that very chastisement of which the argument speaks!

CALLICLES: I do not heed a word of what you are saying, and have only answered hitherto out of civility to Gorgias.

SOCRATES: What are we to do, then? Shall we break off in the middle?

CALLICLES: You shall judge for yourself.

SOCRATES: Well, but people say that 'a tale should have a head and not break off in the middle,' and I should not like to have the argument going about without a head (compare Laws); please then to go on a little longer, and put the head on.

CALLICLES: How tyrannical you are, Socrates! I wish that you and your argument would rest, or that you would get some one else to argue with you.

SOCRATES: But who else is willing?—I want to finish the argument.

CALLICLES: Cannot you finish without my help, either talking straight on, or questioning and answering yourself?

SOCRATES: Must I then say with Epicharmus, 'Two men spoke before, but now one shall be enough'? I suppose that there is absolutely no help. And if I am to carry on the enquiry by myself, I will first of all remark that not only I but all of us should have an ambition to know what is true and what is false in this matter, for the discovery of the truth is a common good. And now I will proceed to argue according to my own notion. But if any of you think that I arrive at conclusions which are untrue you must interpose and refute me, for I do not speak from any knowledge of what I am saying; I am an enquirer like yourselves, and therefore, if my opponent says anything which is of force, I shall be the first to agree with him. I am speaking on the supposition that the argument ought to be completed; but if you think otherwise let us leave off and go our ways.

GORGIAS: I think, Socrates, that we should not go our ways until you have completed the argument; and this appears to me to be the wish of the rest of the company; I myself should very much like to hear what more you have to say.

SOCRATES: I too, Gorgias, should have liked to continue the argument with Callicles, and then I might have given him an 'Amphion' in return for his 'Zethus'; but since you, Callicles, are unwilling to continue, I hope that you will listen, and interrupt me if I seem to you to be in error. And if you refute me, I shall not be angry with you as you are with me, but I shall inscribe you as the greatest of benefactors on the tablets of my soul.

CALLICLES: My good fellow, never mind me, but get on.

SOCRATES: Listen to me, then, while I recapitulate the argument:—Is the pleasant the same as the good? Not the same. Callicles and I are agreed about that. And is the pleasant to be pursued for the sake of the good? or the good for the sake of the pleasant? The pleasant is to be pursued for the sake of the good. And that is pleasant at the presence of which we are pleased, and that is good at the presence of which we are good? To be sure. And we are good, and all good things whatever are good when some virtue is present in us or them? That, Callicles, is my conviction. But the virtue of each thing, whether body or soul, instrument or creature, when given to them in the best way comes to them not by chance but as the result of the order and truth and art which are imparted to them: Am I not right? I maintain that I am. And is not the virtue of each thing dependent on order or arrangement? Yes, I say. And that which makes a thing good is the proper order inhering in each thing? Such is my view. And is not the soul which has an order of her own better than that which has no order? Certainly. And the soul which has order is orderly? Of course. And that which is orderly is temperate? Assuredly. And the temperate soul is good? No other answer can I give, Callicles dear; have you any?

CALLICLES: Go on, my good fellow.

SOCRATES: Then I shall proceed to add, that if the temperate soul is the good soul, the soul which is in the opposite condition, that is, the foolish and intemperate, is the bad soul. Very true.

And will not the temperate man do what is proper, both in relation to the gods and to men;—for he would not be temperate if he did not? Certainly he will do what is proper. In his relation to other men he will do what is just; and in his relation to the gods he will do what is holy; and he who does what is just and holy must be just and holy? Very true. And must he not be courageous? for the duty of a temperate man is not to follow or to avoid what he ought not, but what he ought, whether things or men or pleasures or pains, and patiently to endure when he ought; and therefore, Callicles, the temperate man, being, as we have described, also just and courageous and holy, cannot be other than a perfectly good man, nor can the good man do otherwise than well and perfectly whatever he does; and he who does well must of necessity be happy and blessed, and the evil man who does evil, miserable: now this latter is he whom you were applauding—the intemperate who is the opposite of the temperate. Such is my position, and these things I affirm to be true. And if they are true, then I further affirm that he who desires to be happy must pursue and practise temperance and run away from intemperance as fast as his legs will carry him: he had better order his life so as not to need punishment; but if either he or any of his friends, whether private individual or city, are in need of punishment, then justice must be done and he must suffer punishment, if he would be happy. This appears to me to be the aim which a man ought to have, and towards which he ought to direct all the energies both of himself and of the state, acting so that he may have temperance and justice present with him and be happy, not suffering his lusts to be unrestrained, and in the never-ending desire satisfy them leading a robber's life. Such a one is the friend neither of God nor man, for he is incapable of communion, and he who is incapable of communion is also incapable of friendship. And philosophers tell us, Callicles, that communion and friendship and orderliness and temperance and justice bind together heaven and earth and gods and men, and that this universe is therefore called Cosmos or order, not disorder or misrule, my friend. But although you are a philosopher you seem to me never to have observed that geometrical equality is mighty, both among gods and men; you think that you ought to cultivate inequality or excess, and do not care about geometry.—Well, then, either the principle that the happy are made happy by the possession of justice and temperance, and the miserable miserable by the possession of vice, must be refuted, or, if it is granted, what will be the consequences? All the consequences which I drew before, Callicles, and about which you asked me whether I was in earnest when I said that a man ought to accuse himself and his son and his friend if he did anything wrong, and that to this end he should use his rhetoric—all those consequences are true. And that which you thought that Polus was led to admit out of modesty is true, viz., that, to do injustice, if more disgraceful than to suffer, is in that degree worse; and the other position, which, according to Polus, Gorgias admitted out of modesty, that he who would truly be a rhetorician ought to be just and have a knowledge of justice, has also turned out to be true.

And now, these things being as we have said, let us proceed in the next place to consider whether you are right in throwing in my teeth that I am unable to help myself or any of my friends or kinsmen, or to save them in the extremity of danger, and that I am in the power of another like an outlaw to whom any one may do what he likes,—he may box my ears, which was a brave saying of yours; or take away my goods or banish me, or even do his worst and kill me; a condition which, as you say, is the height of disgrace. My answer to you is one which has been already often repeated, but may as well be repeated once more. I tell you, Callicles, that to be boxed on the ears wrongfully is not the worst evil which can befall a man, nor to have my purse or my body cut open, but that to smite and slay me and mine wrongfully is far more disgraceful and more evil; aye, and to despoil and enslave and pillage, or in any way at all to wrong me and mine, is far more disgraceful and evil to the doer of the wrong than to me who am the sufferer. These truths, which have been already set forth as I state them in the previous discussion, would seem now to have been fixed and riveted by us, if I may use an expression which is certainly bold, in words which are like bonds of iron and adamant; and unless you or some other still more enterprising hero shall break them, there is no possibility of denying what I say. For my position has always been, that I myself am ignorant how these things are, but that I have never met any one who could say otherwise, any more than you can, and not appear ridiculous. This is my position still, and if what I am saying is true, and injustice is the greatest of evils to the doer of injustice, and yet there is if possible a greater than this greatest of evils (compare Republic), in an unjust man not suffering retribution, what is that defence of which the want will make a man truly ridiculous? Must not the defence be one which will avert the greatest of human evils? And will not the worst of all defences be that with which a man is unable to defend himself or his family or his friends?—and next will come that which is unable to avert the next greatest evil; thirdly that which is unable to avert the third greatest evil; and so of other evils. As is the greatness of evil so is the honour of being able to avert them in their several degrees, and the disgrace of not being able to avert them. Am I not right Callicles?

CALLICLES: Yes, quite right.

SOCRATES: Seeing then that there are these two evils, the doing injustice and the suffering injustice—and we affirm that to do injustice is a greater, and to suffer injustice a lesser evil—by what devices can a man succeed in obtaining the two advantages, the one of not doing and the other of not suffering injustice? must he have the power, or only the will to obtain them? I mean to ask whether a man will escape injustice if he has only the will to escape, or must he have provided himself with the power?

CALLICLES: He must have provided himself with the power; that is clear.

SOCRATES: And what do you say of doing injustice? Is the will only sufficient, and will that prevent him from doing injustice, or must he have provided himself with power and art; and if he have not studied and practised, will he be unjust still? Surely you might say, Callicles, whether you think that Polus and I were right in admitting the conclusion that no one does wrong voluntarily, but that all do wrong against their will?

CALLICLES: Granted, Socrates, if you will only have done.

SOCRATES: Then, as would appear, power and art have to be provided in order that we may do no injustice?

CALLICLES: Certainly.

SOCRATES: And what art will protect us from suffering injustice, if not wholly, yet as far as possible? I want to know whether you agree with me; for I think that such an art is the art of one who is either a ruler or even tyrant himself, or the equal and companion of the ruling power.

CALLICLES: Well said, Socrates; and please to observe how ready I am to praise you when you talk sense.

SOCRATES: Think and tell me whether you would approve of another view of mine: To me every man appears to be most the friend of him who is most like to him—like to like, as ancient sages say: Would you not agree to this?

CALLICLES: I should.

SOCRATES: But when the tyrant is rude and uneducated, he may be expected to fear any one who is his superior in virtue, and will never be able to be perfectly friendly with him.

CALLICLES: That is true.

SOCRATES: Neither will he be the friend of any one who is greatly his inferior, for the tyrant will despise him, and will never seriously regard him as a friend.

CALLICLES: That again is true.

SOCRATES: Then the only friend worth mentioning, whom the tyrant can have, will be one who is of the same character, and has the same likes and dislikes, and is at the same time willing to be subject and subservient to him; he is the man who will have power in the state, and no one will injure him with impunity:—is not that so?

CALLICLES: Yes.

SOCRATES: And if a young man begins to ask how he may become great and formidable, this would seem to be the way—he will accustom himself, from his youth upward, to feel sorrow and joy on the same occasions as his master, and will contrive to be as like him as possible?

CALLICLES: Yes.

SOCRATES: And in this way he will have accomplished, as you and your friends would say, the end of becoming a great man and not suffering injury?

CALLICLES: Very true.

SOCRATES: But will he also escape from doing injury? Must not the very opposite be true,—if he is to be like the tyrant in his injustice, and to have influence with him? Will he not rather contrive to do as much wrong as possible, and not be punished?

CALLICLES: True.

SOCRATES: And by the imitation of his master and by the power which he thus acquires will not his soul become bad and corrupted, and will not this be the greatest evil to him?

CALLICLES: You always contrive somehow or other, Socrates, to invert everything: do you not know that he who imitates the tyrant will, if he has a mind, kill him who does not imitate him and take away his goods?

SOCRATES: Excellent Callicles, I am not deaf, and I have heard that a great many times from you and from Polus and from nearly every man in the city, but I wish that you would hear me too. I dare say that he will kill him if he has a mind—the bad man will kill the good and true.

CALLICLES: And is not that just the provoking thing?

SOCRATES: Nay, not to a man of sense, as the argument shows: do you think that all our cares should be directed to prolonging life to the uttermost, and to the study of those arts which secure us from danger always; like that art of rhetoric which saves men in courts of law, and which you advise me to cultivate?

CALLICLES: Yes, truly, and very good advice too.

SOCRATES: Well, my friend, but what do you think of swimming; is that an art of any great pretensions?

CALLICLES: No, indeed.

SOCRATES: And yet surely swimming saves a man from death, and there are occasions on which he must know how to swim. And if you despise the swimmers, I will tell you of another and greater art, the art of the pilot, who not only saves the souls of men, but also their bodies and properties from the extremity of danger, just like rhetoric. Yet his art is modest and unpresuming: it has no airs or pretences of doing anything extraordinary, and, in return for the same salvation which is given by the pleader, demands only two obols, if he brings us from Aegina to Athens, or for the longer voyage from Pontus or Egypt, at the utmost two drachmae, when he has saved, as I was just now saying, the passenger and his wife and children and goods, and safely disembarked them at the Piraeus,—this is the payment which he asks in return for so great a boon; and he who is the master of the art, and has done all this, gets out and walks about on the sea-shore by his ship in an unassuming way. For he is able to reflect and is aware that he cannot tell which of his fellow-passengers he has benefited, and which of them he has injured in not allowing them to be drowned. He knows that they are just the same when he has disembarked them as when they embarked, and not a whit better either in their bodies or in their souls; and he considers that if a man who is afflicted by great and incurable bodily diseases is only to be pitied for having escaped, and is in no way benefited by him in having been saved from drowning, much less he who has great and incurable diseases, not of the body, but of the soul, which is the more valuable part of him; neither is life worth having nor of any profit to the bad man, whether he be delivered from the sea, or the law-courts, or any other devourer;—and so he reflects that such a one had better not live, for he cannot live well. (Compare Republic.)

And this is the reason why the pilot, although he is our saviour, is not usually conceited, any more than the engineer, who is not at all behind either the general, or the pilot, or any one else, in his saving power, for he sometimes saves whole cities. Is there any comparison between him and the pleader? And if he were to talk, Callicles, in your grandiose style, he would bury you under a mountain of words, declaring and insisting that we ought all of us to be engine-makers, and that no other profession is worth thinking about; he would have plenty to say. Nevertheless you despise him and his art, and sneeringly call him an engine-maker, and you will not allow your daughters to marry his son, or marry your son to his daughters. And yet, on your principle, what justice or reason is there in your refusal? What right have you to despise the engine-maker, and the others whom I was just now mentioning? I know that you will say, 'I am better, and better born.' But if the better is not what I say, and virtue consists only in a man saving himself and his, whatever may be his character, then your censure of the engine-maker, and of the physician, and of the other arts of salvation, is ridiculous. O my friend! I want you to see that the noble and the good may possibly be something different from saving and being saved:—May not he who is truly a man cease to care about living a certain time?—he knows, as women say, that no man can escape fate, and therefore he is not fond of life; he leaves all that with God, and considers in what way he can best spend his appointed term;—whether by assimilating himself to the constitution under which he lives, as you at this moment have to consider how you may become as like as possible to the Athenian people, if you mean to be in their good graces, and to have power in the state; whereas I want you to think and see whether this is for the interest of either of us;—I would not have us risk that which is dearest on the acquisition of this power, like the Thessalian enchantresses, who, as they say, bring down the moon from heaven at the risk of their own perdition. But if you suppose that any man will show you the art of becoming great in the city, and yet not conforming yourself to the ways of the city, whether for better or worse, then I can only say that you are mistaken, Callides; for he who would deserve to be the true natural friend of the Athenian Demus, aye, or of Pyrilampes' darling who is called after them, must be by nature like them, and not an imitator only. He, then, who will make you most like them, will make you as you desire, a statesman and orator: for every man is pleased when he is spoken to in his own language and spirit, and dislikes any other. But perhaps you, sweet Callicles, may be of another mind. What do you say?

CALLICLES: Somehow or other your words, Socrates, always appear to me to be good words; and yet, like the rest of the world, I am not quite convinced by them. (Compare Symp.: 1 Alcib.)

SOCRATES: The reason is, Callicles, that the love of Demus which abides in your soul is an adversary to me; but I dare say that if we recur to these same matters, and consider them more thoroughly, you may be convinced for all that. Please, then, to remember that there are two processes of training all things, including body and soul; in the one, as we said, we treat them with a view to pleasure, and in the other with a view to the highest good, and then we do not indulge but resist them: was not that the distinction which we drew?

CALLICLES: Very true.

SOCRATES: And the one which had pleasure in view was just a vulgar flattery:—was not that another of our conclusions?

CALLICLES: Be it so, if you will have it.

SOCRATES: And the other had in view the greatest improvement of that which was ministered to, whether body or soul?

CALLICLES: Quite true.

SOCRATES: And must we not have the same end in view in the treatment of our city and citizens? Must we not try and make them as good as possible? For we have already discovered that there is no use in imparting to them any other good, unless the mind of those who are to have the good, whether money, or office, or any other sort of power, be gentle and good. Shall we say that?

CALLICLES: Yes, certainly, if you like.

SOCRATES: Well, then, if you and I, Callicles, were intending to set about some public business, and were advising one another to undertake buildings, such as walls, docks or temples of the largest size, ought we not to examine ourselves, first, as to whether we know or do not know the art of building, and who taught us?—would not that be necessary, Callicles?

CALLICLES: True.

SOCRATES: In the second place, we should have to consider whether we had ever constructed any private house, either of our own or for our friends, and whether this building of ours was a success or not; and if upon consideration we found that we had had good and eminent masters, and had been successful in constructing many fine buildings, not only with their assistance, but without them, by our own unaided skill—in that case prudence would not dissuade us from proceeding to the construction of public works. But if we had no master to show, and only a number of worthless buildings or none at all, then, surely, it would be ridiculous in us to attempt public works, or to advise one another to undertake them. Is not this true?

CALLICLES: Certainly.

SOCRATES: And does not the same hold in all other cases? If you and I were physicians, and were advising one another that we were competent to practise as state-physicians, should I not ask about you, and would you not ask about me, Well, but how about Socrates himself, has he good health? and was any one else ever known to be cured by him, whether slave or freeman? And I should make the same enquiries about you. And if we arrived at the conclusion that no one, whether citizen or stranger, man or woman, had ever been any the better for the medical skill of either of us, then, by Heaven, Callicles, what an absurdity to think that we or any human being should be so silly as to set up as state-physicians and advise others like ourselves to do the same, without having first practised in private, whether successfully or not, and acquired experience of the art! Is not this, as they say, to begin with the big jar when you are learning the potter's art; which is a foolish thing?

CALLICLES: True.

SOCRATES: And now, my friend, as you are already beginning to be a public character, and are admonishing and reproaching me for not being one, suppose that we ask a few questions of one another. Tell me, then, Callicles, how about making any of the citizens better? Was there ever a man who was once vicious, or unjust, or intemperate, or foolish, and became by the help of Callicles good and noble? Was there ever such a man, whether citizen or stranger, slave or freeman? Tell me, Callicles, if a person were to ask these questions of you, what would you answer? Whom would you say that you had improved by your conversation? There may have been good deeds of this sort which were done by you as a private person, before you came forward in public. Why will you not answer?

CALLICLES: You are contentious, Socrates.

SOCRATES: Nay, I ask you, not from a love of contention, but because I really want to know in what way you think that affairs should be administered among us—whether, when you come to the administration of them, you have any other aim but the improvement of the citizens? Have we not already admitted many times over that such is the duty of a public man? Nay, we have surely said so; for if you will not answer for yourself I must answer for you. But if this is what the good man ought to effect for the benefit of his own state, allow me to recall to you the names of those whom you were just now mentioning, Pericles, and Cimon, and Miltiades, and Themistocles, and ask whether you still think that they were good citizens.

CALLICLES: I do.

SOCRATES: But if they were good, then clearly each of them must have made the citizens better instead of worse?

CALLICLES: Yes.

SOCRATES: And, therefore, when Pericles first began to speak in the assembly, the Athenians were not so good as when he spoke last?

CALLICLES: Very likely.

SOCRATES: Nay, my friend, 'likely' is not the word; for if he was a good citizen, the inference is certain.

CALLICLES: And what difference does that make?

SOCRATES: None; only I should like further to know whether the Athenians are supposed to have been made better by Pericles, or, on the contrary, to have been corrupted by him; for I hear that he was the first who gave the people pay, and made them idle and cowardly, and encouraged them in the love of talk and money.

CALLICLES: You heard that, Socrates, from the laconising set who bruise their ears.

SOCRATES: But what I am going to tell you now is not mere hearsay, but well known both to you and me: that at first, Pericles was glorious and his character unimpeached by any verdict of the Athenians—this was during the time when they were not so good—yet afterwards, when they had been made good and gentle by him, at the very end of his life they convicted him of theft, and almost put him to death, clearly under the notion that he was a malefactor.

CALLICLES: Well, but how does that prove Pericles' badness?

SOCRATES: Why, surely you would say that he was a bad manager of asses or horses or oxen, who had received them originally neither kicking nor butting nor biting him, and implanted in them all these savage tricks? Would he not be a bad manager of any animals who received them gentle, and made them fiercer than they were when he received them? What do you say?

CALLICLES: I will do you the favour of saying 'yes.'

SOCRATES: And will you also do me the favour of saying whether man is an animal?

CALLICLES: Certainly he is.

SOCRATES: And was not Pericles a shepherd of men?

CALLICLES: Yes.

SOCRATES: And if he was a good political shepherd, ought not the animals who were his subjects, as we were just now acknowledging, to have become more just, and not more unjust?

CALLICLES: Quite true.

SOCRATES: And are not just men gentle, as Homer says?—or are you of another mind?

CALLICLES: I agree.

SOCRATES: And yet he really did make them more savage than he received them, and their savageness was shown towards himself; which he must have been very far from desiring.

CALLICLES: Do you want me to agree with you?

SOCRATES: Yes, if I seem to you to speak the truth.

CALLICLES: Granted then.

SOCRATES: And if they were more savage, must they not have been more unjust and inferior?

CALLICLES: Granted again.

SOCRATES: Then upon this view, Pericles was not a good statesman?

CALLICLES: That is, upon your view.

SOCRATES: Nay, the view is yours, after what you have admitted. Take the case of Cimon again. Did not the very persons whom he was serving ostracize him, in order that they might not hear his voice for ten years? and they did just the same to Themistocles, adding the penalty of exile; and they voted that Miltiades, the hero of Marathon, should be thrown into the pit of death, and he was only saved by the Prytanis. And yet, if they had been really good men, as you say, these things would never have happened to them. For the good charioteers are not those who at first keep their place, and then, when they have broken-in their horses, and themselves become better charioteers, are thrown out—that is not the way either in charioteering or in any profession.—What do you think?

CALLICLES: I should think not.

SOCRATES: Well, but if so, the truth is as I have said already, that in the Athenian State no one has ever shown himself to be a good statesman—you admitted that this was true of our present statesmen, but not true of former ones, and you preferred them to the others; yet they have turned out to be no better than our present ones; and therefore, if they were rhetoricians, they did not use the true art of rhetoric or of flattery, or they would not have fallen out of favour.

CALLICLES: But surely, Socrates, no living man ever came near any one of them in his performances.

SOCRATES: O, my dear friend, I say nothing against them regarded as the serving-men of the State; and I do think that they were certainly more serviceable than those who are living now, and better able to gratify the wishes of the State; but as to transforming those desires and not allowing them to have their way, and using the powers which they had, whether of persuasion or of force, in the improvement of their fellow citizens, which is the prime object of the truly good citizen, I do not see that in these respects they were a whit superior to our present statesmen, although I do admit that they were more clever at providing ships and walls and docks, and all that. You and I have a ridiculous way, for during the whole time that we are arguing, we are always going round and round to the same point, and constantly misunderstanding one another. If I am not mistaken, you have admitted and acknowledged more than once, that there are two kinds of operations which have to do with the body, and two which have to do with the soul: one of the two is ministerial, and if our bodies are hungry provides food for them, and if they are thirsty gives them drink, or if they are cold supplies them with garments, blankets, shoes, and all that they crave. I use the same images as before intentionally, in order that you may understand me the better. The purveyor of the articles may provide them either wholesale or retail, or he may be the maker of any of them,—the baker, or the cook, or the weaver, or the shoemaker, or the currier; and in so doing, being such as he is, he is naturally supposed by himself and every one to minister to the body. For none of them know that there is another art—an art of gymnastic and medicine which is the true minister of the body, and ought to be the mistress of all the rest, and to use their results according to the knowledge which she has and they have not, of the real good or bad effects of meats and drinks on the body. All other arts which have to do with the body are servile and menial and illiberal; and gymnastic and medicine are, as they ought to be, their mistresses. Now, when I say that all this is equally true of the soul, you seem at first to know and understand and assent to my words, and then a little while afterwards you come repeating, Has not the State had good and noble citizens? and when I ask you who they are, you reply, seemingly quite in earnest, as if I had asked, Who are or have been good trainers?—and you had replied, Thearion, the baker, Mithoecus, who wrote the Sicilian cookery-book, Sarambus, the vintner: these are ministers of the body, first-rate in their art; for the first makes admirable loaves, the second excellent dishes, and the third capital wine;—to me these appear to be the exact parallel of the statesmen whom you mention. Now you would not be altogether pleased if I said to you, My friend, you know nothing of gymnastics; those of whom you are speaking to me are only the ministers and purveyors of luxury, who have no good or noble notions of their art, and may very likely be filling and fattening men's bodies and gaining their approval, although the result is that they lose their original flesh in the long run, and become thinner than they were before; and yet they, in their simplicity, will not attribute their diseases and loss of flesh to their entertainers; but when in after years the unhealthy surfeit brings the attendant penalty of disease, he who happens to be near them at the time, and offers them advice, is accused and blamed by them, and if they could they would do him some harm; while they proceed to eulogize the men who have been the real authors of the mischief. And that, Callicles, is just what you are now doing. You praise the men who feasted the citizens and satisfied their desires, and people say that they have made the city great, not seeing that the swollen and ulcerated condition of the State is to be attributed to these elder statesmen; for they have filled the city full of harbours and docks and walls and revenues and all that, and have left no room for justice and temperance. And when the crisis of the disorder comes, the people will blame the advisers of the hour, and applaud Themistocles and Cimon and Pericles, who are the real authors of their calamities; and if you are not careful they may assail you and my friend Alcibiades, when they are losing not only their new acquisitions, but also their original possessions; not that you are the authors of these misfortunes of theirs, although you may perhaps be accessories to them. A great piece of work is always being made, as I see and am told, now as of old; about our statesmen. When the State treats any of them as malefactors, I observe that there is a great uproar and indignation at the supposed wrong which is done to them; 'after all their many services to the State, that they should unjustly perish,'—so the tale runs. But the cry is all a lie; for no statesman ever could be unjustly put to death by the city of which he is the head. The case of the professed statesman is, I believe, very much like that of the professed sophist; for the sophists, although they are wise men, are nevertheless guilty of a strange piece of folly; professing to be teachers of virtue, they will often accuse their disciples of wronging them, and defrauding them of their pay, and showing no gratitude for their services. Yet what can be more absurd than that men who have become just and good, and whose injustice has been taken away from them, and who have had justice implanted in them by their teachers, should act unjustly by reason of the injustice which is not in them? Can anything be more irrational, my friends, than this? You, Callicles, compel me to be a mob-orator, because you will not answer.

CALLICLES: And you are the man who cannot speak unless there is some one to answer?

SOCRATES: I suppose that I can; just now, at any rate, the speeches which I am making are long enough because you refuse to answer me. But I adjure you by the god of friendship, my good sir, do tell me whether there does not appear to you to be a great inconsistency in saying that you have made a man good, and then blaming him for being bad?

CALLICLES: Yes, it appears so to me.

SOCRATES: Do you never hear our professors of education speaking in this inconsistent manner?

CALLICLES: Yes, but why talk of men who are good for nothing?

SOCRATES: I would rather say, why talk of men who profess to be rulers, and declare that they are devoted to the improvement of the city, and nevertheless upon occasion declaim against the utter vileness of the city:—do you think that there is any difference between one and the other? My good friend, the sophist and the rhetorician, as I was saying to Polus, are the same, or nearly the same; but you ignorantly fancy that rhetoric is a perfect thing, and sophistry a thing to be despised; whereas the truth is, that sophistry is as much superior to rhetoric as legislation is to the practice of law, or gymnastic to medicine. The orators and sophists, as I am inclined to think, are the only class who cannot complain of the mischief ensuing to themselves from that which they teach others, without in the same breath accusing themselves of having done no good to those whom they profess to benefit. Is not this a fact?

CALLICLES: Certainly it is.

SOCRATES: If they were right in saying that they make men better, then they are the only class who can afford to leave their remuneration to those who have been benefited by them. Whereas if a man has been benefited in any other way, if, for example, he has been taught to run by a trainer, he might possibly defraud him of his pay, if the trainer left the matter to him, and made no agreement with him that he should receive money as soon as he had given him the utmost speed; for not because of any deficiency of speed do men act unjustly, but by reason of injustice.

CALLICLES: Very true.

SOCRATES: And he who removes injustice can be in no danger of being treated unjustly: he alone can safely leave the honorarium to his pupils, if he be really able to make them good—am I not right? (Compare Protag.)

CALLICLES: Yes.

SOCRATES: Then we have found the reason why there is no dishonour in a man receiving pay who is called in to advise about building or any other art?

CALLICLES: Yes, we have found the reason.

SOCRATES: But when the point is, how a man may become best himself, and best govern his family and state, then to say that you will give no advice gratis is held to be dishonourable?

CALLICLES: True.

SOCRATES: And why? Because only such benefits call forth a desire to requite them, and there is evidence that a benefit has been conferred when the benefactor receives a return; otherwise not. Is this true?

CALLICLES: It is.

SOCRATES: Then to which service of the State do you invite me? determine for me. Am I to be the physician of the State who will strive and struggle to make the Athenians as good as possible; or am I to be the servant and flatterer of the State? Speak out, my good friend, freely and fairly as you did at first and ought to do again, and tell me your entire mind.

CALLICLES: I say then that you should be the servant of the State.

SOCRATES: The flatterer? well, sir, that is a noble invitation.

CALLICLES: The Mysian, Socrates, or what you please. For if you refuse, the consequences will be—

SOCRATES: Do not repeat the old story—that he who likes will kill me and get my money; for then I shall have to repeat the old answer, that he will be a bad man and will kill the good, and that the money will be of no use to him, but that he will wrongly use that which he wrongly took, and if wrongly, basely, and if basely, hurtfully.

CALLICLES: How confident you are, Socrates, that you will never come to harm! you seem to think that you are living in another country, and can never be brought into a court of justice, as you very likely may be brought by some miserable and mean person.

SOCRATES: Then I must indeed be a fool, Callicles, if I do not know that in the Athenian State any man may suffer anything. And if I am brought to trial and incur the dangers of which you speak, he will be a villain who brings me to trial—of that I am very sure, for no good man would accuse the innocent. Nor shall I be surprised if I am put to death. Shall I tell you why I anticipate this?

CALLICLES: By all means.

SOCRATES: I think that I am the only or almost the only Athenian living who practises the true art of politics; I am the only politician of my time. Now, seeing that when I speak my words are not uttered with any view of gaining favour, and that I look to what is best and not to what is most pleasant, having no mind to use those arts and graces which you recommend, I shall have nothing to say in the justice court. And you might argue with me, as I was arguing with Polus:—I shall be tried just as a physician would be tried in a court of little boys at the indictment of the cook. What would he reply under such circumstances, if some one were to accuse him, saying, 'O my boys, many evil things has this man done to you: he is the death of you, especially of the younger ones among you, cutting and burning and starving and suffocating you, until you know not what to do; he gives you the bitterest potions, and compels you to hunger and thirst. How unlike the variety of meats and sweets on which I feasted you!' What do you suppose that the physician would be able to reply when he found himself in such a predicament? If he told the truth he could only say, 'All these evil things, my boys, I did for your health,' and then would there not just be a clamour among a jury like that? How they would cry out!

CALLICLES: I dare say.

SOCRATES: Would he not be utterly at a loss for a reply?

CALLICLES: He certainly would.

SOCRATES: And I too shall be treated in the same way, as I well know, if I am brought before the court. For I shall not be able to rehearse to the people the pleasures which I have procured for them, and which, although I am not disposed to envy either the procurers or enjoyers of them, are deemed by them to be benefits and advantages. And if any one says that I corrupt young men, and perplex their minds, or that I speak evil of old men, and use bitter words towards them, whether in private or public, it is useless for me to reply, as I truly might:—'All this I do for the sake of justice, and with a view to your interest, my judges, and to nothing else.' And therefore there is no saying what may happen to me.

CALLICLES: And do you think, Socrates, that a man who is thus defenceless is in a good position?

SOCRATES: Yes, Callicles, if he have that defence, which as you have often acknowledged he should have—if he be his own defence, and have never said or done anything wrong, either in respect of gods or men; and this has been repeatedly acknowledged by us to be the best sort of defence. And if any one could convict me of inability to defend myself or others after this sort, I should blush for shame, whether I was convicted before many, or before a few, or by myself alone; and if I died from want of ability to do so, that would indeed grieve me. But if I died because I have no powers of flattery or rhetoric, I am very sure that you would not find me repining at death. For no man who is not an utter fool and coward is afraid of death itself, but he is afraid of doing wrong. For to go to the world below having one's soul full of injustice is the last and worst of all evils. And in proof of what I say, if you have no objection, I should like to tell you a story.

CALLICLES: Very well, proceed; and then we shall have done.

SOCRATES: Listen, then, as story-tellers say, to a very pretty tale, which I dare say that you may be disposed to regard as a fable only, but which, as I believe, is a true tale, for I mean to speak the truth. Homer tells us (Il.), how Zeus and Poseidon and Pluto divided the empire which they inherited from their father. Now in the days of Cronos there existed a law respecting the destiny of man, which has always been, and still continues to be in Heaven,—that he who has lived all his life in justice and holiness shall go, when he is dead, to the Islands of the Blessed, and dwell there in perfect happiness out of the reach of evil; but that he who has lived unjustly and impiously shall go to the house of vengeance and punishment, which is called Tartarus. And in the time of Cronos, and even quite lately in the reign of Zeus, the judgment was given on the very day on which the men were to die; the judges were alive, and the men were alive; and the consequence was that the judgments were not well given. Then Pluto and the authorities from the Islands of the Blessed came to Zeus, and said that the souls found their way to the wrong places. Zeus said: 'I shall put a stop to this; the judgments are not well given, because the persons who are judged have their clothes on, for they are alive; and there are many who, having evil souls, are apparelled in fair bodies, or encased in wealth or rank, and, when the day of judgment arrives, numerous witnesses come forward and testify on their behalf that they have lived righteously. The judges are awed by them, and they themselves too have their clothes on when judging; their eyes and ears and their whole bodies are interposed as a veil before their own souls. All this is a hindrance to them; there are the clothes of the judges and the clothes of the judged.—What is to be done? I will tell you:—In the first place, I will deprive men of the foreknowledge of death, which they possess at present: this power which they have Prometheus has already received my orders to take from them: in the second place, they shall be entirely stripped before they are judged, for they shall be judged when they are dead; and the judge too shall be naked, that is to say, dead—he with his naked soul shall pierce into the other naked souls; and they shall die suddenly and be deprived of all their kindred, and leave their brave attire strewn upon the earth—conducted in this manner, the judgment will be just. I knew all about the matter before any of you, and therefore I have made my sons judges; two from Asia, Minos and Rhadamanthus, and one from Europe, Aeacus. And these, when they are dead, shall give judgment in the meadow at the parting of the ways, whence the two roads lead, one to the Islands of the Blessed, and the other to Tartarus. Rhadamanthus shall judge those who come from Asia, and Aeacus those who come from Europe. And to Minos I shall give the primacy, and he shall hold a court of appeal, in case either of the two others are in any doubt:—then the judgment respecting the last journey of men will be as just as possible.'

From this tale, Callicles, which I have heard and believe, I draw the following inferences:—Death, if I am right, is in the first place the separation from one another of two things, soul and body; nothing else. And after they are separated they retain their several natures, as in life; the body keeps the same habit, and the results of treatment or accident are distinctly visible in it: for example, he who by nature or training or both, was a tall man while he was alive, will remain as he was, after he is dead; and the fat man will remain fat; and so on; and the dead man, who in life had a fancy to have flowing hair, will have flowing hair. And if he was marked with the whip and had the prints of the scourge, or of wounds in him when he was alive, you might see the same in the dead body; and if his limbs were broken or misshapen when he was alive, the same appearance would be visible in the dead. And in a word, whatever was the habit of the body during life would be distinguishable after death, either perfectly, or in a great measure and for a certain time. And I should imagine that this is equally true of the soul, Callicles; when a man is stripped of the body, all the natural or acquired affections of the soul are laid open to view.—And when they come to the judge, as those from Asia come to Rhadamanthus, he places them near him and inspects them quite impartially, not knowing whose the soul is: perhaps he may lay hands on the soul of the great king, or of some other king or potentate, who has no soundness in him, but his soul is marked with the whip, and is full of the prints and scars of perjuries and crimes with which each action has stained him, and he is all crooked with falsehood and imposture, and has no straightness, because he has lived without truth. Him Rhadamanthus beholds, full of all deformity and disproportion, which is caused by licence and luxury and insolence and incontinence, and despatches him ignominiously to his prison, and there he undergoes the punishment which he deserves.

Now the proper office of punishment is twofold: he who is rightly punished ought either to become better and profit by it, or he ought to be made an example to his fellows, that they may see what he suffers, and fear and become better. Those who are improved when they are punished by gods and men, are those whose sins are curable; and they are improved, as in this world so also in another, by pain and suffering; for there is no other way in which they can be delivered from their evil. But they who have been guilty of the worst crimes, and are incurable by reason of their crimes, are made examples; for, as they are incurable, the time has passed at which they can receive any benefit. They get no good themselves, but others get good when they behold them enduring for ever the most terrible and painful and fearful sufferings as the penalty of their sins—there they are, hanging up as examples, in the prison-house of the world below, a spectacle and a warning to all unrighteous men who come thither. And among them, as I confidently affirm, will be found Archelaus, if Polus truly reports of him, and any other tyrant who is like him. Of these fearful examples, most, as I believe, are taken from the class of tyrants and kings and potentates and public men, for they are the authors of the greatest and most impious crimes, because they have the power. And Homer witnesses to the truth of this; for they are always kings and potentates whom he has described as suffering everlasting punishment in the world below: such were Tantalus and Sisyphus and Tityus. But no one ever described Thersites, or any private person who was a villain, as suffering everlasting punishment, or as incurable. For to commit the worst crimes, as I am inclined to think, was not in his power, and he was happier than those who had the power. No, Callicles, the very bad men come from the class of those who have power (compare Republic). And yet in that very class there may arise good men, and worthy of all admiration they are, for where there is great power to do wrong, to live and to die justly is a hard thing, and greatly to be praised, and few there are who attain to this. Such good and true men, however, there have been, and will be again, at Athens and in other states, who have fulfilled their trust righteously; and there is one who is quite famous all over Hellas, Aristeides, the son of Lysimachus. But, in general, great men are also bad, my friend.

As I was saying, Rhadamanthus, when he gets a soul of the bad kind, knows nothing about him, neither who he is, nor who his parents are; he knows only that he has got hold of a villain; and seeing this, he stamps him as curable or incurable, and sends him away to Tartarus, whither he goes and receives his proper recompense. Or, again, he looks with admiration on the soul of some just one who has lived in holiness and truth; he may have been a private man or not; and I should say, Callicles, that he is most likely to have been a philosopher who has done his own work, and not troubled himself with the doings of other men in his lifetime; him Rhadamanthus sends to the Islands of the Blessed. Aeacus does the same; and they both have sceptres, and judge; but Minos alone has a golden sceptre and is seated looking on, as Odysseus in Homer declares that he saw him:

'Holding a sceptre of gold, and giving laws to the dead.'

Now I, Callicles, am persuaded of the truth of these things, and I consider how I shall present my soul whole and undefiled before the judge in that day. Renouncing the honours at which the world aims, I desire only to know the truth, and to live as well as I can, and, when I die, to die as well as I can. And, to the utmost of my power, I exhort all other men to do the same. And, in return for your exhortation of me, I exhort you also to take part in the great combat, which is the combat of life, and greater than every other earthly conflict. And I retort your reproach of me, and say, that you will not be able to help yourself when the day of trial and judgment, of which I was speaking, comes upon you; you will go before the judge, the son of Aegina, and, when he has got you in his grip and is carrying you off, you will gape and your head will swim round, just as mine would in the courts of this world, and very likely some one will shamefully box you on the ears, and put upon you any sort of insult.

Perhaps this may appear to you to be only an old wife's tale, which you will contemn. And there might be reason in your contemning such tales, if by searching we could find out anything better or truer: but now you see that you and Polus and Gorgias, who are the three wisest of the Greeks of our day, are not able to show that we ought to live any life which does not profit in another world as well as in this. And of all that has been said, nothing remains unshaken but the saying, that to do injustice is more to be avoided than to suffer injustice, and that the reality and not the appearance of virtue is to be followed above all things, as well in public as in private life; and that when any one has been wrong in anything, he is to be chastised, and that the next best thing to a man being just is that he should become just, and be chastised and punished; also that he should avoid all flattery of himself as well as of others, of the few or of the many: and rhetoric and any other art should be used by him, and all his actions should be done always, with a view to justice.

Follow me then, and I will lead you where you will be happy in life and after death, as the argument shows. And never mind if some one despises you as a fool, and insults you, if he has a mind; let him strike you, by Zeus, and do you be of good cheer, and do not mind the insulting blow, for you will never come to any harm in the practice of virtue, if you are a really good and true man. When we have practised virtue together, we will apply ourselves to politics, if that seems desirable, or we will advise about whatever else may seem good to us, for we shall be better able to judge then. In our present condition we ought not to give ourselves airs, for even on the most important subjects we are always changing our minds; so utterly stupid are we! Let us, then, take the argument as our guide, which has revealed to us that the best way of life is to practise justice and every virtue in life and death. This way let us go; and in this exhort all men to follow, not in the way to which you trust and in which you exhort me to follow you; for that way, Callicles, is nothing worth.

ION

By Plato

Translated by Benjamin Jowett

PERSONS OF THE DIALOGUE: Socrates, Ion.

SOCRATES: Welcome, Ion. Are you from your native city of Ephesus?

ION: No, Socrates; but from Epidaurus, where I attended the festival of Asclepius.

SOCRATES: And do the Epidaurians have contests of rhapsodes at the festival?

ION: O yes; and of all sorts of musical performers.

SOCRATES: And were you one of the competitors—and did you succeed?

ION: I obtained the first prize of all, Socrates.

SOCRATES: Well done; and I hope that you will do the same for us at the Panathenaea.

ION: And I will, please heaven.

SOCRATES: I often envy the profession of a rhapsode, Ion; for you have always to wear fine clothes, and to look as beautiful as you can is a part of your art. Then, again, you are obliged to be continually in the company of many good poets; and especially of Homer, who is the best and most divine of them; and to understand him, and not merely learn his words by rote, is a thing greatly to be envied. And no man can be a rhapsode who does not understand the meaning of the poet. For the rhapsode ought to interpret the mind of the poet to his hearers, but how can he interpret him well unless he knows what he means? All this is greatly to be envied.

ION: Very true, Socrates; interpretation has certainly been the most laborious part of my art; and I believe myself able to speak about Homer better than any man; and that neither Metrodorus of Lampsacus, nor Stesimbrotus of Thasos, nor Glaucon, nor any one else who ever was, had as good ideas about Homer as I have, or as many.

SOCRATES: I am glad to hear you say so, Ion; I see that you will not refuse to acquaint me with them.

ION: Certainly, Socrates; and you really ought to hear how exquisitely I render Homer. I think that the Homeridae should give me a golden crown.

SOCRATES: I shall take an opportunity of hearing your embellishments of him at some other time. But just now I should like to ask you a question: Does your art extend to Hesiod and Archilochus, or to Homer only?

ION: To Homer only; he is in himself quite enough.

SOCRATES: Are there any things about which Homer and Hesiod agree?

ION: Yes; in my opinion there are a good many.

SOCRATES: And can you interpret better what Homer says, or what Hesiod says, about these matters in which they agree?

ION: I can interpret them equally well, Socrates, where they agree.

SOCRATES: But what about matters in which they do not agree?—for example, about divination, of which both Homer and Hesiod have something to say,—

ION: Very true:

SOCRATES: Would you or a good prophet be a better interpreter of what these two poets say about divination, not only when they agree, but when they disagree?

ION: A prophet.

SOCRATES: And if you were a prophet, would you not be able to interpret them when they disagree as well as when they agree?

ION: Clearly.

SOCRATES: But how did you come to have this skill about Homer only, and not about Hesiod or the other poets? Does not Homer speak of the same themes which all other poets handle? Is not war his great argument? and does he not speak of human society and of intercourse of men, good and bad, skilled and unskilled, and of the gods conversing with one another and with mankind, and about what happens in heaven and in the world below, and the generations of gods and heroes? Are not these the themes of which Homer sings?

ION: Very true, Socrates.

SOCRATES: And do not the other poets sing of the same?

ION: Yes, Socrates; but not in the same way as Homer.

SOCRATES: What, in a worse way?

ION: Yes, in a far worse.

SOCRATES: And Homer in a better way?

ION: He is incomparably better.

SOCRATES: And yet surely, my dear friend Ion, in a discussion about arithmetic, where many people are speaking, and one speaks better than the rest, there is somebody who can judge which of them is the good speaker?

ION: Yes.

SOCRATES: And he who judges of the good will be the same as he who judges of the bad speakers?

ION: The same.

SOCRATES: And he will be the arithmetician?

ION: Yes.

SOCRATES: Well, and in discussions about the wholesomeness of food, when many persons are speaking, and one speaks better than the rest, will he who recognizes the better speaker be a different person from him who recognizes the worse, or the same?

ION: Clearly the same.

SOCRATES: And who is he, and what is his name?

ION: The physician.

SOCRATES: And speaking generally, in all discussions in which the subject is the same and many men are speaking, will not he who knows the good know the bad speaker also? For if he does not know the bad, neither will he know the good when the same topic is being discussed.

ION: True.

SOCRATES: Is not the same person skilful in both?

ION: Yes.

SOCRATES: And you say that Homer and the other poets, such as Hesiod and Archilochus, speak of the same things, although not in the same way; but the one speaks well and the other not so well?

ION: Yes; and I am right in saying so.

SOCRATES: And if you knew the good speaker, you would also know the inferior speakers to be inferior?

ION: That is true.

SOCRATES: Then, my dear friend, can I be mistaken in saying that Ion is equally skilled in Homer and in other poets, since he himself acknowledges that the same person will be a good judge of all those who speak of the same things; and that almost all poets do speak of the same things?

ION: Why then, Socrates, do I lose attention and go to sleep and have absolutely no ideas of the least value, when any one speaks of any other poet; but when Homer is mentioned, I wake up at once and am all attention and have plenty to say?

SOCRATES: The reason, my friend, is obvious. No one can fail to see that you speak of Homer without any art or knowledge. If you were able to speak of him by rules of art, you would have been able to speak of all other poets; for poetry is a whole.

ION: Yes.

SOCRATES: And when any one acquires any other art as a whole, the same may be said of them. Would you like me to explain my meaning, Ion?

ION: Yes, indeed, Socrates; I very much wish that you would: for I love to hear you wise men talk.

SOCRATES: O that we were wise, Ion, and that you could truly call us so; but you rhapsodes and actors, and the poets whose verses you sing, are wise; whereas I am a common man, who only speak the truth. For consider what a very commonplace and trivial thing is this which I have said—a thing which any man might say: that when a man has acquired a knowledge of a whole art, the enquiry into good and bad is one and the same. Let us consider this matter; is not the art of painting a whole?

ION: Yes.

SOCRATES: And there are and have been many painters good and bad?

ION: Yes.

SOCRATES: And did you ever know any one who was skilful in pointing out the excellences and defects of Polygnotus the son of Aglaophon, but incapable of criticizing other painters; and when the work of any other painter was produced, went to sleep and was at a loss, and had no ideas; but when he had to give his opinion about Polygnotus, or whoever the painter might be, and about him only, woke up and was attentive and had plenty to say?

ION: No indeed, I have never known such a person.

SOCRATES: Or did you ever know of any one in sculpture, who was skilful in expounding the merits of Daedalus the son of Metion, or of Epeius the son of Panopeus, or of Theodorus the Samian, or of any individual sculptor; but when the works of sculptors in general were produced, was at a loss and went to sleep and had nothing to say?

ION: No indeed; no more than the other.

SOCRATES: And if I am not mistaken, you never met with any one among flute-players or harp-players or singers to the harp or rhapsodes who was able to discourse of Olympus or Thamyras or Orpheus, or Phemius the rhapsode of Ithaca, but was at a loss when he came to speak of Ion of Ephesus, and had no notion of his merits or defects?

ION: I cannot deny what you say, Socrates. Nevertheless I am conscious in my own self, and the world agrees with me in thinking that I do speak better and have more to say about Homer than any other man. But I do not speak equally well about others—tell me the reason of this.

SOCRATES: I perceive, Ion; and I will proceed to explain to you what I imagine to be the reason of this. The gift which you possess of speaking excellently about Homer is not an art, but, as I was just saying, an inspiration; there is a divinity moving you, like that contained in the stone which Euripides calls a magnet, but which is commonly known as the stone of Heraclea. This stone not only attracts iron rings, but also imparts to them a similar power of attracting other rings; and sometimes you may see a number of pieces of iron and rings suspended from one another so as to form quite a long chain: and all of them derive their power of suspension from the original stone. In like manner the Muse first of all inspires men herself; and from these inspired persons a chain of other persons is suspended, who take the inspiration. For all good poets, epic as well as lyric, compose their beautiful poems not by art, but because they are inspired and possessed. And as the Corybantian revellers when they dance are not in their right mind, so the lyric poets are not in their right mind when they are composing their beautiful strains: but when falling under the power of music and metre they are inspired and possessed; like Bacchic maidens who draw milk and honey from the rivers when they are under the influence of Dionysus but not when they are in their right mind. And the soul of the lyric poet does the same, as they themselves say; for they tell us that they bring songs from honeyed fountains, culling them out of the gardens and dells of the Muses; they, like the bees, winging their way from flower to flower. And this is true. For the poet is a light and winged and holy thing, and there is no invention in him until he has been inspired and is out of his senses, and the mind is no longer in him: when he has not attained to this state, he is powerless and is unable to utter his oracles. Many are the noble words in which poets speak concerning the actions of men; but like yourself when speaking about Homer, they do not speak of them by any rules of art: they are simply inspired to utter that to which the Muse impels them, and that only; and when inspired, one of them will make dithyrambs, another hymns of praise, another choral strains, another epic or iambic verses—and he who is good at one is not good at any other kind of verse: for not by art does the poet sing, but by power divine. Had he learned by rules of art, he would have known how to speak not of one theme only, but of all; and therefore God takes away the minds of poets, and uses them as his ministers, as he also uses diviners and holy prophets, in order that we who hear them may know them to be speaking not of themselves who utter these priceless words in a state of unconsciousness, but that God himself is the speaker, and that through them he is conversing with us. And Tynnichus the Chalcidian affords a striking instance of what I am saying: he wrote nothing that any one would care to remember but the famous paean which is in every one's mouth, one of the finest poems ever written, simply an invention of the Muses, as he himself says. For in this way the God would seem to indicate to us and not allow us to doubt that these beautiful poems are not human, or the work of man, but divine and the work of God; and that the poets are only the interpreters of the Gods by whom they are severally possessed. Was not this the lesson which the God intended to teach when by the mouth of the worst of poets he sang the best of songs? Am I not right, Ion?

ION: Yes, indeed, Socrates, I feel that you are; for your words touch my soul, and I am persuaded that good poets by a divine inspiration interpret the things of the Gods to us.

SOCRATES: And you rhapsodists are the interpreters of the poets?

ION: There again you are right.

SOCRATES: Then you are the interpreters of interpreters?

ION: Precisely.

SOCRATES: I wish you would frankly tell me, Ion, what I am going to ask of you: When you produce the greatest effect upon the audience in the recitation of some striking passage, such as the apparition of Odysseus leaping forth on the floor, recognized by the suitors and casting his arrows at his feet, or the description of Achilles rushing at Hector, or the sorrows of Andromache, Hecuba, or Priam,—are you in your right mind? Are you not carried out of yourself, and does not your soul in an ecstasy seem to be among the persons or places of which you are speaking, whether they are in Ithaca or in Troy or whatever may be the scene of the poem?

ION: That proof strikes home to me, Socrates. For I must frankly confess that at the tale of pity my eyes are filled with tears, and when I speak of horrors, my hair stands on end and my heart throbs.

SOCRATES: Well, Ion, and what are we to say of a man who at a sacrifice or festival, when he is dressed in holiday attire, and has golden crowns upon his head, of which nobody has robbed him, appears weeping or panic-stricken in the presence of more than twenty thousand friendly faces, when there is no one despoiling or wronging him;—is he in his right mind or is he not?

ION: No indeed, Socrates, I must say that, strictly speaking, he is not in his right mind.

SOCRATES: And are you aware that you produce similar effects on most of the spectators?

ION: Only too well; for I look down upon them from the stage, and behold the various emotions of pity, wonder, sternness, stamped upon their countenances when I am speaking: and I am obliged to give my very best attention to them; for if I make them cry I myself shall laugh, and if I make them laugh I myself shall cry when the time of payment arrives.

SOCRATES: Do you know that the spectator is the last of the rings which, as I am saying, receive the power of the original magnet from one another? The rhapsode like yourself and the actor are intermediate links, and the poet himself is the first of them. Through all these the God sways the souls of men in any direction which he pleases, and makes one man hang down from another. Thus there is a vast chain of dancers and masters and under-masters of choruses, who are suspended, as if from the stone, at the side of the rings which hang down from the Muse. And every poet has some Muse from whom he is suspended, and by whom he is said to be possessed, which is nearly the same thing; for he is taken hold of. And from these first rings, which are the poets, depend others, some deriving their inspiration from Orpheus, others from Musaeus; but the greater number are possessed and held by Homer. Of whom, Ion, you are one, and are possessed by Homer; and when any one repeats the words of another poet you go to sleep, and know not what to say; but when any one recites a strain of Homer you wake up in a moment, and your soul leaps within you, and you have plenty to say; for not by art or knowledge about Homer do you say what you say, but by divine inspiration and by possession; just as the Corybantian revellers too have a quick perception of that strain only which is appropriated to the God by whom they are possessed, and have plenty of dances and words for that, but take no heed of any other. And you, Ion, when the name of Homer is mentioned have plenty to say, and have nothing to say of others. You ask, 'Why is this?' The answer is that you praise Homer not by art but by divine inspiration.

ION: That is good, Socrates; and yet I doubt whether you will ever have eloquence enough to persuade me that I praise Homer only when I am mad and possessed; and if you could hear me speak of him I am sure you would never think this to be the case.

SOCRATES: I should like very much to hear you, but not until you have answered a question which I have to ask. On what part of Homer do you speak well?—not surely about every part.

ION: There is no part, Socrates, about which I do not speak well: of that I can assure you.

SOCRATES: Surely not about things in Homer of which you have no knowledge?

ION: And what is there in Homer of which I have no knowledge?

SOCRATES: Why, does not Homer speak in many passages about arts? For example, about driving; if I can only remember the lines I will repeat them.

ION: I remember, and will repeat them.

SOCRATES: Tell me then, what Nestor says to Antilochus, his son, where he bids him be careful of the turn at the horserace in honour of Patroclus.

ION: 'Bend gently,' he says, 'in the polished chariot to the left of them, and urge the horse on the right hand with whip and voice; and slacken the rein. And when you are at the goal, let the left horse draw near, yet so that the nave of the well-wrought wheel may not even seem to touch the extremity; and avoid catching the stone (Il.).'

SOCRATES: Enough. Now, Ion, will the charioteer or the physician be the better judge of the propriety of these lines?

ION: The charioteer, clearly.

SOCRATES: And will the reason be that this is his art, or will there be any other reason?

ION: No, that will be the reason.

SOCRATES: And every art is appointed by God to have knowledge of a certain work; for that which we know by the art of the pilot we do not know by the art of medicine?

ION: Certainly not.

SOCRATES: Nor do we know by the art of the carpenter that which we know by the art of medicine?

ION: Certainly not.

SOCRATES: And this is true of all the arts;—that which we know with one art we do not know with the other? But let me ask a prior question: You admit that there are differences of arts?

ION: Yes.

SOCRATES: You would argue, as I should, that when one art is of one kind of knowledge and another of another, they are different?

ION: Yes.

SOCRATES: Yes, surely; for if the subject of knowledge were the same, there would be no meaning in saying that the arts were different,—if they both gave the same knowledge. For example, I know that here are five fingers, and you know the same. And if I were to ask whether I and you became acquainted with this fact by the help of the same art of arithmetic, you would acknowledge that we did?

ION: Yes.

SOCRATES: Tell me, then, what I was intending to ask you,—whether this holds universally? Must the same art have the same subject of knowledge, and different arts other subjects of knowledge?

ION: That is my opinion, Socrates.

SOCRATES: Then he who has no knowledge of a particular art will have no right judgment of the sayings and doings of that art?

ION: Very true.

SOCRATES: Then which will be a better judge of the lines which you were reciting from Homer, you or the charioteer?

ION: The charioteer.

SOCRATES: Why, yes, because you are a rhapsode and not a charioteer.

ION: Yes.

SOCRATES: And the art of the rhapsode is different from that of the charioteer?

ION: Yes.

SOCRATES: And if a different knowledge, then a knowledge of different matters?

ION: True.

SOCRATES: You know the passage in which Hecamede, the concubine of Nestor, is described as giving to the wounded Machaon a posset, as he says,

'Made with Pramnian wine; and she grated cheese of goat's milk with a grater of bronze, and at his side placed an onion which gives a relish to drink (Il.).'

Now would you say that the art of the rhapsode or the art of medicine was better able to judge of the propriety of these lines?

ION: The art of medicine.

SOCRATES: And when Homer says,

'And she descended into the deep like a leaden plummet, which, set in the horn of ox that ranges in the fields, rushes along carrying death among the ravenous fishes (Il.),'—

will the art of the fisherman or of the rhapsode be better able to judge whether these lines are rightly expressed or not?

ION: Clearly, Socrates, the art of the fisherman.

SOCRATES: Come now, suppose that you were to say to me: 'Since you, Socrates, are able to assign different passages in Homer to their corresponding arts, I wish that you would tell me what are the passages of which the excellence ought to be judged by the prophet and prophetic art'; and you will see how readily and truly I shall answer you. For there are many such passages, particularly in the Odyssee; as, for example, the passage in which Theoclymenus the prophet of the house of Melampus says to the suitors:—

'Wretched men! what is happening to you? Your heads and your faces and your limbs underneath are shrouded in night; and the voice of lamentation bursts forth, and your cheeks are wet with tears. And the vestibule is full, and the court is full, of ghosts descending into the darkness of Erebus, and the sun has perished out of heaven, and an evil mist is spread abroad (Od.).'

And there are many such passages in the Iliad also; as for example in the description of the battle near the rampart, where he says:—

'As they were eager to pass the ditch, there came to them an omen: a soaring eagle, holding back the people on the left, bore a huge bloody dragon in his talons, still living and panting; nor had he yet resigned the strife, for he bent back and smote the bird which carried him on the breast by the neck, and he in pain let him fall from him to the ground into the midst of the multitude. And the eagle, with a cry, was borne afar on the wings of the wind (Il.).'

These are the sort of things which I should say that the prophet ought to consider and determine.

ION: And you are quite right, Socrates, in saying so.

SOCRATES: Yes, Ion, and you are right also. And as I have selected from the Iliad and Odyssee for you passages which describe the office of the prophet and the physician and the fisherman, do you, who know Homer so much better than I do, Ion, select for me passages which relate to the rhapsode and the rhapsode's art, and which the rhapsode ought to examine and judge of better than other men.

ION: All passages, I should say, Socrates.

SOCRATES: Not all, Ion, surely. Have you already forgotten what you were saying? A rhapsode ought to have a better memory.

ION: Why, what am I forgetting?

SOCRATES: Do you not remember that you declared the art of the rhapsode to be different from the art of the charioteer?

ION: Yes, I remember.

SOCRATES: And you admitted that being different they would have different subjects of knowledge?

ION: Yes.

SOCRATES: Then upon your own showing the rhapsode, and the art of the rhapsode, will not know everything?

ION: I should exclude certain things, Socrates.

SOCRATES: You mean to say that you would exclude pretty much the subjects of the other arts. As he does not know all of them, which of them will he know?

ION: He will know what a man and what a woman ought to say, and what a freeman and what a slave ought to say, and what a ruler and what a subject.

SOCRATES: Do you mean that a rhapsode will know better than the pilot what the ruler of a sea-tossed vessel ought to say?

ION: No; the pilot will know best.

SOCRATES: Or will the rhapsode know better than the physician what the ruler of a sick man ought to say?

ION: He will not.

SOCRATES: But he will know what a slave ought to say?

ION: Yes.

SOCRATES: Suppose the slave to be a cowherd; the rhapsode will know better than the cowherd what he ought to say in order to soothe the infuriated cows?

ION: No, he will not.

SOCRATES: But he will know what a spinning-woman ought to say about the working of wool?

ION: No.

SOCRATES: At any rate he will know what a general ought to say when exhorting his soldiers?

ION: Yes, that is the sort of thing which the rhapsode will be sure to know.

SOCRATES: Well, but is the art of the rhapsode the art of the general?

ION: I am sure that I should know what a general ought to say.

SOCRATES: Why, yes, Ion, because you may possibly have a knowledge of the art of the general as well as of the rhapsode; and you may also have a knowledge of horsemanship as well as of the lyre: and then you would know when horses were well or ill managed. But suppose I were to ask you: By the help of which art, Ion, do you know whether horses are well managed, by your skill as a horseman or as a performer on the lyre—what would you answer?

ION: I should reply, by my skill as a horseman.

SOCRATES: And if you judged of performers on the lyre, you would admit that you judged of them as a performer on the lyre, and not as a horseman?

ION: Yes.

SOCRATES: And in judging of the general's art, do you judge of it as a general or a rhapsode?

ION: To me there appears to be no difference between them.

SOCRATES: What do you mean? Do you mean to say that the art of the rhapsode and of the general is the same?

ION: Yes, one and the same.

SOCRATES: Then he who is a good rhapsode is also a good general?

ION: Certainly, Socrates.

SOCRATES: And he who is a good general is also a good rhapsode?

ION: No; I do not say that.

SOCRATES: But you do say that he who is a good rhapsode is also a good general.

ION: Certainly.

SOCRATES: And you are the best of Hellenic rhapsodes?

ION: Far the best, Socrates.

SOCRATES: And are you the best general, Ion?

ION: To be sure, Socrates; and Homer was my master.

SOCRATES: But then, Ion, what in the name of goodness can be the reason why you, who are the best of generals as well as the best of rhapsodes in all Hellas, go about as a rhapsode when you might be a general? Do you think that the Hellenes want a rhapsode with his golden crown, and do not want a general?

ION: Why, Socrates, the reason is, that my countrymen, the Ephesians, are the servants and soldiers of Athens, and do not need a general; and you and Sparta are not likely to have me, for you think that you have enough generals of your own.

SOCRATES: My good Ion, did you never hear of Apollodorus of Cyzicus?

ION: Who may he be?

SOCRATES: One who, though a foreigner, has often been chosen their general by the Athenians: and there is Phanosthenes of Andros, and Heraclides of Clazomenae, whom they have also appointed to the command of their armies and to other offices, although aliens, after they had shown their merit. And will they not choose Ion the Ephesian to be their general, and honour him, if he prove himself worthy? Were not the Ephesians originally Athenians, and Ephesus is no mean city? But, indeed, Ion, if you are correct in saying that by art and knowledge you are able to praise Homer, you do not deal fairly with me, and after all your professions of knowing many glorious things about Homer, and promises that you would exhibit them, you are only a deceiver, and so far from exhibiting the art of which you are a master, will not, even after my repeated entreaties, explain to me the nature of it. You have literally as many forms as Proteus; and now you go all manner of ways, twisting and turning, and, like Proteus, become all manner of people at once, and at last slip away from me in the disguise of a general, in order that you may escape exhibiting your Homeric lore. And if you have art, then, as I was saying, in falsifying your promise that you would exhibit Homer, you are not dealing fairly with me. But if, as I believe, you have no art, but speak all these beautiful words about Homer unconsciously under his inspiring influence, then I acquit you of dishonesty, and shall only say that you are inspired. Which do you prefer to be thought, dishonest or inspired?

ION: There is a great difference, Socrates, between the two alternatives; and inspiration is by far the nobler.

SOCRATES: Then, Ion, I shall assume the nobler alternative; and attribute to you in your praises of Homer inspiration, and not art.

LACHES

OR COURAGE

By Plato

Translated by Benjamin Jowett

PERSONS OF THE DIALOGUE:

Lysimachus, son of Aristides.

Melesias, son of Thucydides.

Their sons.

Nicias, Laches, Socrates.

LYSIMACHUS: You have seen the exhibition of the man fighting in armour, Nicias and Laches, but we did not tell you at the time the reason why my friend Melesias and I asked you to go with us and see him. I think that we may as well confess what this was, for we certainly ought not to have any reserve with you. The reason was, that we were intending to ask your advice. Some laugh at the very notion of advising others, and when they are asked will not say what they think. They guess at the wishes of the person who asks them, and answer according to his, and not according to their own, opinion. But as we know that you are good judges, and will say exactly what you think, we have taken you into our counsels. The matter about which I am making all this preface is as follows: Melesias and I have two sons; that is his son, and he is named Thucydides, after his grandfather; and this is mine, who is also called after his grandfather, Aristides. Now, we are resolved to take the greatest care of the youths, and not to let them run about as they like, which is too often the way with the young, when they are no longer children, but to begin at once and do the utmost that we can for them. And knowing you to have sons of your own, we thought that you were most likely to have attended to their training and improvement, and, if perchance you have not attended to them, we may remind you that you ought to have done so, and would invite you to assist us in the fulfilment of a common duty. I will tell you, Nicias and Laches, even at the risk of being tedious, how we came to think of this. Melesias and I live together, and our sons live with us; and now, as I was saying at first, we are going to confess to you. Both of us often talk to the lads about the many noble deeds which our own fathers did in war and peace—in the management of the allies, and in the administration of the city; but neither of us has any deeds of his own which he can show. The truth is that we are ashamed of this contrast being seen by them, and we blame our fathers for letting us be spoiled in the days of our youth, while they were occupied with the concerns of others; and we urge all this upon the lads, pointing out to them that they will not grow up to honour if they are rebellious and take no pains about themselves; but that if they take pains they may, perhaps, become worthy of the names which they bear. They, on their part, promise to comply with our wishes; and our care is to discover what studies or pursuits are likely to be most improving to them. Some one commended to us the art of fighting in armour, which he thought an excellent accomplishment for a young man to learn; and he praised the man whose exhibition you have seen, and told us to go and see him. And we determined that we would go, and get you to accompany us; and we were intending at the same time, if you did not object, to take counsel with you about the education of our sons. That is the matter which we wanted to talk over with you; and we hope that you will give us your opinion about this art of fighting in armour, and about any other studies or pursuits which may or may not be desirable for a young man to learn. Please to say whether you agree to our proposal.

NICIAS: As far as I am concerned, Lysimachus and Melesias, I applaud your purpose, and will gladly assist you; and I believe that you, Laches, will be equally glad.

LACHES: Certainly, Nicias; and I quite approve of the remark which Lysimachus made about his own father and the father of Melesias, and which is applicable, not only to them, but to us, and to every one who is occupied with public affairs. As he says, such persons are too apt to be negligent and careless of their own children and their private concerns. There is much truth in that remark of yours, Lysimachus. But why, instead of consulting us, do you not consult our friend Socrates about the education of the youths? He is of the same deme with you, and is always passing his time in places where the youth have any noble study or pursuit, such as you are enquiring after.

LYSIMACHUS: Why, Laches, has Socrates ever attended to matters of this sort?

LACHES: Certainly, Lysimachus.

NICIAS: That I have the means of knowing as well as Laches; for quite lately he supplied me with a teacher of music for my sons,—Damon, the disciple of Agathocles, who is a most accomplished man in every way, as well as a musician, and a companion of inestimable value for young men at their age.

LYSIMACHUS: Those who have reached my time of life, Socrates and Nicias and Laches, fall out of acquaintance with the young, because they are generally detained at home by old age; but you, O son of Sophroniscus, should let your fellow demesman have the benefit of any advice which you are able to give. Moreover I have a claim upon you as an old friend of your father; for I and he were always companions and friends, and to the hour of his death there never was a difference between us; and now it comes back to me, at the mention of your name, that I have heard these lads talking to one another at home, and often speaking of Socrates in terms of the highest praise; but I have never thought to ask them whether the son of Sophroniscus was the person whom they meant. Tell me, my boys, whether this is the Socrates of whom you have often spoken?

SON: Certainly, father, this is he.

LYSIMACHUS: I am delighted to hear, Socrates, that you maintain the name of your father, who was a most excellent man; and I further rejoice at the prospect of our family ties being renewed.

LACHES: Indeed, Lysimachus, you ought not to give him up; for I can assure you that I have seen him maintaining, not only his father's, but also his country's name. He was my companion in the retreat from Delium, and I can tell you that if others had only been like him, the honour of our country would have been upheld, and the great defeat would never have occurred.

LYSIMACHUS: That is very high praise which is accorded to you, Socrates, by faithful witnesses and for actions like those which they praise. Let me tell you the pleasure which I feel in hearing of your fame; and I hope that you will regard me as one of your warmest friends. You ought to have visited us long ago, and made yourself at home with us; but now, from this day forward, as we have at last found one another out, do as I say—come and make acquaintance with me, and with these young men, that I may continue your friend, as I was your father's. I shall expect you to do so, and shall venture at some future time to remind you of your duty. But what say you of the matter of which we were beginning to speak—the art of fighting in armour? Is that a practice in which the lads may be advantageously instructed?

SOCRATES: I will endeavour to advise you, Lysimachus, as far as I can in this matter, and also in every way will comply with your wishes; but as I am younger and not so experienced, I think that I ought certainly to hear first what my elders have to say, and to learn of them, and if I have anything to add, then I may venture to give my opinion to them as well as to you. Suppose, Nicias, that one or other of you begin.

NICIAS: I have no objection, Socrates; and my opinion is that the acquirement of this art is in many ways useful to young men. It is an advantage to them that among the favourite amusements of their leisure hours they should have one which tends to improve and not to injure their bodily health. No gymnastics could be better or harder exercise; and this, and the art of riding, are of all arts most befitting to a freeman; for they only who are thus trained in the use of arms are the athletes of our military profession, trained in that on which the conflict turns. Moreover in actual battle, when you have to fight in a line with a number of others, such an acquirement will be of some use, and will be of the greatest whenever the ranks are broken and you have to fight singly, either in pursuit, when you are attacking some one who is defending himself, or in flight, when you have to defend yourself against an assailant. Certainly he who possessed the art could not meet with any harm at the hands of a single person, or perhaps of several; and in any case he would have a great advantage. Further, this sort of skill inclines a man to the love of other noble lessons; for every man who has learned how to fight in armour will desire to learn the proper arrangement of an army, which is the sequel of the lesson: and when he has learned this, and his ambition is once fired, he will go on to learn the complete art of the general. There is no difficulty in seeing that the knowledge and practice of other military arts will be honourable and valuable to a man; and this lesson may be the beginning of them. Let me add a further advantage, which is by no means a slight one,—that this science will make any man a great deal more valiant and self-possessed in the field. And I will not disdain to mention, what by some may be thought to be a small matter;—he will make a better appearance at the right time; that is to say, at the time when his appearance will strike terror into his enemies. My opinion then, Lysimachus, is, as I say, that the youths should be instructed in this art, and for the reasons which I have given. But Laches may take a different view; and I shall be very glad to hear what he has to say.

LACHES: I should not like to maintain, Nicias, that any kind of knowledge is not to be learned; for all knowledge appears to be a good: and if, as Nicias and as the teachers of the art affirm, this use of arms is really a species of knowledge, then it ought to be learned; but if not, and if those who profess to teach it are deceivers only; or if it be knowledge, but not of a valuable sort, then what is the use of learning it? I say this, because I think that if it had been really valuable, the Lacedaemonians, whose whole life is passed in finding out and practising the arts which give them an advantage over other nations in war, would have discovered this one. And even if they had not, still these professors of the art would certainly not have failed to discover that of all the Hellenes the Lacedaemonians have the greatest interest in such matters, and that a master of the art who was honoured among them would be sure to make his fortune among other nations, just as a tragic poet would who is honoured among ourselves; which is the reason why he who fancies that he can write a tragedy does not go about itinerating in the neighbouring states, but rushes hither straight, and exhibits at Athens; and this is natural. Whereas I perceive that these fighters in armour regard Lacedaemon as a sacred inviolable territory, which they do not touch with the point of their foot; but they make a circuit of the neighbouring states, and would rather exhibit to any others than to the Spartans; and particularly to those who would themselves acknowledge that they are by no means first-rate in the arts of war. Further, Lysimachus, I have encountered a good many of these gentlemen in actual service, and have taken their measure, which I can give you at once; for none of these masters of fence have ever been distinguished in war,—there has been a sort of fatality about them; while in all other arts the men of note have been always those who have practised the art, they appear to be a most unfortunate exception. For example, this very Stesilaus, whom you and I have just witnessed exhibiting in all that crowd and making such great professions of his powers, I have seen at another time making, in sober truth, an involuntary exhibition of himself, which was a far better spectacle. He was a marine on board a ship which struck a transport vessel, and was armed with a weapon, half spear, half scythe; the singularity of this weapon was worthy of the singularity of the man. To make a long story short, I will only tell you what happened to this notable invention of the scythe spear. He was fighting, and the scythe was caught in the rigging of the other ship, and stuck fast; and he tugged, but was unable to get his weapon free. The two ships were passing one another. He first ran along his own ship holding on to the spear; but as the other ship passed by and drew him after as he was holding on, he let the spear slip through his hand until he retained only the end of the handle. The people in the transport clapped their hands, and laughed at his ridiculous figure; and when some one threw a stone, which fell on the deck at his feet, and he quitted his hold of the scythe-spear, the crew of his own trireme also burst out laughing; they could not refrain when they beheld the weapon waving in the air, suspended from the transport. Now I do not deny that there may be something in such an art, as Nicias asserts, but I tell you my experience; and, as I said at first, whether this be an art of which the advantage is so slight, or not an art at all, but only an imposition, in either case such an acquirement is not worth having. For my opinion is, that if the professor of this art be a coward, he will be likely to become rash, and his character will be only more notorious; or if he be brave, and fail ever so little, other men will be on the watch, and he will be greatly traduced; for there is a jealousy of such pretenders; and unless a man be pre-eminent in valour, he cannot help being ridiculous, if he says that he has this sort of skill. Such is my judgment,

Lysimachus, of the desirableness of this art; but, as I said at first, ask Socrates, and do not let him go until he has given you his opinion of the matter.

LYSIMACHUS: I am going to ask this favour of you, Socrates; as is the more necessary because the two councillors disagree, and some one is in a manner still needed who will decide between them. Had they agreed, no arbiter would have been required. But as Laches has voted one way and Nicias another, I should like to hear with which of our two friends you agree.

SOCRATES: What, Lysimachus, are you going to accept the opinion of the majority?

LYSIMACHUS: Why, yes, Socrates; what else am I to do?

SOCRATES: And would you do so too, Melesias? If you were deliberating about the gymnastic training of your son, would you follow the advice of the majority of us, or the opinion of the one who had been trained and exercised under a skilful master?

MELESIAS: The latter, Socrates; as would surely be reasonable.

SOCRATES: His one vote would be worth more than the vote of all us four?

MELESIAS: Certainly.

SOCRATES: And for this reason, as I imagine,—because a good decision is based on knowledge and not on numbers?

MELESIAS: To be sure.

SOCRATES: Must we not then first of all ask, whether there is any one of us who has knowledge of that about which we are deliberating? If there is, let us take his advice, though he be one only, and not mind the rest; if there is not, let us seek further counsel. Is this a slight matter about which you and Lysimachus are deliberating? Are you not risking the greatest of your possessions? For children are your riches; and upon their turning out well or ill depends the whole order of their father's house.

MELESIAS: That is true.

SOCRATES: Great care, then, is required in this matter?

MELESIAS: Certainly.

SOCRATES: Suppose, as I was just now saying, that we were considering, or wanting to consider, who was the best trainer. Should we not select him who knew and had practised the art, and had the best teachers?

MELESIAS: I think that we should.

SOCRATES: But would there not arise a prior question about the nature of the art of which we want to find the masters?

MELESIAS: I do not understand.

SOCRATES: Let me try to make my meaning plainer then. I do not think that we have as yet decided what that is about which we are consulting, when we ask which of us is or is not skilled in the art, and has or has not had a teacher of the art.

NICIAS: Why, Socrates, is not the question whether young men ought or ought not to learn the art of fighting in armour?

SOCRATES: Yes, Nicias; but there is also a prior question, which I may illustrate in this way: When a person considers about applying a medicine to the eyes, would you say that he is consulting about the medicine or about the eyes?

NICIAS: About the eyes.

SOCRATES: And when he considers whether he shall set a bridle on a horse and at what time, he is thinking of the horse and not of the bridle?

NICIAS: True.

SOCRATES: And in a word, when he considers anything for the sake of another thing, he thinks of the end and not of the means?

NICIAS: Certainly.

SOCRATES: And when you call in an adviser, you should see whether he too is skilful in the accomplishment of the end which you have in view?

NICIAS: Most true.

SOCRATES: And at present we have in view some knowledge, of which the end is the soul of youth?

NICIAS: Yes.

SOCRATES: And we are enquiring, Which of us is skilful or successful in the treatment of the soul, and which of us has had good teachers?

LACHES: Well but, Socrates; did you never observe that some persons, who have had no teachers, are more skilful than those who have, in some things?

SOCRATES: Yes, Laches, I have observed that; but you would not be very willing to trust them if they only professed to be masters of their art, unless they could show some proof of their skill or excellence in one or more works.

LACHES: That is true.

SOCRATES: And therefore, Laches and Nicias, as Lysimachus and Melesias, in their anxiety to improve the minds of their sons, have asked our advice about them, we too should tell them who our teachers were, if we say that we have had any, and prove them to be in the first place men of merit and experienced trainers of the minds of youth and also to have been really our teachers. Or if any of us says that he has no teacher, but that he has works of his own to show; then he should point out to them what Athenians or strangers, bond or free, he is generally acknowledged to have improved. But if he can show neither teachers nor works, then he should tell them to look out for others; and not run the risk of spoiling the children of friends, and thereby incurring the most formidable accusation which can be brought against any one by those nearest to him. As for myself, Lysimachus and Melesias, I am the first to confess that I have never had a teacher of the art of virtue; although I have always from my earliest youth desired to have one. But I am too poor to give money to the Sophists, who are the only professors of moral improvement; and to this day I have never been able to discover the art myself, though I should not be surprised if Nicias or Laches may have discovered or learned it; for they are far wealthier than I am, and may therefore have learnt of others. And they are older too; so that they have had more time to make the discovery. And I really believe that they are able to educate a man; for unless they had been confident in their own knowledge, they would never have spoken thus decidedly of the pursuits which are advantageous or hurtful to a young man. I repose confidence in both of them; but I am surprised to find that they differ from one another. And therefore, Lysimachus, as Laches suggested that you should detain me, and not let me go until I answered, I in turn earnestly beseech and advise you to detain Laches and Nicias, and question them. I would have you say to them: Socrates avers that he has no knowledge of the matter—he is unable to decide which of you speaks truly; neither discoverer nor student is he of anything of the kind. But you, Laches and Nicias, should each of you tell us who is the most skilful educator whom you have ever known; and whether you invented the art yourselves, or learned of another; and if you learned, who were your respective teachers, and who were their brothers in the art; and then, if you are too much occupied in politics to teach us yourselves, let us go to them, and present them with gifts, or make interest with them, or both, in the hope that they may be induced to take charge of our children and of yours; and then they will not grow up inferior, and disgrace their ancestors. But if you are yourselves original discoverers in that field, give us some proof of your skill. Who are they who, having been inferior persons, have become under your care good and noble? For if this is your first attempt at education, there is a danger that you may be trying the experiment, not on the 'vile corpus' of a Carian slave, but on your own sons, or the sons of your friend, and, as the proverb says, 'break the large vessel in learning to make pots.' Tell us then, what qualities you claim or do not claim. Make them tell you that, Lysimachus, and do not let them off.

LYSIMACHUS: I very much approve of the words of Socrates, my friends; but you, Nicias and Laches, must determine whether you will be questioned, and give an explanation about matters of this sort. Assuredly, I and Melesias would be greatly pleased to hear you answer the questions which Socrates asks, if you will: for I began by saying that we took you into our counsels because we thought that you would have attended to the subject, especially as you have children who, like our own, are nearly of an age to be educated. Well, then, if you have no objection, suppose that you take Socrates into partnership; and do you and he ask and answer one another's questions: for, as he has well said, we are deliberating about the most important of our concerns. I hope that you will see fit to comply with our request.

NICIAS: I see very clearly, Lysimachus, that you have only known Socrates' father, and have no acquaintance with Socrates himself: at least, you can only have known him when he was a child, and may have met him among his fellow-wardsmen, in company with his father, at a sacrifice, or at some other gathering. You clearly show that you have never known him since he arrived at manhood.

LYSIMACHUS: Why do you say that, Nicias?

NICIAS: Because you seem not to be aware that any one who has an intellectual affinity to Socrates and enters into conversation with him is liable to be drawn into an argument; and whatever subject he may start, he will be continually carried round and round by him, until at last he finds that he has to give an account both of his present and past life; and when he is once entangled, Socrates will not let him go until he has completely and thoroughly sifted him. Now I am used to his ways; and I know that he will certainly do as I say, and also that I myself shall be the sufferer; for I am fond of his conversation, Lysimachus. And I think that there is no harm in being reminded of any wrong thing which we are, or have been, doing: he who does not fly from reproof will be sure to take more heed of his after-life; as Solon says, he will wish and desire to be learning so long as he lives, and will not think that old age of itself brings wisdom. To me, to be cross-examined by Socrates is neither unusual nor unpleasant;

indeed, I knew all along that where Socrates was, the argument would soon pass from our sons to ourselves; and therefore, I say that for my part, I am quite willing to discourse with Socrates in his own manner; but you had better ask our friend Laches what his feeling may be.

LACHES: I have but one feeling, Nicias, or (shall I say?) two feelings, about discussions. Some would think that I am a lover, and to others I may seem to be a hater of discourse; for when I hear a man discoursing of virtue, or of any sort of wisdom, who is a true man and worthy of his theme, I am delighted beyond measure: and I compare the man and his words, and note the harmony and correspondence of them. And such an one I deem to be the true musician, attuned to a fairer harmony than that of the lyre, or any pleasant instrument of music; for truly he has in his own life a harmony of words and deeds arranged, not in the Ionian, or in the Phrygian mode, nor yet in the Lydian, but in the true Hellenic mode, which is the Dorian, and no other. Such an one makes me merry with the sound of his voice; and when I hear him I am thought to be a lover of discourse; so eager am I in drinking in his words. But a man whose actions do not agree with his words is an annoyance to me; and the better he speaks the more I hate him, and then I seem to be a hater of discourse. As to Socrates, I have no knowledge of his words, but of old, as would seem, I have had experience of his deeds; and his deeds show that free and noble sentiments are natural to him. And if his words accord, then I am of one mind with him, and shall be delighted to be interrogated by a man such as he is, and shall not be annoyed at having to learn of him: for I too agree with Solon, 'that I would fain grow old, learning many things.' But I must be allowed to add 'of the good only.' Socrates must be willing to allow that he is a good teacher, or I shall be a dull and uncongenial pupil: but that the teacher is younger, or not as yet in repute—anything of that sort is of no account with me. And therefore, Socrates, I give you notice that you may teach and confute me as much as ever you like, and also learn of me anything which I know. So high is the opinion which I have entertained of you ever since the day on which you were my companion in danger, and gave a proof of your valour such as only the man of merit can give. Therefore, say whatever you like, and do not mind about the difference of our ages.

SOCRATES: I cannot say that either of you show any reluctance to take counsel and advise with me.

LYSIMACHUS: But this is our proper business; and yours as well as ours, for I reckon you as one of us. Please then to take my place, and find out from Nicias and Laches what we want to know, for the sake of the youths, and talk and consult with them: for I am old, and my memory is bad; and I do not remember the questions which I am going to ask, or the answers to them; and if there is any interruption I am quite lost. I will therefore beg of you to carry on the proposed discussion by your selves; and I will listen, and Melesias and I will act upon your conclusions.

SOCRATES: Let us, Nicias and Laches, comply with the request of Lysimachus and Melesias. There will be no harm in asking ourselves the question which was first proposed to us: 'Who have been our own instructors in this sort of training, and whom have we made better?' But the other mode of carrying on the enquiry will bring us equally to the same point, and will be more like proceeding from first principles. For if we knew that the addition of something would improve some other thing, and were able to make the addition, then, clearly, we must know how that about which we are advising may be best and most easily attained. Perhaps you do not understand what I mean. Then let me make my meaning plainer in this way. Suppose we knew that the addition of sight makes better the eyes which possess this gift, and also were able to impart sight to the eyes, then, clearly, we should know the nature of sight, and should be able to advise how this gift of sight may be best and most easily attained; but if we knew neither what sight is, nor what hearing is, we should not be very good medical advisers about the eyes or the ears, or about the best mode of giving sight and hearing to them.

LACHES: That is true, Socrates.

SOCRATES: And are not our two friends, Laches, at this very moment inviting us to consider in what way the gift of virtue may be imparted to their sons for the improvement of their minds?

LACHES: Very true.

SOCRATES: Then must we not first know the nature of virtue? For how can we advise any one about the best mode of attaining something of which we are wholly ignorant?

LACHES: I do not think that we can, Socrates.

SOCRATES: Then, Laches, we may presume that we know the nature of virtue?

LACHES: Yes.

SOCRATES: And that which we know we must surely be able to tell?

LACHES: Certainly.

SOCRATES: I would not have us begin, my friend, with enquiring about the whole of virtue; for that may be more than we can accomplish; let us first consider whether we have a sufficient knowledge of a part; the enquiry will thus probably be made easier to us.

LACHES: Let us do as you say, Socrates.

SOCRATES: Then which of the parts of virtue shall we select? Must we not select that to which the art of fighting in armour is supposed to conduce? And is not that generally thought to be courage?

LACHES: Yes, certainly.

SOCRATES: Then, Laches, suppose that we first set about determining the nature of courage, and in the second place proceed to enquire how the young men may attain this quality by the help of studies and pursuits. Tell me, if you can, what is courage.

LACHES: Indeed, Socrates, I see no difficulty in answering; he is a man of courage who does not run away, but remains at his post and fights against the enemy; there can be no mistake about that.

SOCRATES: Very good, Laches; and yet I fear that I did not express myself clearly; and therefore you have answered not the question which I intended to ask, but another.

LACHES: What do you mean, Socrates?

SOCRATES: I will endeavour to explain; you would call a man courageous who remains at his post, and fights with the enemy?

LACHES: Certainly I should.

SOCRATES: And so should I; but what would you say of another man, who fights flying, instead of remaining?

LACHES: How flying?

SOCRATES: Why, as the Scythians are said to fight, flying as well as pursuing; and as Homer says in praise of the horses of Aeneas, that they knew 'how to pursue, and fly quickly hither and thither'; and he passes an encomium on Aeneas himself, as having a knowledge of fear or flight, and calls him 'an author of fear or flight.'

LACHES: Yes, Socrates, and there Homer is right: for he was speaking of chariots, as you were speaking of the Scythian cavalry, who have that way of fighting; but the heavy-armed Greek fights, as I say, remaining in his rank.

SOCRATES: And yet, Laches, you must except the Lacedaemonians at Plataea, who, when they came upon the light shields of the Persians, are said not to have been willing to stand and fight, and to have fled; but when the ranks of the Persians were broken, they turned upon them like cavalry, and won the battle of Plataea.

LACHES: That is true.

SOCRATES: That was my meaning when I said that I was to blame in having put my question badly, and that this was the reason of your answering badly. For I meant to ask you not only about the courage of heavy-armed soldiers, but about the courage of cavalry and every other style of soldier; and not only who are courageous in war, but who are courageous in perils by sea, and who in disease, or in poverty, or again in politics, are courageous; and not only who are courageous against pain or fear, but mighty to contend against desires and pleasures, either fixed in their rank or turning upon their enemy. There is this sort of courage—is there not, Laches?

LACHES: Certainly, Socrates.

SOCRATES: And all these are courageous, but some have courage in pleasures, and some in pains: some in desires, and some in fears, and some are cowards under the same conditions, as I should imagine.

LACHES: Very true.

SOCRATES: Now I was asking about courage and cowardice in general. And I will begin with courage, and once more ask, What is that common quality, which is the same in all these cases, and which is called courage? Do you now understand what I mean?

LACHES: Not over well.

SOCRATES: I mean this: As I might ask what is that quality which is called quickness, and which is found in running, in playing the lyre, in speaking, in learning, and in many other similar actions, or rather which we possess in nearly every action that is worth mentioning of arms, legs, mouth, voice, mind;—would you not apply the term quickness to all of them?

LACHES: Quite true.

SOCRATES: And suppose I were to be asked by some one: What is that common quality, Socrates, which, in all these uses of the word, you call quickness? I should say the quality which accomplishes much in a little time—whether in running, speaking, or in any other sort of action.

LACHES: You would be quite correct.

SOCRATES: And now, Laches, do you try and tell me in like manner, What is that common quality which is called courage, and which includes all the various uses of the term when applied both to pleasure and pain, and in all the cases to which I was just now referring?

LACHES: I should say that courage is a sort of endurance of the soul, if I am to speak of the universal nature which pervades them all.

SOCRATES: But that is what we must do if we are to answer the question. And yet I cannot say that every kind of endurance is, in my opinion, to be deemed courage. Hear my reason: I am sure, Laches, that you would consider courage to be a very noble quality.

LACHES: Most noble, certainly.

SOCRATES: And you would say that a wise endurance is also good and noble?

LACHES: Very noble.

SOCRATES: But what would you say of a foolish endurance? Is not that, on the other hand, to be regarded as evil and hurtful?

LACHES: True.

SOCRATES: And is anything noble which is evil and hurtful?

LACHES: I ought not to say that, Socrates.

SOCRATES: Then you would not admit that sort of endurance to be courage—for it is not noble, but courage is noble?

LACHES: You are right.

SOCRATES: Then, according to you, only the wise endurance is courage?

LACHES: True.

SOCRATES: But as to the epithet 'wise,'—wise in what? In all things small as well as great? For example, if a man shows the quality of endurance in spending his money wisely, knowing that by spending he will acquire more in the end, do you call him courageous?

LACHES: Assuredly not.

SOCRATES: Or, for example, if a man is a physician, and his son, or some patient of his, has inflammation of the lungs, and begs that he may be allowed to eat or drink something, and the other is firm and refuses; is that courage?

LACHES: No; that is not courage at all, any more than the last.

SOCRATES: Again, take the case of one who endures in war, and is willing to fight, and wisely calculates and knows that others will help him, and that there will be fewer and inferior men against him than there are with him; and suppose that he has also advantages of position; would you say of such a one who endures with all this wisdom and preparation, that he, or some man in the opposing army who is in the opposite circumstances to these and yet endures and remains at his post, is the braver?

LACHES: I should say that the latter, Socrates, was the braver.

SOCRATES: But, surely, this is a foolish endurance in comparison with the other?

LACHES: That is true.

SOCRATES: Then you would say that he who in an engagement of cavalry endures, having the knowledge of horsemanship, is not so courageous as he who endures, having no such knowledge?

LACHES: So I should say.

SOCRATES: And he who endures, having a knowledge of the use of the sling, or the bow, or of any other art, is not so courageous as he who endures, not having such a knowledge?

LACHES: True.

SOCRATES: And he who descends into a well, and dives, and holds out in this or any similar action, having no knowledge of diving, or the like, is, as you would say, more courageous than those who have this knowledge?

LACHES: Why, Socrates, what else can a man say?

SOCRATES: Nothing, if that be what he thinks.

LACHES: But that is what I do think.

SOCRATES: And yet men who thus run risks and endure are foolish, Laches, in comparison of those who do the same things, having the skill to do them.

LACHES: That is true.

SOCRATES: But foolish boldness and endurance appeared before to be base and hurtful to us.

LACHES: Quite true.

SOCRATES: Whereas courage was acknowledged to be a noble quality.

LACHES: True.

SOCRATES: And now on the contrary we are saying that the foolish endurance, which was before held in dishonour, is courage.

LACHES: Very true.

SOCRATES: And are we right in saying so?

LACHES: Indeed, Socrates, I am sure that we are not right.

SOCRATES: Then according to your statement, you and I, Laches, are not attuned to the Dorian mode, which is a harmony of words and deeds; for our deeds are not in accordance with our words. Any one would say that we had courage who saw us in action, but not, I imagine, he who heard us talking about courage just now.

LACHES: That is most true.

SOCRATES: And is this condition of ours satisfactory?

LACHES: Quite the reverse.

SOCRATES: Suppose, however, that we admit the principle of which we are speaking to a certain extent.

LACHES: To what extent and what principle do you mean?

SOCRATES: The principle of endurance. We too must endure and persevere in the enquiry, and then courage will not laugh at our faint-heartedness in searching for courage; which after all may, very likely, be endurance.

LACHES: I am ready to go on, Socrates; and yet I am unused to investigations of this sort. But the spirit of controversy has been aroused in me by what has been said; and I am really grieved at being thus unable to express my meaning. For I fancy that I do know the nature of courage; but, somehow or other, she has slipped away from me, and I cannot get hold of her and tell her nature.

SOCRATES: But, my dear friend, should not the good sportsman follow the track, and not be lazy?

LACHES: Certainly, he should.

SOCRATES: And shall we invite Nicias to join us? he may be better at the sport than we are. What do you say?

LACHES: I should like that.

SOCRATES: Come then, Nicias, and do what you can to help your friends, who are tossing on the waves of argument, and at the last gasp: you see our extremity, and may save us and also settle your own opinion, if you will tell us what you think about courage.

NICIAS: I have been thinking, Socrates, that you and Laches are not defining courage in the right way; for you have forgotten an excellent saying which I have heard from your own lips.

SOCRATES: What is it, Nicias?

NICIAS: I have often heard you say that 'Every man is good in that in which he is wise, and bad in that in which he is unwise.'

SOCRATES: That is certainly true, Nicias.

NICIAS: And therefore if the brave man is good, he is also wise.

SOCRATES: Do you hear him, Laches?

LACHES: Yes, I hear him, but I do not very well understand him.

SOCRATES: I think that I understand him; and he appears to me to mean that courage is a sort of wisdom.

LACHES: What can he possibly mean, Socrates?

SOCRATES: That is a question which you must ask of himself.

LACHES: Yes.

SOCRATES: Tell him then, Nicias, what you mean by this wisdom; for you surely do not mean the wisdom which plays the flute?

NICIAS: Certainly not.

SOCRATES: Nor the wisdom which plays the lyre?

NICIAS: No.

SOCRATES: But what is this knowledge then, and of what?

LACHES: I think that you put the question to him very well, Socrates; and I would like him to say what is the nature of this knowledge or wisdom.

NICIAS: I mean to say, Laches, that courage is the knowledge of that which inspires fear or confidence in war, or in anything.

LACHES: How strangely he is talking, Socrates.

SOCRATES: Why do you say so, Laches?

LACHES: Why, surely courage is one thing, and wisdom another.

SOCRATES: That is just what Nicias denies.

LACHES: Yes, that is what he denies; but he is so silly.

SOCRATES: Suppose that we instruct instead of abusing him?

NICIAS: Laches does not want to instruct me, Socrates; but having been proved to be talking nonsense himself, he wants to prove that I have been doing the same.

LACHES: Very true, Nicias; and you are talking nonsense, as I shall endeavour to show. Let me ask you a question: Do not physicians know the dangers of disease? or do the courageous know them? or are the physicians the same as the courageous?

NICIAS: Not at all.

LACHES: No more than the husbandmen who know the dangers of husbandry, or than other craftsmen, who have a knowledge of that which inspires them with fear or confidence in their own arts, and yet they are not courageous a whit the more for that.

SOCRATES: What is Laches saying, Nicias? He appears to be saying something of importance.

NICIAS: Yes, he is saying something, but it is not true.

SOCRATES: How so?

NICIAS: Why, because he does not see that the physician's knowledge only extends to the nature of health and disease: he can tell the sick man no more than this. Do you imagine, Laches, that the physician knows whether health or disease is the more terrible to a man? Had not many a man better never get up from a sick bed? I should like to know whether you think that life is always better than death. May not death often be the better of the two?

LACHES: Yes certainly so in my opinion.

NICIAS: And do you think that the same things are terrible to those who had better die, and to those who had better live?

LACHES: Certainly not.

NICIAS: And do you suppose that the physician or any other artist knows this, or any one indeed, except he who is skilled in the grounds of fear and hope? And him I call the courageous.

SOCRATES: Do you understand his meaning, Laches?

LACHES: Yes; I suppose that, in his way of speaking, the soothsayers are courageous. For who but one of them can know to whom to die or to live is better? And yet Nicias, would you allow that you are yourself a soothsayer, or are you neither a soothsayer nor courageous?

NICIAS: What! do you mean to say that the soothsayer ought to know the grounds of hope or fear?

LACHES: Indeed I do: who but he?

NICIAS: Much rather I should say he of whom I speak; for the soothsayer ought to know only the signs of things that are about to come to pass, whether death or disease, or loss of property, or victory, or defeat in war, or in any sort of contest; but to whom the suffering or not suffering of these things will be for the best, can no more be decided by the soothsayer than by one who is no soothsayer.

LACHES: I cannot understand what Nicias would be at, Socrates; for he represents the courageous man as neither a soothsayer, nor a physician, nor in any other character, unless he means to say that he is a god. My opinion is that he does not like honestly to confess that he is talking nonsense, but that he shuffles up and down in order to conceal the difficulty into which he has got himself. You and I, Socrates, might have practised a similar shuffle just now, if we had only wanted to avoid the appearance of inconsistency. And if we had been arguing in a court of law there might have been reason in so doing; but why should a man deck himself out with vain words at a meeting of friends such as this?

SOCRATES: I quite agree with you, Laches, that he should not. But perhaps Nicias is serious, and not merely talking for the sake of talking. Let us ask him just to explain what he means, and if he has reason on his side we will agree with him; if not, we will instruct him.

LACHES: Do you, Socrates, if you like, ask him: I think that I have asked enough.

SOCRATES: I do not see why I should not; and my question will do for both of us.

LACHES: Very good.

SOCRATES: Then tell me, Nicias, or rather tell us, for Laches and I are partners in the argument: Do you mean to affirm that courage is the knowledge of the grounds of hope and fear?

NICIAS: I do.

SOCRATES: And not every man has this knowledge; the physician and the soothsayer have it not; and they will not be courageous unless they acquire it—that is what you were saying?

NICIAS: I was.

SOCRATES: Then this is certainly not a thing which every pig would know, as the proverb says, and therefore he could not be courageous.

NICIAS: I think not.

SOCRATES: Clearly not, Nicias; not even such a big pig as the Crommyonian sow would be called by you courageous. And this I say not as a joke, but because I think that he who assents to your doctrine, that courage is the knowledge of the grounds of fear and hope, cannot allow that any wild beast is courageous, unless he admits that a lion, or a leopard, or perhaps a boar, or any other animal, has such a degree of wisdom that he knows things which but a few human beings ever know by reason of their difficulty. He who takes your view of courage must affirm that a lion, and a stag, and a bull, and a monkey, have equally little pretensions to courage.

LACHES: Capital, Socrates; by the gods, that is truly good. And I hope, Nicias, that you will tell us whether these animals, which we all admit to be courageous, are really wiser than mankind; or whether you will have the boldness, in the face of universal opinion, to deny their courage.

NICIAS: Why, Laches, I do not call animals or any other things which have no fear of dangers, because they are ignorant of them, courageous, but only fearless and senseless. Do you imagine that I should call little children courageous, which fear no dangers because they know none? There is a difference, to my way of thinking, between fearlessness and courage. I am of opinion that thoughtful courage is a quality possessed by very few, but that rashness and boldness, and fearlessness, which has no forethought, are very common qualities possessed by many men, many women, many children, many animals. And you, and men in general, call by the term 'courageous' actions which I call rash;—my courageous actions are wise actions.

LACHES: Behold, Socrates, how admirably, as he thinks, he dresses himself out in words, while seeking to deprive of the honour of courage those whom all the world acknowledges to be courageous.

NICIAS: Not so, Laches, but do not be alarmed; for I am quite willing to say of you and also of Lamachus, and of many other Athenians, that you are courageous and therefore wise.

LACHES: I could answer that; but I would not have you cast in my teeth that I am a haughty Aexonian.

SOCRATES: Do not answer him, Laches; I rather fancy that you are not aware of the source from which his wisdom is derived. He has got all this from my friend Damon, and Damon is always with Prodicus, who, of all the Sophists, is considered to be the best puller to pieces of words of this sort.

LACHES: Yes, Socrates; and the examination of such niceties is a much more suitable employment for a Sophist than for a great statesman whom the city chooses to preside over her.

SOCRATES: Yes, my sweet friend, but a great statesman is likely to have a great intelligence. And I think that the view which is implied in Nicias' definition of courage is worthy of examination.

LACHES: Then examine for yourself, Socrates.

SOCRATES: That is what I am going to do, my dear friend. Do not, however, suppose I shall let you out of the partnership; for I shall expect you to apply your mind, and join with me in the consideration of the question.

LACHES: I will if you think that I ought.

SOCRATES: Yes, I do; but I must beg of you, Nicias, to begin again. You remember that we originally considered courage to be a part of virtue.

NICIAS: Very true.

SOCRATES: And you yourself said that it was a part; and there were many other parts, all of which taken together are called virtue.

NICIAS: Certainly.

SOCRATES: Do you agree with me about the parts? For I say that justice, temperance, and the like, are all of them parts of virtue as well as courage. Would you not say the same?

NICIAS: Certainly.

SOCRATES: Well then, so far we are agreed. And now let us proceed a step, and try to arrive at a similar agreement about the fearful and the hopeful: I do not want you to be thinking one thing and myself another. Let me then tell you my own opinion, and if I am wrong you shall set me right: in my opinion the terrible and the hopeful are the things which do or do not create fear, and fear is not of the present, nor of the past, but is of future and expected evil. Do you not agree to that, Laches?

LACHES: Yes, Socrates, entirely.

SOCRATES: That is my view, Nicias; the terrible things, as I should say, are the evils which are future; and the hopeful are the good or not evil things which are future. Do you or do you not agree with me?

NICIAS: I agree.

SOCRATES: And the knowledge of these things you call courage?

NICIAS: Precisely.

SOCRATES: And now let me see whether you agree with Laches and myself as to a third point.

NICIAS: What is that?

SOCRATES: I will tell you. He and I have a notion that there is not one knowledge or science of the past, another of the present, a third of what is likely to be best and what will be best in the future; but that of all three there is one science only: for example, there is one science of medicine which is concerned with the inspection of health equally in all times, present, past, and future; and one science of husbandry in like manner, which is concerned with the productions of the earth in all times. As to the art of the general, you yourselves will be my witnesses that he has an excellent foreknowledge of the future, and that he claims to be the master and not the servant of the soothsayer, because he knows better what is happening or is likely to happen in war: and accordingly the law places the soothsayer under the general, and not the general under the soothsayer. Am I not correct in saying so, Laches?

LACHES: Quite correct.

SOCRATES: And do you, Nicias, also acknowledge that the same science has understanding of the same things, whether future, present, or past?

NICIAS: Yes, indeed Socrates; that is my opinion.

SOCRATES: And courage, my friend, is, as you say, a knowledge of the fearful and of the hopeful?

NICIAS: Yes.

SOCRATES: And the fearful, and the hopeful, are admitted to be future goods and future evils?

NICIAS: True.

SOCRATES: And the same science has to do with the same things in the future or at any time?

NICIAS: That is true.

SOCRATES: Then courage is not the science which is concerned with the fearful and hopeful, for they are future only; courage, like the other sciences, is concerned not only with good and evil of the future, but of the present and past, and of any time?

NICIAS: That, as I suppose, is true.

SOCRATES: Then the answer which you have given, Nicias, includes only a third part of courage; but our question extended to the whole nature of courage: and according to your view, that is, according to your present view, courage is not only the knowledge of the hopeful and the fearful, but seems to include nearly every good and evil without reference to time. What do you say to that alteration in your statement?

NICIAS: I agree, Socrates.

SOCRATES: But then, my dear friend, if a man knew all good and evil, and how they are, and have been, and will be produced, would he not be perfect, and wanting in no virtue, whether justice, or temperance, or holiness? He would possess them all, and he would know which were dangers and which were not, and guard against them whether they were supernatural or natural; and he would provide the good, as he would know how to deal both with gods or men.

NICIAS: I think, Socrates, that there is a great deal of truth in what you say.

SOCRATES: But then, Nicias, courage, according to this new definition of yours, instead of being a part of virtue only, will be all virtue?

NICIAS: It would seem so.

SOCRATES: But we were saying that courage is one of the parts of virtue?

NICIAS: Yes, that was what we were saying.

SOCRATES: And that is in contradiction with our present view?

NICIAS: That appears to be the case.

SOCRATES: Then, Nicias, we have not discovered what courage is.

NICIAS: We have not.

LACHES: And yet, friend Nicias, I imagined that you would have made the discovery, when you were so contemptuous of the answers which I made to Socrates. I had very great hopes that you would have been enlightened by the wisdom of Damon.

NICIAS: I perceive, Laches, that you think nothing of having displayed your ignorance of the nature of courage, but you look only to see whether I have not made a similar display; and if we are both equally ignorant of the things which a man who is good for anything should know, that, I suppose, will be of no consequence. You certainly appear to me very like the rest of the world, looking at your neighbour and not at yourself. I am of opinion that enough has been said on the subject which we have been discussing; and if anything has been imperfectly said, that may be hereafter corrected by the help of Damon, whom you think to laugh down, although you have never seen him, and with the help of others. And when I am satisfied myself, I will freely impart my satisfaction to you, for I think that you are very much in want of knowledge.

LACHES: You are a philosopher, Nicias; of that I am aware: nevertheless I would recommend Lysimachus and Melesias not to take you and me as advisers about the education of their children; but, as I said at first, they should ask Socrates and not let him off; if my own sons were old enough, I would have asked him myself.

NICIAS: To that I quite agree, if Socrates is willing to take them under his charge. I should not wish for any one else to be the tutor of Niceratus. But I observe that when I mention the matter to him he recommends to me some other tutor and refuses himself. Perhaps he may be more ready to listen to you, Lysimachus.

LYSIMACHUS: He ought, Nicias: for certainly I would do things for him which I would not do for many others. What do you say, Socrates—will you comply? And are you ready to give assistance in the improvement of the youths?

SOCRATES: Indeed, Lysimachus, I should be very wrong in refusing to aid in the improvement of anybody. And if I had shown in this conversation that I had a knowledge which Nicias and Laches have not, then I admit that you would be right in inviting me to perform this duty; but as we are all in the same perplexity, why should one of us be preferred to another? I certainly think that no one should; and under these circumstances, let me offer you a piece of advice (and this need not go further than ourselves). I maintain, my friends, that every one of us should seek out the best teacher whom he can find, first for ourselves, who are greatly in need of one, and then for the youth, regardless of expense or anything. But I cannot advise that we remain as we are. And if any one laughs at us for going to school at our age, I would quote to them the authority of Homer, who says, that

'Modesty is not good for a needy man.'

Let us then, regardless of what may be said of us, make the education of the youths our own education.

LYSIMACHUS: I like your proposal, Socrates; and as I am the oldest, I am also the most eager to go to school with the boys. Let me beg a favour of you: Come to my house to-morrow at dawn, and we will advise about these matters. For the present, let us make an end of the conversation.

SOCRATES: I will come to you to-morrow, Lysimachus, as you propose, God willing.

LAWS

By Plato

Translated By Benjamin Jowett

Contents

<u>LAWS</u>

LAWS

BOOK I.

PERSONS OF THE DIALOGUE: An Athenian Stranger, Cleinias (a Cretan), Megillus (a Lacedaemonian).

ATHENIAN: Tell me, Strangers, is a God or some man supposed to be the author of your laws?

CLEINIAS: A God, Stranger; in very truth a God: among us Cretans he is said to have been Zeus, but in Lacedaemon, whence our friend here comes, I believe they would say that Apollo is their lawgiver: would they not, Megillus?

MEGILLUS: Certainly.

ATHENIAN: And do you, Cleinias, believe, as Homer tells, that every ninth year Minos went to converse with his Olympian sire, and was inspired by him to make laws for your cities?

CLEINIAS: Yes, that is our tradition; and there was Rhadamanthus, a brother of his, with whose name you are familiar; he is reputed to have been the justest of men, and we Cretans are of opinion that he earned this reputation from his righteous administration of justice when he was alive.

ATHENIAN: Yes, and a noble reputation it was, worthy of a son of Zeus. As you and Megillus have been trained in these institutions, I dare say that you will not be unwilling to give an account of your government and laws; on our way we can pass the time pleasantly in talking about them, for I am told that the distance from Cnosus to the cave and temple of Zeus is considerable; and doubtless there are shady places under the lofty trees, which will protect us from this scorching sun. Being no longer young, we may often stop to rest beneath them, and get over the whole journey without difficulty, beguiling the time by conversation.

CLEINIAS: Yes, Stranger, and if we proceed onward we shall come to groves of cypresses, which are of rare height and beauty, and there are green meadows, in which we may repose and converse.

ATHENIAN: Very good.

CLEINIAS: Very good, indeed; and still better when we see them; let us move on cheerily.

ATHENIAN: I am willing—And first, I want to know why the law has ordained that you shall have common meals and gymnastic exercises, and wear arms.

CLEINIAS: I think, Stranger, that the aim of our institutions is easily intelligible to any one. Look at the character of our country: Crete is not like Thessaly, a large plain; and for this reason they have horsemen in Thessaly, and we have runners—the inequality of the ground in our country is more adapted to locomotion on foot; but then, if you have runners you must have light arms—no one can carry a heavy weight when running, and bows and arrows are convenient because they are light. Now all these regulations have been made with a view to war, and the legislator appears to me to have looked to this in all his arrangements:—the common meals, if I am not mistaken, were instituted by him for a similar reason, because he saw that while they are in the field the citizens are by the nature of the case compelled to take their meals together for the sake of mutual protection. He seems to me to have thought the world foolish in not understanding that all men are always at war with one another; and if in war there ought to be common meals and certain persons regularly appointed under others to protect an army, they should be continued in peace. For what men in general term peace would be said by him to be only a name; in reality every city is in a natural state of war with every other, not indeed proclaimed by heralds, but everlasting. And if you look closely, you will find that this was the intention of the Cretan legislator; all institutions, private as well as public, were arranged by him with a view to war; in giving them he was under the impression that no possessions or institutions are of any value to him who is defeated in battle; for all the good things of the conquered pass into the hands of the conquerors.

ATHENIAN: You appear to me, Stranger, to have been thoroughly trained in the Cretan institutions, and to be well informed about them; will you tell me a little more explicitly what is the principle of government which you would lay down? You seem to imagine that a well-governed state ought to be so ordered as to conquer all other states in war: am I right in supposing this to be your meaning?

CLEINIAS: Certainly; and our Lacedaemonian friend, if I am not mistaken, will agree with me.

MEGILLUS: Why, my good friend, how could any Lacedaemonian say anything else?

ATHENIAN: And is what you say applicable only to states, or also to villages?

CLEINIAS: To both alike.

ATHENIAN: The case is the same?

CLEINIAS: Yes.

ATHENIAN: And in the village will there be the same war of family against family, and of individual against individual?

CLEINIAS: The same.

ATHENIAN: And should each man conceive himself to be his own enemy:—what shall we say?

CLEINIAS: O Athenian Stranger—inhabitant of Attica I will not call you, for you seem to deserve rather to be named after the goddess herself, because you go back to first principles,—you have thrown a light upon the argument, and will now be better able to understand what I was just saying,—that all men are publicly one another's enemies, and each man privately his own.

(ATHENIAN: My good sir, what do you mean?)—

CLEINIAS:...Moreover, there is a victory and defeat—the first and best of victories, the lowest and worst of defeats—which each man gains or sustains at the hands, not of another, but of himself; this shows that there is a war against ourselves going on within every one of us.

ATHENIAN: Let us now reverse the order of the argument: Seeing that every individual is either his own superior or his own inferior, may we say that there is the same principle in the house, the village, and the state?

CLEINIAS: You mean that in each of them there is a principle of superiority or inferiority to self?

ATHENIAN: Yes.

CLEINIAS: You are quite right in asking the question, for there certainly is such a principle, and above all in states; and the state in which the better citizens win a victory over the mob and over the inferior classes may be truly said to be better than itself, and may be justly praised, where such a victory is gained, or censured in the opposite case.

ATHENIAN: Whether the better is ever really conquered by the worse, is a question which requires more discussion, and may be therefore left for the present. But I now quite understand your meaning when you say that citizens who are of the same race and live in the same cities may unjustly conspire, and having the superiority in numbers may overcome and enslave the few just; and when they prevail, the state may be truly called its own inferior and therefore bad; and when they are defeated, its own superior and therefore good.

CLEINIAS: Your remark, Stranger, is a paradox, and yet we cannot possibly deny it.

ATHENIAN: Here is another case for consideration;—in a family there may be several brothers, who are the offspring of a single pair; very possibly the majority of them may be unjust, and the just may be in a minority.

CLEINIAS: Very possibly.

ATHENIAN: And you and I ought not to raise a question of words as to whether this family and household are rightly said to be superior when they conquer, and inferior when they are conquered; for we are not now considering what may or may not be the proper or customary way of speaking, but we are considering the natural principles of right and wrong in laws.

CLEINIAS: What you say, Stranger, is most true.

MEGILLUS: Quite excellent, in my opinion, as far as we have gone.

ATHENIAN: Again; might there not be a judge over these brethren, of whom we were speaking?

CLEINIAS: Certainly.

ATHENIAN: Now, which would be the better judge—one who destroyed the bad and appointed the good to govern themselves; or one who, while allowing the good to govern, let the bad live, and made them voluntarily submit? Or third, I suppose, in the scale of excellence might be placed a judge, who, finding the family distracted, not only did not destroy any one, but reconciled them to one another for ever after, and gave them laws which they mutually observed, and was able to keep them friends.

CLEINIAS: The last would be by far the best sort of judge and legislator.

ATHENIAN: And yet the aim of all the laws which he gave would be the reverse of war.

CLEINIAS: Very true.

ATHENIAN: And will he who constitutes the state and orders the life of man have in view external war, or that kind of intestine war called civil, which no one, if he could prevent, would like to have occurring in his own state; and when occurring, every one would wish to be quit of as soon as possible?

CLEINIAS: He would have the latter chiefly in view.

ATHENIAN: And would he prefer that this civil war should be terminated by the destruction of one of the parties, and by the victory of the other, or that peace and friendship should be re-established, and that, being reconciled, they should give their attention to foreign enemies?

CLEINIAS: Every one would desire the latter in the case of his own state.

ATHENIAN: And would not that also be the desire of the legislator?

CLEINIAS: Certainly.

ATHENIAN: And would not every one always make laws for the sake of the best?

CLEINIAS: To be sure.

ATHENIAN: But war, whether external or civil, is not the best, and the need of either is to be deprecated; but peace with one another, and good will, are best. Nor is the victory of the state over itself to be regarded as a really good thing, but as a necessity; a man might as well say that the body was in the best state when sick and purged by medicine, forgetting that there is also a state of the body which needs no purge. And in like manner no one can be a true statesman, whether he aims at the happiness of the individual or state, who looks only, or first of all, to external warfare; nor will he ever be a sound legislator who orders peace for the sake of war, and not war for the sake of peace.

CLEINIAS: I suppose that there is truth, Stranger, in that remark of yours; and yet I am greatly mistaken if war is not the entire aim and object of our own institutions, and also of the Lacedaemonian.

ATHENIAN: I dare say; but there is no reason why we should rudely quarrel with one another about your legislators, instead of gently questioning them, seeing that both we and they are equally in earnest. Please follow me and the argument closely:—And first I will put forward Tyrtaeus, an Athenian by birth, but also a Spartan citizen, who of all men was most eager about war: Well, he says,

'I sing not, I care not, about any man,

even if he were the richest of men, and possessed every good (and then he gives a whole list of them), if he be not at all times a brave warrior.' I imagine that you, too, must have heard his poems; our Lacedaemonian friend has probably heard more than enough of them.

MEGILLUS: Very true.

CLEINIAS: And they have found their way from Lacedaemon to Crete.

ATHENIAN: Come now and let us all join in asking this question of Tyrtaeus: O most divine poet, we will say to him, the excellent praise which you have bestowed on those who excel in war sufficiently proves that you are wise and good, and I and

Megillus and Cleinias of Cnosus do, as I believe, entirely agree with you. But we should like to be quite sure that we are speaking of the same men; tell us, then, do you agree with us in thinking that there are two kinds of war; or what would you say? A far inferior man to Tyrtaeus would have no difficulty in replying quite truly, that war is of two kinds,—one which is universally called civil war, and is, as we were just now saying, of all wars the worst; the other, as we should all admit, in which we fall out with other nations who are of a different race, is a far milder form of warfare.

CLEINIAS: Certainly, far milder.

ATHENIAN: Well, now, when you praise and blame war in this high-flown strain, whom are you praising or blaming, and to which kind of war are you referring? I suppose that you must mean foreign war, if I am to judge from expressions of yours in which you say that you abominate those

'Who refuse to look upon fields of blood, and will not draw near and strike at their enemies.'

And we shall naturally go on to say to him,—You, Tyrtaeus, as it seems, praise those who distinguish themselves in external and foreign war; and he must admit this.

CLEINIAS: Evidently.

ATHENIAN: They are good; but we say that there are still better men whose virtue is displayed in the greatest of all battles. And we too have a poet whom we summon as a witness, Theognis, citizen of Megara in Sicily:

'Cyrnus,' he says, 'he who is faithful in a civil broil is worth his weight in gold and silver.'

And such an one is far better, as we affirm, than the other in a more difficult kind of war, much in the same degree as justice and temperance and wisdom, when united with courage, are better than courage only; for a man cannot be faithful and good in civil strife without having all virtue. But in the war of which Tyrtaeus speaks, many a mercenary soldier will take his stand and be ready to die at his post, and yet they are generally and almost without exception insolent, unjust, violent men, and the most senseless of human beings. You will ask what the conclusion is, and what I am seeking to prove: I maintain that the divine legislator of Crete, like any other who is worthy of consideration, will always and above all things in making laws have regard to the greatest virtue; which, according to Theognis, is loyalty in the hour of danger, and may be truly called perfect justice. Whereas, that virtue which Tyrtaeus highly praises is well enough, and was praised by the poet at the right time, yet in place and dignity may be said to be only fourth rate (i.e., it ranks after justice, temperance, and wisdom.).

CLEINIAS: Stranger, we are degrading our inspired lawgiver to a rank which is far beneath him.

ATHENIAN: Nay, I think that we degrade not him but ourselves, if we imagine that Lycurgus and Minos laid down laws both in Lacedaemon and Crete mainly with a view to war.

CLEINIAS: What ought we to say then?

ATHENIAN: What truth and what justice require of us, if I am not mistaken, when speaking in behalf of divine excellence;—that the legislator when making his laws had in view not a part only, and this the lowest part of virtue, but all virtue, and that he devised classes of laws answering to the kinds of virtue; not in the way in which modern inventors of laws make the classes, for they only investigate and offer laws whenever a want is felt, and one man has a class of laws about allotments and heiresses, another about assaults; others about ten thousand other such matters. But we maintain that the right way of examining into laws is to proceed as we have now done, and I admired the spirit of your exposition; for you were quite right in beginning with virtue, and saying that this was the aim of the giver of the law, but I thought that you went wrong when you added that all his legislation had a view only to a part, and the least part of virtue, and this called forth my subsequent remarks. Will you allow me then to explain how I should have liked to have heard you expound the matter?

CLEINIAS: By all means.

ATHENIAN: You ought to have said, Stranger—The Cretan laws are with reason famous among the Hellenes; for they fulfil the object of laws, which is to make those who use them happy; and they confer every sort of good. Now goods are of two kinds: there are human and there are divine goods, and the human hang upon the divine; and the state which attains the greater, at the same time acquires the less, or, not having the greater, has neither. Of the lesser goods the first is health, the second beauty, the third strength, including swiftness in running and bodily agility generally, and the fourth is wealth, not the blind god (Pluto), but one who is keen of sight, if only he has wisdom for his companion. For wisdom is chief and leader of the divine class of goods, and next follows temperance; and from the union of these two with courage springs justice, and fourth in the scale of virtue is courage. All these naturally take precedence of the other goods, and this is the order in which the legislator must place them, and after them he will enjoin the rest of his ordinances on the citizens with a view to these, the human looking to the divine, and the divine looking to their leader mind. Some of his ordinances will relate to contracts of marriage which they make one with another, and then to the procreation and education of children, both male and female; the duty of the lawgiver will be to take charge of his citizens, in youth and age, and at every time of life, and to give them punishments and rewards; and in reference to all their intercourse with one another, he ought to consider their pains and pleasures and desires, and the vehemence of all their passions; he should keep a watch over them, and blame and praise them rightly by the mouth of the laws themselves. Also with regard to anger and terror, and the other perturbations of the soul, which arise out of misfortune, and the deliverances from them which prosperity brings, and the experiences which come to men in diseases, or in war, or poverty, or the opposite of these; in all these states he should determine and teach what is the good and evil of the condition of each. In the next place, the legislator has to be careful how the citizens make their money and in what way they spend it, and to have an eye to their mutual contracts and dissolutions of contracts, whether voluntary or involuntary: he should see how they order all this, and consider where justice as well as injustice is found or is wanting in their several dealings with one another; and honour those who obey the law, and impose fixed penalties on those who disobey, until the round of civil life is ended, and the time has come for the consideration of the proper funeral rites and honours of the dead. And the lawgiver reviewing his work, will appoint guardians to preside over these things,—some who walk by intelligence, others by true opinion only, and then mind will bind together all his ordinances and show them to be in harmony with temperance and justice, and not with wealth or ambition. This is the spirit, Stranger, in which I was and am desirous that you should pursue the subject. And I want to know the nature of all these things, and how they are arranged in the laws of Zeus, as they are termed, and in those of the Pythian Apollo, which Minos and Lycurgus gave; and how the order of them is discovered to his eyes, who has experience in laws gained either by study or habit, although they are far from being self-evident to the rest of mankind like ourselves.

CLEINIAS: How shall we proceed, Stranger?

ATHENIAN: I think that we must begin again as before, and first consider the habit of courage; and then we will go on and discuss another and then another form of virtue, if you please. In this way we shall have a model of the whole; and with these and similar discourses we will beguile the way. And when we have gone through all the virtues, we will show, by the grace of God, that the institutions of which I was speaking look to virtue.

MEGILLUS: Very good; and suppose that you first criticize this praiser of Zeus and the laws of Crete.

ATHENIAN: I will try to criticize you and myself, as well as him, for the argument is a common concern. Tell me,—were not first the syssitia, and secondly the gymnasia, invented by your legislator with a view to war?

MEGILLUS: Yes.

ATHENIAN: And what comes third, and what fourth? For that, I think, is the sort of enumeration which ought to be made of the remaining parts of virtue, no matter whether you call them parts or what their name is, provided the meaning is clear.

MEGILLUS: Then I, or any other Lacedaemonian, would reply that hunting is third in order.

ATHENIAN: Let us see if we can discover what comes fourth and fifth.

MEGILLUS: I think that I can get as far as the fourth head, which is the frequent endurance of pain, exhibited among us Spartans in certain hand-to-hand fights; also in stealing with the prospect of getting a good beating; there is, too, the so-called Crypteia, or secret service, in which wonderful endurance is shown,—our people wander over the whole country by day and by night, and even in winter have not a shoe to their foot, and are without beds to lie upon, and have to attend upon themselves. Marvellous, too, is the endurance which our citizens show in their naked exercises, contending against the violent summer heat; and there are many similar practices, to speak of which in detail would be endless.

ATHENIAN: Excellent, O Lacedaemonian Stranger. But how ought we to define courage? Is it to be regarded only as a combat against fears and pains, or also against desires and pleasures, and against flatteries; which exercise such a tremendous power, that they make the hearts even of respectable citizens to melt like wax?

MEGILLUS: I should say the latter.

ATHENIAN: In what preceded, as you will remember, our Cnosian friend was speaking of a man or a city being inferior to themselves:—Were you not, Cleinias?

CLEINIAS: I was.

ATHENIAN: Now, which is in the truest sense inferior, the man who is overcome by pleasure or by pain?

CLEINIAS: I should say the man who is overcome by pleasure; for all men deem him to be inferior in a more disgraceful sense, than the other who is overcome by pain.

ATHENIAN: But surely the lawgivers of Crete and Lacedaemon have not legislated for a courage which is lame of one leg, able only to meet attacks which come from the left, but impotent against the insidious flatteries which come from the right?

CLEINIAS: Able to meet both, I should say.

ATHENIAN: Then let me once more ask, what institutions have you in either of your states which give a taste of pleasures, and do not avoid them any more than they avoid pains; but which set a person in the midst of them, and compel or induce him by the prospect of reward to get the better of them? Where is an ordinance about pleasure similar to that about pain to be found in your laws? Tell me what there is of this nature among you:—What is there which makes your citizen equally brave against pleasure and pain, conquering what they ought to conquer, and superior to the enemies who are most dangerous and nearest home?

MEGILLUS: I was able to tell you, Stranger, many laws which were directed against pain; but I do not know that I can point out any great or obvious examples of similar institutions which are concerned with pleasure; there are some lesser provisions, however, which I might mention.

CLEINIAS: Neither can I show anything of that sort which is at all equally prominent in the Cretan laws.

ATHENIAN: No wonder, my dear friends; and if, as is very likely, in our search after the true and good, one of us may have to censure the laws of the others, we must not be offended, but take kindly what another says.

CLEINIAS: You are quite right, Athenian Stranger, and we will do as you say.

ATHENIAN: At our time of life, Cleinias, there should be no feeling of irritation.

CLEINIAS: Certainly not.

ATHENIAN: I will not at present determine whether he who censures the Cretan or Lacedaemonian polities is right or wrong. But I believe that I can tell better than either of you what the many say about them. For assuming that you have reasonably good laws, one of the best of them will be the law forbidding any young men to enquire which of them are right or wrong; but with one mouth and one voice they must all agree that the laws are all good, for they came from God; and any one who says the contrary is not to be listened to. But an old man who remarks any defect in your laws may communicate his observation to a ruler or to an equal in years when no young man is present.

CLEINIAS: Exactly so, Stranger; and like a diviner, although not there at the time, you seem to me quite to have hit the meaning of the legislator, and to say what is most true.

ATHENIAN: As there are no young men present, and the legislator has given old men free licence, there will be no impropriety in our discussing these very matters now that we are alone.

CLEINIAS: True. And therefore you may be as free as you like in your censure of our laws, for there is no discredit in knowing what is wrong; he who receives what is said in a generous and friendly spirit will be all the better for it.

ATHENIAN: Very good; however, I am not going to say anything against your laws until to the best of my ability I have examined them, but I am going to raise doubts about them. For you are the only people known to us, whether Greek or barbarian, whom the legislator commanded to eschew all great pleasures and amusements and never to touch them; whereas in the matter of pains or fears which we have just been discussing, he thought that they who from infancy had always avoided pains and fears and sorrows, when they were compelled to face them would run away from those who were hardened in them, and would become their subjects. Now the legislator ought to have considered that this was equally true of pleasure; he should have said to himself, that if our citizens are from their youth upward unacquainted with the greatest pleasures, and unused to endure amid the temptations of pleasure, and are not disciplined to refrain from all things evil, the sweet feeling of pleasure will overcome them just as fear would overcome the former class; and in another, and even a worse manner, they will be the slaves of those who are able to endure amid pleasures, and have had the opportunity of enjoying them, they being often the worst of mankind. One half of their souls will be a slave, the other half free; and they will not be worthy to be called in the true sense men and freemen. Tell me whether you assent to my words?

CLEINIAS: On first hearing, what you say appears to be the truth; but to be hasty in coming to a conclusion about such important matters would be very childish and simple.

ATHENIAN: Suppose, Cleinias and Megillus, that we consider the virtue which follows next of those which we intended to discuss (for after courage comes temperance), what institutions shall we find relating to temperance, either in Crete or Lacedaemon, which, like your military institutions, differ from those of any ordinary state.

MEGILLUS: That is not an easy question to answer; still I should say that the common meals and gymnastic exercises have been excellently devised for the promotion both of temperance and courage.

ATHENIAN: There seems to be a difficulty, Stranger, with regard to states, in making words and facts coincide so that there can be no dispute about them. As in the human body, the regimen which does good in one way does harm in another; and we can hardly say that any one course of treatment is adapted to a particular constitution. Now the gymnasia and common meals do a great deal of good, and yet they are a source of evil in civil troubles; as is shown in the case of the Milesian, and Boeotian, and Thurian youth, among whom these institutions seem always to have had a tendency to degrade the ancient and natural custom of love below the level, not only of man, but of the beasts. The charge may be fairly brought against your cities above all others, and is true also of most other states which especially cultivate gymnastics. Whether such matters are to be regarded jestingly or seriously, I think that the pleasure is to be deemed natural which arises out of the intercourse between men and women; but that the intercourse of men with men, or of women with women, is contrary to nature, and that the bold attempt was originally due to unbridled lust. The Cretans are always accused of having invented the story of Ganymede and Zeus because they wanted to justify themselves in the enjoyment of unnatural pleasures by the practice of the god whom they believe to have been their lawgiver. Leaving the story, we may observe that any speculation about laws turns almost entirely on pleasure and pain, both in states and in individuals: these are two fountains which nature lets flow, and he who draws from them where and when, and as much as he ought, is happy; and this holds of men and animals—of individuals as well as states; and he who indulges in them ignorantly and at the wrong time, is the reverse of happy.

MEGILLUS: I admit, Stranger, that your words are well spoken, and I hardly know what to say in answer to you; but still I think that the Spartan lawgiver was quite right in forbidding pleasure. Of the Cretan laws, I shall leave the defence to my Cnosian friend. But the laws of Sparta, in as far as they relate to pleasure, appear to me to be the best in the world; for that which leads mankind in general into the wildest pleasure and licence, and every other folly, the law has clean driven out; and neither in the country nor in towns which are under the control of Sparta, will you find revelries and the many incitements of every kind of pleasure which accompany them; and any one who meets a drunken and disorderly person, will immediately have him most severely punished, and will not let him off on any pretence, not even at the time of a Dionysiac festival; although I have remarked that this may happen at your performances 'on the cart,' as they are called; and among our Tarentine colonists I have seen the whole city drunk at a Dionysiac festival; but nothing of the sort happens among us.

ATHENIAN: O Lacedaemonian Stranger, these festivities are praiseworthy where there is a spirit of endurance, but are very senseless when they are under no regulations. In order to retaliate, an Athenian has only to point out the licence which exists among your women. To all such accusations, whether they are brought against the Tarentines, or us, or you, there is one answer which exonerates the practice in question from impropriety. When a stranger expresses wonder at the singularity of what he sees, any inhabitant will naturally answer him:—Wonder not, O stranger; this is our custom, and you may very likely have some other custom about the same things. Now we are speaking, my friends, not about men in general, but about the merits and defects of the lawgivers themselves. Let us then discourse a little more at length about intoxication, which is a very important subject, and will seriously task the discrimination of the legislator. I am not speaking of drinking, or not drinking, wine at all, but of intoxication. Are we to follow the custom of the Scythians, and Persians, and Carthaginians, and Celts, and Iberians, and Thracians, who are all warlike nations, or that of your countrymen, for they, as you say, altogether abstain? But the Scythians and Thracians, both men and women, drink unmixed wine, which they pour on their garments, and this they think a happy and glorious institution. The Persians, again, are much given to other practices of luxury which you reject, but they have more moderation in them than the Thracians and Scythians.

MEGILLUS: O best of men, we have only to take arms into our hands, and we send all these nations flying before us.

ATHENIAN: Nay, my good friend, do not say that; there have been, as there always will be, flights and pursuits of which no account can be given, and therefore we cannot say that victory or defeat in battle affords more than a doubtful proof of the goodness or badness of institutions. For when the greater states conquer and enslave the lesser, as the Syracusans have done the Locrians, who appear to be the best-governed people in their part of the world, or as the Athenians have done the Ceans (and there are ten thousand other instances of the same sort of thing), all this is not to the point; let us endeavour rather to form a conclusion about each institution in itself and say nothing, at present, of victories and defeats. Let us only say that such and such a custom is honourable, and another not. And first permit me to tell you how good and bad are to be estimated in reference to these very matters.

MEGILLUS: How do you mean?

ATHENIAN: All those who are ready at a moment's notice to praise or censure any practice which is matter of discussion, seem to me to proceed in a wrong way. Let me give you an illustration of what I mean:—You may suppose a person to be praising wheat as a good kind of food, whereupon another person instantly blames wheat, without ever enquiring into its effect or use, or in what way, or to whom, or with what, or in what state and how, wheat is to be given. And that is just what we are doing in this discussion. At the very mention of the word intoxication, one side is ready with their praises and the other with their censures; which is absurd. For either side adduce their witnesses and approvers, and some of us think that we speak with authority because we have many witnesses; and others because they see those who abstain conquering in battle, and this again is disputed by us. Now I cannot say that I shall be satisfied, if we go on discussing each of the remaining laws in the same way. And about this very point of intoxication I should like to speak in another way, which I hold to be the right one; for if number is to be the criterion, are there not myriads upon myriads of nations ready to dispute the point with you, who are only two cities?

MEGILLUS: I shall gladly welcome any method of enquiry which is right.

ATHENIAN: Let me put the matter thus:—Suppose a person to praise the keeping of goats, and the creatures themselves as capital things to have, and then some one who had seen goats feeding without a goatherd in cultivated spots, and doing mischief, were to censure a goat or any other animal who has no keeper, or a bad keeper, would there be any sense or justice in such censure?

MEGILLUS: Certainly not.

ATHENIAN: Does a captain require only to have nautical knowledge in order to be a good captain, whether he is sea-sick or not? What do you say?

MEGILLUS: I say that he is not a good captain if, although he have nautical skill, he is liable to sea-sickness.

ATHENIAN: And what would you say of the commander of an army? Will he be able to command merely because he has military skill if he be a coward, who, when danger comes, is sick and drunk with fear?

MEGILLUS: Impossible.

ATHENIAN: And what if besides being a coward he has no skill?

MEGILLUS: He is a miserable fellow, not fit to be a commander of men, but only of old women.

ATHENIAN: And what would you say of some one who blames or praises any sort of meeting which is intended by nature to have a ruler, and is well enough when under his presidency? The critic, however, has never seen the society meeting together at an orderly feast under the control of a president, but always without a ruler or with a bad one:—when observers of this class praise or blame such meetings, are we to suppose that what they say is of any value?

MEGILLUS: Certainly not, if they have never seen or been present at such a meeting when rightly ordered.

ATHENIAN: Reflect; may not banqueters and banquets be said to constitute a kind of meeting?

MEGILLUS: Of course.

ATHENIAN: And did any one ever see this sort of convivial meeting rightly ordered? Of course you two will answer that you have never seen them at all, because they are not customary or lawful in your country; but I have come across many of them in many different places, and moreover I have made enquiries about them wherever I went, as I may say, and never did I see or hear of anything of the kind which was carried on altogether rightly; in some few particulars they might be right, but in general they were utterly wrong.

CLEINIAS: What do you mean, Stranger, by this remark? Explain. For we, as you say, from our inexperience in such matters, might very likely not know, even if they came in our way, what was right or wrong in such societies.

ATHENIAN: Likely enough; then let me try to be your instructor: You would acknowledge, would you not, that in all gatherings of mankind, of whatever sort, there ought to be a leader?

CLEINIAS: Certainly I should.

ATHENIAN: And we were saying just now, that when men are at war the leader ought to be a brave man?

CLEINIAS: We were.

ATHENIAN: The brave man is less likely than the coward to be disturbed by fears?

CLEINIAS: That again is true.

ATHENIAN: And if there were a possibility of having a general of an army who was absolutely fearless and imperturbable, should we not by all means appoint him?

CLEINIAS: Assuredly.

ATHENIAN: Now, however, we are speaking not of a general who is to command an army, when foe meets foe in time of war, but of one who is to regulate meetings of another sort, when friend meets friend in time of peace.

CLEINIAS: True.

ATHENIAN: And that sort of meeting, if attended with drunkenness, is apt to be unquiet.

CLEINIAS: Certainly; the reverse of quiet.

ATHENIAN: In the first place, then, the revellers as well as the soldiers will require a ruler?

CLEINIAS: To be sure; no men more so.

ATHENIAN: And we ought, if possible, to provide them with a quiet ruler?

CLEINIAS: Of course.

ATHENIAN: And he should be a man who understands society; for his duty is to preserve the friendly feelings which exist among the company at the time, and to increase them for the future by his use of the occasion.

CLEINIAS: Very true.

ATHENIAN: Must we not appoint a sober man and a wise to be our master of the revels? For if the ruler of drinkers be himself young and drunken, and not over-wise, only by some special good fortune will he be saved from doing some great evil.

CLEINIAS: It will be by a singular good fortune that he is saved.

ATHENIAN: Now suppose such associations to be framed in the best way possible in states, and that some one blames the very fact of their existence—he may very likely be right. But if he blames a practice which he only sees very much mismanaged, he shows in the first place that he is not aware of the mismanagement, and also not aware that everything done in this way will turn out to be wrong, because done without the superintendence of a sober ruler. Do you not see that a drunken pilot or a drunken ruler of any sort will ruin ship, chariot, army—anything, in short, of which he has the direction?

CLEINIAS: The last remark is very true, Stranger; and I see quite clearly the advantage of an army having a good leader—he will give victory in war to his followers, which is a very great advantage; and so of other things. But I do not see any similar advantage which either individuals or states gain from the good management of a feast; and I want you to tell me what great good will be effected, supposing that this drinking ordinance is duly established.

ATHENIAN: If you mean to ask what great good accrues to the state from the right training of a single youth, or of a single chorus—when the question is put in that form, we cannot deny that the good is not very great in any particular instance. But if you ask what is the good of education in general, the answer is easy—that education makes good men, and that good men act nobly, and conquer their enemies in battle, because they are good. Education certainly gives victory, although victory sometimes produces forgetfulness of education; for many have grown insolent from victory in war, and this insolence has engendered in them innumerable evils; and many a victory has been and will be suicidal to the victors; but education is never suicidal.

CLEINIAS: You seem to imply, my friend, that convivial meetings, when rightly ordered, are an important element of education.

ATHENIAN: Certainly I do.

CLEINIAS: And can you show that what you have been saying is true?

ATHENIAN: To be absolutely sure of the truth of matters concerning which there are many opinions, is an attribute of the Gods not given to man, Stranger; but I shall be very happy to tell you what I think, especially as we are now proposing to enter on a discussion concerning laws and constitutions.

CLEINIAS: Your opinion, Stranger, about the questions which are now being raised, is precisely what we want to hear.

ATHENIAN: Very good; I will try to find a way of explaining my meaning, and you shall try to have the gift of understanding me. But first let me make an apology. The Athenian citizen is reputed among all the Hellenes to be a great talker, whereas Sparta is renowned for brevity, and the Cretans have more wit than words. Now I am afraid of appearing to elicit a very long discourse out of very small materials. For drinking indeed may appear to be a slight matter, and yet is one which cannot be rightly ordered according to nature, without correct principles of music; these are necessary to any clear or satisfactory treatment of the subject, and music again runs up into education generally, and there is much to be said about all this. What would you say then to leaving these matters for the present, and passing on to some other question of law?

MEGILLUS: O Athenian Stranger, let me tell you what perhaps you do not know, that our family is the proxenus of your state. I imagine that from their earliest youth all boys, when they are told that they are the proxeni of a particular state, feel kindly towards their second country; and this has certainly been my own feeling. I can well remember from the days of my boyhood, how, when any Lacedaemonians praised or blamed the Athenians, they used to say to me,—'See, Megillus, how ill or how well,' as the case might be, 'has your state treated us'; and having always had to fight your battles against detractors when I heard you assailed, I became warmly attached to you. And I always like to hear the Athenian tongue spoken; the common saying is quite true, that a good Athenian is more than ordinarily good, for he is the only man who is freely and genuinely good by the divine inspiration of his own nature, and is not manufactured. Therefore be assured that I shall like to hear you say whatever you have to say.

CLEINIAS: Yes, Stranger; and when you have heard me speak, say boldly what is in your thoughts. Let me remind you of a tie which unites you to Crete. You must have heard here the story of the prophet Epimenides, who was of my family, and came to Athens ten years before the Persian war, in accordance with the response of the Oracle, and offered certain sacrifices which the God commanded. The Athenians were at that time in dread of the Persian invasion; and he said that for ten years they would not come, and that when they came, they would go away again without accomplishing any of their objects, and would suffer more evil than they inflicted. At that time my forefathers formed ties of hospitality with you; thus ancient is the friendship which I and my parents have had for you.

ATHENIAN: You seem to be quite ready to listen; and I am also ready to perform as much as I can of an almost impossible task, which I will nevertheless attempt. At the outset of the discussion, let me define the nature and power of education; for this is the way by which our argument must travel onwards to the God Dionysus.

CLEINIAS: Let us proceed, if you please.

ATHENIAN: Well, then, if I tell you what are my notions of education, will you consider whether they satisfy you?

CLEINIAS: Let us hear.

ATHENIAN: According to my view, any one who would be good at anything must practise that thing from his youth upwards, both in sport and earnest, in its several branches: for example, he who is to be a good builder, should play at building children's houses; he who is to be a good husbandman, at tilling the ground; and those who have the care of their education should provide them when young with mimic tools. They should learn beforehand the knowledge which they will afterwards require for their art. For example, the future carpenter should learn to measure or apply the line in play; and the future warrior should learn riding, or some other exercise, for amusement, and the teacher should endeavour to direct the children's inclinations and pleasures, by the help of amusements, to their final aim in life. The most important part of education is right training in the nursery. The soul of the child in his play should be guided to the love of that sort of excellence in which when he grows up to manhood he will have to be perfected. Do you agree with me thus far?

CLEINIAS: Certainly.

ATHENIAN: Then let us not leave the meaning of education ambiguous or ill-defined. At present, when we speak in terms of praise or blame about the bringing-up of each person, we call one man educated and another uneducated, although the uneducated man may be sometimes very well educated for the calling of a retail trader, or of a captain of a ship, and the like. For we are not speaking of education in this narrower sense, but of that other education in virtue from youth upwards, which makes a man eagerly pursue the ideal perfection of citizenship, and teaches him how rightly to rule and how to obey. This is the only education which, upon our view, deserves the name; that other sort of training, which aims at the acquisition of wealth or bodily strength, or mere cleverness apart from intelligence and justice, is mean and illiberal, and is not worthy to be called education at all. But let us not quarrel with one another about a word, provided that the proposition which has just been granted hold good: to wit, that those who are rightly educated generally become good men. Neither must we cast a slight upon education, which is the first and fairest thing that the best of men can ever have, and which, though liable to take a wrong direction, is capable of reformation. And this work of reformation is the great business of every man while he lives.

CLEINIAS: Very true; and we entirely agree with you.

ATHENIAN: And we agreed before that they are good men who are able to rule themselves, and bad men who are not.

CLEINIAS: You are quite right.

ATHENIAN: Let me now proceed, if I can, to clear up the subject a little further by an illustration which I will offer you.

CLEINIAS: Proceed.

ATHENIAN: Do we not consider each of ourselves to be one?

CLEINIAS: We do.

ATHENIAN: And each one of us has in his bosom two counsellors, both foolish and also antagonistic; of which we call the one pleasure, and the other pain.

CLEINIAS: Exactly.

ATHENIAN: Also there are opinions about the future, which have the general name of expectations; and the specific name of fear, when the expectation is of pain; and of hope, when of pleasure; and further, there is reflection about the good or evil of them, and this, when embodied in a decree by the State, is called Law.

CLEINIAS: I am hardly able to follow you; proceed, however, as if I were.

MEGILLUS: I am in the like case.

ATHENIAN: Let us look at the matter thus: May we not conceive each of us living beings to be a puppet of the Gods, either their plaything only, or created with a purpose—which of the two we cannot certainly know? But we do know, that these affections in us are like cords and strings, which pull us different and opposite ways, and to opposite actions; and herein lies the difference between virtue and vice.

According to the argument there is one among these cords which every man ought to grasp and never let go, but to pull with it against all the rest; and this is the sacred and golden cord of reason, called by us the common law of the State; there are others which are hard and of iron, but this one is soft because golden; and there are several other kinds. Now we ought always to cooperate with the lead of the best, which is law. For inasmuch as reason is beautiful and gentle, and not violent, her rule must needs have ministers in order to help the golden principle in vanquishing the other principles. And thus the moral of the tale about our being puppets will not have been lost, and the meaning of the expression 'superior or inferior to a man's self' will become clearer; and the individual, attaining to right reason in this matter of pulling the strings of the puppet, should live according to its rule; while the city, receiving the same from some god or from one who has knowledge of these things, should embody it in a law, to be her guide in her dealings with herself and with other states. In this way virtue and vice will be more clearly distinguished by us. And when they have become clearer, education and other institutions will in like manner become clearer; and in particular that question of convivial entertainment, which may seem, perhaps, to have been a very trifling matter, and to have taken a great many more words than were necessary.

CLEINIAS: Perhaps, however, the theme may turn out not to be unworthy of the length of discourse.

ATHENIAN: Very good; let us proceed with any enquiry which really bears on our present object.

CLEINIAS: Proceed.

ATHENIAN: Suppose that we give this puppet of ours drink,—what will be the effect on him?

CLEINIAS: Having what in view do you ask that question?

ATHENIAN: Nothing as yet; but I ask generally, when the puppet is brought to the drink, what sort of result is likely to follow. I will endeavour to explain my meaning more clearly: what I am now asking is this—Does the drinking of wine heighten and increase pleasures and pains, and passions and loves?

CLEINIAS: Very greatly.

ATHENIAN: And are perception and memory, and opinion and prudence, heightened and increased? Do not these qualities entirely desert a man if he becomes saturated with drink?

CLEINIAS: Yes, they entirely desert him.

ATHENIAN: Does he not return to the state of soul in which he was when a young child?

CLEINIAS: He does.

ATHENIAN: Then at that time he will have the least control over himself?

CLEINIAS: The least.

ATHENIAN: And will he not be in a most wretched plight?

CLEINIAS: Most wretched.

ATHENIAN: Then not only an old man but also a drunkard becomes a second time a child?

CLEINIAS: Well said, Stranger.

ATHENIAN: Is there any argument which will prove to us that we ought to encourage the taste for drinking instead of doing all we can to avoid it?

CLEINIAS: I suppose that there is; you at any rate, were just now saying that you were ready to maintain such a doctrine.

ATHENIAN: True, I was; and I am ready still, seeing that you have both declared that you are anxious to hear me.

CLEINIAS: To be sure we are, if only for the strangeness of the paradox, which asserts that a man ought of his own accord to plunge into utter degradation.

ATHENIAN: Are you speaking of the soul?

CLEINIAS: Yes.

ATHENIAN: And what would you say about the body, my friend? Are you not surprised at any one of his own accord bringing upon himself deformity, leanness, ugliness, decrepitude?

CLEINIAS: Certainly.

ATHENIAN: Yet when a man goes of his own accord to a doctor's shop, and takes medicine, is he not aware that soon, and for many days afterwards, he will be in a state of body which he would die rather than accept as the permanent condition of his life? Are not those who train in gymnasia, at first beginning reduced to a state of weakness?

CLEINIAS: Yes, all that is well known.

ATHENIAN: Also that they go of their own accord for the sake of the subsequent benefit?

CLEINIAS: Very good.

ATHENIAN: And we may conceive this to be true in the same way of other practices?

CLEINIAS: Certainly.

ATHENIAN: And the same view may be taken of the pastime of drinking wine, if we are right in supposing that the same good effect follows?

CLEINIAS: To be sure.

ATHENIAN: If such convivialities should turn out to have any advantage equal in importance to that of gymnastic, they are in their very nature to be preferred to mere bodily exercise, inasmuch as they have no accompaniment of pain.

CLEINIAS: True; but I hardly think that we shall be able to discover any such benefits to be derived from them.

ATHENIAN: That is just what we must endeavour to show. And let me ask you a question:—Do we not distinguish two kinds of fear, which are very different?

CLEINIAS: What are they?

ATHENIAN: There is the fear of expected evil.

CLEINIAS: Yes.

ATHENIAN: And there is the fear of an evil reputation; we are afraid of being thought evil, because we do or say some dishonourable thing, which fear we and all men term shame.

CLEINIAS: Certainly.

ATHENIAN: These are the two fears, as I called them; one of which is the opposite of pain and other fears, and the opposite also of the greatest and most numerous sort of pleasures.

CLEINIAS: Very true.

ATHENIAN: And does not the legislator and every one who is good for anything, hold this fear in the greatest honour? This is what he terms reverence, and the confidence which is the reverse of this he terms insolence; and the latter he always deems to be a very great evil both to individuals and to states.

CLEINIAS: True.

ATHENIAN: Does not this kind of fear preserve us in many important ways? What is there which so surely gives victory and safety in war? For there are two things which give victory—confidence before enemies, and fear of disgrace before friends.

CLEINIAS: There are.

ATHENIAN: Then each of us should be fearless and also fearful; and why we should be either has now been determined.

CLEINIAS: Certainly.

ATHENIAN: And when we want to make any one fearless, we and the law bring him face to face with many fears.

CLEINIAS: Clearly.

ATHENIAN: And when we want to make him rightly fearful, must we not introduce him to shameless pleasures, and train him to take up arms against them, and to overcome them? Or does this principle apply to courage only, and must he who would be perfect in valour fight against and overcome his own natural character,—since if he be unpractised and inexperienced in such conflicts, he will not be half the man which he might have been,—and are we to suppose, that with temperance it is otherwise, and that he who has never fought with the shameless and unrighteous temptations of his pleasures and lusts, and conquered them, in earnest and in play, by word, deed, and act, will still be perfectly temperate?

CLEINIAS: A most unlikely supposition.

ATHENIAN: Suppose that some God had given a fear-potion to men, and that the more a man drank of this the more he regarded himself at every draught as a child of misfortune, and that he feared everything happening or about to happen to him; and that at last the most courageous of men utterly lost his presence of mind for a time, and only came to himself again when he had slept off the influence of the draught.

CLEINIAS: But has such a draught, Stranger, ever really been known among men?

ATHENIAN: No; but, if there had been, might not such a draught have been of use to the legislator as a test of courage? Might we not go and say to him, 'O legislator, whether you are legislating for the Cretan, or for any other state, would you not like to have a touchstone of the courage and cowardice of your citizens?'

CLEINIAS: 'I should,' will be the answer of every one.

ATHENIAN: 'And you would rather have a touchstone in which there is no risk and no great danger than the reverse?'

CLEINIAS: In that proposition every one may safely agree.

ATHENIAN: 'And in order to make use of the draught, you would lead them amid these imaginary terrors, and prove them, when the affection of fear was working upon them, and compel them to be fearless, exhorting and admonishing them; and also honouring them, but dishonouring any one who will not be persuaded by you to be in all respects such as you command him; and if he underwent the trial well and manfully, you would let him go unscathed; but if ill, you would inflict a punishment upon him? Or would you abstain from using the potion altogether, although you have no reason for abstaining?'

CLEINIAS: He would be certain, Stranger, to use the potion.

ATHENIAN: This would be a mode of testing and training which would be wonderfully easy in comparison with those now in use, and might be applied to a single person, or to a few, or indeed to any number; and he would do well who provided himself with the potion only, rather than with any number of other things, whether he preferred to be by himself in solitude, and there contend with his fears, because he was ashamed to be seen by the eye of man until he was perfect; or trusting to the force of his own nature and habits, and believing that he had been already disciplined sufficiently, he did not hesitate to train himself in company with any number of others, and display his power in conquering the irresistible change effected by the draught—his virtue being such, that he never in any instance fell into any great unseemliness, but was always himself, and left off before he arrived at the last cup, fearing that he, like all other men, might be overcome by the potion.

CLEINIAS: Yes, Stranger, in that last case, too, he might equally show his self-control.

ATHENIAN: Let us return to the lawgiver, and say to him:—'Well, lawgiver, there is certainly no such fear-potion which man has either received from the Gods or himself discovered; for witchcraft has no place at our board. But is there any potion which might serve as a test of overboldness and excessive and indiscreet boasting?

CLEINIAS: I suppose that he will say, Yes,—meaning that wine is such a potion.

ATHENIAN: Is not the effect of this quite the opposite of the effect of the other? When a man drinks wine he begins to be better pleased with himself, and the more he drinks the more he is filled full of brave hopes, and conceit of his power, and at last the string of his tongue is loosened, and fancying himself wise, he is brimming over with lawlessness, and has no more fear or respect, and is ready to do or say anything.

CLEINIAS: I think that every one will admit the truth of your description.

MEGILLUS: Certainly.

ATHENIAN: Now, let us remember, as we were saying, that there are two things which should be cultivated in the soul: first, the greatest courage; secondly, the greatest fear—

CLEINIAS: Which you said to be characteristic of reverence, if I am not mistaken.

ATHENIAN: Thank you for reminding me. But now, as the habit of courage and fearlessness is to be trained amid fears, let us consider whether the opposite quality is not also to be trained among opposites.

CLEINIAS: That is probably the case.

ATHENIAN: There are times and seasons at which we are by nature more than commonly valiant and bold; now we ought to train ourselves on these occasions to be as free from impudence and shamelessness as possible, and to be afraid to say or suffer or do anything that is base.

CLEINIAS: True.

ATHENIAN: Are not the moments in which we are apt to be bold and shameless such as these?—when we are under the influence of anger, love, pride, ignorance, avarice, cowardice? or when wealth, beauty, strength, and all the intoxicating workings of pleasure madden us? What is better adapted than the festive use of wine, in the first place to test, and in the second place to train the character of a man, if care be taken in the use of it? What is there cheaper, or more innocent? For do but consider which is the greater risk:—Would you rather test a man of a morose and savage nature, which is the source of ten thousand acts of injustice, by making bargains with him at a risk to yourself, or by having him as a companion at the festival of Dionysus? Or would you, if you wanted to apply a touchstone to a man who is prone to love, entrust your wife, or your sons, or daughters to him, perilling your dearest interests in order to have a view of the condition of his soul? I might mention numberless cases, in which the advantage would be manifest of getting to know a character in sport, and without paying dearly for experience. And I do not believe that either a Cretan, or any other man, will doubt that such a test is a fair test, and safer, cheaper, and speedier than any other.

CLEINIAS: That is certainly true.

ATHENIAN: And this knowledge of the natures and habits of men's souls will be of the greatest use in that art which has the management of them; and that art, if I am not mistaken, is politics.

CLEINIAS: Exactly so.

BOOK II.

ATHENIAN: And now we have to consider whether the insight into human nature is the only benefit derived from well-ordered potations, or whether there are not other advantages great and much to be desired. The argument seems to imply that there are. But how and in what way these are to be attained, will have to be considered attentively, or we may be entangled in error.

CLEINIAS: Proceed.

ATHENIAN: Let me once more recall our doctrine of right education; which, if I am not mistaken, depends on the due regulation of convivial intercourse.

CLEINIAS: You talk rather grandly.

ATHENIAN: Pleasure and pain I maintain to be the first perceptions of children, and I say that they are the forms under which virtue and vice are originally present to them. As to wisdom and true and fixed opinions, happy is the man who acquires them, even when declining in years; and we may say that he who possesses them, and the blessings which are contained in them, is a perfect man. Now I mean by education that training which is given by suitable habits to the first instincts of virtue in children;—when pleasure, and friendship, and pain, and hatred, are rightly implanted in souls not yet capable of understanding the nature of them, and who find them, after they have attained reason, to be in harmony with her. This harmony of the soul, taken as a whole, is virtue; but the particular training in respect of pleasure and pain, which leads you always to hate what you ought to hate, and love what you ought to love from the beginning of life to the end, may be separated off; and, in my view, will be rightly called education.

CLEINIAS: I think, Stranger, that you are quite right in all that you have said and are saying about education.

ATHENIAN: I am glad to hear that you agree with me; for, indeed, the discipline of pleasure and pain which, when rightly ordered, is a principle of education, has been often relaxed and corrupted in human life. And the Gods, pitying the toils which our race is born to undergo, have appointed holy festivals, wherein men alternate rest with labour; and have given them the Muses and Apollo, the leader of the Muses, and Dionysus, to be companions in their revels, that they may improve their education by taking part in the festivals of the Gods, and with their help. I should like to know whether a common saying is in our opinion true to nature or not. For men say that the young of all creatures cannot be quiet in their bodies or in their voices; they are always wanting to move and cry out; some leaping and skipping, and overflowing with sportiveness and delight at something, others uttering all sorts of cries. But, whereas the animals have no perception of order or disorder in their movements, that is, of rhythm or harmony, as they are called, to us, the Gods, who, as we say, have been appointed to be our companions in the dance, have given the pleasurable sense of harmony and rhythm; and so they stir us into life, and we follow them, joining hands together in dances and songs; and these they call choruses, which is a term naturally expressive of cheerfulness. Shall we begin, then, with the acknowledgment that education is first given through Apollo and the Muses? What do you say?

CLEINIAS: I assent.

ATHENIAN: And the uneducated is he who has not been trained in the chorus, and the educated is he who has been well trained?

CLEINIAS: Certainly.

ATHENIAN: And the chorus is made up of two parts, dance and song?

CLEINIAS: True.

ATHENIAN: Then he who is well educated will be able to sing and dance well?

CLEINIAS: I suppose that he will.

ATHENIAN: Let us see; what are we saying?

CLEINIAS: What?

ATHENIAN: He sings well and dances well; now must we add that he sings what is good and dances what is good?

CLEINIAS: Let us make the addition.

ATHENIAN: We will suppose that he knows the good to be good, and the bad to be bad, and makes use of them accordingly: which now is the better trained in dancing and music—he who is able to move his body and to use his voice in what is understood to be the right manner, but has no delight in good or hatred of evil; or he who is incorrect in gesture and voice, but is right in his sense of pleasure and pain, and welcomes what is good, and is offended at what is evil?

CLEINIAS: There is a great difference, Stranger, in the two kinds of education.

ATHENIAN: If we three know what is good in song and dance, then we truly know also who is educated and who is uneducated; but if not, then we certainly shall not know wherein lies the safeguard of education, and whether there is any or not.

CLEINIAS: True.

ATHENIAN: Let us follow the scent like hounds, and go in pursuit of beauty of figure, and melody, and song, and dance; if these escape us, there will be no use in talking about true education, whether Hellenic or barbarian.

CLEINIAS: Yes.

ATHENIAN: And what is beauty of figure, or beautiful melody? When a manly soul is in trouble, and when a cowardly soul is in similar case, are they likely to use the same figures and gestures, or to give utterance to the same sounds?

CLEINIAS: How can they, when the very colours of their faces differ?

ATHENIAN: Good, my friend; I may observe, however, in passing, that in music there certainly are figures and there are melodies: and music is concerned with harmony and rhythm, so that you may speak of a melody or figure having good rhythm or good harmony—the term is correct enough; but to speak metaphorically of a melody or figure having a 'good colour,' as the masters of choruses do, is not allowable, although you can speak of the melodies or figures of the brave and the coward, praising the one and censuring the other. And not to be tedious, let us say that the figures and melodies which are expressive of virtue of soul or body, or of images of virtue, are without exception good, and those which are expressive of vice are the reverse of good.

CLEINIAS: Your suggestion is excellent; and let us answer that these things are so.

ATHENIAN: Once more, are all of us equally delighted with every sort of dance?

CLEINIAS: Far otherwise.

ATHENIAN: What, then, leads us astray? Are beautiful things not the same to us all, or are they the same in themselves, but not in our opinion of them? For no one will admit that forms of vice in the dance are more beautiful than forms of virtue, or that he himself delights in the forms of vice, and others in a muse of another character. And yet most persons say, that the excellence of music is to give pleasure to our souls. But this is intolerable and blasphemous; there is, however, a much more plausible account of the delusion.

CLEINIAS: What?

ATHENIAN: The adaptation of art to the characters of men. Choric movements are imitations of manners occurring in various actions, fortunes, dispositions,—each particular is imitated, and those to whom the words, or songs, or dances are suited, either by nature or habit or both, cannot help feeling pleasure in them and applauding them, and calling them beautiful. But those whose natures, or ways, or habits are unsuited to them, cannot delight in them or applaud them, and they call them base. There are others, again, whose natures are right and their habits wrong, or whose habits are right and their natures wrong, and they praise one thing, but are pleased at another. For they say that all these imitations are pleasant, but not good. And in the presence of those whom they think wise, they are ashamed of dancing and singing in the baser manner, or of deliberately lending any countenance to such proceedings; and yet, they have a secret pleasure in them.

CLEINIAS: Very true.

ATHENIAN: And is any harm done to the lover of vicious dances or songs, or any good done to the approver of the opposite sort of pleasure?

CLEINIAS: I think that there is.

ATHENIAN: 'I think' is not the word, but I would say, rather, 'I am certain.' For must they not have the same effect as when a man associates with bad characters, whom he likes and approves rather than dislikes, and only censures playfully because he has a suspicion of his own badness? In that case, he who takes pleasure in them will surely become like those in whom he takes pleasure, even though he be ashamed to praise them. And what greater good or evil can any destiny ever make us undergo?

CLEINIAS: I know of none.

ATHENIAN: Then in a city which has good laws, or in future ages is to have them, bearing in mind the instruction and amusement which are given by music, can we suppose that the poets are to be allowed to teach in the dance anything which they themselves like, in the way of rhythm, or melody, or words, to the young children of any well-conditioned parents? Is the poet to train his choruses as he pleases, without reference to virtue or vice?

CLEINIAS: That is surely quite unreasonable, and is not to be thought of.

ATHENIAN: And yet he may do this in almost any state with the exception of Egypt.

CLEINIAS: And what are the laws about music and dancing in Egypt?

ATHENIAN: You will wonder when I tell you: Long ago they appear to have recognized the very principle of which we are now speaking—that their young citizens must be habituated to forms and strains of virtue. These they fixed, and exhibited the patterns of them in their temples; and no painter or artist is allowed to innovate upon them, or to leave the traditional forms and invent new ones. To this day, no alteration is allowed either in these arts, or in music at all. And you will find that their works of art are painted or moulded in the same forms which they had ten thousand years ago;—this is literally true and no exaggeration,—their ancient paintings and sculptures are not a whit better or worse than the work of to-day, but are made with just the same skill.

CLEINIAS: How extraordinary!

ATHENIAN: I should rather say, How statesmanlike, how worthy of a legislator! I know that other things in Egypt are not so well. But what I am telling you about music is true and deserving of consideration, because showing that a lawgiver may institute melodies which have a natural truth and correctness without any fear of failure. To do this, however, must be the work of God, or of a divine person; in Egypt they have a tradition that their ancient chants which have been preserved for so many ages are the composition of the Goddess Isis. And therefore, as I was saying, if a person can only find in any way the natural melodies, he may confidently embody them in a fixed and legal form. For the love of novelty which arises out of pleasure in the new and weariness of the old, has not strength enough to corrupt the consecrated song and dance, under the plea that they have become antiquated. At any rate, they are far from being corrupted in Egypt.

CLEINIAS: Your arguments seem to prove your point.

ATHENIAN: May we not confidently say that the true use of music and of choral festivities is as follows: We rejoice when we think that we prosper, and again we think that we prosper when we rejoice?

CLEINIAS: Exactly.

ATHENIAN: And when rejoicing in our good fortune, we are unable to be still?

CLEINIAS: True.

ATHENIAN: Our young men break forth into dancing and singing, and we who are their elders deem that we are fulfilling our part in life when we look on at them. Having lost our agility, we delight in their sports and merry-making, because we love to think of our former selves; and gladly institute contests for those who are able to awaken in us the memory of our youth.

CLEINIAS: Very true.

ATHENIAN: Is it altogether unmeaning to say, as the common people do about festivals, that he should be adjudged the wisest of men, and the winner of the palm, who gives us the greatest amount of pleasure and mirth? For on such occasions, and when mirth is the order of the day, ought not he to be honoured most, and, as I was saying, bear the palm, who gives most mirth to the greatest number? Now is this a true way of speaking or of acting?

CLEINIAS: Possibly.

ATHENIAN: But, my dear friend, let us distinguish between different cases, and not be hasty in forming a judgment: One way of considering the question will be to imagine a festival at which there are entertainments of all sorts, including gymnastic, musical, and equestrian contests: the citizens are assembled; prizes are offered, and proclamation is made that any one who likes may enter the lists, and that he is to bear the palm who gives the most pleasure to the spectators—there is to be no regulation about the manner how; but he who is most successful in giving pleasure is to be crowned victor, and deemed to be the pleasantest of the candidates: What is likely to be the result of such a proclamation?

CLEINIAS: In what respect?

ATHENIAN: There would be various exhibitions: one man, like Homer, will exhibit a rhapsody, another a performance on the lute; one will have a tragedy, and another a comedy. Nor would there be anything astonishing in some one imagining that he could gain the prize by exhibiting a puppet-show. Suppose these competitors to meet, and not these only, but innumerable others as well—can you tell me who ought to be the victor?

CLEINIAS: I do not see how any one can answer you, or pretend to know, unless he has heard with his own ears the several competitors; the question is absurd.

ATHENIAN: Well, then, if neither of you can answer, shall I answer this question which you deem so absurd?

CLEINIAS: By all means.

ATHENIAN: If very small children are to determine the question, they will decide for the puppet show.

CLEINIAS: Of course.

ATHENIAN: The older children will be advocates of comedy; educated women, and young men, and people in general, will favour tragedy.

CLEINIAS: Very likely.

ATHENIAN: And I believe that we old men would have the greatest pleasure in hearing a rhapsodist recite well the Iliad and Odyssey, or one of the Hesiodic poems, and would award the victory to him. But, who would really be the victor?—that is the question.

CLEINIAS: Yes.

ATHENIAN: Clearly you and I will have to declare that those whom we old men adjudge victors ought to win; for our ways are far and away better than any which at present exist anywhere in the world.

CLEINIAS: Certainly.

ATHENIAN: Thus far I too should agree with the many, that the excellence of music is to be measured by pleasure. But the pleasure must not be that of chance persons; the fairest music is that which delights the best and best educated, and especially that which delights the one man who is pre-eminent in virtue and education. And therefore the judges must be men of character, for they will require both wisdom and courage; the true judge must not draw his inspiration from the theatre, nor ought he to be unnerved by the clamour of the many and his own incapacity; nor again, knowing the truth, ought he through cowardice and unmanliness carelessly to deliver a lying judgment, with the very same lips which have just appealed to the Gods before he judged. He is sitting not as the disciple of the theatre, but, in his proper place, as their instructor, and he ought to be the enemy of all pandering to the pleasure of the spectators. The ancient and common custom of Hellas, which still prevails in Italy and Sicily, did certainly leave the judgment to the body of spectators, who determined the victor by show of hands. But this custom has been the destruction of the poets; for they are now in the habit of composing with a view to please the bad taste of their judges, and the result is that the spectators instruct themselves;—and also it has been the ruin of the theatre; they ought to be having characters put before them better than their own, and so receiving a higher pleasure, but now by their own act the opposite result follows. What inference is to be drawn from all this? Shall I tell you?

CLEINIAS: What?

ATHENIAN: The inference at which we arrive for the third or fourth time is, that education is the constraining and directing of youth towards that right reason, which the law affirms, and which the experience of the eldest and best has agreed to be truly right. In order, then, that the soul of the child may not be habituated to feel joy and sorrow in a manner at variance with the law, and those who obey the law, but may rather follow the law and rejoice and sorrow at the same things as the aged—in order, I say, to produce this effect, chants appear to have been invented, which really enchant, and are designed to implant that harmony of which we speak. And, because the mind of the child is incapable of enduring serious training, they are called plays and songs, and are performed in play; just as when men are sick and ailing in their bodies, their attendants give them wholesome diet in pleasant meats and drinks, but unwholesome diet in disagreeable things, in order that they may learn, as they ought, to like the one, and to dislike the other. And similarly the true legislator will persuade, and, if he cannot persuade, will compel the poet to express, as he ought, by fair and noble words, in his rhythms, the figures, and in his melodies, the music of temperate and brave and in every way good men.

CLEINIAS: But do you really imagine, Stranger, that this is the way in which poets generally compose in States at the present day? As far as I can observe, except among us and among the Lacedaemonians, there are no regulations like those of which you speak; in other places novelties are always being introduced in dancing and in music, generally not under the authority of any law, but at the instigation of lawless pleasures; and these pleasures are so far from being the same, as you describe the Egyptian to be, or having the same principles, that they are never the same.

ATHENIAN: Most true, Cleinias; and I daresay that I may have expressed myself obscurely, and so led you to imagine that I was speaking of some really existing state of things, whereas I was only saying what regulations I would like to have about music; and hence there occurred a misapprehension on your part. For when evils are far gone and irremediable, the task of censuring them is never pleasant, although at times necessary. But as we do not really differ, will you let me ask you whether you consider such institutions to be more prevalent among the Cretans and Lacedaemonians than among the other Hellenes?

CLEINIAS: Certainly they are.

ATHENIAN: And if they were extended to the other Hellenes, would it be an improvement on the present state of things?

CLEINIAS: A very great improvement, if the customs which prevail among them were such as prevail among us and the Lacedaemonians, and such as you were just now saying ought to prevail.

ATHENIAN: Let us see whether we understand one another:—Are not the principles of education and music which prevail among you as follows: you compel your poets to say that the good man, if he be temperate and just, is fortunate and happy; and this whether he be great and strong or small and weak, and whether he be rich or poor; and, on the other hand, if he have a wealth passing that of Cinyras or Midas, and be unjust, he is wretched and lives in misery? As the poet says, and with truth: I sing not, I care not about him who accomplishes all noble things, not having justice; let him who 'draws near and stretches out his hand against his enemies be a just man.' But if he be unjust, I would not have him 'look calmly upon bloody death,' nor 'surpass in swiftness the Thracian Boreas;' and let no other thing that is called good ever be his. For the goods of which the many speak are not really good: first in the catalogue is placed health, beauty next, wealth third; and then innumerable others, as for example to have a keen eye or a quick ear, and in general to have all the senses perfect; or, again, to be a tyrant and do as you like; and the final consummation of happiness is to have acquired all these things, and when you have acquired them to become at once immortal. But you and I say, that while to the just and holy all these things are the best of possessions, to the unjust they are all, including even health, the greatest of evils. For in truth, to have sight, and hearing, and the use of the senses, or to live at all without justice and virtue, even though a man be rich in all the so-called goods of fortune, is the greatest of evils, if life be immortal; but not so great, if the bad man lives only a very short time. These are the truths which, if I am not mistaken, you will persuade or compel your poets to utter with suitable accompaniments of harmony and rhythm, and in these they must train up your youth. Am I not right? For I plainly declare that evils as they are termed are goods to the unjust, and only evils to the just, and that goods are truly good to the good, but evil to the evil. Let me ask again, Are you and I agreed about this?

CLEINIAS: I think that we partly agree and partly do not.

ATHENIAN: When a man has health and wealth and a tyranny which lasts, and when he is pre-eminent in strength and courage, and has the gift of immortality, and none of the so-called evils which counter-balance these goods, but only the injustice and insolence of his own nature—of such an one you are, I suspect, unwilling to believe that he is miserable rather than happy.

CLEINIAS: That is quite true.

ATHENIAN: Once more: Suppose that he be valiant and strong, and handsome and rich, and does throughout his whole life whatever he likes, still, if he be unrighteous and insolent, would not both of you agree that he will of necessity live basely? You will surely grant so much?

CLEINIAS: Certainly.

ATHENIAN: And an evil life too?

CLEINIAS: I am not equally disposed to grant that.

ATHENIAN: Will he not live painfully and to his own disadvantage?

CLEINIAS: How can I possibly say so?

ATHENIAN: How! Then may Heaven make us to be of one mind, for now we are of two. To me, dear Cleinias, the truth of what I am saying is as plain as the fact that Crete is an island. And, if I were a lawgiver, I would try to make the poets and all the citizens speak in this strain, and I would inflict the heaviest penalties on any one in all the land who should dare to say that there are bad men who lead pleasant lives, or that the profitable and gainful is one thing, and the just another; and there are many other matters about which I should make my citizens speak in a manner different from the Cretans and Lacedaemonians of this age, and I may say, indeed, from the world in general. For tell me, my good friends, by Zeus and Apollo tell me, if I were to ask these same Gods who were your legislators,—Is not the most just life also the pleasantest? or are there two lives, one of which is the justest and the other the pleasantest?—and they were to reply that there are two; and thereupon I proceeded to ask, (that would be the right way of pursuing the enquiry), Which are the happier—those who lead the justest, or those who lead the pleasantest life? and they replied, Those who lead the pleasantest—that would be a very strange answer, which I should not like to put into the mouth of the Gods. The words will come with more propriety from the lips of fathers and legislators, and therefore I will repeat my former questions to one of them, and suppose him to say again that he who leads the pleasantest life is the happiest. And to that I rejoin:—O my father, did you not wish me to live as happily as possible? And yet you also never ceased telling me that I should live as justly as possible. Now, here the giver of the rule, whether he be legislator or father, will be in a dilemma, and will in vain endeavour to be consistent with himself. But if he were to declare that the justest life is also the happiest, every one hearing him would enquire, if I am not mistaken, what is that good and noble principle in life which the law approves, and which is superior to pleasure. For what good can the just man have which is separated from pleasure? Shall we say that glory and fame, coming from Gods and men, though good and noble, are nevertheless unpleasant, and infamy pleasant? Certainly not, sweet legislator. Or shall we say that the not-doing of wrong and there being no wrong done is good and honourable, although there is no pleasure in it, and that the doing wrong is pleasant, but evil and base?

CLEINIAS: Impossible.

ATHENIAN: The view which identifies the pleasant and the pleasant and the just and the good and the noble has an excellent moral and religious tendency. And the opposite view is most at variance with the designs of the legislator, and is, in his opinion, infamous; for no one, if he can help, will be persuaded to do that which gives him more pain than pleasure. But as distant prospects are apt to make us dizzy, especially in childhood, the legislator will try to purge away the darkness and exhibit the truth; he will persuade the citizens, in some way or other, by customs and praises and words, that just and unjust are shadows only, and that injustice, which seems opposed to justice, when contemplated by the unjust and evil man appears pleasant and the just most unpleasant; but that from the just man's point of view, the very opposite is the appearance of both of them.

CLEINIAS: True.

ATHENIAN: And which may be supposed to be the truer judgment—that of the inferior or of the better soul?

CLEINIAS: Surely, that of the better soul.

ATHENIAN: Then the unjust life must not only be more base and depraved, but also more unpleasant than the just and holy life?

CLEINIAS: That seems to be implied in the present argument.

ATHENIAN: And even supposing this were otherwise, and not as the argument has proven, still the lawgiver, who is worth anything, if he ever ventures to tell a lie to the young for their good, could not invent a more useful lie than this, or one which will have a better effect in making them do what is right, not on compulsion but voluntarily.

CLEINIAS: Truth, Stranger, is a noble thing and a lasting, but a thing of which men are hard to be persuaded.

ATHENIAN: And yet the story of the Sidonian Cadmus, which is so improbable, has been readily believed, and also innumerable other tales.

CLEINIAS: What is that story?

ATHENIAN: The story of armed men springing up after the sowing of teeth, which the legislator may take as a proof that he can persuade the minds of the young of anything; so that he has only to reflect and find out what belief will be of the greatest public advantage, and then use all his efforts to make the whole community utter one and the same word in their songs and tales and discourses all their life long. But if you do not agree with me, there is no reason why you should not argue on the other side.

CLEINIAS: I do not see that any argument can fairly be raised by either of us against what you are now saying.

ATHENIAN: The next suggestion which I have to offer is, that all our three choruses shall sing to the young and tender souls of children, reciting in their strains all the noble thoughts of which we have already spoken, or are about to speak; and the sum of them shall be, that the life which is by the Gods deemed to be the happiest is also the best;—we shall affirm this to be a most certain truth; and the minds of our young disciples will be more likely to receive these words of ours than any others which we might address to them.

CLEINIAS: I assent to what you say.

ATHENIAN: First will enter in their natural order the sacred choir composed of children, which is to sing lustily the heaven-taught lay to the whole city. Next will follow the choir of young men under the age of thirty, who will call upon the God Paean to testify to the truth of their words, and will pray him to be gracious to the youth and to turn their hearts. Thirdly, the choir of elder men, who are from thirty to sixty years of age, will also sing. There remain those who are too old to sing, and they will tell stories, illustrating the same virtues, as with the voice of an oracle.

CLEINIAS: Who are those who compose the third choir, Stranger? for I do not clearly understand what you mean to say about them.

ATHENIAN: And yet almost all that I have been saying has been said with a view to them.

CLEINIAS: Will you try to be a little plainer?

ATHENIAN: I was speaking at the commencement of our discourse, as you will remember, of the fiery nature of young creatures: I said that they were unable to keep quiet either in limb or voice, and that they called out and jumped about in a disorderly manner; and that no other animal attained to any perception of order, but man only. Now the order of motion is called rhythm, and the order of the voice, in which high and low are duly mingled, is called harmony; and both together are termed choric song. And I said that the Gods had pity on us, and gave us Apollo and the Muses to be our playfellows and leaders in the dance; and Dionysus, as I dare say that you will remember, was the third.

CLEINIAS: I quite remember.

ATHENIAN: Thus far I have spoken of the chorus of Apollo and the Muses, and I have still to speak of the remaining chorus, which is that of Dionysus.

CLEINIAS: How is that arranged? There is something strange, at any rate on first hearing, in a Dionysiac chorus of old men, if you really mean that those who are above thirty, and may be fifty, or from fifty to sixty years of age, are to dance in his honour.

ATHENIAN: Very true; and therefore it must be shown that there is good reason for the proposal.

CLEINIAS: Certainly.

ATHENIAN: Are we agreed thus far?

CLEINIAS: About what?

ATHENIAN: That every man and boy, slave and free, both sexes, and the whole city, should never cease charming themselves with the strains of which we have spoken; and that there should be every sort of change and variation of them in order to take away the effect of sameness, so that the singers may always receive pleasure from their hymns, and may never weary of them?

CLEINIAS: Every one will agree.

ATHENIAN: Where, then, will that best part of our city which, by reason of age and intelligence, has the greatest influence, sing these fairest of strains, which are to do so much good? Shall we be so foolish as to let them off who would give us the most beautiful and also the most useful of songs?

CLEINIAS: But, says the argument, we cannot let them off.

ATHENIAN: Then how can we carry out our purpose with decorum? Will this be the way?

CLEINIAS: What?

ATHENIAN: When a man is advancing in years, he is afraid and reluctant to sing;—he has no pleasure in his own performances; and if compulsion is used, he will be more and more ashamed, the older and more discreet he grows;—is not this true?

CLEINIAS: Certainly.

ATHENIAN: Well, and will he not be yet more ashamed if he has to stand up and sing in the theatre to a mixed audience?—and if moreover when he is required to do so, like the other choirs who contend for prizes, and have been trained under a singing master, he is pinched and hungry, he will certainly have a feeling of shame and discomfort which will make him very unwilling to exhibit.

CLEINIAS: No doubt.

ATHENIAN: How, then, shall we reassure him, and get him to sing? Shall we begin by enacting that boys shall not taste wine at all until they are eighteen years of age; we will tell them that fire must not be poured upon fire, whether in the body or in the soul, until they begin to go to work—this is a precaution which has to be taken against the excitableness of youth;—afterwards they may taste wine in moderation up to the age of thirty, but while a man is young he should abstain altogether from intoxication and from excess of wine; when, at length, he has reached forty years, after dinner at a public mess, he may invite not only the other Gods, but Dionysus above all, to the mystery and festivity of the elder men, making use of the wine which he has given men to lighten the sourness of old age; that in age we may renew our youth, and forget our sorrows; and also in order that the nature of the soul, like iron melted in the fire, may become softer and so more impressible. In the first place, will not any one who is thus mellowed be more ready and less ashamed to sing—I do not say before a large audience, but before a moderate company; nor yet among strangers, but among his familiars, and, as we have often said, to chant, and to enchant?

CLEINIAS: He will be far more ready.

ATHENIAN: There will be no impropriety in our using such a method of persuading them to join with us in song.

CLEINIAS: None at all.

ATHENIAN: And what strain will they sing, and what muse will they hymn? The strain should clearly be one suitable to them.

CLEINIAS: Certainly.

ATHENIAN: And what strain is suitable for heroes? Shall they sing a choric strain?

CLEINIAS: Truly, Stranger, we of Crete and Lacedaemon know no strain other than that which we have learnt and been accustomed to sing in our chorus.

ATHENIAN: I dare say; for you have never acquired the knowledge of the most beautiful kind of song, in your military way of life, which is modelled after the camp, and is not like that of dwellers in cities; and you have your young men herding and feeding together like young colts. No one takes his own individual colt and drags him away from his fellows against his will, raging and foaming, and gives him a groom to attend to him alone, and trains and rubs him down privately, and gives him the qualities in education which will make him not only a good soldier, but also a governor of a state and of cities. Such an one, as we said at first, would be a greater warrior than he of whom Tyrtaeus sings; and he would honour courage everywhere, but always as the fourth, and not as the first part of virtue, either in individuals or states.

CLEINIAS: Once more, Stranger, I must complain that you depreciate our lawgivers.

ATHENIAN: Not intentionally, if at all, my good friend; but whither the argument leads, thither let us follow; for if there be indeed some strain of song more beautiful than that of the choruses or the public theatres, I should like to impart it to those who, as we say, are ashamed of these, and want to have the best.

CLEINIAS: Certainly.

ATHENIAN: When things have an accompanying charm, either the best thing in them is this very charm, or there is some rightness or utility possessed by them;—for example, I should say that eating and drinking, and the use of food in general, have an accompanying charm which we call pleasure; but that this rightness and utility is just the healthfulness of the things served up to us, which is their true rightness.

CLEINIAS: Just so.

ATHENIAN: Thus, too, I should say that learning has a certain accompanying charm which is the pleasure; but that the right and the profitable, the good and the noble, are qualities which the truth gives to it.

CLEINIAS: Exactly.

ATHENIAN: And so in the imitative arts—if they succeed in making likenesses, and are accompanied by pleasure, may not their works be said to have a charm?

CLEINIAS: Yes.

ATHENIAN: But equal proportions, whether of quality or quantity, and not pleasure, speaking generally, would give them truth or rightness.

CLEINIAS: Yes.

ATHENIAN: Then that only can be rightly judged by the standard of pleasure, which makes or furnishes no utility or truth or likeness, nor on the other hand is productive of any hurtful quality, but exists solely for the sake of the accompanying charm; and the term 'pleasure' is most appropriately applied to it when these other qualities are absent.

CLEINIAS: You are speaking of harmless pleasure, are you not?

ATHENIAN: Yes; and this I term amusement, when doing neither harm nor good in any degree worth speaking of.

CLEINIAS: Very true.

ATHENIAN: Then, if such be our principles, we must assert that imitation is not to be judged of by pleasure and false opinion; and this is true of all equality, for the equal is not equal or the symmetrical symmetrical, because somebody thinks or likes something, but they are to be judged of by the standard of truth, and by no other whatever.

CLEINIAS: Quite true.

ATHENIAN: Do we not regard all music as representative and imitative?

CLEINIAS: Certainly.

ATHENIAN: Then, when any one says that music is to be judged of by pleasure, his doctrine cannot be admitted; and if there be any music of which pleasure is the criterion, such music is not to be sought out or deemed to have any real excellence, but only that other kind of music which is an imitation of the good.

CLEINIAS: Very true.

ATHENIAN: And those who seek for the best kind of song and music ought not to seek for that which is pleasant, but for that which is true; and the truth of imitation consists, as we were saying, in rendering the thing imitated according to quantity and quality.

CLEINIAS: Certainly.

ATHENIAN: And every one will admit that musical compositions are all imitative and representative. Will not poets and spectators and actors all agree in this?

CLEINIAS: They will.

ATHENIAN: Surely then he who would judge correctly must know what each composition is; for if he does not know what is the character and meaning of the piece, and what it represents, he will never discern whether the intention is true or false.

CLEINIAS: Certainly not.

ATHENIAN: And will he who does not know what is true be able to distinguish what is good and bad? My statement is not very clear; but perhaps you will understand me better if I put the matter in another way.

CLEINIAS: How?

ATHENIAN: There are ten thousand likenesses of objects of sight?

CLEINIAS: Yes.

ATHENIAN: And can he who does not know what the exact object is which is imitated, ever know whether the resemblance is truthfully executed? I mean, for example, whether a statue has the proportions of a body, and the true situation of the parts; what those proportions are, and how the parts fit into one another in due order; also their colours and conformations, or whether this is all confused in the execution: do you think that any one can know about this, who does not know what the animal is which has been imitated?

CLEINIAS: Impossible.

ATHENIAN: But even if we know that the thing pictured or sculptured is a man, who has received at the hand of the artist all his proper parts and colours and shapes, must we not also know whether the work is beautiful or in any respect deficient in beauty?

CLEINIAS: If this were not required, Stranger, we should all of us be judges of beauty.

ATHENIAN: Very true; and may we not say that in everything imitated, whether in drawing, music, or any other art, he who is to be a competent judge must possess three things;—he must know, in the first place, of what the imitation is; secondly, he must know that it is true; and thirdly, that it has been well executed in words and melodies and rhythms?

CLEINIAS: Certainly.

ATHENIAN: Then let us not faint in discussing the peculiar difficulty of music. Music is more celebrated than any other kind of imitation, and therefore requires the greatest care of them all. For if a man makes a mistake here, he may do himself the greatest injury by welcoming evil dispositions, and the mistake may be very difficult to discern, because the poets are artists very inferior in character to the Muses themselves, who would never fall into the monstrous error of assigning to the words of men the gestures and songs of women; nor after combining the melodies with the gestures of freemen would they add on the rhythms of slaves and men of the baser sort; nor, beginning with the rhythms and gestures of freemen, would they assign to them a melody or words which are of an opposite character; nor would they mix up the voices and sounds of animals and of men and instruments, and every other sort of noise, as if they were all one. But human poets are fond of introducing this sort of inconsistent mixture, and so make themselves ridiculous in the eyes of those who, as Orpheus says, 'are ripe for true pleasure.' The experienced see all this confusion, and yet the poets go on and make still further havoc by separating the rhythm and the figure of the dance from the melody, setting bare words to metre, and also separating the melody and the rhythm from the words, using the lyre or the flute alone. For when there are no words, it is very difficult to recognize the meaning of the harmony and rhythm, or to see that any worthy object is imitated by them. And we must acknowledge that all this sort of thing, which aims only at swiftness and smoothness and a brutish noise, and uses the flute and the lyre not as the mere accompaniments of the dance and song, is exceedingly coarse and tasteless. The use of either instrument, when unaccompanied, leads to every sort of irregularity and trickery. This is all rational enough. But we are considering not how our choristers, who are from thirty to fifty years of age, and may be over fifty, are not to use the Muses, but how they are to use them. And the considerations which we have urged seem to show in what way these fifty years' old choristers who are to sing, may be expected to be better trained. For they need to have a quick perception and knowledge of harmonies and rhythms; otherwise, how can they ever know whether a melody would be rightly sung to the Dorian mode, or to the rhythm which the poet has assigned to it?

CLEINIAS: Clearly they cannot.

ATHENIAN: The many are ridiculous in imagining that they know what is in proper harmony and rhythm, and what is not, when they can only be made to sing and step in rhythm by force; it never occurs to them that they are ignorant of what they are doing. Now every melody is right when it has suitable harmony and rhythm, and wrong when unsuitable.

CLEINIAS: That is most certain.

ATHENIAN: But can a man who does not know a thing, as we were saying, know that the thing is right?

CLEINIAS: Impossible.

ATHENIAN: Then now, as would appear, we are making the discovery that our newly-appointed choristers, whom we hereby invite and, although they are their own masters, compel to sing, must be educated to such an extent as to be able to follow the steps of the rhythm and the notes of the song, that they may know the harmonies and rhythms, and be able to select what are suitable for men of their age and character to sing; and may sing them, and have innocent pleasure from their own performance, and also lead younger men to welcome with dutiful delight good dispositions. Having such training, they will attain a more accurate knowledge than falls to the lot of the common people, or even of the poets themselves. For the poet need not know the third point, viz., whether the imitation is good or not, though he can hardly help knowing the laws of melody and rhythm. But the aged chorus must know all the three, that they may choose the best, and that which is nearest to the best; for otherwise they will never be able to charm the souls of young men in the way of virtue. And now the original design of the argument which was intended to bring eloquent aid to the

Chorus of Dionysus, has been accomplished to the best of our ability, and let us see whether we were right:—I should imagine that a drinking assembly is likely to become more and more tumultuous as the drinking goes on: this, as we were saying at first, will certainly be the case.

CLEINIAS: Certainly.

ATHENIAN: Every man has a more than natural elevation; his heart is glad within him, and he will say anything and will be restrained by nobody at such a time; he fancies that he is able to rule over himself and all mankind.

CLEINIAS: Quite true.

ATHENIAN: Were we not saying that on such occasions the souls of the drinkers become like iron heated in the fire, and grow softer and younger, and are easily moulded by him who knows how to educate and fashion them, just as when they were young, and that this fashioner of them is the same who prescribed for them in the days of their youth, viz., the good legislator; and that he ought to enact laws of the banquet, which, when a man is confident, bold, and impudent, and unwilling to wait his turn and have his share of silence and speech, and drinking and music, will change his character into the opposite—such laws as will infuse into him a just and noble fear, which will take up arms at the approach of insolence, being that divine fear which we have called reverence and shame?

CLEINIAS: True.

ATHENIAN: And the guardians of these laws and fellow-workers with them are the calm and sober generals of the drinkers; and without their help there is greater difficulty in fighting against drink than in fighting against enemies when the commander of an army is not himself calm; and he who is unwilling to obey them and the commanders of Dionysiac feasts who are more than sixty years of age, shall suffer a disgrace as great as he who disobeys military leaders, or even greater.

CLEINIAS: Right.

ATHENIAN: If, then, drinking and amusement were regulated in this way, would not the companions of our revels be improved? they would part better friends than they were, and not, as now, enemies. Their whole intercourse would be regulated by law and observant of it, and the sober would be the leaders of the drunken.

CLEINIAS: I think so too, if drinking were regulated as you propose.

ATHENIAN: Let us not then simply censure the gift of Dionysus as bad and unfit to be received into the State. For wine has many excellences, and one pre-eminent one, about which there is a difficulty in speaking to the many, from a fear of their misconceiving and misunderstanding what is said.

CLEINIAS: To what do you refer?

ATHENIAN: There is a tradition or story, which has somehow crept about the world, that Dionysus was robbed of his wits by his stepmother Here, and that out of revenge he inspires Bacchic furies and dancing madnesses in others; for which reason he gave men wine. Such traditions concerning the Gods I leave to those who think that they may be safely uttered (compare Euthyph.; Republic); I only know that no animal at birth is mature or perfect in intelligence; and in the intermediate period, in which he has not yet acquired his own proper sense, he rages and roars without rhyme or reason; and when he has once got on his legs he jumps about without rhyme or reason; and this, as you will remember, has been already said by us to be the origin of music and gymnastic.

CLEINIAS: To be sure, I remember.

ATHENIAN: And did we not say that the sense of harmony and rhythm sprang from this beginning among men, and that Apollo and the Muses and Dionysus were the Gods whom we had to thank for them?

CLEINIAS: Certainly.

ATHENIAN: The other story implied that wine was given man out of revenge, and in order to make him mad; but our present doctrine, on the contrary, is, that wine was given him as a balm, and in order to implant modesty in the soul, and health and strength in the body.

CLEINIAS: That, Stranger, is precisely what was said.

ATHENIAN: Then half the subject may now be considered to have been discussed; shall we proceed to the consideration of the other half?

CLEINIAS: What is the other half, and how do you divide the subject?

ATHENIAN: The whole choral art is also in our view the whole of education; and of this art, rhythms and harmonies form the part which has to do with the voice.

CLEINIAS: Yes.

ATHENIAN: The movement of the body has rhythm in common with the movement of the voice, but gesture is peculiar to it, whereas song is simply the movement of the voice.

CLEINIAS: Most true.

ATHENIAN: And the sound of the voice which reaches and educates the soul, we have ventured to term music.

CLEINIAS: We were right.

ATHENIAN: And the movement of the body, when regarded as an amusement, we termed dancing; but when extended and pursued with a view to the excellence of the body, this scientific training may be called gymnastic.

CLEINIAS: Exactly.

ATHENIAN: Music, which was one half of the choral art, may be said to have been completely discussed. Shall we proceed to the other half or not? What would you like?

CLEINIAS: My good friend, when you are talking with a Cretan and Lacedaemonian, and we have discussed music and not gymnastic, what answer are either of us likely to make to such an enquiry?

ATHENIAN: An answer is contained in your question; and I understand and accept what you say not only as an answer, but also as a command to proceed with gymnastic.

CLEINIAS: You quite understand me; do as you say.

ATHENIAN: I will; and there will not be any difficulty in speaking intelligibly to you about a subject with which both of you are far more familiar than with music.

CLEINIAS: There will not.

ATHENIAN: Is not the origin of gymnastics, too, to be sought in the tendency to rapid motion which exists in all animals; man, as we were saying, having attained the sense of rhythm, created and invented dancing; and melody arousing and awakening rhythm, both united formed the choral art?

CLEINIAS: Very true.

ATHENIAN: And one part of this subject has been already discussed by us, and there still remains another to be discussed?

CLEINIAS: Exactly.

ATHENIAN: I have first a final word to add to my discourse about drink, if you will allow me to do so.

CLEINIAS: What more have you to say?

ATHENIAN: I should say that if a city seriously means to adopt the practice of drinking under due regulation and with a view to the enforcement of temperance, and in like manner, and on the same principle, will allow of other pleasures, designing to gain the victory over them—in this way all of them may be used. But if the State makes drinking an amusement only, and whoever likes may drink whenever he likes, and with whom he likes, and add to this any other indulgences, I shall never agree or allow that this city or this man should practise drinking. I would go further than the Cretans and Lacedaemonians, and am disposed rather to the law of the Carthaginians, that no one while he is on a campaign should be allowed to taste wine at all, but that he should drink water during all that time, and that in the city no slave, male or female, should ever drink wine; and that no magistrates should drink during their year of office, nor should pilots of vessels or judges while on duty taste wine at all, nor any one who is going to hold a consultation about any matter of importance; nor in the day-time at all, unless in consequence of exercise or as medicine; nor again at night, when any one, either man or woman, is minded to get children. There are numberless other cases also in which those who have good sense and good laws ought not to drink wine, so that if what I say is true, no city will need many vineyards. Their husbandry and their way of life in general will follow an appointed order, and their cultivation of the vine will be the most limited and the least common of their employments. And this, Stranger, shall be the crown of my discourse about wine, if you agree.

CLEINIAS: Excellent: we agree.

BOOK III.

ATHENIAN: Enough of this. And what, then, is to be regarded as the origin of government? Will not a man be able to judge of it best from a point of view in which he may behold the progress of states and their transitions to good or evil?

CLEINIAS: What do you mean?

ATHENIAN: I mean that he might watch them from the point of view of time, and observe the changes which take place in them during infinite ages.

CLEINIAS: How so?

ATHENIAN: Why, do you think that you can reckon the time which has elapsed since cities first existed and men were citizens of them?

CLEINIAS: Hardly.

ATHENIAN: But are sure that it must be vast and incalculable?

CLEINIAS: Certainly.

ATHENIAN: And have not thousands and thousands of cities come into being during this period and as many perished? And has not each of them had every form of government many times over, now growing larger, now smaller, and again improving or declining?

CLEINIAS: To be sure.

ATHENIAN: Let us endeavour to ascertain the cause of these changes; for that will probably explain the first origin and development of forms of government.

CLEINIAS: Very good. You shall endeavour to impart your thoughts to us, and we will make an effort to understand you.

ATHENIAN: Do you believe that there is any truth in ancient traditions?

CLEINIAS: What traditions?

ATHENIAN: The traditions about the many destructions of mankind which have been occasioned by deluges and pestilences, and in many other ways, and of the survival of a remnant?

CLEINIAS: Every one is disposed to believe them.

ATHENIAN: Let us consider one of them, that which was caused by the famous deluge.

CLEINIAS: What are we to observe about it?

ATHENIAN: I mean to say that those who then escaped would only be hill shepherds,—small sparks of the human race preserved on the tops of mountains.

CLEINIAS: Clearly.

ATHENIAN: Such survivors would necessarily be unacquainted with the arts and the various devices which are suggested to the dwellers in cities by interest or ambition, and with all the wrongs which they contrive against one another.

CLEINIAS: Very true.

ATHENIAN: Let us suppose, then, that the cities in the plain and on the sea-coast were utterly destroyed at that time.

CLEINIAS: Very good.

ATHENIAN: Would not all implements have then perished and every other excellent invention of political or any other sort of wisdom have utterly disappeared?

CLEINIAS: Why, yes, my friend; and if things had always continued as they are at present ordered, how could any discovery have ever been made even in the least particular? For it is evident that the arts were unknown during ten thousand times ten thousand years. And no more than a thousand or two thousand years have elapsed since the discoveries of Daedalus, Orpheus and Palamedes,—since Marsyas and Olympus invented music, and Amphion the lyre—not to speak of numberless other inventions which are but of yesterday.

ATHENIAN: Have you forgotten, Cleinias, the name of a friend who is really of yesterday?

CLEINIAS: I suppose that you mean Epimenides.

ATHENIAN: The same, my friend; he does indeed far overleap the heads of all mankind by his invention; for he carried out in practice, as you declare, what of old Hesiod (Works and Days) only preached.

CLEINIAS: Yes, according to our tradition.

ATHENIAN: After the great destruction, may we not suppose that the state of man was something of this sort:—In the beginning of things there was a fearful illimitable desert and a vast expanse of land; a herd or two of oxen would be the only survivors of the animal world; and there might be a few goats, these too hardly enough to maintain the shepherds who tended them?

CLEINIAS: True.

ATHENIAN: And of cities or governments or legislation, about which we are now talking, do you suppose that they could have any recollection at all?

CLEINIAS: None whatever.

ATHENIAN: And out of this state of things has there not sprung all that we now are and have: cities and governments, and arts and laws, and a great deal of vice and a great deal of virtue?

CLEINIAS: What do you mean?

ATHENIAN: Why, my good friend, how can we possibly suppose that those who knew nothing of all the good and evil of cities could have attained their full development, whether of virtue or of vice?

CLEINIAS: I understand your meaning, and you are quite right.

ATHENIAN: But, as time advanced and the race multiplied, the world came to be what the world is.

CLEINIAS: Very true.

ATHENIAN: Doubtless the change was not made all in a moment, but little by little, during a very long period of time.

CLEINIAS: A highly probable supposition.

ATHENIAN: At first, they would have a natural fear ringing in their ears which would prevent their descending from the heights into the plain.

CLEINIAS: Of course.

ATHENIAN: The fewness of the survivors at that time would have made them all the more desirous of seeing one another; but then the means of travelling either by land or sea had been almost entirely lost, as I may say, with the loss of the arts, and there was great difficulty in getting at one another; for iron and brass and all metals were jumbled together and had disappeared in the chaos; nor was there any possibility of extracting ore from them; and they had scarcely any means of felling timber. Even if you suppose that some implements might have been preserved in the mountains, they must quickly have worn out and vanished, and there would be no more of them until the art of metallurgy had again revived.

CLEINIAS: There could not have been.

ATHENIAN: In how many generations would this be attained?

CLEINIAS: Clearly, not for many generations.

ATHENIAN: During this period, and for some time afterwards, all the arts which require iron and brass and the like would disappear.

CLEINIAS: Certainly.

ATHENIAN: Faction and war would also have died out in those days, and for many reasons.

CLEINIAS: How would that be?

ATHENIAN: In the first place, the desolation of these primitive men would create in them a feeling of affection and goodwill towards one another; and, secondly, they would have no occasion to quarrel about their subsistence, for they would have pasture in abundance, except just at first, and in some particular cases; and from their pasture-land they would obtain the greater part of their food in a primitive age, having plenty of milk and flesh; moreover they would procure other food by the chase, not to be despised either in quantity or quality. They would also have abundance of clothing, and bedding, and dwellings, and utensils either capable of standing on the fire or not; for the plastic and weaving arts do not require any use of iron: and God has given these two arts to man in order to provide him with all such things, that, when reduced to the last extremity, the human race may still grow and increase. Hence in those days mankind were not very poor; nor was poverty a cause of difference among them; and rich they could not have been, having neither gold nor silver:—such at that time was their condition. And the community which has neither poverty nor riches will always have the noblest principles; in it there is no insolence or injustice, nor, again, are there any contentions or envyings. And therefore they were good, and also because they were what is called simple-minded; and when they were told about good and evil, they in their simplicity believed what they heard to be very truth and practised it. No one had the wit to suspect another of a falsehood, as men do now; but what they heard about Gods and men they believed to be true, and lived accordingly; and therefore they were in all respects such as we have described them.

CLEINIAS: That quite accords with my views, and with those of my friend here.

ATHENIAN: Would not many generations living on in a simple manner, although ruder, perhaps, and more ignorant of the arts generally, and in particular of those of land or naval warfare, and likewise of other arts, termed in cities legal practices and party conflicts, and including all conceivable ways of hurting one another in word and deed;—although inferior to those who lived before the deluge, or to the men of our day in these respects, would they not, I say, be simpler and more manly, and also more temperate and altogether more just? The reason has been already explained.

CLEINIAS: Very true.

ATHENIAN: I should wish you to understand that what has preceded and what is about to follow, has been, and will be said, with the intention of explaining what need the men of that time had of laws, and who was their lawgiver.

CLEINIAS: And thus far what you have said has been very well said.

ATHENIAN: They could hardly have wanted lawgivers as yet; nothing of that sort was likely to have existed in their days, for they had no letters at this early period; they lived by habit and the customs of their ancestors, as they are called.

CLEINIAS: Probably.

ATHENIAN: But there was already existing a form of government which, if I am not mistaken, is generally termed a lordship, and this still remains in many places, both among Hellenes and barbarians (compare Arist. Pol.), and is the government which is declared by Homer to have prevailed among the Cyclopes:—

'They have neither councils nor judgments, but they dwell in hollow caves on the tops of high mountains, and every one gives law to his wife and children, and they do not busy themselves about one another.' (Odyss.)

CLEINIAS: That seems to be a charming poet of yours; I have read some other verses of his, which are very clever; but I do not know much of him, for foreign poets are very little read among the Cretans.

MEGILLUS: But they are in Lacedaemon, and he appears to be the prince of them all; the manner of life, however, which he describes is not Spartan, but rather Ionian, and he seems quite to confirm what you are saying, when he traces up the ancient state of mankind by the help of tradition to barbarism.

ATHENIAN: Yes, he does confirm it; and we may accept his witness to the fact that such forms of government sometimes arise.

CLEINIAS: We may.

ATHENIAN: And were not such states composed of men who had been dispersed in single habitations and families by the poverty which attended the devastations; and did not the eldest then rule among them, because with them government originated in the authority of a father and a mother, whom, like a flock of birds, they followed, forming one troop under the patriarchal rule and sovereignty of their parents, which of all sovereignties is the most just?

CLEINIAS: Very true.

ATHENIAN: After this they came together in greater numbers, and increased the size of their cities, and betook themselves to husbandry, first of all at the foot of the mountains, and made enclosures of loose walls and works of defence, in order to keep off wild beasts; thus creating a single large and common habitation.

CLEINIAS: Yes; at least we may suppose so.

ATHENIAN: There is another thing which would probably happen.

CLEINIAS: What?

ATHENIAN: When these larger habitations grew up out of the lesser original ones, each of the lesser ones would survive in the larger; every family would be under the rule of the eldest, and, owing to their separation from one another, would have peculiar customs in things divine and human, which they would have received from their several parents who had educated them; and these customs would incline them to order, when the parents had the element of order in their nature, and to courage, when they had the element of courage. And they would naturally stamp upon their children, and upon their children's children, their own likings; and, as we are saying, they would find their way into the larger society, having already their own peculiar laws.

CLEINIAS: Certainly.

ATHENIAN: And every man surely likes his own laws best, and the laws of others not so well.

CLEINIAS: True.

ATHENIAN: Then now we seem to have stumbled upon the beginnings of legislation.

CLEINIAS: Exactly.

ATHENIAN: The next step will be that these persons who have met together, will select some arbiters, who will review the laws of all of them, and will publicly present such as they approve to the chiefs who lead the tribes, and who are in a manner their kings, allowing them to choose those which they think best. These persons will themselves be called legislators, and will appoint the magistrates, framing some sort of aristocracy, or perhaps monarchy, out of the dynasties or lordships, and in this altered state of the government they will live.

CLEINIAS: Yes, that would be the natural order of things.

ATHENIAN: Then, now let us speak of a third form of government, in which all other forms and conditions of polities and cities concur.

CLEINIAS: What is that?

ATHENIAN: The form which in fact Homer indicates as following the second. This third form arose when, as he says, Dardanus founded Dardania:—

'For not as yet had the holy Ilium been built on the plain to be a city of speaking men; but they were still dwelling at the foot of many-fountained Ida.'

For indeed, in these verses, and in what he said of the Cyclopes, he speaks the words of God and nature; for poets are a divine race, and often in their strains, by the aid of the Muses and the Graces, they attain truth.

CLEINIAS: Yes.

ATHENIAN: Then now let us proceed with the rest of our tale, which will probably be found to illustrate in some degree our proposed design:—Shall we do so?

CLEINIAS: By all means.

ATHENIAN: Ilium was built, when they descended from the mountain, in a large and fair plain, on a sort of low hill, watered by many rivers descending from Ida.

CLEINIAS: Such is the tradition.

ATHENIAN: And we must suppose this event to have taken place many ages after the deluge?

ATHENIAN: A marvellous forgetfulness of the former destruction would appear to have come over them, when they placed their town right under numerous streams flowing from the heights, trusting for their security to not very high hills, either.

CLEINIAS: There must have been a long interval, clearly.

ATHENIAN: And, as population increased, many other cities would begin to be inhabited.

CLEINIAS: Doubtless.

ATHENIAN: Those cities made war against Troy—by sea as well as land—for at that time men were ceasing to be afraid of the sea.

CLEINIAS: Clearly.

ATHENIAN: The Achaeans remained ten years, and overthrew Troy.

CLEINIAS: True.

ATHENIAN: And during the ten years in which the Achaeans were besieging Ilium, the homes of the besiegers were falling into an evil plight. Their youth revolted; and when the soldiers returned to their own cities and families, they did not receive them properly, and as they ought to have done, and numerous deaths, murders, exiles, were the consequence. The exiles came again, under a new name, no longer Achaeans, but Dorians,—a name which they derived from Dorieus; for it was he who gathered them together. The rest of the story is told by you Lacedaemonians as part of the history of Sparta.

MEGILLUS: To be sure.

ATHENIAN: Thus, after digressing from the original subject of laws into music and drinking-bouts, the argument has, providentially, come back to the same point, and presents to us another handle. For we have reached the settlement of Lacedaemon; which, as you truly say, is in laws and in institutions the sister of Crete. And we are all the better for the digression, because we have gone through various governments and settlements, and have been present at the foundation of a first, second, and third state, succeeding one another in infinite time. And now there appears on the horizon a fourth state or nation which was once in process of settlement and has continued settled to this day. If, out of all this, we are able to discern what is well or ill settled, and what laws are the salvation and what are the destruction of cities, and what changes would make a state happy, O Megillus and Cleinias, we may now begin again, unless we have some fault to find with the previous discussion.

MEGILLUS: If some God, Stranger, would promise us that our new enquiry about legislation would be as good and full as the present, I would go a great way to hear such another, and would think that a day as long as this—and we are now approaching the longest day of the year—was too short for the discussion.

ATHENIAN: Then I suppose that we must consider this subject?

MEGILLUS: Certainly.

ATHENIAN: Let us place ourselves in thought at the moment when Lacedaemon and Argos and Messene and the rest of the Peloponnesus were all in complete subjection, Megillus, to your ancestors; for afterwards, as the legend informs us, they divided their army into three portions, and settled three cities, Argos, Messene, Lacedaemon.

MEGILLUS: True.

ATHENIAN: Temenus was the king of Argos, Cresphontes of Messene, Procles and Eurysthenes of Lacedaemon.

MEGILLUS: Certainly.

ATHENIAN: To these kings all the men of that day made oath that they would assist them, if any one subverted their kingdom.

MEGILLUS: True.

ATHENIAN: But can a kingship be destroyed, or was any other form of government ever destroyed, by any but the rulers themselves? No indeed, by Zeus. Have we already forgotten what was said a little while ago?

MEGILLUS: No.

ATHENIAN: And may we not now further confirm what was then mentioned? For we have come upon facts which have brought us back again to the same principle; so that, in resuming the discussion, we shall not be enquiring about an empty theory, but about events which actually happened. The case was as follows:—Three royal heroes made oath to three cities which were under a kingly government, and the cities to the kings, that both rulers and subjects should govern and be governed according to the laws which were common to all of them: the rulers promised that as time and the race went forward they would not make their rule more arbitrary; and the subjects said that, if the rulers observed these conditions, they would never subvert or permit others to subvert those kingdoms; the kings were to assist kings and peoples when injured, and the peoples were to assist peoples and kings in like manner. Is not this the fact?

MEGILLUS: Yes.

ATHENIAN: And the three states to whom these laws were given, whether their kings or any others were the authors of them, had therefore the greatest security for the maintenance of their constitutions?

MEGILLUS: What security?

ATHENIAN: That the other two states were always to come to the rescue against a rebellious third.

MEGILLUS: True.

ATHENIAN: Many persons say that legislators ought to impose such laws as the mass of the people will be ready to receive; but this is just as if one were to command gymnastic masters or physicians to treat or cure their pupils or patients in an agreeable manner.

MEGILLUS: Exactly.

ATHENIAN: Whereas the physician may often be too happy if he can restore health, and make the body whole, without any very great infliction of pain.

MEGILLUS: Certainly.

ATHENIAN: There was also another advantage possessed by the men of that day, which greatly lightened the task of passing laws.

MEGILLUS: What advantage?

ATHENIAN: The legislators of that day, when they equalized property, escaped the great accusation which generally arises in legislation, if a person attempts to disturb the possession of land, or to abolish debts, because he sees that without this reform there can never be any real equality. Now, in general, when the legislator attempts to make a new settlement of such matters, every one meets him with the cry, that 'he is not to disturb vested interests,'—declaring with imprecations that he is introducing agrarian laws and cancelling of debts, until a man is at his wits' end; whereas no one could quarrel with the Dorians for distributing the land,—there was nothing to hinder them; and as for debts, they had none which were considerable or of old standing.

MEGILLUS: Very true.

ATHENIAN: But then, my good friends, why did the settlement and legislation of their country turn out so badly?

MEGILLUS: How do you mean; and why do you blame them?

ATHENIAN: There were three kingdoms, and of these, two quickly corrupted their original constitution and laws, and the only one which remained was the Spartan.

MEGILLUS: The question which you ask is not easily answered.

ATHENIAN: And yet must be answered when we are enquiring about laws, this being our old man's sober game of play, whereby we beguile the way, as I was saying when we first set out on our journey.

MEGILLUS: Certainly; and we must find out why this was.

ATHENIAN: What laws are more worthy of our attention than those which have regulated such cities? or what settlements of states are greater or more famous?

MEGILLUS: I know of none.

ATHENIAN: Can we doubt that your ancestors intended these institutions not only for the protection of Peloponnesus, but of all the Hellenes, in case they were attacked by the barbarian? For the inhabitants of the region about Ilium, when they provoked by their insolence the Trojan war, relied upon the power of the Assyrians and the Empire of Ninus, which still existed and had a great prestige; the people of those days fearing the united Assyrian Empire just as we now fear the Great King. And the second capture of Troy was a serious offence against them, because Troy was a portion of the Assyrian Empire. To meet the danger the single army was distributed between three cities by the royal brothers, sons of Heracles,—a fair device, as it seemed, and a far better arrangement than the expedition against Troy. For, firstly, the people of that day had, as they thought, in the Heraclidae better leaders than the Pelopidae; in the next place, they considered that their army was superior in valour to that which went against Troy; for, although the latter conquered the Trojans, they were themselves conquered by the Heraclidae—Achaeans by Dorians. May we not suppose that this was the intention with which the men of those days framed the constitutions of their states?

MEGILLUS: Quite true.

ATHENIAN: And would not men who had shared with one another many dangers, and were governed by a single race of royal brothers, and had taken the advice of oracles, and in particular of the Delphian Apollo, be likely to think that such states would be firmly and lastingly established?

MEGILLUS: Of course they would.

ATHENIAN: Yet these institutions, of which such great expectations were entertained, seem to have all rapidly vanished away; with the exception, as I was saying, of that small part of them which existed in your land. And this third part has never to this day ceased warring against the two others; whereas, if the original idea had been carried out, and they had agreed to be one, their power would have been invincible in war.

MEGILLUS: No doubt.

ATHENIAN: But what was the ruin of this glorious confederacy? Here is a subject well worthy of consideration.

MEGILLUS: Certainly, no one will ever find more striking instances of laws or governments being the salvation or destruction of great and noble interests, than are here presented to his view.

ATHENIAN: Then now we seem to have happily arrived at a real and important question.

MEGILLUS: Very true.

ATHENIAN: Did you never remark, sage friend, that all men, and we ourselves at this moment, often fancy that they see some beautiful thing which might have effected wonders if any one had only known how to make a right use of it in some way; and yet this mode of looking at things may turn out after all to be a mistake, and not according to nature, either in our own case or in any other?

MEGILLUS: To what are you referring, and what do you mean?

ATHENIAN: I was thinking of my own admiration of the aforesaid Heracleid expedition, which was so noble, and might have had such wonderful results for the Hellenes, if only rightly used; and I was just laughing at myself.

MEGILLUS: But were you not right and wise in speaking as you did, and we in assenting to you?

ATHENIAN: Perhaps; and yet I cannot help observing that any one who sees anything great or powerful, immediately has the feeling that—'If the owner only knew how to use his great and noble possession, how happy would he be, and what great results would he achieve!'

MEGILLUS: And would he not be justified?

ATHENIAN: Reflect; in what point of view does this sort of praise appear just: First, in reference to the question in hand:—If the then commanders had known how to arrange their army properly, how would they have attained success? Would not this have been the way? They would have bound them all firmly together and preserved them for ever, giving them freedom and dominion at pleasure, combined with the power of doing in the whole world, Hellenic and barbarian, whatever they and their descendants desired. What other aim would they have had?

MEGILLUS: Very good.

ATHENIAN: Suppose any one were in the same way to express his admiration at the sight of great wealth or family honour, or the like, he would praise them under the idea that through them he would attain either all or the greater and chief part of what he desires.

MEGILLUS: He would.

ATHENIAN: Well, now, and does not the argument show that there is one common desire of all mankind?

MEGILLUS: What is it?

ATHENIAN: The desire which a man has, that all things, if possible,—at any rate, things human,—may come to pass in accordance with his soul's desire.

MEGILLUS: Certainly.

ATHENIAN: And having this desire always, and at every time of life, in youth, in manhood, in age, he cannot help always praying for the fulfilment of it.

MEGILLUS: No doubt.

ATHENIAN: And we join in the prayers of our friends, and ask for them what they ask for themselves.

MEGILLUS: We do.

ATHENIAN: Dear is the son to the father—the younger to the elder.

MEGILLUS: Of course.

ATHENIAN: And yet the son often prays to obtain things which the father prays that he may not obtain.

MEGILLUS: When the son is young and foolish, you mean?

ATHENIAN: Yes; or when the father, in the dotage of age or the heat of youth, having no sense of right and justice, prays with fervour, under the influence of feelings akin to those of Theseus when he cursed the unfortunate Hippolytus, do you imagine that the son, having a sense of right and justice, will join in his father's prayers?

MEGILLUS: I understand you to mean that a man should not desire or be in a hurry to have all things according to his wish, for his wish may be at variance with his reason. But every state and every individual ought to pray and strive for wisdom.

ATHENIAN: Yes; and I remember, and you will remember, what I said at first, that a statesman and legislator ought to ordain laws with a view to wisdom; while you were arguing that the good lawgiver ought to order all with a view to war. And to this I replied that there were four virtues, but that upon your view one of them only was the aim of legislation; whereas you ought to regard all virtue, and especially that which comes first, and is the leader of all the rest—I mean wisdom and mind and opinion, having affection and desire in their train. And now the argument returns to the same point, and I say once more, in jest if you like, or in earnest if you like, that the prayer of a fool is full of danger, being likely to end in the opposite of what he desires. And if you would rather receive my words in earnest, I am willing that you should; and you will find, I suspect, as I have said already, that not cowardice was the cause of the ruin of the Dorian kings and of their whole design, nor ignorance of military matters, either on the part of the rulers or of their subjects; but their misfortunes were due to their general degeneracy, and especially to their ignorance of the most important human affairs. That was then, and is still, and always will be the case, as I will endeavour, if you will allow me, to make out and demonstrate as well as I am able to you who are my friends, in the course of the argument.

CLEINIAS: Pray go on, Stranger;—compliments are troublesome, but we will show, not in word but in deed, how greatly we prize your words, for we will give them our best attention; and that is the way in which a freeman best shows his approval or disapproval.

MEGILLUS: Excellent, Cleinias; let us do as you say.

CLEINIAS: By all means, if Heaven wills. Go on.

ATHENIAN: Well, then, proceeding in the same train of thought, I say that the greatest ignorance was the ruin of the Dorian power, and that now, as then, ignorance is ruin. And if this be true, the legislator must endeavour to implant wisdom in states, and banish ignorance to the utmost of his power.

CLEINIAS: That is evident.

ATHENIAN: Then now consider what is really the greatest ignorance. I should like to know whether you and Megillus would agree with me in what I am about to say; for my opinion is—

CLEINIAS: What?

ATHENIAN: That the greatest ignorance is when a man hates that which he nevertheless thinks to be good and noble, and loves and embraces that which he knows to be unrighteous and evil. This disagreement between the sense of pleasure and the judgment of reason in the soul is, in my opinion, the worst ignorance; and also the greatest, because affecting the great mass of the human soul; for the principle which feels pleasure and pain in the individual is like the mass or populace in a state. And when the soul is opposed to knowledge, or opinion, or reason, which are her natural lords, that I call folly, just as in the state, when the multitude refuses to obey their rulers and the laws; or, again, in the individual, when fair reasonings have their habitation in the soul and yet do no good, but rather the reverse of good. All these cases I term the worst ignorance, whether in individuals or in states. You will understand, Stranger, that I am speaking of something which is very different from the ignorance of handicraftsmen.

CLEINIAS: Yes, my friend, we understand and agree.

ATHENIAN: Let us, then, in the first place declare and affirm that the citizen who does not know these things ought never to have any kind of authority entrusted to him: he must be stigmatized as ignorant, even though he be versed in calculation and skilled in all sorts of accomplishments, and feats of mental dexterity; and the opposite are to be called wise, even although, in the words of the proverb, they know neither how to read nor how to swim; and to them, as to men of sense, authority is to be committed. For, O my friends, how can there be the least shadow of wisdom when there is no harmony? There is none; but the noblest and greatest of harmonies may be truly said to be the greatest wisdom; and of this he is a partaker who lives according to reason; whereas he who is devoid of reason is the destroyer of his house and the very opposite of a saviour of the state: he is utterly ignorant of political wisdom. Let this, then, as I was saying, be laid down by us.

CLEINIAS: Let it be so laid down.

ATHENIAN: I suppose that there must be rulers and subjects in states?

CLEINIAS: Certainly.

ATHENIAN: And what are the principles on which men rule and obey in cities, whether great or small; and similarly in families? What are they, and how many in number? Is there not one claim of authority which is always just,—that of fathers and mothers and in general of progenitors to rule over their offspring?

CLEINIAS: There is.

ATHENIAN: Next follows the principle that the noble should rule over the ignoble; and, thirdly, that the elder should rule and the younger obey?

CLEINIAS: To be sure.

ATHENIAN: And, fourthly, that slaves should be ruled, and their masters rule?

CLEINIAS: Of course.

ATHENIAN: Fifthly, if I am not mistaken, comes the principle that the stronger shall rule, and the weaker be ruled?

CLEINIAS: That is a rule not to be disobeyed.

ATHENIAN: Yes, and a rule which prevails very widely among all creatures, and is according to nature, as the Theban poet Pindar once said; and the sixth principle, and the greatest of all, is, that the wise should lead and command, and the ignorant follow and obey; and yet, O thou most wise Pindar, as I should reply him, this surely is not contrary to nature, but according to nature, being the rule of law over willing subjects, and not a rule of compulsion.

CLEINIAS: Most true.

ATHENIAN: There is a seventh kind of rule which is awarded by lot, and is dear to the Gods and a token of good fortune: he on whom the lot falls is a ruler, and he who fails in obtaining the lot goes away and is the subject; and this we affirm to be quite just.

CLEINIAS: Certainly.

ATHENIAN: 'Then now,' as we say playfully to any of those who lightly undertake the making of laws, 'you see, legislator, the principles of government, how many they are, and that they are naturally opposed to each other. There we have discovered a fountain-head of seditions, to which you must attend. And, first, we will ask you to consider with us, how and in what respect the kings of Argos and Messene violated these our maxims, and ruined themselves and the great and famous Hellenic power of the olden time. Was it because they did not know how wisely Hesiod spoke when he said that the half is often more than the whole? His meaning was, that when to take the whole would be dangerous, and to take the half would be the safe and moderate course, then the moderate or better was more than the immoderate or worse.'

CLEINIAS: Very true.

ATHENIAN: And may we suppose this immoderate spirit to be more fatal when found among kings than when among peoples?

CLEINIAS: The probability is that ignorance will be a disorder especially prevalent among kings, because they lead a proud and luxurious life.

ATHENIAN: Is it not palpable that the chief aim of the kings of that time was to get the better of the established laws, and that they were not in harmony with the principles which they had agreed to observe by word and oath? This want of harmony may have had the appearance of wisdom, but was really, as we assert, the greatest ignorance, and utterly overthrew the whole empire by dissonance and harsh discord.

CLEINIAS: Very likely.

ATHENIAN: Good; and what measures ought the legislator to have then taken in order to avert this calamity? Truly there is no great wisdom in knowing, and no great difficulty in telling, after the evil has happened; but to have foreseen the remedy at the time would have taken a much wiser head than ours.

MEGILLUS: What do you mean?

ATHENIAN: Any one who looks at what has occurred with you Lacedaemonians, Megillus, may easily know and may easily say what ought to have been done at that time.

MEGILLUS: Speak a little more clearly.

ATHENIAN: Nothing can be clearer than the observation which I am about to make.

MEGILLUS: What is it?

ATHENIAN: That if any one gives too great a power to anything, too large a sail to a vessel, too much food to the body, too much authority to the mind, and does not observe the mean, everything is overthrown, and, in the wantonness of excess, runs in the one case to disorders, and in the other to injustice, which is the child of excess. I mean to say, my dear friends, that there is no soul of man, young and irresponsible, who will be able to sustain the temptation of arbitrary power—no one who will not, under such circumstances, become filled with folly, that worst of diseases, and be hated by his nearest and dearest friends: when this happens his kingdom is undermined, and all his power vanishes from him. And great legislators who know the mean should take heed of the danger. As far as we can guess at this distance of time, what happened was as follows:—

MEGILLUS: What?

ATHENIAN: A God, who watched over Sparta, seeing into the future, gave you two families of kings instead of one; and thus brought you more within the limits of moderation. In the next place, some human wisdom mingled with divine power, observing that the constitution of your government was still feverish and excited, tempered your inborn strength and pride of birth with the moderation which comes of age, making the power of your twenty-eight elders equal with that of the kings in the most important matters. But your third saviour, perceiving that your government was still swelling and foaming, and desirous to impose a curb upon it, instituted the Ephors, whose power he made to resemble that of magistrates elected by lot; and by this arrangement the kingly office, being compounded of the right elements and duly moderated, was preserved, and was the means of preserving all the rest. Since, if there had been only the original legislators, Temenus, Cresphontes, and their contemporaries, as far as they were concerned not even the portion of Aristodemus would have been preserved; for they had no proper experience in legislation, or they would surely not have imagined that oaths would moderate a youthful spirit invested with a power which might be converted into a tyranny. Now that God has instructed us what sort of government would have been or will be lasting, there is no wisdom, as I have already said, in judging after the event; there is no difficulty in learning from an example which has already occurred. But if any one could have foreseen all this at the time, and had been able to moderate the government of the three kingdoms and unite them into one, he might have saved all the excellent institutions which were then conceived; and no Persian or any other armament would have dared to attack us, or would have regarded Hellas as a power to be despised.

CLEINIAS: True.

ATHENIAN: There was small credit to us, Cleinias, in defeating them; and the discredit was, not that the conquerors did not win glorious victories both by land and sea, but what, in my opinion, brought discredit was, first of all, the circumstance that of the three cities one only fought on behalf of Hellas, and the two others were so utterly good for nothing that the one was waging a mighty war against Lacedaemon, and was thus preventing her from rendering assistance, while the city of Argos, which had the precedence at the time of the distribution, when asked to aid in repelling the barbarian, would not answer to the call, or give aid. Many things might be told about Hellas in connexion with that war which are far from honourable; nor, indeed, can we rightly say that Hellas repelled the invader; for the truth is, that unless the Athenians and Lacedaemonians, acting in concert, had warded off the impending yoke, all the tribes of Hellas would have been fused in a chaos of Hellenes mingling with one another, of barbarians mingling with Hellenes, and Hellenes with barbarians; just as nations who are now subject to the Persian power, owing to unnatural separations and combinations of them, are dispersed and scattered, and live miserably. These, Cleinias and Megillus, are the reproaches which we have to make against statesmen and legislators, as they are called, past and present, if we would analyse the causes of their failure, and find out what else might have been done. We said, for instance, just now, that there ought to be no great and unmixed powers; and this was under the idea that a state ought to be free and wise and harmonious, and that a legislator ought to legislate with a view to this end. Nor is there any reason to be surprised at our continually proposing aims for the legislator which appear not to be always the same; but we should consider when we say that temperance is to be the aim, or wisdom is to be the aim, or friendship is to be the aim, that all these aims are really the same; and if so, a variety in the modes of expression ought not to disturb us.

CLEINIAS: Let us resume the argument in that spirit. And now, speaking of friendship and wisdom and freedom, I wish that you would tell me at what, in your opinion, the legislator should aim.

ATHENIAN: Hear me, then: there are two mother forms of states from which the rest may be truly said to be derived; and one of them may be called monarchy and the other democracy: the Persians have the highest form of the one, and we of the other; almost all the rest, as I was saying, are variations of these. Now, if you are to have liberty and the combination of friendship with wisdom, you must have both these forms of government in a measure; the argument emphatically declares that no city can be well governed which is not made up of both.

CLEINIAS: Impossible.

ATHENIAN: Neither the one, if it be exclusively and excessively attached to monarchy, nor the other, if it be similarly attached to freedom, observes moderation; but your states, the Laconian and Cretan, have more of it; and the same was the case with the Athenians and Persians of old time, but now they have less. Shall I tell you why?

CLEINIAS: By all means, if it will tend to elucidate our subject.

ATHENIAN: Hear, then:—There was a time when the Persians had more of the state which is a mean between slavery and freedom. In the reign of Cyrus they were freemen and also lords of many others: the rulers gave a share of freedom to the subjects, and being treated as equals, the soldiers were on better terms with their generals, and showed themselves more ready in the hour of danger. And if there was any wise man among them, who was able to give good counsel, he imparted his wisdom to the public; for the king was not jealous, but allowed him full liberty of speech, and gave honour to those who could advise him in any matter. And the nation waxed in all respects, because there was freedom and friendship and communion of mind among them.

CLEINIAS: That certainly appears to have been the case.

ATHENIAN: How, then, was this advantage lost under Cambyses, and again recovered under Darius? Shall I try to divine?

CLEINIAS: The enquiry, no doubt, has a bearing upon our subject.

ATHENIAN: I imagine that Cyrus, though a great and patriotic general, had never given his mind to education, and never attended to the order of his household.

CLEINIAS: What makes you say so?

ATHENIAN: I think that from his youth upwards he was a soldier, and entrusted the education of his children to the women; and they brought them up from their childhood as the favourites of fortune, who were blessed already, and needed no more blessings. They thought that they were happy enough, and that no one should be allowed to oppose them in any way, and they compelled every one to praise all that they said or did. This was how they brought them up.

CLEINIAS: A splendid education truly!

ATHENIAN: Such an one as women were likely to give them, and especially princesses who had recently grown rich, and in the absence of the men, too, who were occupied in wars and dangers, and had no time to look after them.

CLEINIAS: What would you expect?

ATHENIAN: Their father had possessions of cattle and sheep, and many herds of men and other animals, but he did not consider that those to whom he was about to make them over were not trained in his own calling, which was Persian; for the Persians are shepherds—sons of a rugged land, which is a stern mother, and well fitted to produce a sturdy race able to live in the open air and go without sleep, and also to fight, if fighting is required (compare Arist. Pol.). He did not observe that his sons were trained differently; through the so-called blessing of being royal they were educated in the Median fashion by women and eunuchs, which led to their becoming such as people do become when they are brought up unreproved. And so, after the death of Cyrus, his sons, in the fulness of luxury and licence, took the kingdom, and first one slew the other because he could not endure a rival; and, afterwards, the slayer himself, mad with wine and brutality, lost his kingdom through the Medes and the Eunuch, as they called him, who despised the folly of Cambyses.

CLEINIAS: So runs the tale, and such probably were the facts.

ATHENIAN: Yes; and the tradition says, that the empire came back to the Persians, through Darius and the seven chiefs.

CLEINIAS: True.

ATHENIAN: Let us note the rest of the story. Observe, that Darius was not the son of a king, and had not received a luxurious education. When he came to the throne, being one of the seven, he divided the country into seven portions, and of this arrangement there are some shadowy traces still remaining; he made laws upon the principle of introducing universal equality in the order of the state, and he embodied in his laws the settlement of the tribute which Cyrus promised,—thus creating a feeling of friendship and community among all the Persians, and attaching the people to him with money and gifts. Hence his armies cheerfully acquired for him countries as large as those which Cyrus had left behind him. Darius was succeeded by his son Xerxes; and he again was brought up in the royal and luxurious fashion. Might we not most justly say: 'O Darius, how came you to bring up Xerxes in the same way in which Cyrus brought up Cambyses, and not to see his fatal mistake?' For Xerxes, being the creation of the same education, met with much the same fortune as Cambyses; and from that time until now there has never been a really great king among the Persians, although they are all called Great. And their degeneracy is not to be attributed to chance, as I maintain; the reason is rather the evil life which is generally led by the sons of very rich and royal persons; for never will boy or man, young or old, excel in virtue, who has been thus educated. And this, I say, is what the legislator has to consider, and what at the present moment has to be considered by us. Justly may you, O Lacedaemonians, be praised, in that you do not give special honour or a special education to wealth rather than to poverty, or to a royal rather than to a private station, where the divine and inspired lawgiver has not originally commanded them to be given. For no man ought to have pre-eminent honour in a state because he surpasses others in wealth, any more than because he is swift of foot or fair or strong, unless he have some virtue in him; nor even if he have virtue, unless he have this particular virtue of temperance.

MEGILLUS: What do you mean, Stranger?

ATHENIAN: I suppose that courage is a part of virtue?

MEGILLUS: To be sure.

ATHENIAN: Then, now hear and judge for yourself:—Would you like to have for a fellow-lodger or neighbour a very courageous man, who had no control over himself?

MEGILLUS: Heaven forbid!

ATHENIAN: Or an artist, who was clever in his profession, but a rogue?

MEGILLUS: Certainly not.

ATHENIAN: And surely justice does not grow apart from temperance?

MEGILLUS: Impossible.

ATHENIAN: Any more than our pattern wise man, whom we exhibited as having his pleasures and pains in accordance with and corresponding to true reason, can be intemperate?

MEGILLUS: No.

ATHENIAN: There is a further consideration relating to the due and undue award of honours in states.

MEGILLUS: What is it?

ATHENIAN: I should like to know whether temperance without the other virtues, existing alone in the soul of man, is rightly to be praised or blamed?

MEGILLUS: I cannot tell.

ATHENIAN: And that is the best answer; for whichever alternative you had chosen, I think that you would have gone wrong.

MEGILLUS: I am fortunate.

ATHENIAN: Very good; a quality, which is a mere appendage of things which can be praised or blamed, does not deserve an expression of opinion, but is best passed over in silence.

MEGILLUS: You are speaking of temperance?

ATHENIAN: Yes; but of the other virtues, that which having this appendage is also most beneficial, will be most deserving of honour, and next that which is beneficial in the next degree; and so each of them will be rightly honoured according to a regular order.

MEGILLUS: True.

ATHENIAN: And ought not the legislator to determine these classes?

MEGILLUS: Certainly he should.

ATHENIAN: Suppose that we leave to him the arrangement of details. But the general division of laws according to their importance into a first and second and third class, we who are lovers of law may make ourselves.

MEGILLUS: Very good.

ATHENIAN: We maintain, then, that a State which would be safe and happy, as far as the nature of man allows, must and ought to distribute honour and dishonour in the right way. And the right way is to place the goods of the soul first and highest in the scale, always assuming temperance to be the condition of them; and to assign the second place to the goods of the body; and the third place to money and property. And if any legislator or state departs from this rule by giving money the place of honour, or in any way preferring that which is really last, may we not say, that he or the state is doing an unholy and unpatriotic thing?

MEGILLUS: Yes; let that be plainly declared.

ATHENIAN: The consideration of the Persian governments led us thus far to enlarge. We remarked that the Persians grew worse and worse. And we affirm the reason of this to have been, that they too much diminished the freedom of the people, and introduced too much of despotism, and so destroyed friendship and community of feeling. And when there is an end of these, no longer do the governors govern on behalf of their subjects or of the people, but on behalf of themselves; and if they think that they can gain ever so small an advantage for themselves, they devastate cities, and send fire and desolation among friendly races. And as they hate ruthlessly and horribly, so are they hated; and when they want the people to fight for them, they find no community of feeling or willingness to risk their lives on their behalf; their untold myriads are useless to them on the field of battle, and they think that their salvation depends on the employment of mercenaries and strangers whom they hire, as if they were in want of more men. And they cannot help being stupid, since they proclaim by their actions that the ordinary distinctions of right and wrong which are made in a state are a trifle, when compared with gold and silver.

MEGILLUS: Quite true.

ATHENIAN: And now enough of the Persians, and their present mal-administration of their government, which is owing to the excess of slavery and despotism among them.

MEGILLUS: Good.

ATHENIAN: Next, we must pass in review the government of Attica in like manner, and from this show that entire freedom and the absence of all superior authority is not by any means so good as government by others when properly limited, which was our ancient Athenian constitution at the time when the Persians made their attack on Hellas, or, speaking more correctly, on the whole continent of Europe. There were four classes, arranged according to a property census, and reverence was our queen and mistress, and made us willing to live in obedience to the laws which then prevailed. Also the vastness of the Persian armament, both by sea and on land, caused a helpless terror, which made us more and more the servants of our rulers and of the laws; and for all these reasons an exceeding harmony prevailed among us. About ten years before the naval engagement at Salamis, Datis came, leading a Persian host by command of Darius, which was expressly directed against the Athenians and Eretrians, having orders to carry them away captive; and these orders he was to execute under pain of death. Now Datis and his myriads soon became complete masters of Eretria, and he sent a fearful report to Athens that no Eretrian had escaped him; for the soldiers of Datis had joined hands and netted the whole of Eretria. And this report, whether well or ill founded, was terrible to all the Hellenes, and above all to the Athenians, and they dispatched embassies in all directions, but no one was willing to come to their relief, with the exception of the Lacedaemonians; and they, either because they were detained by the Messenian war, which was then going on, or for some other reason of which we are not told, came a day too late for the battle of Marathon. After a while, the news arrived of mighty preparations being made, and innumerable threats came from the king. Then, as time went on, a rumour reached us that Darius had died, and that his son, who was young and hot-headed, had come to the throne and was persisting in his design. The Athenians were under the impression that the whole expedition was directed against them, in consequence of the battle of Marathon; and hearing of the bridge over the Hellespont, and the canal of Athos, and the host of ships, considering that there was no salvation for them either by land or by sea, for there was no one to help them, and remembering that in the first expedition, when the Persians destroyed Eretria, no one came to their help, or would risk the danger of an alliance with them, they thought that this would happen again, at least on land; nor, when they looked to the sea, could they descry any hope of salvation; for they were attacked by a thousand vessels and more. One chance of safety remained, slight indeed and desperate, but their only one. They saw that on the former occasion they had gained a seemingly impossible victory, and borne up by this hope, they found that their only refuge was in themselves and in the Gods. All these things created in them the spirit of friendship; there was the fear of the moment, and there was that higher fear, which they had acquired by obedience to their ancient laws, and which I have several times in the preceding discourse called reverence, of which the good man ought to be a willing servant, and of which the coward is independent and fearless. If this fear had not possessed them, they would never have met the enemy, or defended their temples and sepulchres and their country, and everything that was near and dear to them, as they did; but little by little they would have been all scattered and dispersed.

MEGILLUS: Your words, Athenian, are quite true, and worthy of yourself and of your country.

ATHENIAN: They are true, Megillus; and to you, who have inherited the virtues of your ancestors, I may properly speak of the actions of that day. And I would wish you and Cleinias to consider whether my words have not also a bearing on legislation; for I am not discoursing only for the pleasure of talking, but for the argument's sake. Please to remark that the experience both of ourselves and the Persians was, in a certain sense, the same; for as they led their people into utter servitude, so we too led ours into all freedom. And now, how shall we proceed? for I would like you to observe that our previous arguments have good deal to say for themselves.

MEGILLUS: True; but I wish that you would give us a fuller explanation.

ATHENIAN: I will. Under the ancient laws, my friends, the people was not as now the master, but rather the willing servant of the laws.

MEGILLUS: What laws do you mean?

ATHENIAN: In the first place, let us speak of the laws about music,—that is to say, such music as then existed—in order that we may trace the growth of the excess of freedom from the beginning. Now music was early divided among us into certain kinds and manners. One sort consisted of prayers to the Gods, which were called hymns; and there was another and opposite sort called lamentations, and another termed paeans, and another, celebrating the birth of Dionysus, called, I believe, 'dithyrambs.' And they used the actual word 'laws,' or nomoi, for another kind of song; and to this they added the term 'citharoedic.' All these and others were duly distinguished, nor were the performers allowed to confuse one style of music with another. And the authority which determined and gave judgment, and punished the disobedient, was not expressed in a hiss, nor in the most unmusical shouts of the multitude, as in our days, nor in applause and clapping of hands. But the directors of public instruction insisted that the spectators should listen in silence to the end; and boys and their tutors, and the multitude in general, were kept quiet by a hint from a stick. Such was the good order which the multitude were willing to observe; they would never have dared to give judgment by noisy cries. And then, as time went on, the poets themselves introduced the reign of vulgar and lawless innovation. They were men of genius, but they had no perception of what is just and lawful in music; raging like Bacchanals and possessed with inordinate delights—mingling lamentations with hymns, and paeans with dithyrambs; imitating the sounds of the flute on the lyre, and making one general confusion; ignorantly affirming that music has no truth, and, whether good or bad, can only be judged of rightly by the pleasure of the hearer (compare Republic). And by composing such licentious works, and adding to them words as licentious, they have inspired the multitude with lawlessness and boldness, and made them fancy that they can judge for themselves about melody and song. And in this way the theatres from being mute have become vocal, as though they had understanding of good and bad in music and poetry; and instead of an aristocracy, an evil sort of theatrocracy has grown up (compare Arist. Pol.). For if the democracy which judged had only consisted of educated persons, no fatal harm would have been done; but in music there first arose the universal conceit of omniscience and general lawlessness;—freedom came following afterwards, and men, fancying that they knew what they did not know, had no longer any fear, and the absence of fear begets shamelessness. For what is this shamelessness, which is so evil a thing, but the insolent refusal to regard the opinion of the better by reason of an over-daring sort of liberty?

MEGILLUS: Very true.

ATHENIAN: Consequent upon this freedom comes the other freedom, of disobedience to rulers (compare Republic); and then the attempt to escape the control and exhortation of father, mother, elders, and when near the end, the control of the laws also; and at the very end there is the contempt of oaths and pledges, and no regard at all for the Gods,—herein they exhibit and imitate the old so-called Titanic nature, and come to the same point as the Titans when they rebelled against God, leading a life of endless evils. But why have I said all this? I ask, because the argument ought to be pulled up from time to time, and not be allowed to run away, but held with bit and bridle, and then we shall not, as the proverb says, fall off our ass. Let us then once more ask the question, To what end has all this been said?

MEGILLUS: Very good.

ATHENIAN: This, then, has been said for the sake—

MEGILLUS: Of what?

ATHENIAN: We were maintaining that the lawgiver ought to have three things in view: first, that the city for which he legislates should be free; and secondly, be at unity with herself; and thirdly, should have understanding;—these were our principles, were they not?

MEGILLUS: Certainly.

ATHENIAN: With a view to this we selected two kinds of government, the one the most despotic, and the other the most free; and now we are considering which of them is the right form: we took a mean in both cases, of despotism in the one, and of liberty in the other, and we saw that in a mean they attained their perfection; but that when they were carried to the extreme of either, slavery or licence, neither party were the gainers.

MEGILLUS: Very true.

ATHENIAN: And that was our reason for considering the settlement of the Dorian army, and of the city built by Dardanus at the foot of the mountains, and the removal of cities to the seashore, and of our mention of the first men, who were the survivors of the deluge. And all that was previously said about music and drinking, and what preceded, was said with the view of seeing how a state might be best administered, and how an individual might best order his own life. And now, Megillus and Cleinias, how can we put to the proof the value of our words?

CLEINIAS: Stranger, I think that I see how a proof of their value may be obtained. This discussion of ours appears to me to have been singularly fortunate, and just what I at this moment want; most auspiciously have you and my friend Megillus come in my way. For I will tell you what has happened to me; and I regard the coincidence as a sort of omen. The greater part of Crete is going to send out a colony, and they have entrusted the management of the affair to the Cnosians; and the Cnosian government to me and nine others. And they desire us to give them any laws which we please, whether taken from the Cretan model or from any other; and they do not mind about their being foreign if they are better. Grant me then this favour, which will also be a gain to yourselves:—Let us make a selection from what has been said, and then let us imagine a State of which we will suppose ourselves to be the original founders. Thus we shall proceed with our enquiry, and, at the same time, I may have the use of the framework which you are constructing, for the city which is in contemplation.

ATHENIAN: Good news, Cleinias; if Megillus has no objection, you may be sure that I will do all in my power to please you.

CLEINIAS: Thank you.

MEGILLUS: And so will I.

CLEINIAS: Excellent; and now let us begin to frame the State.

BOOK IV.

ATHENIAN: And now, what will this city be? I do not mean to ask what is or will hereafter be the name of the place; that may be determined by the accident of locality or of the original settlement—a river or fountain, or some local deity may give the sanction of a name to the newly-founded city; but I do want to know what the situation is, whether maritime or inland.

CLEINIAS: I should imagine, Stranger, that the city of which we are speaking is about eighty stadia distant from the sea.

ATHENIAN: And are there harbours on the seaboard?

CLEINIAS: Excellent harbours, Stranger; there could not be better.

ATHENIAN: Alas! what a prospect! And is the surrounding country productive, or in need of importations?

CLEINIAS: Hardly in need of anything.

ATHENIAN: And is there any neighbouring State?

CLEINIAS: None whatever, and that is the reason for selecting the place; in days of old, there was a migration of the inhabitants, and the region has been deserted from time immemorial.

ATHENIAN: And has the place a fair proportion of hill, and plain, and wood?

CLEINIAS: Like the rest of Crete in that.

ATHENIAN: You mean to say that there is more rock than plain?

CLEINIAS: Exactly.

ATHENIAN: Then there is some hope that your citizens may be virtuous: had you been on the sea, and well provided with harbours, and an importing rather than a producing country, some mighty saviour would have been needed, and lawgivers more than mortal, if you were ever to have a chance of preserving your state from degeneracy and discordance of manners (compare Ar. Pol.). But there is comfort in the eighty stadia; although the sea is too near, especially if, as you say, the harbours are so good. Still we may be content. The sea is pleasant enough as a daily companion, but has indeed also a bitter and brackish quality; filling the streets with merchants and shopkeepers, and begetting in the souls of men uncertain and unfaithful ways—making the state unfriendly and unfaithful both to her own citizens, and also to other nations. There is a consolation, therefore, in the country producing all things at home; and yet, owing to the ruggedness of the soil, not providing anything in great abundance. Had there been abundance, there might have been a great export trade, and a great return of gold and silver; which, as we may safely affirm, has the most fatal results on a State whose aim is the attainment of just and noble sentiments: this was said by us, if you remember, in the previous discussion.

CLEINIAS: I remember, and am of opinion that we both were and are in the right.

ATHENIAN: Well, but let me ask, how is the country supplied with timber for ship-building?

CLEINIAS: There is no fir of any consequence, nor pine, and not much cypress; and you will find very little stone-pine or plane-wood, which shipwrights always require for the interior of ships.

ATHENIAN: These are also natural advantages.

CLEINIAS: Why so?

ATHENIAN: Because no city ought to be easily able to imitate its enemies in what is mischievous.

CLEINIAS: How does that bear upon any of the matters of which we have been speaking?

ATHENIAN: Remember, my good friend, what I said at first about the Cretan laws, that they looked to one thing only, and this, as you both agreed, was war; and I replied that such laws, in so far as they tended to promote virtue, were good; but in that they regarded a part only, and not the whole of virtue, I disapproved of them. And now I hope that you in your turn will follow and watch me if I legislate with a view to anything but virtue, or with a view to a part of virtue only. For I consider that the true lawgiver, like an archer, aims only at that on which some eternal beauty is always attending, and dismisses everything else, whether wealth or any other benefit, when separated from virtue. I was saying that the imitation of enemies was a bad thing; and I was thinking of a case in which a maritime people are harassed by enemies, as the Athenians were by Minos (I do not speak from any desire to recall past grievances); but he, as we know, was a great naval potentate, who compelled the inhabitants of Attica to pay him a cruel tribute; and in those days they had no ships of war as they now have, nor was the country filled with ship-timber, and therefore they could not readily build them. Hence they could not learn how to imitate their enemy at sea, and in this way, becoming sailors themselves, directly repel their enemies. Better for them to have lost many times over the seven youths, than that heavy-armed and stationary troops should have been turned into sailors, and accustomed to be often leaping on shore, and again to come running back to their ships; or should have fancied that there was no disgrace in not awaiting the attack of an enemy and dying boldly; and that there were good reasons, and plenty of them, for a man throwing away his arms, and betaking himself to flight,—which is not dishonourable, as people say, at certain times. This is the language of naval warfare, and is anything but worthy of extraordinary praise. For we should not teach bad habits, least of all to the best part of the citizens. You may learn the evil of such a practice from Homer, by whom Odysseus is introduced, rebuking Agamemnon, because he desires to draw down the ships to the sea at a time when the Achaeans are hard pressed by the Trojans,—he gets angry with him, and says:

'Who, at a time when the battle is in full cry, biddest to drag the well-benched ships into the sea, that the prayers of the Trojans may be accomplished yet more, and high ruin fall upon us. For the Achaeans will not maintain the battle, when the ships are drawn into the sea, but they will look behind and will cease from strife; in that the counsel which you give will prove injurious.'

You see that he quite knew triremes on the sea, in the neighbourhood of fighting men, to be an evil;—lions might be trained in that way to fly from a herd of deer. Moreover, naval powers which owe their safety to ships, do not give honour to that sort of warlike excellence which is most deserving of it. For he who owes his safety to the pilot and the captain, and the oarsman, and all sorts of rather inferior persons, cannot rightly give honour to whom honour is due. But how can a state be in a right condition which cannot justly award honour?

CLEINIAS: It is hardly possible, I admit; and yet, Stranger, we Cretans are in the habit of saying that the battle of Salamis was the salvation of Hellas.

ATHENIAN: Why, yes; and that is an opinion which is widely spread both among Hellenes and barbarians. But Megillus and I say rather, that the battle of Marathon was the beginning, and the battle of Plataea the completion, of the great deliverance, and that these battles by land made the Hellenes better; whereas the sea-fights of Salamis and Artemisium—for I may as well put them both together—made them no better, if I may say so without offence about the battles which helped to save us. And in estimating the goodness of a state, we regard both the situation of the country and the order of the laws, considering that the mere preservation and continuance of life is not the most honourable thing for men, as the vulgar think, but the continuance of the best life, while we live; and that again, if I am not mistaken, is a remark which has been made already.

CLEINIAS: Yes.

ATHENIAN: Then we have only to ask, whether we are taking the course which we acknowledge to be the best for the settlement and legislation of states.

CLEINIAS: The best by far.

ATHENIAN: And now let me proceed to another question: Who are to be the colonists? May any one come out of all Crete; and is the idea that the population in the several states is too numerous for the means of subsistence? For I suppose that you are not going to send out a general invitation to any Hellene who likes to come. And yet I observe that to your country settlers have come from Argos and Aegina and other parts of Hellas. Tell me, then, whence do you draw your recruits in the present enterprise?

CLEINIAS: They will come from all Crete; and of other Hellenes, Peloponnesians will be most acceptable. For, as you truly observe, there are Cretans of Argive descent; and the race of Cretans which has the highest character at the present day is the Gortynian, and this has come from Gortys in the Peloponnesus.

ATHENIAN: Cities find colonization in some respects easier if the colonists are one race, which like a swarm of bees is sent out from a single country, either when friends leave friends, owing to some pressure of population or other similar necessity, or when a portion of a state is driven by factions to emigrate. And there have been whole cities which have taken flight when utterly conquered by a superior power in war. This, however, which is in one way an advantage to the colonist or legislator, in another point of view creates a difficulty. There is an element of friendship in the community of race, and language, and laws, and in common temples and rites of worship; but colonies which are of this homogeneous sort are apt to kick against any laws or any form of constitution differing from that which they had at home; and although the badness of their own laws may have been the cause of the factions which prevailed among them, yet from the force of habit they would fain preserve the very customs which were their ruin, and the leader of the colony, who is their legislator, finds them troublesome and rebellious. On the other hand, the conflux of several populations might be more disposed to listen to new laws; but then, to make them combine and pull together, as they say of horses, is a most difficult task, and the work of years. And yet there is nothing which tends more to the improvement of mankind than legislation and colonization.

CLEINIAS: No doubt; but I should like to know why you say so.

ATHENIAN: My good friend, I am afraid that the course of my speculations is leading me to say something depreciatory of legislators; but if the word be to the purpose, there can be no harm. And yet, why am I disquieted, for I believe that the same principle applies equally to all human things?

CLEINIAS: To what are you referring?

ATHENIAN: I was going to say that man never legislates, but accidents of all sorts, which legislate for us in all sorts of ways. The violence of war and the hard necessity of poverty are constantly overturning governments and changing laws. And the power of disease has often caused innovations in the state, when there have been pestilences, or when there has been a succession of bad seasons continuing during many years. Any one who sees all this, naturally rushes to the conclusion of which I was speaking, that no mortal legislates in anything, but that in human affairs chance is almost everything. And this may be said of the arts of the sailor, and the pilot, and the physician, and the general, and may seem to be well said; and yet there is another thing which may be said with equal truth of all of them.

CLEINIAS: What is it?

ATHENIAN: That God governs all things, and that chance and opportunity co-operate with Him in the government of human affairs. There is, however, a third and less extreme view, that art should be there also; for I should say that in a storm there must surely be a great advantage in having the aid of the pilot's art. You would agree?

CLEINIAS: Yes.

ATHENIAN: And does not a like principle apply to legislation as well as to other things: even supposing all the conditions to be favourable which are needed for the happiness of the state, yet the true legislator must from time to time appear on the scene?

CLEINIAS: Most true.

ATHENIAN: In each case the artist would be able to pray rightly for certain conditions, and if these were granted by fortune, he would then only require to exercise his art?

CLEINIAS: Certainly.

ATHENIAN: And all the other artists just now mentioned, if they were bidden to offer up each their special prayer, would do so?

CLEINIAS: Of course.

ATHENIAN: And the legislator would do likewise?

CLEINIAS: I believe that he would.

ATHENIAN: 'Come, legislator,' we will say to him; 'what are the conditions which you require in a state before you can organize it?' How ought he to answer this question? Shall I give his answer?

CLEINIAS: Yes.

ATHENIAN: He will say—'Give me a state which is governed by a tyrant, and let the tyrant be young and have a good memory; let him be quick at learning, and of a courageous and noble nature; let him have that quality which, as I said before, is the inseparable companion of all the other parts of virtue, if there is to be any good in them.'

CLEINIAS: I suppose, Megillus, that this companion virtue of which the Stranger speaks, must be temperance?

ATHENIAN: Yes, Cleinias, temperance in the vulgar sense; not that which in the forced and exaggerated language of some philosophers is called prudence, but that which is the natural gift of children and animals, of whom some live continently and others incontinently, but when isolated, was, as we said, hardly worth reckoning in the catalogue of goods. I think that you must understand my meaning.

CLEINIAS: Certainly.

ATHENIAN: Then our tyrant must have this as well as the other qualities, if the state is to acquire in the best manner and in the shortest time the form of government which is most conducive to happiness; for there neither is nor ever will be a better or speedier way of establishing a polity than by a tyranny.

CLEINIAS: By what possible arguments, Stranger, can any man persuade himself of such a monstrous doctrine?

ATHENIAN: There is surely no difficulty in seeing, Cleinias, what is in accordance with the order of nature?

CLEINIAS: You would assume, as you say, a tyrant who was young, temperate, quick at learning, having a good memory, courageous, of a noble nature?

ATHENIAN: Yes; and you must add fortunate; and his good fortune must be that he is the contemporary of a great legislator, and that some happy chance brings them together. When this has been accomplished, God has done all that he ever does for a state which he desires to be eminently prosperous; He has done second best for a state in which there are two such rulers, and third best for a state in which there are three. The difficulty increases with the increase, and diminishes with the diminution of the number.

CLEINIAS: You mean to say, I suppose, that the best government is produced from a tyranny, and originates in a good lawgiver and an orderly tyrant, and that the change from such a tyranny into a perfect form of government takes place most easily; less easily when from an oligarchy; and, in the third degree, from a democracy: is not that your meaning?

ATHENIAN: Not so; I mean rather to say that the change is best made out of a tyranny; and secondly, out of a monarchy; and thirdly, out of some sort of democracy: fourth, in the capacity for improvement, comes oligarchy, which has the greatest difficulty in admitting of such a change, because the government is in the hands of a number of potentates. I am supposing that the legislator is by nature of the true sort, and that his strength is united with that of the chief men of the state; and when the ruling element is numerically small, and at the same time very strong, as in a tyranny, there the change is likely to be easiest and most rapid.

CLEINIAS: How? I do not understand.

ATHENIAN: And yet I have repeated what I am saying a good many times; but I suppose that you have never seen a city which is under a tyranny?

CLEINIAS: No, and I cannot say that I have any great desire to see one.

ATHENIAN: And yet, where there is a tyranny, you might certainly see that of which I am now speaking.

CLEINIAS: What do you mean?

ATHENIAN: I mean that you might see how, without trouble and in no very long period of time, the tyrant, if he wishes, can change the manners of a state: he has only to go in the direction of virtue or of vice, whichever he prefers, he himself indicating by his example the lines of conduct, praising and rewarding some actions and reproving others, and degrading those who disobey.

CLEINIAS: But how can we imagine that the citizens in general will at once follow the example set to them; and how can he have this power both of persuading and of compelling them?

ATHENIAN: Let no one, my friends, persuade us that there is any quicker and easier way in which states change their laws than when the rulers lead: such changes never have, nor ever will, come to pass in any other way. The real impossibility or difficulty is of another sort, and is rarely surmounted in the course of ages; but when once it is surmounted, ten thousand or rather all blessings follow.

CLEINIAS: Of what are you speaking?

ATHENIAN: The difficulty is to find the divine love of temperate and just institutions existing in any powerful forms of government, whether in a monarchy or oligarchy of wealth or of birth. You might as well hope to reproduce the character of Nestor, who is said to have excelled all men in the power of speech, and yet more in his temperance. This, however, according to the tradition, was in the times of Troy; in our own days there is nothing of the sort; but if such an one either has or ever shall come into being, or is now among us, blessed is he and blessed are they who hear the wise words that flow from his lips. And this may be said of power in general: When the supreme power in man coincides with the greatest wisdom and temperance, then the best laws and the best constitution come into being; but in no other way. And let what I have been saying be regarded as a kind of sacred legend or oracle, and let this be our proof that, in one point of view, there may be a difficulty for a city to have good laws, but that there is another point of view in which nothing can be easier or sooner effected, granting our supposition.

CLEINIAS: How do you mean?

ATHENIAN: Let us try to amuse ourselves, old boys as we are, by moulding in words the laws which are suitable to your state.

CLEINIAS: Let us proceed without delay.

ATHENIAN: Then let us invoke God at the settlement of our state; may He hear and be propitious to us, and come and set in order the State and the laws!

CLEINIAS: May He come!

ATHENIAN: But what form of polity are we going to give the city?

CLEINIAS: Tell us what you mean a little more clearly. Do you mean some form of democracy, or oligarchy, or aristocracy, or monarchy? For we cannot suppose that you would include tyranny.

ATHENIAN: Which of you will first tell me to which of these classes his own government is to be referred?

MEGILLUS: Ought I to answer first, since I am the elder?

CLEINIAS: Perhaps you should.

MEGILLUS: And yet, Stranger, I perceive that I cannot say, without more thought, what I should call the government of Lacedaemon, for it seems to me to be like a tyranny,—the power of our Ephors is marvellously tyrannical; and sometimes it appears to me to be of all cities the most democratical; and who can reasonably deny that it is an aristocracy (compare Ar. Pol.)? We have also a monarchy which is held for life, and is said by all mankind, and not by ourselves only, to be the most ancient of all monarchies; and, therefore, when asked on a sudden, I cannot precisely say which form of government the Spartan is.

CLEINIAS: I am in the same difficulty, Megillus; for I do not feel confident that the polity of Cnosus is any of these.

ATHENIAN: The reason is, my excellent friends, that you really have polities, but the states of which we were just now speaking are merely aggregations of men dwelling in cities who are the subjects and servants of a part of their own state, and each of them is named after the dominant power; they are not polities at all. But if states are to be named after their rulers, the true state ought to be called by the name of the God who rules over wise men.

CLEINIAS: And who is this God?

ATHENIAN: May I still make use of fable to some extent, in the hope that I may be better able to answer your question: shall I?

CLEINIAS: By all means.

ATHENIAN: In the primeval world, and a long while before the cities came into being whose settlements we have described, there is said to have been in the time of Cronos a blessed rule and life, of which the best-ordered of existing states is a copy (compare Statesman).

CLEINIAS: It will be very necessary to hear about that.

ATHENIAN: I quite agree with you; and therefore I have introduced the subject.

CLEINIAS: Most appropriately; and since the tale is to the point, you will do well in giving us the whole story.

ATHENIAN: I will do as you suggest. There is a tradition of the happy life of mankind in days when all things were spontaneous and abundant. And of this the reason is said to have been as follows:—Cronos knew what we ourselves were declaring, that no human nature invested with supreme power is able to order human affairs and not overflow with insolence and wrong. Which reflection led him to appoint not men but demigods, who are of a higher and more divine race, to be the kings and rulers of our cities; he did as we do with flocks of sheep and other tame animals. For we do not appoint oxen to be the lords of oxen, or goats of goats; but we ourselves are a superior race, and rule over them. In like manner God, in His love of mankind, placed over us the demons, who are a superior race, and they with great ease and pleasure to themselves, and no less to us, taking care of us and giving us peace and reverence and order and justice never failing, made the tribes of men happy and united. And this tradition, which is true, declares that cities of which some mortal man and not God is the ruler, have no escape from evils and toils. Still we must do all that we can to imitate the life which is said to have existed in the days of Cronos, and, as far as the principle of immortality dwells in us, to that we must hearken, both in private and public life, and regulate our cities and houses according to law, meaning by the very term 'law,' the distribution of mind. But if either a single person or an oligarchy or a democracy has a soul eager after pleasures and desires—wanting to be filled with them, yet retaining none of them, and perpetually afflicted with an endless and insatiable disorder; and this evil spirit, having first trampled the laws under foot, becomes the master either of a state or of an individual,—then, as I was saying, salvation is hopeless. And now, Cleinias, we have to consider whether you will or will not accept this tale of mine.

CLEINIAS: Certainly we will.

ATHENIAN: You are aware,—are you not?—that there are often said to be as many forms of laws as there are of governments, and of the latter we have already mentioned all those which are commonly recognized. Now you must regard this as a matter of first-rate importance. For what is to be the standard of just and unjust, is once more the point at issue. Men say that the law ought not to regard either military virtue, or virtue in general, but only the interests and power and preservation of the established form of government; this is thought by them to be the best way of expressing the natural definition of justice.

CLEINIAS: How?

ATHENIAN: Justice is said by them to be the interest of the stronger (Republic).

CLEINIAS: Speak plainer.

ATHENIAN: I will:—'Surely,' they say, 'the governing power makes whatever laws have authority in any state'?

CLEINIAS: True.

ATHENIAN: 'Well,' they would add, 'and do you suppose that tyranny or democracy, or any other conquering power, does not make the continuance of the power which is possessed by them the first or principal object of their laws'?

CLEINIAS: How can they have any other?

ATHENIAN: 'And whoever transgresses these laws is punished as an evil-doer by the legislator, who calls the laws just'?

CLEINIAS: Naturally.

ATHENIAN: 'This, then, is always the mode and fashion in which justice exists.'

CLEINIAS: Certainly, if they are correct in their view.

ATHENIAN: Why, yes, this is one of those false principles of government to which we were referring.

CLEINIAS: Which do you mean?

ATHENIAN: Those which we were examining when we spoke of who ought to govern whom. Did we not arrive at the conclusion that parents ought to govern their children, and the elder the younger, and the noble the ignoble? And there were many other principles, if you remember, and they were not always consistent. One principle was this very principle of might, and we said that Pindar considered violence natural and justified it.

CLEINIAS: Yes; I remember.

ATHENIAN: Consider, then, to whom our state is to be entrusted. For there is a thing which has occurred times without number in states—

CLEINIAS: What thing?

ATHENIAN: That when there has been a contest for power, those who gain the upper hand so entirely monopolize the government, as to refuse all share to the defeated party and their descendants—they live watching one another, the ruling class being in perpetual fear that some one who has a recollection of former wrongs will come into power and rise up against them. Now, according to our view, such governments are not polities at all, nor are laws right which are passed for the good of particular classes and not for the good of the whole state. States which have such laws are not polities but parties, and their notions of justice are simply unmeaning. I say this, because I am going to assert that we must not entrust the government in your state to any one because he is rich, or because he possesses any other advantage, such as strength, or stature, or again birth: but he who is most obedient to the laws of the state, he shall win the palm; and to him who is victorious in the first degree shall be given the highest office and chief ministry of the gods; and the second to him who bears the second palm; and on a similar principle shall all the other offices be assigned to those who come next in order. And when I call the rulers servants or ministers of the law, I give them this name not for the sake of novelty, but because I certainly believe that upon such service or ministry depends the well- or ill-being of the state. For that state in which the law is subject and has no authority, I perceive to be on the highway to ruin; but I see that the state in which the law is above the rulers, and the rulers are the inferiors of the law, has salvation, and every blessing which the Gods can confer.

CLEINIAS: Truly, Stranger, you see with the keen vision of age.

ATHENIAN: Why, yes; every man when he is young has that sort of vision dullest, and when he is old keenest.

CLEINIAS: Very true.

ATHENIAN: And now, what is to be the next step? May we not suppose the colonists to have arrived, and proceed to make our speech to them?

CLEINIAS: Certainly.

ATHENIAN: 'Friends,' we say to them,—'God, as the old tradition declares, holding in his hand the beginning, middle, and end of all that is, travels according to His nature in a straight line towards the accomplishment of His end. Justice always accompanies Him, and is the punisher of those who fall short of the divine law. To justice, he who would be happy holds fast, and follows in her company with all humility and order; but he who is lifted up with pride, or elated by wealth or rank, or beauty, who is young and foolish, and has a soul hot with insolence, and thinks that he has no need of any guide or ruler, but is able himself to be the guide of others, he, I say, is left deserted of God; and being thus deserted, he takes to him others who are like himself, and dances about, throwing all things into confusion, and many think that he is a great man, but in a short time he pays a penalty which justice cannot but approve, and is utterly destroyed, and his family and city with him. Wherefore, seeing that human things are thus ordered, what should a wise man do or think, or not do or think'?

CLEINIAS: Every man ought to make up his mind that he will be one of the followers of God; there can be no doubt of that.

ATHENIAN: Then what life is agreeable to God, and becoming in His followers? One only, expressed once for all in the old saying that 'like agrees with like, with measure measure,' but things which have no measure agree neither with themselves nor with the things which have. Now God ought to be to us the measure of all things, and not man (compare Crat.; Theaet.), as men commonly say (Protagoras): the words are far more true of Him. And he who would be dear to God must, as far as is possible, be like Him and such as He is. Wherefore the temperate man is the friend of God, for he is like Him; and the intemperate man is unlike Him, and different from Him, and unjust. And the same applies to other things; and this is the conclusion, which is also the noblest and truest of all sayings,—that for the good man to offer sacrifice to the Gods, and hold converse with them by means of prayers and offerings and every kind of service, is the noblest and best of all things, and also the most conducive to a happy life, and very fit and meet. But with the bad man, the opposite of this is true: for the bad man has an impure soul, whereas the good is pure; and from one who is polluted, neither a good man nor God can without impropriety receive gifts. Wherefore the unholy do only waste their much service upon the Gods, but when offered by any holy man, such service is most acceptable to them. This is the mark at which we ought to aim. But what weapons shall we use, and how shall we direct them? In the first place, we affirm that next after the Olympian Gods and the Gods of the State, honour should be given to the Gods below; they should receive everything in even numbers, and of the second choice, and ill omen, while the odd numbers, and the first choice, and the things of lucky omen, are given to the Gods above, by him who would rightly hit the mark of piety. Next to these Gods, a wise man will do service to the demons or spirits, and then to the heroes, and after them will follow the private and ancestral Gods, who are worshipped as the law prescribes in the places which are sacred to them. Next comes the honour of living parents, to whom, as is meet, we have to pay the first and greatest and oldest of all debts, considering that all which a man has belongs to those who gave him birth and brought him up, and that he must do all that he can to minister to them, first, in his property, secondly, in his person, and thirdly, in his soul, in return for the endless care and travail which they bestowed upon him of old, in the days of his infancy, and which he is now to pay back to them when they are old and in the extremity of their need. And all his life long he ought never to utter, or to have uttered, an unbecoming word to them; for of light and fleeting words the penalty is most severe; Nemesis, the messenger of justice, is appointed to watch over all such matters. When they are angry and want to satisfy their feelings in word or deed, he should give way to them; for a father who thinks that he has been wronged by his son may be reasonably expected to be very angry. At their death, the most moderate funeral is best, neither exceeding the customary expense, nor yet falling short of the honour which has been usually shown by the former generation to their parents. And let a man not forget to pay the yearly tribute of respect to the dead, honouring them chiefly by omitting nothing that conduces to a perpetual remembrance of them, and giving a reasonable portion of his fortune to the dead. Doing this, and living after this manner, we shall receive our reward from the Gods and those who are above us (i.e. the demons); and we shall spend our days for the most part in good hope. And how a man ought to order what relates to his descendants and his kindred and friends and fellow-citizens, and the rites of hospitality taught by Heaven, and the intercourse which arises out of all these duties, with a view to the embellishment and orderly regulation of his own life—these things, I say, the laws, as we proceed with them, will accomplish, partly persuading, and partly when natures do not yield to the persuasion of custom, chastising them by might and right, and will thus render our state, if the Gods co-operate with us, prosperous and happy. But of what has to be said, and must be said by the legislator who is of my way of thinking, and yet, if said in the form of law, would be out of place—of this I think that he may give a sample for the instruction of himself and of those for whom he is legislating; and then when, as far as he is able, he has gone through all the preliminaries, he may proceed to the work of legislation. Now, what will be the form of such prefaces? There may be a difficulty in including or describing them all under a single form, but I think that we may get some notion of them if we can guarantee one thing.

CLEINIAS: What is that?

ATHENIAN: I should wish the citizens to be as readily persuaded to virtue as possible; this will surely be the aim of the legislator in all his laws.

CLEINIAS: Certainly.

ATHENIAN: The proposal appears to me to be of some value; and I think that a person will listen with more gentleness and good-will to the precepts addressed to him by the legislator, when his soul is not altogether unprepared to receive them. Even a little done in the way of conciliation gains his ear, and is always worth having. For there is no great inclination or readiness on the part of mankind to be made as good, or as quickly good, as possible. The case of the many proves the wisdom of Hesiod, who says that the road to wickedness is smooth and can be travelled without perspiring, because it is so very short:

'But before virtue the immortal Gods have placed the sweat of labour, and long and steep is the way thither, and rugged at first; but when you have reached the top, although difficult before, it is then easy.' (Works and Days.)

CLEINIAS: Yes; and he certainly speaks well.

ATHENIAN: Very true: and now let me tell you the effect which the preceding discourse has had upon me.

CLEINIAS: Proceed.

ATHENIAN: Suppose that we have a little conversation with the legislator, and say to him—'O, legislator, speak; if you know what we ought to say and do, you can surely tell.'

CLEINIAS: Of course he can.

ATHENIAN: 'Did we not hear you just now saying, that the legislator ought not to allow the poets to do what they liked? For that they would not know in which of their words they went against the laws, to the hurt of the state.'

CLEINIAS: That is true.

ATHENIAN: May we not fairly make answer to him on behalf of the poets?

CLEINIAS: What answer shall we make to him?

ATHENIAN: That the poet, according to the tradition which has ever prevailed among us, and is accepted of all men, when he sits down on the tripod of the muse, is not in his right mind; like a fountain, he allows to flow out freely whatever comes in, and his art being imitative, he is often compelled to represent men of opposite dispositions, and thus to contradict himself; neither can he tell whether there is more truth in one thing that he has said than in another. This is not the case in a law; the legislator must give not two rules about the same thing, but one only. Take an example from what you have just been saying. Of three kinds of funerals, there is one which is too extravagant, another is too niggardly, the third in a mean; and you choose and approve and order the last without qualification. But if I had an extremely rich wife, and she bade me bury her and describe her burial in a poem, I should praise the extravagant sort; and a poor miserly man, who had not much money to spend, would approve of the niggardly; and the man of moderate means, who was himself moderate, would praise a moderate funeral. Now you in the capacity of legislator must not barely say 'a moderate funeral,' but you must define what moderation is, and how much; unless you are definite, you must not suppose that you are speaking a language that can become law.

CLEINIAS: Certainly not.

ATHENIAN: And is our legislator to have no preface to his laws, but to say at once Do this, avoid that—and then holding the penalty in terrorem, to go on to another law; offering never a word of advice or exhortation to those for whom he is legislating, after the manner of some doctors? For of doctors, as I may remind you, some have a gentler, others a ruder method of cure; and as children ask the doctor to be gentle with them, so we will ask the legislator to cure our disorders with the gentlest remedies. What I mean to say is, that besides doctors there are doctors' servants, who are also styled doctors.

CLEINIAS: Very true.

ATHENIAN: And whether they are slaves or freemen makes no difference; they acquire their knowledge of medicine by obeying and observing their masters; empirically and not according to the natural way of learning, as the manner of freemen is, who have learned scientifically themselves the art which they impart scientifically to their pupils. You are aware that there are these two classes of doctors?

CLEINIAS: To be sure.

ATHENIAN: And did you ever observe that there are two classes of patients in states, slaves and freemen; and the slave doctors run about and cure the slaves, or wait for them in the dispensaries—practitioners of this sort never talk to their patients individually, or let them talk about their own individual complaints? The slave doctor prescribes what mere experience suggests, as if he had exact knowledge; and when he has given his orders, like a tyrant, he rushes off with equal assurance to some other servant who is ill; and so he relieves the master of the house of the care of his invalid slaves. But the other doctor, who is a freeman, attends and practices upon freemen; and he carries his enquiries far back, and goes into the nature of the disorder; he enters into discourse with the patient and with his friends, and is at once getting information from the sick man, and also instructing him as far as he is able, and he will not prescribe for him until he has first convinced him; at last, when he has brought the patient more and more under his persuasive influences and set him on the road to health, he attempts to effect a cure. Now which is the better way of proceeding in a physician and in a trainer? Is he the better who accomplishes his ends in a double way, or he who works in one way, and that the ruder and inferior?

CLEINIAS: I should say, Stranger, that the double way is far better.

ATHENIAN: Should you like to see an example of the double and single method in legislation?

CLEINIAS: Certainly I should.

ATHENIAN: What will be our first law? Will not the legislator, observing the order of nature, begin by making regulations for states about births?

CLEINIAS: He will.

ATHENIAN: In all states the birth of children goes back to the connexion of marriage?

CLEINIAS: Very true.

ATHENIAN: And, according to the true order, the laws relating to marriage should be those which are first determined in every state?

CLEINIAS: Quite so.

ATHENIAN: Then let me first give the law of marriage in a simple form; it may run as follows:—A man shall marry between the ages of thirty and thirty-five, or, if he does not, he shall pay such and such a fine, or shall suffer the loss of such and such privileges. This would be the simple law about marriage. The double law would run thus:—A man shall marry between the ages of thirty and thirty-five, considering that in a manner the human race naturally partakes of immortality, which every man is by nature inclined to desire to the utmost; for the desire of every man that he may become famous, and not lie in the grave without a name, is only the love of continuance. Now mankind are coeval with all time, and are ever following, and will ever follow, the course of time; and so they are immortal, because they leave children's children behind them, and partake of immortality in the unity of generation. And for a man voluntarily to deprive himself of this gift, as he deliberately does who will not have a wife or children, is impiety. He who obeys the law shall be free, and shall pay no fine; but he who is disobedient, and does not marry, when he has arrived at the age of thirty-five, shall pay a yearly fine of a certain amount, in order that he may not imagine his celibacy to bring ease and profit to him; and he shall not share in the honours which the young men in the state give to the aged. Comparing now the two forms of the law, you will be able to arrive at a judgment about any other laws—whether they should be double in length even when shortest, because they have to persuade as well as threaten, or whether they shall only threaten and be of half the length.

MEGILLUS: The shorter form, Stranger, would be more in accordance with Lacedaemonian custom; although, for my own part, if any one were to ask me which I myself prefer in the state, I should certainly determine in favour of the longer; and I would have every law made after the same pattern, if I had to choose. But I think that

Cleinias is the person to be consulted, for his is the state which is going to use these laws.

CLEINIAS: Thank you, Megillus.

ATHENIAN: Whether, in the abstract, words are to be many or few, is a very foolish question; the best form, and not the shortest, is to be approved; nor is length at all to be regarded. Of the two forms of law which have been recited, the one is not only twice as good in practical usefulness as the other, but the case is like that of the two kinds of doctors, which I was just now mentioning. And yet legislators never appear to have considered that they have two instruments which they might use in legislation—persuasion and force; for in dealing with the rude and uneducated multitude, they use the one only as far as they can; they do not mingle persuasion with coercion, but employ force pure and simple. Moreover, there is a third point, sweet friends, which ought to be, and never is, regarded in our existing laws.

CLEINIAS: What is it?

ATHENIAN: A point arising out of our previous discussion, which comes into my mind in some mysterious way. All this time, from early dawn until noon, have we been talking about laws in this charming retreat: now we are going to promulgate our laws, and what has preceded was only the prelude of them. Why do I mention this? For this reason:—Because all discourses and vocal exercises have preludes and overtures, which are a sort of artistic beginnings intended to help the strain which is to be performed; lyric measures and music of every other kind have preludes framed with wonderful care. But of the truer and higher strain of law and politics, no one has ever yet uttered any prelude, or composed or published any, as though there was no such thing in nature. Whereas our present discussion seems to me to imply that there is;—these double laws, of which we were speaking, are not exactly double, but they are in two parts, the law and the prelude of the law. The arbitrary command, which was compared to the commands of doctors, whom we described as of the meaner sort, was the law pure and simple; and that which preceded, and was described by our friend here as being hortatory only, was, although in fact, an exhortation, likewise analogous to the preamble of a discourse. For I imagine that all this language of conciliation, which the legislator has been uttering in the preface of the law, was intended to create good-will in the person whom he addressed, in order that, by reason of this good-will, he might more intelligently receive his command, that is to say, the law. And therefore, in my way of speaking, this is more rightly described as the preamble than as the matter of the law. And I must further proceed to observe, that to all his laws, and to each separately, the legislator should prefix a preamble; he should remember how great will be the difference between them, according as they have, or have not, such preambles, as in the case already given.

CLEINIAS: The lawgiver, if he asks my opinion, will certainly legislate in the form which you advise.

ATHENIAN: I think that you are right, Cleinias, in affirming that all laws have preambles, and that throughout the whole of this work of legislation every single law should have a suitable preamble at the beginning; for that which is to follow is most important, and it makes all the difference whether we clearly remember the preambles or not. Yet we should be wrong in requiring that all laws, small and great alike, should have preambles of the same kind, any more than all songs or speeches; although they may be natural to all, they are not always necessary, and whether they are to be employed or not has in each case to be left to the judgment of the speaker or the musician, or, in the present instance, of the lawgiver.

CLEINIAS: That I think is most true. And now, Stranger, without delay let us return to the argument, and, as people say in play, make a second and better beginning, if you please, with the principles which we have been laying down, which we never thought of regarding as a preamble before, but of which we may now make a preamble, and not merely consider them to be chance topics of discourse. Let us acknowledge, then, that we have a preamble. About the honour of the Gods and the respect of parents, enough has been already said; and we may proceed to the topics which follow next in order, until the preamble is deemed by you to be complete; and after that you shall go through the laws themselves.

ATHENIAN: I understand you to mean that we have made a sufficient preamble about Gods and demigods, and about parents living or dead; and now you would have us bring the rest of the subject into the light of day?

CLEINIAS: Exactly.

ATHENIAN: After this, as is meet and for the interest of us all, I the speaker, and you the listeners, will try to estimate all that relates to the souls and bodies and properties of the citizens, as regards both their occupations and amusements, and thus arrive, as far as in us lies, at the nature of education. These then are the topics which follow next in order.

CLEINIAS: Very good.

BOOK V.

ATHENIAN: Listen, all ye who have just now heard the laws about Gods, and about our dear forefathers:—Of all the things which a man has, next to the Gods, his soul is the most divine and most truly his own. Now in every man there are two parts: the better and superior, which rules, and the worse and inferior, which serves; and the ruling part of him is always to be preferred to the subject. Wherefore I am right in bidding every one next to the Gods, who are our masters, and those who in order follow them (i.e. the demons), to honour his own soul, which every one seems to honour, but no one honours as he ought; for honour is a divine good, and no evil thing is honourable; and he who thinks that he can honour the soul by word or gift, or any sort of compliance, without making her in any way better, seems to honour her, but honours her not at all. For example, every man, from his very boyhood, fancies that he is able to know everything, and thinks that he honours his soul by praising her, and he is very ready to let her do whatever she may like. But I mean to say that in acting thus he injures his soul, and is far from honouring her; whereas, in our opinion, he ought to honour her as second only to the Gods. Again, when a man thinks that others are to be blamed, and not himself, for the errors which he has committed from time to time, and the many and great evils which befell him in consequence, and is always fancying himself to be exempt and innocent, he is under the idea that he is honouring his soul; whereas the very reverse is the fact, for he is really injuring her. And when, disregarding the word and approval of the legislator, he indulges in pleasure, then again he is far from honouring her; he only dishonours her, and fills her full of evil and remorse; or when he does not endure to the end the labours and fears and sorrows and pains which the legislator approves, but gives way before them, then, by yielding, he does not honour the soul, but by all such conduct he makes her to be dishonourable; nor when he thinks that life at any price is a good, does he honour her, but yet once more he dishonours her; for the soul having a notion that the world below is all evil, he yields to her, and does not resist and teach or convince her that, for aught she knows, the world of the Gods below, instead of being evil, may be the greatest of all goods. Again, when any one prefers beauty to virtue, what is this but the real and utter dishonour of the soul? For such a preference implies that the body is more honourable than the soul; and this is false, for there is nothing of earthly birth which is more honourable than the heavenly, and he who thinks otherwise of the soul has no idea how greatly he undervalues this wonderful possession; nor, again, when a person is willing, or not unwilling, to acquire dishonest gains, does he then honour his soul with gifts—far otherwise; he sells her glory and honour for a small piece of gold; but all the gold which is under or upon the earth is not enough to give in exchange for virtue. In a word, I may say that he who does not estimate the base and evil, the good and noble, according to the standard of the legislator, and abstain in every possible way from the one and practise the other to the utmost of his power, does not know that in all these respects he is most foully and disgracefully abusing his soul, which is the divinest part of man; for no one, as I may say, ever considers that which is declared to be the greatest penalty of evil-doing—namely, to grow into the likeness of bad men, and growing like them to fly from the conversation of the good, and be cut off from them, and cleave to and follow after the company of the bad. And he who is joined to them must do and suffer what such men by nature do and say to one another,—a suffering which is not justice but retribution; for justice and the just are noble, whereas retribution is the suffering which waits upon injustice; and whether a man escape or endure this, he is miserable,—in the former case, because he is not cured; while in the latter, he perishes in order that the rest of mankind may be saved.

Speaking generally, our glory is to follow the better and improve the inferior, which is susceptible of improvement, as far as this is possible. And of all human possessions, the soul is by nature most inclined to avoid the evil, and track out and find the chief good; which when a man has found, he should take up his abode with it during the remainder of his life. Wherefore the soul also is second (or next to God) in honour; and third, as every one will perceive, comes the honour of the body in natural order. Having determined this, we have next to consider that there is a natural honour of the body, and that of honours some are true and some are counterfeit. To decide which are which is the business of the legislator; and he, I suspect, would intimate that they are as follows:—Honour is not to be given to the fair body, or to the strong or the swift or the tall, or to the healthy body (although many may think otherwise), any more than to their opposites; but the mean states of all these habits are by far the safest and most moderate; for the one extreme makes the soul braggart and insolent, and the other, illiberal and base; and money, and property, and distinction all go to the same tune. The excess of any of these things is apt to be a source of hatreds and divisions among states and individuals; and the defect of them is commonly a cause of slavery. And, therefore, I would not have any one fond of heaping up riches for the sake of his children, in order that he may leave them as rich as possible. For the possession of great wealth is of no use, either to them or to the state. The condition of youth which is free from flattery, and at the same time not in need of the necessaries of life, is the best and most harmonious of all, being in accord and agreement with our nature, and making life to be most entirely free from sorrow. Let parents, then, bequeath to their children not a heap of riches, but the spirit of reverence. We, indeed, fancy that they will inherit reverence from us, if we rebuke them when they show a want of reverence. But this quality is not really imparted to them by the present style of admonition, which only tells them that the young ought always to be reverential. A sensible legislator will rather exhort the elders to reverence the younger, and above all to take heed that no young man sees or hears one of themselves doing or saying anything disgraceful; for where old men have no shame, there young men will most certainly be devoid of reverence. The best way of training the young is to train yourself at the same time; not to admonish them, but to be always carrying out your own admonitions in practice. He who honours his kindred, and reveres those who share in the same Gods and are of the same blood and family, may fairly expect that the Gods who preside over generation will be propitious to him, and will quicken his seed. And he who deems the services which his friends and acquaintances do for him, greater and more important than they themselves deem them, and his own favours to them less than theirs to him, will have their good-will in the intercourse of life. And surely in his relations to the state and his fellow citizens, he is by far the best, who rather than the Olympic or any other victory of peace or war, desires to win the palm of obedience to the laws of his country, and who, of all mankind, is the person reputed to have obeyed them best through life. In his relations to strangers, a man should consider that a contract is a most holy thing, and that all concerns and wrongs of strangers are more directly dependent on the protection of God, than wrongs done to citizens; for the stranger, having no kindred and friends, is more to be pitied by Gods and men. Wherefore, also, he who is most able to avenge him is most zealous in his cause; and he who is most able is the genius and the god of the stranger, who follow in the train of Zeus, the god of strangers. And for this reason, he who has a spark of caution in him, will do his best to pass through life without sinning against the stranger. And of offences committed, whether against strangers or fellow-countrymen, that against suppliants is the greatest. For the God who witnessed to the agreement made with the suppliant, becomes in a special manner the guardian of the sufferer; and he will certainly not suffer unavenged.

Thus we have fairly described the manner in which a man is to act about his parents, and himself, and his own affairs; and in relation to the state, and his friends, and kindred, both in what concerns his own countrymen, and in what concerns the stranger. We will now consider what manner of man he must be who would best pass through life in respect of those other things which are not matters of law, but of praise and blame only; in which praise and blame educate a man, and make him more tractable and amenable to the laws which are about to be imposed.

Truth is the beginning of every good thing, both to Gods and men; and he who would be blessed and happy, should be from the first a partaker of the truth, that he may live a true man as long as possible, for then he can be trusted; but he is not to be trusted who loves voluntary falsehood, and he who loves involuntary falsehood is a fool. Neither condition is enviable, for the untrustworthy and ignorant has no friend, and as time advances he becomes known, and lays up in store for himself isolation in crabbed age when life is on the wane: so that, whether his children or friends are alive or not, he is equally solitary.—Worthy of honour is he who does no injustice, and of more than twofold honour, if he not only does no injustice himself, but hinders others from doing any; the first may count as one man, the second is worth many men, because he informs the rulers of the injustice of others. And yet more highly to be esteemed is he who co-operates with the rulers in correcting the citizens as far as he can—he shall be proclaimed the great and perfect citizen, and bear away the palm of virtue. The same praise may be given about temperance and wisdom, and all other goods which may be imparted to others, as well as acquired by a man for himself; he who imparts them shall be honoured as the man of men, and he who is willing, yet is not able, may be allowed the second place; but he who is jealous and will not, if he can help, allow others to partake in a friendly way of any good, is deserving of blame: the good, however, which he has, is not to be undervalued by us because it is possessed by him, but must be acquired by us also to the utmost of our power. Let every man, then, freely strive for the prize of virtue, and let there be no envy. For the unenvious nature increases the greatness of states—he himself contends in the race, blasting the fair fame of no man; but the envious, who thinks that he ought to get the better by defaming others, is less energetic himself in the pursuit of true virtue, and reduces his rivals to despair by his unjust slanders of them. And so he makes the whole city to enter the arena untrained in the practice of virtue, and diminishes her glory as far as in him lies. Now every man should be valiant, but he should also be gentle. From the cruel, or hardly curable, or altogether incurable acts of injustice done to him by others, a man can only escape by fighting and defending himself and conquering, and by never ceasing to punish them; and no man who is not of a noble spirit is able to accomplish this. As to the actions of those who do evil, but whose evil is curable, in the first place, let us remember that the unjust man is not unjust of his own free will. For no man of his own free will would choose to possess the greatest of evils, and least of all in the most honourable part of himself. And the soul, as we said, is of a truth deemed by all men the most honourable. In the soul, then, which is the most honourable part of him, no one, if he could help, would admit, or allow to continue the greatest of evils (compare Republic). The unrighteous and vicious are always to be pitied in any case; and one can afford to forgive as well as pity him who is curable, and refrain and calm one's anger, not getting into a passion, like a woman, and nursing ill-feeling. But upon him who is incapable of reformation and wholly evil, the vials of our wrath should be poured out; wherefore I say that good men ought, when occasion demands, to be both gentle and passionate.

Of all evils the greatest is one which in the souls of most men is innate, and which a man is always excusing in himself and never correcting; I mean, what is expressed in the saying that 'Every man by nature is and ought to be his own friend.' Whereas the excessive love of self is in reality the source to each man of all offences; for the lover is blinded about the beloved, so that he judges wrongly of the just, the good, and the honourable, and thinks that he ought always to prefer himself to the truth. But he who would be a great man ought to regard, not himself or his interests, but what is just, whether the just act be his own or that of another. Through a similar error men are induced to fancy that their own ignorance is wisdom, and thus we who may be truly said to know nothing, think that we know all things; and because we will not let others act for us in what we do not know, we are compelled to act amiss ourselves. Wherefore let every man avoid excess of self-love, and condescend to follow a better man than himself, not allowing any false shame to stand in the way. There are also minor precepts which are often repeated, and are quite as useful; a man should recollect them and remind himself of them. For when a stream is flowing out, there should be water flowing in too; and recollection flows in while wisdom is departing. Therefore I say that a man should refrain from excess either of laughter or tears, and should exhort his neighbour to do the same; he should veil his immoderate sorrow or joy, and seek to behave with propriety, whether the genius of his good fortune remains with him, or whether at the crisis of his fate, when he seems to be mounting high and steep places, the Gods oppose him in some of his enterprises. Still he may ever hope, in the case of good men, that whatever afflictions are to befall them in the future God will lessen, and that present evils He will change for the better; and as to the goods which are the opposite of these evils, he will not doubt that they will be added to them, and that they will be fortunate. Such should be men's hopes, and such should be the exhortations with which they admonish one another, never losing an opportunity, but on every occasion distinctly reminding themselves and others of all these things, both in jest and earnest.

Enough has now been said of divine matters, both as touching the practices which men ought to follow, and as to the sort of persons who they ought severally to be. But of human things we have not as yet spoken, and we must; for to men we are discoursing and not to Gods. Pleasures and pains and desires are a part of human nature, and on them every mortal being must of necessity hang and depend with the most eager interest. And therefore we must praise the noblest life, not only as the fairest in appearance, but as being one which, if a man will only taste, and not, while still in his youth, desert for another, he will find to surpass also in the very thing which we all of us desire,—I mean in having a greater amount of pleasure and less of pain during the whole of life. And this will be plain, if a man has a true taste of them, as will be quickly and clearly seen. But what is a true taste? That we have to learn from the argument—the point being what is according to nature, and what is not according to nature. One life must be compared with another, the more pleasurable with the more painful, after this manner:—We desire to have pleasure, but we neither desire nor choose pain; and the neutral state we are ready to take in exchange, not for pleasure but for pain; and we also wish for less pain and greater pleasure, but less pleasure and greater pain we do not wish for; and an equal balance of either we cannot venture to assert that we should desire. And all these differ or do not differ severally in number and magnitude and intensity and equality, and in the opposites of these when regarded as objects of choice, in relation to desire. And such being the necessary order of things, we wish for that life in which there are many great and intense elements of pleasure and pain, and in which the pleasures are in excess, and do not wish for that in which the opposites exceed; nor, again, do we wish for that in which the elements of either are small and few and feeble, and the pains exceed. And when, as I said before, there is a balance of pleasure and pain in life, this is to be regarded by us as the balanced life; while other lives are preferred by us because they exceed in what we like, or are rejected by us because they exceed in what we dislike. All the lives of men may be regarded by us as bound up in these, and we must also consider what sort of lives we by nature desire. And if we wish for any others, I say that we desire them only through some ignorance and inexperience of the lives which actually exist.

Now, what lives are they, and how many in which, having searched out and beheld the objects of will and desire and their opposites, and making of them a law, choosing, I say, the dear and the pleasant and the best and noblest, a man may live in the happiest way possible? Let us say that the temperate life is one kind of life, and the rational another, and the courageous another, and the healthful another; and to these four let us oppose four other lives—the foolish, the cowardly, the intemperate, the diseased. He who knows the temperate life will describe it as in all things gentle, having gentle pains and gentle pleasures, and placid desires and loves not insane; whereas the intemperate life is impetuous in all things, and has violent pains and pleasures, and vehement and stinging desires, and loves utterly insane; and in the temperate life the pleasures exceed the pains, but in the intemperate life the pains exceed the pleasures in greatness and number and frequency. Hence one of the two lives is naturally and necessarily more pleasant and the other more painful, and he who would live pleasantly cannot possibly choose to live intemperately. And if this is true, the inference clearly is that no man is voluntarily intemperate; but that the whole multitude of men lack temperance in their lives, either from ignorance, or from want of self-control, or both. And the same holds of the diseased and healthy life; they both have pleasures and pains, but in health the pleasure exceeds the pain, and in sickness the pain exceeds the pleasure. Now our intention in choosing the lives is not that the painful should exceed, but the life in which pain is exceeded by pleasure we have determined to be the more pleasant life. And we should say that the temperate life has the elements both of pleasure and pain fewer and smaller and less frequent than the intemperate, and the wise life than the foolish life, and the life of courage than the life of cowardice; one of each pair exceeding in pleasure and the other in pain, the courageous surpassing the cowardly, and the wise exceeding the foolish. And so the one class of lives exceeds the other class in pleasure; the temperate and courageous and wise and healthy exceed the cowardly and foolish and intemperate and diseased lives; and generally speaking, that which has any virtue, whether of body or soul, is pleasanter than the vicious life, and far superior in beauty and rectitude and excellence and reputation, and causes him who lives accordingly to be infinitely happier than the opposite.

Enough of the preamble; and now the laws should follow; or, to speak more correctly, an outline of them. As, then, in the case of a web or any other tissue, the warp and the woof cannot be made of the same materials (compare Statesman), but the warp is necessarily superior as being stronger, and having a certain character of firmness, whereas the woof is softer and has a proper degree of elasticity;—in a similar manner those who are to hold great offices in states, should be distinguished truly in each case from those who have been but slenderly proven by education. Let us suppose that there are two parts in the constitution of a state—one the creation of offices, the other the laws which are assigned to them to administer.

But, before all this, comes the following consideration:—The shepherd or herdsman, or breeder of horses or the like, when he has received his animals will not begin to train them until he has first purified them in a manner which befits a community of animals; he will divide the healthy and unhealthy, and the good breed and the bad breed, and will send away the unhealthy and badly bred to other herds, and tend the rest, reflecting that his labours will be vain and have no effect, either on the souls or bodies of those whom nature and ill nurture have corrupted, and that they will involve in destruction the pure and healthy nature and being of every other animal, if he should neglect to purify them. Now the case of other animals is not so important—they are only worth introducing for the sake of illustration; but what relates to man is of the highest importance; and the legislator should make enquiries, and indicate what is proper for each one in the way of purification and of any other procedure. Take, for example, the purification of a city—there are many kinds of purification, some easier and others more difficult; and some of them, and the best and most difficult of them, the legislator, if he be also a despot, may be able to effect; but the legislator, who, not being a despot, sets up a new government and laws, even if he attempt the mildest of purgations, may think himself happy if he can complete his work. The best kind of purification is painful, like similar cures in medicine, involving righteous punishment and inflicting death or exile in the last resort. For in this way we commonly dispose of great sinners who are incurable, and are the greatest injury of the whole state. But the milder form of purification is as follows:—when men who have nothing, and are in want of food, show a disposition to follow their leaders in an attack on the property of the rich—these, who are the natural plague of the state, are sent away by the legislator in a friendly spirit as far as he is able; and this dismissal of them is euphemistically termed a colony. And every legislator should contrive to do this at once. Our present case, however, is peculiar. For there is no need to devise any colony or purifying separation under the circumstances in which we are placed. But as, when many streams flow together from many sources, whether springs or mountain torrents, into a single lake, we ought to attend and take care that the confluent waters should be perfectly clear, and in order to effect this, should pump and draw off and divert impurities, so in every political arrangement there may be trouble and danger. But, seeing that we are now only discoursing and not acting, let our selection be supposed to be completed, and the desired purity attained. Touching evil men, who want to join and be citizens of our state, after we have tested them by every sort of persuasion and for a sufficient time, we will prevent them from coming; but the good we will to the utmost of our ability receive as friends with open arms.

Another piece of good fortune must not be forgotten, which, as we were saying, the Heraclid colony had, and which is also ours,—that we have escaped division of land and the abolition of debts; for these are always a source of dangerous contention, and a city which is driven by necessity to legislate upon such matters can neither allow the old ways to continue, nor yet venture to alter them. We must have recourse to prayers, so to speak, and hope that a slight change may be cautiously effected in a length of time. And such a change can be accomplished by those who have abundance of land, and having also many debtors, are willing, in a kindly spirit, to share with those who are in want, sometimes remitting and sometimes giving, holding fast in a path of moderation, and deeming poverty to be the increase of a man's desires and not the diminution of his property. For this is the great beginning of salvation to a state, and upon this lasting basis may be erected afterwards whatever political order is suitable under the circumstances; but if the change be based upon an unsound principle, the future administration of the country will be full of difficulties. That is a danger which, as I am saying, is escaped by us, and yet we had better say how, if we had not escaped, we might have escaped; and we may venture now to assert that no other way of escape, whether narrow or broad, can be devised but freedom from avarice and a sense of justice—upon this rock our city shall be built; for there ought to be no disputes among citizens about property. If there are quarrels of long standing among them, no legislator of any degree of sense will proceed a step in the arrangement of the state until they are settled. But that they to whom God has given, as He has to us, to be the founders of a new state as yet free from enmity—that they should create themselves enmities by their mode of distributing lands and houses, would be superhuman folly and wickedness.

How then can we rightly order the distribution of the land? In the first place, the number of the citizens has to be determined, and also the number and size of the divisions into which they will have to be formed; and the land and the houses will then have to be apportioned by us as fairly as we can. The number of citizens can only be estimated satisfactorily in relation to the territory and the neighbouring states. The territory must be sufficient to maintain a certain number of inhabitants in a moderate way of life—more than this is not required; and the number of citizens should be sufficient to defend themselves against the injustice of their neighbours, and also to give them the power of rendering efficient aid to their neighbours when they are wronged. After having taken a survey of their's and their neighbours' territory, we will determine the limits of them in fact as well as in theory. And now, let us proceed to legislate with a view to perfecting the form and outline of our state. The number of our citizens shall be 5040—this will be a convenient number; and these shall be owners of the land and protectors of the allotment. The houses and the land will be divided in the same way, so that every man may correspond to a lot. Let the whole number be first divided into two parts, and then into three; and the number is further capable of being divided into four or five parts, or any number of parts up to ten. Every legislator ought to know so much arithmetic as to be able to tell what number is most likely to be useful to all cities; and we are going to take that number which contains the greatest and most regular and unbroken series of divisions. The whole of number has every possible division, and the number 5040 can be divided by exactly fifty-nine divisors, and ten of these proceed without interval from one to ten: this will furnish numbers for war and peace, and for all contracts and dealings, including taxes and divisions of the land. These properties of number should be ascertained at leisure by those who are bound by law to know them; for they are true, and should be proclaimed at the foundation of the city, with a view to use. Whether the legislator is establishing a new state or restoring an old and decayed one, in respect of Gods and temples,—the temples which are to be built in each city, and the Gods or demi-gods after whom they are to be called,—if he be a man of sense, he will make no change in anything which the oracle of Delphi, or Dodona, or the God Ammon, or any ancient tradition has sanctioned in whatever manner, whether by apparitions or reputed inspiration of Heaven, in obedience to which mankind have established sacrifices in connexion with mystic rites, either originating on the spot, or derived from Tyrrhenia or Cyprus or some other place, and on the strength of which traditions they have consecrated oracles and images, and altars and temples, and portioned out a sacred domain for each of them. The least part of all these ought not to be disturbed by the legislator; but he should assign to the several districts some God, or demi-god, or hero, and, in the distribution of the soil, should give to these first their chosen domain and all things fitting, that the inhabitants of the several districts may meet at fixed times, and that they may readily supply their various wants, and entertain one another with sacrifices, and become friends and acquaintances; for there is no greater good in a state than that the citizens should be known to one another. When not light but darkness and ignorance of each other's characters prevails among them, no one will receive the honour of which he is deserving, or the power or the justice to which he is fairly entitled: wherefore, in every state, above all things, every man should take heed that he have no deceit in him, but that he be always true and simple; and that no deceitful person take any advantage of him.

The next move in our pastime of legislation, like the withdrawal of the stone from the holy line in the game of draughts, being an unusual one, will probably excite wonder when mentioned for the first time. And yet, if a man will only reflect and weigh the matter with care, he will see that our city is ordered in a manner which, if not the best, is the second best. Perhaps also some one may not approve this form, because he thinks that such a constitution is ill adapted to a legislator who has not despotic power. The truth is, that there are three forms of government, the best, the second and the third best, which we may just mention, and then leave the selection to the ruler of the settlement. Following this method in the present instance, let us speak of the states which are respectively first, second, and third in excellence, and then we will leave the choice to Cleinias now, or to any one else who may hereafter have to make a similar choice among constitutions, and may desire to give to his state some feature which is congenial to him and which he approves in his own country.

The first and highest form of the state and of the government and of the law is that in which there prevails most widely the ancient saying, that 'Friends have all things in common.' Whether there is anywhere now, or will ever be, this communion of women and children and of property, in which the private and individual is altogether banished from life, and things which are by nature private, such as eyes and ears and hands, have become common, and in some way see and hear and act in common, and all men express praise and blame and feel joy and sorrow on the same occasions, and whatever laws there are unite the city to the utmost (compare Republic),—whether all this is possible or not, I say that no man, acting upon any other principle, will ever constitute a state which will be truer or better or more exalted in virtue. Whether such a state is governed by Gods or sons of Gods, one, or more than one, happy are the men who, living after this manner, dwell there; and therefore to this we are to look for the pattern of the state, and to cling to this, and to seek with all our might for one which is like this. The state which we have now in hand, when created, will be nearest to immortality and the only one which takes the second place; and after that, by the grace of God, we will complete the third one. And we will begin by speaking of the nature and origin of the second.

Let the citizens at once distribute their land and houses, and not till the land in common, since a community of goods goes beyond their proposed origin, and nurture, and education. But in making the distribution, let the several possessors feel that their particular lots also belong to the whole city; and seeing that the earth is their parent, let them tend her more carefully than children do their mother. For she is a goddess and their queen, and they are her mortal subjects. Such also are the feelings which they ought to entertain to the Gods and demi-gods of the country. And in order that the distribution may always remain, they ought to consider further that the present number of families should be always retained, and neither increased nor diminished. This may be secured for the whole city in the following manner:—Let the possessor of a lot leave the one of his children who is his best beloved, and one only, to be the heir of his dwelling, and his successor in the duty of ministering to the Gods, the state and the family, as well the living members of it as those who are departed when he comes into the inheritance; but of his other children, if he have more than one, he shall give the females in marriage according to the law to be hereafter enacted, and the males he shall distribute as sons to those citizens who have no children, and are disposed to receive them; or if there should be none such, and particular individuals have too many children, male or female, or too few, as in the case of barrenness—in all these cases let the highest and most honourable magistracy created by us judge and determine what is to be done with the redundant or deficient, and devise a means that the number of 5040 houses shall always remain the same. There are many ways of regulating numbers; for they in whom generation is affluent may be made to refrain (compare Arist. Pol.), and, on the other hand, special care may be taken to increase the number of births by rewards and stigmas, or we may meet the evil by the elder men giving advice and administering rebuke to the younger—in this way the object may be attained. And if after all there be very great difficulty about the equal preservation of the 5040 houses, and there be an excess of citizens, owing to the too great love of those who live together, and we are at our wits' end, there is still the old device often mentioned by us of sending out a colony, which will part friends with us, and be composed of suitable persons. If, on the other hand, there come a wave bearing a deluge of disease, or a plague of war, and the inhabitants become much fewer than the appointed number by reason of bereavement, we ought not to introduce citizens of spurious birth and education, if this can be avoided; but even God is said not to be able to fight against necessity.

Wherefore let us suppose this 'high argument' of ours to address us in the following terms:—Best of men, cease not to honour according to nature similarity and equality and sameness and agreement, as regards number and every good and noble quality. And, above all, observe the aforesaid number 5040 throughout life; in the second place, do not disparage the small and modest proportions of the inheritances which you received in the distribution, by buying and selling them to one another. For then neither will the God who gave you the lot be your friend, nor will the legislator; and indeed the law declares to the disobedient that these are the terms upon which he may or may not take the lot. In the first place, the earth as he is informed is sacred to the Gods; and in the next place, priests and priestesses will offer up prayers over a first, and second, and even a third sacrifice, that he who buys or sells the houses or lands which he has received, may suffer the punishment which he deserves; and these their prayers they shall write down in the temples, on tablets of cypress-wood, for the instruction of posterity. Moreover they will set a watch over all these things, that they may be observed;—the magistracy which has the sharpest eyes shall keep watch that any infringement of these commands may be discovered and punished as offences both against the law and the God. How great is the benefit of such an ordinance to all those cities, which obey and are administered accordingly, no bad man can ever know, as the old proverb says; but only a man of experience and good habits. For in such an order of things there will not be much opportunity for making money; no man either ought, or indeed will be allowed, to exercise any ignoble occupation, of which the vulgarity is a matter of reproach to a freeman, and should never want to acquire riches by any such means.

Further, the law enjoins that no private man shall be allowed to possess gold and silver, but only coin for daily use, which is almost necessary in dealing with artisans, and for payment of hirelings, whether slaves or immigrants, by all those persons who require the use of them. Wherefore our citizens, as we say, should have a coin passing current among themselves, but not accepted among the rest of mankind; with a view, however, to expeditions and journeys to other lands,—for embassies, or for any other occasion which may arise of sending out a herald, the state must also possess a common Hellenic currency. If a private person is ever obliged to go abroad, let him have the consent of the magistrates and go; and if when he returns he has any foreign money remaining, let him give the surplus back to the treasury, and receive a corresponding sum in the local currency. And if he is discovered to appropriate it, let it be confiscated, and let him who knows and does not inform be subject to curse and dishonour equally him who brought the money, and also to a fine not less in amount than the foreign money which has been brought back. In marrying and giving in marriage, no one shall give or receive any dowry at all; and no one shall deposit money with another whom he does not trust as a friend, nor shall he lend money upon interest; and the borrower should be under no obligation to repay either capital or interest. That these principles are best, any one may see who compares them with the first principle and intention of a state. The intention, as we affirm, of a reasonable statesman, is not what the many declare to be the object of a good legislator, namely, that the state for the true interests of which he is advising should be as great and as rich as possible, and should possess gold and silver, and have the greatest empire by sea and land;—this they imagine to be the real object of legislation, at the same time adding, inconsistently, that the true legislator desires to have the city the best and happiest possible. But they do not see that some of these things are possible, and some of them are impossible; and he who orders the state will desire what is possible, and will not indulge in vain wishes or attempts to accomplish that which is impossible. The citizen must indeed be happy and good, and the legislator will seek to make him so; but very rich and very good at the same time he cannot be, not, at least, in the sense in which the many speak of riches. For they mean by 'the rich' the few who have the most valuable possessions, although the owner of them may quite well be a rogue. And if this is true, I can never assent to the doctrine that the rich man will be happy—he must be good as well as rich. And good in a high degree, and rich in a high degree at the same time, he cannot be. Some one will ask, why not? And we shall answer—Because acquisitions which come from sources which are just and unjust indifferently, are more than double those which come from just sources only; and the sums which are expended neither honourably nor disgracefully, are only half as great as those which are expended honourably and on honourable purposes. Thus, if the one acquires double and spends half, the other who is in the opposite case and is a good man cannot possibly be wealthier than he. The first—I am speaking of the saver and not of the spender—is not always bad; he may indeed in some cases be utterly bad, but, as I was saying, a good man he never is. For he who receives money unjustly as well as justly, and spends neither nor unjustly, will be a rich man if he be also thrifty. On the other hand, the utterly bad is in general profligate, and therefore very poor; while he who spends on noble objects, and acquires wealth by just means only, can hardly be remarkable for riches, any more than he can be very poor. Our statement, then, is true, that the very rich are not good, and, if they are not good, they are not happy. But the intention of our laws was, that the citizens should be as happy as may be, and as friendly as possible to one another. And men who are always at law with one another, and amongst whom there are many wrongs done, can never be friends to one another, but only those among whom crimes and lawsuits are few and slight. Therefore we say that gold and silver ought not to be allowed in the city, nor much of the vulgar sort of trade which is carried on by lending money, or rearing the meaner kinds of live stock; but only the produce of agriculture, and only so much of this as will not compel us in pursuing it to neglect that for the sake of which riches exist—I mean, soul and body, which without gymnastics, and without education, will never be worth anything; and therefore, as we have said not once but many times, the care of riches should have the last place in our thoughts. For there are in all three things about which every man has an interest; and the interest about money, when rightly regarded, is the third and lowest of them: midway comes the interest of the body; and, first of all, that of the soul; and the state which we are describing will have been rightly constituted if it ordains honours according to this scale. But if, in any of the laws which have been ordained, health has been preferred to temperance, or wealth to health and temperate habits, that law must clearly be wrong. Wherefore, also, the legislator ought often to impress upon himself the question—'What do I want?' and 'Do I attain my aim, or do I miss the mark?' In this way, and in this way only, he may acquit himself and free others from the work of legislation.

Let the allottee then hold his lot upon the conditions which we have mentioned.

It would be well that every man should come to the colony having all things equal; but seeing that this is not possible, and one man will have greater possessions than another, for many reasons and in particular in order to preserve equality in special crises of the state, qualifications of property must be unequal, in order that offices and contributions and distributions may be proportioned to the value of each person's wealth, and not solely to the virtue of his ancestors or himself, nor yet to the strength and beauty of his person, but also to the measure of his wealth or poverty; and so by a law of inequality, which will be in proportion to his wealth, he will receive honours and offices as equally as possible, and there will be no quarrels and disputes. To which end there should be four different standards appointed according to the amount of property: there should be a first and a second and a third and a fourth class, in which the citizens will be placed, and they will be called by these or similar names: they may continue in the same rank, or pass into another in any individual case, on becoming richer from being poorer, or poorer from being richer. The form of law which I should propose as the natural sequel would be as follows:—In a state which is desirous of being saved from the greatest of all plagues—not faction, but rather distraction;—there should exist among the citizens neither extreme poverty, nor, again, excess of wealth, for both are productive of both these evils. Now the legislator should determine what is to be the limit of poverty or wealth. Let the limit of poverty be the value of the lot; this ought to be preserved, and no ruler, nor any one else who aspires after a reputation for virtue, will allow the lot to be impaired in any case. This the legislator gives as a measure, and he will permit a man to acquire double or triple, or as much as four times the amount of this (compare Arist. Pol.). But if a person have yet greater riches, whether he has found them, or they have been given to him, or he has made them in business, or has acquired by any stroke of fortune that which is in excess of the measure, if he give back the surplus to the state, and to the Gods who are the patrons of the state, he shall suffer no penalty or loss of reputation; but if he disobeys this our law, any one who likes may inform against him and receive half the value of the excess, and the delinquent shall pay a sum equal to the excess out of his own property, and the other half of the excess shall belong to the Gods. And let every possession of every man, with the exception of the lot, be publicly registered before the magistrates whom the law appoints, so that all suits about money may be easy and quite simple.

The next thing to be noted is, that the city should be placed as nearly as possible in the centre of the country; we should choose a place which possesses what is suitable for a city, and this may easily be imagined and described. Then we will divide the city into twelve portions, first founding temples to Hestia, to Zeus and to Athene, in a spot which we will call the Acropolis, and surround with a circular wall, making the division of the entire city and country radiate from this point. The twelve portions shall be equalized by the provision that those which are of good land shall be smaller, while those of inferior quality shall be larger. The number of the lots shall be 5040, and each of them shall be divided into two, and every allotment shall be composed of two such sections; one of land near the city, the other of land which is at a distance (compare Arist. Pol.). This arrangement shall be carried out in the following manner: The section which is near the city shall be added to that which is on the borders, and form one lot, and the portion which is next nearest shall be added to the portion which is next farthest; and so of the rest. Moreover, in the two sections of the lots the same principle of equalization of the soil ought to be maintained; the badness and goodness shall be compensated by more and less. And the legislator shall divide the citizens into twelve parts, and arrange the rest of their property, as far as possible, so as to form twelve equal parts; and there shall be a registration of all. After this they shall assign twelve lots to twelve Gods, and call them by their names, and dedicate to each God their several portions, and call the tribes after them. And they shall distribute the twelve divisions of the city in the same way in which they divided the country; and every man shall have two habitations, one in the centre of the country, and the other at the extremity. Enough of the manner of settlement.

Now we ought by all means to consider that there can never be such a happy concurrence of circumstances as we have described; neither can all things coincide as they are wanted. Men who will not take offence at such a mode of living together, and will endure all their life long to have their property fixed at a moderate limit, and to beget children in accordance with our ordinances, and will allow themselves to be deprived of gold and other things which the legislator, as is evident from these enactments, will certainly forbid them; and will endure, further, the situation of the land with the city in the middle and dwellings round about;—all this is as if the legislator were telling his dreams, or making a city and citizens of wax. There is truth in these objections, and therefore every one should take to heart what I am going to say. Once more, then, the legislator shall appear and address us:—'O my friends,' he will say to us, 'do not suppose me ignorant that there is a certain degree of truth in your words; but I am of opinion that, in matters which are not present but future, he who exhibits a pattern of that at which he aims, should in nothing fall short of the fairest and truest; and that if he finds any part of this work impossible of execution he should avoid and not execute it, but he should contrive to carry out that which is nearest and most akin to it; you must allow the legislator to perfect his design, and when it is perfected, you should join with him in considering what part of his legislation is expedient and what will arouse opposition; for surely the artist who is to be deemed worthy of any regard at all, ought always to make his work self-consistent.'

Having determined that there is to be a distribution into twelve parts, let us now see in what way this may be accomplished. There is no difficulty in perceiving that the twelve parts admit of the greatest number of divisions of that which they include, or in seeing the other numbers which are consequent upon them, and are produced out of them up to 5040; wherefore the law ought to order phratries and demes and villages, and also military ranks and movements, as well as coins and measures, dry and liquid, and weights, so as to be commensurable and agreeable to one another. Nor should we fear the appearance of minuteness, if the law commands that all the vessels which a man possesses should have a common measure, when we consider generally that the divisions and variations of numbers have a use in respect of all the variations of which they are susceptible, both in themselves and as measures of height and depth, and in all sounds, and in motions, as well those which proceed in a straight direction, upwards or downwards, as in those which go round and round. The legislator is to consider all these things and to bid the citizens, as far as possible, not to lose sight of numerical order; for no single instrument of youthful education has such mighty power, both as regards domestic economy and politics, and in the arts, as the study of arithmetic. Above all, arithmetic stirs up him who is by nature sleepy and dull, and makes him quick to learn, retentive, shrewd, and aided by art divine he makes progress quite beyond his natural powers (compare Republic). All such things, if only the legislator, by other laws and institutions, can banish meanness and covetousness from the souls of men, so that they can use them properly and to their own good, will be excellent and suitable instruments of education. But if he cannot, he will unintentionally create in them, instead of wisdom, the habit of craft, which evil tendency may be observed in the Egyptians and Phoenicians, and many other races, through the general vulgarity of their pursuits and acquisitions, whether some unworthy legislator of theirs has been the cause, or some impediment of chance or nature. For we must not fail to observe, O Megillus and Cleinias, that there is a difference in places, and that some beget better men and others worse; and we must legislate accordingly. Some places are subject to strange and fatal influences by reason of diverse winds and violent heats, some by reason of waters; or, again, from the character of the food given by the earth, which not only affects the bodies of men for good or evil, but produces similar results in their souls. And in all such qualities those spots excel in which there is a divine inspiration, and in which the demigods have their appointed lots, and are propitious, not adverse, to the settlers in them. To all these matters the legislator, if he have any sense in him, will attend as far as man can, and frame his laws accordingly. And this is what you, Cleinias, must do, and to matters of this kind you must turn your mind since you are going to colonize a new country.

CLEINIAS: Your words, Athenian Stranger, are excellent, and I will do as you say.

BOOK VI.

ATHENIAN: And now having made an end of the preliminaries we will proceed to the appointment of magistracies.

CLEINIAS: Very good.

ATHENIAN: In the ordering of a state there are two parts: first, the number of the magistracies, and the mode of establishing them; and, secondly, when they have been established, laws again will have to be provided for each of them, suitable in nature and number. But before electing the magistrates let us stop a little and say a word in season about the election of them.

CLEINIAS: What have you got to say?

ATHENIAN: This is what I have to say;—every one can see, that although the work of legislation is a most important matter, yet if a well-ordered city superadd to good laws unsuitable offices, not only will there be no use in having the good laws,—not only will they be ridiculous and useless, but the greatest political injury and evil will accrue from them.

CLEINIAS: Of course.

ATHENIAN: Then now, my friend, let us observe what will happen in the constitution of out intended state. In the first place, you will acknowledge that those who are duly appointed to magisterial power, and their families, should severally have given satisfactory proof of what they are, from youth upward until the time of election; in the next place, those who are to elect should have been trained in habits of law, and be well educated, that they may have a right judgment, and may be able to select or reject men whom they approve or disapprove, as they are worthy of either. But how can we imagine that those who are brought together for the first time, and are strangers to one another, and also uneducated, will avoid making mistakes in the choice of magistrates?

CLEINIAS: Impossible.

ATHENIAN: The matter is serious, and excuses will not serve the turn. I will tell you, then, what you and I will have to do, since you, as you tell me, with nine others, have offered to settle the new state on behalf of the people of Crete, and I am to help you by the invention of the present romance. I certainly should not like to leave the tale wandering all over the world without a head;—a headless monster is such a hideous thing.

CLEINIAS: Excellent, Stranger.

ATHENIAN: Yes; and I will be as good as my word.

CLEINIAS: Let us by all means do as you propose.

ATHENIAN: That we will, by the grace of God, if old age will only permit us.

CLEINIAS: But God will be gracious.

ATHENIAN: Yes; and under his guidance let us consider a further point.

CLEINIAS: What is it?

ATHENIAN: Let us remember what a courageously mad and daring creation this our city is.

CLEINIAS: What had you in your mind when you said that?

ATHENIAN: I had in my mind the free and easy manner in which we are ordaining that the inexperienced colonists shall receive our laws. Now a man need not be very wise, Cleinias, in order to see that no one can easily receive laws at their first imposition. But if we could anyhow wait until those who have been imbued with them from childhood, and have been nurtured in them, and become habituated to them, take their part in the public elections of the state; I say, if this could be accomplished, and rightly accomplished by any way or contrivance—then, I think that there would be very little danger, at the end of the time, of a state thus trained not being permanent.

CLEINIAS: A reasonable supposition.

ATHENIAN: Then let us consider if we can find any way out of the difficulty; for I maintain, Cleinias, that the Cnosians, above all the other Cretans, should not be satisfied with barely discharging their duty to the colony, but they ought to take the utmost pains to establish the offices which are first created by them in the best and surest manner. Above all, this applies to the selection of the guardians of the law, who must be chosen first of all, and with the greatest care; the others are of less importance.

CLEINIAS: What method can we devise of electing them?

ATHENIAN: This will be the method:—Sons of the Cretans, I shall say to them, inasmuch as the Cnosians have precedence over the other states, they should, in common with those who join this settlement, choose a body of thirty-seven in all, nineteen of them being taken from the settlers, and the remainder from the citizens of Cnosus. Of these latter the Cnosians shall make a present to your colony, and you yourself shall be one of the eighteen, and shall become a citizen of the new state; and if you and they cannot be persuaded to go, the Cnosians may fairly use a little violence in order to make you.

CLEINIAS: But why, Stranger, do not you and Megillus take a part in our new city?

ATHENIAN: O, Cleinias, Athens is proud, and Sparta too; and they are both a long way off. But you and likewise the other colonists are conveniently situated as you describe. I have been speaking of the way in which the new citizens may be best managed under present circumstances; but in after-ages, if the city continues to exist, let the election be on this wise. All who are horse or foot soldiers, or have seen military service at the proper ages when they were severally fitted for it (compare Arist. Pol.), shall share in the election of magistrates; and the election shall be held in whatever temple the state deems most venerable, and every one shall carry his vote to the altar of the God, writing down on a tablet the name of the person for whom he votes, and his father's name, and his tribe, and ward; and at the side he shall write his own name in like manner. Any one who pleases may take away any tablet which he does not think properly filled up, and exhibit it in the Agora for a period of not less than thirty days. The tablets which are judged to be first, to the number of 300, shall be shown by the magistrates to the whole city, and the citizens shall in like manner select from these the candidates whom they prefer; and this second selection, to the number of 100, shall be again exhibited to the citizens; in the third, let any one who pleases select whom he pleases out of the 100, walking through the parts of victims, and let them choose for magistrates and proclaim the seven-and-thirty who have the greatest number of votes. But who, Cleinias and Megillus, will order for us in the colony all this matter of the magistrates, and the scrutinies of them? If we reflect, we shall see that cities which are in process of construction like ours must have some such persons, who cannot possibly be elected before there are any magistrates; and yet they must be elected in some way, and they are not to be inferior men, but the best possible. For as the proverb says, 'a good beginning is half the business'; and 'to have begun well' is praised by all, and in my opinion is a great deal more than half the business, and has never been praised by any one enough.

CLEINIAS: That is very true.

ATHENIAN: Then let us recognize the difficulty, and make clear to our own minds how the beginning is to be accomplished. There is only one proposal which I have to offer, and that is one which, under our circumstances, is both necessary and expedient.

CLEINIAS: What is it?

ATHENIAN: I maintain that this colony of ours has a father and mother, who are no other than the colonizing state. Well I know that many colonies have been, and will be, at enmity with their parents. But in early days the child, as in a family, loves and is beloved; even if there come a time later when the tie is broken, still, while he is in want of education, he naturally loves his parents and is beloved by them, and flies to his relatives for protection, and finds in them his only natural allies in time of need; and this parental feeling already exists in the Cnosians, as is shown by their care of the new city; and there is a similar feeling on the part of the young city towards Cnosus. And I repeat what I was saying—for there is no harm in repeating a good thing—that the Cnosians should take a common interest in all these matters, and choose, as far as they can, the eldest and best of the colonists, to the number of not less than a hundred; and let there be another hundred of the Cnosians themselves. These, I say, on their arrival, should have a joint care that the magistrates should be appointed according to law, and that when they are appointed they should undergo a scrutiny. When this has been effected, the Cnosians shall return home, and the new city do the best she can for her own preservation and happiness. I would have the seven-and-thirty now, and in all future time, chosen to fulfil the following duties:—Let them, in the first place, be the guardians of the law; and, secondly, of the registers in which each one registers before the magistrate the amount of his property, excepting four minae which are allowed to citizens of the first class, three allowed to the second, two to the third, and a single mina to the fourth. And if any one, despising the laws for the sake of gain, be found to possess anything more which has not been registered, let all that he has in excess be confiscated, and let him be liable to a suit which shall be the reverse of honourable or fortunate. And let any one who will, indict him on the charge of loving base gains, and proceed against him before the guardians of the law. And if he be cast, let him lose his share of the public possessions, and when there is any public distribution, let him have nothing but his original lot; and let him be written down a condemned man as long as he lives, in some place in which any one who pleases can read about his offences. The guardian of the law shall not hold office longer than twenty years, and shall not be less than fifty years of age when he is elected; or if he is elected when he is sixty years of age, he shall hold office for ten years only; and upon the same principle, he must not imagine that he will be permitted to hold such an important office as that of guardian of the laws after he is seventy years of age, if he live so long.

These are the three first ordinances about the guardians of the law; as the work of legislation progresses, each law in turn will assign to them their further duties. And now we may proceed in order to speak of the election of other officers; for generals have to be elected, and these again must have their ministers, commanders, and colonels of horse, and commanders of brigades of foot, who would be more rightly called by their popular name of brigadiers. The guardians of the law shall propose as generals men who are natives of the city, and a selection from the candidates proposed shall be made by those who are or have been of the age for military service. And if one who is not proposed is thought by somebody to be better than one who is, let him name whom he prefers in the place of whom, and make oath that he is better, and propose him; and whichever of them is approved by vote shall be admitted to the final selection; and the three who have the greatest number of votes shall be appointed generals, and superintendents of military affairs, after previously undergoing a scrutiny, like the guardians of the law. And let the generals thus elected propose twelve brigadiers, one for each tribe; and there shall be a right of counter-proposal as in the case of the generals, and the voting and decision shall take place in the same way. Until the prytanes and council are elected, the guardians of the law shall convene the assembly in some holy spot which is suitable to the purpose, placing the hoplites by themselves, and the cavalry by themselves, and in a third division all the rest of the army. All are to vote for the generals (and for the colonels of horse), but the brigadiers are to be voted for only by those who carry shields (i.e. the hoplites). Let the body of cavalry choose phylarchs for the generals; but captains of light troops, or archers, or any other division of the army, shall be appointed by the generals for themselves. There only remains the appointment of officers of cavalry: these shall be proposed by the same persons who proposed the generals, and the election and the counter-proposal of other candidates shall be arranged in the same way as in the case of the generals, and let the cavalry vote and the infantry look on at the election; the two who have the greatest number of votes shall be the leaders of all the horse. Disputes about the voting may be raised once or twice; but if the dispute be raised a third time, the officers who preside at the several elections shall decide.

The council shall consist of 30 x 12 members—360 will be a convenient number for sub-division. If we divide the whole number into four parts of ninety each, we get ninety counsellors for each class. First, all the citizens shall select candidates from the first class; they shall be compelled to vote, and, if they do not, shall be duly fined. When the candidates have been selected, some one shall mark them down; this shall be the business of the first day. And on the following day, candidates shall be selected from the second class in the same manner and under the same conditions as on the previous day; and on the third day a selection shall be made from the third class, at which every one may, if he likes vote, and the three first classes shall be compelled to vote; but the fourth and lowest class shall be under no compulsion, and any member of this class who does not vote shall not be punished. On the fourth day candidates shall be selected from the fourth and smallest class; they shall be selected by all, but he who is of the fourth class shall suffer no penalty, nor he who is of the third, if he be not willing to vote; but he who is of the first or second class, if he does not vote shall be punished;—he who is of the second class shall pay a fine of triple the amount which was exacted at first, and he who is of the first class quadruple. On the fifth day the rulers shall bring out the names noted down, for all the citizens to see, and every man shall choose out of them, under pain, if he do not, of suffering the first penalty;

and when they have chosen 180 out of each of the classes, they shall choose one-half of them by lot, who shall undergo a scrutiny:—These are to form the council for the year.

The mode of election which has been described is in a mean between monarchy and democracy, and such a mean the state ought always to observe; for servants and masters never can be friends, nor good and bad, merely because they are declared to have equal privileges. For to unequals equals become unequal, if they are not harmonised by measure; and both by reason of equality, and by reason of inequality, cities are filled with seditions. The old saying, that 'equality makes friendship,' is happy and also true; but there is obscurity and confusion as to what sort of equality is meant. For there are two equalities which are called by the same name, but are in reality in many ways almost the opposite of one another; one of them may be introduced without difficulty, by any state or any legislator in the distribution of honours: this is the rule of measure, weight, and number, which regulates and apportions them. But there is another equality, of a better and higher kind, which is not so easily recognized. This is the judgment of Zeus; among men it avails but little; that little, however, is the source of the greatest good to individuals and states. For it gives to the greater more, and to the inferior less and in proportion to the nature of each; and, above all, greater honour always to the greater virtue, and to the less less; and to either in proportion to their respective measure of virtue and education. And this is justice, and is ever the true principle of states, at which we ought to aim, and according to this rule order the new city which is now being founded, and any other city which may be hereafter founded. To this the legislator should look,—not to the interests of tyrants one or more, or to the power of the people, but to justice always; which, as I was saying, is the distribution of natural equality among unequals in each case. But there are times at which every state is compelled to use the words, 'just,' 'equal,' in a secondary sense, in the hope of escaping in some degree from factions. For equity and indulgence are infractions of the perfect and strict rule of justice. And this is the reason why we are obliged to use the equality of the lot, in order to avoid the discontent of the people; and so we invoke God and fortune in our prayers, and beg that they themselves will direct the lot with a view to supreme justice. And therefore, although we are compelled to use both equalities, we should use that into which the element of chance enters as seldom as possible.

Thus, O my friends, and for the reasons given, should a state act which would endure and be saved. But as a ship sailing on the sea has to be watched night and day, in like manner a city also is sailing on a sea of politics, and is liable to all sorts of insidious assaults; and therefore from morning to night, and from night to morning, rulers must join hands with rulers, and watchers with watchers, receiving and giving up their trust in a perpetual succession. Now a multitude can never fulfil a duty of this sort with anything like energy. Moreover, the greater number of the senators will have to be left during the greater part of the year to order their concerns at their own homes. They will therefore have to be arranged in twelve portions, answering to the twelve months, and furnish guardians of the state, each portion for a single month. Their business is to be at hand and receive any foreigner or citizen who comes to them, whether to give information, or to put one of those questions, to which, when asked by other cities, a city should give an answer, and to which, if she ask them herself, she should receive an answer; or again, when there is a likelihood of internal commotions, which are always liable to happen in some form or other, they will, if they can, prevent their occurring; or if they have already occurred, will lose no time in making them known to the city, and healing the evil. Wherefore, also, this which is the presiding body of the state ought always to have the control of their assemblies, and of the dissolutions of them, ordinary as well as extraordinary. All this is to be ordered by the twelfth part of the council, which is always to keep watch together with the other officers of the state during one portion of the year, and to rest during the remaining eleven portions.

Thus will the city be fairly ordered. And now, who is to have the superintendence of the country, and what shall be the arrangement? Seeing that the whole city and the entire country have been both of them divided into twelve portions, ought there not to be appointed superintendents of the streets of the city, and of the houses, and buildings, and harbours, and the agora, and fountains, and sacred domains, and temples, and the like?

CLEINIAS: To be sure there ought.

ATHENIAN: Let us assume, then, that there ought to be servants of the temples, and priests and priestesses. There must also be superintendents of roads and buildings, who will have a care of men, that they may do no harm, and also of beasts, both within the enclosure and in the suburbs. Three kinds of officers will thus have to be appointed, in order that the city may be suitably provided according to her needs. Those who have the care of the city shall be called wardens of the city; and those who have the care of the agora shall be called wardens of the agora; and those who have the care of the temples shall be called priests. Those who hold hereditary offices as priests or priestesses, shall not be disturbed; but if there be few or none such, as is probable at the foundation of a new city, priests and priestesses shall be appointed to be servants of the Gods who have no servants. Some of our officers shall be elected, and others appointed by lot, those who are of the people and those who are not of the people mingling in a friendly manner in every place and city, that the state may be as far as possible of one mind. The officers of the temples shall be appointed by lot; in this way their election will be committed to God, that He may do what is agreeable to Him. And he who obtains a lot shall undergo a scrutiny, first, as to whether he is sound of body and of legitimate birth; and in the second place, in order to show that he is of a perfectly pure family, not stained with homicide or any similar impiety in his own person, and also that his father and mother have led a similar unstained life. Now the laws about all divine things should be brought from Delphi, and interpreters appointed, under whose direction they should be used. The tenure of the priesthood should always be for a year and no longer; and he who will duly execute the sacred office, according to the laws of religion, must be not less than sixty years of age—the laws shall be the same about priestesses. As for the interpreters, they shall be appointed thus:—Let the twelve tribes be distributed into groups of four, and let each group select four, one out of each tribe within the group, three times; and let the three who have the greatest number of votes (out of the twelve appointed by each group), after undergoing a scrutiny, nine in all, be sent to Delphi, in order that the God may return one out of each triad; their age shall be the same as that of the priests, and the scrutiny of them shall be conducted in the same manner; let them be interpreters for life, and when any one dies let the four tribes select another from the tribe of the deceased. Moreover, besides priests and interpreters, there must be treasurers, who will take charge of the property of the several temples, and of the sacred domains, and shall have authority over the produce and the letting of them; and three of them shall be chosen from the highest classes for the greater temples, and two for the lesser, and one for the least of all; the manner of their election and the scrutiny of them shall be the same as that of the generals. This shall be the order of the temples.

Let everything have a guard as far as possible. Let the defence of the city be commited to the generals, and taxiarchs, and hipparchs, and phylarchs, and prytanes, and the wardens of the city, and of the agora, when the election of them has been completed. The defence of the country shall be provided for as follows:—The entire land has been already distributed into twelve as nearly as possible equal parts, and let the tribe allotted to a division provide annually for it five wardens of the country and commanders of the watch; and let each body of five have the power of selecting twelve others out of the youth of their own tribe,—these shall be not less than twenty-five years of age, and not more than thirty. And let there be allotted to them severally every month the various districts, in order that they may all acquire knowledge and experience of the whole country. The term of service for commanders and for watchers shall continue during two years. After having had their stations allotted to them, they will go from place to place in regular order, making their round from left to right as their commanders direct them; (when I speak of going to the right, I mean that they are to go to the east). And at the commencement of the second year, in order that as many as possible of the guards may not only get a knowledge of the country at any one season of the year, but may also have experience of the manner in which different places are affected at different seasons of the year, their then commanders shall lead them again towards the left, from place to place in succession, until they have completed the second year. In the third year other wardens of the country shall be chosen and commanders of the watch, five for each division, who are to be the superintendents of the bands of twelve. While on service at each station, their attention shall be directed to the following points:—In the first place, they shall see that the country is well protected against enemies; they shall trench and dig wherever this is required, and, as far as they can, they shall by fortifications keep off the evil-disposed, in order to prevent them from doing any harm to the country or the property; they shall use the beasts of burden and the labourers whom they find on the spot: these will be their instruments whom they will superintend, taking them, as far as possible, at the times when they are not engaged in their regular business. They shall make every part of the country inaccessible to enemies, and as accessible as possible to friends (compare Arist. Pol.); there shall be ways for man and beasts of burden and for cattle, and they shall take care to have them always as smooth as they can; and shall provide against the rains doing harm instead of good to the land, when they come down from the mountains into the hollow dells; and shall keep in the overflow by the help of works and ditches, in order that the valleys, receiving and drinking up the rain from heaven, and providing fountains and streams in the fields and regions which lie underneath, may furnish even to the dry places plenty of good water. The fountains of water, whether of rivers or of springs, shall be ornamented with plantations and buildings for beauty; and let them bring together the streams in subterraneous channels, and make all things plenteous; and if there be a sacred grove or dedicated precinct in the neighbourhood, they shall conduct the water to the actual temples of the Gods, and so beautify them at all seasons of the year. Everywhere in such places the youth shall make gymnasia for themselves, and warm baths for the aged, placing by them abundance of dry wood, for the benefit of those labouring under disease—there the weary frame of the rustic, worn with toil, will receive a kindly welcome, far better than he would at the hands of a not over-wise doctor.

The building of these and the like works will be useful and ornamental; they will provide a pleasing amusement, but they will be a serious employment too; for the sixty wardens will have to guard their several divisions, not only with a view to enemies, but also with an eye to professing friends. When a quarrel arises among neighbours or citizens, and any one whether slave or freeman wrongs another, let the five wardens decide small matters on their own authority; but where the charge against another relates to greater matters, the seventeen composed of the fives and twelves, shall determine any charges which one man brings against another, not involving more than three minae. Every judge and magistrate shall be liable to give an account of his conduct in office, except those who, like kings, have the final decision. Moreover, as regards the aforesaid wardens of the country, if they do any wrong to those of whom they have the care, whether by imposing upon them unequal tasks, or by taking the produce of the soil or implements of husbandry without their consent; also if they receive anything in the way of a bribe, or decide suits unjustly, or if they yield to the influences of flattery, let them be publicly dishonoured; and in regard to any other wrong which they do to the inhabitants of the country, if the question be of a mina, let them submit to the decision of the villagers in the neighbourhood; but in suits of greater amount, or in case of lesser, if they refuse to submit, trusting that their monthly removal into another part of the country will enable them to escape—in such cases the injured party may bring his suit in the common court, and if he obtain a verdict he may exact from the defendant, who refused to submit, a double penalty.

The wardens and the overseers of the country, while on their two years' service, shall have common meals at their several stations, and shall all live together; and he who is absent from the common meal, or sleeps out, if only for one day or night, unless by order of his commanders, or by reason of absolute necessity, if the five denounce him and inscribe his name in the agora as not having kept his guard, let him be deemed to have betrayed the city, as far as lay in his power, and let him be disgraced and beaten with impunity by any one who meets him and is willing to punish him. If any of the commanders is guilty of such an irregularity, the whole company of sixty shall see to it, and he who is cognisant of the offence, and does not bring the offender to trial, shall be amenable to the same laws as the younger offender himself, and shall pay a heavier fine, and be incapable of ever commanding the young. The guardians of the law are to be careful inspectors of these matters, and shall either prevent or punish offenders. Every man should remember the universal rule, that he who is not a good servant will not be a good master; a man should pride himself more upon serving well than upon commanding well: first upon serving the laws, which is also the service of the Gods; in the second place, upon having served ancient and honourable men in the days of his youth. Furthermore, during the two years in which any one is a warden of the country, his daily food ought to be of a simple and humble kind. When the twelve have been chosen, let them and the five meet together, and determine that they will be their own servants, and, like servants, will not have other slaves and servants for their own use, neither will they use those of the villagers and husbandmen for their private advantage, but for the public service only; and in general they should make up their minds to live independently by themselves, servants of each other and of themselves. Further, at all seasons of the year, summer and winter alike, let them be under arms and survey minutely the whole country; thus they will at once keep guard, and at the same time acquire a perfect knowledge of every locality. There can be no more important kind of information than the exact knowledge of a man's own country; and for this as well as for more general reasons of pleasure and advantage, hunting with dogs and other kinds of sports should be pursued by the young. The service to whom this is committed may be called the secret police or wardens of the country; the name does not much signify, but every one who has the safety of the state at heart will use his utmost diligence in this service.

After the wardens of the country, we have to speak of the election of wardens of the agora and of the city. The wardens of the country were sixty in number, and the wardens of the city will be three, and will divide the twelve parts of the city into three; like the former, they shall have care of the ways, and of the different high roads which lead out of the country into the city, and of the buildings, that they may be all made according to law;—also of the waters, which the guardians of the supply preserve and convey to them, care being taken that they may reach the fountains pure and abundant, and be both an ornament and a benefit to the city. These also should be men of influence, and at leisure to take care of the public interest. Let every man propose as warden of the city any one whom he likes out of the highest class, and when the vote has been given on them, and the number is reduced to the six who have the greatest number of votes, let the electing officers choose by lot three out of the six, and when they have undergone a scrutiny let them hold office according to the laws laid down for them. Next, let the wardens of the agora be elected in like manner, out of the first and second class, five in number: ten are to be first elected, and out of the ten five are to be chosen by lot, as in the election of the wardens of the city:—these when they have undergone a scrutiny are to be declared magistrates. Every one shall vote for every one, and he who will not vote, if he be informed against before the magistrates, shall be fined fifty drachmae, and shall also be deemed a bad citizen. Let any one who likes go to the assembly and to the general council; it shall be compulsory to go on citizens of the first and second class, and they shall pay a fine of ten drachmae if they be found not answering to their names at the assembly. But the third and fourth class shall be under no compulsion, and shall be let off without a fine, unless the magistrates have commanded all to be present, in consequence of some urgent necessity. The wardens of the agora shall observe the order appointed by law for the agora, and shall have the charge of the temples and fountains which are in the agora; and they shall see that no one injures anything, and punish him who does, with stripes and bonds, if he be a slave or stranger; but if he be a citizen who misbehaves in this way, they shall have the power themselves of inflicting a fine upon him to the amount of a hundred drachmae, or with the consent of the wardens of the city up to double that amount. And let the wardens of the city have a similar power of imposing punishments and fines in their own department; and let them impose fines by their own department; and let them impose fines by their own authority, up to a mina, or up to two minae with the consent of the wardens of the agora.

In the next place, it will be proper to appoint directors of music and gymnastic, two kinds of each—of the one kind the business will be education, of the other, the superintendence of contests. In speaking of education, the law means to speak of those who have the care of order and instruction in gymnasia and schools, and of the going to school, and of school buildings for boys and girls; and in speaking of contests, the law refers to the judges of gymnastics and of music; these again are divided into two classes, the one having to do with music, the other with gymnastics; and the same who judge of the gymnastic contests of men, shall judge of horses; but in music there shall be one set of judges of solo singing, and of imitation—I mean of rhapsodists, players on the harp, the flute and the like, and another who shall judge of choral song. First of all, we must choose directors for the choruses of boys, and men, and maidens, whom they shall follow in the amusement of the dance, and for our other musical arrangements;—one director will be enough for the choruses, and he should be not less than forty years of age. One director will also be enough to introduce the solo singers, and to give judgment on the competitors, and he ought not to be less than thirty years of age. The director and manager of the choruses shall be elected after the following manner:—Let any persons who commonly take an interest in such matters go to the meeting, and be fined if they do not go (the guardians of the law shall judge of their fault), but those who have no interest shall not be compelled.

The elector shall propose as director some one who understands music, and he in the scrutiny may be challenged on the one part by those who say he has no skill, and defended on the other hand by those who say that he has. Ten are to be elected by vote, and he of the ten who is chosen by lot shall undergo a scrutiny, and lead the choruses for a year according to law. And in like manner the competitor who wins the lot shall be leader of the solo and concert music for that year; and he who is thus elected shall deliver the award to the judges. In the next place, we have to choose judges in the contests of horses and of men; these shall be selected from the third and also from the second class of citizens, and three first classes shall be compelled to go to the election, but the lowest may stay away with impunity; and let there be three elected by lot out of the twenty who have been chosen previously, and they must also have the vote and approval of the examiners. But if any one is rejected in the scrutiny at any ballot or decision, others shall be chosen in the same manner, and undergo a similar scrutiny.

There remains the minister of the education of youth, male and female; he too will rule according to law; one such minister will be sufficient, and he must be fifty years old, and have children lawfully begotten, both boys and girls by preference, at any rate, one or the other. He who is elected, and he who is the elector, should consider that of all the great offices of state this is the greatest; for the first shoot of any plant, if it makes a good start towards the attainment of its natural excellence, has the greatest effect on its maturity; and this is not only true of plants, but of animals wild and tame, and also of men. Man, as we say, is a tame or civilized animal; nevertheless, he requires proper instruction and a fortunate nature, and then of all animals he becomes the most divine and most civilized (Arist. Pol.); but if he be insufficiently or ill educated he is the most savage of earthly creatures. Wherefore the legislator ought not to allow the education of children to become a secondary or accidental matter. In the first place, he who would be rightly provident about them, should begin by taking care that he is elected, who of all the citizens is in every way best; him the legislator shall do his utmost to appoint guardian and superintendent. To this end all the magistrates, with the exception of the council and prytanes, shall go to the temple of Apollo, and elect by ballot him of the guardians of the law whom they severally think will be the best superintendent of education. And he who has the greatest number of votes, after he has undergone a scrutiny at the hands of all the magistrates who have been his electors, with the exception of the guardians of the law,—shall hold office for five years; and in the sixth year let another be chosen in like manner to fill his office.

If any one dies while he is holding a public office, and more than thirty days before his term of office expires, let those whose business it is elect another to the office in the same manner as before. And if any one who is entrusted with orphans dies, let the relations both on the father's and mother's side, who are residing at home, including cousins, appoint another guardian within ten days, or be fined a drachma a day for neglect to do so.

A city which has no regular courts of law ceases to be a city; and again, if a judge is silent and says no more in preliminary proceedings than the litigants, as is the case in arbitrations, he will never be able to decide justly; wherefore a multitude of judges will not easily judge well, nor a few if they are bad. The point in dispute between the parties should be made clear; and time, and deliberation, and repeated examination, greatly tend to clear up doubts. For this reason, he who goes to law with another, should go first of all to his neighbours and friends who know best the questions at issue. And if he be unable to obtain from them a satisfactory decision, let him have recourse to another court; and if the two courts cannot settle the matter, let a third put an end to the suit.

Now the establishment of courts of justice may be regarded as a choice of magistrates, for every magistrate must also be a judge of some things; and the judge, though he be not a magistrate, yet in certain respects is a very important magistrate on the day on which he is determining a suit. Regarding then the judges also as magistrates, let us say who are fit to be judges, and of what they are to be judges, and how many of them are to judge in each suit. Let that be the supreme tribunal which the litigants appoint in common for themselves, choosing certain persons by agreement. And let there be two other tribunals: one for private causes, when a citizen accuses another of wronging him and wishes to get a decision; the other for public causes, in which some citizen is of opinion that the public has been wronged by an individual, and is willing to vindicate the common interests. And we must not forget to mention how the judges are to be qualified, and who they are to be. In the first place, let there be a tribunal open to all private persons who are trying causes one against another for the third time, and let this be composed as follows:—All the officers of state, as well annual as those holding office for a longer period, when the new year is about to commence, in the month following after the summer solstice, on the last day but one of the year, shall meet in some temple, and calling God to witness, shall dedicate one judge from every magistracy to be their first-fruits, choosing in each office him who seems to them to be the best, and whom they deem likely to decide the causes of his fellow-citizens during the ensuing year in the best and holiest manner. And when the election is completed, a scrutiny shall be held in the presence of the electors themselves, and if any one be rejected another shall be chosen in the same manner. Those who have undergone the scrutiny shall judge the causes of those who have declined the inferior courts, and shall give their vote openly. The councillors and other magistrates who have elected them shall be required to be hearers and spectators of the causes; and any one else may be present who pleases. If one man charges another with having intentionally decided wrong, let him go to the guardians of the law and lay his accusation before them, and he who is found guilty in such a case shall pay damages to the injured party equal to half the injury; but if he shall appear to deserve a greater penalty, the judges shall determine what additional punishment he shall suffer, and how much more he ought to pay to the public treasury, and to the party who brought the suit.

In the judgment of offences against the state, the people ought to participate, for when any one wrongs the state all are wronged, and may reasonably complain if they are not allowed to share in the decision. Such causes ought to originate with the people, and the ought also to have the final decision of them, but the trial of them shall take place before three of the highest magistrates, upon whom the plaintiff and the defendant shall agree; and if they are not able to come to an agreement themselves, the council shall choose one of the two proposed. And in private suits, too, as far as is possible, all should have a share; for he who has no share in the administration of justice, is apt to imagine that he has no share in the state at all. And for this reason there shall be a court of law in every tribe, and the judges shall be chosen by lot;—they shall give their decisions at once, and shall be inaccessible to entreaties. The final judgment shall rest with that court which, as we maintain, has been established in the most incorruptible form of which human things admit: this shall be the court established for those who are unable to get rid of their suits either in the courts of neighbours or of the tribes.

Thus much of the courts of law, which, as I was saying, cannot be precisely defined either as being or not being offices; a superficial sketch has been given of them, in which some things have been told and others omitted. For the right place of an exact statement of the laws respecting suits, under their several heads, will be at the end of the body of legislation;—let us then expect them at the end. Hitherto our legislation has been chiefly occupied with the appointment of offices. Perfect unity and exactness, extending to the whole and every particular of political administration, cannot be attained to the full, until the discussion shall have a beginning, middle, and end, and is complete in every part. At present we have reached the election of magistrates, and this may be regarded as a sufficient termination of what preceded. And now there need no longer be any delay or hesitation in beginning the work of legislation.

CLEINIAS: I like what you have said, Stranger; and I particularly like your manner of tacking on the beginning of your new discourse to the end of the former one.

ATHENIAN: Thus far, then, the old men's rational pastime has gone off well.

CLEINIAS: You mean, I suppose, their serious and noble pursuit?

ATHENIAN: Perhaps; but I should like to know whether you and I are agreed about a certain thing.

CLEINIAS: About what thing?

ATHENIAN: You know the endless labour which painters expend upon their pictures—they are always putting in or taking out colours, or whatever be the term which artists employ; they seem as if they would never cease touching up their works, which are always being made brighter and more beautiful.

CLEINIAS: I know something of these matters from report, although I have never had any great acquaintance with the art.

ATHENIAN: No matter; we may make use of the illustration notwithstanding:—Suppose that some one had a mind to paint a figure in the most beautiful manner, in the hope that his work instead of losing would always improve as time went on—do you not see that being a mortal, unless he leaves some one to succeed him who will correct the flaws which time may introduce, and be able to add what is left imperfect through the defect of the artist, and who will further brighten up and improve the picture, all his great labour will last but a short time?

CLEINIAS: True.

ATHENIAN: And is not the aim of the legislator similar? First, he desires that his laws should be written down with all possible exactness; in the second place, as time goes on and he has made an actual trial of his decrees, will he not find omissions? Do you imagine that there ever was a legislator so foolish as not to know that many things are necessarily omitted, which some one coming after him must correct, if the constitution and the order of government is not to deteriorate, but to improve in the state which he has established?

CLEINIAS: Assuredly, that is the sort of thing which every one would desire.

ATHENIAN: And if any one possesses any means of accomplishing this by word or deed, or has any way great or small by which he can teach a person to understand how he can maintain and amend the laws, he should finish what he has to say, and not leave the work incomplete.

CLEINIAS: By all means.

ATHENIAN: And is not this what you and I have to do at the present moment?

CLEINIAS: What have we to do?

ATHENIAN: As we are about to legislate and have chosen our guardians of the law, and are ourselves in the evening of life, and they as compared with us are young men, we ought not only to legislate for them, but to endeavour to make them not only guardians of the law but legislators themselves, as far as this is possible.

CLEINIAS: Certainly; if we can.

ATHENIAN: At any rate, we must do our best.

CLEINIAS: Of course.

ATHENIAN: We will say to them—O friends and saviours of our laws, in laying down any law, there are many particulars which we shall omit, and this cannot be helped; at the same time, we will do our utmost to describe what is important, and will give an outline which you shall fill up. And I will explain on what principle you are to act. Megillus and Cleinias and I have often spoken to one another touching these matters, and we are of opinion that we have spoken well. And we hope that you will be of the same mind with us, and become our disciples, and keep in view the things which in our united opinion the legislator and guardian of the law ought to keep in view. There was one main point about which we were agreed—that a man's whole energies throughout life should be devoted to the acquisition of the virtue proper to a man, whether this was to be gained by study, or habit, or some mode of acquisition, or desire, or opinion, or knowledge—and this applies equally to men and women, old and young—the aim of all should always be such as I have described; anything which may be an impediment, the good man ought to show that he utterly disregards. And if at last necessity plainly compels him to be an outlaw from his native land, rather than bow his neck to the yoke of slavery and be ruled by inferiors, and he has to fly, an exile he must be and endure all such trials, rather than accept another form of government, which is likely to make men worse. These are our original principles; and do you now, fixing your eyes upon the standard of what a man and a citizen ought or ought not to be, praise and blame the laws—blame those which have not this power of making the citizen better, but embrace those which have; and with gladness receive and live in them; bidding a long farewell to other institutions which aim at goods, as they are termed, of a different kind.

Let us proceed to another class of laws, beginning with their foundation in religion. And we must first return to the number 5040—the entire number had, and has, a great many convenient divisions, and the number of the tribes which was a twelfth part of the whole, being correctly formed by 21 x 20 (5040/(21 x 20), i.e., 5040/420 = 12), also has them. And not only is the whole number divisible by twelve, but also the number of each tribe is divisible by twelve. Now every portion should be regarded by us as a sacred gift of Heaven, corresponding to the months and to the revolution of the universe (compare Tim.). Every city has a guiding and sacred principle given by nature, but in some the division or distribution has been more right than in others, and has been more sacred and fortunate. In our opinion, nothing can be more right than the selection of the number 5040, which may be divided by all numbers from one to twelve with the single exception of eleven, and that admits of a very easy correction; for if, turning to the dividend (5040), we deduct two families, the defect in the division is cured. And the truth of this may be easily proved when we have leisure. But for the present, trusting to the mere assertion of this principle, let us divide the state; and assigning to each portion some God or son of a God, let us give them altars and sacred rites, and at the altars let us hold assemblies for sacrifice twice in the month—twelve assemblies for the tribes, and twelve for the city, according to their divisions; the first in honour of the Gods and divine things, and the second to promote friendship and 'better acquaintance,' as the phrase is, and every sort of good fellowship with one another. For people must be acquainted with those into whose families and whom they marry and with those to whom they give in marriage; in such matters, as far as possible, a man should deem it all important to avoid a mistake, and with this serious purpose let games be instituted (compare Republic) in which youths and maidens shall dance together, seeing one another and being seen naked, at a proper age, and on a suitable occasion, not transgressing the rules of modesty.

The directors of choruses will be the superintendents and regulators of these games, and they, together with the guardians of the law, will legislate in any matters which we have omitted; for, as we said, where there are numerous and minute details, the legislator must leave out something. And the annual officers who have experience, and know what is wanted, must make arrangements and improvements year by year, until such enactments and provisions are sufficiently determined. A ten years' experience of sacrifices and dances, if extending to all particulars, will be quite sufficient; and if the legislator be alive they shall communicate with him, but if he be dead then the several officers shall refer the omissions which come under their notice to the guardians of the law, and correct them, until all is perfect; and from that time there shall be no more change, and they shall establish and use the new laws with the others which the legislator originally gave them, and of which they are never, if they can help, to change aught; or, if some necessity overtakes them, the magistrates must be called into counsel, and the whole people, and they must go to all the oracles of the Gods; and if they are all agreed, in that case they may make the change, but if they are not agreed, by no manner of means, and any one who dissents shall prevail, as the law ordains.

Whenever any one over twenty-five years of age, having seen and been seen by others, believes himself to have found a marriage connexion which is to his mind, and suitable for the procreation of children, let him marry if he be still under the age of five-and-thirty years; but let him first hear how he ought to seek after what is suitable and appropriate (compare Arist. Pol.). For, as Cleinias says, every law should have a suitable prelude.

CLEINIAS: You recollect at the right moment, Stranger, and do not miss the opportunity which the argument affords of saying a word in season.

ATHENIAN: I thank you. We will say to him who is born of good parents—O my son, you ought to make such a marriage as wise men would approve. Now they would advise you neither to avoid a poor marriage, nor specially to desire a rich one; but if other things are equal, always to honour inferiors, and with them to form connexions;—this will be for the benefit of the city and of the families which are united; for the equable and symmetrical tends infinitely more to virtue than the unmixed. And he who is conscious of being too headstrong, and carried away more than is fitting in all his actions, ought to desire to become the relation of orderly parents; and he who is of the opposite temper ought to seek the opposite alliance. Let there be one word concerning all marriages:—Every man shall follow, not after the marriage which is most pleasing to himself, but after that which is most beneficial to the state. For somehow every one is by nature prone to that which is likest to himself, and in this way the whole city becomes unequal in property and in disposition; and hence there arise in most states the very results which we least desire to happen. Now, to add to the law an express provision, not only that the rich man shall not marry into the rich family, nor the powerful into the family of the powerful, but that the slower natures shall be compelled to enter into marriage with the quicker, and the quicker with the slower, may awaken anger as well as laughter in the minds of many; for there is a difficulty in perceiving that the city ought to be well mingled like a cup, in which the maddening wine is hot and fiery, but when chastened by a soberer God, receives a fair associate and becomes an excellent and temperate drink (compare Statesman). Yet in marriage no one is able to see that the same result occurs. Wherefore also the law must let alone such matters, but we should try to charm the spirits of men into believing the equability of their children's disposition to be of more importance than equality in excessive fortune when they marry; and him who is too desirous of making a rich marriage we should endeavour to turn aside by reproaches, not, however, by any compulsion of written law.

Let this then be our exhortation concerning marriage, and let us remember what was said before—that a man should cling to immortality, and leave behind him children's children to be the servants of God in his place for ever. All this and much more may be truly said by way of prelude about the duty of marriage. But if a man will not listen, and remains unsocial and alien among his fellow-citizens, and is still unmarried at thirty-five years of age, let him pay a yearly fine;—he who of the highest class shall pay a fine of a hundred drachmae, and he who is of the second class a fine of seventy drachmae; the third class shall pay sixty drachmae, and the fourth thirty drachmae, and let the money be sacred to Here; he who does not pay the fine annually shall owe ten times the sum, which the treasurer of the goddess shall exact; and if he fails in doing so, let him be answerable and give an account of the money at his audit. He who refuses to marry shall be thus punished in money, and also be deprived of all honour which the younger show to the elder; let no young man voluntarily obey him, and, if he attempt to punish any one, let every one come to the rescue and defend the injured person, and he who is present and does not come to the rescue, shall be pronounced by the law to be a coward and a bad citizen. Of the marriage portion I have already spoken; and again I say for the instruction of poor men that he who neither gives nor receives a dowry on account of poverty, has a compensation; for the citizens of our state are provided with the necessaries of life, and wives will be less likely to be insolent, and husbands to be mean and subservient to them on account of property. And he who obeys this law will do a noble action; but he who will not obey, and gives or receives more than fifty drachmae as the price of the marriage garments if he be of the lowest, or more than a mina, or a mina-and-a-half, if he be of the third or second classes, or two minae if he be of the highest class, shall owe to the public treasury a similar sum, and that which is given or received shall be sacred to Here and Zeus; and let the treasurers of these Gods exact the money, as was said before about the unmarried—that the treasurers of Here were to exact the money, or pay the fine themselves.

The betrothal by a father shall be valid in the first degree, that by a grandfather in the second degree, and in the third degree, betrothal by brothers who have the same father; but if there are none of these alive, the betrothal by a mother shall be valid in like manner; in cases of unexampled fatality, the next of kin and the guardians shall have authority. What are to be the rites before marriages, or any other sacred acts, relating either to future, present, or past marriages, shall be referred to the interpreters; and he who follows their advice may be satisfied. Touching the marriage festival, they shall assemble not more than five male and five female friends of both families; and a like number of members of the family of either sex, and no man shall spend more than his means will allow; he who is of the richest class may spend a mina,—he who is of the second, half a mina, and in the same proportion as the census of each decreases: all men shall praise him who is obedient to the law; but he who is disobedient shall be punished by the guardians of the law as a man wanting in true taste, and uninstructed in the laws of bridal song. Drunkenness is always improper, except at the festivals of the God who gave wine; and peculiarly dangerous, when a man is engaged in the business of marriage; at such a crisis of their lives a bride and bridegroom ought to have all their wits about them—they ought to take care that their offspring may be born of reasonable beings; for on what day or night Heaven will give them increase, who can say? Moreover, they ought not to begetting children when their bodies are dissipated by intoxication, but their offspring should be compact and solid, quiet and compounded properly; whereas the drunkard is all abroad in all his actions, and beside himself both in body and soul. Wherefore, also, the drunken man is bad and unsteady in sowing the seed of increase, and is likely to beget offspring who will be unstable and untrustworthy, and cannot be expected to walk straight either in body or mind. Hence during the whole year and all his life long, and especially while he is begetting children, he ought to take care and not intentionally do what is injurious to health, or what involves insolence and wrong; for he cannot help leaving the impression of himself on the souls and bodies of his offspring, and he begets children in every way inferior. And especially on the day and night of marriage should a man abstain from such things. For the beginning, which is also a God dwelling in man, preserves all things, if it meet with proper respect from each individual. He who marries is further to consider, that one of the two houses in the lot is the nest and nursery of his young, and there he is to marry and make a home for himself and bring up his children, going away from his father and mother. For in friendships there must be some degree of desire, in order to cement and bind together diversities of character; but excessive intercourse not having the desire which is created by time, insensibly dissolves friendships from a feeling of satiety; wherefore a man and his wife shall leave to his and her father and mother their own dwelling-places, and themselves go as to a colony and dwell there, and visit and be visited by their parents; and they shall beget and bring up children, handing on the torch of life from one generation to another, and worshipping the Gods according to law for ever.

In the next place, we have to consider what sort of property will be most convenient. There is no difficulty either in understanding or acquiring most kinds of property, but there is great difficulty in what relates to slaves. And the reason is, that we speak about them in a way which is right and which is not right; for what we say about our slaves is consistent and also inconsistent with our practice about them.

MEGILLUS: I do not understand, Stranger, what you mean.

ATHENIAN: I am not surprised, Megillus, for the state of the Helots among the Lacedaemonians is of all Hellenic forms of slavery the most controverted and disputed about, some approving and some condemning it; there is less dispute about the slavery which exists among the Heracleots, who have subjugated the Mariandynians, and about the Thessalian Penestae. Looking at these and the like examples, what ought we to do concerning property in slaves? I made a remark, in passing, which naturally elicited a question about my meaning from you. It was this:—We know that all would agree that we should have the best and most attached slaves whom we can get. For many a man has found his slaves better in every way than brethren or sons, and many times they have saved the lives and property of their masters and their whole house—such tales are well known.

MEGILLUS: To be sure.

ATHENIAN: But may we not also say that the soul of the slave is utterly corrupt, and that no man of sense ought to trust them? And the wisest of our poets, speaking of Zeus, says:

'Far-seeing Zeus takes away half the understanding of men whom the day of slavery subdues.'

Different persons have got these two different notions of slaves in their minds—some of them utterly distrust their servants, and, as if they were wild beasts, chastise them with goads and whips, and make their souls three times, or rather many times, as slavish as they were before;—and others do just the opposite.

MEGILLUS: True.

CLEINIAS: Then what are we to do in our own country, Stranger, seeing that there are such differences in the treatment of slaves by their owners?

ATHENIAN: Well, Cleinias, there can be no doubt that man is a troublesome animal, and therefore he is not very manageable, nor likely to become so, when you attempt to introduce the necessary division of slave, and freeman, and master.

CLEINIAS: That is obvious.

ATHENIAN: He is a troublesome piece of goods, as has been often shown by the frequent revolts of the Messenians, and the great mischiefs which happen in states having many slaves who speak the same language, and the numerous robberies and lawless life of the Italian banditti, as they are called. A man who considers all this is fairly at a loss. Two remedies alone remain to us,—not to have the slaves of the same country, nor if possible, speaking the same language (compare Aris. Pol.); in this way they will more easily be held in subjection: secondly, we should tend them carefully, not only out of regard to them, but yet more out of respect to ourselves. And the right treatment of slaves is to behave properly to them, and to do to them, if possible, even more justice than to those who are our equals; for he who naturally and genuinely reverences justice, and hates injustice, is discovered in his dealings with any class of men to whom he can easily be unjust. And he who in regard to the natures and actions of his slaves is undefiled by impiety and injustice, will best sow the seeds of virtue in them; and this may be truly said of every master, and tyrant, and of every other having authority in relation to his inferiors. Slaves ought to be punished as they deserve, and not admonished as if they were freemen, which will only make them conceited. The language used to a servant ought always to be that of a command (compare Arist. Pol.), and we ought not to jest with them, whether they are males or females—this is a foolish way which many people have of setting up their slaves, and making the life of servitude more disagreeable both for them and for their masters.

CLEINIAS: True.

ATHENIAN: Now that each of the citizens is provided, as far as possible, with a sufficient number of suitable slaves who can help him in what he has to do, we may next proceed to describe their dwellings.

CLEINIAS: Very good.

ATHENIAN: The city being new and hitherto uninhabited, care ought to be taken of all the buildings, and the manner of building each of them, and also of the temples and walls. These, Cleinias, were matters which properly came before the marriages;—but, as we are only talking, there is no objection to changing the order. If, however, our plan of legislation is ever to take effect, then the house shall precede the marriage if God so will, and afterwards we will come to the regulations about marriage; but at present we are only describing these matters in a general outline.

CLEINIAS: Quite true.

ATHENIAN: The temples are to be placed all round the agora, and the whole city built on the heights in a circle (compare Arist. Pol.), for the sake of defence and for the sake of purity. Near the temples are to be placed buildings for the magistrates and the courts of law; in these plaintiff and defendant will receive their due, and the places will be regarded as most holy, partly because they have to do with holy things: and partly because they are the dwelling-places of holy Gods: and in them will be held the courts in which cases of homicide and other trials of capital offences may fitly take place. As to the walls, Megillus, I agree with Sparta in thinking that they should be allowed to sleep in the earth, and that we should not attempt to disinter them (compare Arist. Pol.); there is a poetical saying, which is finely expressed, that 'walls ought to be of steel and iron, and not of earth;' besides, how ridiculous of us to be sending out our young men annually into the country to dig and to trench, and to keep off the enemy by fortifications, under the idea that they are not to be allowed to set foot in our territory, and then, that we should surround ourselves with a wall, which, in the first place, is by no means conducive to the health of cities, and is also apt to produce a certain effeminacy in the minds of the inhabitants, inviting men to run thither instead of repelling their enemies, and leading them to imagine that their safety is due not to their keeping guard day and night, but that when they are protected by walls and gates, then they may sleep in safety; as if they were not meant to labour, and did not know that true repose comes from labour, and that disgraceful indolence and a careless temper of mind is only the renewal of trouble. But if men must have walls, the private houses ought to be so arranged from the first that the whole city may be one wall, having all the houses capable of defence by reason of their uniformity and equality towards the streets (compare Arist. Pol.). The form of the city being that of a single dwelling will have an agreeable aspect, and being easily guarded will be infinitely better for security. Until the original building is completed, these should be the principal objects of the inhabitants; and the wardens of the city should superintend the work, and should impose a fine on him who is negligent; and in all that relates to the city they should have a care of cleanliness, and not allow a private person to encroach upon any public property either by buildings or excavations. Further, they ought to take care that the rains from heaven flow off easily, and of any other matters which may have to be administered either within or without the city. The guardians of the law shall pass any further enactments which their experience may show to be necessary, and supply any other points in which the law may be deficient. And now that these matters, and the buildings about the agora, and the gymnasia, and places of instruction, and theatres, are all ready and waiting for scholars and spectators, let us proceed to the subjects which follow marriage in the order of legislation.

CLEINIAS: By all means.

ATHENIAN: Assuming that marriages exist already, Cleinias, the mode of life during the year after marriage, before children are born, will follow next in order. In what way bride and bridegroom ought to live in a city which is to be superior to other cities, is a matter not at all easy for us to determine. There have been many difficulties already, but this will be the greatest of them, and the most disagreeable to the many. Still I cannot but say what appears to me to be right and true, Cleinias.

CLEINIAS: Certainly.

ATHENIAN: He who imagines that he can give laws for the public conduct of states, while he leaves the private life of citizens wholly to take care of itself; who thinks that individuals may pass the day as they please, and that there is no necessity of order in all things; he, I say, who gives up the control of their private lives, and supposes that they will conform to law in their common and public life, is making a great mistake. Why have I made this remark? Why, because I am going to enact that the bridegrooms should live at the common tables, just as they did before marriage. This was a singularity when first enacted by the legislator in your parts of the world, Megillus and Cleinias, as I should suppose, on the occasion of some war or other similar danger, which caused the passing of the law, and which would be likely to occur in thinly-peopled places, and in times of pressure. But when men had once tried and been accustomed to a common table, experience showed that the institution greatly conduced to security; and in some such manner the custom of having common tables arose among you.

CLEINIAS: Likely enough.

ATHENIAN: I said that there may have been singularity and danger in imposing such a custom at first, but that now there is not the same difficulty. There is, however, another institution which is the natural sequel to this, and would be excellent, if it existed anywhere, but at present it does not. The institution of which I am about to speak is not easily described or executed; and would be like the legislator 'combing wool into the fire,' as people say, or performing any other impossible and useless feat.

CLEINIAS: What is the cause, Stranger, of this extreme hesitation?

ATHENIAN: You shall hear without any fruitless loss of time. That which has law and order in a state is the cause of every good, but that which is disordered or ill-ordered is often the ruin of that which is well-ordered; and at this point the argument is now waiting. For with you, Cleinias and Megillus, the common tables of men are, as I said, a heaven-born and admirable institution, but you are mistaken in leaving the women unregulated by law. They have no similar institution of public tables in the light of day, and just that part of the human race which is by nature prone to secrecy and stealth on account of their weakness—I mean the female sex—has been left without regulation by the legislator, which is a great mistake. And, in consequence of this neglect, many things have grown lax among you, which might have been far better, if they had been only regulated by law; for the neglect of regulations about women may not only be regarded as a neglect of half the entire matter (Arist. Pol.), but in proportion as woman's nature is inferior to that of men in capacity for virtue, in that degree the consequence of such neglect is more than twice as important. The careful consideration of this matter, and the arranging and ordering on a common principle of all our institutions relating both to men and women, greatly conduces to the happiness of the state. But at present, such is the unfortunate condition of mankind, that no man of sense will even venture to speak of common tables in places and cities in which they have never been established at all; and how can any one avoid being utterly ridiculous, who attempts to compel women to show in public how much they eat and drink? There is nothing at which the sex is more likely to take offence. For women are accustomed to creep into dark places, and when dragged out into the light they will exert their utmost powers of resistance, and be far too much for the legislator. And therefore, as I said before, in most places they will not endure to have the truth spoken without raising a tremendous outcry, but in this state perhaps they may. And if we may assume that our whole discussion about the state has not been mere idle talk, I should like to prove to you, if you will consent to listen, that this institution is good and proper; but if you had rather not, I will refrain.

CLEINIAS: There is nothing which we should both of us like better, Stranger, than to hear what you have to say.

ATHENIAN: Very good; and you must not be surprised if I go back a little, for we have plenty of leisure, and there is nothing to prevent us from considering in every point of view the subject of law.

CLEINIAS: True.

ATHENIAN: Then let us return once more to what we were saying at first. Every man should understand that the human race either had no beginning at all, and will never have an end, but always will be and has been; or that it began an immense while ago.

CLEINIAS: Certainly.

ATHENIAN: Well, and have there not been constitutions and destructions of states, and all sorts of pursuits both orderly and disorderly, and diverse desires of meats and drinks always, and in all the world, and all sorts of changes of the seasons in which animals may be expected to have undergone innumerable transformations of themselves?

CLEINIAS: No doubt.

ATHENIAN: And may we not suppose that vines appeared, which had previously no existence, and also olives, and the gifts of Demeter and her daughter, of which one Triptolemus was the minister, and that, before these existed, animals took to devouring each other as they do still?

CLEINIAS: True.

ATHENIAN: Again, the practice of men sacrificing one another still exists among many nations; while, on the other hand, we hear of other human beings who did not even venture to taste the flesh of a cow and had no animal sacrifices, but only cakes and fruits dipped in honey, and similar pure offerings, but no flesh of animals; from these they abstained under the idea that they ought not to eat them, and might not stain the altars of the Gods with blood. For in those days men are said to have lived a sort of Orphic life, having the use of all lifeless things, but abstaining from all living things.

CLEINIAS: Such has been the constant tradition, and is very likely true.

ATHENIAN: Some one might say to us, What is the drift of all this?

CLEINIAS: A very pertinent question, Stranger.

ATHENIAN: And therefore I will endeavour, Cleinias, if I can, to draw the natural inference.

CLEINIAS: Proceed.

ATHENIAN: I see that among men all things depend upon three wants and desires, of which the end is virtue, if they are rightly led by them, or the opposite if wrongly. Now these are eating and drinking, which begin at birth—every animal has a natural desire for them, and is violently excited, and rebels against him who says that he must not satisfy all his pleasures and appetites, and get rid of all the corresponding pains—and the third and greatest and sharpest want and desire breaks out last, and is the fire of sexual lust, which kindles in men every species of wantonness and madness. And these three disorders we must endeavour to master by the three great principles of fear and law and right reason; turning them away from that which is called pleasantest to the best, using the Muses and the Gods who preside over contests to extinguish their increase and influx.

But to return:—After marriage let us speak of the birth of children, and after their birth of their nurture and education. In the course of discussion the several laws will be perfected, and we shall at last arrive at the common tables. Whether such associations are to be confined to men, or extended to women also, we shall see better when we approach and take a nearer view of them; and we may then determine what previous institutions are required and will have to precede them. As I said before, we shall see them more in detail, and shall be better able to lay down the laws which are proper or suited to them.

CLEINIAS: Very true.

ATHENIAN: Let us keep in mind the words which have now been spoken; for hereafter there may be need of them.

CLEINIAS: What do you bid us keep in mind?

ATHENIAN: That which we comprehended under the three words—first, eating, secondly, drinking, thirdly, the excitement of love.

CLEINIAS: We shall be sure to remember, Stranger.

ATHENIAN: Very good. Then let us now proceed to marriage, and teach persons in what way they shall beget children, threatening them, if they disobey, with the terrors of the law.

CLEINIAS: What do you mean?

ATHENIAN: The bride and bridegroom should consider that they are to produce for the state the best and fairest specimens of children which they can. Now all men who are associated in any action always succeed when they attend and give their mind to what they are doing, but when they do not give their mind or have no mind, they fail; wherefore let the bridegroom give his mind to the bride and to the begetting of children, and the bride in like manner give her mind to the bridegroom, and particularly at the time when their children are not yet born. And let the women whom we have chosen be the overseers of such matters, and let them in whatever number, large or small, and at whatever time the magistrates may command, assemble every day in the temple of Eileithyia during a third part of the day, and being there assembled, let them inform one another of any one whom they see, whether man or woman, of those who are begetting children, disregarding the ordinances given at the time when the nuptial sacrifices and ceremonies were performed. Let the begetting of children and the supervision of those who are begetting them continue ten years and no longer, during the time when marriage is fruitful. But if any continue without children up to this time, let them take counsel with their kindred and with the women holding the office of overseer and be divorced for their mutual benefit. If, however, any dispute arises about what is proper and for the interest of either party, they shall choose ten of the guardians of the law and abide by their permission and appointment. The women who preside over these matters shall enter into the houses of the young, and partly by admonitions and partly by threats make them give over their folly and error: if they persist, let the women go and tell the guardians of the law, and the guardians shall prevent them. But if they too cannot prevent them, they shall bring the matter before the people; and let them write up their names and make oath that they cannot reform such and such an one; and let him who is thus written up, if he cannot in a court of law convict those who have inscribed his name, be deprived of the privileges of a citizen in the following respects:—let him not go to weddings nor to the thanksgivings after the birth of children; and if he go, let any one who pleases strike him with impunity; and let the same regulations hold about women: let not a woman be allowed to appear abroad, or receive honour, or go to nuptial and birthday festivals, if she in like manner be written up as acting disorderly and cannot obtain a verdict. And if, when they themselves have done begetting children according to the law, a man or woman have connexion with another man or woman who are still begetting children, let the same penalties be inflicted upon them as upon those who are still having a family; and when the time for procreation has passed let the man or woman who refrains in such matters be held in esteem, and let those who do not refrain be held in the contrary of esteem—that is to say, disesteem. Now, if the greater part of mankind behave modestly, the enactments of law may be left to slumber; but, if they are disorderly, the enactments having been passed, let them be carried into execution. To every man the first year is the beginning of life, and the time of birth ought to be written down in the temples of their fathers as the beginning of existence to every child, whether boy or girl. Let every phratria have inscribed on a whited wall the names of the successive archons by whom the years are reckoned. And near to them let the living members of the phratria be inscribed, and when they depart life let them be erased. The limit of marriageable ages for a woman shall be from sixteen to twenty years at the longest,—for a man, from thirty to thirty-five years; and let a woman hold office at forty, and a man at thirty years. Let a man go out to war from twenty to sixty years, and for a woman, if there appear any need to make use of her in military service, let the time of service be after she shall have brought forth children up to fifty years of age; and let regard be had to what is possible and suitable to each.

BOOK VII.

And now, assuming children of both sexes to have been born, it will be proper for us to consider, in the next place, their nurture and education; this cannot be left altogether unnoticed, and yet may be thought a subject fitted rather for precept and admonition than for law. In private life there are many little things, not always apparent, arising out of the pleasures and pains and desires of individuals, which run counter to the intention of the legislator, and make the characters of the citizens various and dissimilar:—this is an evil in states; for by reason of their smallness and frequent occurrence, there would be an unseemliness and want of propriety in making them penal by law; and if made penal, they are the destruction of the written law because mankind get the habit of frequently transgressing the law in small matters. The result is that you cannot legislate about them, and still less can you be silent. I speak somewhat darkly, but I shall endeavour also to bring my wares into the light of day, for I acknowledge that at present there is a want of clearness in what I am saying.

CLEINIAS: Very true.

ATHENIAN. Am I not right in maintaining that a good education is that which tends most to the improvement of mind and body?

CLEINIAS: Undoubtedly.

ATHENIAN: And nothing can be plainer than that the fairest bodies are those which grow up from infancy in the best and straightest manner?

CLEINIAS: Certainly.

ATHENIAN: And do we not further observe that the first shoot of every living thing is by far the greatest and fullest? Many will even contend that a man at twenty-five does not reach twice the height which he attained at five.

CLEINIAS: True.

ATHENIAN: Well, and is not rapid growth without proper and abundant exercise the source endless evils in the body?

CLEINIAS: Yes.

ATHENIAN: And the body should have the most exercise when it receives most nourishment?

CLEINIAS: But, Stranger, are we to impose this great amount of exercise upon newly-born infants?

ATHENIAN: Nay, rather on the bodies of infants still unborn.

CLEINIAS: What do you mean, my good sir? In the process of gestation?

ATHENIAN: Exactly. I am not at all surprised that you have never heard of this very peculiar sort of gymnastic applied to such little creatures, which, although strange, I will endeavour to explain to you.

CLEINIAS: By all means.

ATHENIAN: The practice is more easy for us to understand than for you, by reason of certain amusements which are carried to excess by us at Athens. Not only boys, but often older persons, are in the habit of keeping quails and cocks (compare Republic), which they train to fight one another. And they are far from thinking that the contests in which they stir them up to fight with one another are sufficient exercise; for, in addition to this, they carry them about tucked beneath their armpits, holding the smaller birds in their hands, the larger under their arms, and go for a walk of a great many miles for the sake of health, that is to say, not their own health, but the health of the birds; whereby they prove to any intelligent person, that all bodies are benefited by shakings and movements, when they are moved without weariness, whether the motion proceeds from themselves, or is caused by a swing, or at sea, or on horseback, or by other bodies in whatever way moving, and that thus gaining the mastery over food and drink, they are able to impart beauty and health and strength. But admitting all this, what follows? Shall we make a ridiculous law that the pregnant woman shall walk about and fashion the embryo within as we fashion wax before it hardens, and after birth swathe the infant for two years? Suppose that we compel nurses, under penalty of a legal fine, to be always carrying the children somewhere or other, either to the temples, or into the country, or to their relations' houses, until they are well able to stand, and to take care that their limbs are not distorted by leaning on them when they are too young (compare Arist. Pol.),—they should continue to carry them until the infant has completed its third year; the nurses should be strong, and there should be more than one of them. Shall these be our rules, and shall we impose a penalty for the neglect of them? No, no; the penalty of which we were speaking will fall upon our own heads more than enough.

CLEINIAS: What penalty?

ATHENIAN: Ridicule, and the difficulty of getting the feminine and servant-like dispositions of the nurses to comply.

CLEINIAS: Then why was there any need to speak of the matter at all?

ATHENIAN: The reason is, that masters and freemen in states, when they hear of it, are very likely to arrive at a true conviction that without due regulation of private life in cities, stability in the laying down of laws is hardly to be expected (compare Republic); and he who makes this reflection may himself adopt the laws just now mentioned, and, adopting them, may order his house and state well and be happy.

CLEINIAS: Likely enough.

ATHENIAN: And therefore let us proceed with our legislation until we have determined the exercises which are suited to the souls of young children, in the same manner in which we have begun to go through the rules relating to their bodies.

CLEINIAS: By all means.

ATHENIAN: Let us assume, then, as a first principle in relation both to the body and soul of very young creatures, that nursing and moving about by day and night is good for them all, and that the younger they are, the more they will need it (compare Arist. Pol.); infants should live, if that were possible, as if they were always rocking at sea. This is the lesson which we may gather from the experience of nurses, and likewise from the use of the remedy of motion in the rites of the Corybantes; for when mothers want their restless children to go to sleep they do not employ rest, but, on the contrary, motion—rocking them in their arms; nor do they give them silence, but they sing to them and lap them in sweet strains; and the Bacchic women are cured of their frenzy in the same manner by the use of the dance and of music.

CLEINIAS: Well, Stranger, and what is the reason of this?

ATHENIAN: The reason is obvious.

CLEINIAS: What?

ATHENIAN: The affection both of the Bacchantes and of the children is an emotion of fear, which springs out of an evil habit of the soul. And when some one applies external agitation to affections of this sort, the motion coming from without gets the better of the terrible and violent internal one, and produces a peace and calm in the soul, and quiets the restless palpitation of the heart, which is a thing much to be desired, sending the children to sleep, and making the Bacchantes, although they remain awake, to dance to the pipe with the help of the Gods to whom they offer acceptable sacrifices, and producing in them a sound mind, which takes the place of their frenzy. And, to express what I mean in a word, there is a good deal to be said in favour of this treatment.

CLEINIAS: Certainly.

ATHENIAN: But if fear has such a power we ought to infer from these facts, that every soul which from youth upward has been familiar with fears, will be made more liable to fear (compare Republic), and every one will allow that this is the way to form a habit of cowardice and not of courage.

CLEINIAS: No doubt.

ATHENIAN: And, on the other hand, the habit of overcoming, from our youth upwards, the fears and terrors which beset us, may be said to be an exercise of courage.

CLEINIAS: True.

ATHENIAN: And we may say that the use of exercise and motion in the earliest years of life greatly contributes to create a part of virtue in the soul.

CLEINIAS: Quite true.

ATHENIAN: Further, a cheerful temper, or the reverse, may be regarded as having much to do with high spirit on the one hand, or with cowardice on the other.

CLEINIAS: To be sure.

ATHENIAN: Then now we must endeavour to show how and to what extent we may, if we please, without difficulty implant either character in the young.

CLEINIAS: Certainly.

ATHENIAN: There is a common opinion, that luxury makes the disposition of youth discontented and irascible and vehemently excited by trifles; that on the other hand excessive and savage servitude makes men mean and abject, and haters of their kind, and therefore makes them undesirable associates.

CLEINIAS: But how must the state educate those who do not as yet understand the language of the country, and are therefore incapable of appreciating any sort of instruction?

ATHENIAN: I will tell you how:—Every animal that is born is wont to utter some cry, and this is especially the case with man, and he is also affected with the inclination to weep more than any other animal.

CLEINIAS: Quite true.

ATHENIAN: Do not nurses, when they want to know what an infant desires, judge by these signs?—when anything is brought to the infant and he is silent, then he is supposed to be pleased, but, when he weeps and cries out, then he is not pleased. For tears and cries are the inauspicious signs by which children show what they love and hate. Now the time which is thus spent is no less than three years, and is a very considerable portion of life to be passed ill or well.

CLEINIAS: True.

ATHENIAN: Does not the discontented and ungracious nature appear to you to be full of lamentations and sorrows more than a good man ought to be?

CLEINIAS: Certainly.

ATHENIAN: Well, but if during these three years every possible care were taken that our nursling should have as little of sorrow and fear, and in general of pain as was possible, might we not expect in early childhood to make his soul more gentle and cheerful? (Compare Arist. Pol.)

CLEINIAS: To be sure, Stranger—more especially if we could procure him a variety of pleasures.

ATHENIAN: There I can no longer agree, Cleinias: you amaze me. To bring him up in such a way would be his utter ruin; for the beginning is always the most critical part of education. Let us see whether I am right.

CLEINIAS: Proceed.

ATHENIAN: The point about which you and I differ is of great importance, and I hope that you, Megillus, will help to decide between us. For I maintain that the true life should neither seek for pleasures, nor, on the other hand, entirely avoid pains, but should embrace the middle state (compare Republic), which I just spoke of as gentle and benign, and is a state which we by some divine presage and inspiration rightly ascribe to God. Now, I say, he among men, too, who would be divine ought to pursue after this mean habit—he should not rush headlong into pleasures, for he will not be free from pains; nor should we allow any one, young or old, male or female, to be thus given any more than ourselves, and least of all the newly-born infant, for in infancy more than at any other time the character is engrained by habit. Nay, more, if I were not afraid of appearing to be ridiculous, I would say that a woman during her year of pregnancy should of all women be most carefully tended, and kept from violent or excessive pleasures and pains, and should at that time cultivate gentleness and benevolence and kindness.

CLEINIAS: You need not ask Megillus, Stranger, which of us has most truly spoken; for I myself agree that all men ought to avoid the life of unmingled pain or pleasure, and pursue always a middle course. And having spoken well, may I add that you have been well answered?

ATHENIAN: Very good, Cleinias; and now let us all three consider a further point.

CLEINIAS: What is it?

ATHENIAN: That all the matters which we are now describing are commonly called by the general name of unwritten customs, and what are termed the laws of our ancestors are all of similar nature. And the reflection which lately arose in our minds, that we can neither call these things laws, nor yet leave them unmentioned, is justified; for they are the bonds of the whole state, and come in between the written laws which are or are hereafter to be laid down; they are just ancestral customs of great antiquity, which, if they are rightly ordered and made habitual, shield and preserve the previously existing written law; but if they depart from right and fall into disorder, then they are like the props of builders which slip away out of their place and cause a universal ruin—one part drags another down, and the fair super-structure falls because the old foundations are undermined. Reflecting upon this, Cleinias, you ought to bind together the new state in every possible way, omitting nothing, whether great or small, of what are called laws or manners or pursuits, for by these means a city is bound together, and all these things are only lasting when they depend upon one another; and, therefore, we must not wonder if we find that many apparently trifling customs or usages come pouring in and lengthening out our laws.

CLEINIAS: Very true: we are disposed to agree with you.

ATHENIAN: Up to the age of three years, whether of boy or girl, if a person strictly carries out our previous regulations and makes them a principal aim, he will do much for the advantage of the young creatures. But at three, four, five, and even six years the childish nature will require sports; now is the time to get rid of self-will in him, punishing him, but not so as to disgrace him. We were saying about slaves, that we ought neither to add insult to punishment so as to anger them, nor yet to leave them unpunished lest they become self-willed; and a like rule is to be observed in the case of the free-born. Children at that age have certain natural modes of amusement which they find out for themselves when they meet. And all the children who are between the ages of three and six ought to meet at the temples of the villages, the several families of a village uniting on one spot. The nurses are to see that the children behave properly and orderly—they themselves and all their companies are to be under the control of twelve matrons, one for each company, who are annually selected to inspect them from the women previously mentioned [i.e. the women who have authority over marriage], whom the guardians of the law appoint. These matrons shall be chosen by the women who have authority over marriage, one out of each tribe; all are to be of the same age; and let each of them, as soon as she is appointed, hold office and go to the temples every day, punishing all offenders, male or female, who are slaves or strangers, by the help of some of the public slaves; but if any citizen disputes the punishment, let her bring him before the wardens of the city; or, if there be no dispute, let her punish him herself. After the age of six years the time has arrived for the separation of the sexes—let boys live with boys, and girls in like manner with girls. Now they must begin to learn—the boys going to teachers of horsemanship and the use of the bow, the javelin, and sling, and the girls too, if they do not object, at any rate until they know how to manage these weapons, and especially how to handle heavy arms; for I may note, that the practice which now prevails is almost universally misunderstood.

CLEINIAS: In what respect?

ATHENIAN: In that the right and left hand are supposed to be by nature differently suited for our various uses of them; whereas no difference is found in the use of the feet and the lower limbs; but in the use of the hands we are, as it were, maimed by the folly of nurses and mothers; for although our several limbs are by nature balanced, we create a difference in them by bad habit. In some cases this is of no consequence, as, for example, when we hold the lyre in the left hand, and the plectrum in the right, but it is downright folly to make the same distinction in other cases. The custom of the Scythians proves our error; for they not only hold the bow from them with the left hand and draw the arrow to them with their right, but use either hand for both purposes. And there are many similar examples in charioteering and other things, from which we may learn that those who make the left side weaker than the right act contrary to nature. In the case of the plectrum, which is of horn only, and similar instruments, as I was saying, it is of no consequence, but makes a great difference, and may be of very great importance to the warrior who has to use iron weapons, bows and javelins, and the like; above all, when in heavy armour, he has to fight against heavy armour. And there is a very great difference between one who has learnt and one who has not, and between one who has been trained in gymnastic exercises and one who has not been. For as he who is perfectly skilled in the Pancratium or boxing or wrestling, is not unable to fight from his left side, and does not limp and draggle in confusion when his opponent makes him change his position, so in heavy-armed fighting, and in all other things, if I am not mistaken, the like holds—he who has these double powers of attack and defence ought not in any case to leave them either unused or untrained, if he can help; and if a person had the nature of Geryon or Briareus he ought to be able with his hundred hands to throw a hundred darts. Now, the magistrates, male and female, should see to all these things, the women superintending the nursing and amusements of the children, and the men superintending their education, that all of them, boys and girls alike, may be sound hand and foot, and may not, if they can help, spoil the gifts of nature by bad habits.

Education has two branches—one of gymnastic, which is concerned with the body, and the other of music, which is designed for the improvement of the soul. And gymnastic has also two branches—dancing and wrestling; and one sort of dancing imitates musical recitation, and aims at preserving dignity and freedom, the other aims at producing health, agility, and beauty in the limbs and parts of the body, giving the proper flexion and extension to each of them, a harmonious motion being diffused everywhere, and forming a suitable accompaniment to the dance. As regards wrestling, the tricks which Antaeus and Cercyon devised in their systems out of a vain spirit of competition, or the tricks of boxing which Epeius or Amycus invented, are useless and unsuitable for war, and do not deserve to have much said about them; but the art of wrestling erect and keeping free the neck and hands and sides, working with energy and constancy, with a composed strength, for the sake of health—these are always useful, and are not to be neglected, but to be enjoined alike on masters and scholars, when we reach that part of legislation; and we will desire the one to give their instructions freely, and the others to receive them thankfully. Nor, again, must we omit suitable imitations of war in our choruses; here in Crete you have the armed dances of the Curetes, and the Lacedaemonians have those of the Dioscuri. And our virgin lady, delighting in the amusement of the dance, thought it not fit to amuse herself with empty hands; she must be clothed in a complete suit of armour, and in this attire go through the dance; and youths and maidens should in every respect imitate her, esteeming highly the favour of the Goddess, both with a view to the necessities of war, and to festive occasions: it will be right also for the boys, until such time as they go out to war, to make processions and supplications to all the Gods in goodly array, armed and on horseback, in dances and marches, fast or slow, offering up prayers to the Gods and to the sons of Gods; and also engaging in contests and preludes of contests, if at all, with these objects. For these sorts of exercises, and no others, are useful both in peace and war, and are beneficial alike to states and to private houses. But other labours and sports and exercises of the body are unworthy of freemen, O Megillus and Cleinias.

I have now completely described the kind of gymnastic which I said at first ought to be described; if you know of any better, will you communicate your thoughts?

CLEINIAS: It is not easy, Stranger, to put aside these principles of gymnastic and wrestling and to enunciate better ones.

ATHENIAN: Now we must say what has yet to be said about the gifts of the Muses and of Apollo: before, we fancied that we had said all, and that gymnastic alone remained; but now we see clearly what points have been omitted, and should be first proclaimed; of these, then, let us proceed to speak.

CLEINIAS: By all means.

ATHENIAN: Let me tell you once more—although you have heard me say the same before—that caution must be always exercised, both by the speaker and by the hearer, about anything that is very singular and unusual. For my tale is one which many a man would be afraid to tell, and yet I have a confidence which makes me go on.

CLEINIAS: What have you to say, Stranger?

ATHENIAN: I say that in states generally no one has observed that the plays of childhood have a great deal to do with the permanence or want of permanence in legislation. For when plays are ordered with a view to children having the same plays, and amusing themselves after the same manner, and finding delight in the same playthings, the more solemn institutions of the state are allowed to remain undisturbed. Whereas if sports are disturbed, and innovations are made in them, and they constantly change, and the young never speak of their having the same likings, or the same established notions of good and bad taste, either in the bearing of their bodies or in their dress, but he who devises something new and out of the way in figures and colours and the like is held in special honour, we may truly say that no greater evil can happen in a state; for he who changes the sports is secretly changing the manners of the young, and making the old to be dishonoured among them and the new to be honoured. And I affirm that there is nothing which is a greater injury to all states than saying or thinking thus. Will you hear me tell how great I deem the evil to be?

CLEINIAS: You mean the evil of blaming antiquity in states?

ATHENIAN: Exactly.

CLEINIAS: If you are speaking of that, you will find in us hearers who are disposed to receive what you say not unfavourably but most favourably.

ATHENIAN: I should expect so.

CLEINIAS: Proceed.

ATHENIAN: Well, then, let us give all the greater heed to one another's words. The argument affirms that any change whatever except from evil is the most dangerous of all things; this is true in the case of the seasons and of the winds, in the management of our bodies and the habits of our minds—true of all things except, as I said before, of the bad. He who looks at the constitution of individuals accustomed to eat any sort of meat, or drink any drink, or to do any work which they can get, may see that they are at first disordered by them, but afterwards, as time goes on, their bodies grow adapted to them, and they learn to know and like variety, and have good health and enjoyment of life; and if ever afterwards they are confined again to a superior diet, at first they are troubled with disorders, and with difficulty become habituated to their new food. A similar principle we may imagine to hold good about the minds of men and the natures of their souls. For when they have been brought up in certain laws, which by some Divine Providence have remained unchanged during long ages, so that no one has any memory or tradition of their ever having been otherwise than they are, then every one is afraid and ashamed to change that which is established. The legislator must somehow find a way of implanting this reverence for antiquity, and I would propose the following way: People are apt to fancy, as I was saying before, that when the plays of children are altered they are merely plays, not seeing that the most serious and detrimental consequences arise out of the change; and they readily comply with the child's wishes instead of deterring him, not considering that these children who make innovations in their games, when they grow up to be men, will be different from the last generation of children, and, being different, will desire a different sort of life, and under the influence of this desire will want other institutions and laws; and no one of them reflects that there will follow what I just now called the greatest of evils to states. Changes in bodily fashions are no such serious evils, but frequent changes in the praise and censure of manners are the greatest of evils, and require the utmost prevision.

CLEINIAS: To be sure.

ATHENIAN: And now do we still hold to our former assertion, that rhythms and music in general are imitations of good and evil characters in men? What say you?

CLEINIAS: That is the only doctrine which we can admit.

ATHENIAN: Must we not, then, try in every possible way to prevent our youth from even desiring to imitate new modes either in dance or song? nor must any one be allowed to offer them varieties of pleasures.

CLEINIAS: Most true.

ATHENIAN: Can any of us imagine a better mode of effecting this object than that of the Egyptians?

CLEINIAS: What is their method?

ATHENIAN: To consecrate every sort of dance or melody. First we should ordain festivals—calculating for the year what they ought to be, and at what time, and in honour of what Gods, sons of Gods, and heroes they ought to be celebrated; and, in the next place, what hymns ought to be sung at the several sacrifices, and with what dances the particular festival is to be honoured. This has to be arranged at first by certain persons, and, when arranged, the whole assembly of the citizens are to offer sacrifices and libations to the Fates and all the other Gods, and to consecrate the several odes to Gods and heroes: and if any one offers any other hymns or dances to any one of the Gods, the priests and priestesses, acting in concert with the guardians of the law, shall, with the sanction of religion and the law, exclude him, and he who is excluded, if he do not submit, shall be liable all his life long to have a suit of impiety brought against him by any one who likes.

CLEINIAS: Very good.

ATHENIAN: In the consideration of this subject, let us remember what is due to ourselves.

CLEINIAS: To what are you referring?

ATHENIAN: I mean that any young man, and much more any old one, when he sees or hears anything strange or unaccustomed, does not at once run to embrace the paradox, but he stands considering, like a person who is at a place where three paths meet, and does not very well know his way—he may be alone or he may be walking with others, and he will say to himself and them, 'Which is the way?' and will not move forward until he is satisfied that he is going right. And this is what we must do in the present instance: A strange discussion on the subject of law has arisen, which requires the utmost consideration, and we should not at our age be too ready to speak about such great matters, or be confident that we can say anything certain all in a moment.

CLEINIAS: Most true.

ATHENIAN: Then we will allow time for reflection, and decide when we have given the subject sufficient consideration. But that we may not be hindered from completing the natural arrangement of our laws, let us proceed to the conclusion of them in due order; for very possibly, if God will, the exposition of them, when completed, may throw light on our present perplexity.

CLEINIAS: Excellent, Stranger; let us do as you propose.

ATHENIAN: Let us then affirm the paradox that strains of music are our laws (nomoi), and this latter being the name which the ancients gave to lyric songs, they probably would not have very much objected to our proposed application of the word. Some one, either asleep or awake, must have had a dreamy suspicion of their nature. And let our decree be as follows: No one in singing or dancing shall offend against public and consecrated models, and the general fashion among the youth, any more than he would offend against any other law. And he who observes this law shall be blameless; but he who is disobedient, as I was saying, shall be punished by the guardians of the laws, and by the priests and priestesses. Suppose that we imagine this to be our law.

CLEINIAS: Very good.

ATHENIAN: Can any one who makes such laws escape ridicule? Let us see. I think that our only safety will be in first framing certain models for composers. One of these models shall be as follows: If when a sacrifice is going on, and the victims are being burnt according to law—if, I say, any one who may be a son or brother, standing by another at the altar and over the victims, horribly blasphemes, will not his words inspire despondency and evil omens and forebodings in the mind of his father and of his other kinsmen?

CLEINIAS: Of course.

ATHENIAN: And this is just what takes place in almost all our cities. A magistrate offers a public sacrifice, and there come in not one but many choruses, who take up a position a little way from the altar, and from time to time pour forth all sorts of horrible blasphemies on the sacred rites, exciting the souls of the audience with words and rhythms and melodies most sorrowful to hear; and he who at the moment when the city is offering sacrifice makes the citizens weep most, carries away the palm of victory. Now, ought we not to forbid such strains as these? And if ever our citizens must hear such lamentations, then on some unblest and inauspicious day let there be choruses of foreign and hired minstrels, like those hirelings who accompany the departed at funerals with barbarous Carian chants. That is the sort of thing which will be appropriate if we have such strains at all; and let the apparel of the singers be, not circlets and ornaments of gold, but the reverse. Enough of all this. I will simply ask once more whether we shall lay down as one of our principles of song—

CLEINIAS: What?

ATHENIAN: That we should avoid every word of evil omen; let that kind of song which is of good omen be heard everywhere and always in our state. I need hardly ask again, but shall assume that you agree with me.

CLEINIAS: By all means; that law is approved by the suffrages of us all.

ATHENIAN: But what shall be our next musical law or type? Ought not prayers to be offered up to the Gods when we sacrifice?

CLEINIAS: Certainly.

ATHENIAN: And our third law, if I am not mistaken, will be to the effect that our poets, understanding prayers to be requests which we make to the Gods, will take especial heed that they do not by mistake ask for evil instead of good. To make such a prayer would surely be too ridiculous.

CLEINIAS: Very true.

ATHENIAN: Were we not a little while ago quite convinced that no silver or golden Plutus should dwell in our state?

CLEINIAS: To be sure.

ATHENIAN: And what has it been the object of our argument to show? Did we not imply that the poets are not always quite capable of knowing what is good or evil? And if one of them utters a mistaken prayer in song or words, he will make our citizens pray for the opposite of what is good in matters of the highest import; than which, as I was saying, there can be few greater mistakes. Shall we then propose as one of our laws and models relating to the Muses—

CLEINIAS: What? will you explain the law more precisely?

ATHENIAN: Shall we make a law that the poet shall compose nothing contrary to the ideas of the lawful, or just, or beautiful, or good, which are allowed in the state? nor shall he be permitted to communicate his compositions to any private individuals, until he shall have shown them to the appointed judges and the guardians of the law, and they are satisfied with them. As to the persons whom we appoint to be our legislators about music and as to the director of education, these have been already indicated. Once more then, as I have asked more than once, shall this be our third law, and type, and model—What do you say?

CLEINIAS: Let it be so, by all means.

ATHENIAN: Then it will be proper to have hymns and praises of the Gods, intermingled with prayers; and after the Gods prayers and praises should be offered in like manner to demigods and heroes, suitable to their several characters.

CLEINIAS: Certainly.

ATHENIAN: In the next place there will be no objection to a law, that citizens who are departed and have done good and energetic deeds, either with their souls or with their bodies, and have been obedient to the laws, should receive eulogies; this will be very fitting.

CLEINIAS: Quite true.

ATHENIAN: But to honour with hymns and panegyrics those who are still alive is not safe; a man should run his course, and make a fair ending, and then we will praise him; and let praise be given equally to women as well as men who have been distinguished in virtue. The order of songs and dances shall be as follows: There are many ancient musical compositions and dances which are excellent, and from these the newly-founded city may freely select what is proper and suitable; and they shall choose judges of not less than fifty years of age, who shall make the selection, and any of the old poems which they deem sufficient they shall include; any that are deficient or altogether unsuitable, they shall either utterly throw aside, or examine and amend, taking into their counsel poets and musicians, and making use of their poetical genius; but explaining to them the wishes of the legislator in order that they may regulate dancing, music, and all choral strains, according to the mind of the judges; and not allowing them to indulge, except in some few matters, their individual pleasures and fancies. Now the irregular strain of music is always made ten thousand times better by attaining to law and order, and rejecting the honeyed Muse—not however that we mean wholly to exclude pleasure, which is the characteristic of all music. And if a man be brought up from childhood to the age of discretion and maturity in the use of the orderly and severe music, when he hears the opposite he detests it, and calls it illiberal; but if trained in the sweet and vulgar music, he deems the severer kind cold and displeasing. So that, as I was saying before, while he who hears them gains no more pleasure from the one than from the other, the one has the advantage of making those who are trained in it better men, whereas the other makes them worse.

CLEINIAS: Very true.

ATHENIAN: Again, we must distinguish and determine on some general principle what songs are suitable to women, and what to men, and must assign to them their proper melodies and rhythms. It is shocking for a whole harmony to be inharmonical, or for a rhythm to be unrhythmical, and this will happen when the melody is inappropriate to them. And therefore the legislator must assign to these also their forms. Now both sexes have melodies and rhythms which of necessity belong to them; and those of women are clearly enough indicated by their natural difference. The grand, and that which tends to courage, may be fairly called manly; but that which inclines to moderation and temperance, may be declared both in law and in ordinary speech to be the more womanly quality. This, then, will be the general order of them.

Let us now speak of the manner of teaching and imparting them, and the persons to whom, and the time when, they are severally to be imparted. As the shipwright first lays down the lines of the keel, and thus, as it were, draws the ship in outline, so do I seek to distinguish the patterns of life, and lay down their keels according to the nature of different men's souls; seeking truly to consider by what means, and in what ways, we may go through the voyage of life best. Now human affairs are hardly worth considering in earnest, and yet we must be in earnest about them—a sad necessity constrains us. And having got thus far, there will be a fitness in our completing the matter, if we can only find some suitable method of doing so. But what do I mean? Some one may ask this very question, and quite rightly, too.

CLEINIAS: Certainly.

ATHENIAN: I say that about serious matters a man should be serious, and about a matter which is not serious he should not be serious; and that God is the natural and worthy object of our most serious and blessed endeavours, for man, as I said before, is made to be the plaything of God, and this, truly considered, is the best of him; wherefore also every man and woman should walk seriously, and pass life in the noblest of pastimes, and be of another mind from what they are at present.

CLEINIAS: In what respect?

ATHENIAN: At present they think that their serious pursuits should be for the sake of their sports, for they deem war a serious pursuit, which must be managed well for the sake of peace; but the truth is, that there neither is, nor has been, nor ever will be, either amusement or instruction in any degree worth speaking of in war, which is nevertheless deemed by us to be the most serious of our pursuits. And therefore, as we say, every one of us should live the life of peace as long and as well as he can. And what is the right way of living? Are we to live in sports always? If so, in what kind of sports? We ought to live sacrificing, and singing, and dancing, and then a man will be able to propitiate the Gods, and to defend himself against his enemies and conquer them in battle. The type of song or dance by which he will propitiate them has been described, and the paths along which he is to proceed have been cut for him. He will go forward in the spirit of the poet:

'Telemachus, some things thou wilt thyself find in thy heart, but other things God will suggest; for I deem that thou wast not born or brought up without the will of the Gods.'

And this ought to be the view of our alumni; they ought to think that what has been said is enough for them, and that any other things their Genius and God will suggest to them—he will tell them to whom, and when, and to what Gods severally they are to sacrifice and perform dances, and how they may propitiate the deities, and live according to the appointment of nature; being for the most part puppets, but having some little share of reality.

MEGILLUS: You have a low opinion of mankind, Stranger.

ATHENIAN: Nay, Megillus, be not amazed, but forgive me: I was comparing them with the Gods; and under that feeling I spoke. Let us grant, if you wish, that the human race is not to be despised, but is worthy of some consideration.

Next follow the buildings for gymnasia and schools open to all; these are to be in three places in the midst of the city; and outside the city and in the surrounding country, also in three places, there shall be schools for horse exercise, and large grounds arranged with a view to archery and the throwing of missiles, at which young men may learn and practise. Of these mention has already been made; and if the mention be not sufficiently explicit, let us speak further of them and embody them in laws. In these several schools let there be dwellings for teachers, who shall be brought from foreign parts by pay, and let them teach those who attend the schools the art of war and the art of music, and the children shall come not only if their parents please, but if they do not please; there shall be compulsory education, as the saying is, of all and sundry, as far as this is possible; and the pupils shall be regarded as belonging to the state rather than to their parents. My law would apply to females as well as males; they shall both go through the same exercises. I assert without fear of contradiction that gymnastic and horsemanship are as suitable to women as to men. Of the truth of this I am persuaded from ancient tradition, and at the present day there are said to be countless myriads of women in the neighbourhood of the Black Sea, called Sauromatides, who not only ride on horseback like men, but have enjoined upon them the use of bows and other weapons equally with the men. And I further affirm, that if these things are possible, nothing can be more absurd than the practice which prevails in our own country, of men and women not following the same pursuits with all their strength and with one mind, for thus the state, instead of being a whole, is reduced to a half, but has the same imposts to pay and the same toils to undergo; and what can be a greater mistake for any legislator to make than this?

CLEINIAS: Very true; yet much of what has been asserted by us, Stranger, is contrary to the custom of states; still, in saying that the discourse should be allowed to proceed, and that when the discussion is completed, we should choose what seems best, you spoke very properly, and I now feel compunction for what I have said. Tell me, then, what you would next wish to say.

ATHENIAN: I should wish to say, Cleinias, as I said before, that if the possibility of these things were not sufficiently proven in fact, then there might be an objection to the argument, but the fact being as I have said, he who rejects the law must find some other ground of objection; and, failing this, our exhortation will still hold good, nor will any one deny that women ought to share as far as possible in education and in other ways with men. For consider; if women do not share in their whole life with men, then they must have some other order of life.

CLEINIAS: Certainly.

ATHENIAN: And what arrangement of life to be found anywhere is preferable to this community which we are now assigning to them? Shall we prefer that which is adopted by the Thracians and many other races who use their women to till the ground and to be shepherds of their herds and flocks, and to minister to them like slaves? Or shall we do as we and people in our part of the world do—getting together, as the phrase is, all our goods and chattels into one dwelling, we entrust them to our women, who are the stewards of them, and who also preside over the shuttles and the whole art of spinning? Or shall we take a middle course, as in Lacedaemon, Megillus—letting the girls share in gymnastic and music, while the grown-up women, no longer employed in spinning wool, are hard at work weaving the web of life, which will be no cheap or mean employment, and in the duty of serving and taking care of the household and bringing up the children, in which they will observe a sort of mean, not participating in the toils of war; and if there were any necessity that they should fight for their city and families, unlike the Amazons, they would be unable to take part in archery or any other skilled use of missiles, nor could they, after the example of the Goddess, carry shield or spear, or stand up nobly for their country when it was being destroyed, and strike terror into their enemies, if only because they were seen in regular order? Living as they do, they would never dare at all to imitate the Sauromatides, who, when compared with ordinary women, would appear to be like men. Let him who will, praise your legislators, but I must say what I think. The legislator ought to be whole and perfect, and not half a man only; he ought not to let the female sex live softly and waste money and have no order of life, while he takes the utmost care of the male sex, and leaves half of life only blest with happiness, when he might have made the whole state happy.

MEGILLUS: What shall we do, Cleinias? Shall we allow a stranger to run down Sparta in this fashion?

CLEINIAS: Yes; for as we have given him liberty of speech we must let him go on until we have perfected the work of legislation.

MEGILLUS: Very true.

ATHENIAN: Then now I may proceed?

CLEINIAS: By all means.

ATHENIAN: What will be the manner of life among men who may be supposed to have their food and clothing provided for them in moderation, and who have entrusted the practice of the arts to others, and whose husbandry committed to slaves paying a part of the produce, brings them a return sufficient for men living temperately; who, moreover, have common tables in which the men are placed apart, and near them are the common tables of their families, of their daughters and mothers, which day by day, the officers, male and female, are to inspect—they shall see to the behaviour of the company, and so dismiss them; after which the presiding magistrate and his attendants shall honour with libations those Gods to whom that day and night are dedicated, and then go home? To men whose lives are thus ordered, is there no work remaining to be done which is necessary and fitting, but shall each one of them live fattening like a beast? Such a life is neither just nor honourable, nor can he who lives it fail of meeting his due; and the due reward of the idle fatted beast is that he should be torn in pieces by some other valiant beast whose fatness is worn down by brave deeds and toil. These regulations, if we duly consider them, will never be exactly carried into execution under present circumstances, nor as long as women and children and houses and all other things are the private property of individuals; but if we can attain the second-best form of polity, we shall be very well off. And to men living under this second polity there remains a work to be accomplished which is far from being small or insignificant, but is the greatest of all works, and ordained by the appointment of righteous law. For the life which may be truly said to be concerned with the virtue of body and soul is twice, or more than twice, as full of toil and trouble as the pursuit after Pythian and Olympic victories, which debars a man from every employment of life. For there ought to be no bye-work interfering with the greater work of providing the necessary exercise and nourishment for the body, and instruction and education for the soul. Night and day are not long enough for the accomplishment of their perfection and consummation; and therefore to this end all freemen ought to arrange the way in which they will spend their time during the whole course of the day, from morning till evening and from evening till the morning of the next sunrise. There may seem to be some impropriety in the legislator determining minutely the numberless details of the management of the house, including such particulars as the duty of wakefulness in those who are to be perpetual watchmen of the whole city; for that any citizen should continue during the whole of any night in sleep, instead of being seen by all his servants, always the first to awake and get up—this, whether the regulation is to be called a law or only a practice, should be deemed base and unworthy of a freeman; also that the mistress of the house should be awakened by her hand-maidens instead of herself first awakening them, is what the slaves, male and female, and the serving-boys, and, if that were possible, everybody and everything in the house should regard as base. If they rise early, they may all of them do much of their public and of their household business, as magistrates in the city, and masters and mistresses in their private houses, before the sun is up. Much sleep is not required by nature, either for our souls or bodies, or for the actions which they perform. For no one who is asleep is good for anything, any more than if he were dead; but he of us who has the most regard for life and reason keeps awake as long as he can, reserving only so much time for sleep as is expedient for health; and much sleep is not required, if the habit of moderation be once rightly formed. Magistrates in states who keep awake at night are terrible to the bad, whether enemies or citizens, and are honoured and reverenced by the just and temperate, and are useful to themselves and to the whole state.

A night which is passed in such a manner, in addition to all the above-mentioned advantages, infuses a sort of courage into the minds of the citizens. When the day breaks, the time has arrived for youth to go to their schoolmasters. Now neither sheep nor any other animals can live without a shepherd, nor can children be left without tutors, or slaves without masters. And of all animals the boy is the most unmanageable, inasmuch as he has the fountain of reason in him not yet regulated; he is the most insidious, sharp-witted, and insubordinate of animals. Wherefore he must be bound with many bridles; in the first place, when he gets away from mothers and nurses, he must be under the management of tutors on account of his childishness and foolishness; then, again, being a freeman, he must be controlled by teachers, no matter what they teach, and by studies; but he is also a slave, and in that regard any freeman who comes in his way may punish him and his tutor and his instructor, if any of them does anything wrong; and he who comes across him and does not inflict upon him the punishment which he deserves, shall incur the greatest disgrace; and let the guardian of the law, who is the director of education, see to him who coming in the way of the offences which we have mentioned, does not chastise them when he ought, or chastises them in a way which he ought not; let him keep a sharp look-out, and take especial care of the training of our children, directing their natures, and always turning them to good according to the law.

But how can our law sufficiently train the director of education himself; for as yet all has been imperfect, and nothing has been said either clear or satisfactory? Now, as far as possible, the law ought to leave nothing to him, but to explain everything, that he may be an interpreter and tutor to others. About dances and music and choral strains, I have already spoken both as to the character of the selection of them, and the manner in which they are to be amended and consecrated. But we have not as yet spoken, O illustrious guardian of education, of the manner in which your pupils are to use those strains which are written in prose, although you have been informed what martial strains they are to learn and practise; what relates in the first place to the learning of letters, and secondly, to the lyre, and also to calculation, which, as we were saying, is needful for them all to learn, and any other things which are required with a view to war and the management of house and city, and, looking to the same object, what is useful in the revolutions of the heavenly bodies—the stars and sun and moon, and the various regulations about these matters which are necessary for the whole state—I am speaking of the arrangements of days in periods of months, and of months in years, which are to be observed, in order that seasons and sacrifices and festivals may have their regular and natural order, and keep the city alive and awake, the Gods receiving the honours due to them, and men having a better understanding about them: all these things, O my friend, have not yet been sufficiently declared to you by the legislator. Attend, then, to what I am now going to say: We were telling you, in the first place, that you were not sufficiently informed about letters, and the objection was to this effect—that you were never told whether he who was meant to be a respectable citizen should apply himself in detail to that sort of learning, or not apply himself at all; and the same remark holds good of the study of the lyre. But now we say that he ought to attend to them. A fair time for a boy of ten years old to spend in letters is three years; the age of thirteen is the proper time for him to begin to handle the lyre, and he may continue at this for another three years, neither more nor less, and whether his father or himself like or dislike the study, he is not to be allowed to spend more or less time in learning music than the law allows. And let him who disobeys the law be deprived of those youthful honours of which we shall hereafter speak. Hear, however, first of all, what the young ought to learn in the early years of life, and what their instructors ought to teach them. They ought to be occupied with their letters until they are able to read and write; but the acquisition of perfect beauty or quickness in writing, if nature has not stimulated them to acquire these accomplishments in the given number of years, they should let alone. And as to the learning of compositions committed to writing which are not set to the lyre, whether metrical or without rhythmical divisions, compositions in prose, as they are termed, having no rhythm or harmony—seeing how dangerous are the writings handed down to us by many writers of this class—what will you do with them, O most excellent guardians of the law? or how can the lawgiver rightly direct you about them? I believe that he will be in great difficulty.

CLEINIAS: What troubles you, Stranger? and why are you so perplexed in your mind?

ATHENIAN: You naturally ask, Cleinias, and to you and Megillus, who are my partners in the work of legislation, I must state the more difficult as well as the easier parts of the task.

CLEINIAS: To what do you refer in this instance?

ATHENIAN: I will tell you. There is a difficulty in opposing many myriads of mouths.

CLEINIAS: Well, and have we not already opposed the popular voice in many important enactments?

ATHENIAN: That is quite true; and you mean to imply that the road which we are taking may be disagreeable to some but is agreeable to as many others, or if not to as many, at any rate to persons not inferior to the others, and in company with them you bid me, at whatever risk, to proceed along the path of legislation which has opened out of our present discourse, and to be of good cheer, and not to faint.

CLEINIAS: Certainly.

ATHENIAN: And I do not faint; I say, indeed, that we have a great many poets writing in hexameter, trimeter, and all sorts of measures—some who are serious, others who aim only at raising a laugh—and all mankind declare that the youth who are rightly educated should be brought up in them and saturated with them; some insist that they should be constantly hearing them read aloud, and always learning them, so as to get by heart entire poets; while others select choice passages and long speeches, and make compendiums of them, saying that these ought to be committed to memory, if a man is to be made good and wise by experience and learning of many things. And you want me now to tell them plainly in what they are right and in what they are wrong.

CLEINIAS: Yes, I do.

ATHENIAN: But how can I in one word rightly comprehend all of them? I am of opinion, and, if I am not mistaken, there is a general agreement, that every one of these poets has said many things well and many things the reverse of well; and if this be true, then I do affirm that much learning is dangerous to youth.

CLEINIAS: How would you advise the guardian of the law to act?

ATHENIAN: In what respect?

CLEINIAS: I mean to what pattern should he look as his guide in permitting the young to learn some things and forbidding them to learn others. Do not shrink from answering.

ATHENIAN: My good Cleinias, I rather think that I am fortunate.

CLEINIAS: How so?

ATHENIAN: I think that I am not wholly in want of a pattern, for when I consider the words which we have spoken from early dawn until now, and which, as I believe, have been inspired by Heaven, they appear to me to be quite like a poem. When I reflected upon all these words of ours, I naturally felt pleasure, for of all the discourses which I have ever learnt or heard, either in poetry or prose, this seemed to me to be the justest, and most suitable for young men to hear; I cannot imagine any better pattern than this which the guardian of the law who is also the director of education can have. He cannot do better than advise the teachers to teach the young these words and any which are of a like nature, if he should happen to find them, either in poetry or prose, or if he come across unwritten discourses akin to ours, he should certainly preserve them, and commit them to writing. And, first of all, he shall constrain the teachers themselves to learn and approve them, and any of them who will not, shall not be employed by him, but those whom he finds agreeing in his judgment, he shall make use of and shall commit to them the instruction and education of youth. And here and on this wise let my fanciful tale about letters and teachers of letters come to an end.

CLEINIAS: I do not think, Stranger, that we have wandered out of the proposed limits of the argument; but whether we are right or not in our whole conception, I cannot be very certain.

ATHENIAN: The truth, Cleinias, may be expected to become clearer when, as we have often said, we arrive at the end of the whole discussion about laws.

CLEINIAS: Yes.

ATHENIAN: And now that we have done with the teacher of letters, the teacher of the lyre has to receive orders from us.

CLEINIAS: Certainly.

ATHENIAN: I think that we have only to recollect our previous discussions, and we shall be able to give suitable regulations touching all this part of instruction and education to the teachers of the lyre.

CLEINIAS: To what do you refer?

ATHENIAN: We were saying, if I remember rightly, that the sixty years old choristers of Dionysus were to be specially quick in their perceptions of rhythm and musical composition, that they might be able to distinguish good and bad imitation, that is to say, the imitation of the good or bad soul when under the influence of passion, rejecting the one and displaying the other in hymns and songs, charming the souls of youth, and inviting them to follow and attain virtue by the way of imitation.

CLEINIAS: Very true.

ATHENIAN: And with this view the teacher and the learner ought to use the sounds of the lyre, because its notes are pure, the player who teaches and his pupil rendering note for note in unison; but complexity, and variation of notes, when the strings give one sound and the poet or composer of the melody gives another—also when they make concords and harmonies in which lesser and greater intervals, slow and quick, or high and low notes, are combined—or, again, when they make complex variations of rhythms, which they adapt to the notes of the lyre—all that sort of thing is not suited to those who have to acquire speedy and useful knowledge of music in three years; for opposite principles are confusing, and create a difficulty in learning, and our young men should learn quickly, and their mere necessary acquirements are not few or trifling, as will be shown in due course. Let the director of education attend to the principles concerning music which we are laying down. As to the songs and words themselves which the masters of choruses are to teach and the character of them, they have been already described by us, and are the same which, when consecrated and adapted to the different festivals, we said were to benefit cities by affording them an innocent amusement.

CLEINIAS: That, again, is true.

ATHENIAN: Then let him who has been elected a director of music receive these rules from us as containing the very truth; and may he prosper in his office! Let us now proceed to lay down other rules in addition to the preceding about dancing and gymnastic exercise in general. Having said what remained to be said about the teaching of music, let us speak in like manner about gymnastic. For boys and girls ought to learn to dance and practise gymnastic exercises—ought they not?

CLEINIAS: Yes.

ATHENIAN: Then the boys ought to have dancing masters, and the girls dancing mistresses to exercise them.

CLEINIAS: Very good.

ATHENIAN: Then once more let us summon him who has the chief concern in the business, the superintendent of youth [i.e. the director of education]; he will have plenty to do, if he is to have the charge of music and gymnastic.

CLEINIAS: But how will an old man be able to attend to such great charges?

ATHENIAN: O my friend, there will be no difficulty, for the law has already given and will give him permission to select as his assistants in this charge any citizens, male or female, whom he desires; and he will know whom he ought to choose, and will be anxious not to make a mistake, from a due sense of responsibility, and from a consciousness of the importance of his office, and also because he will consider that if young men have been and are well brought up, then all things go swimmingly, but if not, it is not meet to say, nor do we say, what will follow, lest the regarders of omens should take alarm about our infant state. Many things have been said by us about dancing and about gymnastic movements in general; for we include under gymnastics all military exercises, such as archery, and all hurling of weapons, and the use of the light shield, and all fighting with heavy arms, and military evolutions, and movements of armies, and encampings, and all that relates to horsemanship. Of all these things there ought to be public teachers, receiving pay from the state, and their pupils should be the men and boys in the state, and also the girls and women, who are to know all these things. While they are yet girls they should have practised dancing in arms and the whole art of fighting—when grown-up women, they should apply themselves to evolutions and tactics, and the mode of grounding and taking up arms; if for no other reason, yet in case the whole military force should have to leave the city and carry on operations of war outside, that those who will have to guard the young and the rest of the city may be equal to the task; and, on the other hand, when enemies, whether barbarian or Hellenic, come from without with mighty force and make a violent assault upon them, and thus compel them to fight for the possession of the city, which is far from being an impossibility, great would be the disgrace to the state, if the women had been so miserably trained that they could not fight for their young, as birds will, against any creature however strong, and die or undergo any danger, but must instantly rush to the temples and crowd at the altars and shrines, and bring upon human nature the reproach, that of all animals man is the most cowardly!

CLEINIAS: Such a want of education, Stranger, is certainly an unseemly thing to happen in a state, as well as a great misfortune.

ATHENIAN: Suppose that we carry our law to the extent of saying that women ought not to neglect military matters, but that all citizens, male and female alike, shall attend to them?

CLEINIAS: I quite agree.

ATHENIAN: Of wrestling we have spoken in part, but of what I should call the most important part we have not spoken, and cannot easily speak without showing at the same time by gesture as well as in word what we mean; when word and action combine, and not till then, we shall explain clearly what has been said, pointing out that of all movements wrestling is most akin to the military art, and is to be pursued for the sake of this, and not this for the sake of wrestling.

CLEINIAS: Excellent. ATHENIAN: Enough of wrestling; we will now proceed to speak of other movements of the body. Such motion may be in general called dancing, and is of two kinds: one of nobler figures, imitating the honourable, the other of the more ignoble figures, imitating the mean; and of both these there are two further subdivisions. Of the serious, one kind is of those engaged in war and vehement action, and is the exercise of a noble person and a manly heart; the other exhibits a temperate soul in the enjoyment of prosperity and modest pleasures, and may be truly called and is the dance of peace. The warrior dance is different from the peaceful one, and may be rightly termed Pyrrhic; this imitates the modes of avoiding blows and missiles by dropping or giving way, or springing aside, or rising up or falling down; also the opposite postures which are those of action, as, for example, the imitation of archery and the hurling of javelins, and of all sorts of blows. And when the imitation is of brave bodies and souls, and the action is direct and muscular, giving for the most part a straight movement to the limbs of the body—that, I say, is the true sort; but the opposite is not right. In the dance of peace what we have to consider is whether a man bears himself naturally and gracefully, and after the manner of men who duly conform to the law. But before proceeding I must distinguish the dancing about which there is any doubt, from that about which there is no doubt. Which is the doubtful kind, and how are the two to be distinguished? There are dances of the Bacchic sort, both those in which, as they say, they imitate drunken men, and which are named after the Nymphs, and Pan, and Silenuses, and Satyrs; and also those in which purifications are made or mysteries celebrated—all this sort of dancing cannot be rightly defined as having either a peaceful or a warlike character, or indeed as having any meaning whatever, and may, I think, be most truly described as distinct from the warlike dance, and distinct from the peaceful, and not suited for a city at all. There let it lie; and so leaving it to lie, we will proceed to the dances of war and peace, for with these we are undoubtedly concerned. Now the unwarlike muse, which honours in dance the Gods and the sons of the Gods, is entirely associated with the consciousness of prosperity; this class may be subdivided into two lesser classes, of which one is expressive of an escape from some labour or danger into good, and has greater pleasures, the other expressive of preservation and increase of former good, in which the pleasure is less exciting—in all these cases, every man when the pleasure is greater, moves his body more, and less when the pleasure is less; and, again, if he be more orderly and has learned courage from discipline he moves less, but if he be a coward, and has no training or self-control, he makes greater and more violent movements, and in general when he is speaking or singing he is not altogether able to keep his body still; and so out of the imitation of words in gestures the whole art of dancing has arisen. And in these various kinds of imitation one man moves in an orderly, another in a disorderly manner; and as the ancients may be observed to have given many names which are according to nature and deserving of praise, so there is an excellent one which they have given to the dances of men who in their times of prosperity are moderate in their pleasures—the giver of names, whoever he was, assigned to them a very true, and poetical, and rational name, when he called them Emmeleiai, or dances of order, thus establishing two kinds of dances of the nobler sort, the dance of war which he called the Pyrrhic, and the dance of peace which he called Emmeleia, or the dance of order; giving to each their appropriate and becoming name. These things the legislator should indicate in general outline, and the guardian of the law should enquire into them and search them out, combining dancing with music, and assigning to the several sacrificial feasts that which is suitable to them; and when he has consecrated all of them in due order, he shall for the future change nothing, whether of dance or song. Thenceforward the city and the citizens shall continue to have the same pleasures, themselves being as far as possible alike, and shall live well and happily.

I have described the dances which are appropriate to noble bodies and generous souls. But it is necessary also to consider and know uncomely persons and thoughts, and those which are intended to produce laughter in comedy, and have a comic character in respect of style, song, and dance, and of the imitations which these afford. For serious things cannot be understood without laughable things, nor opposites at all without opposites, if a man is really to have intelligence of either; but he cannot carry out both in action, if he is to have any degree of virtue. And for this very reason he should learn them both, in order that he may not in ignorance do or say anything which is ridiculous and out of place—he should command slaves and hired strangers to imitate such things, but he should never take any serious interest in them himself, nor should any freeman or freewoman be discovered taking pains to learn them; and there should always be some element of novelty in the imitation. Let these then be laid down, both in law and in our discourse, as the regulations of laughable amusements which are generally called comedy. And, if any of the serious poets, as they are termed, who write tragedy, come to us and say—'O strangers, may we go to your city and country or may we not, and shall we bring with us our poetry—what is your will about these matters?'—how shall we answer the divine men? I think that our answer should be as follows: Best of strangers, we will say to them, we also according to our ability are tragic poets, and our tragedy is the best and noblest; for our whole state is an imitation of the best and noblest life, which we affirm to be indeed the very truth of tragedy. You are poets and we are poets, both makers of the same strains, rivals and antagonists in the noblest of dramas, which true law can alone perfect, as our hope is. Do not then suppose that we shall all in a moment allow you to erect your stage in the agora, or introduce the fair voices of your actors, speaking above our own, and permit you to harangue our women and children, and the common people, about our institutions, in language other than our own, and very often the opposite of our own. For a state would be mad which gave you this licence, until the magistrates had determined whether your poetry might be recited, and was fit for publication or not. Wherefore, O ye sons and scions of the softer Muses, first of all show your songs to the magistrates, and let them compare them with our own, and if they are the same or better we will give you a chorus; but if not, then, my friends, we cannot. Let these, then, be the customs ordained by law about all dances and the teaching of them, and let matters relating to slaves be separated from those relating to masters, if you do not object.

CLEINIAS: We can have no hesitation in assenting when you put the matter thus.

ATHENIAN: There still remain three studies suitable for freemen. Arithmetic is one of them; the measurement of length, surface, and depth is the second; and the third has to do with the revolutions of the stars in relation to one another. Not every one has need to toil through all these things in a strictly scientific manner, but only a few, and who they are to be we will hereafter indicate at the end, which will be the proper place; not to know what is necessary for mankind in general, and what is the truth, is disgraceful to every one: and yet to enter into these matters minutely is neither easy, nor at all possible for every one; but there is something in them which is necessary and cannot be set aside, and probably he who made the proverb about God originally had this in view when he said, that 'not even God himself can fight against necessity;' he meant, if I am not mistaken, divine necessity; for as to the human necessities of which the many speak, when they talk in this manner, nothing can be more ridiculous than such an application of the words.

CLEINIAS: And what necessities of knowledge are there, Stranger, which are divine and not human?

ATHENIAN: I conceive them to be those of which he who has no use nor any knowledge at all cannot be a God, or demi-god, or hero to mankind, or able to take any serious thought or charge of them. And very unlike a divine man would he be, who is unable to count one, two, three, or to distinguish odd and even numbers, or is unable to count at all, or reckon night and day, and who is totally unacquainted with the revolution of the sun and moon, and the other stars. There would be great folly in supposing that all these are not necessary parts of knowledge to him who intends to know anything about the highest kinds of knowledge; but which these are, and how many there are of them, and when they are to be learned, and what is to be learned together and what apart, and the whole correlation of them, must be rightly apprehended first; and these leading the way we may proceed to the other parts of knowledge. For so necessity grounded in nature constrains us, against which we say that no God contends, or ever will contend.

CLEINIAS: I think, Stranger, that what you have now said is very true and agreeable to nature.

ATHENIAN: Yes, Cleinias, that is so. But it is difficult for the legislator to begin with these studies; at a more convenient time we will make regulations for them.

CLEINIAS: You seem, Stranger, to be afraid of our habitual ignorance of the subject: there is no reason why that should prevent you from speaking out.

ATHENIAN: I certainly am afraid of the difficulties to which you allude, but I am still more afraid of those who apply themselves to this sort of knowledge, and apply themselves badly. For entire ignorance is not so terrible or extreme an evil, and is far from being the greatest of all; too much cleverness and too much learning, accompanied with an ill bringing up, are far more fatal.

CLEINIAS: True.

ATHENIAN: All freemen I conceive, should learn as much of these branches of knowledge as every child in Egypt is taught when he learns the alphabet. In that country arithmetical games have been invented for the use of mere children, which they learn as a pleasure and amusement. They have to distribute apples and garlands, using the same number sometimes for a larger and sometimes for a lesser number of persons; and they arrange pugilists and wrestlers as they pair together by lot or remain over, and show how their turns come in natural order. Another mode of amusing them is to distribute vessels, sometimes of gold, brass, silver, and the like, intermixed with one another, sometimes of one metal only; as I was saying they adapt to their amusement the numbers in common use, and in this way make more intelligible to their pupils the arrangements and movements of armies and expeditions, and in the management of a household they make people more useful to themselves, and more wide awake; and again in measurements of things which have length, and breadth, and depth, they free us from that natural ignorance of all these things which is so ludicrous and disgraceful.

CLEINIAS: What kind of ignorance do you mean?

ATHENIAN: O my dear Cleinias, I, like yourself, have late in life heard with amazement of our ignorance in these matters; to me we appear to be more like pigs than men, and I am quite ashamed, not only of myself, but of all Hellenes.

CLEINIAS: About what? Say, Stranger, what you mean.

ATHENIAN: I will; or rather I will show you my meaning by a question, and do you please to answer me: You know, I suppose, what length is?

CLEINIAS: Certainly.

ATHENIAN: And what breadth is?

CLEINIAS: To be sure.

ATHENIAN: And you know that these are two distinct things, and that there is a third thing called depth?

CLEINIAS: Of course.

ATHENIAN: And do not all these seem to you to be commensurable with themselves?

CLEINIAS: Yes.

ATHENIAN: That is to say, length is naturally commensurable with length, and breadth with breadth, and depth in like manner with depth?

CLEINIAS: Undoubtedly.

ATHENIAN: But if some things are commensurable and others wholly incommensurable, and you think that all things are commensurable, what is your position in regard to them?

CLEINIAS: Clearly, far from good.

ATHENIAN: Concerning length and breadth when compared with depth, or breadth and length when compared with one another, are not all the Hellenes agreed that these are commensurable with one another in some way?

CLEINIAS: Quite true.

ATHENIAN: But if they are absolutely incommensurable, and yet all of us regard them as commensurable, have we not reason to be ashamed of our compatriots; and might we not say to them: O ye best of Hellenes, is not this one of the things of which we were saying that not to know them is disgraceful, and of which to have a bare knowledge only is no great distinction?

CLEINIAS: Certainly.

ATHENIAN: And there are other things akin to these, in which there spring up other errors of the same family.

CLEINIAS: What are they?

ATHENIAN: The natures of commensurable and incommensurable quantities in their relation to one another. A man who is good for anything ought to be able, when he thinks, to distinguish them; and different persons should compete with one another in asking questions, which will be a far better and more graceful way of passing their time than the old man's game of draughts.

CLEINIAS: I dare say; and these pastimes are not so very unlike a game of draughts.

ATHENIAN: And these, as I maintain, Cleinias, are the studies which our youth ought to learn, for they are innocent and not difficult; the learning of them will be an amusement, and they will benefit the state. If any one is of another mind, let him say what he has to say.

CLEINIAS: Certainly.

ATHENIAN: Then if these studies are such as we maintain, we will include them; if not, they shall be excluded.

CLEINIAS: Assuredly: but may we not now, Stranger, prescribe these studies as necessary, and so fill up the lacunae of our laws?

ATHENIAN: They shall be regarded as pledges which may be hereafter redeemed and removed from our state, if they do not please either us who give them, or you who accept them.

CLEINIAS: A fair condition.

ATHENIAN: Next let us see whether we are or are not willing that the study of astronomy shall be proposed for our youth.

CLEINIAS: Proceed.

ATHENIAN: Here occurs a strange phenomenon, which certainly cannot in any point of view be tolerated.

CLEINIAS: To what are you referring?

ATHENIAN: Men say that we ought not to enquire into the supreme God and the nature of the universe, nor busy ourselves in searching out the causes of things, and that such enquiries are impious; whereas the very opposite is the truth.

CLEINIAS: What do you mean?

ATHENIAN: Perhaps what I am saying may seem paradoxical, and at variance with the usual language of age. But when any one has any good and true notion which is for the advantage of the state and in every way acceptable to God, he cannot abstain from expressing it.

CLEINIAS: Your words are reasonable enough; but shall we find any good or true notion about the stars?

ATHENIAN: My good friends, at this hour all of us Hellenes tell lies, if I may use such an expression, about those great Gods, the Sun and the Moon.

CLEINIAS: Lies of what nature?

ATHENIAN: We say that they and divers other stars do not keep the same path, and we call them planets or wanderers.

CLEINIAS: Very true, Stranger; and in the course of my life I have often myself seen the morning star and the evening star and divers others not moving in their accustomed course, but wandering out of their path in all manner of ways, and I have seen the sun and moon doing what we all know that they do.

ATHENIAN: Just so, Megillus and Cleinias; and I maintain that our citizens and our youth ought to learn about the nature of the Gods in heaven, so far as to be able to offer sacrifices and pray to them in pious language, and not to blaspheme about them.

CLEINIAS: There you are right, if such a knowledge be only attainable; and if we are wrong in our mode of speaking now, and can be better instructed and learn to use better language, then I quite agree with you that such a degree of knowledge as will enable us to speak rightly should be acquired by us. And now do you try to explain to us your whole meaning, and we, on our part, will endeavour to understand you.

ATHENIAN: There is some difficulty in understanding my meaning, but not a very great one, nor will any great length of time be required. And of this I am myself a proof; for I did not know these things long ago, nor in the days of my youth, and yet I can explain them to you in a brief space of time; whereas if they had been difficult I could certainly never have explained them all, old as I am, to old men like yourselves.

CLEINIAS: True; but what is this study which you describe as wonderful and fitting for youth to learn, but of which we are ignorant? Try and explain the nature of it to us as clearly as you can.

ATHENIAN: I will. For, O my good friends, that other doctrine about the wandering of the sun and the moon and the other stars is not the truth, but the very reverse of the truth. Each of them moves in the same path—not in many paths, but in one only, which is circular, and the varieties are only apparent. Nor are we right in supposing that the swiftest of them is the slowest, nor conversely, that the slowest is the quickest. And if what I say is true, only just imagine that we had a similar notion about horses running at Olympia, or about men who ran in the long course, and that we addressed the swiftest as the slowest and the slowest as the swiftest, and sang the praises of the vanquished as though he were the victor—in that case our praises would not be true, nor very agreeable to the runners, though they be but men; and now, to commit the same error about the Gods which would have been ludicrous and erroneous in the case of men—is not that ludicrous and erroneous?

CLEINIAS: Worse than ludicrous, I should say.

ATHENIAN: At all events, the Gods cannot like us to be spreading a false report of them.

CLEINIAS: Most true, if such is the fact.

ATHENIAN: And if we can show that such is really the fact, then all these matters ought to be learned so far as is necessary for the avoidance of impiety; but if we cannot, they may be let alone, and let this be our decision.

CLEINIAS: Very good.

ATHENIAN: Enough of laws relating to education and learning. But hunting and similar pursuits in like manner claim our attention. For the legislator appears to have a duty imposed upon him which goes beyond mere legislation. There is something over and above law which lies in a region between admonition and law, and has several times occurred to us in the course of discussion; for example, in the education of very young children there were things, as we maintain, which are not to be defined, and to regard them as matters of positive law is a great absurdity. Now, our laws and the whole constitution of our state having been thus delineated, the praise of the virtuous citizen is not complete when he is described as the person who serves the laws best and obeys them most, but the higher form of praise is that which describes him as the good citizen who passes through life undefiled and is obedient to the words of the legislator, both when he is giving laws and when he assigns praise and blame. This is the truest word that can be spoken in praise of a citizen; and the true legislator ought not only to write his laws, but also to interweave with them all such things as seem to him honourable and dishonourable. And the perfect citizen ought to seek to strengthen these no less than the principles of law which are sanctioned by punishments. I will adduce an example which will clear up my meaning, and will be a sort of witness to my words. Hunting is of wide extent, and has a name under which many things are included, for there is a hunting of creatures in the water, and of creatures in the air, and there is a great deal of hunting of land animals of all kinds, and not of wild beasts only. The hunting after man is also worthy of consideration; there is the hunting after him in war, and there is often a hunting after him in the way of friendship, which is praised and also blamed; and there is thieving, and the hunting which is practised by robbers, and that of armies against armies. Now the legislator, in laying down laws about hunting, can neither abstain from noting these things, nor can he make threatening ordinances which will assign rules and penalties about all of them. What is he to do? He will have to praise and blame hunting with a view to the exercise and pursuits of youth. And, on the other hand, the young man must listen obediently; neither pleasure nor pain should hinder him, and he should regard as his standard of action the praises and injunctions of the legislator rather than the punishments which he imposes by law. This being premised, there will follow next in order moderate praise and censure of hunting; the praise being assigned to that kind which will make the souls of young men better, and the censure to that which has the opposite effect. And now let us address young men in the form of a prayer for their welfare: O friends, we will say to them, may no desire or love of hunting in the sea, or of angling or of catching the creatures in the waters, ever take possession of you, either when you are awake or when you are asleep, by hook or with weels, which latter is a very lazy contrivance; and let not any desire of catching men and of piracy by sea enter into your souls and make you cruel and lawless hunters. And as to the desire of thieving in town or country, may it never enter into your most passing thoughts; nor let the insidious fancy of catching birds, which is hardly worthy of freemen, come into the head of any youth. There remains therefore for our athletes only the hunting and catching of land animals, of which the one sort is called hunting by night, in which the hunters sleep in turn and are lazy; this is not to be commended any more than that which has intervals of rest, in which the wild strength of beasts is subdued by nets and snares, and not by the victory of a laborious spirit. Thus, only the best kind of hunting is allowed at all—that of quadrupeds, which is carried on with horses and dogs and men's own persons, and they get the victory over the animals by running them down and striking them and hurling at them, those who have a care of godlike manhood taking them with their own hands. The praise and blame which is assigned to all these things has now been declared; and let the law be as follows: Let no one hinder these who verily are sacred hunters from following the chase wherever and whithersoever they will; but the hunter by night, who trusts to his nets and gins, shall not be allowed to hunt anywhere. The fowler in the mountains and waste places shall be permitted, but on cultivated ground and on consecrated wilds he shall not be permitted; and any one who meets him may stop him. As to the hunter in waters, he may hunt anywhere except in harbours or sacred streams or marshes or pools, provided only that he do not pollute the water with poisonous juices. And now we may say that all our enactments about education are complete.

CLEINIAS: Very good.

BOOK VIII.

ATHENIAN: Next, with the help of the Delphian oracle, we have to institute festivals and make laws about them, and to determine what sacrifices will be for the good of the city, and to what Gods they shall be offered; but when they shall be offered, and how often, may be partly regulated by us.

CLEINIAS: The number—yes.

ATHENIAN: Then we will first determine the number; and let the whole number be 365—one for every day—so that one magistrate at least will sacrifice daily to some God or demi-god on behalf of the city, and the citizens, and their possessions. And the interpreters, and priests, and priestesses, and prophets shall meet, and, in company with the guardians of the law, ordain those things which the legislator of necessity omits; and I may remark that they are the very persons who ought to take note of what is omitted. The law will say that there are twelve feasts dedicated to the twelve Gods, after whom the several tribes are named; and that to each of them they shall sacrifice every month, and appoint choruses, and musical and gymnastic contests, assigning them so as to suit the Gods and seasons of the year. And they shall have festivals for women, distinguishing those which ought to be separated from the men's festivals, and those which ought not. Further, they shall not confuse the infernal deities and their rites with the Gods who are termed heavenly and their rites, but shall separate them, giving to Pluto his own in the twelfth month, which is sacred to him, according to the law. To such a deity warlike men should entertain no aversion, but they should honour him as being always the best friend of man. For the connexion of soul and body is no way better than the dissolution of them, as I am ready to maintain quite seriously. Moreover, those who would regulate these matters rightly should consider, that our city among existing cities has no fellow, either in respect of leisure or command of the necessaries of life, and that like an individual she ought to live happily. And those who would live happily should in the first place do no wrong to one another, and ought not themselves to be wronged by others; to attain the first is not difficult, but there is great difficulty in acquiring the power of not being wronged. No man can be perfectly secure against wrong, unless he has become perfectly good; and cities are like individuals in this, for a city if good has a life of peace, but if evil, a life of war within and without. Wherefore the citizens ought to practise war—not in time of war, but rather while they are at peace. And every city which has any sense, should take the field at least for one day in every month, and for more if the magistrates think fit, having no regard to winter cold or summer heat; and they should go out en masse, including their wives and their children, when the magistrates determine to lead forth the whole people, or in separate portions when summoned by them; and they should always provide that there should be games and sacrificial feasts, and they should have tournaments, imitating in as lively a manner as they can real battles. And they should distribute prizes of victory and valour to the competitors, passing censures and encomiums on one another according to the characters which they bear in the contests and in their whole life, honouring him who seems to be the best, and blaming him who is the opposite. And let poets celebrate the victors—not however every poet, but only one who in the first place is not less than fifty years of age; nor should he be one who, although he may have musical and poetical gifts, has never in his life done any noble or illustrious action; but those who are themselves good and also honourable in the state, creators of noble actions—let their poems be sung, even though they be not very musical. And let the judgment of them rest with the instructor of youth and the other guardians of the laws, who shall give them this privilege, and they alone shall be free to sing; but the rest of the world shall not have this liberty. Nor shall any one dare to sing a song which has not been approved by the judgment of the guardians of the laws, not even if his strain be sweeter than the songs of Thamyras and Orpheus; but only such poems as have been judged sacred and dedicated to the Gods, and such as are the works of good men, in which praise or blame has been awarded and which have been deemed to fulfil their design fairly.

The regulations about war, and about liberty of speech in poetry, ought to apply equally to men and women. The legislator may be supposed to argue the question in his own mind: Who are my citizens for whom I have set in order the city? Are they not competitors in the greatest of all contests, and have they not innumerable rivals? To be sure, will be the natural reply. Well, but if we were training boxers, or pancratiasts, or any other sort of athletes, would they never meet until the hour of contest arrived; and should we do nothing to prepare ourselves previously by daily practice? Surely, if we were boxers, we should have been learning to fight for many days before, and exercising ourselves in imitating all those blows and wards which we were intending to use in the hour of conflict; and in order that we might come as near to reality as possible, instead of cestuses we should put on boxing-gloves, that the blows and the wards might be practised by us to the utmost of our power. And if there were a lack of competitors, the ridicule of fools would not deter us from hanging up a lifeless image and practising at that. Or if we had no adversary at all, animate or inanimate, should we not venture in the dearth of antagonists to spar by ourselves? In what other manner could we ever study the art of self-defence?

CLEINIAS: The way which you mention, Stranger, would be the only way.

ATHENIAN: And shall the warriors of our city, who are destined when occasion calls to enter the greatest of all contests, and to fight for their lives, and their children, and their property, and the whole city, be worse prepared than boxers? And will the legislator, because he is afraid that their practising with one another may appear to some ridiculous, abstain from commanding them to go out and fight; will he not ordain that soldiers shall perform lesser exercises without arms every day, making dancing and all gymnastic tend to this end; and also will he not require that they shall practise some gymnastic exercises, greater as well as lesser, as often as every month; and that they shall have contests one with another in every part of the country, seizing upon posts and lying in ambush, and imitating in every respect the reality of war; fighting with boxing-gloves and hurling javelins, and using weapons somewhat dangerous, and as nearly as possible like the true ones, in order that the sport may not be altogether without fear, but may have terrors and to a certain degree show the man who has and who has not courage; and that the honour and dishonour which are assigned to them respectively, may prepare the whole city for the true conflict of life? If any one dies in these mimic contests, the homicide is involuntary, and we will make the slayer, when he has been purified according to law, to be pure of blood, considering that if a few men should die, others as good as they will be born; but that if fear is dead, then the citizens will never find a test of superior and inferior natures, which is a far greater evil to the state than the loss of a few.

CLEINIAS: We are quite agreed, Stranger, that we should legislate about such things, and that the whole state should practise them.

ATHENIAN: And what is the reason that dances and contests of this sort hardly ever exist in states, at least not to any extent worth speaking of? Is this due to the ignorance of mankind and their legislators?

CLEINIAS: Perhaps.

ATHENIAN: Certainly not, sweet Cleinias; there are two causes, which are quite enough to account for the deficiency.

CLEINIAS: What are they?

ATHENIAN: One cause is the love of wealth, which wholly absorbs men, and never for a moment allows them to think of anything but their own private possessions; on this the soul of every citizen hangs suspended, and can attend to nothing but his daily gain; mankind are ready to learn any branch of knowledge, and to follow any pursuit which tends to this end, and they laugh at every other: that is one reason why a city will not be in earnest about such contests or any other good and honourable pursuit. But from an insatiable love of gold and silver, every man will stoop to any art or contrivance, seemly or unseemly, in the hope of becoming rich; and will make no objection to performing any action, holy, or unholy and utterly base; if only like a beast he have the power of eating and drinking all kinds of things, and procuring for himself in every sort of way the gratification of his lusts.

CLEINIAS: True.

ATHENIAN: Let this, then, be deemed one of the causes which prevent states from pursuing in an efficient manner the art of war, or any other noble aim, but makes the orderly and temperate part of mankind into merchants, and captains of ships, and servants, and converts the valiant sort into thieves and burglars, and robbers of temples, and violent, tyrannical persons; many of whom are not without ability, but they are unfortunate.

CLEINIAS: What do you mean?

ATHENIAN: Must not they be truly unfortunate whose souls are compelled to pass through life always hungering?

CLEINIAS: Then that is one cause, Stranger; but you spoke of another.

ATHENIAN: Thank you for reminding me.

CLEINIAS: The insatiable lifelong love of wealth, as you were saying, is one cause which absorbs mankind, and prevents them from rightly practising the arts of war: Granted; and now tell me, what is the other?

ATHENIAN: Do you imagine that I delay because I am in a perplexity?

CLEINIAS: No; but we think that you are too severe upon the money-loving temper, of which you seem in the present discussion to have a peculiar dislike.

ATHENIAN: That is a very fair rebuke, Cleinias; and I will now proceed to the second cause.

CLEINIAS: Proceed.

ATHENIAN: I say that governments are a cause—democracy, oligarchy, tyranny, concerning which I have often spoken in the previous discourse; or rather governments they are not, for none of them exercises a voluntary rule over voluntary subjects; but they may be truly called states of discord, in which while the government is voluntary, the subjects always obey against their will, and have to be coerced; and the ruler fears the subject, and will not, if he can help, allow him to become either noble, or rich, or strong, or valiant, or warlike at all. These two are the chief causes of almost all evils, and of the evils of which I have been speaking they are notably the causes. But our state has escaped both of them; for her citizens have the greatest leisure, and they are not subject to one another, and will, I think, be made by these laws the reverse of lovers of money. Such a constitution may be reasonably supposed to be the only one existing which will accept the education which we have described, and the martial pastimes which have been perfected according to our idea.

CLEINIAS: True.

ATHENIAN: Then next we must remember, about all gymnastic contests, that only the warlike sort of them are to be practised and to have prizes of victory; and those which are not military are to be given up. The military sort had better be completely described and established by law; and first, let us speak of running and swiftness.

CLEINIAS: Very good.

ATHENIAN: Certainly the most military of all qualities is general activity of body, whether of foot or hand. For escaping or for capturing an enemy, quickness of foot is required; but hand-to-hand conflict and combat need vigour and strength.

CLEINIAS: Very true.

ATHENIAN: Neither of them can attain their greatest efficiency without arms.

CLEINIAS: How can they?

ATHENIAN: Then our herald, in accordance with the prevailing practice, will first summon the runner—he will appear armed, for to an unarmed competitor we will not give a prize. And he shall enter first who is to run the single course bearing arms; next, he who is to run the double course; third, he who is to run the horse-course; and fourthly, he who is to run the long course; the fifth whom we start, shall be the first sent forth in heavy armour, and shall run a course of sixty stadia to some temple of Ares—and we will send forth another, whom we will style the more heavily armed, to run over smoother ground. There remains the archer; and he shall run in the full equipments of an archer a distance of 100 stadia over mountains, and across every sort of country, to a temple of Apollo and Artemis; this shall be the order of the contest, and we will wait for them until they return, and will give a prize to the conqueror in each.

CLEINIAS: Very good.

ATHENIAN: Let us suppose that there are three kinds of contests—one of boys, another of beardless youths, and a third of men. For the youths we will fix the length of the contest at two-thirds, and for the boys at half of the entire course, whether they contend as archers or as heavy-armed. Touching the women, let the girls who are not grown up compete naked in the stadium and the double course, and the horse-course and the long course, and let them run on the race-ground itself; those who are thirteen years of age and upwards until their marriage shall continue to share in contests if they are not more than twenty, and shall be compelled to run up to eighteen; and they shall descend into the arena in suitable dresses. Let these be the regulations about contests in running both for men and women.

Respecting contests of strength, instead of wrestling and similar contests of the heavier sort, we will institute conflicts in armour of one against one, and two against two, and so on up to ten against ten. As to what a man ought not to suffer or do, and to what extent, in order to gain the victory—as in wrestling, the masters of the art have laid down what is fair and what is not fair, so in fighting in armour—we ought to call in skilful persons, who shall judge for us and be our assessors in the work of legislation; they shall say who deserves to be victor in combats of this sort, and what he is not to do or have done to him, and in like manner what rule determines who is defeated; and let these ordinances apply to women until they are married as well as to men. The pancration shall have a counterpart in a combat of the light-armed; they shall contend with bows and with light shields and with javelins and in the throwing of stones by slings and by hand: and laws shall be made about it, and rewards and prizes given to him who best fulfils the ordinances of the law.

Next in order we shall have to legislate about the horse contests. Now we do not need many horses, for they cannot be of much use in a country like Crete, and hence we naturally do not take great pains about the rearing of them or about horse races. There is no one who keeps a chariot among us, and any rivalry in such matters would be altogether out of place; there would be no sense nor any shadow of sense in instituting contests which are not after the manner of our country. And therefore we give our prizes for single horses—for colts who have not yet cast their teeth, and for those who are intermediate, and for the full-grown horses themselves; and thus our equestrian games will accord with the nature of the country. Let them have conflict and rivalry in these matters in accordance with the law, and let the colonels and generals of horse decide together about all courses and about the armed competitors in them. But we have nothing to say to the unarmed either in gymnastic exercises or in these contests. On the other hand, the Cretan bowman or javelin-man who fights in armour on horseback is useful, and therefore we may as well place a competition of this sort among our amusements. Women are not to be forced to compete by laws and ordinances; but if from previous training they have acquired the habit and are strong enough and like to take part, let them do so, girls as well as boys, and no blame to them.

Thus the competition in gymnastic and the mode of learning it have been described; and we have spoken also of the toils of the contest, and of daily exercises under the superintendence of masters. Likewise, what relates to music has been, for the most part, completed. But as to rhapsodes and the like, and the contests of choruses which are to perform at feasts, all this shall be arranged when the months and days and years have been appointed for Gods and demi-gods, whether every third year, or again every fifth year, or in whatever way or manner the Gods may put into men's minds the distribution and order of them. At the same time, we may expect that the musical contests will be celebrated in their turn by the command of the judges and the director of education and the guardians of the law meeting together for this purpose, and themselves becoming legislators of the times and nature and conditions of the choral contests and of dancing in general. What they ought severally to be in language and song, and in the admixture of harmony with rhythm and the dance, has been often declared by the original legislator; and his successors ought to follow him, making the games and sacrifices duly to correspond at fitting times, and appointing public festivals. It is not difficult to determine how these and the like matters may have a regular order; nor, again, will the alteration of them do any great good or harm to the state. There is, however, another matter of great importance and difficulty, concerning which God should legislate, if there were any possibility of obtaining from Him an ordinance about it. But seeing that divine aid is not to be had, there appears to be a need of some bold man who specially honours plainness of speech, and will say outright what he thinks best for the city and citizens—ordaining what is good and convenient for the whole state amid the corruptions of human souls, opposing the mightiest lusts, and having no man his helper but himself standing alone and following reason only.

CLEINIAS: What is this, Stranger, that you are saying? For we do not as yet understand your meaning.

ATHENIAN: Very likely; I will endeavour to explain myself more clearly. When I came to the subject of education, I beheld young men and maidens holding friendly intercourse with one another. And there naturally arose in my mind a sort of apprehension—I could not help thinking how one is to deal with a city in which youths and maidens are well nurtured, and have nothing to do, and are not undergoing the excessive and servile toils which extinguish wantonness, and whose only cares during their whole life are sacrifices and festivals and dances. How, in such a state as this, will they abstain from desires which thrust many a man and woman into perdition; and from which reason, assuming the functions of law, commands them to abstain? The ordinances already made may possibly get the better of most of these desires; the prohibition of excessive wealth is a very considerable gain in the direction of temperance, and the whole education of our youth imposes a law of moderation on them; moreover, the eye of the rulers is required always to watch over the young, and never to lose sight of them; and these provisions do, as far as human means can effect anything, exercise a regulating influence upon the desires in general. But how can we take precautions against the unnatural loves of either sex, from which innumerable evils have come upon individuals and cities? How shall we devise a remedy and way of escape out of so great a danger? Truly, Cleinias, here is a difficulty. In many ways Crete and Lacedaemon furnish a great help to those who make peculiar laws; but in the matter of love, as we are alone, I must confess that they are quite against us. For if any one following nature should lay down the law which existed before the days of Laius, and denounce these lusts as contrary to nature, adducing the animals as a proof that such unions were monstrous, he might prove his point, but he would be wholly at variance with the custom of your states. Further, they are repugnant to a principle which we say that a legislator should always observe; for we are always enquiring which of our enactments tends to virtue and which not. And suppose we grant that these loves are accounted by law to the honourable, or at least not disgraceful, in what degree will they contribute to virtue? Will such passions implant in the soul of him who is seduced the habit of courage, or in the soul of the seducer the principle of temperance? Who will ever believe this? or rather, who will not blame the effeminacy of him who yields to pleasures and is unable to hold out against them? Will not all men censure as womanly him who imitates the woman? And who would ever think of establishing such a practice by law? certainly no one who had in his mind the image of true law. How can we prove that what I am saying is true? He who would rightly consider these matters must see the nature of friendship and desire, and of these so-called loves, for they are of two kinds, and out of the two arises a third kind, having the same name; and this similarity of name causes all the difficulty and obscurity.

CLEINIAS: How is that?

ATHENIAN: Dear is the like in virtue to the like, and the equal to the equal; dear also, though unlike, is he who has abundance to him who is in want. And when either of these friendships becomes excessive, we term the excess love.

CLEINIAS: Very true.

ATHENIAN: The friendship which arises from contraries is horrible and coarse, and has often no tie of communion; but that which arises from likeness is gentle, and has a tie of communion which lasts through life. As to the mixed sort which is made up of them both, there is, first of all, a difficulty in determining what he who is possessed by this third love desires; moreover, he is drawn different ways, and is in doubt between the two principles; the one exhorting him to enjoy the beauty of youth, and the other forbidding him. For the one is a lover of the body, and hungers after beauty, like ripe fruit, and would fain satisfy himself without any regard to the character of the beloved; the other holds the desire of the body to be a secondary matter, and looking rather than loving and with his soul desiring the soul of the other in a becoming manner, regards the satisfaction of the bodily love as wantonness; he reverences and respects temperance and courage and magnanimity and wisdom, and wishes to live chastely with the chaste object of his affection. Now the sort of love which is made up of the other two is that which we have described as the third. Seeing then that there are these three sorts of love, ought the law to prohibit and forbid them all to exist among us? Is it not rather clear that we should wish to have in the state the love which is of virtue and which desires the beloved youth to be the best possible; and the other two, if possible, we should hinder? What do you say, friend Megillus?

MEGILLUS: I think, Stranger, that you are perfectly right in what you have been now saying.

Athenian: I knew well, my friend, that I should obtain your assent, which I accept, and therefore have no need to analyze your custom any further. Cleinias shall be prevailed upon to give me his assent at some other time. Enough of this; and now let us proceed to the laws.

MEGILLUS: Very good.

ATHENIAN: Upon reflection I see a way of imposing the law, which, in one respect, is easy, but, in another, is of the utmost difficulty.

MEGILLUS: What do you mean?

ATHENIAN: We are all aware that most men, in spite of their lawless natures, are very strictly and precisely restrained from intercourse with the fair, and this is not at all against their will, but entirely with their will.

MEGILLUS: When do you mean?

ATHENIAN: When any one has a brother or sister who is fair; and about a son or daughter the same unwritten law holds, and is a most perfect safeguard, so that no open or secret connexion ever takes place between them. Nor does the thought of such a thing ever enter at all into the minds of most of them.

MEGILLUS: Very true.

ATHENIAN: Does not a little word extinguish all pleasures of that sort?

MEGILLUS: What word?

ATHENIAN: The declaration that they are unholy, hated of God, and most infamous; and is not the reason of this that no one has ever said the opposite, but every one from his earliest childhood has heard men speaking in the same manner about them always and everywhere, whether in comedy or in the graver language of tragedy? When the poet introduces on the stage a Thyestes or an Oedipus, or a Macareus having secret intercourse with his sister, he represents him, when found out, ready to kill himself as the penalty of his sin.

MEGILLUS: You are very right in saying that tradition, if no breath of opposition ever assails it, has a marvellous power.

ATHENIAN: Am I not also right in saying that the legislator who wants to master any of the passions which master man may easily know how to subdue them? He will consecrate the tradition of their evil character among all, slaves and freemen, women and children, throughout the city: that will be the surest foundation of the law which he can make.

MEGILLUS: Yes; but will he ever succeed in making all mankind use the same language about them?

ATHENIAN: A good objection; but was I not just now saying that I had a way to make men use natural love and abstain from unnatural, not intentionally destroying the seeds of human increase, or sowing them in stony places, in which they will take no root; and that I would command them to abstain too from any female field of increase in which that which is sown is not likely to grow? Now if a law to this effect could only be made perpetual, and gain an authority such as already prevents intercourse of parents and children—such a law, extending to other sensual desires, and conquering them, would be the source of ten thousand blessings. For, in the first place, moderation is the appointment of nature, and deters men from all frenzy and madness of love, and from all adulteries and immoderate use of meats and drinks, and makes them good friends to their own wives. And innumerable other benefits would result if such a law could only be enforced. I can imagine some lusty youth who is standing by, and who, on hearing this enactment, declares in scurrilous terms that we are making foolish and impossible laws, and fills the world with his outcry. And therefore I said that I knew a way of enacting and perpetuating such a law, which was very easy in one respect, but in another most difficult. There is no difficulty in seeing that such a law is possible, and in what way; for, as I was saying, the ordinance once consecrated would master the soul of every man, and terrify him into obedience. But matters have now come to such a pass that even then the desired result seems as if it could not be attained, just as the continuance of an entire state in the practice of common meals is also deemed impossible. And although this latter is partly disproven by the fact of their existence among you, still even in your cities the common meals of women would be regarded as unnatural and impossible. I was thinking of the rebelliousness of the human heart when I said that the permanent establishment of these things is very difficult.

MEGILLUS: Very true.

ATHENIAN: Shall I try and find some sort of persuasive argument which will prove to you that such enactments are possible, and not beyond human nature?

CLEINIAS: By all means.

ATHENIAN: Is a man more likely to abstain from the pleasures of love and to do what he is bidden about them, when his body is in a good condition, or when he is in an ill condition, and out of training?

CLEINIAS: He will be far more temperate when he is in training.

ATHENIAN: And have we not heard of Iccus of Tarentum, who, with a view to the Olympic and other contests, in his zeal for his art, and also because he was of a manly and temperate disposition, never had any connexion with a woman or a youth during the whole time of his training? And the same is said of Crison and Astylus and Diopompus and many others; and yet, Cleinias, they were far worse educated in their minds than your and my citizens, and in their bodies far more lusty.

CLEINIAS: No doubt this fact has been often affirmed positively by the ancients of these athletes.

ATHENIAN: And had they the courage to abstain from what is ordinarily deemed a pleasure for the sake of a victory in wrestling, running, and the like; and shall our young men be incapable of a similar endurance for the sake of a much nobler victory, which is the noblest of all, as from their youth upwards we will tell them, charming them, as we hope, into the belief of this by tales and sayings and songs?

CLEINIAS: Of what victory are you speaking?

ATHENIAN: Of the victory over pleasure, which if they win, they will live happily; or if they are conquered, the reverse of happily. And, further, may we not suppose that the fear of impiety will enable them to master that which other inferior people have mastered?

CLEINIAS: I dare say.

ATHENIAN: And since we have reached this point in our legislation, and have fallen into a difficulty by reason of the vices of mankind, I affirm that our ordinance should simply run in the following terms: Our citizens ought not to fall below the nature of birds and beasts in general, who are born in great multitudes, and yet remain until the age for procreation virgin and unmarried, but when they have reached the proper time of life are coupled, male and female, and lovingly pair together, and live the rest of their lives in holiness and innocence, abiding firmly in their original compact: surely, we will say to them, you should be better than the animals. But if they are corrupted by the other Hellenes and the common practice of barbarians, and they see with their eyes and hear with their ears of the so-called free love everywhere prevailing among them, and they themselves are not able to get the better of the temptation, the guardians of the law, exercising the functions of lawgivers, shall devise a second law against them.

CLEINIAS: And what law would you advise them to pass if this one failed?

ATHENIAN: Clearly, Cleinias, the one which would naturally follow.

CLEINIAS: What is that?

ATHENIAN: Our citizens should not allow pleasures to strengthen with indulgence, but should by toil divert the aliment and exuberance of them into other parts of the body; and this will happen if no immodesty be allowed in the practice of love. Then they will be ashamed of frequent intercourse, and they will find pleasure, if seldom enjoyed, to be a less imperious mistress. They should not be found out doing anything of the sort. Concealment shall be honourable, and sanctioned by custom and made law by unwritten prescription; on the other hand, to be detected shall be esteemed dishonourable, but not, to abstain wholly. In this way there will be a second legal standard of honourable and dishonourable, involving a second notion of right. Three principles will comprehend all those corrupt natures whom we call inferior to themselves, and who form but one class, and will compel them not to transgress.

CLEINIAS: What are they?

ATHENIAN: The principle of piety, the love of honour, and the desire of beauty, not in the body but in the soul. These are, perhaps, romantic aspirations; but they are the noblest of aspirations, if they could only be realised in all states, and, God willing, in the matter of love we may be able to enforce one of two things—either that no one shall venture to touch any person of the freeborn or noble class except his wedded wife, or sow the unconsecrated and bastard seed among harlots, or in barren and unnatural lusts; or at least we may abolish altogether the connection of men with men; and as to women, if any man has to do with any but those who come into his house duly married by sacred rites, whether they be bought or acquired in any other way, and he offends publicly in the face of all mankind, we shall be right in enacting that he be deprived of civic honours and privileges, and be deemed to be, as he truly is, a stranger. Let this law, then, whether it is one, or ought rather to be called two, be laid down respecting love in general, and the intercourse of the sexes which arises out of the desires, whether rightly or wrongly indulged.

MEGILLUS: I, for my part, Stranger, would gladly receive this law. Cleinias shall speak for himself, and tell you what is his opinion.

CLEINIAS: I will, Megillus, when an opportunity offers; at present, I think that we had better allow the Stranger to proceed with his laws.

MEGILLUS: Very good.

ATHENIAN: We had got about as far as the establishment of the common tables, which in most places would be difficult, but in Crete no one would think of introducing any other custom. There might arise a question about the manner of them—whether they shall be such as they are here in Crete, or such as they are in Lacedaemon—or is there a third kind which may be better than either of them? The answer to this question might be easily discovered, but the discovery would do no great good, for at present they are very well ordered.

Leaving the common tables, we may therefore proceed to the means of providing food. Now, in cities the means of life are gained in many ways and from divers sources, and in general from two sources, whereas our city has only one. For most of the Hellenes obtain their food from sea and land, but our citizens from land only. And this makes the task of the legislator less difficult—half as many laws will be enough, and much less than half; and they will be of a kind better suited to free men. For he has nothing to do with laws about shipowners and merchants and retailers and inn-keepers and tax collectors and mines and moneylending and compound interest and innumerable other things—bidding good-bye to these, he gives laws to husbandmen and shepherds and bee-keepers, and to the guardians and superintendents of their implements; and he has already legislated for greater matters, as for example, respecting marriage and the procreation and nurture of children, and for education, and the establishment of offices—and now he must direct his laws to those who provide food and labour in preparing it.

Let us first of all, then, have a class of laws which shall be called the laws of husbandmen. And let the first of them be the law of Zeus, the God of boundaries. Let no one shift the boundary line either of a fellow-citizen who is a neighbour, or, if he dwells at the extremity of the land, of any stranger who is conterminous with him, considering that this is truly 'to move the immovable,' and every one should be more willing to move the largest rock which is not a landmark, than the least stone which is the sworn mark of friendship and hatred between neighbours; for Zeus, the god of kindred, is the witness of the citizen, and Zeus, the god of strangers, of the stranger, and when aroused, terrible are the wars which they stir up. He who obeys the law will never know the fatal consequences of disobedience, but he who despises the law shall be liable to a double penalty, the first coming from the Gods, and the second from the law. For let no one wilfully remove the boundaries of his neighbour's land, and if any one does, let him who will inform the landowners, and let them bring him into court, and if he be convicted of re-dividing the land by stealth or by force, let the court determine what he ought to suffer or pay. In the next place, many small injuries done by neighbours to one another, through their multiplication, may cause a weight of enmity, and make neighbourhood a very disagreeable and bitter thing. Wherefore a man ought to be very careful of committing any offence against his neighbour, and especially of encroaching on his neighbour's land; for any man may easily do harm, but not every man can do good to another. He who encroaches on his neighbour's land, and transgresses his boundaries, shall make good the damage, and, to cure him of his impudence and also of his meanness, he shall pay a double penalty to the injured party. Of these and the like matters the wardens of the country shall take cognizance, and be the judges of them and assessors of the damage; in the more important cases, as has been already said, the whole number of them belonging to any one of the twelve divisions shall decide, and in the lesser cases the commanders: or, again, if any one pastures his cattle on his neighbour's land, they shall see the injury, and adjudge the penalty. And if any one, by decoying the bees, gets possession of another's swarms, and draws them to himself by making noises, he shall pay the damage; or if any one sets fire to his own wood and takes no care of his neighbour's property, he shall be fined at the discretion of the magistrates. And if in planting he does not leave a fair distance between his own and his neighbour's land, he shall be punished, in accordance with the enactments of many lawgivers, which we may use, not deeming it necessary that the great legislator of our state should determine all the trifles which might be decided by any body; for example, husbandmen have had of old excellent laws about waters, and there is no reason why we should propose to divert their course: He who likes may draw water from the fountain-head of the common stream on to his own land, if he do not cut off the spring which clearly belongs to some other owner; and he may take the water in any direction which he pleases, except through a house or temple or sepulchre, but he must be careful to do no harm beyond the channel. And if there be in any place a natural dryness of the earth, which keeps in the rain from heaven, and causes a deficiency in the supply of water, let him dig down on his own land as far as the clay, and if at this depth he finds no water, let him obtain water from his neighbours, as much as is required for his servants' drinking, and if his neighbours, too, are limited in their supply, let him have a fixed measure, which shall be determined by the wardens of the country. This he shall receive each day, and on these terms have a share of his neighbours' water. If there be heavy rain, and one of those on the lower ground injures some tiller of the upper ground, or some one who has a common wall, by refusing to give them an outlet for water; or, again, if some one living on the higher ground recklessly lets off the water on his lower neighbour, and they cannot come to terms with one another, let him who will call in a warden of the city, if he be in the city, or if he be in the country, a warden of the country, and let him obtain a decision determining what each of them is to do. And he who will not abide by the decision shall suffer for his malignant and morose temper, and pay a fine to the injured party, equivalent to double the value of the injury, because he was unwilling to submit to the magistrates.

Now the participation of fruits shall be ordered on this wise. The goddess of Autumn has two gracious gifts: one the joy of Dionysus which is not treasured up; the other, which nature intends to be stored. Let this be the law, then, concerning the fruits of autumn: He who tastes the common or storing fruits of autumn, whether grapes or figs, before the season of vintage which coincides with Arcturus, either on his own land or on that of others—let him pay fifty drachmae, which shall be sacred to Dionysus, if he pluck them from his own land; and if from his neighbour's land, a mina, and if from any others', two-thirds of a mina. And he who would gather the 'choice' grapes or the 'choice' figs, as they are now termed, if he take them off his own land, let him pluck them how and when he likes; but if he take them from the ground of others without their leave, let him in that case be always punished in accordance with the law which ordains that he should not move what he has not laid down. And if a slave touches any fruit of this sort, without the consent of the owner of the land, he shall be beaten with as many blows as there are grapes on the bunch, or figs on the fig-tree. Let a metic purchase the 'choice' autumnal fruit, and then, if he pleases, he may gather it; but if a stranger is passing along the road, and desires to eat, let him take of the 'choice' grape for himself and a single follower without payment, as a tribute of hospitality. The law however forbids strangers from sharing in the sort which is not used for eating; and if any one, whether he be master or slave, takes of them in ignorance, let the slave be beaten, and the freeman dismissed with admonitions, and instructed to take of the other autumnal fruits which are unfit for making raisins and wine, or for laying by as dried figs. As to pears, and apples, and pomegranates, and similar fruits, there shall be no disgrace in taking them secretly; but he who is caught, if he be of less than thirty years of age, shall be struck and beaten off, but not wounded; and no freeman shall have any right of satisfaction for such blows. Of these fruits the stranger may partake, just as he may of the fruits of autumn. And if an elder, who is more than thirty years of age, eat of them on the spot, let him, like the stranger, be allowed to partake of all such fruits, but he must carry away nothing. If, however, he will not obey the law, let him run the risk of failing in the competition of virtue, in case any one takes notice of his actions before the judges at the time.

Water is the greatest element of nutrition in gardens, but is easily polluted. You cannot poison the soil, or the sun, or the air, which are the other elements of nutrition in plants, or divert them, or steal them; but all these things may very likely happen in regard to water, which must therefore be protected by law. And let this be the law: If any one intentionally pollutes the water of another, whether the water of a spring, or collected in reservoirs, either by poisonous substances, or by digging, or by theft, let the injured party bring the cause before the wardens of the city, and claim in writing the value of the loss; if the accused be found guilty of injuring the water by deleterious substances, let him not only pay damages, but purify the stream or the cistern which contains the water, in such manner as the laws of the interpreters order the purification to be made by the offender in each case.

With respect to the gathering in of the fruits of the soil, let a man, if he pleases, carry his own fruits through any place in which he either does no harm to any one, or himself gains three times as much as his neighbour loses. Now of these things the magistrates should be cognizant, as of all other things in which a man intentionally does injury to another or to the property of another, by fraud or force, in the use which he makes of his own property. All these matters a man should lay before the magistrates, and receive damages, supposing the injury to be not more than three minae; or if he have a charge against another which involves a larger amount, let him bring his suit into the public courts and have the evil-doer punished. But if any of the magistrates appear to adjudge the penalties which he imposes in an unjust spirit, let him be liable to pay double to the injured party. Any one may bring the offences of magistrates, in any particular case, before the public courts. There are innumerable little matters relating to the modes of punishment, and applications for suits, and summonses and the witnesses to summonses—for example, whether two witnesses should be required for a summons, or how many—and all such details, which cannot be omitted in legislation, but are beneath the wisdom of an aged legislator. These lesser matters, as they indeed are in comparison with the greater ones, let a younger generation regulate by law, after the patterns which have preceded, and according to their own experience of the usefulness and necessity of such laws; and when they are duly regulated let there be no alteration, but let the citizens live in the observance of them.

Now of artisans, let the regulations be as follows: In the first place, let no citizen or servant of a citizen be occupied in handicraft arts; for he who is to secure and preserve the public order of the state, has an art which requires much study and many kinds of knowledge, and does not admit of being made a secondary occupation; and hardly any human being is capable of pursuing two professions or two arts rightly, or of practising one art himself, and superintending some one else who is practising another. Let this, then, be our first principle in the state: No one who is a smith shall also be a carpenter, and if he be a carpenter, he shall not superintend the smith's art rather than his own, under the pretext that in superintending many servants who are working for him, he is likely to superintend them better, because more revenue will accrue to him from them than from his own art; but let every man in the state have one art, and get his living by that. Let the wardens of the city labour to maintain this law, and if any citizen incline to any other art rather than the study of virtue, let them punish him with disgrace and infamy, until they bring him back into his own right course; and if any stranger profess two arts, let them chastise him with bonds and money penalties, and expulsion from the state, until they compel him to be one only and not many.

But as touching payments for hire, and contracts of work, or in case any one does wrong to any of the citizens, or they do wrong to any other, up to fifty drachmae, let the wardens of the city decide the case; but if a greater amount be involved, then let the public courts decide according to law. Let no one pay any duty either on the importation or exportation of goods; and as to frankincense and similar perfumes, used in the service of the Gods, which come from abroad, and purple and other dyes which are not produced in the country, or the materials of any art which have to be imported, and which are not necessary—no one should import them; nor, again, should any one export anything which is wanted in the country. Of all these things let there be inspectors and superintendents, taken from the guardians of the law; and they shall be the twelve next in order to the five seniors. Concerning arms, and all implements which are required for military purposes, if there be need of introducing any art, or plant, or metal, or chains of any kind, or animals for use in war, let the commanders of the horse and the generals have authority over their importation and exportation; the city shall send them out and also receive them, and the guardians of the law shall make fit and proper laws about them. But let there be no retail trade for the sake of moneymaking, either in these or any other articles, in the city or country at all.

With respect to food and the distribution of the produce of the country, the right and proper way seems to be nearly that which is the custom of Crete; for all should be required to distribute the fruits of the soil into twelve parts, and in this way consume them. Let the twelfth portion of each as for instance of wheat and barley, to which the rest of the fruits of the earth shall be added, as well as the animals which are for sale in each of the twelve divisions, be divided in due proportion into three parts; one part for freemen, another for their servants, and a third for craftsmen and in general for strangers, whether sojourners who may be dwelling in the city, and like other men must live, or those who come on some business which they have with the state, or with some individual. Let only this third part of all necessaries be required to be sold; out of the other two-thirds no one shall be compelled to sell. And how will they be best distributed? In the first place, we see clearly that the distribution will be of equals in one point of view, and in another point of view of unequals.

CLEINIAS: What do you mean?

ATHENIAN: I mean that the earth of necessity produces and nourishes the various articles of food, sometimes better and sometimes worse.

CLEINIAS: Of course.

ATHENIAN: Such being the case, let no one of the three portions be greater than either of the other two—neither that which is assigned to masters or to slaves, nor again that of the stranger; but let the distribution to all be equal and alike, and let every citizen take his two portions and distribute them among slaves and freemen, he having power to determine the quantity and quality. And what remains he shall distribute by measure and number among the animals who have to be sustained from the earth, taking the whole number of them.

In the second place, our citizens should have separate houses duly ordered; and this will be the order proper for men like them. There shall be twelve hamlets, one in the middle of each twelfth portion, and in each hamlet they shall first set apart a market-place, and the temples of the Gods, and of their attendant demi-gods; and if there be any local deities of the Magnetes, or holy seats of other ancient deities, whose memory has been preserved, to these let them pay their ancient honours. But Hestia, and Zeus, and Athene will have temples everywhere together with the God who presides in each of the twelve districts. And the first erection of houses shall be around these temples, where the ground is highest, in order to provide the safest and most defensible place of retreat for the guards. All the rest of the country they shall settle in the following manner: They shall make thirteen divisions of the craftsmen; one of them they shall establish in the city, and this, again, they shall subdivide into twelve lesser divisions, among the twelve districts of the city, and the remainder shall be distributed in the country round about; and in each village they shall settle various classes of craftsmen, with a view to the convenience of the husbandmen. And the chief officers of the wardens of the country shall superintend all these matters, and see how many of them, and which class of them, each place requires; and fix them where they are likely to be least troublesome, and most useful to the husbandman. And the wardens of the city shall see to similar matters in the city.

Now the wardens of the agora ought to see to the details of the agora. Their first care, after the temples which are in the agora have been seen to, should be to prevent any one from doing any wrong in dealings between man and man; in the second place, as being inspectors of temperance and violence, they should chastise him who requires chastisement. Touching articles of sale, they should first see whether the articles which the citizens are under regulations to sell to strangers are sold to them, as the law ordains. And let the law be as follows: On the first day of the month, the persons in charge, whoever they are, whether strangers or slaves, who have the charge on behalf of the citizens, shall produce to the strangers the portion which falls to them, in the first place, a twelfth portion of the corn—the stranger shall purchase corn for the whole month, and other cereals, on the first market day; and on the tenth day of the month the one party shall sell, and the other buy, liquids sufficient to last during the whole month; and on the twenty-third day there shall be a sale of animals by those who are willing to sell to the people who want to buy, and of implements and other things which husbandmen sell, (such as skins and all kinds of clothing, either woven or made of felt and other goods of the same sort) and which strangers are compelled to buy and purchase of others. As to the retail trade in these things, whether of barley or wheat set apart for meal and flour, or any other kind of food, no one shall sell them to citizens or their slaves, nor shall any one buy of a citizen; but let the stranger sell them in the market of strangers, to artisans and their slaves, making an exchange of wine and food, which is commonly called retail trade. And butchers shall offer for sale parts of dismembered animals to the strangers, and artisans, and their servants. Let any stranger who likes buy fuel from day to day wholesale, from those who have the care of it in the country, and let him sell to the strangers as much as he pleases and when he pleases. As to other goods and implements which are likely to be wanted, they shall sell them in the common market, at any place which the guardians of the law and the wardens of the market and city, choosing according to their judgment, shall determine; at such places they shall exchange money for goods, and goods for money, neither party giving credit to the other; and he who gives credit must be satisfied, whether he obtain his money or not, for in such exchanges he will not be protected by law. But whenever property has been bought or sold, greater in quantity or value than is allowed by the law, which has determined within what limits a man may increase and diminish his possessions, let the excess be registered in the books of the guardians of the law; or in case of diminution, let there be an erasure made. And let the same rule be observed about the registration of the property of the metics. Any one who likes may come and be a metic on certain conditions; a foreigner, if he likes, and is able to settle, may dwell in the land, but he must practise an art, and not abide more than twenty years from the time at which he has registered himself; and he shall pay no sojourner's tax, however small, except good conduct, nor any other tax for buying and selling. But when the twenty years have expired, he shall take his property with him and depart. And if in the course of these years he should chance to distinguish himself by any considerable benefit which he confers on the state, and he thinks that he can persuade the council and assembly, either to grant him delay in leaving the country, or to allow him to remain for the whole of his life, let him go and persuade the city, and whatever they assent to at his instance shall take effect. For the children of the metics, being artisans, and of fifteen years of age, let the time of their sojourn commence after their fifteenth year; and let them remain for twenty years, and then go where they like; but any of them who wishes to remain, may do so, if he can persuade the council and assembly. And if he depart, let him erase all the entries which have been made by him in the register kept by the magistrates.

BOOK IX.

Next to all the matters which have preceded in the natural order of legislation will come suits of law. Of suits those which relate to agriculture have been already described, but the more important have not been described. Having mentioned them severally under their usual names, we will proceed to say what punishments are to be inflicted for each offence, and who are to be the judges of them.

CLEINIAS: Very good.

ATHENIAN: There is a sense of disgrace in legislating, as we are about to do, for all the details of crime in a state which, as we say, is to be well regulated and will be perfectly adapted to the practice of virtue. To assume that in such a state there will arise some one who will be guilty of crimes as heinous as any which are ever perpetrated in other states, and that we must legislate for him by anticipation, and threaten and make laws against him if he should arise, in order to deter him, and punish his acts, under the idea that he will arise—this, as I was saying, is in a manner disgraceful. Yet seeing that we are not like the ancient legislators, who gave laws to heroes and sons of gods, being, according to the popular belief, themselves the offspring of the gods, and legislating for others, who were also the children of divine parents, but that we are only men who are legislating for the sons of men, there is no uncharitableness in apprehending that some one of our citizens may be like a seed which has touched the ox's horn, having a heart so hard that it cannot be softened any more than those seeds can be softened by fire. Among our citizens there may be those who cannot be subdued by all the strength of the laws; and for their sake, though an ungracious task, I will proclaim my first law about the robbing of temples, in case any one should dare to commit such a crime. I do not expect or imagine that any well-brought-up citizen will ever take the infection, but their servants, and strangers, and strangers' servants may be guilty of many impieties. And with a view to them especially, and yet not without a provident eye to the weakness of human nature generally, I will proclaim the law about robbers of temples and similar incurable, or almost incurable, criminals. Having already agreed that such enactments ought always to have a short prelude, we may speak to the criminal, whom some tormenting desire by night and by day tempts to go and rob a temple, the fewest possible words of admonition and exhortation: O sir, we will say to him, the impulse which moves you to rob temples is not an ordinary human malady, nor yet a visitation of heaven, but a madness which is begotten in a man from ancient and unexpiated crimes of his race, an ever-recurring curse—against this you must guard with all your might, and how you are to guard we will explain to you. When any such thought comes into your mind, go and perform expiations, go as a suppliant to the temples of the Gods who avert evils, go to the society of those who are called good men among you; hear them tell and yourself try to repeat after them, that every man should honour the noble and the just. Fly from the company of the wicked—fly and turn not back; and if your disorder is lightened by these remedies, well and good, but if not, then acknowledge death to be nobler than life, and depart hence.

Such are the preludes which we sing to all who have thoughts of unholy and treasonable actions, and to him who hearkens to them the law has nothing to say. But to him who is disobedient when the prelude is over, cry with a loud voice—He who is taken in the act of robbing temples, if he be a slave or stranger, shall have his evil deed engraven on his face and hands, and shall be beaten with as many stripes as may seem good to the judges, and be cast naked beyond the borders of the land. And if he suffers this punishment he will probably return to his right mind and be improved; for no penalty which the law inflicts is designed for evil, but always makes him who suffers either better or not so much worse as he would have been. But if any citizen be found guilty of any great or unmentionable wrong, either in relation to the Gods, or his parents, or the state, let the judge deem him to be incurable, remembering that after receiving such an excellent education and training from youth upward, he has not abstained from the greatest of crimes. His punishment shall be death, which to him will be the least of evils; and his example will benefit others, if he perish ingloriously, and be cast beyond the borders of the land. But let his children and family, if they avoid the ways of their father, have glory, and let honourable mention be made of them, as having nobly and manfully escaped out of evil into good. None of them should have their goods confiscated to the state, for the lots of the citizens ought always to continue the same and equal.

Touching the exaction of penalties, when a man appears to have done anything which deserves a fine, he shall pay the fine, if he have anything in excess of the lot which is assigned to him; but more than that he shall not pay. And to secure exactness, let the guardians of the law refer to the registers, and inform the judges of the precise truth, in order that none of the lots may go uncultivated for want of money. But if any one seems to deserve a greater penalty, let him undergo a long and public imprisonment and be dishonoured, unless some of his friends are willing to be surety for him, and liberate him by assisting him to pay the fine. No criminal shall go unpunished, not even for a single offence, nor if he have fled the country; but let the penalty be according to his deserts—death, or bonds, or blows, or degrading places of sitting or standing, or removal to some temple on the borders of the land; or let him pay fines, as we said before. In cases of death, let the judges be the guardians of the law, and a court selected by merit from the last year's magistrates. But how the causes are to be brought into court, how the summonses are to be served, and the like, these things may be left to the younger generation of legislators to determine; the manner of voting we must determine ourselves.

Let the vote be given openly; but before they come to the vote let the judges sit in order of seniority over against plaintiff and defendant, and let all the citizens who can spare time hear and take a serious interest in listening to such causes. First of all the plaintiff shall make one speech, and then the defendant shall make another; and after the speeches have been made the eldest judge shall begin to examine the parties, and proceed to make an adequate enquiry into what has been said; and after the oldest has spoken, the rest shall proceed in order to examine either party as to what he finds defective in the evidence, whether of statement or omission; and he who has nothing to ask shall hand over the examination to another. And on so much of what has been said as is to the purpose all the judges shall set their seals, and place the writings on the altar of Hestia. On the next day they shall meet again, and in like manner put their questions and go through the cause, and again set their seals upon the evidence; and when they have three times done this, and have had witnesses and evidence enough, they shall each of them give a holy vote, after promising by Hestia that they will decide justly and truly to the utmost of their power; and so they shall put an end to the suit.

Next, after what relates to the Gods, follows what relates to the dissolution of the state: Whoever by permitting a man to power enslaves the laws, and subjects the city to factions, using violence and stirring up sedition contrary to law, him we will deem the greatest enemy of the whole state. But he who takes no part in such proceedings, and, being one of the chief magistrates of the state, has no knowledge of treason, or, having knowledge of it, by reason of cowardice does not interfere on behalf of his country, such an one we must consider nearly as bad. Every man who is worth anything will inform the magistrates, and bring the conspirator to trial for making a violent and illegal attempt to change the government. The judges of such cases shall be the same as of the robbers of temples; and let the whole proceeding be carried on in the same way, and the vote of the majority condemn to death. But let there be a general rule, that the disgrace and punishment of the father is not to be visited on the children, except in the case of some one whose father, grandfather, and great-grandfather have successively undergone the penalty of death. Such persons the city shall send away with all their possessions to the city and country of their ancestors, retaining only and wholly their appointed lot. And out of the citizens who have more than one son of not less than ten years of age, they shall select ten whom their father or grandfather by the mother's or father's side shall appoint, and let them send to Delphi the names of those who are selected, and him whom the God chooses they shall establish as heir of the house which has failed; and may he have better fortune than his predecessors!

CLEINIAS: Very good.

ATHENIAN: Once more let there be a third general law respecting the judges who are to give judgment, and the manner of conducting suits against those who are tried on an accusation of treason; and as concerning the remaining or departure of their descendants—there shall be one law for all three, for the traitor, and the robber of temples, and the subverter by violence of the laws of the state. For a thief, whether he steal much or little, let there be one law, and one punishment for all alike: in the first place, let him pay double the amount of the theft if he be convicted, and if he have so much over and above the allotment—if he have not, he shall be bound until he pay the penalty, or persuade him who has obtained the sentence against him to forgive him. But if a person be convicted of a theft against the state, then if he can persuade the city, or if he will pay back twice the amount of the theft, he shall be set free from his bonds.

CLEINIAS: What makes you say, Stranger, that a theft is all one, whether the thief may have taken much or little, and either from sacred or secular places—and these are not the only differences in thefts—seeing, then, that they are of many kinds, ought not the legislator to adapt himself to them, and impose upon them entirely different penalties?

ATHENIAN: Excellent. I was running on too fast, Cleinias, and you impinged upon me, and brought me to my senses, reminding me of what, indeed, had occurred to my mind already, that legislation was never yet rightly worked out, as I may say in passing. Do you remember the image in which I likened the men for whom laws are now made to slaves who are doctored by slaves? For of this you may be very sure, that if one of those empirical physicians, who practise medicine without science, were to come upon the gentleman physician talking to his gentleman patient, and using the language almost of philosophy, beginning at the beginning of the disease and discoursing about the whole nature of the body, he would burst into a hearty laugh—he would say what most of those who are called doctors always have at their tongue's end: Foolish fellow, he would say, you are not healing the sick man, but you are educating him; and he does not want to be made a doctor, but to get well.

CLEINIAS: And would he not be right?

ATHENIAN: Perhaps he would; and he might remark upon us, that he who discourses about laws, as we are now doing, is giving the citizens education and not laws; that would be rather a telling observation.

CLEINIAS: Very true.

ATHENIAN: But we are fortunate.

CLEINIAS: In what way?

ATHENIAN: Inasmuch as we are not compelled to give laws, but we may take into consideration every form of government, and ascertain what is best and what is most needful, and how they may both be carried into execution; and we may also, if we please, at this very moment choose what is best, or, if we prefer, what is most necessary—which shall we do?

CLEINIAS: There is something ridiculous, Stranger, in our proposing such an alternative, as if we were legislators, simply bound under some great necessity which cannot be deferred to the morrow. But we, as I may by the grace of Heaven affirm, like gatherers of stones or beginners of some composite work, may gather a heap of materials, and out of this, at our leisure, select what is suitable for our projected construction. Let us then suppose ourselves to be at leisure, not of necessity building, but rather like men who are partly providing materials, and partly putting them together. And we may truly say that some of our laws, like stones, are already fixed in their places, and others lie at hand.

ATHENIAN: Certainly, in that case, Cleinias, our view of law will be more in accordance with nature. For there is another matter affecting legislators, which I must earnestly entreat you to consider.

CLEINIAS: What is it?

ATHENIAN: There are many writings to be found in cities, and among them there are discourses composed by legislators as well as by other persons.

CLEINIAS: To be sure.

ATHENIAN: Shall we give heed rather to the writings of those others—poets and the like, who either in metre or out of metre have recorded their advice about the conduct of life, and not to the writings of legislators? or shall we give heed to them above all?

CLEINIAS: Yes; to them far above all others.

ATHENIAN: And ought the legislator alone among writers to withhold his opinion about the beautiful, the good, and the just, and not to teach what they are, and how they are to be pursued by those who intend to be happy?

CLEINIAS: Certainly not.

ATHENIAN: And is it disgraceful for Homer and Tyrtaeus and other poets to lay down evil precepts in their writings respecting life and the pursuits of men, but not so disgraceful for Lycurgus and Solon and others who were legislators as well as writers? Is it not true that of all the writings to be found in cities, those which relate to laws, when you unfold and read them, ought to be by far the noblest and the best? and should not other writings either agree with them, or if they disagree, be deemed ridiculous? We should consider whether the laws of states ought not to have the character of loving and wise parents, rather than of tyrants and masters, who command and threaten, and, after writing their decrees on walls, go their ways; and whether, in discoursing of laws, we should not take the gentler view of them which may or may not be attainable—at any rate, we will show our readiness to entertain such a view, and be prepared to undergo whatever may be the result. And may the result be good, and if God be gracious, it will be good!

CLEINIAS: Excellent; let us do as you say.

ATHENIAN: Then we will now consider accurately, as we proposed, what relates to robbers of temples, and all kinds of thefts, and offences in general; and we must not be annoyed if, in the course of legislation, we have enacted some things, and have not made up our minds about some others; for as yet we are not legislators, but we may soon be. Let us, if you please, consider these matters.

CLEINIAS: By all means.

ATHENIAN: Concerning all things honourable and just, let us then endeavour to ascertain how far we are consistent with ourselves, and how far we are inconsistent, and how far the many, from whom at any rate we should profess a desire to differ, agree and disagree among themselves.

CLEINIAS: What are the inconsistencies which you observe in us?

ATHENIAN: I will endeavour to explain. If I am not mistaken, we are all agreed that justice, and just men and things and actions, are all fair, and, if a person were to maintain that just men, even when they are deformed in body, are still perfectly beautiful in respect of the excellent justice of their minds, no one would say that there was any inconsistency in this.

CLEINIAS: They would be quite right.

ATHENIAN: Perhaps; but let us consider further, that if all things which are just are fair and honourable, in the term 'all' we must include just sufferings which are the correlatives of just actions.

CLEINIAS: And what is the inference?

ATHENIAN: The inference is, that a just action in partaking of the just partakes also in the same degree of the fair and honourable.

CLEINIAS: Certainly.

ATHENIAN: And must not a suffering which partakes of the just principle be admitted to be in the same degree fair and honourable, if the argument is consistently carried out?

CLEINIAS: True.

ATHENIAN: But then if we admit suffering to be just and yet dishonourable, and the term 'dishonourable' is applied to justice, will not the just and the honourable disagree?

CLEINIAS: What do you mean?

ATHENIAN: A thing not difficult to understand; the laws which have been already enacted would seem to announce principles directly opposed to what we are saying.

CLEINIAS: To what?

ATHENIAN: We had enacted, if I am not mistaken, that the robber of temples, and he who was the enemy of law and order, might justly be put to death, and we were proceeding to make divers other enactments of a similar nature. But we stopped short, because we saw that these sufferings are infinite in number and degree, and that they are, at once, the most just and also the most dishonourable of all sufferings. And if this be true, are not the just and the honourable at one time all the same, and at another time in the most diametrical opposition?

CLEINIAS: Such appears to be the case.

ATHENIAN: In this discordant and inconsistent fashion does the language of the many rend asunder the honourable and just.

CLEINIAS: Very true, Stranger.

ATHENIAN: Then now, Cleinias, let us see how far we ourselves are consistent about these matters.

CLEINIAS: Consistent in what?

ATHENIAN: I think that I have clearly stated in the former part of the discussion, but if I did not, let me now state—

CLEINIAS: What?

ATHENIAN: That all bad men are always involuntarily bad; and from this I must proceed to draw a further inference.

CLEINIAS: What is it?

ATHENIAN: That the unjust man may be bad, but that he is bad against his will. Now that an action which is voluntary should be done involuntarily is a contradiction; wherefore he who maintains that injustice is involuntary will deem that the unjust does injustice involuntarily. I too admit that all men do injustice involuntarily, and if any contentious or disputatious person says that men are unjust against their will, and yet that many do injustice willingly, I do not agree with him. But, then, how can I avoid being inconsistent with myself, if you, Cleinias, and you, Megillus, say to me—Well, Stranger, if all this be as you say, how about legislating for the city of the Magnetes—shall we legislate or not—what do you advise? Certainly we will, I should reply. Then will you determine for them what are voluntary and what are involuntary crimes, and shall we make the punishments greater of voluntary errors and crimes and less for the involuntary? or shall we make the punishment of all to be alike, under the idea that there is no such thing as voluntary crime?

CLEINIAS: Very good, Stranger; and what shall we say in answer to these objections?

ATHENIAN: That is a very fair question. In the first place, let us—

CLEINIAS: Do what?

ATHENIAN: Let us remember what has been well said by us already, that our ideas of justice are in the highest degree confused and contradictory. Bearing this in mind, let us proceed to ask ourselves once more whether we have discovered a way out of the difficulty. Have we ever determined in what respect these two classes of actions differ from one another? For in all states and by all legislators whatsoever, two kinds of actions have been distinguished—the one, voluntary, the other, involuntary; and they have legislated about them accordingly. But shall this new word of ours, like an oracle of God, be only spoken, and get away without giving any explanation or verification of itself? How can a word not understood be the basis of legislation? Impossible. Before proceeding to legislate, then, we must prove that they are two, and what is the difference between them, that when we impose the penalty upon either, every one may understand our proposal, and be able in some way to judge whether the penalty is fitly or unfitly inflicted.

CLEINIAS: I agree with you, Stranger; for one of two things is certain: either we must not say that all unjust acts are involuntary, or we must show the meaning and truth of this statement.

ATHENIAN: Of these two alternatives, the one is quite intolerable—not to speak what I believe to be the truth would be to me unlawful and unholy. But if acts of injustice cannot be divided into voluntary and involuntary, I must endeavour to find some other distinction between them.

CLEINIAS: Very true, Stranger; there cannot be two opinions among us upon that point.

ATHENIAN: Reflect, then; there are hurts of various kinds done by the citizens to one another in the intercourse of life, affording plentiful examples both of the voluntary and involuntary.

CLEINIAS: Certainly.

ATHENIAN: I would not have any one suppose that all these hurts are injuries, and that these injuries are of two kinds—one, voluntary, and the other, involuntary; for the involuntary hurts of all men are quite as many and as great as the voluntary. And please to consider whether I am right or quite wrong in what I am going to say; for I deny, Cleinias and Megillus, that he who harms another involuntarily does him an injury involuntarily, nor should I legislate about such an act under the idea that I am legislating for an involuntary injury. But I should rather say that such a hurt, whether great or small, is not an injury at all; and, on the other hand, if I am right, when a benefit is wrongly conferred, the author of the benefit may often be said to injure. For I maintain, O my friends, that the mere giving or taking away of anything is not to be described either as just or unjust; but the legislator has to consider whether mankind do good or harm to one another out of a just principle and intention. On the distinction between injustice and hurt he must fix his eye; and when there is hurt, he must, as far as he can, make the hurt good by law, and save that which is ruined, and raise up that which is fallen, and make that which is dead or wounded whole. And when compensation has been given for injustice, the law must always seek to win over the doers and sufferers of the several hurts from feelings of enmity to those of friendship.

CLEINIAS: Very good.

ATHENIAN: Then as to unjust hurts (and gains also, supposing the injustice to bring gain), of these we may heal as many as are capable of being healed, regarding them as diseases of the soul; and the cure of injustice will take the following direction.

CLEINIAS: What direction?

ATHENIAN: When any one commits any injustice, small or great, the law will admonish and compel him either never at all to do the like again, or never voluntarily, or at any rate in a far less degree; and he must in addition pay for the hurt. Whether the end is to be attained by word or action, with pleasure or pain, by giving or taking away privileges, by means of fines or gifts, or in whatsoever way the law shall proceed to make a man hate injustice, and love or not hate the nature of the just—this is quite the noblest work of law. But if the legislator sees any one who is incurable, for him he will appoint a law and a penalty. He knows quite well that to such men themselves there is no profit in the continuance of their lives, and that they would do a double good to the rest of mankind if they would take their departure, inasmuch as they would be an example to other men not to offend, and they would relieve the city of bad citizens. In such cases, and in such cases only, the legislator ought to inflict death as the punishment of offences.

CLEINIAS: What you have said appears to me to be very reasonable, but will you favour me by stating a little more clearly the difference between hurt and injustice, and the various complications of the voluntary and involuntary which enter into them?

ATHENIAN: I will endeavour to do as you wish: Concerning the soul, thus much would be generally said and allowed, that one element in her nature is passion, which may be described either as a state or a part of her, and is hard to be striven against and contended with, and by irrational force overturns many things.

CLEINIAS: Very true.

ATHENIAN: And pleasure is not the same with passion, but has an opposite power, working her will by persuasion and by the force of deceit in all things.

CLEINIAS: Quite true.

ATHENIAN: A man may truly say that ignorance is a third cause of crimes. Ignorance, however, may be conveniently divided by the legislator into two sorts: there is simple ignorance, which is the source of lighter offences, and double ignorance, which is accompanied by a conceit of wisdom; and he who is under the influence of the latter fancies that he knows all about matters of which he knows nothing. This second kind of ignorance, when possessed of power and strength, will be held by the legislator to be the source of great and monstrous crimes, but when attended with weakness, will only result in the errors of children and old men; and these he will treat as errors, and will make laws accordingly for those who commit them, which will be the mildest and most merciful of all laws.

CLEINIAS: You are perfectly right.

ATHENIAN: We all of us remark of one man that he is superior to pleasure and passion, and of another that he is inferior to them; and this is true.

CLEINIAS: Certainly.

ATHENIAN: But no one was ever yet heard to say that one of us is superior and another inferior to ignorance.

CLEINIAS: Very true.

ATHENIAN: We are speaking of motives which incite men to the fulfilment of their will; although an individual may be often drawn by them in opposite directions at the same time.

CLEINIAS: Yes, often.

ATHENIAN: And now I can define to you clearly, and without ambiguity, what I mean by the just and unjust, according to my notion of them: When anger and fear, and pleasure and pain, and jealousies and desires, tyrannize over the soul, whether they do any harm or not—I call all this injustice. But when the opinion of the best, in whatever part of human nature states or individuals may suppose that to dwell, has dominion in the soul and orders the life of every man, even if it be sometimes mistaken, yet what is done in accordance therewith, and the principle in individuals which obeys this rule, and is best for the whole life of man, is to be called just; although the hurt done by mistake is thought by many to be involuntary injustice. Leaving the question of names, about which we are not going to quarrel, and having already delineated three sources of error, we may begin by recalling them somewhat more vividly to our memory: One of them was of the painful sort, which we denominate anger and fear.

CLEINIAS: Quite right.

ATHENIAN: There was a second consisting of pleasures and desires, and a third of hopes, which aimed at true opinion about the best. The latter being subdivided into three, we now get five sources of actions, and for these five we will make laws of two kinds.

CLEINIAS: What are the two kinds?

ATHENIAN: There is one kind of actions done by violence and in the light of day, and another kind of actions which are done in darkness and with secret deceit, or sometimes both with violence and deceit; the laws concerning these last ought to have a character of severity.

CLEINIAS: Naturally.

ATHENIAN: And now let us return from this digression and complete the work of legislation. Laws have been already enacted by us concerning the robbers of the Gods, and concerning traitors, and also concerning those who corrupt the laws for the purpose of subverting the government. A man may very likely commit some of these crimes, either in a state of madness or when affected by disease, or under the influence of extreme old age, or in a fit of childish wantonness, himself no better than a child. And if this be made evident to the judges elected to try the cause, on the appeal of the criminal or his advocate, and he be judged to have been in this state when he committed the offence, he shall simply pay for the hurt which he may have done to another; but he shall be exempt from other penalties, unless he have slain some one, and have on his hands the stain of blood. And in that case he shall go to another land and country, and there dwell for a year; and if he return before the expiration of the time which the law appoints, or even set his foot at all on his native land, he shall be bound by the guardians of the law in the public prison for two years, and then go free.

Having begun to speak of homicide, let us endeavour to lay down laws concerning every different kind of homicide; and, first of all, concerning violent and involuntary homicides. If any one in an athletic contest, and at the public games, involuntarily kills a friend, and he dies either at the time or afterwards of the blows which he has received; or if the like misfortune happens to any one in war, or military exercises, or mimic contests of which the magistrates enjoin the practice, whether with or without arms, when he has been purified according to the law brought from Delphi relating to these matters, he shall be innocent. And so in the case of physicians: if their patient dies against their will, they shall be held guiltless by the law. And if one slay another with his own hand, but unintentionally, whether he be unarmed or have some instrument or dart in his hand; or if he kill him by administering food or drink, or by the application of fire or cold, or by suffocating him, whether he do the deed by his own hand, or by the agency of others, he shall be deemed the agent, and shall suffer one of the following penalties: If he kill the slave of another in the belief that he is his own, he shall bear the master of the dead man harmless from loss, or shall pay a penalty of twice the value of the dead man, which the judges shall assess; but purifications must be used greater and more numerous than for those who committed homicide at the games—what they are to be, the interpreters whom the God appoints shall be authorised to declare. And if a man kills his own slave, when he has been purified according to law, he shall be quit of the homicide. And if a man kills a freeman unintentionally, he shall undergo the same purification as he did who killed the slave. But let him not forget also a tale of olden time, which is to this effect: He who has suffered a violent end, when newly dead, if he has had the soul of a freeman in life, is angry with the author of his death; and being himself full of fear and panic by reason of his violent end, when he sees his murderer walking about in his own accustomed haunts, he is stricken with terror and becomes disordered, and this disorder of his, aided by the guilty recollection of the other, is communicated by him with overwhelming force to the murderer and his deeds. Wherefore also the murderer must go out of the way of his victim for the entire period of a year, and not himself be found in any spot which was familiar to him throughout the country. And if the dead man be a stranger, the homicide shall be kept from the country of the stranger during a like period. If any one voluntarily obeys this law, the next of kin to the deceased, seeing all that has happened, shall take pity on him, and make peace with him, and show him all gentleness. But if any one is disobedient, and either ventures to go to any of the temples and sacrifice unpurified, or will not continue in exile during the appointed time, the next of kin to the deceased shall proceed against him for murder; and if he be convicted, every part of his punishment shall be doubled. And if the next of kin do not proceed against the perpetrator of the crime, then the pollution shall be deemed to fall upon his own head—the murdered man will fix the guilt upon his kinsman, and he who has a mind to proceed against him may compel him to be absent from his country during five years, according to law. If a stranger unintentionally kill a stranger who is dwelling in the city, he who likes shall prosecute the cause according to the same rules. If he be a metic, let him be absent for a year, or if he be an entire stranger, in addition to the purification, whether he have slain a stranger, or a metic, or a citizen, he shall be banished for life from the country which is in possession of our laws. And if he return contrary to law, let the guardians of the law punish him with death; and let them hand over his property, if he have any, to him who is next of kin to the sufferer. And if he be wrecked, and driven on the coast against his will, he shall take up his abode on the seashore, wetting his feet in the sea, and watching for an opportunity of sailing; but if he be brought by land, and is not his own master, let the magistrate whom he first comes across in the city, release him and send him unharmed over the border.

If any one slays a freeman with his own hand, and the deed be done in passion, in the case of such actions we must begin by making a distinction. For a deed is done from passion either when men suddenly, and without intention to kill, cause the death of another by blows and the like on a momentary impulse, and are sorry for the deed immediately afterwards; or again, when after having been insulted in deed or word, men pursue revenge, and kill a person intentionally, and are not sorry for the act. And, therefore, we must assume that these homicides are of two kinds, both of them arising from passion, which may be justly said to be in a mean between the voluntary and involuntary; at the same time, they are neither of them anything more than a likeness or shadow of either. He who treasures up his anger, and avenges himself, not immediately and at the moment, but with insidious design, and after an interval, is like the voluntary; but he who does not treasure up his anger, and takes vengeance on the instant, and without malice prepense, approaches to the involuntary; and yet even he is not altogether involuntary, but is only the image or shadow of the involuntary; wherefore about homicides committed in hot blood, there is a difficulty in determining whether in legislating we shall reckon them as voluntary or as partly involuntary. The best and truest view is to regard them respectively as likenesses only of the voluntary and involuntary, and to distinguish them accordingly as they are done with or without premeditation. And we should make the penalties heavier for those who commit homicide with angry premeditation, and lighter for those who do not premeditate, but smite upon the instant; for that which is like a greater evil should be punished more severely, and that which is like a less evil should be punished less severely: this shall be the rule of our laws.

CLEINIAS: Certainly.

ATHENIAN: Let us proceed: If any one slays a freeman with his own hand, and the deed be done in a moment of anger, and without premeditation, let the offender suffer in other respects as the involuntary homicide would have suffered, and also undergo an exile of two years, that he may learn to school his passions. But he who slays another from passion, yet with premeditation, shall in other respects suffer as the former; and to this shall be added an exile of three instead of two years—his punishment is to be longer because his passion is greater. The manner of their return shall be on this wise: (and here the law has difficulty in determining exactly; for in some cases the murderer who is judged by the law to be the worse may really be the less cruel, and he who is judged the less cruel may be really the worse, and may have executed the murder in a more savage manner, whereas the other may have been gentler. But in general the degrees of guilt will be such as we have described them. Of all these things the guardians of the law must take cognizance): When a homicide of either kind has completed his term of exile, the guardians shall send twelve judges to the borders of the land; these during the interval shall have informed themselves of the actions of the criminals, and they shall judge respecting their pardon and reception; and the homicides shall abide by their judgment. But if after they have returned home, any one of them in a moment of anger repeats the deed, let him be an exile, and return no more; or if he returns, let him suffer as the stranger was to suffer in a similar case. He who kills his own slave shall undergo a purification, but if he kills the slave of another in anger, he shall pay twice the amount of the loss to his owner. And if any homicide is disobedient to the law, and without purification pollutes the agora, or the games, or the temples, he who pleases may bring to trial the next of kin to the dead man for permitting him, and the murderer with him, and may compel the one to exact and the other to suffer a double amount of fines and purifications; and the accuser shall himself receive the fine in accordance with the law. If a slave in a fit of passion kills his master, the kindred of the deceased man may do with the murderer (provided only they do not spare his life) whatever they please, and they will be pure; or if he kills a freeman, who is not his master, the owner shall give up the slave to the relatives of the deceased, and they shall be under an obligation to put him to death, but this may be done in any manner which they please. And if (which is a rare occurrence, but does sometimes happen) a father or a mother in a moment of passion slays a son or daughter by blows, or some other violence, the slayer shall undergo the same purification as in other cases, and be exiled during three years; but when the exile returns the wife shall separate from the husband, and the husband from the wife, and they shall never afterwards beget children together, or live under the same roof, or partake of the same sacred rites with those whom they have deprived of a child or of a brother. And he who is impious and disobedient in such a case shall be brought to trial for impiety by any one who pleases. If in a fit of anger a husband kills his wedded wife, or the wife her husband, the slayer shall undergo the same purification, and the term of exile shall be three years. And when he who has committed any such crime returns, let him have no communication in sacred rites with his children, neither let him sit at the same table with them, and the father or son who disobeys shall be liable to be brought to trial for impiety by any one who pleases. If a brother or a sister in a fit of passion kills a brother or a sister, they shall undergo purification and exile, as was the case with parents who killed their offspring: they shall not come under the same roof, or share in the sacred rites of those whom they have deprived of their brethren, or of their children. And he who is disobedient shall be justly liable to the law concerning impiety, which relates to these matters. If any one is so violent in his passion against his parents, that in the madness of his anger he dares to kill one of them, if the murdered person before dying freely forgives the murderer, let him undergo the purification which is assigned to those who have been guilty of involuntary homicide, and do as they do, and he shall be pure. But if he be not acquitted, the perpetrator of such a deed shall be amenable to many laws—he shall be amenable to the extreme punishments for assault, and impiety, and robbing of temples, for he has robbed his parent of life; and if a man could be slain more than once, most justly would he who in a fit of passion has slain father or mother, undergo many deaths. How can he, whom, alone of all men, even in defence of his life, and when about to suffer death at the hands of his parents, no law will allow to kill his father or his mother who are the authors of his being, and whom the legislator will command to endure any extremity rather than do this—how can he, I say, lawfully receive any other punishment? Let death then be the appointed punishment of him who in a fit of passion slays his father or his mother. But if brother kills brother in a civil broil, or under other like circumstances, if the other has begun, and he only defends himself, let him be free from guilt, as he would be if he had slain an enemy; and the same rule will apply if a citizen kill a citizen, or a stranger a stranger. Or if a stranger kill a citizen or a citizen a stranger in self-defence, let him be free from guilt in like manner; and so in the case of a slave who has killed a slave; but if a slave have killed a freeman in self-defence, let him be subject to the same law as he who has killed a father; and let the law about the remission of penalties in the case of parricide apply equally to every other remission. Whenever any sufferer of his own accord remits the guilt of homicide to another, under the idea that his act was involuntary, let the perpetrator of the deed undergo a purification and remain in exile for a year, according to law.

Enough has been said of murders violent and involuntary and committed in passion: we have now to speak of voluntary crimes done with injustice of every kind and with premeditation, through the influence of pleasures, and desires, and jealousies.

CLEINIAS: Very good.

ATHENIAN: Let us first speak, as far as we are able, of their various kinds. The greatest cause of them is lust, which gets the mastery of the soul maddened by desire; and this is most commonly found to exist where the passion reigns which is strongest and most prevalent among the mass of mankind: I mean where the power of wealth breeds endless desires of never-to-be-satisfied acquisition, originating in natural disposition, and a miserable want of education. Of this want of education, the false praise of wealth which is bruited about both among Hellenes and barbarians is the cause; they deem that to be the first of goods which in reality is only the third. And in this way they wrong both posterity and themselves, for nothing can be nobler and better than that the truth about wealth should be spoken in all states—namely, that riches are for the sake of the body, as the body is for the sake of the soul. They are good, and wealth is intended by nature to be for the sake of them, and is therefore inferior to them both, and third in order of excellence. This argument teaches us that he who would be happy ought not to seek to be rich, or rather he should seek to be rich justly and temperately, and then there would be no murders in states requiring to be purged away by other murders. But now, as I said at first, avarice is the chiefest cause and source of the worst trials for voluntary homicide. A second cause is ambition: this creates jealousies, which are troublesome companions, above all to the jealous man himself, and in a less degree to the chiefs of the state. And a third cause is cowardly and unjust fear, which has been the occasion of many murders. When a man is doing or has done something which he desires that no one should know him to be doing or to have done, he will take the life of those who are likely to inform of such things, if he have no other means of getting rid of them. Let this be said as a prelude concerning crimes of violence in general; and I must not omit to mention a tradition which is firmly believed by many, and has been received by them from those who are learned in the mysteries: they say that such deeds will be punished in the world below, and also that when the perpetrators return to this world they will pay the natural penalty which is due to the sufferer, and end their lives in like manner by the hand of another. If he who is about to commit murder believes this, and is made by the mere prelude to dread such a penalty, there is no need to proceed with the proclamation of the law. But if he will not listen, let the following law be declared and registered against him: Whoever shall wrongfully and of design slay with his own hand any of his kinsmen, shall in the first place be deprived of legal privileges; and he shall not pollute the temples, or the agora, or the harbours, or any other place of meeting, whether he is forbidden of men or not; for the law, which represents the whole state, forbids him, and always is and will be in the attitude of forbidding him. And if a cousin or nearer relative of the deceased, whether on the male or female side, does not prosecute the homicide when he ought, and have him proclaimed an outlaw, he shall in the first place be involved in the pollution, and incur the hatred of the Gods, even as the curse of the law stirs up the voices of men against him; and in the second place he shall be liable to be prosecuted by any one who is willing to inflict retribution on behalf of the dead. And he who would avenge a murder shall observe all the precautionary ceremonies of lavation, and any others which the God commands in cases of this kind. Let him have proclamation made, and then go forth and compel the perpetrator to suffer the execution of justice according to the law. Now the legislator may easily show that these things must be accomplished by prayers and sacrifices to certain Gods, who are concerned with the prevention of murders in states. But who these Gods are, and what should be the true manner of instituting such trials with due regard to religion, the guardians of the law, aided by the interpreters, and the prophets, and the God, shall determine, and when they have determined let them carry on the prosecution at law. The cause shall have the same judges who are appointed to decide in the case of those who plunder temples. Let him who is convicted be punished with death, and let him not be buried in the country of the murdered man, for this would be shameless as well as impious. But if he fly and will not stand his trial, let him fly for ever; or, if he set foot anywhere on any part of the murdered man's country, let any relation of the deceased, or any other citizen who may first happen to meet with him, kill him with impunity, or bind and deliver him to those among the judges of the case who are magistrates, that they may put him to death. And let the prosecutor demand surety of him whom he prosecutes; three sureties sufficient in the opinion of the magistrates who try the cause shall be provided by him, and they shall undertake to produce him at the trial. But if he be unwilling or unable to provide sureties, then the magistrates shall take him and keep him in bonds, and produce him at the day of trial.

If a man do not commit a murder with his own hand, but contrives the death of another, and is the author of the deed in intention and design, and he continues to dwell in the city, having his soul not pure of the guilt of murder, let him be tried in the same way, except in what relates to the sureties; and also, if he be found guilty, his body after execution may have burial in his native land, but in all other respects his case shall be as the former; and whether a stranger shall kill a citizen, or a citizen a stranger, or a slave a slave, there shall be no difference as touching murder by one's own hand or by contrivance, except in the matter of sureties; and these, as has been said, shall be required of the actual murderer only, and he who brings the accusation shall bind them over at the time. If a slave be convicted of slaying a freeman voluntarily, either by his own hand or by contrivance, let the public executioner take him in the direction of the sepulchre, to a place whence he can see the tomb of the dead man, and inflict upon him as many stripes as the person who caught him orders, and if he survive, let him put him to death. And if any one kills a slave who has done no wrong, because he is afraid that he may inform of some base and evil deeds of his own, or for any similar reason, in such a case let him pay the penalty of murder, as he would have done if he had slain a citizen. There are things about which it is terrible and unpleasant to legislate, but impossible not to legislate. If, for example, there should be murders of kinsmen, either perpetrated by the hands of kinsmen, or by their contrivance, voluntary and purely malicious, which most often happen in ill-regulated and ill-educated states, and may perhaps occur even in a country where a man would not expect to find them, we must repeat once more the tale which we narrated a little while ago, in the hope that he who hears us will be the more disposed to abstain voluntarily on these grounds from murders which are utterly abominable. For the myth, or saying, or whatever we ought to call it, has been plainly set forth by priests of old; they have pronounced that the justice which guards and avenges the blood of kindred, follows the law of retaliation, and ordains that he who has done any murderous act should of necessity suffer that which he has done. He who has slain a father shall himself be slain at some time or other by his children—if a mother, he shall of necessity take a woman's nature, and lose his life at the hands of his offspring in after ages; for where the blood of a family has been polluted there is no other purification, nor can the pollution be washed out until the homicidal soul which did the deed has given life for life, and has propitiated and laid to sleep the wrath of the whole family. These are the retributions of Heaven, and by such punishments men should be deterred. But if they are not deterred, and any one should be incited by some fatality to deprive his father, or mother, or brethren, or children, of life voluntarily and of purpose, for him the earthly lawgiver legislates as follows: There shall be the same proclamations about outlawry, and there shall be the same sureties which have been enacted in the former cases. But in his case, if he be convicted, the servants of the judges and the magistrates shall slay him at an appointed place without the city where three ways meet, and there expose his body naked, and each of the magistrates on behalf of the whole city shall take a stone and cast it upon the head of the dead man, and so deliver the city from pollution; after that, they shall bear him to the borders of the land, and cast him forth unburied, according to law. And what shall he suffer who slays him who of all men, as they say, is his own best friend? I mean the suicide, who deprives himself by violence of his appointed share of life, not because the law of the state requires him, nor yet under the compulsion of some painful and inevitable misfortune which has come upon him, nor because he has had to suffer from irremediable and intolerable shame, but who from sloth or want of manliness imposes upon himself an unjust penalty. For him, what ceremonies there are to be of purification and burial God knows, and about these the next of kin should enquire of the interpreters and of the laws thereto relating, and do according to their injunctions. They who meet their death in this way shall be buried alone, and none shall be laid by their side; they shall be buried ingloriously in the borders of the twelve portions of the land, in such places as are uncultivated and nameless, and no column or inscription shall mark the place of their interment. And if a beast of burden or other animal cause the death of any one, except in the case of anything of that kind happening to a competitor in the public contests, the kinsmen of the deceased shall prosecute the slayer for murder, and the wardens of the country, such, and so many as the kinsmen appoint, shall try the cause, and let the beast when condemned be slain by them, and let them cast it beyond the borders. And if any lifeless thing deprive a man of life, except in the case of a thunderbolt or other fatal dart sent from the Gods—whether a man is killed by lifeless objects falling upon him, or by his falling upon them, the nearest of kin shall appoint the nearest neighbour to be a judge, and thereby acquit himself and the whole family of guilt. And he shall cast forth the guilty thing beyond the border, as has been said about the animals.

If a man is found dead, and his murderer be unknown, and after a diligent search cannot be detected, there shall be the same proclamation as in the previous cases, and the same interdict on the murderer; and having proceeded against him, they shall proclaim in the agora by a herald, that he who has slain such and such a person, and has been convicted of murder, shall not set his foot in the temples, nor at all in the country of the murdered man, and if he appears and is discovered, he shall die, and be cast forth unburied beyond the border. Let this one law then be laid down by us about murder; and let cases of this sort be so regarded.

And now let us say in what cases and under what circumstances the murderer is rightly free from guilt: If a man catch a thief coming into his house by night to steal, and he take and kill him, or if he slay a footpad in self-defence, he shall be guiltless. And any one who does violence to a free woman or a youth, shall be slain with impunity by the injured person, or by his or her father or brothers or sons. If a man find his wife suffering violence, he may kill the violator, and be guiltless in the eye of the law; or if a person kill another in warding off death from his father or mother or children or brethren or wife who are doing no wrong, he shall assuredly be guiltless.

Thus much as to the nurture and education of the living soul of man, having which, he can, and without which, if he unfortunately be without them, he cannot live; and also concerning the punishments which are to be inflicted for violent deaths, let thus much be enacted. Of the nurture and education of the body we have spoken before, and next in order we have to speak of deeds of violence, voluntary and involuntary, which men do to one another; these we will now distinguish, as far as we are able, according to their nature and number, and determine what will be the suitable penalties of each, and so assign to them their proper place in the series of our enactments. The poorest legislator will have no difficulty in determining that wounds and mutilations arising out of wounds should follow next in order after deaths. Let wounds be divided as homicides were divided—into those which are involuntary, and which are given in passion or from fear, and those inflicted voluntarily and with premeditation.

Concerning all this, we must make some such proclamation as the following: Mankind must have laws, and conform to them, or their life would be as bad as that of the most savage beast. And the reason of this is that no man's nature is able to know what is best for human society; or knowing, always able and willing to do what is best. In the first place, there is a difficulty in apprehending that the true art of politics is concerned, not with private but with public good (for public good binds together states, but private only distracts them); and that both the public and private good as well of individuals as of states is greater when the state and not the individual is first considered. In the second place, although a person knows in the abstract that this is true, yet if he be possessed of absolute and irresponsible power, he will never remain firm in his principles or persist in regarding the public good as primary in the state, and the private good as secondary. Human nature will be always drawing him into avarice and selfishness, avoiding pain and pursuing pleasure without any reason, and will bring these to the front, obscuring the juster and better; and so working darkness in his soul will at last fill with evils both him and the whole city. For if a man were born so divinely gifted that he could naturally apprehend the truth, he would have no need of laws to rule over him; for there is no law or order which is above knowledge, nor can mind, without impiety, be deemed the subject or slave of any man, but rather the lord of all. I speak of mind, true and free, and in harmony with nature. But then there is no such mind anywhere, or at least not much; and therefore we must choose law and order, which are second best. These look at things as they exist for the most part only, and are unable to survey the whole of them. And therefore I have spoken as I have.

And now we will determine what penalty he ought to pay or suffer who has hurt or wounded another. Any one may easily imagine the questions which have to be asked in all such cases: What did he wound, or whom, or how, or when? for there are innumerable particulars of this sort which greatly vary from one another. And to allow courts of law to determine all these things, or not to determine any of them, is alike impossible. There is one particular which they must determine in all cases—the question of fact. And then, again, that the legislator should not permit them to determine what punishment is to be inflicted in any of these cases, but should himself decide about all of them, small or great, is next to impossible.

CLEINIAS: Then what is to be the inference?

ATHENIAN: The inference is, that some things should be left to courts of law; others the legislator must decide for himself.

CLEINIAS: And what ought the legislator to decide, and what ought he to leave to the courts of law?

ATHENIAN: I may reply, that in a state in which the courts are bad and mute, because the judges conceal their opinions and decide causes clandestinely; or what is worse, when they are disorderly and noisy, as in a theatre, clapping or hooting in turn this or that orator—I say that then there is a very serious evil, which affects the whole state. Unfortunate is the necessity of having to legislate for such courts, but where the necessity exists, the legislator should only allow them to ordain the penalties for the smallest offences; if the state for which he is legislating be of this character, he must take most matters into his own hands and speak distinctly. But when a state has good courts, and the judges are well trained and scrupulously tested, the determination of the penalties or punishments which shall be inflicted on the guilty may fairly and with advantage be left to them. And we are not to be blamed for not legislating concerning all that large class of matters which judges far worse educated than ours would be able to determine, assigning to each offence what is due both to the perpetrator and to the sufferer. We believe those for whom we are legislating to be best able to judge, and therefore to them the greater part may be left. At the same time, as I have often said, we should exhibit to the judges, as we have done, the outline and form of the punishments to be inflicted, and then they will not transgress the just rule. That was an excellent practice, which we observed before, and which now that we are resuming the work of legislation, may with advantage be repeated by us.

Let the enactment about wounding be in the following terms: If any one has a purpose and intention to slay another who is not his enemy, and whom the law does not permit him to slay, and he wounds him, but is unable to kill him, he who had the intent and has wounded him is not to be pitied—he deserves no consideration, but should be regarded as a murderer and be tried for murder. Still having respect to the fortune which has in a manner favoured him, and to the providence which in pity to him and to the wounded man saved the one from a fatal blow, and the other from an accursed fate and calamity—as a thank-offering to this deity, and in order not to oppose his will—in such a case the law will remit the punishment of death, and only compel the offender to emigrate to a neighbouring city for the rest of his life, where he shall remain in the enjoyment of all his possessions. But if he have injured the wounded man, he shall make such compensation for the injury as the court deciding the cause shall assess, and the same judges shall decide who would have decided if the man had died of his wounds. And if a child intentionally wound his parents, or a servant his master, death shall be the penalty. And if a brother or a sister intentionally wound a brother or a sister, and is found guilty, death shall be the penalty. And if a husband wound a wife, or a wife a husband, with intent to kill, let him or her undergo perpetual exile; if they have sons or daughters who are still young, the guardians shall take care of their property, and have charge of the children as orphans. If their sons are grown up, they shall be under no obligation to support the exiled parent, but they shall possess the property themselves. And if he who meets with such a misfortune has no children, the kindred of the exiled man to the degree of sons of cousins, both on the male and female side, shall meet together, and after taking counsel with the guardians of the law and the priests, shall appoint a 5040th citizen to be the heir of the house, considering and reasoning that no house of all the 5040 belongs to the inhabitant or to the whole family, but is the public and private property of the state. Now the state should seek to have its houses as holy and happy as possible. And if any one of the houses be unfortunate, and stained with impiety, and the owner leave no posterity, but dies unmarried, or married and childless, having suffered death as the penalty of murder or some other crime committed against the Gods or against his fellow-citizens, of which death is the penalty distinctly laid down in the law; or if any of the citizens be in perpetual exile, and also childless, that house shall first of all be purified and undergo expiation according to law; and then let the kinsmen of the house, as we were just now saying, and the guardians of the law, meet and consider what family there is in the state which is of the highest repute for virtue and also for good fortune, in which there are a number of sons; from that family let them take one and introduce him to the father and forefathers of the dead man as their son, and, for the sake of the omen, let him be called so, that he may be the continuer of their family, the keeper of their hearth, and the minister of their sacred rites with better fortune than his father had; and when they have made this supplication, they shall make him heir according to law, and the offending person they shall leave nameless and childless and portionless when calamities such as these overtake him.

Now the boundaries of some things do not touch one another, but there is a borderland which comes in between, preventing them from touching. And we were saying that actions done from passion are of this nature, and come in between the voluntary and involuntary. If a person be convicted of having inflicted wounds in a passion, in the first place he shall pay twice the amount of the injury, if the wound be curable, or, if incurable, four times the amount of the injury; or if the wound be curable, and at the same time cause great and notable disgrace to the wounded person, he shall pay fourfold. And whenever any one in wounding another injures not only the sufferer, but also the city, and makes him incapable of defending his country against the enemy, he, besides the other penalties, shall pay a penalty for the loss which the state has incurred. And the penalty shall be, that in addition to his own times of service, he shall serve on behalf of the disabled person, and shall take his place in war; or, if he refuse, he shall be liable to be convicted by law of refusal to serve. The compensation for the injury, whether to be twofold or threefold or fourfold, shall be fixed by the judges who convict him. And if, in like manner, a brother wounds a brother, the parents and kindred of either sex, including the children of cousins, whether on the male or female side, shall meet, and when they have judged the cause, they shall entrust the assessment of damages to the parents, as is natural; and if the estimate be disputed, then the kinsmen on the male side shall make the estimate, or if they cannot, they shall commit the matter to the guardians of the law. And when similar charges of wounding are brought by children against their parents, those who are more than sixty years of age, having children of their own, not adopted, shall be required to decide; and if any one is convicted, they shall determine whether he or she ought to die, or suffer some other punishment either greater than death, or, at any rate, not much less. A kinsman of the offender shall not be allowed to judge the cause, not even if he be of the age which is prescribed by the law. If a slave in a fit of anger wound a freeman, the owner of the slave shall give him up to the wounded man, who may do as he pleases with him, and if he do not give him up he shall himself make good the injury. And if any one says that the slave and the wounded man are conspiring together, let him argue the point, and if he is cast, he shall pay for the wrong three times over, but if he gains his case, the freeman who conspired with the slave shall be liable to an action for kidnapping. And if any one unintentionally wounds another he shall simply pay for the harm, for no legislator is able to control chance. In such a case the judges shall be the same as those who are appointed in the case of children suing their parents; and they shall estimate the amount of the injury.

All the preceding injuries and every kind of assault are deeds of violence; and every man, woman, or child ought to consider that the elder has the precedence of the younger in honour, both among the Gods and also among men who would live in security and happiness. Wherefore it is a foul thing and hateful to the Gods to see an elder man assaulted by a younger in the city, and it is reasonable that a young man when struck by an elder should lightly endure his anger, laying up in store for himself a like honour when he is old. Let this be the law: Every one shall reverence his elder in word and deed; he shall respect any one who is twenty years older than himself, whether male or female, regarding him or her as his father or mother; and he shall abstain from laying hands on any one who is of an age to have been his father or mother, out of reverence to the Gods who preside over birth; similarly he shall keep his hands from a stranger, whether he be an old inhabitant or newly arrived; he shall not venture to correct such an one by blows, either as the aggressor or in self-defence. If he thinks that some stranger has struck him out of wantonness or insolence, and ought to be punished, he shall take him to the wardens of the city, but let him not strike him, that the stranger may be kept far away from the possibility of lifting up his hand against a citizen, and let the wardens of the city take the offender and examine him, not forgetting their duty to the God of Strangers, and in case the stranger appears to have struck the citizen unjustly, let them inflict upon him as many blows with the scourge as he was himself inflicted, and quell his presumption. But if he be innocent, they shall threaten and rebuke the man who arrested him, and let them both go. If a person strikes another of the same age or somewhat older than himself, who has no children, whether he be an old man who strikes an old man or a young man who strikes a young man, let the person struck defend himself in the natural way without a weapon and with his hands only. He who, being more than forty years of age, dares to fight with another, whether he be the aggressor or in self-defence, shall be regarded as rude and ill-mannered and slavish—this will be a disgraceful punishment, and therefore suitable to him. The obedient nature will readily yield to such exhortations, but the disobedient, who heeds not the prelude, shall have the law ready for him: If any man smite another who is older than himself, either by twenty or by more years, in the first place, he who is at hand, not being younger than the combatants, nor their equal in age, shall separate them, or be disgraced according to law; but if he be the equal in age of the person who is struck or younger, he shall defend the person injured as he would a brother or father or still older relative. Further, let him who dares to smite an elder be tried for assault, as I have said, and if he be found guilty, let him be imprisoned for a period of not less than a year, or if the judges approve of a longer period, their decision shall be final. But if a stranger or metic smite one who is older by twenty years or more, the same law shall hold about the bystanders assisting, and he who is found guilty in such a suit, if he be a stranger but not resident, shall be imprisoned during a period of two years; and a metic who disobeys the laws shall be imprisoned for three years, unless the court assign him a longer term. And let him who was present in any of these cases and did not assist according to law be punished, if he be of the highest class, by paying a fine of a mina; or if he be of the second class, of fifty drachmas; or if of the third class, by a fine of thirty drachmas; or if he be of the fourth class, by a fine of twenty drachmas; and the generals and taxiarchs and phylarchs and hipparchs shall form the court in such cases.

Laws are partly framed for the sake of good men, in order to instruct them how they may live on friendly terms with one another, and partly for the sake of those who refuse to be instructed, whose spirit cannot be subdued, or softened, or hindered from plunging into evil. These are the persons who cause the word to be spoken which I am about to utter; for them the legislator legislates of necessity, and in the hope that there may be no need of his laws. He who shall dare to lay violent hands upon his father or mother, or any still older relative, having no fear either of the wrath of the Gods above, or of the punishments that are spoken of in the world below, but transgresses in contempt of ancient and universal traditions as though he were too wise to believe in them, requires some extreme measure of prevention. Now death is not the worst that can happen to men; far worse are the punishments which are said to pursue them in the world below. But although they are most true tales, they work on such souls no prevention; for if they had any effect there would be no slayers of mothers, or impious hands lifted up against parents; and therefore the punishments of this world which are inflicted during life ought not in such cases to fall short, if possible, of the terrors of the world below. Let our enactment then be as follows: If a man dare to strike his father or his mother, or their fathers or mothers, he being at the time of sound mind, then let any one who is at hand come to the rescue as has been already said, and the metic or stranger who comes to the rescue shall be called to the first place in the games; but if he do not come he shall suffer the punishment of perpetual exile. He who is not a metic, if he comes to the rescue, shall have praise, and if he do not come, blame. And if a slave come to the rescue, let him be made free, but if he do not come to the rescue, let him receive 100 strokes of the whip, by order of the wardens of the agora, if the occurrence take place in the agora; or if somewhere in the city beyond the limits of the agora, any warden of the city who is in residence shall punish him; or if in the country, then the commanders of the wardens of the country. If those who are near at the time be inhabitants of the same place, whether they be youths, or men, or women, let them come to the rescue and denounce him as the impious one; and he who does not come to the rescue shall fall under the curse of Zeus, the God of kindred and of ancestors, according to law. And if any one is found guilty of assaulting a parent, let him in the first place be forever banished from the city into the country, and let him abstain from the temples; and if he do not abstain, the wardens of the country shall punish him with blows, or in any way which they please, and if he return he shall be put to death. And if any freeman eat or drink, or have any other sort of intercourse with him, or only meeting him have voluntarily touched him, he shall not enter into any temple, nor into the agora, nor into the city, until he is purified; for he should consider that he has become tainted by a curse. And if he disobeys the law, and pollutes the city and the temples contrary to law, and one of the magistrates sees him and does not indict him, when he gives in his account this omission shall be a most serious charge.

If a slave strike a freeman, whether a stranger or a citizen, let any one who is present come to the rescue, or pay the penalty already mentioned; and let the bystanders bind him, and deliver him up to the injured person, and he receiving him shall put him in chains, and inflict on him as many stripes as he pleases; but having punished him he must surrender him to his master according to law, and not deprive him of his property. Let the law be as follows: The slave who strikes a freeman, not at the command of the magistrates, his owner shall receive bound from the man whom he has stricken, and not release him until the slave has persuaded the man whom he has stricken that he ought to be released. And let there be the same laws about women in relation to women, and about men and women in relation to one another.

BOOK X.

And now having spoken of assaults, let us sum up all acts of violence under a single law, which shall be as follows: No one shall take or carry away any of his neighbour's goods, neither shall he use anything which is his neighbour's without the consent of the owner; for these are the offences which are and have been, and will ever be, the source of all the aforesaid evils. The greatest of them are excesses and insolences of youth, and are offences against the greatest when they are done against religion; and especially great when in violation of public and holy rites, or of the partly-common rites in which tribes and phratries share; and in the second degree great when they are committed against private rites and sepulchres, and in the third degree (not to repeat the acts formerly mentioned), when insults are offered to parents; the fourth kind of violence is when any one, regardless of the authority of the rulers, takes or carries away or makes use of anything which belongs to them, not having their consent; and the fifth kind is when the violation of the civil rights of an individual demands reparation. There should be a common law embracing all these cases. For we have already said in general terms what shall be the punishment of sacrilege, whether fraudulent or violent, and now we have to determine what is to be the punishment of those who speak or act insolently toward the Gods. But first we must give them an admonition which may be in the following terms: No one who in obedience to the laws believed that there were Gods, ever intentionally did any unholy act, or uttered any unlawful word; but he who did must have supposed one of three things—either that they did not exist—which is the first possibility, or secondly, that, if they did, they took no care of man, or thirdly, that they were easily appeased and turned aside from their purpose by sacrifices and prayers.

CLEINIAS: What shall we say or do to these persons?

ATHENIAN: My good friend, let us first hear the jests which I suspect that they in their superiority will utter against us.

CLEINIAS: What jests?

ATHENIAN: They will make some irreverent speech of this sort: 'O inhabitants of Athens, and Sparta, and Cnosus,' they will reply, 'in that you speak truly; for some of us deny the very existence of the Gods, while others, as you say, are of opinion that they do not care about us; and others that they are turned from their course by gifts. Now we have a right to claim, as you yourself allowed, in the matter of laws, that before you are hard upon us and threaten us, you should argue with us and convince us—you should first attempt to teach and persuade us that there are Gods by reasonable evidences, and also that they are too good to be unrighteous, or to be propitiated, or turned from their course by gifts. For when we hear such things said of them by those who are esteemed to be the best of poets, and orators, and prophets, and priests, and by innumerable others, the thoughts of most of us are not set upon abstaining from unrighteous acts, but upon doing them and atoning for them. When lawgivers profess that they are gentle and not stern, we think that they should first of all use persuasion to us, and show us the existence of Gods, if not in a better manner than other men, at any rate in a truer; and who knows but that we shall hearken to you? If then our request is a fair one, please to accept our challenge.

CLEINIAS: But is there any difficulty in proving the existence of the Gods?

ATHENIAN: How would you prove it?

CLEINIAS: How? In the first place, the earth and the sun, and the stars and the universe, and the fair order of the seasons, and the division of them into years and months, furnish proofs of their existence, and also there is the fact that all Hellenes and barbarians believe in them.

ATHENIAN: I fear, my sweet friend, though I will not say that I much regard, the contempt with which the profane will be likely to assail us. For you do not understand the nature of their complaint, and you fancy that they rush into impiety only from a love of sensual pleasure.

CLEINIAS: Why, Stranger, what other reason is there?

ATHENIAN: One which you who live in a different atmosphere would never guess.

CLEINIAS: What is it?

ATHENIAN: A very grievous sort of ignorance which is imagined to be the greatest wisdom.

CLEINIAS: What do you mean?

ATHENIAN: At Athens there are tales preserved in writing which the virtue of your state, as I am informed, refuses to admit. They speak of the Gods in prose as well as verse, and the oldest of them tell of the origin of the heavens and of the world, and not far from the beginning of their story they proceed to narrate the birth of the Gods, and how after they were born they behaved to one another. Whether these stories have in other ways a good or a bad influence, I should not like to be severe upon them, because they are ancient; but, looking at them with reference to the duties of children to their parents, I cannot praise them, or think that they are useful, or at all true. Of the words of the ancients I have nothing more to say; and I should wish to say of them only what is pleasing to the Gods. But as to our younger generation and their wisdom, I cannot let them off when they do mischief. For do but mark the effect of their words: when you and I argue for the existence of the Gods, and produce the sun, moon, stars, and earth, claiming for them a divine being, if we would listen to the aforesaid philosophers we should say that they are earth and stones only, which can have no care at all of human affairs, and that all religion is a cooking up of words and a make-believe.

CLEINIAS: One such teacher, O stranger, would be bad enough, and you imply that there are many of them, which is worse.

ATHENIAN: Well, then; what shall we say or do? Shall we assume that some one is accusing us among unholy men, who are trying to escape from the effect of our legislation; and that they say of us—How dreadful that you should legislate on the supposition that there are Gods! Shall we make a defence of ourselves? or shall we leave them and return to our laws, lest the prelude should become longer than the law? For the discourse will certainly extend to great length, if we are to treat the impiously disposed as they desire, partly demonstrating to them at some length the things of which they demand an explanation, partly making them afraid or dissatisfied, and then proceed to the requisite enactments.

CLEINIAS: Yes, Stranger; but then how often have we repeated already that on the present occasion there is no reason why brevity should be preferred to length; for who is 'at our heels?' as the saying goes, and it would be paltry and ridiculous to prefer the shorter to the better. It is a matter of no small consequence, in some way or other to prove that there are Gods, and that they are good, and regard justice more than men do. The demonstration of this would be the best and noblest prelude of all our laws. And therefore, without impatience, and without hurry, let us unreservedly consider the whole matter, summoning up all the power of persuasion which we possess.

ATHENIAN: Seeing you thus in earnest, I would fain offer up a prayer that I may succeed: but I must proceed at once. Who can be calm when he is called upon to prove the existence of the Gods? Who can avoid hating and abhorring the men who are and have been the cause of this argument; I speak of those who will not believe the tales which they have heard as babes and sucklings from their mothers and nurses, repeated by them both in jest and earnest, like charms, who have also heard them in the sacrificial prayers, and seen sights accompanying them—sights and sounds delightful to children—and their parents during the sacrifices showing an intense earnestness on behalf of their children and of themselves, and with eager interest talking to the Gods, and beseeching them, as though they were firmly convinced of their existence; who likewise see and hear the prostrations and invocations which are made by Hellenes and barbarians at the rising and setting of the sun and moon, in all the vicissitudes of life, not as if they thought that there were no Gods, but as if there could be no doubt of their existence, and no suspicion of their non-existence; when men, knowing all these things, despise them on no real grounds, as would be admitted by all who have any particle of intelligence, and when they force us to say what we are now saying, how can any one in gentle terms remonstrate with the like of them, when he has to begin by proving to them the very existence of the Gods? Yet the attempt must be made; for it would be unseemly that one half of mankind should go mad in their lust of pleasure, and the other half in their indignation at such persons. Our address to these lost and perverted natures should not be spoken in passion; let us suppose ourselves to select some one of them, and gently reason with him, smothering our anger: O my son, we will say to him, you are young, and the advance of time will make you reverse many of the opinions which you now hold. Wait awhile, and do not attempt to judge at present of the highest things; and that is the highest of which you now think nothing—to know the Gods rightly and to live accordingly. And in the first place let me indicate to you one point which is of great importance, and about which I cannot be deceived: You and your friends are not the first who have held this opinion about the Gods. There have always been persons more or less numerous who have had the same disorder. I have known many of them, and can tell you, that no one who had taken up in youth this opinion, that the Gods do not exist, ever continued in the same until he was old; the two other notions certainly do continue in some cases, but not in many; the notion, I mean, that the Gods exist, but take no heed of human things, and the other notion that they do take heed of them, but are easily propitiated with sacrifices and prayers. As to the opinion about the Gods which may some day become clear to you, I advise you to wait and consider if it be true or not; ask of others, and above all of the legislator. In the meantime take care that you do not offend against the Gods. For the duty of the legislator is and always will be to teach you the truth of these matters.

CLEINIAS: Our address, Stranger, thus far, is excellent.

ATHENIAN: Quite true, Megillus and Cleinias, but I am afraid that we have unconsciously lighted on a strange doctrine.

CLEINIAS: What doctrine do you mean?

ATHENIAN: The wisest of all doctrines, in the opinion of many.

CLEINIAS: I wish that you would speak plainer.

ATHENIAN: The doctrine that all things do become, have become, and will become, some by nature, some by art, and some by chance.

CLEINIAS: Is not that true?

ATHENIAN: Well, philosophers are probably right; at any rate we may as well follow in their track, and examine what is the meaning of them and their disciples.

CLEINIAS: By all means.

ATHENIAN: They say that the greatest and fairest things are the work of nature and of chance, the lesser of art, which, receiving from nature the greater and primeval creations, moulds and fashions all those lesser works which are generally termed artificial.

CLEINIAS: How is that?

ATHENIAN: I will explain my meaning still more clearly. They say that fire and water, and earth and air, all exist by nature and chance, and none of them by art, and that as to the bodies which come next in order—earth, and sun, and moon, and stars—they have been created by means of these absolutely inanimate existences. The elements are severally moved by chance and some inherent force according to certain affinities among them—of hot with cold, or of dry with moist, or of soft with hard, and according to all the other accidental admixtures of opposites which have been formed by necessity. After this fashion and in this manner the whole heaven has been created, and all that is in the heaven, as well as animals and all plants, and all the seasons come from these elements, not by the action of mind, as they say, or of any God, or from art, but as I was saying, by nature and chance only. Art sprang up afterwards and out of these, mortal and of mortal birth, and produced in play certain images and very partial imitations of the truth, having an affinity to one another, such as music and painting create and their companion arts. And there are other arts which have a serious purpose, and these co-operate with nature, such, for example, as medicine, and husbandry, and gymnastic. And they say that politics co-operate with nature, but in a less degree, and have more of art; also that legislation is entirely a work of art, and is based on assumptions which are not true.

CLEINIAS: How do you mean?

ATHENIAN: In the first place, my dear friend, these people would say that the Gods exist not by nature, but by art, and by the laws of states, which are different in different places, according to the agreement of those who make them; and that the honourable is one thing by nature and another thing by law, and that the principles of justice have no existence at all in nature, but that mankind are always disputing about them and altering them; and that the alterations which are made by art and by law have no basis in nature, but are of authority for the moment and at the time at which they are made. These, my friends, are the sayings of wise men, poets and prose writers, which find a way into the minds of youth. They are told by them that the highest right is might, and in this way the young fall into impieties, under the idea that the Gods are not such as the law bids them imagine; and hence arise factions, these philosophers inviting them to lead a true life according to nature, that is, to live in real dominion over others, and not in legal subjection to them.

CLEINIAS: What a dreadful picture, Stranger, have you given, and how great is the injury which is thus inflicted on young men to the ruin both of states and families!

ATHENIAN: True, Cleinias; but then what should the lawgiver do when this evil is of long standing? should he only rise up in the state and threaten all mankind, proclaiming that if they will not say and think that the Gods are such as the law ordains (and this may be extended generally to the honourable, the just, and to all the highest things, and to all that relates to virtue and vice), and if they will not make their actions conform to the copy which the law gives them, then he who refuses to obey the law shall die, or suffer stripes and bonds, or privation of citizenship, or in some cases be punished by loss of property and exile? Should he not rather, when he is making laws for men, at the same time infuse the spirit of persuasion into his words, and mitigate the severity of them as far as he can?

CLEINIAS: Why, Stranger, if such persuasion be at all possible, then a legislator who has anything in him ought never to weary of persuading men; he ought to leave nothing unsaid in support of the ancient opinion that there are Gods, and of all those other truths which you were just now mentioning; he ought to support the law and also art, and acknowledge that both alike exist by nature, and no less than nature, if they are the creations of mind in accordance with right reason, as you appear to me to maintain, and I am disposed to agree with you in thinking.

ATHENIAN: Yes, my enthusiastic Cleinias; but are not these things when spoken to a multitude hard to be understood, not to mention that they take up a dismal length of time?

CLEINIAS: Why, Stranger, shall we, whose patience failed not when drinking or music were the themes of discourse, weary now of discoursing about the Gods, and about divine things? And the greatest help to rational legislation is that the laws when once written down are always at rest; they can be put to the test at any future time, and therefore, if on first hearing they seem difficult, there is no reason for apprehension about them, because any man however dull can go over them and consider them again and again; nor if they are tedious but useful, is there any reason or religion, as it seems to me, in any man refusing to maintain the principles of them to the utmost of his power.

MEGILLUS: Stranger, I like what Cleinias is saying.

ATHENIAN: Yes, Megillus, and we should do as he proposes; for if impious discourses were not scattered, as I may say, throughout the world, there would have been no need for any vindication of the existence of the Gods—but seeing that they are spread far and wide, such arguments are needed; and who should come to the rescue of the greatest laws, when they are being undermined by bad men, but the legislator himself?

MEGILLUS: There is no more proper champion of them.

ATHENIAN: Well, then, tell me, Cleinias—for I must ask you to be my partner—does not he who talks in this way conceive fire and water and earth and air to be the first elements of all things? these he calls nature, and out of these he supposes the soul to be formed afterwards; and this is not a mere conjecture of ours about his meaning, but is what he really means.

CLEINIAS: Very true.

ATHENIAN: Then, by Heaven, we have discovered the source of this vain opinion of all those physical investigators; and I would have you examine their arguments with the utmost care, for their impiety is a very serious matter; they not only make a bad and mistaken use of argument, but they lead away the minds of others: that is my opinion of them.

CLEINIAS: You are right; but I should like to know how this happens.

ATHENIAN: I fear that the argument may seem singular.

CLEINIAS: Do not hesitate, Stranger; I see that you are afraid of such a discussion carrying you beyond the limits of legislation. But if there be no other way of showing our agreement in the belief that there are Gods, of whom the law is said now to approve, let us take this way, my good sir.

ATHENIAN: Then I suppose that I must repeat the singular argument of those who manufacture the soul according to their own impious notions; they affirm that which is the first cause of the generation and destruction of all things, to be not first, but last, and that which is last to be first, and hence they have fallen into error about the true nature of the Gods.

CLEINIAS: Still I do not understand you.

ATHENIAN: Nearly all of them, my friends, seem to be ignorant of the nature and power of the soul, especially in what relates to her origin: they do not know that she is among the first of things, and before all bodies, and is the chief author of their changes and transpositions. And if this is true, and if the soul is older than the body, must not the things which are of the soul's kindred be of necessity prior to those which appertain to the body?

CLEINIAS: Certainly.

ATHENIAN: Then thought and attention and mind and art and law will be prior to that which is hard and soft and heavy and light; and the great and primitive works and actions will be works of art; they will be the first, and after them will come nature and works of nature, which however is a wrong term for men to apply to them; these will follow, and will be under the government of art and mind.

CLEINIAS: But why is the word 'nature' wrong?

ATHENIAN: Because those who use the term mean to say that nature is the first creative power; but if the soul turn out to be the primeval element, and not fire or air, then in the truest sense and beyond other things the soul may be said to exist by nature; and this would be true if you proved that the soul is older than the body, but not otherwise.

CLEINIAS: You are quite right.

ATHENIAN: Shall we, then, take this as the next point to which our attention should be directed?

CLEINIAS: By all means.

ATHENIAN: Let us be on our guard lest this most deceptive argument with its youthful looks, beguiling us old men, give us the slip and make a laughing-stock of us. Who knows but we may be aiming at the greater, and fail of attaining the lesser? Suppose that we three have to pass a rapid river, and I, being the youngest of the three and experienced in rivers, take upon me the duty of making the attempt first by myself; leaving you in safety on the bank, I am to examine whether the river is passable by older men like yourselves, and if such appears to be the case then I shall invite you to follow, and my experience will help to convey you across; but if the river is impassable by you, then there will have been no danger to anybody but myself—would not that seem to be a very fair proposal? I mean to say that the argument in prospect is likely to be too much for you, out of your depth and beyond your strength, and I should be afraid that the stream of my questions might create in you who are not in the habit of answering, giddiness and confusion of mind, and hence a feeling of unpleasantness and unsuitableness might arise. I think therefore that I had better first ask the questions and then answer them myself while you listen in safety; in that way I can carry on the argument until I have completed the proof that the soul is prior to the body.

CLEINIAS: Excellent, Stranger, and I hope that you will do as you propose.

ATHENIAN: Come, then, and if ever we are to call upon the Gods, let us call upon them now in all seriousness to come to the demonstration of their own existence. And so holding fast to the rope we will venture upon the depths of the argument. When questions of this sort are asked of me, my safest answer would appear to be as follows: Some one says to me, 'O Stranger, are all things at rest and nothing in motion, or is the exact opposite of this true, or are some things in motion and others at rest?' To this I shall reply that some things are in motion and others at rest. 'And do not things which move move in a place, and are not the things which are at rest at rest in a place?' Certainly. 'And some move or rest in one place and some in more places than one?' You mean to say, we shall rejoin, that those things which rest at the centre move in one place, just as the circumference goes round of globes which are said to be at rest? 'Yes.' And we observe that, in the revolution, the motion which carries round the larger and the lesser circle at the same time is proportionally distributed to greater and smaller, and is greater and smaller in a certain proportion. Here is a wonder which might be thought an impossibility, that the same motion should impart swiftness and slowness in due proportion to larger and lesser circles. 'Very true.' And when you speak of bodies moving in many places, you seem to me to mean those which move from one place to another, and sometimes have one centre of motion and sometimes more than one because they turn upon their axis; and whenever they meet anything, if it be stationary, they are divided by it; but if they get in the midst between bodies which are approaching and moving towards the same spot from opposite directions, they unite with them. 'I admit the truth of what you are saying.' Also when they unite they grow, and when they are divided they waste away—that is, supposing the constitution of each to remain, or if that fails, then there is a second reason of their dissolution. 'And when are all things created and how?' Clearly, they are created when the first principle receives increase and attains to the second dimension, and from this arrives at the one which is neighbour to this, and after reaching the third becomes perceptible to sense. Everything which is thus changing and moving is in process of generation; only when at rest has it real existence, but when passing into another state it is destroyed utterly. Have we not mentioned all motions that there are, and comprehended them under their kinds and numbered them with the exception, my friends, of two?

CLEINIAS: Which are they?

ATHENIAN: Just the two, with which our present enquiry is concerned.

CLEINIAS: Speak plainer.

ATHENIAN: I suppose that our enquiry has reference to the soul?

CLEINIAS: Very true.

ATHENIAN: Let us assume that there is a motion able to move other things, but not to move itself; that is one kind; and there is another kind which can move itself as well as other things, working in composition and decomposition, by increase and diminution and generation and destruction—that is also one of the many kinds of motion.

CLEINIAS: Granted.

ATHENIAN: And we will assume that which moves other, and is changed by other, to be the ninth, and that which changes itself and others, and is coincident with every action and every passion, and is the true principle of change and motion in all that is—that we shall be inclined to call the tenth.

CLEINIAS: Certainly.

ATHENIAN: And which of these ten motions ought we to prefer as being the mightiest and most efficient?

CLEINIAS: I must say that the motion which is able to move itself is ten thousand times superior to all the others.

ATHENIAN: Very good; but may I make one or two corrections in what I have been saying?

CLEINIAS: What are they?

ATHENIAN: When I spoke of the tenth sort of motion, that was not quite correct.

CLEINIAS: What was the error?

ATHENIAN: According to the true order, the tenth was really the first in generation and power; then follows the second, which was strangely enough termed the ninth by us.

CLEINIAS: What do you mean?

ATHENIAN: I mean this: when one thing changes another, and that another, of such will there be any primary changing element? How can a thing which is moved by another ever be the beginning of change? Impossible. But when the self-moved changes other, and that again other, and thus thousands upon tens of thousands of bodies are set in motion, must not the beginning of all this motion be the change of the self-moving principle?

CLEINIAS: Very true, and I quite agree.

ATHENIAN: Or, to put the question in another way, making answer to ourselves: If, as most of these philosophers have the audacity to affirm, all things were at rest in one mass, which of the above-mentioned principles of motion would first spring up among them?

CLEINIAS: Clearly the self-moving; for there could be no change in them arising out of any external cause; the change must first take place in themselves.

ATHENIAN: Then we must say that self-motion being the origin of all motions, and the first which arises among things at rest as well as among things in motion, is the eldest and mightiest principle of change, and that which is changed by another and yet moves other is second.

CLEINIAS: Quite true.

ATHENIAN: At this stage of the argument let us put a question.

CLEINIAS: What question?

ATHENIAN: If we were to see this power existing in any earthy, watery, or fiery substance, simple or compound—how should we describe it?

CLEINIAS: You mean to ask whether we should call such a self-moving power life?

ATHENIAN: I do.

CLEINIAS: Certainly we should.

ATHENIAN: And when we see soul in anything, must we not do the same—must we not admit that this is life?

CLEINIAS: We must.

ATHENIAN: And now, I beseech you, reflect—you would admit that we have a threefold knowledge of things?

CLEINIAS: What do you mean?

ATHENIAN: I mean that we know the essence, and that we know the definition of the essence, and the name—these are the three; and there are two questions which may be raised about anything.

CLEINIAS: How two?

ATHENIAN: Sometimes a person may give the name and ask the definition; or he may give the definition and ask the name. I may illustrate what I mean in this way.

CLEINIAS: How?

ATHENIAN: Number like some other things is capable of being divided into equal parts; when thus divided, number is named 'even,' and the definition of the name 'even' is 'number divisible into two equal parts'?

CLEINIAS: True.

ATHENIAN: I mean, that when we are asked about the definition and give the name, or when we are asked about the name and give the definition—in either case, whether we give name or definition, we speak of the same thing, calling 'even' the number which is divided into two equal parts.

CLEINIAS: Quite true.

ATHENIAN: And what is the definition of that which is named 'soul'? Can we conceive of any other than that which has been already given—the motion which can move itself?

CLEINIAS: You mean to say that the essence which is defined as the self-moved is the same with that which has the name soul?

ATHENIAN: Yes; and if this is true, do we still maintain that there is anything wanting in the proof that the soul is the first origin and moving power of all that is, or has become, or will be, and their contraries, when she has been clearly shown to be the source of change and motion in all things?

CLEINIAS: Certainly not; the soul as being the source of motion, has been most satisfactorily shown to be the oldest of all things.

ATHENIAN: And is not that motion which is produced in another, by reason of another, but never has any self-moving power at all, being in truth the change of an inanimate body, to be reckoned second, or by any lower number which you may prefer?

CLEINIAS: Exactly.

ATHENIAN: Then we are right, and speak the most perfect and absolute truth, when we say that the soul is prior to the body, and that the body is second and comes afterwards, and is born to obey the soul, which is the ruler?

CLEINIAS: Nothing can be more true.

ATHENIAN: Do you remember our old admission, that if the soul was prior to the body the things of the soul were also prior to those of the body?

CLEINIAS: Certainly.

ATHENIAN: Then characters and manners, and wishes and reasonings, and true opinions, and reflections, and recollections are prior to length and breadth and depth and strength of bodies, if the soul is prior to the body.

CLEINIAS: To be sure.

ATHENIAN: In the next place, we must not of necessity admit that the soul is the cause of good and evil, base and honourable, just and unjust, and of all other opposites, if we suppose her to be the cause of all things?

CLEINIAS: We must.

ATHENIAN: And as the soul orders and inhabits all things that move, however moving, must we not say that she orders also the heavens?

CLEINIAS: Of course.

ATHENIAN: One soul or more? More than one—I will answer for you; at any rate, we must not suppose that there are less than two—one the author of good, and the other of evil.

CLEINIAS: Very true.

ATHENIAN: Yes, very true; the soul then directs all things in heaven, and earth, and sea by her movements, and these are described by the terms—will, consideration, attention, deliberation, opinion true and false, joy and sorrow, confidence, fear, hatred, love, and other primary motions akin to these; which again receive the secondary motions of corporeal substances, and guide all things to growth and decay, to composition and decomposition, and to the qualities which accompany them, such as heat and cold, heaviness and lightness, hardness and softness, blackness and whiteness, bitterness and sweetness, and all those other qualities which the soul uses, herself a goddess, when truly receiving the divine mind she disciplines all things rightly to their happiness; but when she is the companion of folly, she does the very contrary of all this. Shall we assume so much, or do we still entertain doubts?

CLEINIAS: There is no room at all for doubt.

ATHENIAN: Shall we say then that it is the soul which controls heaven and earth, and the whole world? that it is a principle of wisdom and virtue, or a principle which has neither wisdom nor virtue? Suppose that we make answer as follows:

CLEINIAS: How would you answer?

ATHENIAN: If, my friend, we say that the whole path and movement of heaven, and of all that is therein, is by nature akin to the movement and revolution and calculation of mind, and proceeds by kindred laws, then, as is plain, we must say that the best soul takes care of the world and guides it along the good path.

CLEINIAS: True.

ATHENIAN: But if the world moves wildly and irregularly, then the evil soul guides it.

CLEINIAS: True again.

ATHENIAN: Of what nature is the movement of mind? To this question it is not easy to give an intelligent answer; and therefore I ought to assist you in framing one.

CLEINIAS: Very good.

ATHENIAN: Then let us not answer as if we would look straight at the sun, making ourselves darkness at midday—I mean as if we were under the impression that we could see with mortal eyes, or know adequately the nature of mind—it will be safer to look at the image only.

CLEINIAS: What do you mean?

ATHENIAN: Let us select of the ten motions the one which mind chiefly resembles; this I will bring to your recollection, and will then make the answer on behalf of us all.

CLEINIAS: That will be excellent.

ATHENIAN: You will surely remember our saying that all things were either at rest or in motion?

CLEINIAS: I do.

ATHENIAN: And that of things in motion some were moving in one place, and others in more than one?

CLEINIAS: Yes.

ATHENIAN: Of these two kinds of motion, that which moves in one place must move about a centre like globes made in a lathe, and is most entirely akin and similar to the circular movement of mind.

CLEINIAS: What do you mean?

ATHENIAN: In saying that both mind and the motion which is in one place move in the same and like manner, in and about the same, and in relation to the same, and according to one proportion and order, and are like the motion of a globe, we invented a fair image, which does no discredit to our ingenuity.

CLEINIAS: It does us great credit.

ATHENIAN: And the motion of the other sort which is not after the same manner, nor in the same, nor about the same, nor in relation to the same, nor in one place, nor in order, nor according to any rule or proportion, may be said to be akin to senselessness and folly?

CLEINIAS: That is most true.

ATHENIAN: Then, after what has been said, there is no difficulty in distinctly stating, that since soul carries all things round, either the best soul or the contrary must of necessity carry round and order and arrange the revolution of the heaven.

CLEINIAS: And judging from what has been said, Stranger, there would be impiety in asserting that any but the most perfect soul or souls carries round the heavens.

ATHENIAN: You have understood my meaning right well, Cleinias, and now let me ask you another question.

CLEINIAS: What are you going to ask?

ATHENIAN: If the soul carries round the sun and moon, and the other stars, does she not carry round each individual of them?

CLEINIAS: Certainly.

ATHENIAN: Then of one of them let us speak, and the same argument will apply to all.

CLEINIAS: Which will you take?

ATHENIAN: Every one sees the body of the sun, but no one sees his soul, nor the soul of any other body living or dead; and yet there is great reason to believe that this nature, unperceived by any of our senses, is circumfused around them all, but is perceived by mind; and therefore by mind and reflection only let us apprehend the following point.

CLEINIAS: What is that?

ATHENIAN: If the soul carries round the sun, we shall not be far wrong in supposing one of three alternatives.

CLEINIAS: What are they?

ATHENIAN: Either the soul which moves the sun this way and that, resides within the circular and visible body, like the soul which carries us about every way; or the soul provides herself with an external body of fire or air, as some affirm, and violently propels body by body; or thirdly, she is without such a body, but guides the sun by some extraordinary and wonderful power.

CLEINIAS: Yes, certainly; the soul can only order all things in one of these three ways.

ATHENIAN: And this soul of the sun, which is therefore better than the sun, whether taking the sun about in a chariot to give light to men, or acting from without, or in whatever way, ought by every man to be deemed a God.

CLEINIAS: Yes, by every man who has the least particle of sense.

ATHENIAN: And of the stars too, and of the moon, and of the years and months and seasons, must we not say in like manner, that since a soul or souls having every sort of excellence are the causes of all of them, those souls are Gods, whether they are living beings and reside in bodies, and in this way order the whole heaven, or whatever be the place and mode of their existence—and will any one who admits all this venture to deny that all things are full of Gods?

CLEINIAS: No one, Stranger, would be such a madman.

ATHENIAN: And now, Megillus and Cleinias, let us offer terms to him who has hitherto denied the existence of the Gods, and leave him.

CLEINIAS: What terms?

ATHENIAN: Either he shall teach us that we were wrong in saying that the soul is the original of all things, and arguing accordingly; or, if he be not able to say anything better, then he must yield to us and live for the remainder of his life in the belief that there are Gods. Let us see, then, whether we have said enough or not enough to those who deny that there are Gods.

CLEINIAS: Certainly, quite enough, Stranger.

ATHENIAN: Then to them we will say no more. And now we are to address him who, believing that there are Gods, believes also that they take no heed of human affairs: To him we say—O thou best of men, in believing that there are Gods you are led by some affinity to them, which attracts you towards your kindred and makes you honour and believe in them. But the fortunes of evil and unrighteous men in private as well as public life, which, though not really happy, are wrongly counted happy in the judgment of men, and are celebrated both by poets and prose writers—these draw you aside from your natural piety. Perhaps you have seen impious men growing old and leaving their children's children in high offices, and their prosperity shakes your faith—you have known or heard or been yourself an eyewitness of many monstrous impieties, and have beheld men by such criminal means from small beginnings attaining to sovereignty and the pinnacle of greatness; and considering all these things you do not like to accuse the Gods of them, because they are your relatives; and so from some want of reasoning power, and also from an unwillingness to find fault with them, you have come to believe that they exist indeed, but have no thought or care of human things. Now, that your present evil opinion may not grow to still greater impiety, and that we may if possible use arguments which may conjure away the evil before it arrives, we will add another argument to that originally addressed to him who utterly denied the existence of the Gods. And do you, Megillus and Cleinias, answer for the young man as you did before; and if any impediment comes in our way, I will take the word out of your mouths, and carry you over the river as I did just now.

CLEINIAS: Very good; do as you say, and we will help you as well as we can.

ATHENIAN: There will probably be no difficulty in proving to him that the Gods care about the small as well as about the great. For he was present and heard what was said, that they are perfectly good, and that the care of all things is most entirely natural to them.

CLEINIAS: No doubt he heard that.

ATHENIAN: Let us consider together in the next place what we mean by this virtue which we ascribe to them. Surely we should say that to be temperate and to possess mind belongs to virtue, and the contrary to vice?

CLEINIAS: Certainly.

ATHENIAN: Yes; and courage is a part of virtue, and cowardice of vice?

CLEINIAS: True.

ATHENIAN: And the one is honourable, and the other dishonourable?

CLEINIAS: To be sure.

ATHENIAN: And the one, like other meaner things, is a human quality, but the Gods have no part in anything of the sort?

CLEINIAS: That again is what everybody will admit.

ATHENIAN: But do we imagine carelessness and idleness and luxury to be virtues? What do you think?

CLEINIAS: Decidedly not.

ATHENIAN: They rank under the opposite class?

CLEINIAS: Yes.

ATHENIAN: And their opposites, therefore, would fall under the opposite class?

CLEINIAS: Yes.

ATHENIAN: But are we to suppose that one who possesses all these good qualities will be luxurious and heedless and idle, like those whom the poet compares to stingless drones?

CLEINIAS: And the comparison is a most just one.

ATHENIAN: Surely God must not be supposed to have a nature which He Himself hates? he who dares to say this sort of thing must not be tolerated for a moment.

CLEINIAS: Of course not. How could he have?

ATHENIAN: Should we not on any principle be entirely mistaken in praising any one who has some special business entrusted to him, if he have a mind which takes care of great matters and no care of small ones? Reflect; he who acts in this way, whether he be God or man, must act from one of two principles.

CLEINIAS: What are they?

ATHENIAN: Either he must think that the neglect of the small matters is of no consequence to the whole, or if he knows that they are of consequence, and he neglects them, his neglect must be attributed to carelessness and indolence. Is there any other way in which his neglect can be explained? For surely, when it is impossible for him to take care of all, he is not negligent if he fails to attend to these things great or small, which a God or some inferior being might be wanting in strength or capacity to manage?

CLEINIAS: Certainly not.

ATHENIAN: Now, then, let us examine the offenders, who both alike confess that there are Gods, but with a difference—the one saying that they may be appeased, and the other that they have no care of small matters: there are three of us and two of them, and we will say to them—In the first place, you both acknowledge that the Gods hear and see and know all things, and that nothing can escape them which is matter of sense and knowledge: do you admit this?

CLEINIAS: Yes.

ATHENIAN: And do you admit also that they have all power which mortals and immortals can have?

CLEINIAS: They will, of course, admit this also.

ATHENIAN: And surely we three and they two—five in all—have acknowledged that they are good and perfect?

CLEINIAS: Assuredly.

ATHENIAN: But, if they are such as we conceive them to be, can we possibly suppose that they ever act in the spirit of carelessness and indolence? For in us inactivity is the child of cowardice, and carelessness of inactivity and indolence.

CLEINIAS: Most true.

ATHENIAN: Then not from inactivity and carelessness is any God ever negligent; for there is no cowardice in them.

CLEINIAS: That is very true.

ATHENIAN: Then the alternative which remains is, that if the Gods neglect the lighter and lesser concerns of the universe, they neglect them because they know that they ought not to care about such matters—what other alternative is there but the opposite of their knowing?

CLEINIAS: There is none.

ATHENIAN: And, O most excellent and best of men, do I understand you to mean that they are careless because they are ignorant, and do not know that they ought to take care, or that they know, and yet like the meanest sort of men, knowing the better, choose the worse because they are overcome by pleasures and pains?

CLEINIAS: Impossible.

ATHENIAN: Do not all human things partake of the nature of soul? And is not man the most religious of all animals?

CLEINIAS: That is not to be denied.

ATHENIAN: And we acknowledge that all mortal creatures are the property of the Gods, to whom also the whole of heaven belongs?

CLEINIAS: Certainly.

ATHENIAN: And, therefore, whether a person says that these things are to the Gods great or small—in either case it would not be natural for the Gods who own us, and who are the most careful and the best of owners, to neglect us. There is also a further consideration.

CLEINIAS: What is it?

ATHENIAN: Sensation and power are in an inverse ratio to each other in respect to their ease and difficulty.

CLEINIAS: What do you mean?

ATHENIAN: I mean that there is greater difficulty in seeing and hearing the small than the great, but more facility in moving and controlling and taking care of small and unimportant things than of their opposites.

CLEINIAS: Far more.

ATHENIAN: Suppose the case of a physician who is willing and able to cure some living thing as a whole—how will the whole fare at his hands if he takes care only of the greater and neglects the parts which are lesser?

CLEINIAS: Decidedly not well.

ATHENIAN: No better would be the result with pilots or generals, or householders or statesmen, or any other such class, if they neglected the small and regarded only the great—as the builders say, the larger stones do not lie well without the lesser.

CLEINIAS: Of course not.

ATHENIAN: Let us not, then, deem God inferior to human workmen, who, in proportion to their skill, finish and perfect their works, small as well as great, by one and the same art; or that God, the wisest of beings, who is both willing and able to take care, is like a lazy good-for-nothing, or a coward, who turns his back upon labour and gives no thought to smaller and easier matters, but to the greater only.

CLEINIAS: Never, Stranger, let us admit a supposition about the Gods which is both impious and false.

ATHENIAN: I think that we have now argued enough with him who delights to accuse the Gods of neglect.

CLEINIAS: Yes.

ATHENIAN: He has been forced to acknowledge that he is in error, but he still seems to me to need some words of consolation.

CLEINIAS: What consolation will you offer him?

ATHENIAN: Let us say to the youth: The ruler of the universe has ordered all things with a view to the excellence and preservation of the whole, and each part, as far as may be, has an action and passion appropriate to it. Over these, down to the least fraction of them, ministers have been appointed to preside, who have wrought out their perfection with infinitesimal exactness. And one of these portions of the universe is thine own, unhappy man, which, however little, contributes to the whole; and you do not seem to be aware that this and every other creation is for the sake of the whole, and in order that the life of the whole may be blessed; and that you are created for the sake of the whole, and not the whole for the sake of you. For every physician and every skilled artist does all things for the sake of the whole, directing his effort towards the common good, executing the part for the sake of the whole, and not the whole for the sake of the part. And you are annoyed because you are ignorant how what is best for you happens to you and to the universe, as far as the laws of the common creation admit. Now, as the soul combining first with one body and then with another undergoes all sorts of changes, either of herself, or through the influence of another soul, all that remains to the player of the game is that he should shift the pieces; sending the better nature to the better place, and the worse to the worse, and so assigning to them their proper portion.

CLEINIAS: In what way do you mean?

ATHENIAN: In a way which may be supposed to make the care of all things easy to the Gods. If any one were to form or fashion all things without any regard to the whole—if, for example, he formed a living element of water out of fire, instead of forming many things out of one or one out of many in regular order attaining to a first or second or third birth, the transmutation would have been infinite; but now the ruler of the world has a wonderfully easy task.

CLEINIAS: How so?

ATHENIAN: I will explain: When the king saw that our actions had life, and that there was much virtue in them and much vice, and that the soul and body, although not, like the Gods of popular opinion, eternal, yet having once come into existence, were indestructible (for if either of them had been destroyed, there would have been no generation of living beings); and when he observed that the good of the soul was ever by nature designed to profit men, and the evil to harm them—he, seeing all this, contrived so to place each of the parts that their position might in the easiest and best manner procure the victory of good and the defeat of evil in the whole. And he contrived a general plan by which a thing of a certain nature found a certain seat and room. But the formation of qualities he left to the wills of individuals. For every one of us is made pretty much what he is by the bent of his desires and the nature of his soul.

CLEINIAS: Yes, that is probably true.

ATHENIAN: Then all things which have a soul change, and possess in themselves a principle of change, and in changing move according to law and to the order of destiny: natures which have undergone a lesser change move less and on the earth's surface, but those which have suffered more change and have become more criminal sink into the abyss, that is to say, into Hades and other places in the world below, of which the very names terrify men, and which they picture to themselves as in a dream, both while alive and when released from the body. And whenever the soul receives more of good or evil from her own energy and the strong influence of others—when she has communion with divine virtue and becomes divine, she is carried into another and better place, which is perfect in holiness; but when she has communion with evil, then she also changes the place of her life.

'This is the justice of the Gods who inhabit Olympus.'

O youth or young man, who fancy that you are neglected by the Gods, know that if you become worse you shall go to the worse souls, or if better to the better, and in every succession of life and death you will do and suffer what like may fitly suffer at the hands of like. This is the justice of heaven, which neither you nor any other unfortunate will ever glory in escaping, and which the ordaining powers have specially ordained; take good heed thereof, for it will be sure to take heed of you. If you say: I am small and will creep into the depths of the earth, or I am high and will fly up to heaven, you are not so small or so high but that you shall pay the fitting penalty, either here or in the world below or in some still more savage place whither you shall be conveyed. This is also the explanation of the fate of those whom you saw, who had done unholy and evil deeds, and from small beginnings had grown great, and you fancied that from being miserable they had become happy; and in their actions, as in a mirror, you seemed to see the universal neglect of the Gods, not knowing how they make all things work together and contribute to the great whole. And thinkest thou, bold man, that thou needest not to know this? he who knows it not can never form any true idea of the happiness or unhappiness of life or hold any rational discourse respecting either. If Cleinias and this our reverend company succeed in proving to you that you know not what you say of the Gods, then will God help you; but should you desire to hear more, listen to what we say to the third opponent, if you have any understanding whatsoever. For I think that we have sufficiently proved the existence of the Gods, and that they care for men: The other notion that they are appeased by the wicked, and take gifts, is what we must not concede to any one, and what every man should disprove to the utmost of his power.

CLEINIAS: Very good; let us do as you say.

ATHENIAN: Well, then, by the Gods themselves I conjure you to tell me—if they are to be propitiated, how are they to be propitiated? Who are they, and what is their nature? Must they not be at least rulers who have to order unceasingly the whole heaven?

CLEINIAS: True.

ATHENIAN: And to what earthly rulers can they be compared, or who to them? How in the less can we find an image of the greater? Are they charioteers of contending pairs of steeds, or pilots of vessels? Perhaps they might be compared to the generals of armies, or they might be likened to physicians providing against the diseases which make war upon the body, or to husbandmen observing anxiously the effects of the seasons on the growth of plants; or perhaps to shepherds of flocks. For as we acknowledge the world to be full of many goods and also of evils, and of more evils than goods, there is, as we affirm, an immortal conflict going on among us, which requires marvellous watchfulness; and in that conflict the Gods and demigods are our allies, and we are their property. Injustice and insolence and folly are the destruction of us, and justice and temperance and wisdom are our salvation; and the place of these latter is in the life of the Gods, although some vestige of them may occasionally be discerned among mankind. But upon this earth we know that there dwell souls possessing an unjust spirit, who may be compared to brute animals, which fawn upon their keepers, whether dogs or shepherds, or the best and most perfect masters; for they in like manner, as the voices of the wicked declare, prevail by flattery and prayers and incantations, and are allowed to make their gains with impunity. And this sin, which is termed dishonesty, is an evil of the same kind as what is termed disease in living bodies or pestilence in years or seasons of the year, and in cities and governments has another name, which is injustice.

CLEINIAS: Quite true.

ATHENIAN: What else can he say who declares that the Gods are always lenient to the doers of unjust acts, if they divide the spoil with them? As if wolves were to toss a portion of their prey to the dogs, and they, mollified by the gift, suffered them to tear the flocks. Must not he who maintains that the Gods can be propitiated argue thus?

CLEINIAS: Precisely so.

ATHENIAN: And to which of the above-mentioned classes of guardians would any man compare the Gods without absurdity? Will he say that they are like pilots, who are themselves turned away from their duty by 'libations of wine and the savour of fat,' and at last overturn both ship and sailors?

CLEINIAS: Assuredly not.

ATHENIAN: And surely they are not like charioteers who are bribed to give up the victory to other chariots?

CLEINIAS: That would be a fearful image of the Gods.

ATHENIAN: Nor are they like generals, or physicians, or husbandmen, or shepherds; and no one would compare them to dogs who have been silenced by wolves.

CLEINIAS: A thing not to be spoken of.

ATHENIAN: And are not all the Gods the chiefest of all guardians, and do they not guard our highest interests?

CLEINIAS: Yes; the chiefest.

ATHENIAN: And shall we say that those who guard our noblest interests, and are the best of guardians, are inferior in virtue to dogs, and to men even of moderate excellence, who would never betray justice for the sake of gifts which unjust men impiously offer them?

CLEINIAS: Certainly not; nor is such a notion to be endured, and he who holds this opinion may be fairly singled out and characterized as of all impious men the wickedest and most impious.

ATHENIAN: Then are the three assertions—that the Gods exist, and that they take care of men, and that they can never be persuaded to do injustice, now sufficiently demonstrated? May we say that they are?

CLEINIAS: You have our entire assent to your words.

ATHENIAN: I have spoken with vehemence because I am zealous against evil men; and I will tell you, dear Cleinias, why I am so. I would not have the wicked think that, having the superiority in argument, they may do as they please and act according to their various imaginations about the Gods; and this zeal has led me to speak too vehemently; but if we have at all succeeded in persuading the men to hate themselves and love their opposites, the prelude of our laws about impiety will not have been spoken in vain.

CLEINIAS: So let us hope; and even if we have failed, the style of our argument will not discredit the lawgiver.

ATHENIAN: After the prelude shall follow a discourse, which will be the interpreter of the law; this shall proclaim to all impious persons that they must depart from their ways and go over to the pious. And to those who disobey, let the law about impiety be as follows: If a man is guilty of any impiety in word or deed, any one who happens to be present shall give information to the magistrates, in aid of the law; and let the magistrates who first receive the information bring him before the appointed court according to the law; and if a magistrate, after receiving information, refuses to act, he shall be tried for impiety at the instance of any one who is willing to vindicate the laws; and if any one be cast, the court shall estimate the punishment of each act of impiety; and let all such criminals be imprisoned. There shall be three prisons in the state: the first of them is to be the common prison in the neighbourhood of the agora for the safe-keeping of the generality of offenders; another is to be in the neighbourhood of the nocturnal council, and is to be called the 'House of Reformation'; another, to be situated in some wild and desolate region in the centre of the country, shall be called by some name expressive of retribution. Now, men fall into impiety from three causes, which have been already mentioned, and from each of these causes arise two sorts of impiety, in all six, which are worth distinguishing, and should not all have the same punishment. For he who does not believe in the Gods, and yet has a righteous nature, hates the wicked and dislikes and refuses to do injustice, and avoids unrighteous men, and loves the righteous. But they who besides believing that the world is devoid of Gods are intemperate, and have at the same time good memories and quick wits, are worse; although both of them are unbelievers, much less injury is done by the one than by the other. The one may talk loosely about the Gods and about sacrifices and oaths, and perhaps by laughing at other men he may make them like himself, if he be not punished. But the other who holds the same opinions and is called a clever man, is full of stratagem and deceit—men of this class deal in prophecy and jugglery of all kinds, and out of their ranks sometimes come tyrants and demagogues and generals and hierophants of private mysteries and the Sophists, as they are termed, with their ingenious devices. There are many kinds of unbelievers, but two only for whom legislation is required; one the hypocritical sort, whose crime is deserving of death many times over, while the other needs only bonds and admonition. In like manner also the notion that the Gods take no thought of men produces two other sorts of crimes, and the notion that they may be propitiated produces two more. Assuming these divisions, let those who have been made what they are only from want of understanding, and not from malice or an evil nature, be placed by the judge in the House of Reformation, and ordered to suffer imprisonment during a period of not less than five years. And in the meantime let them have no intercourse with the other citizens, except with members of the nocturnal council, and with them let them converse with a view to the improvement of their soul's health. And when the time of their imprisonment has expired, if any of them be of sound mind let him be restored to sane company, but if not, and if he be condemned a second time, let him be punished with death. As to that class of monstrous natures who not only believe that there are no Gods, or that they are negligent, or to be propitiated, but in contempt of mankind conjure the souls of the living and say that they can conjure the dead and promise to charm the Gods with sacrifices and prayers, and will utterly overthrow individuals and whole houses and states for the sake of money—let him who is guilty of any of these things be condemned by the court to be bound according to law in the prison which is in the centre of the land, and let no freeman ever approach him, but let him receive the rations of food appointed by the guardians of the law from the hands of the public slaves; and when he is dead let him be cast beyond the borders unburied, and if any freeman assist in burying him, let him pay the penalty of impiety to any one who is willing to bring a suit against him. But if he leaves behind him children who are fit to be citizens, let the guardians of orphans take care of them, just as they would of any other orphans, from the day on which their father is convicted.

In all these cases there should be one law, which will make men in general less liable to transgress in word or deed, and less foolish, because they will not be allowed to practise religious rites contrary to law. And let this be the simple form of the law: No man shall have sacred rites in a private house. When he would sacrifice, let him go to the temples and hand over his offerings to the priests and priestesses, who see to the sanctity of such things, and let him pray himself, and let any one who pleases join with him in prayer. The reason of this is as follows: Gods and temples are not easily instituted, and to establish them rightly is the work of a mighty intellect. And women especially, and men too, when they are sick or in danger, or in any sort of difficulty, or again on their receiving any good fortune, have a way of consecrating the occasion, vowing sacrifices, and promising shrines to Gods, demigods, and sons of Gods; and when they are awakened by terrible apparitions and dreams or remember visions, they find in altars and temples the remedies of them, and will fill every house and village with them, placing them in the open air, or wherever they may have had such visions; and with a view to all these cases we should obey the law. The law has also regard to the impious, and would not have them fancy that by the secret performance of these actions—by raising temples and by building altars in private houses, they can propitiate the God secretly with sacrifices and prayers, while they are really multiplying their crimes infinitely, bringing guilt from heaven upon themselves, and also upon those who permit them, and who are better men than they are; and the consequence is that the whole state reaps the fruit of their impiety, which, in a certain sense, is deserved. Assuredly God will not blame the legislator, who will enact the following law: No one shall possess shrines of the Gods in private houses, and he who is found to possess them, and perform any sacred rites not publicly authorised—supposing the offender to be some man or woman who is not guilty of any other great and impious crime—shall be informed against by him who is acquainted with the fact, which shall be announced by him to the guardians of the law; and let them issue orders that he or she shall carry away their private rites to the public temples, and if they do not persuade them, let them inflict a penalty on them until they comply. And if a person be proven guilty of impiety, not merely from childish levity, but such as grown-up men may be guilty of, whether he have sacrificed publicly or privately to any Gods, let him be punished with death, for his sacrifice is impure. Whether the deed has been done in earnest, or only from childish levity, let the guardians of the law determine, before they bring the matter into court and prosecute the offender for impiety.

BOOK XI.

In the next place, dealings between man and man require to be suitably regulated. The principle of them is very simple: Thou shalt not, if thou canst help, touch that which is mine, or remove the least thing which belongs to me without my consent; and may I be of a sound mind, and do to others as I would that they should do to me. First, let us speak of treasure-trove: May I never pray the Gods to find the hidden treasure, which another has laid up for himself and his family, he not being one of my ancestors, nor lift, if I should find, such a treasure. And may I never have any dealings with those who are called diviners, and who in any way or manner counsel me to take up the deposit entrusted to the earth, for I should not gain so much in the increase of my possessions, if I take up the prize, as I should grow in justice and virtue of soul, if I abstain; and this will be a better possession to me than the other in a better part of myself; for the possession of justice in the soul is preferable to the possession of wealth. And of many things it is well said—'Move not the immovables,' and this may be regarded as one of them. And we shall do well to believe the common tradition which says, that such deeds prevent a man from having a family. Now as to him who is careless about having children and regardless of the legislator, taking up that which neither he deposited, nor any ancestor of his, without the consent of the depositor, violating the simplest and noblest of laws which was the enactment of no mean man: 'Take not up that which was not laid down by thee'—of him, I say, who despises these two legislators, and takes up, not some small matter which he has not deposited, but perhaps a great heap of treasure, what he ought to suffer at the hands of the Gods, God only knows; but I would have the first person who sees him go and tell the wardens of the city, if the occurrence has taken place in the city, or if the occurrence has taken place in the agora he shall tell the wardens of the agora, or if in the country he shall tell the wardens of the country and their commanders. When information has been received the city shall send to Delphi, and, whatever the God answers about the money and the remover of the money, that the city shall do in obedience to the oracle; the informer, if he be a freeman, shall have the honour of doing rightly, and he who informs not, the dishonour of doing wrongly; and if he be a slave who gives information, let him be freed, as he ought to be, by the state, which shall give his master the price of him; but if he do not inform he shall be punished with death. Next in order shall follow a similar law, which shall apply equally to matters great and small: If a man happens to leave behind him some part of his property, whether intentionally or unintentionally, let him who may come upon the left property suffer it to remain, reflecting that such things are under the protection of the Goddess of ways, and are dedicated to her by the law. But if any one defies the law, and takes the property home with him, let him, if the thing is of little worth, and the man who takes it a slave, be beaten with many stripes by him who meets him, being a person of not less than thirty years of age. Or if he be a freeman, in addition to being thought a mean person and a despiser of the laws, let him pay ten times the value of the treasure which he has moved to the leaver. And if some one accuses another of having anything which belongs to him, whether little or much, and the other admits that he has this thing, but denies that the property in dispute belongs to the other, if the property be registered with the magistrates according to law, the claimant shall summon the possessor, who shall bring it before the magistrates; and when it is brought into court, if it be registered in the public registers, to which of the litigants it belonged, let him take it and go his way. Or if the property be registered as belonging to some one who is not present, whoever will offer sufficient surety on behalf of the absent person that he will give it up to him, shall take it away as the representative of the other. But if the property which is deposited be not registered with the magistrates, let it remain until the time of trial with three of the eldest of the magistrates; and if it be an animal which is deposited, then he who loses the suit shall pay the magistrates for its keep, and they shall determine the cause within three days.

Any one who is of sound mind may arrest his own slave, and do with him whatever he will of such things as are lawful; and he may arrest the runaway slave of any of his friends or kindred with a view to his safe-keeping. And if any one takes away him who is being carried off as a slave, intending to liberate him, he who is carrying him off shall let him go; but he who takes him away shall give three sufficient sureties; and if he give them, and not without giving them, he may take him away, but if he take him away after any other manner he shall be deemed guilty of violence, and being convicted shall pay as a penalty double the amount of the damages claimed to him who has been deprived of the slave. Any man may also carry off a freedman, if he do not pay respect or sufficient respect to him who freed him. Now the respect shall be, that the freedman go three times in the month to the hearth of the person who freed him, and offer to do whatever he ought, so far as he can; and he shall agree to make such a marriage as his former master approves. He shall not be permitted to have more property than he who gave him liberty, and what more he has shall belong to his master. The freedman shall not remain in the state more than twenty years, but like other foreigners shall go away, taking his entire property with him, unless he has the consent of the magistrates and of his former master to remain. If a freedman or any other stranger has a property greater than the census of the third class, at the expiration of thirty days from the day on which this comes to pass, he shall take that which is his and go his way, and in this case he shall not be allowed to remain any longer by the magistrates. And if any one disobeys this regulation, and is brought into court and convicted, he shall be punished with death, and his property shall be confiscated. Suits about these matters shall take place before the tribes, unless the plaintiff and defendant have got rid of the accusation either before their neighbours or before judges chosen by them. If a man lay claim to any animal or anything else which he declares to be his, let the possessor refer to the seller or to some honest and trustworthy person, who has given, or in some legitimate way made over the property to him; if he be a citizen or a metic, sojourning in the city, within thirty days, or, if the property have been delivered to him by a stranger, within five months, of which the middle month shall include the summer solstice. When goods are exchanged by selling and buying, a man shall deliver them, and receive the price of them, at a fixed place in the agora, and have done with the matter; but he shall not buy or sell anywhere else, nor give credit. And if in any other manner or in any other place there be an exchange of one thing for another, and the seller give credit to the man who buys from him, he must do this on the understanding that the law gives no protection in cases of things sold not in accordance with these regulations. Again, as to contributions, any man who likes may go about collecting contributions as a friend among friends, but if any difference arises about the collection, he is to act on the understanding that the law gives no protection in such cases. He who sells anything above the value of fifty drachmas shall be required to remain in the city for ten days, and the purchaser shall be informed of the house of the seller, with a view to the sort of charges which are apt to arise in such cases, and the restitutions which the law allows. And let legal restitution be on this wise: If a man sells a slave who is in a consumption, or who has the disease of the stone, or of strangury, or epilepsy, or some other tedious and incurable disorder of body or mind, which is not discernible to the ordinary man, if the purchaser be a physician or trainer, he shall have no right of restitution; nor shall there be any right of restitution if the seller has told the truth beforehand to the buyer. But if a skilled person sells to another who is not skilled, let the buyer appeal for restitution within six months, except in the case of epilepsy, and then the appeal may be made within a year. The cause shall be determined by such physicians as the parties may agree to choose; and the defendant, if he lose the suit, shall pay double the price at which he sold. If a private person sell to another private person, he shall have the right of restitution, and the decision shall be given as before, but the defendant, if he be cast, shall only pay back the price of the slave. If a person sells a homicide to another, and they both know of the fact, let there be no restitution in such a case, but if he do not know of the fact, there shall be a right of restitution, whenever the buyer makes the discovery; and the decision shall rest with the five youngest guardians of the law, and if the decision be that the seller was cognisant of the fact, he shall purify the house of the purchaser, according to the law of the interpreters, and shall pay back three times the purchase-money.

If a man exchanges either money for money, or anything whatever for anything else, either with or without life, let him give and receive them genuine and unadulterated, in accordance with the law. And let us have a prelude about all this sort of roguery, like the preludes of our other laws. Every man should regard adulteration as of one and the same class with falsehood and deceit, concerning which the many are too fond of saying that at proper times and places the practice may often be right. But they leave the occasion, and the when, and the where, undefined and unsettled, and from this want of definiteness in their language they do a great deal of harm to themselves and to others. Now a legislator ought not to leave the matter undetermined; he ought to prescribe some limit, either greater or less. Let this be the rule prescribed: No one shall call the Gods to witness, when he says or does anything false or deceitful or dishonest, unless he would be the most hateful of mankind to them. And he is most hateful to them who takes a false oath, and pays no heed to the Gods; and in the next degree, he who tells a falsehood in the presence of his superiors. Now better men are the superiors of worse men, and in general elders are the superiors of the young; wherefore also parents are the superiors of their offspring, and men of women and children, and rulers of their subjects; for all men ought to reverence any one who is in any position of authority, and especially those who are in state offices. And this is the reason why I have spoken of these matters. For every one who is guilty of adulteration in the agora tells a falsehood, and deceives, and when he invokes the Gods, according to the customs and cautions of the wardens of the agora, he does but swear without any respect for God or man. Certainly, it is an excellent rule not lightly to defile the names of the Gods, after the fashion of men in general, who care little about piety and purity in their religious actions. But if a man will not conform to this rule, let the law be as follows: He who sells anything in the agora shall not ask two prices for that which he sells, but he shall ask one price, and if he do not obtain this, he shall take away his goods; and on that day he shall not value them either at more or less; and there shall be no praising of any goods, or oath taken about them. If a person disobeys this command, any citizen who is present, not being less than thirty years of age, may with impunity chastise and beat the swearer, but if instead of obeying the laws he takes no heed, he shall be liable to the charge of having betrayed them. If a man sells any adulterated goods and will not obey these regulations, he who knows and can prove the fact, and does prove it in the presence of the magistrates, if he be a slave or a metic, shall have the adulterated goods; but if he be a citizen, and do not pursue the charge, he shall be called a rogue, and deemed to have robbed the Gods of the agora; or if he proves the charge, he shall dedicate the goods to the Gods of the agora. He who is proved to have sold any adulterated goods, in addition to losing the goods themselves, shall be beaten with stripes—a stripe for a drachma, according to the price of the goods; and the herald shall proclaim in the agora the offence for which he is going to be beaten. The wardens of the agora and the guardians of the law shall obtain information from experienced persons about the rogueries and adulterations of the sellers, and shall write up what the seller ought and ought not to do in each case; and let them inscribe their laws on a column in front of the court of the wardens of the agora, that they may be clear instructors of those who have business in the agora. Enough has been said in what has preceded about the wardens of the city, and if anything seems to be wanting, let them communicate with the guardians of the law, and write down the omission, and place on a column in the court of the wardens of the city the primary and secondary regulations which are laid down for them about their office.

After the practices of adulteration naturally follow the practices of retail trade. Concerning these, we will first of all give a word of counsel and reason, and the law shall come afterwards. Retail trade in a city is not by nature intended to do any harm, but quite the contrary; for is not he a benefactor who reduces the inequalities and incommensurabilities of goods to equality and common measure? And this is what the power of money accomplishes, and the merchant may be said to be appointed for this purpose. The hireling and the tavern-keeper, and many other occupations, some of them more and others less seemly—all alike have this object—they seek to satisfy our needs and equalize our possessions. Let us then endeavour to see what has brought retail trade into ill-odour, and wherein lies the dishonour and unseemliness of it, in order that if not entirely, we may yet partially, cure the evil by legislation. To effect this is no easy matter, and requires a great deal of virtue.

CLEINIAS: What do you mean?

ATHENIAN: Dear Cleinias, the class of men is small—they must have been rarely gifted by nature, and trained by education—who, when assailed by wants and desires, are able to hold out and observe moderation, and when they might make a great deal of money are sober in their wishes, and prefer a moderate to a large gain. But the mass of mankind are the very opposite: their desires are unbounded, and when they might gain in moderation they prefer gains without limit; wherefore all that relates to retail trade, and merchandise, and the keeping of taverns, is denounced and numbered among dishonourable things. For if what I trust may never be and will not be, we were to compel, if I may venture to say a ridiculous thing, the best men everywhere to keep taverns for a time, or carry on retail trade, or do anything of that sort; or if, in consequence of some fate or necessity, the best women were compelled to follow similar callings, then we should know how agreeable and pleasant all these things are; and if all such occupations were managed on incorrupt principles, they would be honoured as we honour a mother or a nurse. But now that a man goes to desert places and builds houses which can only be reached by long journeys, for the sake of retail trade, and receives strangers who are in need at the welcome resting-place, and gives them peace and calm when they are tossed by the storm, or cool shade in the heat; and then instead of behaving to them as friends, and showing the duties of hospitality to his guests, treats them as enemies and captives who are at his mercy, and will not release them until they have paid the most unjust, abominable, and extortionate ransom—these are the sort of practises, and foul evils they are, which cast a reproach upon the succour of adversity. And the legislator ought always to be devising a remedy for evils of this nature. There is an ancient saying, which is also a true one—'To fight against two opponents is a difficult thing,' as is seen in diseases and in many other cases. And in this case also the war is against two enemies—wealth and poverty; one of whom corrupts the soul of man with luxury, while the other drives him by pain into utter shamelessness. What remedy can a city of sense find against this disease? In the first place, they must have as few retail traders as possible; and in the second place, they must assign the occupation to that class of men whose corruption will be the least injury to the state; and in the third place, they must devise some way whereby the followers of these occupations themselves will not readily fall into habits of unbridled shamelessness and meanness.

After this preface let our law run as follows, and may fortune favour us: No landowner among the Magnetes, whose city the God is restoring and resettling—no one, that is, of the 5040 families, shall become a retail trader either voluntarily or involuntarily; neither shall he be a merchant, or do any service for private persons unless they equally serve him, except for his father or his mother, and their fathers and mothers; and in general for his elders who are freemen, and whom he serves as a freeman. Now it is difficult to determine accurately the things which are worthy or unworthy of a freeman, but let those who have obtained the prize of virtue give judgment about them in accordance with their feelings of right and wrong. He who in any way shares in the illiberality of retail trades may be indicted for dishonouring his race by any one who likes, before those who have been judged to be the first in virtue; and if he appear to throw dirt upon his father's house by an unworthy occupation, let him be imprisoned for a year and abstain from that sort of thing; and if he repeat the offence, for two years; and every time that he is convicted let the length of his imprisonment be doubled. This shall be the second law: He who engages in retail trade must be either a metic or a stranger. And a third law shall be: In order that the retail trader who dwells in our city may be as good or as little bad as possible, the guardians of the law shall remember that they are not only guardians of those who may be easily watched and prevented from becoming lawless or bad, because they are well-born and bred; but still more should they have a watch over those who are of another sort, and follow pursuits which have a very strong tendency to make men bad. And, therefore, in respect of the multifarious occupations of retail trade, that is to say, in respect of such of them as are allowed to remain, because they seem to be quite necessary in a state—about these the guardians of the law should meet and take counsel with those who have experience of the several kinds of retail trade, as we before commanded concerning adulteration (which is a matter akin to this), and when they meet they shall consider what amount of receipts, after deducting expenses, will produce a moderate gain to the retail trades, and they shall fix in writing and strictly maintain what they find to be the right percentage of profit; this shall be seen to by the wardens of the agora, and by the wardens of the city, and by the wardens of the country. And so retail trade will benefit every one, and do the least possible injury to those in the state who practise it.

When a man makes an agreement which he does not fulfil, unless the agreement be of a nature which the law or a vote of the assembly does not allow, or which he has made under the influence of some unjust compulsion, or which he is prevented from fulfilling against his will by some unexpected chance, the other party may go to law with him in the courts of the tribes, for not having completed his agreement, if the parties are not able previously to come to terms before arbiters or before their neighbours. The class of craftsmen who have furnished human life with the arts is dedicated to Hephaestus and Athene; and there is a class of craftsmen who preserve the works of all craftsmen by arts of defence, the votaries of Ares and Athene, to which divinities they too are rightly dedicated. All these continue through life serving the country and the people; some of them are leaders in battle; others make for hire implements and works, and they ought not to deceive in such matters, out of respect to the Gods who are their ancestors. If any craftsman through indolence omit to execute his work in a given time, not reverencing the God who gives him the means of life, but considering, foolish fellow, that he is his own God and will let him off easily, in the first place, he shall suffer at the hands of the God, and in the second place, the law shall follow in a similar spirit. He shall owe to him who contracted with him the price of the works which he has failed in performing, and he shall begin again and execute them gratis in the given time. When a man undertakes a work, the law gives him the same advice which was given to the seller, that he should not attempt to raise the price, but simply ask the value; this the law enjoins also on the contractor; for the craftsman assuredly knows the value of his work. Wherefore, in free states the man of art ought not to attempt to impose upon private individuals by the help of his art, which is by nature a true thing; and he who is wronged in a matter of this sort, shall have a right of action against the party who has wronged him. And if any one lets out work to a craftsman, and does not pay him duly according to the lawful agreement, disregarding Zeus the guardian of the city and Athene, who are the partners of the state, and overthrows the foundations of society for the sake of a little gain, in his case let the law and the Gods maintain the common bonds of the state. And let him who, having already received the work in exchange, does not pay the price in the time agreed, pay double the price; and if a year has elapsed, although interest is not to be taken on loans, yet for every drachma which he owes to the contractor let him pay a monthly interest of an obol. Suits about these matters are to be decided by the courts of the tribes; and by the way, since we have mentioned craftsmen at all, we must not forget that other craft of war, in which generals and tacticians are the craftsmen, who undertake voluntarily or involuntarily the work of our safety, as other craftsmen undertake other public works—if they execute their work well the law will never tire of praising him who gives them those honours which are the just rewards of the soldier; but if any one, having already received the benefit of any noble service in war, does not make the due return of honour, the law will blame him. Let this then be the law, having an ingredient of praise, not compelling but advising the great body of the citizens to honour the brave men who are the saviours of the whole state, whether by their courage or by their military skill—they should honour them, I say, in the second place; for the first and highest tribute of respect is to be given to those who are able above other men to honour the words of good legislators.

The greater part of the dealings between man and man have been now regulated by us with the exception of those that relate to orphans and the supervision of orphans by their guardians. These follow next in order, and must be regulated in some way. But to arrive at them we must begin with the testamentary wishes of the dying and the case of those who may have happened to die intestate. When I said, Cleinias, that we must regulate them, I had in my mind the difficulty and perplexity in which all such matters are involved. You cannot leave them unregulated, for individuals would make regulations at variance with one another, and repugnant to the laws and habits of the living and to their own previous habits, if a person were simply allowed to make any will which he pleased, and this were to take effect in whatever state he may have been at the end of his life; for most of us lose our senses in a manner, and feel crushed when we think that we are about to die.

CLEINIAS: What do you mean, Stranger?

ATHENIAN: O Cleinias, a man when he is about to die is an intractable creature, and is apt to use language which causes a great deal of anxiety and trouble to the legislator.

CLEINIAS: In what way?

ATHENIAN: He wants to have the entire control of all his property, and will use angry words.

CLEINIAS: Such as what?

ATHENIAN: O ye Gods, he will say, how monstrous that I am not allowed to give, or not to give, my own to whom I will—less to him who has been bad to me, and more to him who has been good to me, and whose badness and goodness have been tested by me in time of sickness or in old age and in every other sort of fortune!

CLEINIAS: Well, Stranger, and may he not very fairly say so?

ATHENIAN: In my opinion, Cleinias, the ancient legislators were too good-natured, and made laws without sufficient observation or consideration of human things.

CLEINIAS: What do you mean?

ATHENIAN: I mean, my friend, that they were afraid of the testator's reproaches, and so they passed a law to the effect that a man should be allowed to dispose of his property in all respects as he liked; but you and I, if I am not mistaken, will have something better to say to our departing citizens.

CLEINIAS: What?

ATHENIAN: O my friends, we will say to them, hard is it for you, who are creatures of a day, to know what is yours—hard too, as the Delphic oracle says, to know yourselves at this hour. Now I, as the legislator, regard you and your possessions, not as belonging to yourselves, but as belonging to your whole family, both past and future, and yet more do I regard both family and possessions as belonging to the state; wherefore, if some one steals upon you with flattery, when you are tossed on the sea of disease or old age, and persuades you to dispose of your property in a way that is not for the best, I will not, if I can help, allow this; but I will legislate with a view to the whole, considering what is best both for the state and for the family, esteeming as I ought the feelings of an individual at a lower rate; and I hope that you will depart in peace and kindness towards us, as you are going the way of all mankind; and we will impartially take care of all your concerns, not neglecting any of them, if we can possibly help. Let this be our prelude and consolation to the living and dying, Cleinias, and let the law be as follows: He who makes a disposition in a testament, if he be the father of a family, shall first of all inscribe as his heir any one of his sons whom he may think fit; and if he gives any of his children to be adopted by another citizen, let the adoption be inscribed. And if he has a son remaining over and above who has not been adopted upon any lot, and who may be expected to be sent out to a colony according to law, to him his father may give as much as he pleases of the rest of his property, with the exception of the paternal lot and the fixtures on the lot. And if there are other sons, let him distribute among them what there is more than the lot in such portions as he pleases. And if one of the sons has already a house of his own, he shall not give him of the money, nor shall he give money to a daughter who has been betrothed, but if she is not betrothed he may give her money. And if any of the sons or daughters shall be found to have another lot of land in the country, which has accrued after the testament has been made, they shall leave the lot which they have inherited to the heir of the man who has made the will. If the testator has no sons, but only daughters, let him choose the husband of any one of his daughters whom he pleases, and leave and inscribe him as his son and heir. And if a man have lost his son, when he was a child, and before he could be reckoned among grown up men, whether his own or an adopted son, let the testator make mention of the circumstance and inscribe whom he will to be his second son in hope of better fortune. If the testator has no children at all, he may select and give to any one whom he pleases the tenth part of the property which he has acquired; but let him not be blamed if he gives all the rest to his adopted son, and makes a friend of him according to the law. If the sons of a man require guardians, and the father when he dies leaves a will appointing guardians, those who have been named by him, whoever they are and whatever their number be, if they are able and willing to take charge of the children, shall be recognised according to the provisions of the will. But if he dies and has made no will, or a will in which he has appointed no guardians, then the next of kin, two on the father's and two on the mother's side, and one of the friends of the deceased, shall have the authority of guardians, whom the guardians of the law shall appoint when the orphans require guardians. And the fifteen eldest guardians of the law shall have the whole care and charge of the orphans, divided into threes according to seniority—a body of three for one year, and then another body of three for the next year, until the cycle of the five periods is complete; and this, as far as possible, is to continue always. If a man dies, having made no will at all, and leaves sons who require the care of guardians, they shall share in the protection which is afforded by these laws. And if a man dying by some unexpected fate leaves daughters behind him, let him pardon the legislator if when he gives them in marriage, he have a regard only to two out of three conditions—nearness of kin and the preservation of the lot, and omits the third condition, which a father would naturally consider, for he would choose out of all the citizens a son for himself, and a husband for his daughter, with a view to his character and disposition—the father, I say, shall forgive the legislator if he disregards this, which to him is an impossible consideration. Let the law about these matters where practicable be as follows: If a man dies without making a will, and leaves behind him daughters, let his brother, being the son of the same father or of the same mother, having no lot, marry the daughter and have the lot of the dead man. And if he have no brother, but only a brother's son, in like manner let them marry, if they be of a suitable age; and if there be not even a brother's son, but only the son of a sister, let them do likewise, and so in the fourth degree, if there be only the testator's father's brother, or in the fifth degree, his father's brother's son, or in the sixth degree, the child of his father's sister. Let kindred be always reckoned in this way: if a person leaves daughters the relationship shall proceed upwards through brothers and sisters, and brothers' and sisters' children, and first the males shall come, and after them the females in the same family. The judge shall consider and determine the suitableness or unsuitableness of age in marriage; he shall make an inspection of the males naked, and of the women naked down to the navel. And if there be a lack of kinsmen in a family extending to grandchildren of a brother, or to the grandchildren of a grandfather's children, the maiden may choose with the consent of her guardians any one of the citizens who is willing and whom she wills, and he shall be the heir of the dead man, and the husband of his daughter. Circumstances vary, and there may sometimes be a still greater lack of relations within the limits of the state; and if any maiden has no kindred living in the city, and there is some one who has been sent out to a colony, and she is disposed to make him the heir of her father's possessions, if he be indeed of her kindred, let him proceed to take the lot according to the regulation of the law; but if he be not of her kindred, she having no kinsmen within the city, and he be chosen by the daughter of the dead man, and empowered to marry by the guardians, let him return home and take the lot of him who died intestate. And if a man has no children, either male or female, and dies without making a will, let the previous law in general hold; and let a man and a woman go forth from the family and share the deserted house, and let the lot belong absolutely to them; and let the heiress in the first degree be a sister, and in a second degree a daughter of a brother, and in the third, a daughter of a sister, in the fourth degree the sister of a father, and in the fifth degree the daughter of a father's brother, and in a sixth degree of a father's sister; and these shall dwell with their male kinsmen, according to the degree of relationship and right, as we enacted before. Now we must not conceal from ourselves that such laws are apt to be oppressive and that there may sometimes be a hardship in the lawgiver commanding the kinsman of the dead man to marry his relation; he may be thought not to have considered the innumerable hindrances which may arise among men in the execution of such ordinances; for there may be cases in which the parties refuse to obey, and are ready to do anything rather than marry, when there is some bodily or mental malady or defect among those who are bidden to marry or be married. Persons may fancy that the legislator never thought of this, but they are mistaken; wherefore let us make a common prelude on behalf of the lawgiver and of his subjects, the law begging the latter to forgive the legislator, in that he, having to take care of the common weal, cannot order at the same time the various circumstances of individuals, and begging him to pardon them if naturally they are sometimes unable to fulfil the act which he in his ignorance imposes upon them.

CLEINIAS: And how, Stranger, can we act most fairly under the circumstances?

ATHENIAN: There must be arbiters chosen to deal with such laws and the subjects of them.

CLEINIAS: What do you mean?

ATHENIAN: I mean to say, that a case may occur in which the nephew, having a rich father, will be unwilling to marry the daughter of his uncle; he will have a feeling of pride, and he will wish to look higher. And there are cases in which the legislator will be imposing upon him the greatest calamity, and he will be compelled to disobey the law, if he is required, for example, to take a wife who is mad, or has some other terrible malady of soul or body, such as makes life intolerable to the sufferer. Then let what we are saying concerning these cases be embodied in a law: If any one finds fault with the established laws respecting testaments, both as to other matters and especially in what relates to marriage, and asserts that the legislator, if he were alive and present, would not compel him to obey—that is to say, would not compel those who are by our law required to marry or be given in marriage, to do either—and some kinsman or guardian dispute this, the reply is that the legislator left fifteen of the guardians of the law to be arbiters and fathers of orphans, male or female, and to them let the disputants have recourse, and by their aid determine any matters of the kind, admitting their decision to be final. But if any one thinks that too great power is thus given to the guardians of the law, let him bring his adversaries into the court of the select judges, and there have the points in dispute determined. And he who loses the cause shall have censure and blame from the legislator, which, by a man of sense, is felt to be a penalty far heavier than a great loss of money.

Thus will orphan children have a second birth. After their first birth we spoke of their nurture and education, and after their second birth, when they have lost their parents, we ought to take measures that the misfortune of orphanhood may be as little sad to them as possible. In the first place, we say that the guardians of the law are lawgivers and fathers to them, not inferior to their natural fathers. Moreover, they shall take charge of them year by year as of their own kindred; and we have given both to them and to the children's own guardians as suitable admonition concerning the nurture of orphans. And we seem to have spoken opportunely in our former discourse, when we said that the souls of the dead have the power after death of taking an interest in human affairs, about which there are many tales and traditions, long indeed, but true; and seeing that they are so many and so ancient, we must believe them, and we must also believe the lawgivers, who tell us that these things are true, if they are not to be regarded as utter fools. But if these things are really so, in the first place men should have a fear of the Gods above, who regard the loneliness of the orphans; and in the second place of the souls of the departed, who by nature incline to take an especial care of their own children, and are friendly to those who honour, and unfriendly to those who dishonour them. Men should also fear the souls of the living who are aged and high in honour; wherever a city is well ordered and prosperous, their descendants cherish them, and so live happily; old persons are quick to see and hear all that relates to them, and are propitious to those who are just in the fulfilment of such duties, and they punish those who wrong the orphan and the desolate, considering that they are the greatest and most sacred of trusts. To all which matters the guardian and magistrate ought to apply his mind, if he has any, and take heed of the nurture and education of the orphans, seeking in every possible way to do them good, for he is making a contribution to his own good and that of his children. He who obeys the tale which precedes the law, and does no wrong to an orphan, will never experience the wrath of the legislator. But he who is disobedient, and wrongs any one who is bereft of father or mother, shall pay twice the penalty which he would have paid if he had wronged one whose parents had been alive. As touching other legislation concerning guardians in their relation to orphans, or concerning magistrates and their superintendence of the guardians, if they did not possess examples of the manner in which children of freemen would be brought up in the bringing up of their own children, and of the care of their property in the care of their own, or if they had not just laws fairly stated about these very things—there would have been reason in making laws for them, under the idea that they were a peculiar class, and we might distinguish and make separate rules for the life of those who are orphans and of those who are not orphans. But as the case stands, the condition of orphans with us is not different from the case of those who have a father, though in regard to honour and dishonour, and the attention given to them, the two are not usually placed upon a level. Wherefore, touching the legislation about orphans, the law speaks in serious accents, both of persuasion and threatening, and such a threat as the following will be by no means out of place: He who is the guardian of an orphan of either sex, and he among the guardians of the law to whom the superintendence of this guardian has been assigned, shall love the unfortunate orphan as though he were his own child, and he shall be as careful and diligent in the management of his possessions as he would be if they were his own, or even more careful and diligent. Let every one who has the care of an orphan observe this law. But any one who acts contrary to the law on these matters, if he be a guardian of the child, may be fined by a magistrate, or, if he be himself a magistrate, the guardian may bring him before the court of select judges, and punish him, if convicted, by exacting a fine of double the amount of that inflicted by the court. And if a guardian appears to the relations of the orphan, or to any other citizen, to act negligently or dishonestly, let them bring him before the same court, and whatever damages are given against him, let him pay fourfold, and let half belong to the orphan and half to him who procured the conviction. If any orphan arrives at years of discretion, and thinks that he has been ill-used by his guardians, let him within five years of the expiration of the guardianship be allowed to bring them to trial; and if any of them be convicted, the court shall determine what he shall pay or suffer. And if a magistrate shall appear to have wronged the orphan by neglect, and he be convicted, let the court determine what he shall suffer or pay to the orphan, and if there be dishonesty in addition to neglect, besides paying the fine, let him be deposed from his office of guardian of the law, and let the state appoint another guardian of the law for the city and for the country in his room.

Greater differences than there ought to be sometimes arise between fathers and sons, on the part either of fathers who will be of opinion that the legislator should enact that they may, if they wish, lawfully renounce their son by the proclamation of a herald in the face of the world, or of sons who think that they should be allowed to indict their fathers on the charge of imbecility when they are disabled by disease or old age. These things only happen, as a matter of fact, where the natures of men are utterly bad; for where only half is bad, as, for example, if the father be not bad, but the son be bad, or conversely, no great calamity is the result of such an amount of hatred as this. In another state, a son disowned by his father would not of necessity cease to be a citizen, but in our state, of which these are to be the laws, the disinherited must necessarily emigrate into another country, for no addition can be made even of a single family to the 5040 households; and, therefore, he who deserves to suffer these things must be renounced not only by his father, who is a single person, but by the whole family, and what is done in these cases must be regulated by some such law as the following: He who in the sad disorder of his soul has a mind, justly or unjustly, to expel from his family a son whom he has begotten and brought up, shall not lightly or at once execute his purpose; but first of all he shall collect together his own kinsmen, extending to cousins, and in like manner his son's kinsmen by the mother's side, and in their presence he shall accuse his son, setting forth that he deserves at the hands of them all to be dismissed from the family; and the son shall be allowed to address them in a similar manner, and show that he does not deserve to suffer any of these things. And if the father persuades them, and obtains the suffrages of more than half of his kindred, exclusive of the father and mother and the offender himself—I say, if he obtains more than half the suffrages of all the other grown-up members of the family, of both sexes, the father shall be permitted to put away his son, but not otherwise. And if any other citizen is willing to adopt the son who is put away, no law shall hinder him; for the characters of young men are subject to many changes in the course of their lives. And if he has been put away, and in a period of ten years no one is willing to adopt him, let those who have the care of the superabundant population which is sent out into colonies, see to him, in order that he may be suitably provided for in the colony. And if disease or age or harshness of temper, or all these together, makes a man to be more out of his mind than the rest of the world are—but this is not observable, except to those who live with him—and he, being master of his property, is the ruin of the house, and his son doubts and hesitates about indicting his father for insanity, let the law in that case ordain that he shall first of all go to the eldest guardians of the law and tell them of his father's misfortune, and they shall duly look into the matter, and take counsel as to whether he shall indict him or not. And if they advise him to proceed, they shall be both his witnesses and his advocates; and if the father is cast, he shall henceforth be incapable of ordering the least particular of his life; let him be as a child dwelling in the house for the remainder of his days. And if a man and his wife have an unfortunate incompatibility of temper, ten of the guardians of the law, who are impartial, and ten of the women who regulate marriages, shall look to the matter, and if they are able to reconcile them they shall be formally reconciled; but if their souls are too much tossed with passion, they shall endeavour to find other partners. Now they are not likely to have very gentle tempers; and, therefore, we must endeavour to associate with them deeper and softer natures. Those who have no children, or only a few, at the time of their separation, should choose their new partners with a view to the procreation of children; but those who have a sufficient number of children should separate and marry again in order that they may have some one to grow old with and that the pair may take care of one another in age. If a woman dies, leaving children, male or female, the law will advise rather than compel the husband to bring up the children without introducing into the house a stepmother. But if he have no children, then he shall be compelled to marry until he has begotten a sufficient number of sons to his family and to the state. And if a man dies leaving a sufficient number of children, the mother of his children shall remain with them and bring them up. But if she appears to be too young to live virtuously without a husband, let her relations communicate with the women who superintend marriage, and let both together do what they think best in these matters; if there is a lack of children, let the choice be made with a view to having them; two children, one of either sex, shall be deemed sufficient in the eye of the law. When a child is admitted to be the offspring of certain parents and is acknowledged by them, but there is need of a decision as to which parent the child is to follow—in case a female slave have intercourse with a male slave, or with a freeman or freedman, the offspring shall always belong to the master of the female slave. Again, if a free woman have intercourse with a male slave, the offspring shall belong to the master of the slave; but if a child be born either of a slave by her master, or of his mistress by a slave—and this be proven—the offspring of the woman and its father shall be sent away by the women who superintend marriage into another country, and the guardians of the law shall send away the offspring of the man and its mother.

Neither God, nor a man who has understanding, will ever advise any one to neglect his parents. To a discourse concerning the honour and dishonour of parents, a prelude such as the following, about the service of the Gods, will be a suitable introduction: There are ancient customs about the Gods which are universal, and they are of two kinds: some of the Gods we see with our eyes and we honour them, of others we honour the images, raising statues of them which we adore; and though they are lifeless, yet we imagine that the living Gods have a good will and gratitude to us on this account. Now, if a man has a father or mother, or their fathers or mothers treasured up in his house stricken in years, let him consider that no statue can be more potent to grant his requests than they are, who are sitting at his hearth, if only he knows how to show true service to them.

CLEINIAS: And what do you call the true mode of service?

ATHENIAN: I will tell you, O my friend, for such things are worth listening to.

CLEINIAS: Proceed.

ATHENIAN: Oedipus, as tradition says, when dishonoured by his sons, invoked on them curses which every one declares to have been heard and ratified by the Gods, and Amyntor in his wrath invoked curses on his son Phoenix, and Theseus upon Hippolytus, and innumerable others have also called down wrath upon their children, whence it is clear that the Gods listen to the imprecations of parents; for the curses of parents are, as they ought to be, mighty against their children as no others are. And shall we suppose that the prayers of a father or mother who is specially dishonoured by his or her children, are heard by the Gods in accordance with nature; and that if a parent is honoured by them, and in the gladness of his heart earnestly entreats the Gods in his prayers to do them good, he is not equally heard, and that they do not minister to his request? If not, they would be very unjust ministers of good, and that we affirm to be contrary to their nature.

CLEINIAS: Certainly.

ATHENIAN: May we not think, as I was saying just now, that we can possess no image which is more honoured by the Gods, than that of a father or grandfather, or of a mother stricken in years? whom when a man honours, the heart of the God rejoices, and he is ready to answer their prayers. And, truly, the figure of an ancestor is a wonderful thing, far higher than that of a lifeless image. For the living, when they are honoured by us, join in our prayers, and when they are dishonoured, they utter imprecations against us; but lifeless objects do neither. And therefore, if a man makes a right use of his father and grandfather and other aged relations, he will have images which above all others will win him the favour of the Gods.

CLEINIAS: Excellent.

ATHENIAN: Every man of any understanding fears and respects the prayers of parents, knowing well that many times and to many persons they have been accomplished. Now these things being thus ordered by nature, good men think it a blessing from heaven if their parents live to old age and reach the utmost limit of human life, or if taken away before their time they are deeply regretted by them; but to bad men parents are always a cause of terror. Wherefore let every man honour with every sort of lawful honour his own parents, agreeably to what has now been said. But if this prelude be an unmeaning sound in the ears of any one, let the law follow, which may be rightly imposed in these terms: If any one in this city be not sufficiently careful of his parents, and do not regard and gratify in every respect their wishes more than those of his sons and of his other offspring or of himself—let him who experiences this sort of treatment either come himself, or send some one to inform the three eldest guardians of the law, and three of the women who have the care of marriages; and let them look to the matter and punish youthful evil-doers with stripes and bonds if they are under thirty years of age, that is to say, if they be men, or if they be women, let them undergo the same punishment up to forty years of age. But if, when they are still more advanced in years, they continue the same neglect of their parents, and do any hurt to any of them, let them be brought before a court in which every single one of the eldest citizens shall be the judges, and if the offender be convicted, let the court determine what he ought to pay or suffer, and any penalty may be imposed on him which a man can pay or suffer. If the person who has been wronged be unable to inform the magistrates, let any freeman who hears of his case inform, and if he do not, he shall be deemed base, and shall be liable to have a suit for damage brought against him by any one who likes. And if a slave inform, he shall receive freedom; and if he be the slave of the injurer or injured party, he shall be set free by the magistrates, or if he belong to any other citizen, the public shall pay a price on his behalf to the owner; and let the magistrates take heed that no one wrongs him out of revenge, because he has given information.

Cases in which one man injures another by poisons, and which prove fatal, have been already discussed; but about other cases in which a person intentionally and of malice harms another with meats, or drinks, or ointments, nothing has as yet been determined. For there are two kinds of poisons used among men, which cannot clearly be distinguished. There is the kind just now explicitly mentioned, which injures bodies by the use of other bodies according to a natural law; there is also another kind which persuades the more daring class that they can do injury by sorceries, and incantations, and magic knots, as they are termed, and makes others believe that they above all persons are injured by the powers of the magician. Now it is not easy to know the nature of all these things; nor if a man do know can he readily persuade others to believe him. And when men are disturbed in their minds at the sight of waxen images fixed either at their doors, or in a place where three ways meet, or on the sepulchres of parents, there is no use in trying to persuade them that they should despise all such things because they have no certain knowledge about them. But we must have a law in two parts, concerning poisoning, in whichever of the two ways the attempt is made, and we must entreat, and exhort, and advise men not to have recourse to such practises, by which they scare the multitude out of their wits, as if they were children, compelling the legislator and the judge to heal the fears which the sorcerer arouses, and to tell them in the first place, that he who attempts to poison or enchant others knows not what he is doing, either as regards the body (unless he has a knowledge of medicine), or as regards his enchantments (unless he happens to be a prophet or diviner). Let the law, then, run as follows about poisoning or witchcraft: He who employs poison to do any injury, not fatal, to a man himself, or to his servants, or any injury, whether fatal or not, to his cattle or his bees, if he be a physician, and be convicted of poisoning, shall be punished with death; or if he be a private person, the court shall determine what he is to pay or suffer. But he who seems to be the sort of man who injures others by magic knots, or enchantments, or incantations, or any of the like practices, if he be a prophet or diviner, let him die; and if, not being a prophet, he be convicted of witchcraft, as in the previous case, let the court fix what he ought to pay or suffer.

When a man does another any injury by theft or violence, for the greater injury let him pay greater damages to the injured man, and less for the smaller injury; but in all cases, whatever the injury may have been, as much as will compensate the loss. And besides the compensation of the wrong, let a man pay a further penalty for the chastisement of his offence: he who has done the wrong instigated by the folly of another, through the lightheartedness of youth or the like, shall pay a lighter penalty; but he who has injured another through his own folly, when overcome by pleasure or pain, in cowardly fear, or lust, or envy, or implacable anger, shall endure a heavier punishment. Not that he is punished because he did wrong, for that which is done can never be undone, but in order that in future times, he, and those who see him corrected, may utterly hate injustice, or at any rate abate much of their evil-doing. Having an eye to all these things, the law, like a good archer, should aim at the right measure of punishment, and in all cases at the deserved punishment. In the attainment of this the judge shall be a fellow-worker with the legislator, whenever the law leaves to him to determine what the offender shall suffer or pay; and the legislator, like a painter, shall give a rough sketch of the cases in which the law is to be applied. This is what we must do, Megillus and Cleinias, in the best and fairest manner that we can, saying what the punishments are to be of all actions of theft and violence, and giving laws of such a kind as the Gods and sons of Gods would have us give.

If a man is mad he shall not be at large in the city, but his relations shall keep him at home in any way which they can; or if not, let them pay a penalty—he who is of the highest class shall pay a penalty of one hundred drachmas, whether he be a slave or a freeman whom he neglects; and he of the second class shall pay four-fifths of a mina; and he of the third class three-fifths; and he of the fourth class two-fifths. Now there are many sorts of madness, some arising out of disease, which we have already mentioned; and there are other kinds, which originate in an evil and passionate temperament, and are increased by bad education; out of a slight quarrel this class of madmen will often raise a storm of abuse against one another, and nothing of that sort ought to be allowed to occur in a well-ordered state. Let this, then, be the law about abuse, which shall relate to all cases: No one shall speak evil of another; and when a man disputes with another he shall teach and learn of the disputant and the company, but he shall abstain from evil-speaking; for out of the imprecations which men utter against one another, and the feminine habit of casting aspersions on one another, and using foul names, out of words light as air, in very deed the greatest enmities and hatreds spring up. For the speaker gratifies his anger, which is an ungracious element of his nature; and nursing up his wrath by the entertainment of evil thoughts, and exacerbating that part of his soul which was formerly civilised by education, he lives in a state of savageness and moroseness, and pays a bitter penalty for his anger. And in such cases almost all men take to saying something ridiculous about their opponent, and there is no man who is in the habit of laughing at another who does not miss virtue and earnestness altogether, or lose the better half of greatness. Wherefore let no one utter any taunting word at a temple, or at the public sacrifices, or at the games, or in the agora, or in a court of justice, or in any public assembly. And let the magistrate who presides on these occasions chastise an offender, and he shall be blameless; but if he fails in doing so, he shall not claim the prize of virtue; for he is one who heeds not the laws, and does not do what the legislator commands. And if in any other place any one indulges in these sort of revilings, whether he has begun the quarrel or is only retaliating, let any elder who is present support the law, and control with blows those who indulge in passion, which is another great evil; and if he do not, let him be liable to pay the appointed penalty. And we say now, that he who deals in reproaches against others cannot reproach them without attempting to ridicule them; and this, when done in a moment of anger, is what we make matter of reproach against him. But then, do we admit into our state the comic writers who are so fond of making mankind ridiculous, if they attempt in a good-natured manner to turn the laugh against our citizens? or do we draw the distinction of jest and earnest, and allow a man to make use of ridicule in jest and without anger about any thing or person; though as we were saying, not if he be angry and have a set purpose? We forbid earnest—that is unalterably fixed; but we have still to say who are to be sanctioned or not to be sanctioned by the law in the employment of innocent humour. A comic poet, or maker of iambic or satirical lyric verse, shall not be permitted to ridicule any of the citizens, either by word or likeness, either in anger or without anger. And if any one is disobedient, the judges shall either at once expel him from the country, or he shall pay a fine of three minae, which shall be dedicated to the God who presides over the contests. Those only who have received permission shall be allowed to write verses at one another, but they shall be without anger and in jest; in anger and in serious earnest they shall not be allowed. The decision of this matter shall be left to the superintendent of the general education of the young, and whatever he may license, the writer shall be allowed to produce, and whatever he rejects let not the poet himself exhibit, or ever teach anybody else, slave or freeman, under the penalty of being dishonoured, and held disobedient to the laws.

Now he is not to be pitied who is hungry, or who suffers any bodily pain, but he who is temperate, or has some other virtue, or part of a virtue, and at the same time suffers from misfortune; it would be an extraordinary thing if such an one, whether slave or freeman, were utterly forsaken and fell into the extremes of poverty in any tolerably well-ordered city or government. Wherefore the legislator may safely make a law applicable to such cases in the following terms: Let there be no beggars in our state; and if anybody begs, seeking to pick up a livelihood by unavailing prayers, let the wardens of the agora turn him out of the agora, and the wardens of the city out of the city, and the wardens of the country send him out of any other parts of the land across the border, in order that the land may be cleared of this sort of animal.

If a slave of either sex injure anything, which is not his or her own, through inexperience, or some improper practice, and the person who suffers damage be not himself in part to blame, the master of the slave who has done the harm shall either make full satisfaction, or give up the slave who has done the injury. But if the master argue that the charge has arisen by collusion between the injured party and the injurer, with the view of obtaining the slave, let him sue the person, who says that he has been injured, for malpractices. And if he gain a conviction, let him receive double the value which the court fixes as the price of the slave; and if he lose his suit, let him make amends for the injury, and give up the slave. And if a beast of burden, or horse, or dog, or any other animal, injure the property of a neighbour, the owner shall in like manner pay for the injury.

If any man refuses to be a witness, he who wants him shall summon him, and he who is summoned shall come to the trial; and if he knows and is willing to bear witness, let him bear witness, but if he says he does not know let him swear by the three divinities Zeus, and Apollo, and Themis, that he does not, and have no more to do with the cause. And he who is summoned to give witness and does not answer to his summoner, shall be liable for the harm which ensues according to law. And if a person calls up as a witness any one who is acting as a judge, let him give his witness, but he shall not afterwards vote in the cause. A free woman may give her witness and plead, if she be more than forty years of age, and may bring an action if she have no husband; but if her husband be alive she shall only be allowed to bear witness. A slave of either sex and a child shall be allowed to give evidence and to plead, but only in cases of murder; and they must produce sufficient sureties that they will certainly remain until the trial, in case they should be charged with false witness. And either of the parties in a cause may bring an accusation of perjury against witnesses, touching their evidence in whole or in part, if he asserts that such evidence has been given; but the accusation must be brought previous to the final decision of the cause. The magistrates shall preserve the accusations of false witness, and have them kept under the seal of both parties, and produce them on the day when the trial for false witness takes place. If a man be twice convicted of false witness, he shall not be required, and if thrice, he shall not be allowed to bear witness; and if he dare to witness after he has been convicted three times, let any one who pleases inform against him to the magistrates, and let the magistrates hand him over to the court, and if he be convicted he shall be punished with death. And in any case in which the evidence is rightly found to be false, and yet to have given the victory to him who wins the suit, and more than half the witnesses are condemned, the decision which was gained by these means shall be rescinded, and there shall be a discussion and a decision as to whether the suit was determined by that false evidence or not; and in whichever way the decision may be given, the previous suit shall be determined accordingly.

There are many noble things in human life, but to most of them attach evils which are fated to corrupt and spoil them. Is not justice noble, which has been the civiliser of humanity? How then can the advocate of justice be other than noble? And yet upon this profession which is presented to us under the fair name of art has come an evil reputation. In the first place, we are told that by ingenious pleas and the help of an advocate the law enables a man to win a particular cause, whether just or unjust; and that both the art, and the power of speech which is thereby imparted, are at the service of him who is willing to pay for them. Now in our state this so-called art, whether really an art or only an experience and practice destitute of any art, ought if possible never to come into existence, or if existing among us should listen to the request of the legislator and go away into another land, and not speak contrary to justice. If the offenders obey we say no more; but for those who disobey, the voice of the law is as follows: If any one thinks that he will pervert the power of justice in the minds of the judges, and unseasonably litigate or advocate, let any one who likes indict him for malpractices of law and dishonest advocacy, and let him be judged in the court of select judges; and if he be convicted, let the court determine whether he may be supposed to act from a love of money or from contentiousness. And if he is supposed to act from contentiousness, the court shall fix a time during which he shall not be allowed to institute or plead a cause; and if he is supposed to act as he does from love of money, in case he be a stranger, he shall leave the country, and never return under penalty of death; but if he be a citizen, he shall die, because he is a lover of money, in whatever manner gained; and equally, if he be judged to have acted more than once from contentiousness, he shall die.

BOOK XII.

If a herald or an ambassador carry a false message from our city to any other, or bring back a false message from the city to which he is sent, or be proved to have brought back, whether from friends or enemies, in his capacity of herald or ambassador, what they have never said, let him be indicted for having violated, contrary to the law, the commands and duties imposed upon him by Hermes and Zeus, and let there be a penalty fixed, which he shall suffer or pay if he be convicted.

Theft is a mean, and robbery a shameless thing; and none of the sons of Zeus delight in fraud and violence, or ever practised either. Wherefore let no one be deluded by poets or mythologers into a mistaken belief of such things, nor let him suppose, when he thieves or is guilty of violence, that he is doing nothing base, but only what the Gods themselves do. For such tales are untrue and improbable; and he who steals or robs contrary to the law, is never either a God or the son of a God; of this the legislator ought to be better informed than all the poets put together. Happy is he and may he be for ever happy, who is persuaded and listens to our words; but he who disobeys shall have to contend against the following law: If a man steal anything belonging to the public, whether that which he steals be much or little, he shall have the same punishment. For he who steals a little steals with the same wish as he who steals much, but with less power, and he who takes up a greater amount, not having deposited it, is wholly unjust. Wherefore the law is not disposed to inflict a less penalty on the one than on the other because his theft is less, but on the ground that the thief may possibly be in one case still curable, and may in another case be incurable. If any one convict in a court of law a stranger or a slave of a theft of public property, let the court determine what punishment he shall suffer, or what penalty he shall pay, bearing in mind that he is probably not incurable. But the citizen who has been brought up as our citizens will have been, if he be found guilty of robbing his country by fraud or violence, whether he be caught in the act or not, shall be punished with death; for he is incurable.

Now for expeditions of war much consideration and many laws are required; the great principle of all is that no one of either sex should be without a commander; nor should the mind of any one be accustomed to do anything, either in jest or earnest, of his own motion, but in war and in peace he should look to and follow his leader, even in the least things being under his guidance; for example, he should stand or move, or exercise, or wash, or take his meals, or get up in the night to keep guard and deliver messages when he is bidden; and in the hour of danger he should not pursue and not retreat except by order of his superior; and in a word, not teach the soul or accustom her to know or understand how to do anything apart from others. Of all soldiers the life should be always and in all things as far as possible in common and together; there neither is nor ever will be a higher, or better, or more scientific principle than this for the attainment of salvation and victory in war. And we ought in time of peace from youth upwards to practise this habit of commanding others, and of being commanded by others; anarchy should have no place in the life of man or of the beasts who are subject to man. I may add that all dances ought to be performed with a view to military excellence; and agility and ease should be cultivated for the same object, and also endurance of the want of meats and drinks, and of winter cold and summer heat, and of hard couches; and, above all, care should be taken not to destroy the peculiar qualities of the head and the feet by surrounding them with extraneous coverings, and so hindering their natural growth of hair and soles. For these are the extremities, and of all the parts of the body, whether they are preserved or not is of the greatest consequence; the one is the servant of the whole body, and the other the master, in whom all the ruling senses are by nature set. Let the young men imagine that he hears in what has preceded the praises of the military life; the law shall be as follows: He shall serve in war who is on the roll or appointed to some special service, and if any one is absent from cowardice, and without the leave of the generals, he shall be indicted before the military commanders for failure of service when the army comes home; and the soldiers shall be his judges; the heavy-armed, and the cavalry, and the other arms of the service shall form separate courts; and they shall bring the heavy-armed before the heavy-armed, and the horsemen before the horsemen, and the others in like manner before their peers; and he who is found guilty shall never be allowed to compete for any prize of valour, or indict another for not serving on an expedition, or be an accuser at all in any military matters. Moreover, the court shall further determine what punishment he shall suffer, or what penalty he shall pay. When the suits for failure of service are completed, the leaders of the several kinds of troops shall again hold an assembly, and they shall adjudge the prizes of valour; and he who likes searching for judgment in his own branch of the service, saying nothing about any former expedition, nor producing any proof or witnesses to confirm his statement, but speaking only of the present occasion. The crown of victory shall be an olive wreath which the victor shall offer up at the temple of any war-god whom he likes, adding an inscription for a testimony to last during life, that such an one has received the first, the second, or the third prize. If any one goes on an expedition, and returns home before the appointed time, when the generals have not withdrawn the army, he shall be indicted for desertion before the same persons who took cognizance of failure of service, and if he be found guilty, the same punishment shall be inflicted on him. Now every man who is engaged in any suit ought to be very careful of bringing false witness against any one, either intentionally or unintentionally, if he can help; for justice is truly said to be an honourable maiden, and falsehood is naturally repugnant to honour and justice. A witness ought to be very careful not to sin against justice, as for example in what relates to the throwing away of arms—he must distinguish the throwing them away when necessary, and not make that a reproach, or bring an action against some innocent person on that account. To make the distinction may be difficult; but still the law must attempt to define the different kinds in some way. Let me endeavour to explain my meaning by an ancient tale: If Patroclus had been brought to the tent still alive but without his arms (and this has happened to innumerable persons), the original arms, which the poet says were presented to Peleus by the Gods as a nuptial gift when he married Thetis, remaining in the hands of Hector, then the base spirits of that day might have reproached the son of Menoetius with having cast away his arms. Again, there is the case of those who have been thrown down precipices and lost their arms; and of those who at sea, and in stormy places, have been suddenly overwhelmed by floods of water; and there are numberless things of this kind which one might adduce by way of extenuation, and with the view of justifying a misfortune which is easily misrepresented. We must, therefore, endeavour to divide to the best of our power the greater and more serious evil from the lesser. And a distinction may be drawn in the use of terms of reproach. A man does not always deserve to be called the thrower away of his shield; he may be only the loser of his arms. For there is a great or rather absolute difference between him who is deprived of his arms by a sufficient force, and him who voluntarily lets his shield go. Let the law then be as follows: If a person having arms is overtaken by the enemy and does not turn round and defend himself, but lets them go voluntarily or throws them away, choosing a base life and a swift escape rather than a courageous and noble and blessed death—in such a case of the throwing away of arms let justice be done, but the judge need take no note of the case just now mentioned; for the bad men ought always to be punished, in the hope that he may be improved, but not the unfortunate, for there is no advantage in that. And what shall be the punishment suited to him who has thrown away his weapons of defence? Tradition says that Caeneus, the Thessalian, was changed by a God from a woman into a man; but the converse miracle cannot now be wrought, or no punishment would be more proper than that the man who throws away his shield should be changed into a woman. This however is impossible, and therefore let us make a law as nearly like this as we can—that he who loves his life too well shall be in no danger for the remainder of his days, but shall live for ever under the stigma of cowardice. And let the law be in the following terms: When a man is found guilty of disgracefully throwing away his arms in war, no general or military officer shall allow him to serve as a soldier, or give him any place at all in the ranks of soldiers; and the officer who gives the coward any place, shall suffer a penalty which the public examiner shall exact of him; and if he be of the highest class, he shall pay a thousand drachmae; or if he be of the second class, five minae; or if he be of the third, three minae; or if he be of the fourth class, one mina. And he who is found guilty of cowardice, shall not only be dismissed from manly dangers, which is a disgrace appropriate to his nature, but he shall pay a thousand drachmae, if he be of the highest class, and five minae if he be of the second class, and three if he be of the third class, and a mina, like the preceding, if he be of the fourth class.

What regulations will be proper about examiners, seeing that some of our magistrates are elected by lot, and for a year, and some for a longer time and from selected persons? Of such magistrates, who will be a sufficient censor or examiner, if any of them, weighed down by the pressure of office or his own inability to support the dignity of his office, be guilty of any crooked practice? It is by no means easy to find a magistrate who excels other magistrates in virtue, but still we must endeavour to discover some censor or examiner who is more than man. For the truth is, that there are many elements of dissolution in a state, as there are also in a ship, or in an animal; they all have their cords, and girders, and sinews—one nature diffused in many places, and called by many names; and the office of examiner is a most important element in the preservation and dissolution of states. For if the examiners are better than the magistrates, and their duty is fulfilled justly and without blame, then the whole state and country flourishes and is happy; but if the examination of the magistrates is carried on in a wrong way, then, by the relaxation of that justice which is the uniting principle of all constitutions, every power in the state is rent asunder from every other; they no longer incline in the same direction, but fill the city with faction, and make many cities out of one, and soon bring all to destruction. Wherefore the examiners ought to be admirable in every sort of virtue. Let us invent a mode of creating them, which shall be as follows: Every year, after the summer solstice, the whole city shall meet in the common precincts of Helios and Apollo, and shall present to the God three men out of their own number in the manner following: Each citizen shall select, not himself, but some other citizen whom he deems in every way the best, and who is not less than fifty years of age. And out of the selected persons who have the greatest number of votes, they shall make a further selection until they reduce them to one-half, if they are an even number; but if they are not an even number, they shall subtract the one who has the smallest number of votes, and make them an even number, and then leave the half which have the greater number of votes. And if two persons have an equal number of votes, and thus increase the number beyond one-half, they shall withdraw the younger of the two and do away the excess; and then including all the rest they shall again vote, until there are left three having an unequal number of votes. But if all the three, or two out of the three, have equal votes, let them commit the election to good fate and fortune, and separate off by lot the first, and the second, and the third; these they shall crown with an olive wreath and give them the prize of excellence, at the same time proclaiming to all the world that the city of the Magnetes, by the providence of the Gods, is again preserved, and presents to the Sun and to Apollo her three best men as first-fruits, to be a common offering to them, according to the ancient law, as long as their lives answer to the judgment formed of them. And these shall appoint in their first year twelve examiners, to continue until each has completed seventy-five years, to whom three shall afterwards be added yearly; and let these divide all the magistracies into twelve parts, and prove the holders of them by every sort of test to which a freeman may be subjected; and let them live while they hold office in the precinct of Helios and Apollo, in which they were chosen, and let each one form a judgment of some things individually, and of others in company with his colleagues; and let him place a writing in the agora about each magistracy, and what the magistrate ought to suffer or pay, according to the decision of the examiners. And if a magistrate does not admit that he has been justly judged, let him bring the examiners before the select judges, and if he be acquitted by their decision, let him, if he will, accuse the examiners themselves; if, however, he be convicted, and have been condemned to death by the examiners, let him die (and of course he can only die once): but any other penalties which admit of being doubled let him suffer twice over.

And now let us pass under review the examiners themselves; what will their examination be, and how conducted? During the life of these men, whom the whole state counts worthy of the rewards of virtue, they shall have the first seat at all public assemblies, and at all Hellenic sacrifices and sacred missions, and other public and holy ceremonies in which they share. The chiefs of each sacred mission shall be selected from them, and they only of all the citizens shall be adorned with a crown of laurel; they shall all be priests of Apollo and Helios; and one of them, who is judged first of the priests created in that year, shall be high priest; and they shall write up his name in each year to be a measure of time as long as the city lasts; and after their death they shall be laid out and carried to the grave and entombed in a manner different from the other citizens. They shall be decked in a robe all of white, and there shall be no crying or lamentation over them; but a chorus of fifteen maidens, and another of boys, shall stand around the bier on either side, hymning the praises of the departed priests in alternate responses, declaring their blessedness in song all day long; and at dawn a hundred of the youths who practise gymnastic exercises, and whom the relations of the departed shall choose, shall carry the bier to the sepulchre, the young men marching first, dressed in the garb of warriors—the cavalry with their horses, the heavy-armed with their arms, and the others in like manner. And boys near the bier and in front of it shall sing their national hymn, and maidens shall follow behind, and with them the women who have passed the age of child-bearing; next, although they are interdicted from other burials, let priests and priestesses follow, unless the Pythian oracle forbid them; for this burial is free from pollution. The place of burial shall be an oblong vaulted chamber underground, constructed of tufa, which will last for ever, having stone couches placed side by side. And here they will lay the blessed person, and cover the sepulchre with a circular mound of earth and plant a grove of trees around on every side but one; and on that side the sepulchre shall be allowed to extend for ever, and a new mound will not be required. Every year they shall have contests in music and gymnastics, and in horsemanship, in honour of the dead. These are the honours which shall be given to those who at the examination are found blameless; but if any of them, trusting to the scrutiny being over, should, after the judgment has been given, manifest the wickedness of human nature, let the law ordain that he who pleases shall indict him, and let the cause be tried in the following manner. In the first place, the court shall be composed of the guardians of the law, and to them the surviving examiners shall be added, as well as the court of select judges; and let the pursuer lay his indictment in this form—he shall say that so-and-so is unworthy of the prize of virtue and of his office; and if the defendant be convicted let him be deprived of his office, and of the burial, and of the other honours given him. But if the prosecutor do not obtain the fifth part of the votes, let him, if he be of the first-class, pay twelve minae, and eight if he be of the second class, and six if he be of the third class, and two minae if he be of the fourth class.

The so-called decision of Rhadamanthus is worthy of all admiration. He knew that the men of his own time believed and had no doubt that there were Gods, which was a reasonable belief in those days, because most men were the sons of Gods, and according to tradition he was one himself. He appears to have thought that he ought to commit judgment to no man, but to the Gods only, and in this way suits were simply and speedily decided by him. For he made the two parties take an oath respecting the points in dispute, and so got rid of the matter speedily and safely. But now that a certain portion of mankind do not believe at all in the existence of the Gods, and others imagine that they have no care of us, and the opinion of most men, and of the worst men, is that in return for a small sacrifice and a few flattering words they will be their accomplices in purloining large sums and save them from many terrible punishments, the way of Rhadamanthus is no longer suited to the needs of justice; for as the opinions of men about the Gods are changed, the laws should also be changed—in the granting of suits a rational legislation ought to do away with the oaths of the parties on either side—he who obtains leave to bring an action should write down the charges, but should not add an oath; and the defendant in like manner should give his denial to the magistrates in writing, and not swear; for it is a dreadful thing to know, when many lawsuits are going on in a state, that almost half the people who meet one another quite unconcernedly at the public meals and in other companies and relations of private life are perjured. Let the law, then, be as follows: A judge who is about to give judgment shall take an oath, and he who is choosing magistrates for the state shall either vote on oath or with a voting tablet which he brings from a temple; so too the judge of dances and of all music, and the superintendents and umpires of gymnastic and equestrian contests, and any matters in which, as far as men can judge, there is nothing to be gained by a false oath; but all cases in which a denial confirmed by an oath clearly results in a great advantage to the taker of the oath, shall be decided without the oath of the parties to the suit, and the presiding judges shall not permit either of them to use an oath for the sake of persuading, nor to call down curses on himself and his race, nor to use unseemly supplications or womanish laments. But they shall ever be teaching and learning what is just in auspicious words; and he who does otherwise shall be supposed to speak beside the point, and the judges shall again bring him back to the question at issue. On the other hand, strangers in their dealings with strangers shall as at present have power to give and receive oaths, for they will not often grow old in the city or leave a fry of young ones like themselves to be the sons and heirs of the land.

As to the initiation of private suits, let the manner of deciding causes between all citizens be the same as in cases in which any freeman is disobedient to the state in minor matters, of which the penalty is not stripes, imprisonment, or death. But as regards attendance at choruses or processions or other shows, and as regards public services, whether the celebration of sacrifice in peace, or the payment of contributions in war—in all these cases, first comes the necessity of providing a remedy for the loss; and by those who will not obey, there shall be security given to the officers whom the city and the law empower to exact the sum due; and if they forfeit their security, let the goods which they have pledged be sold and the money given to the city; but if they ought to pay a larger sum, the several magistrates shall impose upon the disobedient a suitable penalty, and bring them before the court, until they are willing to do what they are ordered.

Now a state which makes money from the cultivation of the soil only, and has no foreign trade, must consider what it will do about the emigration of its own people to other countries, and the reception of strangers from elsewhere. About these matters the legislator has to consider, and he will begin by trying to persuade men as far as he can. The intercourse of cities with one another is apt to create a confusion of manners; strangers are always suggesting novelties to strangers. When states are well governed by good laws the mixture causes the greatest possible injury; but seeing that most cities are the reverse of well-ordered, the confusion which arises in them from the reception of strangers, and from the citizens themselves rushing off into other cities, when any one either young or old desires to travel anywhere abroad at whatever time, is of no consequence. On the other hand, the refusal of states to receive others, and for their own citizens never to go to other places, is an utter impossibility, and to the rest of the world is likely to appear ruthless and uncivilised; it is a practice adopted by people who use harsh words, such as xenelasia or banishment of strangers, and who have harsh and morose ways, as men think. And to be thought or not to be thought well of by the rest of the world is no light matter; for the many are not so far wrong in their judgment of who are bad and who are good, as they are removed from the nature of virtue in themselves. Even bad men have a divine instinct which guesses rightly, and very many who are utterly depraved form correct notions and judgments of the differences between the good and bad. And the generality of cities are quite right in exhorting us to value a good reputation in the world, for there is no truth greater and more important than this—that he who is really good (I am speaking of the men who would be perfect) seeks for reputation with, but not without, the reality of goodness. And our Cretan colony ought also to acquire the fairest and noblest reputation for virtue from other men; and there is every reason to expect that, if the reality answers to the idea, she will be one of the few well-ordered cities which the sun and the other Gods behold. Wherefore, in the matter of journeys to other countries and the reception of strangers, we enact as follows: In the first place, let no one be allowed to go anywhere at all into a foreign country who is less than forty years of age; and no one shall go in a private capacity, but only in some public one, as a herald, or on an embassy, or on a sacred mission. Going abroad on an expedition or in war is not to be included among travels of the class authorised by the state. To Apollo at Delphi and to Zeus at Olympia and to Nemea and to the Isthmus, citizens should be sent to take part in the sacrifices and games there dedicated to the Gods; and they should send as many as possible, and the best and fairest that can be found, and they will make the city renowned at holy meetings in time of peace, procuring a glory which shall be the converse of that which is gained in war; and when they come home they shall teach the young that the institutions of other states are inferior to their own. And they shall send spectators of another sort, if they have the consent of the guardians, being such citizens as desire to look a little more at leisure at the doings of other men; and these no law shall hinder. For a city which has no experience of good and bad men or intercourse with them, can never be thoroughly and perfectly civilised, nor, again, can the citizens of a city properly observe the laws by habit only, and without an intelligent understanding of them. And there always are in the world a few inspired men whose acquaintance is beyond price, and who spring up quite as much in ill-ordered as in well-ordered cities. These are they whom the citizens of a well-ordered city should be ever seeking out, going forth over sea and over land to find him who is incorruptible—that he may establish more firmly institutions in his own state which are good already, and amend what is deficient; for without this examination and enquiry a city will never continue perfect any more than if the examination is ill-conducted.

CLEINIAS: How can we have an examination and also a good one?

ATHENIAN: In this way: In the first place, our spectator shall be of not less than fifty years of age; he must be a man of reputation, especially in war, if he is to exhibit to other cities a model of the guardians of the law, but when he is more than sixty years of age he shall no longer continue in his office of spectator. And when he has carried on his inspection during as many out of the ten years of his office as he pleases, on his return home let him go to the assembly of those who review the laws. This shall be a mixed body of young and old men, who shall be required to meet daily between the hour of dawn and the rising of the sun. They shall consist, in the first place, of the priests who have obtained the rewards of virtue; and, in the second place, of guardians of the law, the ten eldest being chosen; the general superintendent of education shall also be a member, as well as the last appointed as those who have been released from the office; and each of them shall take with him as his companion a young man, whomsoever he chooses, between the ages of thirty and forty. These shall be always holding conversation and discourse about the laws of their own city or about any specially good ones which they may hear to be existing elsewhere; also about kinds of knowledge which may appear to be of use and will throw light upon the examination, or of which the want will make the subject of laws dark and uncertain to them. Any knowledge of this sort which the elders approve, the younger men shall learn with all diligence; and if any one of those who have been invited appear to be unworthy, the whole assembly shall blame him who invited him. The rest of the city shall watch over those among the young men who distinguish themselves, having an eye upon them, and especially honouring them if they succeed, but dishonouring them above the rest if they turn out to be inferior. This is the assembly to which he who has visited the institutions of other men, on his return home shall straightway go, and if he have discovered any one who has anything to say about the enactment of laws or education or nurture, or if he have himself made any observations, let him communicate his discoveries to the whole assembly. And if he be seen to have come home neither better nor worse, let him be praised at any rate for his enthusiasm; and if he be much better, let him be praised so much the more; and not only while he lives but after his death let the assembly honour him with fitting honours. But if on his return home he appear to have been corrupted, pretending to be wise when he is not, let him hold no communication with any one, whether young or old; and if he will hearken to the rulers, then he shall be permitted to live as a private individual; but if he will not, let him die, if he be convicted in a court of law of interfering about education and the laws. And if he deserve to be indicted, and none of the magistrates indict him, let that be counted as a disgrace to them when the rewards of virtue are decided.

Let such be the character of the person who goes abroad, and let him go abroad under these conditions. In the next place, the stranger who comes from abroad should be received in a friendly spirit. Now there are four kinds of strangers, of whom we must make some mention—the first is he who comes and stays throughout the summer; this class are like birds of passage, taking wing in pursuit of commerce, and flying over the sea to other cities, while the season lasts; he shall be received in market-places and harbours and public buildings, near the city but outside, by those magistrates who are appointed to superintend these matters; and they shall take care that a stranger, whoever he be, duly receives justice; but he shall not be allowed to make any innovation. They shall hold the intercourse with him which is necessary, and this shall be as little as possible. The second kind is just a spectator who comes to see with his eyes and hear with his ears the festivals of the Muses; such ought to have entertainment provided them at the temples by hospitable persons, and the priests and ministers of the temples should see and attend to them. But they should not remain more than a reasonable time; let them see and hear that for the sake of which they came, and then go away, neither having suffered nor done any harm. The priests shall be their judges, if any of them receive or do any wrong up to the sum of fifty drachmae, but if any greater charge be brought, in such cases the suit shall come before the wardens of the agora. The third kind of stranger is he who comes on some public business from another land, and is to be received with public honours. He is to be received only by the generals and commanders of horse and foot, and the host by whom he is entertained, in conjunction with the Prytanes, shall have the sole charge of what concerns him. There is a fourth class of persons answering to our spectators, who come from another land to look at ours. In the first place, such visits will be rare, and the visitor should be at least fifty years of age; he may possibly be wanting to see something that is rich and rare in other states, or himself to show something in like manner to another city. Let such an one, then, go unbidden to the doors of the wise and rich, being one of them himself: let him go, for example, to the house of the superintendent of education, confident that he is a fitting guest of such a host, or let him go to the house of some of those who have gained the prize of virtue and hold discourse with them, both learning from them, and also teaching them; and when he has seen and heard all, he shall depart, as a friend taking leave of friends, and be honoured by them with gifts and suitable tributes of respect. These are the customs, according to which our city should receive all strangers of either sex who come from other countries, and should send forth her own citizens, showing respect to Zeus, the God of hospitality, not forbidding strangers at meals and sacrifices, as is the manner which prevails among the children of the Nile, nor driving them away by savage proclamations.

When a man becomes surety, let him give the security in a distinct form, acknowledging the whole transaction in a written document, and in the presence of not less than three witnesses if the sum be under a thousand drachmae, and of not less than five witnesses if the sum be above a thousand drachmae. The agent of a dishonest or untrustworthy seller shall himself be responsible; both the agent and the principal shall be equally liable. If a person wishes to find anything in the house of another, he shall enter naked, or wearing only a short tunic and without a girdle, having first taken an oath by the customary Gods that he expects to find it there; he shall then make his search, and the other shall throw open his house and allow him to search things both sealed and unsealed. And if a person will not allow the searcher to make his search, he who is prevented shall go to law with him, estimating the value of the goods after which he is searching, and if the other be convicted he shall pay twice the value of the article. If the master be absent from home, the dwellers in the house shall let him search the unsealed property, and on the sealed property the searcher shall set another seal, and shall appoint any one whom he likes to guard them during five days; and if the master of the house be absent during a longer time, he shall take with him the wardens of the city, and so make his search, opening the sealed property as well as the unsealed, and then, together with the members of the family and the wardens of the city, he shall seal them up again as they were before. There shall be a limit of time in the case of disputed things, and he who has had possession of them during a certain time shall no longer be liable to be disturbed. As to houses and lands there can be no dispute in this state of ours; but if a man has any other possessions which he has used and openly shown in the city and in the agora and in the temples, and no one has put in a claim to them, and some one says that he was looking for them during this time, and the possessor is proved to have made no concealment, if they have continued for a year, the one having the goods and the other looking for them, the claim of the seeker shall not be allowed after the expiration of the year; or if he does not use or show the lost property in the market or in the city, but only in the country, and no one offers himself as the owner during five years, at the expiration of the five years the claim shall be barred for ever after; or if he uses them in the city but within the house, then the appointed time of claiming the goods shall be three years, or ten years if he has them in the country in private. And if he has them in another land, there shall be no limit of time or prescription, but whenever the owner finds them he may claim them.

If any one prevents another by force from being present at a trial, whether a principal party or his witnesses; if the person prevented be a slave, whether his own or belonging to another, the suit shall be incomplete and invalid; but if he who is prevented be a freeman, besides the suit being incomplete, the other who has prevented him shall be imprisoned for a year, and shall be prosecuted for kidnapping by any one who pleases. And if any one hinders by force a rival competitor in gymnastic or music, or any other sort of contest, from being present at the contest, let him who has a mind inform the presiding judges, and they shall liberate him who is desirous of competing; and if they are not able, and he who hinders the other from competing wins the prize, then they shall give the prize of victory to him who is prevented, and inscribe him as the conqueror in any temples which he pleases; and he who hinders the other shall not be permitted to make any offering or inscription having reference to that contest, and in any case he shall be liable for damages, whether he be defeated or whether he conquer.

If any one knowingly receives anything which has been stolen, he shall undergo the same punishment as the thief, and if a man receives an exile he shall be punished with death. Every man should regard the friend and enemy of the state as his own friend and enemy; and if any one makes peace or war with another on his own account, and without the authority of the state, he, like the receiver of the exile, shall undergo the penalty of death. And if any fraction of the city declare war or peace against any, the generals shall indict the authors of this proceeding, and if they are convicted death shall be the penalty. Those who serve their country ought to serve without receiving gifts, and there ought to be no excusing or approving the saying, 'Men should receive gifts as the reward of good, but not of evil deeds'; for to know which we are doing, and to stand fast by our knowledge, is no easy matter. The safest course is to obey the law which says, 'Do no service for a bribe,' and let him who disobeys, if he be convicted, simply die. With a view to taxation, for various reasons, every man ought to have had his property valued: and the tribesmen should likewise bring a register of the yearly produce to the wardens of the country, that in this way there may be two valuations; and the public officers may use annually whichever on consideration they deem the best, whether they prefer to take a certain portion of the whole value, or of the annual revenue, after subtracting what is paid to the common tables.

Touching offerings to the Gods, a moderate man should observe moderation in what he offers. Now the land and the hearth of the house of all men is sacred to all Gods; wherefore let no man dedicate them a second time to the Gods. Gold and silver, whether possessed by private persons or in temples, are in other cities provocative of envy, and ivory, the product of a dead body, is not a proper offering; brass and iron, again, are instruments of war; but of wood let a man bring what offering he likes, provided it be a single block, and in like manner of stone, to the public temples; of woven work let him not offer more than one woman can execute in a month. White is a colour suitable to the Gods, especially in woven works, but dyes should only be used for the adornments of war. The most divine of gifts are birds and images, and they should be such as one painter can execute in a single day. And let all other offerings follow a similar rule.

Now that the whole city has been divided into parts of which the nature and number have been described, and laws have been given about all the most important contracts as far as this was possible, the next thing will be to have justice done. The first of the courts shall consist of elected judges, who shall be chosen by the plaintiff and the defendant in common: these shall be called arbiters rather than judges. And in the second court there shall be judges of the villages and tribes corresponding to the twelvefold division of the land, and before these the litigants shall go to contend for greater damages, if the suit be not decided before the first judges; the defendant, if he be defeated the second time, shall pay a fifth more than the damages mentioned in the indictment; and if he find fault with his judges and would try a third time, let him carry the suit before the select judges, and if he be again defeated, let him pay the whole of the damages and half as much again. And the plaintiff, if when defeated before the first judges he persist in going on to the second, shall if he wins receive in addition to the damages a fifth part more, and if defeated he shall pay a like sum; but if he is not satisfied with the previous decision, and will insist on proceeding to a third court, then if he win he shall receive from the defendant the amount of the damages and, as I said before, half as much again, and the plaintiff, if he lose, shall pay half of the damages claimed. Now the assignment by lot of judges to courts and the completion of the number of them, and the appointment of servants to the different magistrates, and the times at which the several causes should be heard, and the votings and delays, and all the things that necessarily concern suits, and the order of causes, and the time in which answers have to be put in and parties are to appear—of these and other things akin to these we have indeed already spoken, but there is no harm in repeating what is right twice or thrice: All lesser and easier matters which the elder legislator has omitted may be supplied by the younger one. Private courts will be sufficiently regulated in this way, and the public and state courts, and those which the magistrates must use in the administration of their several offices, exist in many other states. Many very respectable institutions of this sort have been framed by good men, and from them the guardians of the law may by reflection derive what is necessary for the order of our new state, considering and correcting them, and bringing them to the test of experience, until every detail appears to be satisfactorily determined; and then putting the final seal upon them, and making them irreversible, they shall use them for ever afterwards. As to what relates to the silence of judges and the abstinence from words of evil omen and the reverse, and the different notions of the just and good and honourable which exist in our own as compared with other states, they have been partly mentioned already, and another part of them will be mentioned hereafter as we draw near the end. To all these matters he who would be an equal judge shall justly look, and he shall possess writings about them that he may learn them. For of all kinds of knowledge the knowledge of good laws has the greatest power of improving the learner; otherwise there would be no meaning in the divine and admirable law possessing a name akin to mind (nous, nomos). And of all other words, such as the praises and censures of individuals which occur in poetry and also in prose, whether written down or uttered in daily conversation, whether men dispute about them in the spirit of contention or weakly assent to them, as is often the case—of all these the one sure test is the writings of the legislator, which the righteous judge ought to have in his mind as the antidote of all other words, and thus make himself and the city stand upright, procuring for the good the continuance and increase of justice, and for the bad, on the other hand, a conversion from ignorance and intemperance, and in general from all unrighteousness, as far as their evil minds can be healed, but to those whose web of life is in reality finished, giving death, which is the only remedy for souls in their condition, as I may say truly again and again. And such judges and chiefs of judges will be worthy of receiving praise from the whole city.

When the suits of the year are completed the following laws shall regulate their execution: In the first place, the judge shall assign to the party who wins the suit the whole property of him who loses, with the exception of mere necessaries, and the assignment shall be made through the herald immediately after each decision in the hearing of the judges; and when the month arrives following the month in which the courts are sitting, (unless the gainer of the suit has been previously satisfied) the court shall follow up the case, and hand over to the winner the goods of the loser; but if they find that he has not the means of paying, and the sum deficient is not less than a drachma, the insolvent person shall not have any right of going to law with any other man until he have satisfied the debt of the winning party; but other persons shall still have the right of bringing suits against him. And if any one after he is condemned refuses to acknowledge the authority which condemned him, let the magistrates who are thus deprived of their authority bring him before the court of the guardians of the law, and if he be cast, let him be punished with death, as a subverter of the whole state and of the laws.

Thus a man is born and brought up, and after this manner he begets and brings up his own children, and has his share of dealings with other men, and suffers if he has done wrong to any one, and receives satisfaction if he has been wronged, and so at length in due time he grows old under the protection of the laws, and his end comes in the order of nature. Concerning the dead of either sex, the religious ceremonies which may fittingly be performed, whether appertaining to the Gods of the under-world or of this, shall be decided by the interpreters with absolute authority. Their sepulchres are not to be in places which are fit for cultivation, and there shall be no monuments in such spots, either large or small, but they shall occupy that part of the country which is naturally adapted for receiving and concealing the bodies of the dead with as little hurt as possible to the living. No man, living or dead, shall deprive the living of the sustenance which the earth, their foster-parent, is naturally inclined to provide for them. And let not the mound be piled higher than would be the work of five men completed in five days; nor shall the stone which is placed over the spot be larger than would be sufficient to receive the praises of the dead included in four heroic lines. Nor shall the laying out of the dead in the house continue for a longer time than is sufficient to distinguish between him who is in a trance only and him who is really dead, and speaking generally, the third day after death will be a fair time for carrying out the body to the sepulchre. Now we must believe the legislator when he tells us that the soul is in all respects superior to the body, and that even in life what makes each one of us to be what we are is only the soul; and that the body follows us about in the likeness of each of us, and therefore, when we are dead, the bodies of the dead are quite rightly said to be our shades or images; for the true and immortal being of each one of us which is called the soul goes on her way to other Gods, before them to give an account—which is an inspiring hope to the good, but very terrible to the bad, as the laws of our fathers tell us; and they also say that not much can be done in the way of helping a man after he is dead. But the living—he should be helped by all his kindred, that while in life he may be the holiest and justest of men, and after death may have no great sins to be punished in the world below. If this be true, a man ought not to waste his substance under the idea that all this lifeless mass of flesh which is in process of burial is connected with him; he should consider that the son, or brother, or the beloved one, whoever he may be, whom he thinks he is laying in the earth, has gone away to complete and fulfil his own destiny, and that his duty is rightly to order the present, and to spend moderately on the lifeless altar of the Gods below. But the legislator does not intend moderation to be taken in the sense of meanness. Let the law, then, be as follows: The expenditure on the entire funeral of him who is of the highest class, shall not exceed five minae; and for him who is of the second class, three minae, and for him who is of the third class, two minae, and for him who is of the fourth class, one mina, will be a fair limit of expense. The guardians of the law ought to take especial care of the different ages of life, whether childhood, or manhood, or any other age. And at the end of all, let there be some one guardian of the law presiding, who shall be chosen by the friends of the deceased to superintend, and let it be glory to him to manage with fairness and moderation what relates to the dead, and a discredit to him if they are not well managed. Let the laying out and other ceremonies be in accordance with custom, but to the statesman who adopts custom as his law we must give way in certain particulars. It would be monstrous for example that he should command any man to weep or abstain from weeping over the dead; but he may forbid cries of lamentation, and not allow the voice of the mourner to be heard outside the house; also, he may forbid the bringing of the dead body into the open streets, or the processions of mourners in the streets, and may require that before daybreak they should be outside the city. Let these, then, be our laws relating to such matters, and let him who obeys be free from penalty; but he who disobeys even a single guardian of the law shall be punished by them all with a fitting penalty. Other modes of burial, or again the denial of burial, which is to be refused in the case of robbers of temples and parricides and the like, have been devised and are embodied in the preceding laws, so that now our work of legislation is pretty nearly at an end; but in all cases the end does not consist in doing something or acquiring something or establishing something—the end will be attained and finally accomplished, when we have provided for the perfect and lasting continuance of our institutions; until then our creation is incomplete.

CLEINIAS: That is very good, Stranger; but I wish you would tell me more clearly what you mean.

ATHENIAN: O Cleinias, many things of old time were well said and sung; and the saying about the Fates was one of them.

CLEINIAS: What is it?

ATHENIAN: The saying that Lachesis or the giver of the lots is the first of them, and that Clotho or the spinster is the second of them, and that Atropos or the unchanging one is the third of them; and that she is the preserver of the things which we have spoken, and which have been compared in a figure to things woven by fire, they both (i.e. Atropos and the fire) producing the quality of unchangeableness. I am speaking of the things which in a state and government give not only health and salvation to the body, but law, or rather preservation of the law, in the soul; and, if I am not mistaken, this seems to be still wanting in our laws: we have still to see how we can implant in them this irreversible nature.

CLEINIAS: It will be no small matter if we can only discover how such a nature can be implanted in anything.

ATHENIAN: But it certainly can be; so much I clearly see.

CLEINIAS: Then let us not think of desisting until we have imparted this quality to our laws; for it is ridiculous, after a great deal of labour has been spent, to place a thing at last on an insecure foundation.

ATHENIAN: I approve of your suggestion, and am quite of the same mind with you.

CLEINIAS: Very good: And now what, according to you, is to be the salvation of our government and of our laws, and how is it to be effected?

ATHENIAN: Were we not saying that there must be in our city a council which was to be of this sort: The ten oldest guardians of the law, and all those who have obtained prizes of virtue, were to meet in the same assembly, and the council was also to include those who had visited foreign countries in the hope of hearing something that might be of use in the preservation of the laws, and who, having come safely home, and having been tested in these same matters, had proved themselves to be worthy to take part in the assembly—each of the members was to select some young man of not less than thirty years of age, he himself judging in the first instance whether the young man was worthy by nature and education, and then suggesting him to the others, and if he seemed to them also to be worthy they were to adopt him; but if not, the decision at which they arrived was to be kept a secret from the citizens at large, and, more especially, from the rejected candidate. The meeting of the council was to be held early in the morning, when everybody was most at leisure from all other business, whether public or private—was not something of this sort said by us before?

CLEINIAS: True.

ATHENIAN: Then, returning to the council, I would say further, that if we let it down to be the anchor of the state, our city, having everything which is suitable to her, will preserve all that we wish to preserve.

CLEINIAS: What do you mean?

ATHENIAN: Now is the time for me to speak the truth in all earnestness.

CLEINIAS: Well said, and I hope that you will fulfil your intention.

ATHENIAN: Know, Cleinias, that everything, in all that it does, has a natural saviour, as of an animal the soul and the head are the chief saviours.

CLEINIAS: Once more, what do you mean?

ATHENIAN: The well-being of those two is obviously the preservation of every living thing.

CLEINIAS: How is that?

ATHENIAN: The soul, besides other things, contains mind, and the head, besides other things, contains sight and hearing; and the mind, mingling with the noblest of the senses, and becoming one with them, may be truly called the salvation of all.

CLEINIAS: Yes, quite so.

ATHENIAN: Yes, indeed; but with what is that intellect concerned which, mingling with the senses, is the salvation of ships in storms as well as in fair weather? In a ship, when the pilot and the sailors unite their perceptions with the piloting mind, do they not save both themselves and their craft?

CLEINIAS: Very true.

ATHENIAN: We do not want many illustrations about such matters: What aim would the general of an army, or what aim would a physician propose to himself, if he were seeking to attain salvation?

CLEINIAS: Very good.

ATHENIAN: Does not the general aim at victory and superiority in war, and do not the physician and his assistants aim at producing health in the body?

CLEINIAS: Certainly.

ATHENIAN: And a physician who is ignorant about the body, that is to say, who knows not that which we just now called health, or a general who knows not victory, or any others who are ignorant of the particulars of the arts which we mentioned, cannot be said to have understanding about any of these matters.

CLEINIAS: They cannot.

ATHENIAN: And what would you say of the state? If a person proves to be ignorant of the aim to which the statesman should look, ought he, in the first place, to be called a ruler at all; and further, will he ever be able to preserve that of which he does not even know the aim?

CLEINIAS: Impossible.

ATHENIAN: And therefore, if our settlement of the country is to be perfect, we ought to have some institution, which, as I was saying, will tell what is the aim of the state, and will inform us how we are to attain this, and what law or what man will advise us to that end. Any state which has no such institution is likely to be devoid of mind and sense, and in all her actions will proceed by mere chance.

CLEINIAS: Very true.

ATHENIAN: In which, then, of the parts or institutions of the state is any such guardian power to be found? Can we say?

CLEINIAS: I am not quite certain, Stranger; but I have a suspicion that you are referring to the assembly which you just now said was to meet at night.

ATHENIAN: You understand me perfectly, Cleinias; and we must assume, as the argument implies, that this council possesses all virtue; and the beginning of virtue is not to make mistakes by guessing many things, but to look steadily at one thing, and on this to fix all our aims.

CLEINIAS: Quite true.

ATHENIAN: Then now we shall see why there is nothing wonderful in states going astray—the reason is that their legislators have such different aims; nor is there anything wonderful in some laying down as their rule of justice, that certain individuals should bear rule in the state, whether they be good or bad, and others that the citizens should be rich, not caring whether they are the slaves of other men or not. The tendency of others, again, is towards freedom; and some legislate with a view to two things at once—they want to be at the same time free and the lords of other states; but the wisest men, as they deem themselves to be, look to all these and similar aims, and there is no one of them which they exclusively honour, and to which they would have all things look.

CLEINIAS: Then, Stranger, our former assertion will hold; for we were saying that laws generally should look to one thing only; and this, as we admitted, was rightly said to be virtue.

ATHENIAN: Yes.

CLEINIAS: And we said that virtue was of four kinds?

ATHENIAN: Quite true.

CLEINIAS: And that mind was the leader of the four, and that to her the three other virtues and all other things ought to have regard?

ATHENIAN: You follow me capitally, Cleinias, and I would ask you to follow me to the end, for we have already said that the mind of the pilot, the mind of the physician and of the general look to that one thing to which they ought to look; and now we may turn to mind political, of which, as of a human creature, we will ask a question: O wonderful being, and to what are you looking? The physician is able to tell his single aim in life, but you, the superior, as you declare yourself to be, of all intelligent beings, when you are asked are not able to tell. Can you, Megillus, and you, Cleinias, say distinctly what is the aim of mind political, in return for the many explanations of things which I have given you?

CLEINIAS: We cannot, Stranger.

ATHENIAN: Well, but ought we not to desire to see it, and to see where it is to be found?

CLEINIAS: For example, where?

ATHENIAN: For example, we were saying that there are four kinds of virtue, and as there are four of them, each of them must be one.

CLEINIAS: Certainly.

ATHENIAN: And further, all four of them we call one; for we say that courage is virtue, and that prudence is virtue, and the same of the two others, as if they were in reality not many but one, that is, virtue.

CLEINIAS: Quite so.

ATHENIAN: There is no difficulty in seeing in what way the two differ from one another, and have received two names, and so of the rest. But there is more difficulty in explaining why we call these two and the rest of them by the single name of virtue.

CLEINIAS: How do you mean?

ATHENIAN: I have no difficulty in explaining what I mean. Let us distribute the subject into questions and answers.

CLEINIAS: Once more, what do you mean?

ATHENIAN: Ask me what is that one thing which I call virtue, and then again speak of as two, one part being courage and the other wisdom. I will tell you how that occurs: One of them has to do with fear; in this the beasts also participate, and quite young children—I mean courage; for a courageous temper is a gift of nature and not of reason. But without reason there never has been, or is, or will be a wise and understanding soul; it is of a different nature.

CLEINIAS: That is true.

ATHENIAN: I have now told you in what way the two are different, and do you in return tell me in what way they are one and the same. Suppose that I ask you in what way the four are one, and when you have answered me, you will have a right to ask of me in return in what way they are four; and then let us proceed to enquire whether in the case of things which have a name and also a definition to them, true knowledge consists in knowing the name only and not the definition. Can he who is good for anything be ignorant of all this without discredit where great and glorious truths are concerned?

CLEINIAS: I suppose not.

ATHENIAN: And is there anything greater to the legislator and the guardian of the law, and to him who thinks that he excels all other men in virtue, and has won the palm of excellence, than these very qualities of which we are now speaking—courage, temperance, wisdom, justice?

CLEINIAS: How can there be anything greater?

ATHENIAN: And ought not the interpreters, the teachers, the lawgivers, the guardians of the other citizens, to excel the rest of mankind, and perfectly to show him who desires to learn and know or whose evil actions require to be punished and reproved, what is the nature of virtue and vice? Or shall some poet who has found his way into the city, or some chance person who pretends to be an instructor of youth, show himself to be better than him who has won the prize for every virtue? And can we wonder that when the guardians are not adequate in speech or action, and have no adequate knowledge of virtue, the city being unguarded should experience the common fate of cities in our day?

CLEINIAS: Wonder! no.

ATHENIAN: Well, then, must we do as we said? Or can we give our guardians a more precise knowledge of virtue in speech and action than the many have? or is there any way in which our city can be made to resemble the head and senses of rational beings because possessing such a guardian power?

CLEINIAS: What, Stranger, is the drift of your comparison?

ATHENIAN: Do we not see that the city is the trunk, and are not the younger guardians, who are chosen for their natural gifts, placed in the head of the state, having their souls all full of eyes, with which they look about the whole city? They keep watch and hand over their perceptions to the memory, and inform the elders of all that happens in the city; and those whom we compared to the mind, because they have many wise thoughts—that is to say, the old men—take counsel, and making use of the younger men as their ministers, and advising with them—in this way both together truly preserve the whole state: Shall this or some other be the order of our state? Are all our citizens to be equal in acquirements, or shall there be special persons among them who have received a more careful training and education?

CLEINIAS: That they should be equal, my good sir, is impossible.

ATHENIAN: Then we ought to proceed to some more exact training than any which has preceded.

CLEINIAS: Certainly.

ATHENIAN: And must not that of which we are in need be the one to which we were just now alluding?

CLEINIAS: Very true.

ATHENIAN: Did we not say that the workman or guardian, if he be perfect in every respect, ought not only to be able to see the many aims, but he should press onward to the one? This he should know, and knowing, order all things with a view to it.

CLEINIAS: True.

ATHENIAN: And can any one have a more exact way of considering or contemplating anything, than the being able to look at one idea gathered from many different things?

CLEINIAS: Perhaps not.

ATHENIAN: Not 'Perhaps not,' but 'Certainly not,' my good sir, is the right answer. There never has been a truer method than this discovered by any man.

CLEINIAS: I bow to your authority, Stranger; let us proceed in the way which you propose.

ATHENIAN: Then, as would appear, we must compel the guardians of our divine state to perceive, in the first place, what that principle is which is the same in all the four—the same, as we affirm, in courage and in temperance, and in justice and in prudence, and which, being one, we call as we ought, by the single name of virtue. To this, my friends, we will, if you please, hold fast, and not let go until we have sufficiently explained what that is to which we are to look, whether to be regarded as one, or as a whole, or as both, or in whatever way. Are we likely ever to be in a virtuous condition, if we cannot tell whether virtue is many, or four, or one? Certainly, if we take counsel among ourselves, we shall in some way contrive that this principle has a place amongst us; but if you have made up your mind that we should let the matter alone, we will.

CLEINIAS: We must not, Stranger, by the God of strangers I swear that we must not, for in our opinion you speak most truly; but we should like to know how you will accomplish your purpose.

ATHENIAN: Wait a little before you ask; and let us, first of all, be quite agreed with one another that the purpose has to be accomplished.

CLEINIAS: Certainly, it ought to be, if it can be.

ATHENIAN: Well, and about the good and the honourable, are we to take the same view? Are our guardians only to know that each of them is many, or also how and in what way they are one?

CLEINIAS: They must consider also in what sense they are one.

ATHENIAN: And are they to consider only, and to be unable to set forth what they think?

CLEINIAS: Certainly not; that would be the state of a slave.

ATHENIAN: And may not the same be said of all good things—that the true guardians of the laws ought to know the truth about them, and to be able to interpret them in words, and carry them out in action, judging of what is and of what is not well, according to nature?

CLEINIAS: Certainly.

ATHENIAN: Is not the knowledge of the Gods which we have set forth with so much zeal one of the noblest sorts of knowledge—to know that they are, and know how great is their power, as far as in man lies? We do indeed excuse the mass of the citizens, who only follow the voice of the laws, but we refuse to admit as guardians any who do not labour to obtain every possible evidence that there is respecting the Gods; our city is forbidden and not allowed to choose as a guardian of the law, or to place in the select order of virtue, him who is not an inspired man, and has not laboured at these things.

CLEINIAS: It is certainly just, as you say, that he who is indolent about such matters or incapable should be rejected, and that things honourable should be put away from him.

ATHENIAN: Are we assured that there are two things which lead men to believe in the Gods, as we have already stated?

CLEINIAS: What are they?

ATHENIAN: One is the argument about the soul, which has been already mentioned—that it is the eldest and most divine of all things, to which motion attaining generation gives perpetual existence; the other was an argument from the order of the motion of the stars, and of all things under the dominion of the mind which ordered the universe. If a man look upon the world not lightly or ignorantly, there was never any one so godless who did not experience an effect opposite to that which the many imagine. For they think that those who handle these matters by the help of astronomy, and the accompanying arts of demonstration, may become godless, because they see, as far as they can see, things happening by necessity, and not by an intelligent will accomplishing good.

CLEINIAS: But what is the fact?

ATHENIAN: Just the opposite, as I said, of the opinion which once prevailed among men, that the sun and stars are without soul. Even in those days men wondered about them, and that which is now ascertained was then conjectured by some who had a more exact knowledge of them—that if they had been things without soul, and had no mind, they could never have moved with numerical exactness so wonderful; and even at that time some ventured to hazard the conjecture that mind was the orderer of the universe. But these same persons again mistaking the nature of the soul, which they conceived to be younger and not older than the body, once more overturned the world, or rather, I should say, themselves; for the bodies which they saw moving in heaven all appeared to be full of stones, and earth, and many other lifeless substances, and to these they assigned the causes of all things. Such studies gave rise to much atheism and perplexity, and the poets took occasion to be abusive—comparing the philosophers to she-dogs uttering vain howlings, and talking other nonsense of the same sort. But now, as I said, the case is reversed.

CLEINIAS: How so?

ATHENIAN: No man can be a true worshipper of the Gods who does not know these two principles—that the soul is the eldest of all things which are born, and is immortal and rules over all bodies; moreover, as I have now said several times, he who has not contemplated the mind of nature which is said to exist in the stars, and gone through the previous training, and seen the connexion of music with these things, and harmonized them all with laws and institutions, is not able to give a reason of such things as have a reason. And he who is unable to acquire this in addition to the ordinary virtues of a citizen, can hardly be a good ruler of a whole state; but he should be the subordinate of other rulers. Wherefore, Cleinias and Megillus, let us consider whether we may not add to all the other laws which we have discussed this further one—that the nocturnal assembly of the magistrates, which has also shared in the whole scheme of education proposed by us, shall be a guard set according to law for the salvation of the state. Shall we propose this?

CLEINIAS: Certainly, my good friend, we will if the thing is in any degree possible.

ATHENIAN: Let us make a common effort to gain such an object; for I too will gladly share in the attempt. Of these matters I have had much experience, and have often considered them, and I dare say that I shall be able to find others who will also help.

CLEINIAS: I agree, Stranger, that we should proceed along the road in which God is guiding us; and how we can proceed rightly has now to be investigated and explained.

ATHENIAN: O Megillus and Cleinias, about these matters we cannot legislate further until the council is constituted; when that is done, then we will determine what authority they shall have of their own; but the explanation of how this is all to be ordered would only be given rightly in a long discourse.

CLEINIAS: What do you mean, and what new thing is this?

ATHENIAN: In the first place, a list would have to be made out of those who by their ages and studies and dispositions and habits are well fitted for the duty of a guardian. In the next place, it will not be easy for them to discover themselves what they ought to learn, or become the disciple of one who has already made the discovery. Furthermore, to write down the times at which, and during which, they ought to receive the several kinds of instruction, would be a vain thing; for the learners themselves do not know what is learned to advantage until the knowledge which is the result of learning has found a place in the soul of each. And so these details, although they could not be truly said to be secret, might be said to be incapable of being stated beforehand, because when stated they would have no meaning.

CLEINIAS: What then are we to do, Stranger, under these circumstances?

ATHENIAN: As the proverb says, the answer is no secret, but open to all of us: We must risk the whole on the chance of throwing, as they say, thrice six or thrice ace, and I am willing to share with you the danger by stating and explaining to you my views about education and nurture, which is the question coming to the surface again. The danger is not a slight or ordinary one, and I would advise you, Cleinias, in particular, to see to the matter; for if you order rightly the city of the Magnetes, or whatever name God may give it, you will obtain the greatest glory; or at any rate you will be thought the most courageous of men in the estimation of posterity. Dear companions, if this our divine assembly can only be established, to them we will hand over the city; none of the present company of legislators, as I may call them, would hesitate about that. And the state will be perfected and become a waking reality, which a little while ago we attempted to create as a dream and in idea only, mingling together reason and mind in one image, in the hope that our citizens might be duly mingled and rightly educated; and being educated, and dwelling in the citadel of the land, might become perfect guardians, such as we have never seen in all our previous life, by reason of the saving virtue which is in them.

MEGILLUS: Dear Cleinias, after all that has been said, either we must detain the Stranger, and by supplications and in all manner of ways make him share in the foundation of the city, or we must give up the undertaking.

CLEINIAS: Very true, Megillus; and you must join with me in detaining him.

MEGILLUS: I will.

LYSIS, OR FRIENDSHIP

By Plato

Translated by Benjamin Jowett

PERSONS OF THE DIALOGUE:

Socrates, who is the narrator, Menexenus, Hippothales, Lysis, Ctesippus.

SCENE: A newly-erected Palaestra outside the walls of Athens.

I was going from the Academy straight to the Lyceum, intending to take the outer road, which is close under the wall. When I came to the postern gate of the city, which is by the fountain of Panops, I fell in with Hippothales, the son of Hieronymus, and Ctesippus the Paeanian, and a company of young men who were standing with them. Hippothales, seeing me approach, asked whence I came and whither I was going.

I am going, I replied, from the Academy straight to the Lyceum.

Then come straight to us, he said, and put in here; you may as well.

Who are you, I said; and where am I to come?

He showed me an enclosed space and an open door over against the wall. And there, he said, is the building at which we all meet: and a goodly company we are.

And what is this building, I asked; and what sort of entertainment have you?

The building, he replied, is a newly erected Palaestra; and the entertainment is generally conversation, to which you are welcome.

Thank you, I said; and is there any teacher there?

Yes, he said, your old friend and admirer, Miccus.

Indeed, I replied; he is a very eminent professor.

Are you disposed, he said, to go with me and see them?

Yes, I said; but I should like to know first, what is expected of me, and who is the favourite among you?

Some persons have one favourite, Socrates, and some another, he said.

And who is yours? I asked: tell me that, Hippothales.

At this he blushed; and I said to him, O Hippothales, thou son of Hieronymus! do not say that you are, or that you are not, in love; the confession is too late; for I see that you are not only in love, but are already far gone in your love. Simple and foolish as I am, the Gods have given me the power of understanding affections of this kind.

Whereupon he blushed more and more.

Ctesippus said: I like to see you blushing, Hippothales, and hesitating to tell Socrates the name; when, if he were with you but for a very short time, you would have plagued him to death by talking about nothing else. Indeed, Socrates, he has literally deafened us, and stopped our ears with the praises of Lysis; and if he is a little intoxicated, there is every likelihood that we may have our sleep murdered with a cry of Lysis. His performances in prose are bad enough, but nothing at all in comparison with his verse; and when he drenches us with his poems and other compositions, it is really too bad; and worse still is his manner of singing them to his love; he has a voice which is truly appalling, and we cannot help hearing him: and now having a question put to him by you, behold he is blushing.

Who is Lysis? I said: I suppose that he must be young; for the name does not recall any one to me.

Why, he said, his father being a very well-known man, he retains his patronymic, and is not as yet commonly called by his own name; but, although you do not know his name, I am sure that you must know his face, for that is quite enough to distinguish him.

But tell me whose son he is, I said.

He is the eldest son of Democrates, of the deme of Aexone.

Ah, Hippothales, I said; what a noble and really perfect love you have found! I wish that you would favour me with the exhibition which you have been making to the rest of the company, and then I shall be able to judge whether you know what a lover ought to say about his love, either to the youth himself, or to others.

Nay, Socrates, he said; you surely do not attach any importance to what he is saying.

Do you mean, I said, that you disown the love of the person whom he says that you love?

No; but I deny that I make verses or address compositions to him.

He is not in his right mind, said Ctesippus; he is talking nonsense, and is stark mad.

O Hippothales, I said, if you have ever made any verses or songs in honour of your favourite, I do not want to hear them; but I want to know the purport of them, that I may be able to judge of your mode of approaching your fair one.

Ctesippus will be able to tell you, he said; for if, as he avers, the sound of my words is always dinning in his ears, he must have a very accurate knowledge and recollection of them.

Yes, indeed, said Ctesippus; I know only too well; and very ridiculous the tale is: for although he is a lover, and very devotedly in love, he has nothing particular to talk about to his beloved which a child might not say. Now is not that ridiculous? He can only speak of the wealth of Democrates, which the whole city celebrates, and grandfather Lysis, and the other ancestors of the youth, and their stud of horses, and their victory at the Pythian games, and at the Isthmus, and at Nemea with four horses and single horses—these are the tales which he composes and repeats. And there is greater twaddle still. Only the day before yesterday he made a poem in which he described the entertainment of Heracles, who was a connexion of the family, setting forth how in virtue of this relationship he was hospitably received by an ancestor of Lysis; this ancestor was himself begotten of Zeus by the daughter of the founder of the deme. And these are the sort of old wives' tales which he sings and recites to us, and we are obliged to listen to him.

When I heard this, I said: O ridiculous Hippothales! how can you be making and singing hymns in honour of yourself before you have won?

But my songs and verses, he said, are not in honour of myself, Socrates.

You think not? I said.

Nay, but what do you think? he replied.

Most assuredly, I said, those songs are all in your own honour; for if you win your beautiful love, your discourses and songs will be a glory to you, and may be truly regarded as hymns of praise composed in honour of you who have conquered and won such a love; but if he slips away from you, the more you have praised him, the more ridiculous you will look at having lost this fairest and best of blessings; and therefore the wise lover does not praise his beloved until he has won him, because he is afraid of accidents. There is also another danger; the fair, when any one praises or magnifies them, are filled with the spirit of pride and vain-glory. Do you not agree with me?

Yes, he said.

And the more vain-glorious they are, the more difficult is the capture of them?

I believe you.

What should you say of a hunter who frightened away his prey, and made the capture of the animals which he is hunting more difficult?

He would be a bad hunter, undoubtedly.

Yes; and if, instead of soothing them, he were to infuriate them with words and songs, that would show a great want of wit: do you not agree.

Yes.

And now reflect, Hippothales, and see whether you are not guilty of all these errors in writing poetry. For I can hardly suppose that you will affirm a man to be a good poet who injures himself by his poetry.

Assuredly not, he said; such a poet would be a fool. And this is the reason why I take you into my counsels, Socrates, and I shall be glad of any further advice which you may have to offer. Will you tell me by what words or actions I may become endeared to my love?

That is not easy to determine, I said; but if you will bring your love to me, and will let me talk with him, I may perhaps be able to show you how to converse with him, instead of singing and reciting in the fashion of which you are accused.

There will be no difficulty in bringing him, he replied; if you will only go with Ctesippus into the Palaestra, and sit down and talk, I believe that he will come of his own accord; for he is fond of listening, Socrates. And as this is the festival of the Hermaea, the young men and boys are all together, and there is no separation between them. He will be sure to come: but if he does not, Ctesippus with whom he is familiar, and whose relation Menexenus is his great friend, shall call him.

That will be the way, I said. Thereupon I led Ctesippus into the Palaestra, and the rest followed.

Upon entering we found that the boys had just been sacrificing; and this part of the festival was nearly at an end. They were all in their white array, and games at dice were going on among them. Most of them were in the outer court amusing themselves; but some were in a corner of the Apodyterium playing at odd and even with a number of dice, which they took out of little wicker baskets. There was also a circle of lookers-on; among them was Lysis. He was standing with the other boys and youths, having a crown upon his head, like a fair vision, and not less worthy of praise for his goodness than for his beauty. We left them, and went over to the opposite side of the room, where, finding a quiet place, we sat down; and then we began to talk. This attracted Lysis, who was constantly turning round to look at us—he was evidently wanting to come to us. For a time he hesitated and had not the courage to come alone; but first of all, his friend Menexenus, leaving his play, entered the Palaestra from the court, and when he saw Ctesippus and myself, was going to take a seat by us; and then Lysis, seeing him, followed, and sat down by his side; and the other boys joined. I should observe that Hippothales, when he saw the crowd, got behind them, where he thought that he would be out of sight of Lysis, lest he should anger him; and there he stood and listened.

I turned to Menexenus, and said: Son of Demophon, which of you two youths is the elder?

That is a matter of dispute between us, he said.

And which is the nobler? Is that also a matter of dispute?

Yes, certainly.

And another disputed point is, which is the fairer?

The two boys laughed.

I shall not ask which is the richer of the two, I said; for you are friends, are you not?

Certainly, they replied.

And friends have all things in common, so that one of you can be no richer than the other, if you say truly that you are friends.

They assented. I was about to ask which was the juster of the two, and which was the wiser of the two; but at this moment Menexenus was called away by some one who came and said that the gymnastic-master wanted him. I supposed that he had to offer sacrifice. So he went away, and I asked Lysis some more questions. I dare say, Lysis, I said, that your father and mother love you very much.

Certainly, he said.

And they would wish you to be perfectly happy.

Yes.

But do you think that any one is happy who is in the condition of a slave, and who cannot do what he likes?

I should think not indeed, he said.

And if your father and mother love you, and desire that you should be happy, no one can doubt that they are very ready to promote your happiness.

Certainly, he replied.

And do they then permit you to do what you like, and never rebuke you or hinder you from doing what you desire?

Yes, indeed, Socrates; there are a great many things which they hinder me from doing.

What do you mean? I said. Do they want you to be happy, and yet hinder you from doing what you like? for example, if you want to mount one of your father's chariots, and take the reins at a race, they will not allow you to do so—they will prevent you?

Certainly, he said, they will not allow me to do so.

Whom then will they allow?

There is a charioteer, whom my father pays for driving.

And do they trust a hireling more than you? and may he do what he likes with the horses? and do they pay him for this?

They do.

But I dare say that you may take the whip and guide the mule-cart if you like;—they will permit that?

Permit me! indeed they will not.

Then, I said, may no one use the whip to the mules?

Yes, he said, the muleteer.

And is he a slave or a free man?

A slave, he said.

And do they esteem a slave of more value than you who are their son? And do they entrust their property to him rather than to you? and allow him to do what he likes, when they prohibit you? Answer me now: Are you your own master, or do they not even allow that?

Nay, he said; of course they do not allow it.

Then you have a master?

Yes, my tutor; there he is.

And is he a slave?

To be sure; he is our slave, he replied.

Surely, I said, this is a strange thing, that a free man should be governed by a slave. And what does he do with you?

He takes me to my teachers.

You do not mean to say that your teachers also rule over you?

Of course they do.

Then I must say that your father is pleased to inflict many lords and masters on you. But at any rate when you go home to your mother, she will let you have your own way, and will not interfere with your happiness; her wool, or the piece of cloth which she is weaving, are at your disposal: I am sure that there is nothing to hinder you from touching her wooden spathe, or her comb, or any other of her spinning implements.

Nay, Socrates, he replied, laughing; not only does she hinder me, but I should be beaten if I were to touch one of them.

Well, I said, this is amazing. And did you ever behave ill to your father or your mother?

No, indeed, he replied.

But why then are they so terribly anxious to prevent you from being happy, and doing as you like?—keeping you all day long in subjection to another, and, in a word, doing nothing which you desire; so that you have no good, as would appear, out of their great possessions, which are under the control of anybody rather than of you, and have no use of your own fair person, which is tended and taken care of by another; while you, Lysis, are master of nobody, and can do nothing?

Why, he said, Socrates, the reason is that I am not of age.

I doubt whether that is the real reason, I said; for I should imagine that your father Democrates, and your mother, do permit you to do many things already, and do not wait until you are of age: for example, if they want anything read or written, you, I presume, would be the first person in the house who is summoned by them.

Very true.

And you would be allowed to write or read the letters in any order which you please, or to take up the lyre and tune the notes, and play with the fingers, or strike with the plectrum, exactly as you please, and neither father nor mother would interfere with you.

That is true, he said.

Then what can be the reason, Lysis, I said, why they allow you to do the one and not the other?

I suppose, he said, because I understand the one, and not the other.

Yes, my dear youth, I said, the reason is not any deficiency of years, but a deficiency of knowledge; and whenever your father thinks that you are wiser than he is, he will instantly commit himself and his possessions to you.

I think so.

Aye, I said; and about your neighbour, too, does not the same rule hold as about your father? If he is satisfied that you know more of housekeeping than he does, will he continue to administer his affairs himself, or will he commit them to you?

I think that he will commit them to me.

Will not the Athenian people, too, entrust their affairs to you when they see that you have wisdom enough to manage them?

Yes.

And oh! let me put another case, I said: There is the great king, and he has an eldest son, who is the Prince of Asia;—suppose that you and I go to him and establish to his satisfaction that we are better cooks than his son, will he not entrust to us the prerogative of making soup, and putting in anything that we like while the pot is boiling, rather than to the Prince of Asia, who is his son?

To us, clearly.

And we shall be allowed to throw in salt by handfuls, whereas the son will not be allowed to put in as much as he can take up between his fingers?

Of course.

Or suppose again that the son has bad eyes, will he allow him, or will he not allow him, to touch his own eyes if he thinks that he has no knowledge of medicine?

He will not allow him.

Whereas, if he supposes us to have a knowledge of medicine, he will allow us to do what we like with him—even to open the eyes wide and sprinkle ashes upon them, because he supposes that we know what is best?

That is true.

And everything in which we appear to him to be wiser than himself or his son he will commit to us?

That is very true, Socrates, he replied.

Then now, my dear Lysis, I said, you perceive that in things which we know every one will trust us,—Hellenes and barbarians, men and women,—and we may do as we please about them, and no one will like to interfere with us; we shall be free, and masters of others; and these things will be really ours, for we shall be benefited by them. But in things of which we have no understanding, no one will trust us to do as seems good to us—they will hinder us as far as they can; and not only strangers, but father and mother, and the friend, if there be one, who is dearer still, will also hinder us; and we shall be subject to others; and these things will not be ours, for we shall not be benefited by them. Do you agree?

He assented.

And shall we be friends to others, and will any others love us, in as far as we are useless to them?

Certainly not.

Neither can your father or mother love you, nor can anybody love anybody else, in so far as they are useless to them?

No.

And therefore, my boy, if you are wise, all men will be your friends and kindred, for you will be useful and good; but if you are not wise, neither father, nor mother, nor kindred, nor any one else, will be your friends. And in matters of which you have as yet no knowledge, can you have any conceit of knowledge?

That is impossible, he replied.

And you, Lysis, if you require a teacher, have not yet attained to wisdom.

True.

And therefore you are not conceited, having nothing of which to be conceited.

Indeed, Socrates, I think not.

When I heard him say this, I turned to Hippothales, and was very nearly making a blunder, for I was going to say to him: That is the way, Hippothales, in which you should talk to your beloved, humbling and lowering him, and not as you do, puffing him up and spoiling him. But I saw that he was in great excitement and confusion at what had been said, and I remembered that, although he was in the neighbourhood, he did not want to be seen by Lysis; so upon second thoughts I refrained.

In the meantime Menexenus came back and sat down in his place by Lysis; and Lysis, in a childish and affectionate manner, whispered privately in my ear, so that Menexenus should not hear: Do, Socrates, tell Menexenus what you have been telling me.

Suppose that you tell him yourself, Lysis, I replied; for I am sure that you were attending.

Certainly, he replied.

Try, then, to remember the words, and be as exact as you can in repeating them to him, and if you have forgotten anything, ask me again the next time that you see me.

I will be sure to do so, Socrates; but go on telling him something new, and let me hear, as long as I am allowed to stay.

I certainly cannot refuse, I said, since you ask me; but then, as you know, Menexenus is very pugnacious, and therefore you must come to the rescue if he attempts to upset me.

Yes, indeed, he said; he is very pugnacious, and that is the reason why I want you to argue with him.

That I may make a fool of myself?

No, indeed, he said; but I want you to put him down.

That is no easy matter, I replied; for he is a terrible fellow—a pupil of Ctesippus. And there is Ctesippus himself: do you see him?

Never mind, Socrates, you shall argue with him.

Well, I suppose that I must, I replied.

Hereupon Ctesippus complained that we were talking in secret, and keeping the feast to ourselves.

I shall be happy, I said, to let you have a share. Here is Lysis, who does not understand something that I was saying, and wants me to ask Menexenus, who, as he thinks, is likely to know.

And why do you not ask him? he said.

Very well, I said, I will; and do you, Menexenus, answer. But first I must tell you that I am one who from my childhood upward have set my heart upon a certain thing. All people have their fancies; some desire horses, and others dogs; and some are fond of gold, and others of honour. Now, I have no violent desire of any of these things; but I have a passion for friends; and I would rather have a good friend than the best cock or quail in the world: I would even go further, and say the best horse or dog. Yea, by the dog of Egypt, I should greatly prefer a real friend to all the gold of Darius, or even to Darius himself: I am such a lover of friends as that. And when I see you and Lysis, at your early age, so easily possessed of this treasure, and so soon, he of you, and you of him, I am amazed and delighted, seeing that I myself, although I am now advanced in years, am so far from having made a similar acquisition, that I do not even know in what way a friend is acquired. But I want to ask you a question about this, for you have experience: tell me then, when one loves another, is the lover or the beloved the friend; or may either be the friend?

Either may, I should think, be the friend of either.

Do you mean, I said, that if only one of them loves the other, they are mutual friends?

Yes, he said; that is my meaning.

But what if the lover is not loved in return? which is a very possible case.

Yes.

Or is, perhaps, even hated? which is a fancy which sometimes is entertained by lovers respecting their beloved. Nothing can exceed their love; and yet they imagine either that they are not loved in return, or that they are hated. Is not that true?

Yes, he said, quite true.

In that case, the one loves, and the other is loved?

Yes.

Then which is the friend of which? Is the lover the friend of the beloved, whether he be loved in return, or hated; or is the beloved the friend; or is there no friendship at all on either side, unless they both love one another?

There would seem to be none at all.

Then this notion is not in accordance with our previous one. We were saying that both were friends, if one only loved; but now, unless they both love, neither is a friend.

That appears to be true.

Then nothing which does not love in return is beloved by a lover?

I think not.

Then they are not lovers of horses, whom the horses do not love in return; nor lovers of quails, nor of dogs, nor of wine, nor of gymnastic exercises, who have no return of love; no, nor of wisdom, unless wisdom loves them in return. Or shall we say that they do love them, although they are not beloved by them; and that the poet was wrong who sings—

'Happy the man to whom his children are dear, and steeds having single hoofs, and dogs of chase, and the stranger of another land'?

I do not think that he was wrong.

You think that he is right?

Yes.

Then, Menexenus, the conclusion is, that what is beloved, whether loving or hating, may be dear to the lover of it: for example, very young children, too young to love, or even hating their father or mother when they are punished by them, are never dearer to them than at the time when they are being hated by them.

I think that what you say is true.

And, if so, not the lover, but the beloved, is the friend or dear one?

Yes.

And the hated one, and not the hater, is the enemy?

Clearly.

Then many men are loved by their enemies, and hated by their friends, and are the friends of their enemies, and the enemies of their friends. Yet how absurd, my dear friend, or indeed impossible is this paradox of a man being an enemy to his friend or a friend to his enemy.

I quite agree, Socrates, in what you say.

But if this cannot be, the lover will be the friend of that which is loved?

True.

And the hater will be the enemy of that which is hated?

Certainly.

Yet we must acknowledge in this, as in the preceding instance, that a man may be the friend of one who is not his friend, or who may be his enemy, when he loves that which does not love him or which even hates him. And he may be the enemy of one who is not his enemy, and is even his friend: for example, when he hates that which does not hate him, or which even loves him.

That appears to be true.

But if the lover is not a friend, nor the beloved a friend, nor both together, what are we to say? Whom are we to call friends to one another? Do any remain?

Indeed, Socrates, I cannot find any.

But, O Menexenus! I said, may we not have been altogether wrong in our conclusions?

I am sure that we have been wrong, Socrates, said Lysis. And he blushed as he spoke, the words seeming to come from his lips involuntarily, because his whole mind was taken up with the argument; there was no mistaking his attentive look while he was listening.

I was pleased at the interest which was shown by Lysis, and I wanted to give Menexenus a rest, so I turned to him and said, I think, Lysis, that what you say is true, and that, if we had been right, we should never have gone so far wrong; let us proceed no further in this direction (for the road seems to be getting troublesome), but take the other path into which we turned, and see what the poets have to say; for they are to us in a manner the fathers and authors of wisdom, and they speak of friends in no light or trivial manner, but God himself, as they say, makes them and draws them to one another; and this they express, if I am not mistaken, in the following words:—

'God is ever drawing like towards like, and making them acquainted.'

I dare say that you have heard those words.

Yes, he said; I have.

And have you not also met with the treatises of philosophers who say that like must love like? they are the people who argue and write about nature and the universe.

Very true, he replied.

And are they right in saying this?

They may be.

Perhaps, I said, about half, or possibly, altogether, right, if their meaning were rightly apprehended by us. For the more a bad man has to do with a bad man, and the more nearly he is brought into contact with him, the more he will be likely to hate him, for he injures him; and injurer and injured cannot be friends. Is not that true?

Yes, he said.

Then one half of the saying is untrue, if the wicked are like one another?

That is true.

But the real meaning of the saying, as I imagine, is, that the good are like one another, and friends to one another; and that the bad, as is often said of them, are never at unity with one another or with themselves; for they are passionate and restless, and anything which is at variance and enmity with itself is not likely to be in union or harmony with any other thing. Do you not agree?

Yes, I do.

Then, my friend, those who say that the like is friendly to the like mean to intimate, if I rightly apprehend them, that the good only is the friend of the good, and of him only; but that the evil never attains to any real friendship, either with good or evil. Do you agree?

He nodded assent.

Then now we know how to answer the question 'Who are friends?' for the argument declares 'That the good are friends.'

Yes, he said, that is true.

Yes, I replied; and yet I am not quite satisfied with this answer. By heaven, and shall I tell you what I suspect? I will. Assuming that like, inasmuch as he is like, is the friend of like, and useful to him—or rather let me try another way of putting the matter: Can like do any good or harm to like which he could not do to himself, or suffer anything from his like which he would not suffer from himself? And if neither can be of any use to the other, how can they be loved by one another? Can they now?

They cannot.

And can he who is not loved be a friend?

Certainly not.

But say that the like is not the friend of the like in so far as he is like; still the good may be the friend of the good in so far as he is good?

True.

But then again, will not the good, in so far as he is good, be sufficient for himself? Certainly he will. And he who is sufficient wants nothing—that is implied in the word sufficient.

Of course not.

And he who wants nothing will desire nothing?

He will not.

Neither can he love that which he does not desire?

He cannot.

And he who loves not is not a lover or friend?

Clearly not.

What place then is there for friendship, if, when absent, good men have no need of one another (for even when alone they are sufficient for themselves), and when present have no use of one another? How can such persons ever be induced to value one another?

They cannot.

And friends they cannot be, unless they value one another?

Very true.

But see now, Lysis, whether we are not being deceived in all this—are we not indeed entirely wrong?

How so? he replied.

Have I not heard some one say, as I just now recollect, that the like is the greatest enemy of the like, the good of the good?—Yes, and he quoted the authority of Hesiod, who says:

'Potter quarrels with potter, bard with bard, Beggar with beggar;'

and of all other things he affirmed, in like manner, 'That of necessity the most like are most full of envy, strife, and hatred of one another, and the most unlike, of friendship. For the poor man is compelled to be the friend of the rich, and the weak requires the aid of the strong, and the sick man of the physician; and every one who is ignorant, has to love and court him who knows.' And indeed he went on to say in grandiloquent language, that the idea of friendship existing between similars is not the truth, but the very reverse of the truth, and that the most opposed are the most friendly; for that everything desires not like but that which is most unlike: for example, the dry desires the moist, the cold the hot, the bitter the sweet, the sharp the blunt, the void the full, the full the void, and so of all other things; for the opposite is the food of the opposite, whereas like receives nothing from like. And I thought that he who said this was a charming man, and that he spoke well. What do the rest of you say?

I should say, at first hearing, that he is right, said Menexenus.

Then we are to say that the greatest friendship is of opposites?

Exactly.

Yes, Menexenus; but will not that be a monstrous answer? and will not the all-wise eristics be down upon us in triumph, and ask, fairly enough, whether love is not the very opposite of hate; and what answer shall we make to them—must we not admit that they speak the truth?

We must.

They will then proceed to ask whether the enemy is the friend of the friend, or the friend the friend of the enemy?

Neither, he replied.

Well, but is a just man the friend of the unjust, or the temperate of the intemperate, or the good of the bad?

I do not see how that is possible.

And yet, I said, if friendship goes by contraries, the contraries must be friends.

They must.

Then neither like and like nor unlike and unlike are friends.

I suppose not.

And yet there is a further consideration: may not all these notions of friendship be erroneous? but may not that which is neither good nor evil still in some cases be the friend of the good?

How do you mean? he said.

Why really, I said, the truth is that I do not know; but my head is dizzy with thinking of the argument, and therefore I hazard the conjecture, that 'the beautiful is the friend,' as the old proverb says. Beauty is certainly a soft, smooth, slippery thing, and therefore of a nature which easily slips in and permeates our souls. For I affirm that the good is the beautiful. You will agree to that?

Yes.

This I say from a sort of notion that what is neither good nor evil is the friend of the beautiful and the good, and I will tell you why I am inclined to think so: I assume that there are three principles—the good, the bad, and that which is neither good nor bad. You would agree—would you not?

I agree.

And neither is the good the friend of the good, nor the evil of the evil, nor the good of the evil;—these alternatives are excluded by the previous argument; and therefore, if there be such a thing as friendship or love at all, we must infer that what is neither good nor evil must be the friend, either of the good, or of that which is neither good nor evil, for nothing can be the friend of the bad.

True.

But neither can like be the friend of like, as we were just now saying.

True.

And if so, that which is neither good nor evil can have no friend which is neither good nor evil.

Clearly not.

Then the good alone is the friend of that only which is neither good nor evil.

That may be assumed to be certain.

And does not this seem to put us in the right way? Just remark, that the body which is in health requires neither medical nor any other aid, but is well enough; and the healthy man has no love of the physician, because he is in health.

He has none.

But the sick loves him, because he is sick?

Certainly.

And sickness is an evil, and the art of medicine a good and useful thing?

Yes.

But the human body, regarded as a body, is neither good nor evil?

True.

And the body is compelled by reason of disease to court and make friends of the art of medicine?

Yes.

Then that which is neither good nor evil becomes the friend of good, by reason of the presence of evil?

So we may infer.

And clearly this must have happened before that which was neither good nor evil had become altogether corrupted with the element of evil—if itself had become evil it would not still desire and love the good; for, as we were saying, the evil cannot be the friend of the good.

Impossible.

Further, I must observe that some substances are assimilated when others are present with them; and there are some which are not assimilated: take, for example, the case of an ointment or colour which is put on another substance.

Very good.

In such a case, is the substance which is anointed the same as the colour or ointment?

What do you mean? he said.

This is what I mean: Suppose that I were to cover your auburn locks with white lead, would they be really white, or would they only appear to be white?

They would only appear to be white, he replied.

And yet whiteness would be present in them?

True.

But that would not make them at all the more white, notwithstanding the presence of white in them—they would not be white any more than black?

No.

But when old age infuses whiteness into them, then they become assimilated, and are white by the presence of white.

Certainly.

Now I want to know whether in all cases a substance is assimilated by the presence of another substance; or must the presence be after a peculiar sort?

The latter, he said.

Then that which is neither good nor evil may be in the presence of evil, but not as yet evil, and that has happened before now?

Yes.

And when anything is in the presence of evil, not being as yet evil, the presence of good arouses the desire of good in that thing; but the presence of evil, which makes a thing evil, takes away the desire and friendship of the good; for that which was once both good and evil has now become evil only, and the good was supposed to have no friendship with the evil?

None.

And therefore we say that those who are already wise, whether Gods or men, are no longer lovers of wisdom; nor can they be lovers of wisdom who are ignorant to the extent of being evil, for no evil or ignorant person is a lover of wisdom. There remain those who have the misfortune to be ignorant, but are not yet hardened in their ignorance, or void of understanding, and do not as yet fancy that they know what they do not know: and therefore those who are the lovers of wisdom are as yet neither good nor bad. But the bad do not love wisdom any more than the good; for, as we have already seen, neither is unlike the friend of unlike, nor like of like. You remember that?

Yes, they both said.

And so, Lysis and Menexenus, we have discovered the nature of friendship—there can be no doubt of it: Friendship is the love which by reason of the presence of evil the neither good nor evil has of the good, either in the soul, or in the body, or anywhere.

They both agreed and entirely assented, and for a moment I rejoiced and was satisfied like a huntsman just holding fast his prey. But then a most unaccountable suspicion came across me, and I felt that the conclusion was untrue. I was pained, and said, Alas! Lysis and Menexenus, I am afraid that we have been grasping at a shadow only.

Why do you say so? said Menexenus.

I am afraid, I said, that the argument about friendship is false: arguments, like men, are often pretenders.

How do you mean? he asked.

Well, I said; look at the matter in this way: a friend is the friend of some one; is he not?

Certainly he is.

And has he a motive and object in being a friend, or has he no motive and object?

He has a motive and object.

And is the object which makes him a friend, dear to him, or neither dear nor hateful to him?

I do not quite follow you, he said.

I do not wonder at that, I said. But perhaps, if I put the matter in another way, you will be able to follow me, and my own meaning will be clearer to myself. The sick man, as I was just now saying, is the friend of the physician—is he not?

Yes.

And he is the friend of the physician because of disease, and for the sake of health?

Yes.

And disease is an evil?

Certainly.

And what of health? I said. Is that good or evil, or neither?

Good, he replied.

And we were saying, I believe, that the body being neither good nor evil, because of disease, that is to say because of evil, is the friend of medicine, and medicine is a good: and medicine has entered into this friendship for the sake of health, and health is a good.

True.

And is health a friend, or not a friend?

A friend.

And disease is an enemy?

Yes.

Then that which is neither good nor evil is the friend of the good because of the evil and hateful, and for the sake of the good and the friend?

Clearly.

Then the friend is a friend for the sake of the friend, and because of the enemy?

That is to be inferred.

Then at this point, my boys, let us take heed, and be on our guard against deceptions. I will not again repeat that the friend is the friend of the friend, and the like of the like, which has been declared by us to be an impossibility; but, in order that this new statement may not delude us, let us attentively examine another point, which I will proceed to explain: Medicine, as we were saying, is a friend, or dear to us for the sake of health?

Yes.

And health is also dear?

Certainly.

And if dear, then dear for the sake of something?

Yes.

And surely this object must also be dear, as is implied in our previous admissions?

Yes.

And that something dear involves something else dear?

Yes.

But then, proceeding in this way, shall we not arrive at some first principle of friendship or dearness which is not capable of being referred to any other, for the sake of which, as we maintain, all other things are dear, and, having there arrived, we shall stop?

True.

My fear is that all those other things, which, as we say, are dear for the sake of another, are illusions and deceptions only, but where that first principle is, there is the true ideal of friendship. Let me put the matter thus: Suppose the case of a great treasure (this may be a son, who is more precious to his father than all his other treasures); would not the father, who values his son above all things, value other things also for the sake of his son? I mean, for instance, if he knew that his son had drunk hemlock, and the father thought that wine would save him, he would value the wine?

He would.

And also the vessel which contains the wine?

Certainly.

But does he therefore value the three measures of wine, or the earthen vessel which contains them, equally with his son? Is not this rather the true state of the case? All his anxiety has regard not to the means which are provided for the sake of an object, but to the object for the sake of which they are provided. And although we may often say that gold and silver are highly valued by us, that is not the truth; for there is a further object, whatever it may be, which we value most of all, and for the sake of which gold and all our other possessions are acquired by us. Am I not right?

Yes, certainly.

And may not the same be said of the friend? That which is only dear to us for the sake of something else is improperly said to be dear, but the truly dear is that in which all these so-called dear friendships terminate.

That, he said, appears to be true.

And the truly dear or ultimate principle of friendship is not for the sake of any other or further dear.

True.

Then we have done with the notion that friendship has any further object. May we then infer that the good is the friend?

I think so.

And the good is loved for the sake of the evil? Let me put the case in this way: Suppose that of the three principles, good, evil, and that which is neither good nor evil, there remained only the good and the neutral, and that evil went far away, and in no way affected soul or body, nor ever at all that class of things which, as we say, are neither good nor evil in themselves;—would the good be of any use, or other than useless to us? For if there were nothing to hurt us any longer, we should have no need of anything that would do us good. Then would be clearly seen that we did but love and desire the good because of the evil, and as the remedy of the evil, which was the disease; but if there had been no disease, there would have been no need of a remedy. Is not this the nature of the good—to be loved by us who are placed between the two, because of the evil? but there is no use in the good for its own sake.

I suppose not.

Then the final principle of friendship, in which all other friendships terminated, those, I mean, which are relatively dear and for the sake of something else, is of another and a different nature from them. For they are called dear because of another dear or friend. But with the true friend or dear, the case is quite the reverse; for that is proved to be dear because of the hated, and if the hated were away it would be no longer dear.

Very true, he replied: at any rate not if our present view holds good.

But, oh! will you tell me, I said, whether if evil were to perish, we should hunger any more, or thirst any more, or have any similar desire? Or may we suppose that hunger will remain while men and animals remain, but not so as to be hurtful? And the same of thirst and the other desires,—that they will remain, but will not be evil because evil has perished? Or rather shall I say, that to ask what either will be then or will not be is ridiculous, for who knows? This we do know, that in our present condition hunger may injure us, and may also benefit us:—Is not that true?

Yes.

And in like manner thirst or any similar desire may sometimes be a good and sometimes an evil to us, and sometimes neither one nor the other?

To be sure.

But is there any reason why, because evil perishes, that which is not evil should perish with it?

None.

Then, even if evil perishes, the desires which are neither good nor evil will remain?

Clearly they will.

And must not a man love that which he desires and affects?

He must.

Then, even if evil perishes, there may still remain some elements of love or friendship?

Yes.

But not if evil is the cause of friendship: for in that case nothing will be the friend of any other thing after the destruction of evil; for the effect cannot remain when the cause is destroyed.

True.

And have we not admitted already that the friend loves something for a reason? and at the time of making the admission we were of opinion that the neither good nor evil loves the good because of the evil?

Very true.

But now our view is changed, and we conceive that there must be some other cause of friendship?

I suppose so.

May not the truth be rather, as we were saying just now, that desire is the cause of friendship; for that which desires is dear to that which is desired at the time of desiring it? and may not the other theory have been only a long story about nothing?

Likely enough.

But surely, I said, he who desires, desires that of which he is in want?

Yes.

And that of which he is in want is dear to him?

True.

And he is in want of that of which he is deprived?

Certainly.

Then love, and desire, and friendship would appear to be of the natural or congenial. Such, Lysis and Menexenus, is the inference.

They assented.

Then if you are friends, you must have natures which are congenial to one another?

Certainly, they both said.

And I say, my boys, that no one who loves or desires another would ever have loved or desired or affected him, if he had not been in some way congenial to him, either in his soul, or in his character, or in his manners, or in his form.

Yes, yes, said Menexenus. But Lysis was silent.

Then, I said, the conclusion is, that what is of a congenial nature must be loved.

It follows, he said.

Then the lover, who is true and no counterfeit, must of necessity be loved by his love.

Lysis and Menexenus gave a faint assent to this; and Hippothales changed into all manner of colours with delight.

Here, intending to revise the argument, I said: Can we point out any difference between the congenial and the like? For if that is possible, then I think, Lysis and Menexenus, there may be some sense in our argument about friendship. But if the congenial is only the like, how will you get rid of the other argument, of the uselessness of like to like in as far as they are like; for to say that what is useless is dear, would be absurd? Suppose, then, that we agree to distinguish between the congenial and the like—in the intoxication of argument, that may perhaps be allowed.

Very true.

And shall we further say that the good is congenial, and the evil uncongenial to every one? Or again that the evil is congenial to the evil, and the good to the good; and that which is neither good nor evil to that which is neither good nor evil?

They agreed to the latter alternative.

Then, my boys, we have again fallen into the old discarded error; for the unjust will be the friend of the unjust, and the bad of the bad, as well as the good of the good.

That appears to be the result.

But again, if we say that the congenial is the same as the good, in that case the good and he only will be the friend of the good.

True.

But that too was a position of ours which, as you will remember, has been already refuted by ourselves.

We remember.

Then what is to be done? Or rather is there anything to be done? I can only, like the wise men who argue in courts, sum up the arguments:—If neither the beloved, nor the lover, nor the like, nor the unlike, nor the good, nor the congenial, nor any other of whom we spoke—for there were such a number of them that I cannot remember all—if none of these are friends, I know not what remains to be said.

Here I was going to invite the opinion of some older person, when suddenly we were interrupted by the tutors of Lysis and Menexenus, who came upon us like an evil apparition with their brothers, and bade them go home, as it was getting late. At first, we and the by-standers drove them off; but afterwards, as they would not mind, and only went on shouting in their barbarous dialect, and got angry, and kept calling the boys—they appeared to us to have been drinking rather too much at the Hermaea, which made them difficult to manage—we fairly gave way and broke up the company.

I said, however, a few words to the boys at parting: O Menexenus and Lysis, how ridiculous that you two boys, and I, an old boy, who would fain be one of you, should imagine ourselves to be friends—this is what the by-standers will go away and say—and as yet we have not been able to discover what is a friend!

MENEXENUS

by Plato

Translated by Benjamin Jowett

PERSONS OF THE DIALOGUE:

Socrates and Menexenus.

SOCRATES: Whence come you, Menexenus? Are you from the Agora?

MENEXENUS: Yes, Socrates; I have been at the Council.

SOCRATES: And what might you be doing at the Council? And yet I need hardly ask, for I see that you, believing yourself to have arrived at the end of education and of philosophy, and to have had enough of them, are mounting upwards to things higher still, and, though rather young for the post, are intending to govern us elder men, like the rest of your family, which has always provided some one who kindly took care of us.

MENEXENUS: Yes, Socrates, I shall be ready to hold office, if you allow and advise that I should, but not if you think otherwise. I went to the council chamber because I heard that the Council was about to choose some one who was to speak over the dead. For you know that there is to be a public funeral?

SOCRATES: Yes, I know. And whom did they choose?

MENEXENUS: No one; they delayed the election until tomorrow, but I believe that either Archinus or Dion will be chosen.

SOCRATES: O Menexenus! Death in battle is certainly in many respects a noble thing. The dead man gets a fine and costly funeral, although he may have been poor, and an elaborate speech is made over him by a wise man who has long ago prepared what he has to say, although he who is praised may not have been good for much. The speakers praise him for what he has done and for what he has not done—that is the beauty of them—and they steal away our souls with their embellished words; in every conceivable form they praise the city; and they praise those who died in war, and all our ancestors who went before us; and they praise ourselves also who are still alive, until I feel quite elevated by their laudations, and I stand listening to their words, Menexenus, and become enchanted by them, and all in a moment I imagine myself to have become a greater and nobler and finer man than I was before. And if, as often happens, there are any foreigners who accompany me to the speech, I become suddenly conscious of having a sort of triumph over them, and they seem to experience a corresponding feeling of admiration at me, and at the greatness of the city, which appears to them, when they are under the influence of the speaker, more wonderful than ever. This consciousness of dignity lasts me more than three days, and not until the fourth or fifth day do I come to my senses and know where I am; in the meantime I have been living in the Islands of the Blest. Such is the art of our rhetoricians, and in such manner does the sound of their words keep ringing in my ears.

MENEXENUS: You are always making fun of the rhetoricians, Socrates; this time, however, I am inclined to think that the speaker who is chosen will not have much to say, for he has been called upon to speak at a moment's notice, and he will be compelled almost to improvise.

SOCRATES: But why, my friend, should he not have plenty to say? Every rhetorician has speeches ready made; nor is there any difficulty in improvising that sort of stuff. Had the orator to praise Athenians among Peloponnesians, or Peloponnesians among Athenians, he must be a good rhetorician who could succeed and gain credit. But there is no difficulty in a man's winning applause when he is contending for fame among the persons whom he is praising.

MENEXENUS: Do you think not, Socrates?

SOCRATES: Certainly 'not.'

MENEXENUS: Do you think that you could speak yourself if there should be a necessity, and if the Council were to choose you?

SOCRATES: That I should be able to speak is no great wonder, Menexenus, considering that I have an excellent mistress in the art of rhetoric,—she who has made so many good speakers, and one who was the best among all the Hellenes—Pericles, the son of Xanthippus.

MENEXENUS: And who is she? I suppose that you mean Aspasia.

SOCRATES: Yes, I do; and besides her I had Connus, the son of Metrobius, as a master, and he was my master in music, as she was in rhetoric. No wonder that a man who has received such an education should be a finished speaker; even the pupil of very inferior masters, say, for example, one who had learned music of Lamprus, and rhetoric of Antiphon the Rhamnusian, might make a figure if he were to praise the Athenians among the Athenians.

MENEXENUS: And what would you be able to say if you had to speak?

SOCRATES: Of my own wit, most likely nothing; but yesterday I heard Aspasia composing a funeral oration about these very dead. For she had been told, as you were saying, that the Athenians were going to choose a speaker, and she repeated to me the sort of speech which he should deliver, partly improvising and partly from previous thought, putting together fragments of the funeral oration which Pericles spoke, but which, as I believe, she composed.

MENEXENUS: And can you remember what Aspasia said?

SOCRATES: I ought to be able, for she taught me, and she was ready to strike me because I was always forgetting.

MENEXENUS: Then why will you not rehearse what she said?

SOCRATES: Because I am afraid that my mistress may be angry with me if I publish her speech.

MENEXENUS: Nay, Socrates, let us have the speech, whether Aspasia's or any one else's, no matter. I hope that you will oblige me.

SOCRATES: But I am afraid that you will laugh at me if I continue the games of youth in old age.

MENEXENUS: Far otherwise, Socrates; let us by all means have the speech.

SOCRATES: Truly I have such a disposition to oblige you, that if you bid me dance naked I should not like to refuse, since we are alone. Listen then: If I remember rightly, she began as follows, with the mention of the dead:—(Thucyd.)

There is a tribute of deeds and of words. The departed have already had the first, when going forth on their destined journey they were attended on their way by the state and by their friends; the tribute of words remains to be given to them, as is meet and by law ordained. For noble words are a memorial and a crown of noble actions, which are given to the doers of them by the hearers. A word is needed which will duly praise the dead and gently admonish the living, exhorting the brethren and descendants of the departed to imitate their virtue, and consoling their fathers and mothers and the survivors, if any, who may chance to be alive of the previous generation. What sort of a word will this be, and how shall we rightly begin the praises of these brave men? In their life they rejoiced their own friends with their valour, and their death they gave in exchange for the salvation of the living. And I think that we should praise them in the order in which nature made them good, for they were good because they were sprung from good fathers. Wherefore let us first of all praise the goodness of their birth; secondly, their nurture and education; and then let us set forth how noble their actions were, and how worthy of the education which they had received.

And first as to their birth. Their ancestors were not strangers, nor are these their descendants sojourners only, whose fathers have come from another country; but they are the children of the soil, dwelling and living in their own land. And the country which brought them up is not like other countries, a stepmother to her children, but their own true mother; she bore them and nourished them and received them, and in her bosom they now repose. It is meet and right, therefore, that we should begin by praising the land which is their mother, and that will be a way of praising their noble birth.

The country is worthy to be praised, not only by us, but by all mankind; first, and above all, as being dear to the Gods. This is proved by the strife and contention of the Gods respecting her. And ought not the country which the Gods praise to be praised by all mankind? The second praise which may be fairly claimed by her, is that at the time when the whole earth was sending forth and creating diverse animals, tame and wild, she our mother was free and pure from savage monsters, and out of all animals selected and brought forth man, who is superior to the rest in understanding, and alone has justice and religion. And a great proof that she brought forth the common ancestors of us and of the departed, is that she provided the means of support for her offspring. For as a woman proves her motherhood by giving milk to her young ones (and she who has no fountain of milk is not a mother), so did this our land prove that she was the mother of men, for in those days she alone and first of all brought forth wheat and barley for human food, which is the best and noblest sustenance for man, whom she regarded as her true offspring. And these are truer proofs of motherhood in a country than in a woman, for the woman in her conception and generation is but the imitation of the earth, and not the earth of the woman. And of the fruit of the earth she gave a plenteous supply, not only to her own, but to others also; and afterwards she made the olive to spring up to be a boon to her children, and to help them in their toils. And when she had herself nursed them and brought them up to manhood, she gave them Gods to be their rulers and teachers, whose names are well known, and need not now be repeated. They are the Gods who first ordered our lives, and instructed us in the arts for the supply of our daily needs, and taught us the acquisition and use of arms for the defence of the country.

Thus born into the world and thus educated, the ancestors of the departed lived and made themselves a government, which I ought briefly to commemorate. For government is the nurture of man, and the government of good men is good, and of bad men bad. And I must show that our ancestors were trained under a good government, and for this reason they were good, and our contemporaries are also good, among whom our departed friends are to be reckoned. Then as now, and indeed always, from that time to this, speaking generally, our government was an aristocracy—a form of government which receives various names, according to the fancies of men, and is sometimes called democracy, but is really an aristocracy or government of the best which has the approval of the many. For kings we have always had, first hereditary and then elected, and authority is mostly in the hands of the people, who dispense offices and power to those who appear to be most deserving of them. Neither is a man rejected from weakness or poverty or obscurity of origin, nor honoured by reason of the opposite, as in other states, but there is one principle—he who appears to be wise and good is a governor and ruler. The basis of this our government is equality of birth; for other states are made up of all sorts and unequal conditions of men, and therefore their governments are unequal; there are tyrannies and there are oligarchies, in which the one party are slaves and the others masters. But we and our citizens are brethren, the children all of one mother, and we do not think it right to be one another's masters or servants; but the natural equality of birth compels us to seek for legal equality, and to recognize no superiority except in the reputation of virtue and wisdom.

And so their and our fathers, and these, too, our brethren, being nobly born and having been brought up in all freedom, did both in their public and private capacity many noble deeds famous over the whole world. They were the deeds of men who thought that they ought to fight both against Hellenes for the sake of Hellenes on behalf of freedom, and against barbarians in the common interest of Hellas. Time would fail me to tell of their defence of their country against the invasion of Eumolpus and the Amazons, or of their defence of the Argives against the Cadmeians, or of the Heracleids against the Argives; besides, the poets have already declared in song to all mankind their glory, and therefore any commemoration of their deeds in prose which we might attempt would hold a second place. They already have their reward, and I say no more of them; but there are other worthy deeds of which no poet has worthily sung, and which are still wooing the poet's muse. Of these I am bound to make honourable mention, and shall invoke others to sing of them also in lyric and other strains, in a manner becoming the actors. And first I will tell how the Persians, lords of Asia, were enslaving Europe, and how the children of this land, who were our fathers, held them back. Of these I will speak first, and praise their valour, as is meet and fitting. He who would rightly estimate them should place himself in thought at that time, when the whole of Asia was subject to the third king of Persia. The first king, Cyrus, by his valour freed the Persians, who were his countrymen, and subjected the Medes, who were their lords, and he ruled over the rest of Asia, as far as Egypt; and after him came his son, who ruled all the accessible part of Egypt and Libya; the third king was Darius, who extended the land boundaries of the empire to Scythia, and with his fleet held the sea and the islands. None presumed to be his equal; the minds of all men were enthralled by him—so many and mighty and warlike nations had the power of Persia subdued. Now Darius had a quarrel against us and the Eretrians, because, as he said, we had conspired against Sardis, and he sent 500,000 men in transports and vessels of war, and 300 ships, and Datis as commander, telling him to bring the Eretrians and Athenians to the king, if he wished to keep his head on his shoulders. He sailed against the Eretrians, who were reputed to be amongst the noblest and most warlike of the Hellenes of that day, and they were numerous, but he conquered them all in three days; and when he had conquered them, in order that no one might escape, he searched the whole country after this manner: his soldiers, coming to the borders of Eretria and spreading from sea to sea, joined hands and passed through the whole country, in order that they might be able to tell the king that no one had escaped them. And from Eretria they went to Marathon with a like intention, expecting to bind the Athenians in the same yoke of necessity in which they had bound the Eretrians. Having effected one-half of their purpose, they were in the act of attempting the other, and none of the Hellenes dared to assist either the Eretrians or the Athenians, except the Lacedaemonians, and they arrived a day too late for the battle; but the rest were panic-stricken and kept quiet, too happy in having escaped for a time. He who has present to his mind that conflict will know what manner of men they were who received the onset of the barbarians at Marathon, and chastened the pride of the whole of Asia, and by the victory which they gained over the barbarians first taught other men that the power of the Persians was not invincible, but that hosts of men and the multitude of riches alike yield to valour. And I assert that those men are the fathers not only of ourselves, but of our liberties and of the liberties of all who are on the continent, for that was the action to which the Hellenes looked back when they ventured to fight for their own safety in the battles which ensued: they became disciples of the men of Marathon. To them, therefore, I assign in my speech the first place, and the second to those who fought and conquered in the sea fights at Salamis and Artemisium; for of them, too, one might have many things to say—of the assaults which they endured by sea and land, and how they repelled them. I will mention only that act of theirs which appears to me to be the noblest, and which followed that of Marathon and came nearest to it; for the men of Marathon only showed the Hellenes that it was possible to ward off the barbarians by land, the many by the few; but there was no proof that they could be defeated by ships, and at sea the Persians retained the reputation of being invincible in numbers and wealth and skill and strength. This is the glory of the men who fought at sea, that they dispelled the second terror which had hitherto possessed the Hellenes, and so made the fear of numbers, whether of ships or men, to cease among them. And so the soldiers of Marathon and the sailors of Salamis became the schoolmasters of Hellas; the one teaching and habituating the Hellenes not to fear the barbarians at sea, and the others not to fear them by land. Third in order, for the number and valour of the combatants, and third in the salvation of Hellas, I place the battle of Plataea. And now the Lacedaemonians as well as the Athenians took part in the struggle; they were all united in this greatest and most terrible conflict of all; wherefore their virtues will be celebrated in times to come, as they are now celebrated by us. But at a later period many Hellenic tribes were still on the side of the barbarians, and there was a report that the great king was going to make a new attempt upon the Hellenes, and therefore justice requires that we should also make mention of those who crowned the previous work of our salvation, and drove and purged away all barbarians from the sea. These were the men who fought by sea at the river Eurymedon, and who went on the expedition to Cyprus, and who sailed to Egypt and divers other places; and they should be gratefully remembered by us, because they compelled the king in fear for himself to look to his own safety instead of plotting the destruction of Hellas.

And so the war against the barbarians was fought out to the end by the whole city on their own behalf, and on behalf of their countrymen. There was peace, and our city was held in honour; and then, as prosperity makes men jealous, there succeeded a jealousy of her, and jealousy begat envy, and so she became engaged against her will in a war with the Hellenes. On the breaking out of war, our citizens met the Lacedaemonians at Tanagra, and fought for the freedom of the Boeotians; the issue was doubtful, and was decided by the engagement which followed. For when the Lacedaemonians had gone on their way, leaving the Boeotians, whom they were aiding, on the third day after the battle of Tanagra, our countrymen conquered at Oenophyta, and righteously restored those who had been unrighteously exiled. And they were the first after the Persian war who fought on behalf of liberty in aid of Hellenes against Hellenes; they were brave men, and freed those whom they aided, and were the first too who were honourably interred in this sepulchre by the state. Afterwards there was a mighty war, in which all the Hellenes joined, and devastated our country, which was very ungrateful of them; and our countrymen, after defeating them in a naval engagement and taking their leaders, the Spartans, at Sphagia, when they might have destroyed them, spared their lives, and gave them back, and made peace, considering that they should war with the fellow-countrymen only until they gained a victory over them, and not because of the private anger of the state destroy the common interest of Hellas; but that with barbarians they should war to the death. Worthy of praise are they also who waged this war, and are here interred; for they proved, if any one doubted the superior prowess of the Athenians in the former war with the barbarians, that their doubts had no foundation—showing by their victory in the civil war with Hellas, in which they subdued the other chief state of the Hellenes, that they could conquer single-handed those with whom they had been allied in the war against the barbarians. After the peace there followed a third war, which was of a terrible and desperate nature, and in this many brave men who are here interred lost their lives—many of them had won victories in Sicily, whither they had gone over the seas to fight for the liberties of the Leontines, to whom they were bound by oaths; but, owing to the distance, the city was unable to help them, and they lost heart and came to misfortune, their very enemies and opponents winning more renown for valour and temperance than the friends of others. Many also fell in naval engagements at the Hellespont, after having in one day taken all the ships of the enemy, and defeated them in other naval engagements. And what I call the terrible and desperate nature of the war, is that the other Hellenes, in their extreme animosity towards the city, should have entered into negotiations with their bitterest enemy, the king of Persia, whom they, together with us, had expelled;—him, without us, they again brought back, barbarian against Hellenes, and all the hosts, both of Hellenes and barbarians, were united against Athens. And then shone forth the power and valour of our city. Her enemies had supposed that she was exhausted by the war, and our ships were blockaded at Mitylene. But the citizens themselves embarked, and came to the rescue with sixty other ships, and their valour was confessed of all men, for they conquered their enemies and delivered their friends. And yet by some evil fortune they were left to perish at sea, and therefore are not interred here. Ever to be remembered and honoured are they, for by their valour not only that sea-fight was won for us, but the entire war was decided by them, and through them the city gained the reputation of being invincible, even though attacked by all mankind. And that reputation was a true one, for the defeat which came upon us was our own doing. We were never conquered by others, and to this day we are still unconquered by them; but we were our own conquerors, and received defeat at our own hands. Afterwards there was quiet and peace abroad, but there sprang up war at home; and, if men are destined to have civil war, no one could have desired that his city should take the disorder in a milder form. How joyful and natural was the reconciliation of those who came from the Piraeus and those who came from the city; with what moderation did they order the war against the tyrants in Eleusis, and in a manner how unlike what the other Hellenes expected! And the reason of this gentleness was the veritable tie of blood, which created among them a friendship as of kinsmen, faithful not in word only, but in deed. And we ought also to remember those who then fell by one another's hands, and on such occasions as these to reconcile them with sacrifices and prayers, praying to those who have power over them, that they may be reconciled even as we are reconciled. For they did not attack one another out of malice or enmity, but they were unfortunate. And that such was the fact we ourselves are witnesses, who are of the same race with them, and have mutually received and granted forgiveness of what we have done and suffered. After this there was perfect peace, and the city had rest; and her feeling was that she forgave the barbarians, who had severely suffered at her hands and severely retaliated, but that she was indignant at the ingratitude of the Hellenes, when she remembered how they had received good from her and returned evil, having made common cause with the barbarians, depriving her of the ships which had once been their salvation, and dismantling our walls, which had preserved their own from falling. She thought that she would no longer defend the Hellenes, when enslaved either by one another or by the barbarians, and did accordingly. This was our feeling, while the Lacedaemonians were thinking that we who were the champions of liberty had fallen, and that their business was to subject the remaining Hellenes. And why should I say more? for the events of which I am speaking happened not long ago and we can all of us remember how the chief peoples of Hellas, Argives and Boeotians and Corinthians, came to feel the need of us, and, what is the greatest miracle of all, the Persian king himself was driven to such extremity as to come round to the opinion, that from this city, of which he was the destroyer, and from no other, his salvation would proceed.

And if a person desired to bring a deserved accusation against our city, he would find only one charge which he could justly urge—that she was too compassionate and too favourable to the weaker side. And in this instance she was not able to hold out or keep her resolution of refusing aid to her injurers when they were being enslaved, but she was softened, and did in fact send out aid, and delivered the Hellenes from slavery, and they were free until they afterwards enslaved themselves. Whereas, to the great king she refused to give the assistance of the state, for she could not forget the trophies of Marathon and Salamis and Plataea; but she allowed exiles and volunteers to assist him, and they were his salvation. And she herself, when she was compelled, entered into the war, and built walls and ships, and fought with the Lacedaemonians on behalf of the Parians. Now the king fearing this city and wanting to stand aloof, when he saw the Lacedaemonians growing weary of the war at sea, asked of us, as the price of his alliance with us and the other allies, to give up the Hellenes in Asia, whom the Lacedaemonians had previously handed over to him, he thinking that we should refuse, and that then he might have a pretence for withdrawing from us. About the other allies he was mistaken, for the Corinthians and Argives and Boeotians, and the other states, were quite willing to let them go, and swore and covenanted, that, if he would pay them money, they would make over to him the Hellenes of the continent, and we alone refused to give them up and swear. Such was the natural nobility of this city, so sound and healthy was the spirit of freedom among us, and the instinctive dislike of the barbarian, because we are pure Hellenes, having no admixture of barbarism in us. For we are not like many others, descendants of Pelops or Cadmus or Egyptus or Danaus, who are by nature barbarians, and yet pass for Hellenes, and dwell in the midst of us; but we are pure Hellenes, uncontaminated by any foreign element, and therefore the hatred of the foreigner has passed unadulterated into the life-blood of the city. And so, notwithstanding our noble sentiments, we were again isolated, because we were unwilling to be guilty of the base and unholy act of giving up Hellenes to barbarians. And we were in the same case as when we were subdued before; but, by the favour of Heaven, we managed better, for we ended the war without the loss of our ships or walls or colonies; the enemy was only too glad to be quit of us. Yet in this war we lost many brave men, such as were those who fell owing to the ruggedness of the ground at the battle of Corinth, or by treason at Lechaeum. Brave men, too, were those who delivered the Persian king, and drove the Lacedaemonians from the sea. I remind you of them, and you must celebrate them together with me, and do honour to their memories.

Such were the actions of the men who are here interred, and of others who have died on behalf of their country; many and glorious things I have spoken of them, and there are yet many more and more glorious things remaining to be told—many days and nights would not suffice to tell of them. Let them not be forgotten, and let every man remind their descendants that they also are soldiers who must not desert the ranks of their ancestors, or from cowardice fall behind. Even as I exhort you this day, and in all future time, whenever I meet with any of you, shall continue to remind and exhort you, O ye sons of heroes, that you strive to be the bravest of men. And I think that I ought now to repeat what your fathers desired to have said to you who are their survivors, when they went out to battle, in case anything happened to them. I will tell you what I heard them say, and what, if they had only speech, they would fain be saying, judging from what they then said. And you must imagine that you hear them saying what I now repeat to you:—

'Sons, the event proves that your fathers were brave men; for we might have lived dishonourably, but have preferred to die honourably rather than bring you and your children into disgrace, and rather than dishonour our own fathers and forefathers; considering that life is not life to one who is a dishonour to his race, and that to such a one neither men nor Gods are friendly, either while he is on the earth or after death in the world below. Remember our words, then, and whatever is your aim let virtue be the condition of the attainment of your aim, and know that without this all possessions and pursuits are dishonourable and evil. For neither does wealth bring honour to the owner, if he be a coward; of such a one the wealth belongs to another, and not to himself. Nor does beauty and strength of body, when dwelling in a base and cowardly man, appear comely, but the reverse of comely, making the possessor more conspicuous, and manifesting forth his cowardice. And all knowledge, when separated from justice and virtue, is seen to be cunning and not wisdom; wherefore make this your first and last and constant and all-absorbing aim, to exceed, if possible, not only us but all your ancestors in virtue; and know that to excel you in virtue only brings us shame, but that to be excelled by you is a source of happiness to us. And we shall most likely be defeated, and you will most likely be victors in the contest, if you learn so to order your lives as not to abuse or waste the reputation of your ancestors, knowing that to a man who has any self-respect, nothing is more dishonourable than to be honoured, not for his own sake, but on account of the reputation of his ancestors. The honour of parents is a fair and noble treasure to their posterity, but to have the use of a treasure of wealth and honour, and to leave none to your successors, because you have neither money nor reputation of your own, is alike base and dishonourable. And if you follow our precepts you will be received by us as friends, when the hour of destiny brings you hither; but if you neglect our words and are disgraced in your lives, no one will welcome or receive you. This is the message which is to be delivered to our children.

'Some of us have fathers and mothers still living, and we would urge them, if, as is likely, we shall die, to bear the calamity as lightly as possible, and not to condole with one another; for they have sorrows enough, and will not need any one to stir them up. While we gently heal their wounds, let us remind them that the Gods have heard the chief part of their prayers; for they prayed, not that their children might live for ever, but that they might be brave and renowned. And this, which is the greatest good, they have attained. A mortal man cannot expect to have everything in his own life turning out according to his will; and they, if they bear their misfortunes bravely, will be truly deemed brave fathers of the brave. But if they give way to their sorrows, either they will be suspected of not being our parents, or we of not being such as our panegyrists declare. Let not either of the two alternatives happen, but rather let them be our chief and true panegyrists, who show in their lives that they are true men, and had men for their sons. Of old the saying, "Nothing too much," appeared to be, and really was, well said. For he whose happiness rests with himself, if possible, wholly, and if not, as far as is possible,—who is not hanging in suspense on other men, or changing with the vicissitude of their fortune,—has his life ordered for the best. He is the temperate and valiant and wise; and when his riches come and go, when his children are given and taken away, he will remember the proverb—"Neither rejoicing overmuch nor grieving overmuch," for he relies upon himself. And such we would have our parents to be—that is our word and wish, and as such we now offer ourselves, neither lamenting overmuch, nor fearing overmuch, if we are to die at this time. And we entreat our fathers and mothers to retain these feelings throughout their future life, and to be assured that they will not please us by sorrowing and lamenting over us. But, if the dead have any knowledge of the living, they will displease us most by making themselves miserable and by taking their misfortunes too much to heart, and they will please us best if they bear their loss lightly and temperately. For our life will have the noblest end which is vouchsafed to man, and should be glorified rather than lamented. And if they will direct their minds to the care and nurture of our wives and children, they will soonest forget their misfortunes, and live in a better and nobler way, and be dearer to us.

'This is all that we have to say to our families: and to the state we would say—Take care of our parents and of our sons: let her worthily cherish the old age of our parents, and bring up our sons in the right way. But we know that she will of her own accord take care of them, and does not need any exhortation of ours.'

This, O ye children and parents of the dead, is the message which they bid us deliver to you, and which I do deliver with the utmost seriousness. And in their name I beseech you, the children, to imitate your fathers, and you, parents, to be of good cheer about yourselves; for we will nourish your age, and take care of you both publicly and privately in any place in which one of us may meet one of you who are the parents of the dead. And the care of you which the city shows, you know yourselves; for she has made provision by law concerning the parents and children of those who die in war; the highest authority is specially entrusted with the duty of watching over them above all other citizens, and they will see that your fathers and mothers have no wrong done to them. The city herself shares in the education of the children, desiring as far as it is possible that their orphanhood may not be felt by them; while they are children she is a parent to them, and when they have arrived at man's estate she sends them to their several duties, in full armour clad; and bringing freshly to their minds the ways of their fathers, she places in their hands the instruments of their fathers' virtues; for the sake of the omen, she would have them from the first begin to rule over their own houses arrayed in the strength and arms of their fathers. And as for the dead, she never ceases honouring them, celebrating in common for all rites which become the property of each; and in addition to this, holding gymnastic and equestrian contests, and musical festivals of every sort. She is to the dead in the place of a son and heir, and to their sons in the place of a father, and to their parents and elder kindred in the place of a guardian—ever and always caring for them. Considering this, you ought to bear your calamity the more gently; for thus you will be most endeared to the dead and to the living, and your sorrows will heal and be healed. And now do you and all, having lamented the dead in common according to the law, go your ways.

You have heard, Menexenus, the oration of Aspasia the Milesian.

MENEXENUS: Truly, Socrates, I marvel that Aspasia, who is only a woman, should be able to compose such a speech; she must be a rare one.

SOCRATES: Well, if you are incredulous, you may come with me and hear her.

MENEXENUS: I have often met Aspasia, Socrates, and know what she is like.

SOCRATES: Well, and do you not admire her, and are you not grateful for her speech?

MENEXENUS: Yes, Socrates, I am very grateful to her or to him who told you, and still more to you who have told me.

SOCRATES: Very good. But you must take care not to tell of me, and then at some future time I will repeat to you many other excellent political speeches of hers.

MENEXENUS: Fear not, only let me hear them, and I will keep the secret.

SOCRATES: Then I will keep my promise.

MENO

by Plato

Translated by Benjamin Jowett

PERSONS OF THE DIALOGUE:

Meno, Socrates, A Slave of Meno (Boy), Anytus.

MENO: Can you tell me, Socrates, whether virtue is acquired by teaching or by practice; or if neither by teaching nor by practice, then whether it comes to man by nature, or in what other way?

SOCRATES: O Meno, there was a time when the Thessalians were famous among the other Hellenes only for their riches and their riding; but now, if I am not mistaken, they are equally famous for their wisdom, especially at Larisa, which is the native city of your friend Aristippus. And this is Gorgias' doing; for when he came there, the flower of the Aleuadae, among them your admirer Aristippus, and the other chiefs of the Thessalians, fell in love with his wisdom. And he has taught you the habit of answering questions in a grand and bold style, which becomes those who know, and is the style in which he himself answers all comers; and any Hellene who likes may ask him anything. How different is our lot! my dear Meno. Here at Athens there is a dearth of the commodity, and all wisdom seems to have emigrated from us to you. I am certain that if you were to ask any Athenian whether virtue was natural or acquired, he would laugh in your face, and say: 'Stranger, you have far too good an opinion of me, if you think that I can answer your question. For I literally do not know what virtue is, and much less whether it is acquired by teaching or not.' And I myself, Meno, living as I do in this region of poverty, am as poor as the rest of the world; and I confess with shame that I know literally nothing about virtue; and when I do not know the 'quid' of anything how can I know the 'quale'? How, if I knew nothing at all of Meno, could I tell if he was fair, or the opposite of fair; rich and noble, or the reverse of rich and noble? Do you think that I could?

MENO: No, indeed. But are you in earnest, Socrates, in saying that you do not know what virtue is? And am I to carry back this report of you to Thessaly?

SOCRATES: Not only that, my dear boy, but you may say further that I have never known of any one else who did, in my judgment.

MENO: Then you have never met Gorgias when he was at Athens?

SOCRATES: Yes, I have.

MENO: And did you not think that he knew?

SOCRATES: I have not a good memory, Meno, and therefore I cannot now tell what I thought of him at the time. And I dare say that he did know, and that you know what he said: please, therefore, to remind me of what he said; or, if you would rather, tell me your own view; for I suspect that you and he think much alike.

MENO: Very true.

SOCRATES: Then as he is not here, never mind him, and do you tell me: By the gods, Meno, be generous, and tell me what you say that virtue is; for I shall be truly delighted to find that I have been mistaken, and that you and Gorgias do really have this knowledge; although I have been just saying that I have never found anybody who had.

MENO: There will be no difficulty, Socrates, in answering your question. Let us take first the virtue of a man—he should know how to administer the state, and in the administration of it to benefit his friends and harm his enemies; and he must also be careful not to suffer harm himself. A woman's virtue, if you wish to know about that, may also be easily described: her duty is to order her house, and keep what is indoors, and obey her husband. Every age, every condition of life, young or old, male or female, bond or free, has a different virtue: there are virtues numberless, and no lack of definitions of them; for virtue is relative to the actions and ages of each of us in all that we do. And the same may be said of vice, Socrates (Compare Arist. Pol.).

SOCRATES: How fortunate I am, Meno! When I ask you for one virtue, you present me with a swarm of them (Compare Theaet.), which are in your keeping. Suppose that I carry on the figure of the swarm, and ask of you, What is the nature of the bee? and you answer that there are many kinds of bees, and I reply: But do bees differ as bees, because there are many and different kinds of them; or are they not rather to be distinguished by some other quality, as for example beauty, size, or shape? How would you answer me?

MENO: I should answer that bees do not differ from one another, as bees.

SOCRATES: And if I went on to say: That is what I desire to know, Meno; tell me what is the quality in which they do not differ, but are all alike;—would you be able to answer?

MENO: I should.

SOCRATES: And so of the virtues, however many and different they may be, they have all a common nature which makes them virtues; and on this he who would answer the question, 'What is virtue?' would do well to have his eye fixed: Do you understand?

MENO: I am beginning to understand; but I do not as yet take hold of the question as I could wish.

SOCRATES: When you say, Meno, that there is one virtue of a man, another of a woman, another of a child, and so on, does this apply only to virtue, or would you say the same of health, and size, and strength? Or is the nature of health always the same, whether in man or woman?

MENO: I should say that health is the same, both in man and woman.

SOCRATES: And is not this true of size and strength? If a woman is strong, she will be strong by reason of the same form and of the same strength subsisting in her which there is in the man. I mean to say that strength, as strength, whether of man or woman, is the same. Is there any difference?

MENO: I think not.

SOCRATES: And will not virtue, as virtue, be the same, whether in a child or in a grown-up person, in a woman or in a man?

MENO: I cannot help feeling, Socrates, that this case is different from the others.

SOCRATES: But why? Were you not saying that the virtue of a man was to order a state, and the virtue of a woman was to order a house?

MENO: I did say so.

SOCRATES: And can either house or state or anything be well ordered without temperance and without justice?

MENO: Certainly not.

SOCRATES: Then they who order a state or a house temperately or justly order them with temperance and justice?

MENO: Certainly.

SOCRATES: Then both men and women, if they are to be good men and women, must have the same virtues of temperance and justice?

MENO: True.

SOCRATES: And can either a young man or an elder one be good, if they are intemperate and unjust?

MENO: They cannot.

SOCRATES: They must be temperate and just?

MENO: Yes.

SOCRATES: Then all men are good in the same way, and by participation in the same virtues?

MENO: Such is the inference.

SOCRATES: And they surely would not have been good in the same way, unless their virtue had been the same?

MENO: They would not.

SOCRATES: Then now that the sameness of all virtue has been proven, try and remember what you and Gorgias say that virtue is.

MENO: Will you have one definition of them all?

SOCRATES: That is what I am seeking.

MENO: If you want to have one definition of them all, I know not what to say, but that virtue is the power of governing mankind.

SOCRATES: And does this definition of virtue include all virtue? Is virtue the same in a child and in a slave, Meno? Can the child govern his father, or the slave his master; and would he who governed be any longer a slave?

MENO: I think not, Socrates.

SOCRATES: No, indeed; there would be small reason in that. Yet once more, fair friend; according to you, virtue is 'the power of governing;' but do you not add 'justly and not unjustly'?

MENO: Yes, Socrates; I agree there; for justice is virtue.

SOCRATES: Would you say 'virtue,' Meno, or 'a virtue'?

MENO: What do you mean?

SOCRATES: I mean as I might say about anything; that a round, for example, is 'a figure' and not simply 'figure,' and I should adopt this mode of speaking, because there are other figures.

MENO: Quite right; and that is just what I am saying about virtue—that there are other virtues as well as justice.

SOCRATES: What are they? tell me the names of them, as I would tell you the names of the other figures if you asked me.

MENO: Courage and temperance and wisdom and magnanimity are virtues; and there are many others.

SOCRATES: Yes, Meno; and again we are in the same case: in searching after one virtue we have found many, though not in the same way as before; but we have been unable to find the common virtue which runs through them all.

MENO: Why, Socrates, even now I am not able to follow you in the attempt to get at one common notion of virtue as of other things.

SOCRATES: No wonder; but I will try to get nearer if I can, for you know that all things have a common notion. Suppose now that some one asked you the question which I asked before: Meno, he would say, what is figure? And if you answered 'roundness,' he would reply to you, in my way of speaking, by asking whether you would say that roundness is 'figure' or 'a figure;' and you would answer 'a figure.'

MENO: Certainly.

SOCRATES: And for this reason—that there are other figures?

MENO: Yes.

SOCRATES: And if he proceeded to ask, What other figures are there? you would have told him.

MENO: I should.

SOCRATES: And if he similarly asked what colour is, and you answered whiteness, and the questioner rejoined, Would you say that whiteness is colour or a colour? you would reply, A colour, because there are other colours as well.

MENO: I should.

SOCRATES: And if he had said, Tell me what they are?—you would have told him of other colours which are colours just as much as whiteness.

MENO: Yes.

SOCRATES: And suppose that he were to pursue the matter in my way, he would say: Ever and anon we are landed in particulars, but this is not what I want; tell me then, since you call them by a common name, and say that they are all figures, even when opposed to one another, what is that common nature which you designate as figure—which contains straight as well as round, and is no more one than the other—that would be your mode of speaking?

MENO: Yes.

SOCRATES: And in speaking thus, you do not mean to say that the round is round any more than straight, or the straight any more straight than round?

MENO: Certainly not.

SOCRATES: You only assert that the round figure is not more a figure than the straight, or the straight than the round?

MENO: Very true.

SOCRATES: To what then do we give the name of figure? Try and answer. Suppose that when a person asked you this question either about figure or colour, you were to reply, Man, I do not understand what you want, or know what you are saying; he would look rather astonished and say: Do you not understand that I am looking for the 'simile in multis'? And then he might put the question in another form: Meno, he might say, what is that 'simile in multis' which you call figure, and which includes not only round and straight figures, but all? Could you not answer that question, Meno? I wish that you would try; the attempt will be good practice with a view to the answer about virtue.

MENO: I would rather that you should answer, Socrates.

SOCRATES: Shall I indulge you?

MENO: By all means.

SOCRATES: And then you will tell me about virtue?

MENO: I will.

SOCRATES: Then I must do my best, for there is a prize to be won.

MENO: Certainly.

SOCRATES: Well, I will try and explain to you what figure is. What do you say to this answer?—Figure is the only thing which always follows colour. Will you be satisfied with it, as I am sure that I should be, if you would let me have a similar definition of virtue?

MENO: But, Socrates, it is such a simple answer.

SOCRATES: Why simple?

MENO: Because, according to you, figure is that which always follows colour.

(SOCRATES: Granted.)

MENO: But if a person were to say that he does not know what colour is, any more than what figure is—what sort of answer would you have given him?

SOCRATES: I should have told him the truth. And if he were a philosopher of the eristic and antagonistic sort, I should say to him: You have my answer, and if I am wrong, your business is to take up the argument and refute me. But if we were friends, and were talking as you and I are now, I should reply in a milder strain and more in the dialectician's vein; that is to say, I should not only speak the truth, but I should make use of premises which the person interrogated would be willing to admit. And this is the way in which I shall endeavour to approach you. You will acknowledge, will you not, that there is such a thing as an end, or termination, or extremity?—all which words I use in the same sense, although I am aware that Prodicus might draw distinctions about them: but still you, I am sure, would speak of a thing as ended or terminated—that is all which I am saying—not anything very difficult.

MENO: Yes, I should; and I believe that I understand your meaning.

SOCRATES: And you would speak of a surface and also of a solid, as for example in geometry.

MENO: Yes.

SOCRATES: Well then, you are now in a condition to understand my definition of figure. I define figure to be that in which the solid ends; or, more concisely, the limit of solid.

MENO: And now, Socrates, what is colour?

SOCRATES: You are outrageous, Meno, in thus plaguing a poor old man to give you an answer, when you will not take the trouble of remembering what is Gorgias' definition of virtue.

MENO: When you have told me what I ask, I will tell you, Socrates.

SOCRATES: A man who was blindfolded has only to hear you talking, and he would know that you are a fair creature and have still many lovers.

MENO: Why do you think so?

SOCRATES: Why, because you always speak in imperatives: like all beauties when they are in their prime, you are tyrannical; and also, as I suspect, you have found out that I have weakness for the fair, and therefore to humour you I must answer.

MENO: Please do.

SOCRATES: Would you like me to answer you after the manner of Gorgias, which is familiar to you?

MENO: I should like nothing better.

SOCRATES: Do not he and you and Empedocles say that there are certain effluences of existence?

MENO: Certainly.

SOCRATES: And passages into which and through which the effluences pass?

MENO: Exactly.

SOCRATES: And some of the effluences fit into the passages, and some of them are too small or too large?

MENO: True.

SOCRATES: And there is such a thing as sight?

MENO: Yes.

SOCRATES: And now, as Pindar says, 'read my meaning:'—colour is an effluence of form, commensurate with sight, and palpable to sense.

MENO: That, Socrates, appears to me to be an admirable answer.

SOCRATES: Why, yes, because it happens to be one which you have been in the habit of hearing: and your wit will have discovered, I suspect, that you may explain in the same way the nature of sound and smell, and of many other similar phenomena.

MENO: Quite true.

SOCRATES: The answer, Meno, was in the orthodox solemn vein, and therefore was more acceptable to you than the other answer about figure.

MENO: Yes.

SOCRATES: And yet, O son of Alexidemus, I cannot help thinking that the other was the better; and I am sure that you would be of the same opinion, if you would only stay and be initiated, and were not compelled, as you said yesterday, to go away before the mysteries.

MENO: But I will stay, Socrates, if you will give me many such answers.

SOCRATES: Well then, for my own sake as well as for yours, I will do my very best; but I am afraid that I shall not be able to give you very many as good: and now, in your turn, you are to fulfil your promise, and tell me what virtue is in the universal; and do not make a singular into a plural, as the facetious say of those who break a thing, but deliver virtue to me whole and sound, and not broken into a number of pieces: I have given you the pattern.

MENO: Well then, Socrates, virtue, as I take it, is when he, who desires the honourable, is able to provide it for himself; so the poet says, and I say too—

'Virtue is the desire of things honourable and the power of attaining them.'

SOCRATES: And does he who desires the honourable also desire the good?

MENO: Certainly.

SOCRATES: Then are there some who desire the evil and others who desire the good? Do not all men, my dear sir, desire good?

MENO: I think not.

SOCRATES: There are some who desire evil?

MENO: Yes.

SOCRATES: Do you mean that they think the evils which they desire, to be good; or do they know that they are evil and yet desire them?

MENO: Both, I think.

SOCRATES: And do you really imagine, Meno, that a man knows evils to be evils and desires them notwithstanding?

MENO: Certainly I do.

SOCRATES: And desire is of possession?

MENO: Yes, of possession.

SOCRATES: And does he think that the evils will do good to him who possesses them, or does he know that they will do him harm?

MENO: There are some who think that the evils will do them good, and others who know that they will do them harm.

SOCRATES: And, in your opinion, do those who think that they will do them good know that they are evils?

MENO: Certainly not.

SOCRATES: Is it not obvious that those who are ignorant of their nature do not desire them; but they desire what they suppose to be goods although they are really evils; and if they are mistaken and suppose the evils to be goods they really desire goods?

MENO: Yes, in that case.

SOCRATES: Well, and do those who, as you say, desire evils, and think that evils are hurtful to the possessor of them, know that they will be hurt by them?

MENO: They must know it.

SOCRATES: And must they not suppose that those who are hurt are miserable in proportion to the hurt which is inflicted upon them?

MENO: How can it be otherwise?

SOCRATES: But are not the miserable ill-fated?

MENO: Yes, indeed.

SOCRATES: And does any one desire to be miserable and ill-fated?

MENO: I should say not, Socrates.

SOCRATES: But if there is no one who desires to be miserable, there is no one, Meno, who desires evil; for what is misery but the desire and possession of evil?

MENO: That appears to be the truth, Socrates, and I admit that nobody desires evil.

SOCRATES: And yet, were you not saying just now that virtue is the desire and power of attaining good?

MENO: Yes, I did say so.

SOCRATES: But if this be affirmed, then the desire of good is common to all, and one man is no better than another in that respect?

MENO: True.

SOCRATES: And if one man is not better than another in desiring good, he must be better in the power of attaining it?

MENO: Exactly.

SOCRATES: Then, according to your definition, virtue would appear to be the power of attaining good?

MENO: I entirely approve, Socrates, of the manner in which you now view this matter.

SOCRATES: Then let us see whether what you say is true from another point of view; for very likely you may be right:—You affirm virtue to be the power of attaining goods?

MENO: Yes.

SOCRATES: And the goods which you mean are such as health and wealth and the possession of gold and silver, and having office and honour in the state—those are what you would call goods?

MENO: Yes, I should include all those.

SOCRATES: Then, according to Meno, who is the hereditary friend of the great king, virtue is the power of getting silver and gold; and would you add that they must be gained piously, justly, or do you deem this to be of no consequence? And is any mode of acquisition, even if unjust and dishonest, equally to be deemed virtue?

MENO: Not virtue, Socrates, but vice.

SOCRATES: Then justice or temperance or holiness, or some other part of virtue, as would appear, must accompany the acquisition, and without them the mere acquisition of good will not be virtue.

MENO: Why, how can there be virtue without these?

SOCRATES: And the non-acquisition of gold and silver in a dishonest manner for oneself or another, or in other words the want of them, may be equally virtue?

MENO: True.

SOCRATES: Then the acquisition of such goods is no more virtue than the non-acquisition and want of them, but whatever is accompanied by justice or honesty is virtue, and whatever is devoid of justice is vice.

MENO: It cannot be otherwise, in my judgment.

SOCRATES: And were we not saying just now that justice, temperance, and the like, were each of them a part of virtue?

MENO: Yes.

SOCRATES: And so, Meno, this is the way in which you mock me.

MENO: Why do you say that, Socrates?

SOCRATES: Why, because I asked you to deliver virtue into my hands whole and unbroken, and I gave you a pattern according to which you were to frame your answer; and you have forgotten already, and tell me that virtue is the power of attaining good justly, or with justice; and justice you acknowledge to be a part of virtue.

MENO: Yes.

SOCRATES: Then it follows from your own admissions, that virtue is doing what you do with a part of virtue; for justice and the like are said by you to be parts of virtue.

MENO: What of that?

SOCRATES: What of that! Why, did not I ask you to tell me the nature of virtue as a whole? And you are very far from telling me this; but declare every action to be virtue which is done with a part of virtue; as though you had told me and I must already know the whole of virtue, and this too when frittered away into little pieces. And, therefore, my dear Meno, I fear that I must begin again and repeat the same question: What is virtue? for otherwise, I can only say, that every action done with a part of virtue is virtue; what else is the meaning of saying that every action done with justice is virtue? Ought I not to ask the question over again; for can any one who does not know virtue know a part of virtue?

MENO: No; I do not say that he can.

SOCRATES: Do you remember how, in the example of figure, we rejected any answer given in terms which were as yet unexplained or unadmitted?

MENO: Yes, Socrates; and we were quite right in doing so.

SOCRATES: But then, my friend, do not suppose that we can explain to any one the nature of virtue as a whole through some unexplained portion of virtue, or anything at all in that fashion; we should only have to ask over again the old question, What is virtue? Am I not right?

MENO: I believe that you are.

SOCRATES: Then begin again, and answer me, What, according to you and your friend Gorgias, is the definition of virtue?

MENO: O Socrates, I used to be told, before I knew you, that you were always doubting yourself and making others doubt; and now you are casting your spells over me, and I am simply getting bewitched and enchanted, and am at my wits' end. And if I may venture to make a jest upon you, you seem to me both in your appearance and in your power over others to be very like the flat torpedo fish, who torpifies those who come near him and touch him, as you have now torpified me, I think. For my soul and my tongue are really torpid, and I do not know how to answer you; and though I have been delivered of an infinite variety of speeches about virtue before now, and to many persons—and very good ones they were, as I thought—at this moment I cannot even say what virtue is. And I think that you are very wise in not voyaging and going away from home, for if you did in other places as you do in Athens, you would be cast into prison as a magician.

SOCRATES: You are a rogue, Meno, and had all but caught me.

MENO: What do you mean, Socrates?

SOCRATES: I can tell why you made a simile about me.

MENO: Why?

SOCRATES: In order that I might make another simile about you. For I know that all pretty young gentlemen like to have pretty similes made about them—as well they may—but I shall not return the compliment. As to my being a torpedo, if the torpedo is torpid as well as the cause of torpidity in others, then indeed I am a torpedo, but not otherwise; for I perplex others, not because I am clear, but because I am utterly perplexed myself. And now I know not what virtue is, and you seem to be in the same case, although you did once perhaps know before you touched me. However, I have no objection to join with you in the enquiry.

MENO: And how will you enquire, Socrates, into that which you do not know? What will you put forth as the subject of enquiry? And if you find what you want, how will you ever know that this is the thing which you did not know?

SOCRATES: I know, Meno, what you mean; but just see what a tiresome dispute you are introducing. You argue that a man cannot enquire either about that which he knows, or about that which he does not know; for if he knows, he has no need to enquire; and if not, he cannot; for he does not know the very subject about which he is to enquire (Compare Aristot. Post. Anal.).

MENO: Well, Socrates, and is not the argument sound?

SOCRATES: I think not.

MENO: Why not?

SOCRATES: I will tell you why: I have heard from certain wise men and women who spoke of things divine that—

MENO: What did they say?

SOCRATES: They spoke of a glorious truth, as I conceive.

MENO: What was it? and who were they?

SOCRATES: Some of them were priests and priestesses, who had studied how they might be able to give a reason of their profession: there have been poets also, who spoke of these things by inspiration, like Pindar, and many others who were inspired. And they say—mark, now, and see whether their words are true—they say that the soul of man is immortal, and at one time has an end, which is termed dying, and at another time is born again, but is never destroyed. And the moral is, that a man ought to live always in perfect holiness. 'For in the ninth year Persephone sends the souls of those from whom she has received the penalty of ancient crime back again from beneath into the light of the sun above, and these are they who become noble kings and mighty men and great in wisdom and are called saintly heroes in after ages.' The soul, then, as being immortal, and having been born again many times, and having seen all things that exist, whether in this world or in the world below, has knowledge of them all; and it is no wonder that she should be able to call to remembrance all that she ever knew about virtue, and about everything; for as all nature is akin, and the soul has learned all things; there is no difficulty in her eliciting or as men say learning, out of a single recollection all the rest, if a man is strenuous and does not faint; for all enquiry and all learning is but recollection. And therefore we ought not to listen to this sophistical argument about the impossibility of enquiry: for it will make us idle; and is sweet only to the sluggard; but the other saying will make us active and inquisitive. In that confiding, I will gladly enquire with you into the nature of virtue.

MENO: Yes, Socrates; but what do you mean by saying that we do not learn, and that what we call learning is only a process of recollection? Can you teach me how this is?

SOCRATES: I told you, Meno, just now that you were a rogue, and now you ask whether I can teach you, when I am saying that there is no teaching, but only recollection; and thus you imagine that you will involve me in a contradiction.

MENO: Indeed, Socrates, I protest that I had no such intention. I only asked the question from habit; but if you can prove to me that what you say is true, I wish that you would.

SOCRATES: It will be no easy matter, but I will try to please you to the utmost of my power. Suppose that you call one of your numerous attendants, that I may demonstrate on him.

MENO: Certainly. Come hither, boy.

SOCRATES: He is Greek, and speaks Greek, does he not?

MENO: Yes, indeed; he was born in the house.

SOCRATES: Attend now to the questions which I ask him, and observe whether he learns of me or only remembers.

MENO: I will.

SOCRATES: Tell me, boy, do you know that a figure like this is a square?

BOY: I do.

SOCRATES: And you know that a square figure has these four lines equal?

BOY: Certainly.

SOCRATES: And these lines which I have drawn through the middle of the square are also equal?

BOY: Yes.

SOCRATES: A square may be of any size?

BOY: Certainly.

SOCRATES: And if one side of the figure be of two feet, and the other side be of two feet, how much will the whole be? Let me explain: if in one direction the space was of two feet, and in the other direction of one foot, the whole would be of two feet taken once?

BOY: Yes.

SOCRATES: But since this side is also of two feet, there are twice two feet?

BOY: There are.

SOCRATES: Then the square is of twice two feet?

BOY: Yes.

SOCRATES: And how many are twice two feet? count and tell me.

BOY: Four, Socrates.

SOCRATES: And might there not be another square twice as large as this, and having like this the lines equal?

BOY: Yes.

SOCRATES: And of how many feet will that be?

BOY: Of eight feet.

SOCRATES: And now try and tell me the length of the line which forms the side of that double square: this is two feet—what will that be?

BOY: Clearly, Socrates, it will be double.

SOCRATES: Do you observe, Meno, that I am not teaching the boy anything, but only asking him questions; and now he fancies that he knows how long a line is necessary in order to produce a figure of eight square feet; does he not?

MENO: Yes.

SOCRATES: And does he really know?

MENO: Certainly not.

SOCRATES: He only guesses that because the square is double, the line is double.

MENO: True.

SOCRATES: Observe him while he recalls the steps in regular order. (To the Boy:) Tell me, boy, do you assert that a double space comes from a double line? Remember that I am not speaking of an oblong, but of a figure equal every way, and twice the size of this—that is to say of eight feet; and I want to know whether you still say that a double square comes from double line?

BOY: Yes.

SOCRATES: But does not this line become doubled if we add another such line here?

BOY: Certainly.

SOCRATES: And four such lines will make a space containing eight feet?

BOY: Yes.

SOCRATES: Let us describe such a figure: Would you not say that this is the figure of eight feet?

BOY: Yes.

SOCRATES: And are there not these four divisions in the figure, each of which is equal to the figure of four feet?

BOY: True.

SOCRATES: And is not that four times four?

BOY: Certainly.

SOCRATES: And four times is not double?

BOY: No, indeed.

SOCRATES: But how much?

BOY: Four times as much.

SOCRATES: Therefore the double line, boy, has given a space, not twice, but four times as much.

BOY: True.

SOCRATES: Four times four are sixteen—are they not?

BOY: Yes.

SOCRATES: What line would give you a space of eight feet, as this gives one of sixteen feet;—do you see?

BOY: Yes.

SOCRATES: And the space of four feet is made from this half line?

BOY: Yes.

SOCRATES: Good; and is not a space of eight feet twice the size of this, and half the size of the other?

BOY: Certainly.

SOCRATES: Such a space, then, will be made out of a line greater than this one, and less than that one?

BOY: Yes; I think so.

SOCRATES: Very good; I like to hear you say what you think. And now tell me, is not this a line of two feet and that of four?

BOY: Yes.

SOCRATES: Then the line which forms the side of eight feet ought to be more than this line of two feet, and less than the other of four feet?

BOY: It ought.

SOCRATES: Try and see if you can tell me how much it will be.

BOY: Three feet.

SOCRATES: Then if we add a half to this line of two, that will be the line of three. Here are two and there is one; and on the other side, here are two also and there is one: and that makes the figure of which you speak?

BOY: Yes.

SOCRATES: But if there are three feet this way and three feet that way, the whole space will be three times three feet?

BOY: That is evident.

SOCRATES: And how much are three times three feet?

BOY: Nine.

SOCRATES: And how much is the double of four?

BOY: Eight.

SOCRATES: Then the figure of eight is not made out of a line of three?

BOY: No.

SOCRATES: But from what line?—tell me exactly; and if you would rather not reckon, try and show me the line.

BOY: Indeed, Socrates, I do not know.

SOCRATES: Do you see, Meno, what advances he has made in his power of recollection? He did not know at first, and he does not know now, what is the side of a figure of eight feet: but then he thought that he knew, and answered confidently as if he knew, and had no difficulty; now he has a difficulty, and neither knows nor fancies that he knows.

MENO: True.

SOCRATES: Is he not better off in knowing his ignorance?

MENO: I think that he is.

SOCRATES: If we have made him doubt, and given him the 'torpedo's shock,' have we done him any harm?

MENO: I think not.

SOCRATES: We have certainly, as would seem, assisted him in some degree to the discovery of the truth; and now he will wish to remedy his ignorance, but then he would have been ready to tell all the world again and again that the double space should have a double side.

MENO: True.

SOCRATES: But do you suppose that he would ever have enquired into or learned what he fancied that he knew, though he was really ignorant of it, until he had fallen into perplexity under the idea that he did not know, and had desired to know?

MENO: I think not, Socrates.

SOCRATES: Then he was the better for the torpedo's touch?

MENO: I think so.

SOCRATES: Mark now the farther development. I shall only ask him, and not teach him, and he shall share the enquiry with me: and do you watch and see if you find me telling or explaining anything to him, instead of eliciting his opinion. Tell me, boy, is not this a square of four feet which I have drawn?

BOY: Yes.

SOCRATES: And now I add another square equal to the former one?

BOY: Yes.

SOCRATES: And a third, which is equal to either of them?

BOY: Yes.

SOCRATES: Suppose that we fill up the vacant corner?

BOY: Very good.

SOCRATES: Here, then, there are four equal spaces?

BOY: Yes.

SOCRATES: And how many times larger is this space than this other?

BOY: Four times.

SOCRATES: But it ought to have been twice only, as you will remember.

BOY: True.

SOCRATES: And does not this line, reaching from corner to corner, bisect each of these spaces?

BOY: Yes.

SOCRATES: And are there not here four equal lines which contain this space?

BOY: There are.

SOCRATES: Look and see how much this space is.

BOY: I do not understand.

SOCRATES: Has not each interior line cut off half of the four spaces?

BOY: Yes.

SOCRATES: And how many spaces are there in this section?

BOY: Four.

SOCRATES: And how many in this?

BOY: Two.

SOCRATES: And four is how many times two?

BOY: Twice.

SOCRATES: And this space is of how many feet?

BOY: Of eight feet.

SOCRATES: And from what line do you get this figure?

BOY: From this.

SOCRATES: That is, from the line which extends from corner to corner of the figure of four feet?

BOY: Yes.

SOCRATES: And that is the line which the learned call the diagonal. And if this is the proper name, then you, Meno's slave, are prepared to affirm that the double space is the square of the diagonal?

BOY: Certainly, Socrates.

SOCRATES: What do you say of him, Meno? Were not all these answers given out of his own head?

MENO: Yes, they were all his own.

SOCRATES: And yet, as we were just now saying, he did not know?

MENO: True.

SOCRATES: But still he had in him those notions of his—had he not?

MENO: Yes.

SOCRATES: Then he who does not know may still have true notions of that which he does not know?

MENO: He has.

SOCRATES: And at present these notions have just been stirred up in him, as in a dream; but if he were frequently asked the same questions, in different forms, he would know as well as any one at last?

MENO: I dare say.

SOCRATES: Without any one teaching him he will recover his knowledge for himself, if he is only asked questions?

MENO: Yes.

SOCRATES: And this spontaneous recovery of knowledge in him is recollection?

MENO: True.

SOCRATES: And this knowledge which he now has must he not either have acquired or always possessed?

MENO: Yes.

SOCRATES: But if he always possessed this knowledge he would always have known; or if he has acquired the knowledge he could not have acquired it in this life, unless he has been taught geometry; for he may be made to do the same with all geometry and every other branch of knowledge. Now, has any one ever taught him all this? You must know about him, if, as you say, he was born and bred in your house.

MENO: And I am certain that no one ever did teach him.

SOCRATES: And yet he has the knowledge?

MENO: The fact, Socrates, is undeniable.

SOCRATES: But if he did not acquire the knowledge in this life, then he must have had and learned it at some other time?

MENO: Clearly he must.

SOCRATES: Which must have been the time when he was not a man?

MENO: Yes.

SOCRATES: And if there have been always true thoughts in him, both at the time when he was and was not a man, which only need to be awakened into knowledge by putting questions to him, his soul must have always possessed this knowledge, for he always either was or was not a man?

MENO: Obviously.

SOCRATES: And if the truth of all things always existed in the soul, then the soul is immortal. Wherefore be of good cheer, and try to recollect what you do not know, or rather what you do not remember.

MENO: I feel, somehow, that I like what you are saying.

SOCRATES: And I, Meno, like what I am saying. Some things I have said of which I am not altogether confident. But that we shall be better and braver and less helpless if we think that we ought to enquire, than we should have been if we indulged in the idle fancy that there was no knowing and no use in seeking to know what we do not know;—that is a theme upon which I am ready to fight, in word and deed, to the utmost of my power.

MENO: There again, Socrates, your words seem to me excellent.

SOCRATES: Then, as we are agreed that a man should enquire about that which he does not know, shall you and I make an effort to enquire together into the nature of virtue?

MENO: By all means, Socrates. And yet I would much rather return to my original question, Whether in seeking to acquire virtue we should regard it as a thing to be taught, or as a gift of nature, or as coming to men in some other way?

SOCRATES: Had I the command of you as well as of myself, Meno, I would not have enquired whether virtue is given by instruction or not, until we had first ascertained 'what it is.' But as you think only of controlling me who am your slave, and never of controlling yourself,—such being your notion of freedom, I must yield to you, for you are irresistible. And therefore I have now to enquire into the qualities of a thing of which I do not as yet know the nature. At any rate, will you condescend a little, and allow the question 'Whether virtue is given by instruction, or in any other way,' to be argued upon hypothesis? As the geometrician, when he is asked whether a certain triangle is capable being inscribed in a certain circle (Or, whether a certain area is capable of being inscribed as a triangle in a certain circle.), will reply: 'I cannot tell you as yet; but I will offer a hypothesis which may assist us in forming a conclusion: If the figure be such that when you have produced a given side of it (Or, when you apply it to the given line, i.e. the diameter of the circle (autou).), the given area of the triangle falls short by an area corresponding to the part produced (Or, similar to the area so applied.), then one consequence follows, and if this is impossible then some other; and therefore I wish to assume a hypothesis before I tell you whether this triangle is capable of being inscribed in the circle':—that is a geometrical hypothesis. And we too, as we know not the nature and qualities of virtue, must ask, whether virtue is or is not taught, under a hypothesis: as thus, if virtue is of such a class of mental goods, will it be taught or not? Let the first hypothesis be that virtue is or is not knowledge,—in that case will it be taught or not? or, as we were just now saying, 'remembered'? For there is no use in disputing about the name. But is virtue taught or not? or rather, does not every one see that knowledge alone is taught?

MENO: I agree.

SOCRATES: Then if virtue is knowledge, virtue will be taught?

MENO: Certainly.

SOCRATES: Then now we have made a quick end of this question: if virtue is of such a nature, it will be taught; and if not, not?

MENO: Certainly.

SOCRATES: The next question is, whether virtue is knowledge or of another species?

MENO: Yes, that appears to be the question which comes next in order.

SOCRATES: Do we not say that virtue is a good?—This is a hypothesis which is not set aside.

MENO: Certainly.

SOCRATES: Now, if there be any sort of good which is distinct from knowledge, virtue may be that good; but if knowledge embraces all good, then we shall be right in thinking that virtue is knowledge?

MENO: True.

SOCRATES: And virtue makes us good?

MENO: Yes.

SOCRATES: And if we are good, then we are profitable; for all good things are profitable?

MENO: Yes.

SOCRATES: Then virtue is profitable?

MENO: That is the only inference.

SOCRATES: Then now let us see what are the things which severally profit us. Health and strength, and beauty and wealth—these, and the like of these, we call profitable?

MENO: True.

SOCRATES: And yet these things may also sometimes do us harm: would you not think so?

MENO: Yes.

SOCRATES: And what is the guiding principle which makes them profitable or the reverse? Are they not profitable when they are rightly used, and hurtful when they are not rightly used?

MENO: Certainly.

SOCRATES: Next, let us consider the goods of the soul: they are temperance, justice, courage, quickness of apprehension, memory, magnanimity, and the like?

MENO: Surely.

SOCRATES: And such of these as are not knowledge, but of another sort, are sometimes profitable and sometimes hurtful; as, for example, courage wanting prudence, which is only a sort of confidence? When a man has no sense he is harmed by courage, but when he has sense he is profited?

MENO: True.

SOCRATES: And the same may be said of temperance and quickness of apprehension; whatever things are learned or done with sense are profitable, but when done without sense they are hurtful?

MENO: Very true.

SOCRATES: And in general, all that the soul attempts or endures, when under the guidance of wisdom, ends in happiness; but when she is under the guidance of folly, in the opposite?

MENO: That appears to be true.

SOCRATES: If then virtue is a quality of the soul, and is admitted to be profitable, it must be wisdom or prudence, since none of the things of the soul are either profitable or hurtful in themselves, but they are all made profitable or hurtful by the addition of wisdom or of folly; and therefore if virtue is profitable, virtue must be a sort of wisdom or prudence?

MENO: I quite agree.

SOCRATES: And the other goods, such as wealth and the like, of which we were just now saying that they are sometimes good and sometimes evil, do not they also become profitable or hurtful, accordingly as the soul guides and uses them rightly or wrongly; just as the things of the soul herself are benefited when under the guidance of wisdom and harmed by folly?

MENO: True.

SOCRATES: And the wise soul guides them rightly, and the foolish soul wrongly.

MENO: Yes.

SOCRATES: And is not this universally true of human nature? All other things hang upon the soul, and the things of the soul herself hang upon wisdom, if they are to be good; and so wisdom is inferred to be that which profits—and virtue, as we say, is profitable?

MENO: Certainly.

SOCRATES: And thus we arrive at the conclusion that virtue is either wholly or partly wisdom?

MENO: I think that what you are saying, Socrates, is very true.

SOCRATES: But if this is true, then the good are not by nature good?

MENO: I think not.

SOCRATES: If they had been, there would assuredly have been discerners of characters among us who would have known our future great men; and on their showing we should have adopted them, and when we had got them, we should have kept them in the citadel out of the way of harm, and set a stamp upon them far rather than upon a piece of gold, in order that no one might tamper with them; and when they grew up they would have been useful to the state?

MENO: Yes, Socrates, that would have been the right way.

SOCRATES: But if the good are not by nature good, are they made good by instruction?

MENO: There appears to be no other alternative, Socrates. On the supposition that virtue is knowledge, there can be no doubt that virtue is taught.

SOCRATES: Yes, indeed; but what if the supposition is erroneous?

MENO: I certainly thought just now that we were right.

SOCRATES: Yes, Meno; but a principle which has any soundness should stand firm not only just now, but always.

MENO: Well; and why are you so slow of heart to believe that knowledge is virtue?

SOCRATES: I will try and tell you why, Meno. I do not retract the assertion that if virtue is knowledge it may be taught; but I fear that I have some reason in doubting whether virtue is knowledge: for consider now and say whether virtue, and not only virtue but anything that is taught, must not have teachers and disciples?

MENO: Surely.

SOCRATES: And conversely, may not the art of which neither teachers nor disciples exist be assumed to be incapable of being taught?

MENO: True; but do you think that there are no teachers of virtue?

SOCRATES: I have certainly often enquired whether there were any, and taken great pains to find them, and have never succeeded; and many have assisted me in the search, and they were the persons whom I thought the most likely to know. Here at the moment when he is wanted we fortunately have sitting by us Anytus, the very person of whom we should make enquiry; to him then let us repair. In the first place, he is the son of a wealthy and wise father, Anthemion, who acquired his wealth, not by accident or gift, like Ismenias the Theban (who has recently made himself as rich as Polycrates), but by his own skill and industry, and who is a well-conditioned, modest man, not insolent, or overbearing, or annoying; moreover, this son of his has received a good education, as the Athenian people certainly appear to think, for they choose him to fill the highest offices. And these are the sort of men from whom you are likely to learn whether there are any teachers of virtue, and who they are. Please, Anytus, to help me and your friend Meno in answering our question, Who are the teachers? Consider the matter thus: If we wanted Meno to be a good physician, to whom should we send him? Should we not send him to the physicians?

ANYTUS: Certainly.

SOCRATES: Or if we wanted him to be a good cobbler, should we not send him to the cobblers?

ANYTUS: Yes.

SOCRATES: And so forth?

ANYTUS: Yes.

SOCRATES: Let me trouble you with one more question. When we say that we should be right in sending him to the physicians if we wanted him to be a physician, do we mean that we should be right in sending him to those who profess the art, rather than to those who do not, and to those who demand payment for teaching the art, and profess to teach it to any one who will come and learn? And if these were our reasons, should we not be right in sending him?

ANYTUS: Yes.

SOCRATES: And might not the same be said of flute-playing, and of the other arts? Would a man who wanted to make another a flute-player refuse to send him to those who profess to teach the art for money, and be plaguing other persons to give him instruction, who are not professed teachers and who never had a single disciple in that branch of knowledge which he wishes him to acquire—would not such conduct be the height of folly?

ANYTUS: Yes, by Zeus, and of ignorance too.

SOCRATES: Very good. And now you are in a position to advise with me about my friend Meno. He has been telling me, Anytus, that he desires to attain that kind of wisdom and virtue by which men order the state or the house, and honour their parents, and know when to receive and when to send away citizens and strangers, as a good man should. Now, to whom should he go in order that he may learn this virtue? Does not the previous argument imply clearly that we should send him to those who profess and avouch that they are the common teachers of all Hellas, and are ready to impart instruction to any one who likes, at a fixed price?

ANYTUS: Whom do you mean, Socrates?

SOCRATES: You surely know, do you not, Anytus, that these are the people whom mankind call Sophists?

ANYTUS: By Heracles, Socrates, forbear! I only hope that no friend or kinsman or acquaintance of mine, whether citizen or stranger, will ever be so mad as to allow himself to be corrupted by them; for they are a manifest pest and corrupting influence to those who have to do with them.

SOCRATES: What, Anytus? Of all the people who profess that they know how to do men good, do you mean to say that these are the only ones who not only do them no good, but positively corrupt those who are entrusted to them, and in return for this disservice have the face to demand money? Indeed, I cannot believe you; for I know of a single man, Protagoras, who made more out of his craft than the illustrious Pheidias, who created such noble works, or any ten other statuaries. How could that be? A mender of old shoes, or patcher up of clothes, who made the shoes or clothes worse than he received them, could not have remained thirty days undetected, and would very soon have starved; whereas during more than forty years, Protagoras was corrupting all Hellas, and sending his disciples from him worse than he received them, and he was never found out. For, if I am not mistaken, he was about seventy years old at his death, forty of which were spent in the practice of his profession; and during all that time he had a good reputation, which to this day he retains: and not only Protagoras, but many others are well spoken of; some who lived before him, and others who are still living. Now, when you say that they deceived and corrupted the youth, are they to be supposed to have corrupted them consciously or unconsciously? Can those who were deemed by many to be the wisest men of Hellas have been out of their minds?

ANYTUS: Out of their minds! No, Socrates; the young men who gave their money to them were out of their minds, and their relations and guardians who entrusted their youth to the care of these men were still more out of their minds, and most of all, the cities who allowed them to come in, and did not drive them out, citizen and stranger alike.

SOCRATES: Has any of the Sophists wronged you, Anytus? What makes you so angry with them?

ANYTUS: No, indeed, neither I nor any of my belongings has ever had, nor would I suffer them to have, anything to do with them.

SOCRATES: Then you are entirely unacquainted with them?

ANYTUS: And I have no wish to be acquainted.

SOCRATES: Then, my dear friend, how can you know whether a thing is good or bad of which you are wholly ignorant?

ANYTUS: Quite well; I am sure that I know what manner of men these are, whether I am acquainted with them or not.

SOCRATES: You must be a diviner, Anytus, for I really cannot make out, judging from your own words, how, if you are not acquainted with them, you know about them. But I am not enquiring of you who are the teachers who will corrupt Meno (let them be, if you please, the Sophists); I only ask you to tell him who there is in this great city who will teach him how to become eminent in the virtues which I was just now describing. He is the friend of your family, and you will oblige him.

ANYTUS: Why do you not tell him yourself?

SOCRATES: I have told him whom I supposed to be the teachers of these things; but I learn from you that I am utterly at fault, and I dare say that you are right. And now I wish that you, on your part, would tell me to whom among the Athenians he should go. Whom would you name?

ANYTUS: Why single out individuals? Any Athenian gentleman, taken at random, if he will mind him, will do far more good to him than the Sophists.

SOCRATES: And did those gentlemen grow of themselves; and without having been taught by any one, were they nevertheless able to teach others that which they had never learned themselves?

ANYTUS: I imagine that they learned of the previous generation of gentlemen. Have there not been many good men in this city?

SOCRATES: Yes, certainly, Anytus; and many good statesmen also there always have been and there are still, in the city of Athens. But the question is whether they were also good teachers of their own virtue;—not whether there are, or have been, good men in this part of the world, but whether virtue can be taught, is the question which we have been discussing. Now, do we mean to say that the good men of our own and of other times knew how to impart to others that virtue which they had themselves; or is virtue a thing incapable of being communicated or imparted by one man to another? That is the question which I and Meno have been arguing. Look at the matter in your own way: Would you not admit that Themistocles was a good man?

ANYTUS: Certainly; no man better.

SOCRATES: And must not he then have been a good teacher, if any man ever was a good teacher, of his own virtue?

ANYTUS: Yes certainly,—if he wanted to be so.

SOCRATES: But would he not have wanted? He would, at any rate, have desired to make his own son a good man and a gentleman; he could not have been jealous of him, or have intentionally abstained from imparting to him his own virtue. Did you never hear that he made his son Cleophantus a famous horseman; and had him taught to stand upright on horseback and hurl a javelin, and to do many other marvellous things; and in anything which could be learned from a master he was well trained? Have you not heard from our elders of him?

ANYTUS: I have.

SOCRATES: Then no one could say that his son showed any want of capacity?

ANYTUS: Very likely not.

SOCRATES: But did any one, old or young, ever say in your hearing that Cleophantus, son of Themistocles, was a wise or good man, as his father was?

ANYTUS: I have certainly never heard any one say so.

SOCRATES: And if virtue could have been taught, would his father Themistocles have sought to train him in these minor accomplishments, and allowed him who, as you must remember, was his own son, to be no better than his neighbours in those qualities in which he himself excelled?

ANYTUS: Indeed, indeed, I think not.

SOCRATES: Here was a teacher of virtue whom you admit to be among the best men of the past. Let us take another,—Aristides, the son of Lysimachus: would you not acknowledge that he was a good man?

ANYTUS: To be sure I should.

SOCRATES: And did not he train his son Lysimachus better than any other Athenian in all that could be done for him by the help of masters? But what has been the result? Is he a bit better than any other mortal? He is an acquaintance of yours, and you see what he is like. There is Pericles, again, magnificent in his wisdom; and he, as you are aware, had two sons, Paralus and Xanthippus.

ANYTUS: I know.

SOCRATES: And you know, also, that he taught them to be unrivalled horsemen, and had them trained in music and gymnastics and all sorts of arts—in these respects they were on a level with the best—and had he no wish to make good men of them? Nay, he must have wished it. But virtue, as I suspect, could not be taught. And that you may not suppose the incompetent teachers to be only the meaner sort of Athenians and few in number, remember again that Thucydides had two sons, Melesias and Stephanus, whom, besides giving them a good education in other things, he trained in wrestling, and they were the best wrestlers in Athens: one of them he committed to the care of Xanthias, and the other of Eudorus, who had the reputation of being the most celebrated wrestlers of that day. Do you remember them?

ANYTUS: I have heard of them.

SOCRATES: Now, can there be a doubt that Thucydides, whose children were taught things for which he had to spend money, would have taught them to be good men, which would have cost him nothing, if virtue could have been taught? Will you reply that he was a mean man, and had not many friends among the Athenians and allies? Nay, but he was of a great family, and a man of influence at Athens and in all Hellas, and, if virtue could have been taught, he would have found out some Athenian or foreigner who would have made good men of his sons, if he could not himself spare the time from cares of state. Once more, I suspect, friend Anytus, that virtue is not a thing which can be taught?

ANYTUS: Socrates, I think that you are too ready to speak evil of men: and, if you will take my advice, I would recommend you to be careful. Perhaps there is no city in which it is not easier to do men harm than to do them good, and this is certainly the case at Athens, as I believe that you know.

SOCRATES: O Meno, think that Anytus is in a rage. And he may well be in a rage, for he thinks, in the first place, that I am defaming these gentlemen; and in the second place, he is of opinion that he is one of them himself. But some day he will know what is the meaning of defamation, and if he ever does, he will forgive me. Meanwhile I will return to you, Meno; for I suppose that there are gentlemen in your region too?

MENO: Certainly there are.

SOCRATES: And are they willing to teach the young? and do they profess to be teachers? and do they agree that virtue is taught?

MENO: No indeed, Socrates, they are anything but agreed; you may hear them saying at one time that virtue can be taught, and then again the reverse.

SOCRATES: Can we call those teachers who do not acknowledge the possibility of their own vocation?

MENO: I think not, Socrates.

SOCRATES: And what do you think of these Sophists, who are the only professors? Do they seem to you to be teachers of virtue?

MENO: I often wonder, Socrates, that Gorgias is never heard promising to teach virtue: and when he hears others promising he only laughs at them; but he thinks that men should be taught to speak.

SOCRATES: Then do you not think that the Sophists are teachers?

MENO: I cannot tell you, Socrates; like the rest of the world, I am in doubt, and sometimes I think that they are teachers and sometimes not.

SOCRATES: And are you aware that not you only and other politicians have doubts whether virtue can be taught or not, but that Theognis the poet says the very same thing?

MENO: Where does he say so?

SOCRATES: In these elegiac verses (Theog.):

'Eat and drink and sit with the mighty, and make yourself agreeable to them; for from the good you will learn what is good, but if you mix with the bad you will lose the intelligence which you already have.'

Do you observe that here he seems to imply that virtue can be taught?

MENO: Clearly.

SOCRATES: But in some other verses he shifts about and says (Theog.):

'If understanding could be created and put into a man, then they' (who were able to perform this feat) 'would have obtained great rewards.'

And again:—

'Never would a bad son have sprung from a good sire, for he would have heard the voice of instruction; but not by teaching will you ever make a bad man into a good one.'

And this, as you may remark, is a contradiction of the other.

MENO: Clearly.

SOCRATES: And is there anything else of which the professors are affirmed not only not to be teachers of others, but to be ignorant themselves, and bad at the knowledge of that which they are professing to teach? or is there anything about which even the acknowledged 'gentlemen' are sometimes saying that 'this thing can be taught,' and sometimes the opposite? Can you say that they are teachers in any true sense whose ideas are in such confusion?

MENO: I should say, certainly not.

SOCRATES: But if neither the Sophists nor the gentlemen are teachers, clearly there can be no other teachers?

MENO: No.

SOCRATES: And if there are no teachers, neither are there disciples?

MENO: Agreed.

SOCRATES: And we have admitted that a thing cannot be taught of which there are neither teachers nor disciples?

MENO: We have.

SOCRATES: And there are no teachers of virtue to be found anywhere?

MENO: There are not.

SOCRATES: And if there are no teachers, neither are there scholars?

MENO: That, I think, is true.

SOCRATES: Then virtue cannot be taught?

MENO: Not if we are right in our view. But I cannot believe, Socrates, that there are no good men: And if there are, how did they come into existence?

SOCRATES: I am afraid, Meno, that you and I are not good for much, and that Gorgias has been as poor an educator of you as Prodicus has been of me. Certainly we shall have to look to ourselves, and try to find some one who will help in some way or other to improve us. This I say, because I observe that in the previous discussion none of us remarked that right and good action is possible to man under other guidance than that of knowledge (episteme);—and indeed if this be denied, there is no seeing how there can be any good men at all.

MENO: How do you mean, Socrates?

SOCRATES: I mean that good men are necessarily useful or profitable. Were we not right in admitting this? It must be so.

MENO: Yes.

SOCRATES: And in supposing that they will be useful only if they are true guides to us of action—there we were also right?

MENO: Yes.

SOCRATES: But when we said that a man cannot be a good guide unless he have knowledge (phrhonesis), this we were wrong.

MENO: What do you mean by the word 'right'?

SOCRATES: I will explain. If a man knew the way to Larisa, or anywhere else, and went to the place and led others thither, would he not be a right and good guide?

MENO: Certainly.

SOCRATES: And a person who had a right opinion about the way, but had never been and did not know, might be a good guide also, might he not?

MENO: Certainly.

SOCRATES: And while he has true opinion about that which the other knows, he will be just as good a guide if he thinks the truth, as he who knows the truth?

MENO: Exactly.

SOCRATES: Then true opinion is as good a guide to correct action as knowledge; and that was the point which we omitted in our speculation about the nature of virtue, when we said that knowledge only is the guide of right action; whereas there is also right opinion.

MENO: True.

SOCRATES: Then right opinion is not less useful than knowledge?

MENO: The difference, Socrates, is only that he who has knowledge will always be right; but he who has right opinion will sometimes be right, and sometimes not.

SOCRATES: What do you mean? Can he be wrong who has right opinion, so long as he has right opinion?

MENO: I admit the cogency of your argument, and therefore, Socrates, I wonder that knowledge should be preferred to right opinion—or why they should ever differ.

SOCRATES: And shall I explain this wonder to you?

MENO: Do tell me.

SOCRATES: You would not wonder if you had ever observed the images of Daedalus (Compare Euthyphro); but perhaps you have not got them in your country?

MENO: What have they to do with the question?

SOCRATES: Because they require to be fastened in order to keep them, and if they are not fastened they will play truant and run away.

MENO: Well, what of that?

SOCRATES: I mean to say that they are not very valuable possessions if they are at liberty, for they will walk off like runaway slaves; but when fastened, they are of great value, for they are really beautiful works of art. Now this is an illustration of the nature of true opinions: while they abide with us they are beautiful and fruitful, but they run away out of the human soul, and do not remain long, and therefore they are not of much value until they are fastened by the tie of the cause; and this fastening of them, friend Meno, is recollection, as you and I have agreed to call it. But when they are bound, in the first place, they have the nature of knowledge; and, in the second place, they are abiding. And this is why knowledge is more honourable and excellent than true opinion, because fastened by a chain.

MENO: What you are saying, Socrates, seems to be very like the truth.

SOCRATES: I too speak rather in ignorance; I only conjecture. And yet that knowledge differs from true opinion is no matter of conjecture with me. There are not many things which I profess to know, but this is most certainly one of them.

MENO: Yes, Socrates; and you are quite right in saying so.

SOCRATES: And am I not also right in saying that true opinion leading the way perfects action quite as well as knowledge?

MENO: There again, Socrates, I think you are right.

SOCRATES: Then right opinion is not a whit inferior to knowledge, or less useful in action; nor is the man who has right opinion inferior to him who has knowledge?

MENO: True.

SOCRATES: And surely the good man has been acknowledged by us to be useful?

MENO: Yes.

SOCRATES: Seeing then that men become good and useful to states, not only because they have knowledge, but because they have right opinion, and that neither knowledge nor right opinion is given to man by nature or acquired by him—(do you imagine either of them to be given by nature?

MENO: Not I.)

SOCRATES: Then if they are not given by nature, neither are the good by nature good?

MENO: Certainly not.

SOCRATES: And nature being excluded, then came the question whether virtue is acquired by teaching?

MENO: Yes.

SOCRATES: If virtue was wisdom (or knowledge), then, as we thought, it was taught?

MENO: Yes.

SOCRATES: And if it was taught it was wisdom?

MENO: Certainly.

SOCRATES: And if there were teachers, it might be taught; and if there were no teachers, not?

MENO: True.

SOCRATES: But surely we acknowledged that there were no teachers of virtue?

MENO: Yes.

SOCRATES: Then we acknowledged that it was not taught, and was not wisdom?

MENO: Certainly.

SOCRATES: And yet we admitted that it was a good?

MENO: Yes.

SOCRATES: And the right guide is useful and good?

MENO: Certainly.

SOCRATES: And the only right guides are knowledge and true opinion—these are the guides of man; for things which happen by chance are not under the guidance of man: but the guides of man are true opinion and knowledge.

MENO: I think so too.

SOCRATES: But if virtue is not taught, neither is virtue knowledge.

MENO: Clearly not.

SOCRATES: Then of two good and useful things, one, which is knowledge, has been set aside, and cannot be supposed to be our guide in political life.

MENO: I think not.

SOCRATES: And therefore not by any wisdom, and not because they were wise, did Themistocles and those others of whom Anytus spoke govern states. This was the reason why they were unable to make others like themselves—because their virtue was not grounded on knowledge.

MENO: That is probably true, Socrates.

SOCRATES: But if not by knowledge, the only alternative which remains is that statesmen must have guided states by right opinion, which is in politics what divination is in religion; for diviners and also prophets say many things truly, but they know not what they say.

MENO: So I believe.

SOCRATES: And may we not, Meno, truly call those men 'divine' who, having no understanding, yet succeed in many a grand deed and word?

MENO: Certainly.

SOCRATES: Then we shall also be right in calling divine those whom we were just now speaking of as diviners and prophets, including the whole tribe of poets. Yes, and statesmen above all may be said to be divine and illumined, being inspired and possessed of God, in which condition they say many grand things, not knowing what they say.

MENO: Yes.

SOCRATES: And the women too, Meno, call good men divine—do they not? and the Spartans, when they praise a good man, say 'that he is a divine man.'

MENO: And I think, Socrates, that they are right; although very likely our friend Anytus may take offence at the word.

SOCRATES: I do not care; as for Anytus, there will be another opportunity of talking with him. To sum up our enquiry—the result seems to be, if we are at all right in our view, that virtue is neither natural nor acquired, but an instinct given by God to the virtuous. Nor is the instinct accompanied by reason, unless there may be supposed to be among statesmen some one who is capable of educating statesmen. And if there be such an one, he may be said to be among the living what Homer says that Tiresias was among the dead, 'he alone has understanding; but the rest are flitting shades'; and he and his virtue in like manner will be a reality among shadows.

MENO: That is excellent, Socrates.

SOCRATES: Then, Meno, the conclusion is that virtue comes to the virtuous by the gift of God. But we shall never know the certain truth until, before asking how virtue is given, we enquire into the actual nature of virtue. I fear that I must go away, but do you, now that you are persuaded yourself, persuade our friend Anytus. And do not let him be so exasperated; if you can conciliate him, you will have done good service to the Athenian people.

PARMENIDES

By Plato

Translated by Benjamin Jowett

PERSONS OF THE DIALOGUE:

Cephalus, Adeimantus, Glaucon, Antiphon, Pythodorus, Socrates, Zeno, Parmenides, Aristoteles.

Cephalus rehearses a dialogue which is supposed to have been narrated in his presence by Antiphon, the half-brother of Adeimantus and Glaucon, to certain Clazomenians.

We had come from our home at Clazomenae to Athens, and met Adeimantus and Glaucon in the Agora. Welcome, Cephalus, said Adeimantus, taking me by the hand; is there anything which we can do for you in Athens?

Yes; that is why I am here; I wish to ask a favour of you.

What may that be? he said.

I want you to tell me the name of your half brother, which I have forgotten; he was a mere child when I last came hither from Clazomenae, but that was a long time ago; his father's name, if I remember rightly, was Pyrilampes?

Yes, he said, and the name of our brother, Antiphon; but why do you ask?

Let me introduce some countrymen of mine, I said; they are lovers of philosophy, and have heard that Antiphon was intimate with a certain Pythodorus, a friend of Zeno, and remembers a conversation which took place between Socrates, Zeno, and Parmenides many years ago, Pythodorus having often recited it to him.

Quite true.

And could we hear it? I asked.

Nothing easier, he replied; when he was a youth he made a careful study of the piece; at present his thoughts run in another direction; like his grandfather Antiphon he is devoted to horses. But, if that is what you want, let us go and look for him; he dwells at Melita, which is quite near, and he has only just left us to go home.

Accordingly we went to look for him; he was at home, and in the act of giving a bridle to a smith to be fitted. When he had done with the smith, his brothers told him the purpose of our visit; and he saluted me as an acquaintance whom he remembered from my former visit, and we asked him to repeat the dialogue. At first he was not very willing, and complained of the trouble, but at length he consented. He told us that Pythodorus had described to him the appearance of Parmenides and Zeno; they came to Athens, as he said, at the great Panathenaea; the former was, at the time of his visit, about 65 years old, very white with age, but well favoured. Zeno was nearly 40 years of age, tall and fair to look upon; in the days of his youth he was reported to have been beloved by Parmenides. He said that they lodged with Pythodorus in the Ceramicus, outside the wall, whither Socrates, then a very young man, came to see them, and many others with him; they wanted to hear the writings of Zeno, which had been brought to Athens for the first time on the occasion of their visit. These Zeno himself read to them in the absence of Parmenides, and had very nearly finished when Pythodorus entered, and with him Parmenides and Aristoteles who was afterwards one of the Thirty, and heard the little that remained of the dialogue. Pythodorus had heard Zeno repeat them before.

When the recitation was completed, Socrates requested that the first thesis of the first argument might be read over again, and this having been done, he said: What is your meaning, Zeno? Do you maintain that if being is many, it must be both like and unlike, and that this is impossible, for neither can the like be unlike, nor the unlike like—is that your position?

Just so, said Zeno.

And if the unlike cannot be like, or the like unlike, then according to you, being could not be many; for this would involve an impossibility. In all that you say have you any other purpose except to disprove the being of the many? and is not each division of your treatise intended to furnish a separate proof of this, there being in all as many proofs of the not-being of the many as you have composed arguments? Is that your meaning, or have I misunderstood you?

No, said Zeno; you have correctly understood my general purpose.

I see, Parmenides, said Socrates, that Zeno would like to be not only one with you in friendship but your second self in his writings too; he puts what you say in another way, and would fain make believe that he is telling us something which is new. For you, in your poems, say The All is one, and of this you adduce excellent proofs; and he on the other hand says There is no many; and on behalf of this he offers overwhelming evidence. You affirm unity, he denies plurality. And so you deceive the world into believing that you are saying different things when really you are saying much the same. This is a strain of art beyond the reach of most of us.

Yes, Socrates, said Zeno. But although you are as keen as a Spartan hound in pursuing the track, you do not fully apprehend the true motive of the composition, which is not really such an artificial work as you imagine; for what you speak of was an accident; there was no pretence of a great purpose; nor any serious intention of deceiving the world. The truth is, that these writings of mine were meant to protect the arguments of Parmenides against those who make fun of him and seek to show the many ridiculous and contradictory results which they suppose to follow from the affirmation of the one. My answer is addressed to the partisans of the many, whose attack I return with interest by retorting upon them that their hypothesis of the being of many, if carried out, appears to be still more ridiculous than the hypothesis of the being of one. Zeal for my master led me to write the book in the days of my youth, but some one stole the copy; and therefore I had no choice whether it should be published or not; the motive, however, of writing, was not the ambition of an elder man, but the pugnacity of a young one. This you do not seem to see, Socrates; though in other respects, as I was saying, your notion is a very just one.

I understand, said Socrates, and quite accept your account. But tell me, Zeno, do you not further think that there is an idea of likeness in itself, and another idea of unlikeness, which is the opposite of likeness, and that in these two, you and I and all other things to which we apply the term many, participate—things which participate in likeness become in that degree and manner like; and so far as they participate in unlikeness become in that degree unlike, or both like and unlike in the degree in which they participate in both? And may not all things partake of both opposites, and be both like and unlike, by reason of this participation?—Where is the wonder? Now if a person could prove the absolute like to become unlike, or the absolute unlike to become like, that, in my opinion, would indeed be a wonder; but there is nothing extraordinary, Zeno, in showing that the things which only partake of likeness and unlikeness experience both. Nor, again, if a person were to show that all is one by partaking of one, and at the same time many by partaking of many, would that be very astonishing. But if he were to show me that the absolute one was many, or the absolute many one, I should be truly amazed. And so of all the rest: I should be surprised to hear that the natures or ideas themselves had these opposite qualities; but not if a person wanted to prove of me that I was many and also one. When he wanted to show that I was many he would say that I have a right and a left side, and a front and a back, and an upper and a lower half, for I cannot deny that I partake of multitude; when, on the other hand, he wants to prove that I am one, he will say, that we who are here assembled are seven, and that I am one and partake of the one. In both instances he proves his case. So again, if a person shows that such things as wood, stones, and the like, being many are also one, we admit that he shows the coexistence of the one and many, but he does not show that the many are one or the one many; he is uttering not a paradox but a truism. If however, as I just now suggested, some one were to abstract simple notions of like, unlike, one, many, rest, motion, and similar ideas, and then to show that these admit of admixture and separation in themselves, I should be very much astonished. This part of the argument appears to be treated by you, Zeno, in a very spirited manner; but, as I was saying, I should be far more amazed if any one found in the ideas themselves which are apprehended by reason, the same puzzle and entanglement which you have shown to exist in visible objects.

While Socrates was speaking, Pythodorus thought that Parmenides and Zeno were not altogether pleased at the successive steps of the argument; but still they gave the closest attention, and often looked at one another, and smiled as if in admiration of him. When he had finished, Parmenides expressed their feelings in the following words:—

Socrates, he said, I admire the bent of your mind towards philosophy; tell me now, was this your own distinction between ideas in themselves and the things which partake of them? and do you think that there is an idea of likeness apart from the likeness which we possess, and of the one and many, and of the other things which Zeno mentioned?

I think that there are such ideas, said Socrates.

Parmenides proceeded: And would you also make absolute ideas of the just and the beautiful and the good, and of all that class?

Yes, he said, I should.

And would you make an idea of man apart from us and from all other human creatures, or of fire and water?

I am often undecided, Parmenides, as to whether I ought to include them or not.

And would you feel equally undecided, Socrates, about things of which the mention may provoke a smile?—I mean such things as hair, mud, dirt, or anything else which is vile and paltry; would you suppose that each of these has an idea distinct from the actual objects with which we come into contact, or not?

Certainly not, said Socrates; visible things like these are such as they appear to us, and I am afraid that there would be an absurdity in assuming any idea of them, although I sometimes get disturbed, and begin to think that there is nothing without an idea; but then again, when I have taken up this position, I run away, because I am afraid that I may fall into a bottomless pit of nonsense, and perish; and so I return to the ideas of which I was just now speaking, and occupy myself with them.

Yes, Socrates, said Parmenides; that is because you are still young; the time will come, if I am not mistaken, when philosophy will have a firmer grasp of you, and then you will not despise even the meanest things; at your age, you are too much disposed to regard the opinions of men. But I should like to know whether you mean that there are certain ideas of which all other things partake, and from which they derive their names; that similars, for example, become similar, because they partake of similarity; and great things become great, because they partake of greatness; and that just and beautiful things become just and beautiful, because they partake of justice and beauty?

Yes, certainly, said Socrates that is my meaning.

Then each individual partakes either of the whole of the idea or else of a part of the idea? Can there be any other mode of participation?

There cannot be, he said.

Then do you think that the whole idea is one, and yet, being one, is in each one of the many?

Why not, Parmenides? said Socrates.

Because one and the same thing will exist as a whole at the same time in many separate individuals, and will therefore be in a state of separation from itself.

Nay, but the idea may be like the day which is one and the same in many places at once, and yet continuous with itself; in this way each idea may be one and the same in all at the same time.

I like your way, Socrates, of making one in many places at once. You mean to say, that if I were to spread out a sail and cover a number of men, there would be one whole including many—is not that your meaning?

I think so.

And would you say that the whole sail includes each man, or a part of it only, and different parts different men?

The latter.

Then, Socrates, the ideas themselves will be divisible, and things which participate in them will have a part of them only and not the whole idea existing in each of them?

That seems to follow.

Then would you like to say, Socrates, that the one idea is really divisible and yet remains one?

Certainly not, he said.

Suppose that you divide absolute greatness, and that of the many great things, each one is great in virtue of a portion of greatness less than absolute greatness—is that conceivable?

No.

Or will each equal thing, if possessing some small portion of equality less than absolute equality, be equal to some other thing by virtue of that portion only?

Impossible.

Or suppose one of us to have a portion of smallness; this is but a part of the small, and therefore the absolutely small is greater; if the absolutely small be greater, that to which the part of the small is added will be smaller and not greater than before.

How absurd!

Then in what way, Socrates, will all things participate in the ideas, if they are unable to participate in them either as parts or wholes?

Indeed, he said, you have asked a question which is not easily answered.

Well, said Parmenides, and what do you say of another question?

What question?

I imagine that the way in which you are led to assume one idea of each kind is as follows:—You see a number of great objects, and when you look at them there seems to you to be one and the same idea (or nature) in them all; hence you conceive of greatness as one.

Very true, said Socrates.

And if you go on and allow your mind in like manner to embrace in one view the idea of greatness and of great things which are not the idea, and to compare them, will not another greatness arise, which will appear to be the source of all these?

It would seem so.

Then another idea of greatness now comes into view over and above absolute greatness, and the individuals which partake of it; and then another, over and above all these, by virtue of which they will all be great, and so each idea instead of being one will be infinitely multiplied.

But may not the ideas, asked Socrates, be thoughts only, and have no proper existence except in our minds, Parmenides? For in that case each idea may still be one, and not experience this infinite multiplication.

And can there be individual thoughts which are thoughts of nothing?

Impossible, he said.

The thought must be of something?

Yes.

Of something which is or which is not?

Of something which is.

Must it not be of a single something, which the thought recognizes as attaching to all, being a single form or nature?

Yes.

And will not the something which is apprehended as one and the same in all, be an idea?

From that, again, there is no escape.

Then, said Parmenides, if you say that everything else participates in the ideas, must you not say either that everything is made up of thoughts, and that all things think; or that they are thoughts but have no thought?

The latter view, Parmenides, is no more rational than the previous one. In my opinion, the ideas are, as it were, patterns fixed in nature, and other things are like them, and resemblances of them—what is meant by the participation of other things in the ideas, is really assimilation to them.

But if, said he, the individual is like the idea, must not the idea also be like the individual, in so far as the individual is a resemblance of the idea? That which is like, cannot be conceived of as other than the like of like.

Impossible.

And when two things are alike, must they not partake of the same idea?

They must.

And will not that of which the two partake, and which makes them alike, be the idea itself?

Certainly.

Then the idea cannot be like the individual, or the individual like the idea; for if they are alike, some further idea of likeness will always be coming to light, and if that be like anything else, another; and new ideas will be always arising, if the idea resembles that which partakes of it?

Quite true.

The theory, then, that other things participate in the ideas by resemblance, has to be given up, and some other mode of participation devised?

It would seem so.

Do you see then, Socrates, how great is the difficulty of affirming the ideas to be absolute?

Yes, indeed.

And, further, let me say that as yet you only understand a small part of the difficulty which is involved if you make of each thing a single idea, parting it off from other things.

What difficulty? he said.

There are many, but the greatest of all is this:—If an opponent argues that these ideas, being such as we say they ought to be, must remain unknown, no one can prove to him that he is wrong, unless he who denies their existence be a man of great ability and knowledge, and is willing to follow a long and laborious demonstration; he will remain unconvinced, and still insist that they cannot be known.

What do you mean, Parmenides? said Socrates.

In the first place, I think, Socrates, that you, or any one who maintains the existence of absolute essences, will admit that they cannot exist in us.

No, said Socrates; for then they would be no longer absolute.

True, he said; and therefore when ideas are what they are in relation to one another, their essence is determined by a relation among themselves, and has nothing to do with the resemblances, or whatever they are to be termed, which are in our sphere, and from which we receive this or that name when we partake of them. And the things which are within our sphere and have the same names with them, are likewise only relative to one another, and not to the ideas which have the same names with them, but belong to themselves and not to them.

What do you mean? said Socrates.

I may illustrate my meaning in this way, said Parmenides:—A master has a slave; now there is nothing absolute in the relation between them, which is simply a relation of one man to another. But there is also an idea of mastership in the abstract, which is relative to the idea of slavery in the abstract. These natures have nothing to do with us, nor we with them; they are concerned with themselves only, and we with ourselves. Do you see my meaning?

Yes, said Socrates, I quite see your meaning.

And will not knowledge—I mean absolute knowledge—answer to absolute truth?

Certainly.

And each kind of absolute knowledge will answer to each kind of absolute being?

Yes.

But the knowledge which we have, will answer to the truth which we have; and again, each kind of knowledge which we have, will be a knowledge of each kind of being which we have?

Certainly.

But the ideas themselves, as you admit, we have not, and cannot have?

No, we cannot.

And the absolute natures or kinds are known severally by the absolute idea of knowledge?

Yes.

And we have not got the idea of knowledge?

No.

Then none of the ideas are known to us, because we have no share in absolute knowledge?

I suppose not.

Then the nature of the beautiful in itself, and of the good in itself, and all other ideas which we suppose to exist absolutely, are unknown to us?

It would seem so.

I think that there is a stranger consequence still.

What is it?

Would you, or would you not say, that absolute knowledge, if there is such a thing, must be a far more exact knowledge than our knowledge; and the same of beauty and of the rest?

Yes.

And if there be such a thing as participation in absolute knowledge, no one is more likely than God to have this most exact knowledge?

Certainly.

But then, will God, having absolute knowledge, have a knowledge of human things?

Why not?

Because, Socrates, said Parmenides, we have admitted that the ideas are not valid in relation to human things; nor human things in relation to them; the relations of either are limited to their respective spheres.

Yes, that has been admitted.

And if God has this perfect authority, and perfect knowledge, his authority cannot rule us, nor his knowledge know us, or any human thing; just as our authority does not extend to the gods, nor our knowledge know anything which is divine, so by parity of reason they, being gods, are not our masters, neither do they know the things of men.

Yet, surely, said Socrates, to deprive God of knowledge is monstrous.

These, Socrates, said Parmenides, are a few, and only a few of the difficulties in which we are involved if ideas really are and we determine each one of them to be an absolute unity. He who hears what may be said against them will deny the very existence of them—and even if they do exist, he will say that they must of necessity be unknown to man; and he will seem to have reason on his side, and as we were remarking just now, will be very difficult to convince; a man must be gifted with very considerable ability before he can learn that everything has a class and an absolute essence; and still more remarkable will he be who discovers all these things for himself, and having thoroughly investigated them is able to teach them to others.

I agree with you, Parmenides, said Socrates; and what you say is very much to my mind.

And yet, Socrates, said Parmenides, if a man, fixing his attention on these and the like difficulties, does away with ideas of things and will not admit that every individual thing has its own determinate idea which is always one and the same, he will have nothing on which his mind can rest; and so he will utterly destroy the power of reasoning, as you seem to me to have particularly noted.

Very true, he said.

But, then, what is to become of philosophy? Whither shall we turn, if the ideas are unknown?

I certainly do not see my way at present.

Yes, said Parmenides; and I think that this arises, Socrates, out of your attempting to define the beautiful, the just, the good, and the ideas generally, without sufficient previous training. I noticed your deficiency, when I heard you talking here with your friend Aristoteles, the day before yesterday. The impulse that carries you towards philosophy is assuredly noble and divine; but there is an art which is called by the vulgar idle talking, and which is often imagined to be useless; in that you must train and exercise yourself, now that you are young, or truth will elude your grasp.

And what is the nature of this exercise, Parmenides, which you would recommend?

That which you heard Zeno practising; at the same time, I give you credit for saying to him that you did not care to examine the perplexity in reference to visible things, or to consider the question that way; but only in reference to objects of thought, and to what may be called ideas.

Why, yes, he said, there appears to me to be no difficulty in showing by this method that visible things are like and unlike and may experience anything.

Quite true, said Parmenides; but I think that you should go a step further, and consider not only the consequences which flow from a given hypothesis, but also the consequences which flow from denying the hypothesis; and that will be still better training for you.

What do you mean? he said.

I mean, for example, that in the case of this very hypothesis of Zeno's about the many, you should inquire not only what will be the consequences to the many in relation to themselves and to the one, and to the one in relation to itself and the many, on the hypothesis of the being of the many, but also what will be the consequences to the one and the many in their relation to themselves and to each other, on the opposite hypothesis. Or, again, if likeness is or is not, what will be the consequences in either of these cases to the subjects of the hypothesis, and to other things, in relation both to themselves and to one another, and so of unlikeness; and the same holds good of motion and rest, of generation and destruction, and even of being and not-being. In a word, when you suppose anything to be or not to be, or to be in any way affected, you must look at the consequences in relation to the thing itself, and to any other things which you choose,—to each of them singly, to more than one, and to all; and so of other things, you must look at them in relation to themselves and to anything else which you suppose either to be or not to be, if you would train yourself perfectly and see the real truth.

That, Parmenides, is a tremendous business of which you speak, and I do not quite understand you; will you take some hypothesis and go through the steps?—then I shall apprehend you better.

That, Socrates, is a serious task to impose on a man of my years.

Then will you, Zeno? said Socrates.

Zeno answered with a smile:—Let us make our petition to Parmenides himself, who is quite right in saying that you are hardly aware of the extent of the task which you are imposing on him; and if there were more of us I should not ask him, for these are not subjects which any one, especially at his age, can well speak of before a large audience; most people are not aware that this roundabout progress through all things is the only way in which the mind can attain truth and wisdom. And therefore, Parmenides, I join in the request of Socrates, that I may hear the process again which I have not heard for a long time.

When Zeno had thus spoken, Pythodorus, according to Antiphon's report of him, said, that he himself and Aristoteles and the whole company entreated Parmenides to give an example of the process. I cannot refuse, said Parmenides; and yet I feel rather like Ibycus, who, when in his old age, against his will, he fell in love, compared himself to an old racehorse, who was about to run in a chariot race, shaking with fear at the course he knew so well—this was his simile of himself. And I also experience a trembling when I remember through what an ocean of words I have to wade at my time of life. But I must indulge you, as Zeno says that I ought, and we are alone. Where shall I begin? And what shall be our first hypothesis, if I am to attempt this laborious pastime? Shall I begin with myself, and take my own hypothesis the one? and consider the consequences which follow on the supposition either of the being or of the not-being of one?

By all means, said Zeno.

And who will answer me? he said. Shall I propose the youngest? He will not make difficulties and will be the most likely to say what he thinks; and his answers will give me time to breathe.

I am the one whom you mean, Parmenides, said Aristoteles; for I am the youngest and at your service. Ask, and I will answer.

Parmenides proceeded: 1.a. If one is, he said, the one cannot be many?

Impossible.

Then the one cannot have parts, and cannot be a whole?

Why not?

Because every part is part of a whole; is it not?

Yes.

And what is a whole? would not that of which no part is wanting be a whole?

Certainly.

Then, in either case, the one would be made up of parts; both as being a whole, and also as having parts?

To be sure.

And in either case, the one would be many, and not one?

True.

But, surely, it ought to be one and not many?

It ought.

Then, if the one is to remain one, it will not be a whole, and will not have parts?

No.

But if it has no parts, it will have neither beginning, middle, nor end; for these would of course be parts of it.

Right.

But then, again, a beginning and an end are the limits of everything?

Certainly.

Then the one, having neither beginning nor end, is unlimited?

Yes, unlimited.

And therefore formless; for it cannot partake either of round or straight.

But why?

Why, because the round is that of which all the extreme points are equidistant from the centre?

Yes.

And the straight is that of which the centre intercepts the view of the extremes?

True.

Then the one would have parts and would be many, if it partook either of a straight or of a circular form?

Assuredly.

But having no parts, it will be neither straight nor round?

Right.

And, being of such a nature, it cannot be in any place, for it cannot be either in another or in itself.

How so?

Because if it were in another, it would be encircled by that in which it was, and would touch it at many places and with many parts; but that which is one and indivisible, and does not partake of a circular nature, cannot be touched all round in many places.

Certainly not.

But if, on the other hand, one were in itself, it would also be contained by nothing else but itself; that is to say, if it were really in itself; for nothing can be in anything which does not contain it.

Impossible.

But then, that which contains must be other than that which is contained? for the same whole cannot do and suffer both at once; and if so, one will be no longer one, but two?

True.

Then one cannot be anywhere, either in itself or in another?

No.

Further consider, whether that which is of such a nature can have either rest or motion.

Why not?

Why, because the one, if it were moved, would be either moved in place or changed in nature; for these are the only kinds of motion.

Yes.

And the one, when it changes and ceases to be itself, cannot be any longer one.

It cannot.

It cannot therefore experience the sort of motion which is change of nature?

Clearly not.

Then can the motion of the one be in place?

Perhaps.

But if the one moved in place, must it not either move round and round in the same place, or from one place to another?

It must.

And that which moves in a circle must rest upon a centre; and that which goes round upon a centre must have parts which are different from the centre; but that which has no centre and no parts cannot possibly be carried round upon a centre?

Impossible.

But perhaps the motion of the one consists in change of place?

Perhaps so, if it moves at all.

And have we not already shown that it cannot be in anything?

Yes.

Then its coming into being in anything is still more impossible; is it not?

I do not see why.

Why, because anything which comes into being in anything, can neither as yet be in that other thing while still coming into being, nor be altogether out of it, if already coming into being in it.

Certainly not.

And therefore whatever comes into being in another must have parts, and then one part may be in, and another part out of that other; but that which has no parts can never be at one and the same time neither wholly within nor wholly without anything.

True.

And is there not a still greater impossibility in that which has no parts, and is not a whole, coming into being anywhere, since it cannot come into being either as a part or as a whole?

Clearly.

Then it does not change place by revolving in the same spot, nor by going somewhere and coming into being in something; nor again, by change in itself?

Very true.

Then in respect of any kind of motion the one is immoveable?

Immoveable.

But neither can the one be in anything, as we affirm?

Yes, we said so.

Then it is never in the same?

Why not?

Because if it were in the same it would be in something.

Certainly.

And we said that it could not be in itself, and could not be in other?

True.

Then one is never in the same place?

It would seem not.

But that which is never in the same place is never quiet or at rest?

Never.

One then, as would seem, is neither at rest nor in motion?

It certainly appears so.

Neither will it be the same with itself or other; nor again, other than itself or other.

How is that?

If other than itself it would be other than one, and would not be one.

True.

And if the same with other, it would be that other, and not itself; so that upon this supposition too, it would not have the nature of one, but would be other than one?

It would.

Then it will not be the same with other, or other than itself?

It will not.

Neither will it be other than other, while it remains one; for not one, but only other, can be other than other, and nothing else.

True.

Then not by virtue of being one will it be other?

Certainly not.

But if not by virtue of being one, not by virtue of itself; and if not by virtue of itself, not itself, and itself not being other at all, will not be other than anything?

Right.

Neither will one be the same with itself.

How not?

Surely the nature of the one is not the nature of the same.

Why not?

It is not when anything becomes the same with anything that it becomes one.

What of that?

Anything which becomes the same with the many, necessarily becomes many and not one.

True.

But, if there were no difference between the one and the same, when a thing became the same, it would always become one; and when it became one, the same?

Certainly.

And, therefore, if one be the same with itself, it is not one with itself, and will therefore be one and also not one.

Surely that is impossible.

And therefore the one can neither be other than other, nor the same with itself.

Impossible.

And thus the one can neither be the same, nor other, either in relation to itself or other?

No.

Neither will the one be like anything or unlike itself or other.

Why not?

Because likeness is sameness of affections.

Yes.

And sameness has been shown to be of a nature distinct from oneness?

That has been shown.

But if the one had any other affection than that of being one, it would be affected in such a way as to be more than one; which is impossible.

True.

Then the one can never be so affected as to be the same either with another or with itself?

Clearly not.

Then it cannot be like another, or like itself?

No.

Nor can it be affected so as to be other, for then it would be affected in such a way as to be more than one.

It would.

That which is affected otherwise than itself or another, will be unlike itself or another, for sameness of affections is likeness.

True.

But the one, as appears, never being affected otherwise, is never unlike itself or other?

Never.

Then the one will never be either like or unlike itself or other?

Plainly not.

Again, being of this nature, it can neither be equal nor unequal either to itself or to other.

How is that?

Why, because the one if equal must be of the same measures as that to which it is equal.

True.

And if greater or less than things which are commensurable with it, the one will have more measures than that which is less, and fewer than that which is greater?

Yes.

And so of things which are not commensurate with it, the one will have greater measures than that which is less and smaller than that which is greater.

Certainly.

But how can that which does not partake of sameness, have either the same measures or have anything else the same?

Impossible.

And not having the same measures, the one cannot be equal either with itself or with another?

It appears so.

But again, whether it have fewer or more measures, it will have as many parts as it has measures; and thus again the one will be no longer one but will have as many parts as measures.

Right.

And if it were of one measure, it would be equal to that measure; yet it has been shown to be incapable of equality.

It has.

Then it will neither partake of one measure, nor of many, nor of few, nor of the same at all, nor be equal to itself or another; nor be greater or less than itself, or other?

Certainly.

Well, and do we suppose that one can be older, or younger than anything, or of the same age with it?

Why not?

Why, because that which is of the same age with itself or other, must partake of equality or likeness of time; and we said that the one did not partake either of equality or of likeness?

We did say so.

And we also said, that it did not partake of inequality or unlikeness.

Very true.

How then can one, being of this nature, be either older or younger than anything, or have the same age with it?

In no way.

Then one cannot be older or younger, or of the same age, either with itself or with another?

Clearly not.

Then the one, being of this nature, cannot be in time at all; for must not that which is in time, be always growing older than itself?

Certainly.

And that which is older, must always be older than something which is younger?

True.

Then, that which becomes older than itself, also becomes at the same time younger than itself, if it is to have something to become older than.

What do you mean?

I mean this:—A thing does not need to become different from another thing which is already different; it IS different, and if its different has become, it has become different; if its different will be, it will be different; but of that which is becoming different, there cannot have been, or be about to be, or yet be, a different—the only different possible is one which is becoming.

That is inevitable.

But, surely, the elder is a difference relative to the younger, and to nothing else.

True.

Then that which becomes older than itself must also, at the same time, become younger than itself?

Yes.

But again, it is true that it cannot become for a longer or for a shorter time than itself, but it must become, and be, and have become, and be about to be, for the same time with itself?

That again is inevitable.

Then things which are in time, and partake of time, must in every case, I suppose, be of the same age with themselves; and must also become at once older and younger than themselves?

Yes.

But the one did not partake of those affections?

Not at all.

Then it does not partake of time, and is not in any time?

So the argument shows.

Well, but do not the expressions 'was,' and 'has become,' and 'was becoming,' signify a participation of past time?

Certainly.

And do not 'will be,' 'will become,' 'will have become,' signify a participation of future time?

Yes.

And 'is,' or 'becomes,' signifies a participation of present time?

Certainly.

And if the one is absolutely without participation in time, it never had become, or was becoming, or was at any time, or is now become or is becoming, or is, or will become, or will have become, or will be, hereafter.

Most true.

But are there any modes of partaking of being other than these?

There are none.

Then the one cannot possibly partake of being?

That is the inference.

Then the one is not at all?

Clearly not.

Then the one does not exist in such way as to be one; for if it were and partook of being, it would already be; but if the argument is to be trusted, the one neither is nor is one?

True.

But that which is not admits of no attribute or relation?

Of course not.

Then there is no name, nor expression, nor perception, nor opinion, nor knowledge of it?

Clearly not.

Then it is neither named, nor expressed, nor opined, nor known, nor does anything that is perceive it.

So we must infer.

But can all this be true about the one?

I think not.

1.b. Suppose, now, that we return once more to the original hypothesis; let us see whether, on a further review, any new aspect of the question appears.

I shall be very happy to do so.

We say that we have to work out together all the consequences, whatever they may be, which follow, if the one is?

Yes.

Then we will begin at the beginning:—If one is, can one be, and not partake of being?

Impossible.

Then the one will have being, but its being will not be the same with the one; for if the same, it would not be the being of the one; nor would the one have participated in being, for the proposition that one is would have been identical with the proposition that one is one; but our hypothesis is not if one is one, what will follow, but if one is:—am I not right?

Quite right.

We mean to say, that being has not the same significance as one?

Of course.

And when we put them together shortly, and say 'One is,' that is equivalent to saying, 'partakes of being'?

Quite true.

Once more then let us ask, if one is what will follow. Does not this hypothesis necessarily imply that one is of such a nature as to have parts?

How so?

In this way:—If being is predicated of the one, if the one is, and one of being, if being is one; and if being and one are not the same; and since the one, which we have assumed, is, must not the whole, if it is one, itself be, and have for its parts, one and being?

Certainly.

And is each of these parts—one and being—to be simply called a part, or must the word 'part' be relative to the word 'whole'?

The latter.

Then that which is one is both a whole and has a part?

Certainly.

Again, of the parts of the one, if it is—I mean being and one—does either fail to imply the other? is the one wanting to being, or being to the one?

Impossible.

Thus, each of the parts also has in turn both one and being, and is at the least made up of two parts; and the same principle goes on for ever, and every part whatever has always these two parts; for being always involves one, and one being; so that one is always disappearing, and becoming two.

Certainly.

And so the one, if it is, must be infinite in multiplicity?

Clearly.

Let us take another direction.

What direction?

We say that the one partakes of being and therefore it is?

Yes.

And in this way, the one, if it has being, has turned out to be many?

True.

But now, let us abstract the one which, as we say, partakes of being, and try to imagine it apart from that of which, as we say, it partakes—will this abstract one be one only or many?

One, I think.

Let us see:—Must not the being of one be other than one? for the one is not being, but, considered as one, only partook of being?

Certainly.

If being and the one be two different things, it is not because the one is one that it is other than being; nor because being is being that it is other than the one; but they differ from one another in virtue of otherness and difference.

Certainly.

So that the other is not the same—either with the one or with being?

Certainly not.

And therefore whether we take being and the other, or being and the one, or the one and the other, in every such case we take two things, which may be rightly called both.

How so.

In this way—you may speak of being?

Yes.

And also of one?

Yes.

Then now we have spoken of either of them?

Yes.

Well, and when I speak of being and one, I speak of them both?

Certainly.

And if I speak of being and the other, or of the one and the other,—in any such case do I not speak of both?

Yes.

And must not that which is correctly called both, be also two?

Undoubtedly.

And of two things how can either by any possibility not be one?

It cannot.

Then, if the individuals of the pair are together two, they must be severally one?

Clearly.

And if each of them is one, then by the addition of any one to any pair, the whole becomes three?

Yes.

And three are odd, and two are even?

Of course.

And if there are two there must also be twice, and if there are three there must be thrice; that is, if twice one makes two, and thrice one three?

Certainly.

There are two, and twice, and therefore there must be twice two; and there are three, and there is thrice, and therefore there must be thrice three?

Of course.

If there are three and twice, there is twice three; and if there are two and thrice, there is thrice two?

Undoubtedly.

Here, then, we have even taken even times, and odd taken odd times, and even taken odd times, and odd taken even times.

True.

And if this is so, does any number remain which has no necessity to be?

None whatever.

Then if one is, number must also be?

It must.

But if there is number, there must also be many, and infinite multiplicity of being; for number is infinite in multiplicity, and partakes also of being: am I not right?

Certainly.

And if all number participates in being, every part of number will also participate?

Yes.

Then being is distributed over the whole multitude of things, and nothing that is, however small or however great, is devoid of it? And, indeed, the very supposition of this is absurd, for how can that which is, be devoid of being?

In no way.

And it is divided into the greatest and into the smallest, and into being of all sizes, and is broken up more than all things; the divisions of it have no limit.

True.

Then it has the greatest number of parts?

Yes, the greatest number.

Is there any of these which is a part of being, and yet no part?

Impossible.

But if it is at all and so long as it is, it must be one, and cannot be none?

Certainly.

Then the one attaches to every single part of being, and does not fail in any part, whether great or small, or whatever may be the size of it?

True.

But reflect:—Can one, in its entirety, be in many places at the same time?

No; I see the impossibility of that.

And if not in its entirety, then it is divided; for it cannot be present with all the parts of being, unless divided.

True.

And that which has parts will be as many as the parts are?

Certainly.

Then we were wrong in saying just now, that being was distributed into the greatest number of parts. For it is not distributed into parts more than the one, into parts equal to the one; the one is never wanting to being, or being to the one, but being two they are co-equal and co-extensive.

Certainly that is true.

The one itself, then, having been broken up into parts by being, is many and infinite?

True.

Then not only the one which has being is many, but the one itself distributed by being, must also be many?

Certainly.

Further, inasmuch as the parts are parts of a whole, the one, as a whole, will be limited; for are not the parts contained by the whole?

Certainly.

And that which contains, is a limit?

Of course.

Then the one if it has being is one and many, whole and parts, having limits and yet unlimited in number?

Clearly.

And because having limits, also having extremes?

Certainly.

And if a whole, having beginning and middle and end. For can anything be a whole without these three? And if any one of them is wanting to anything, will that any longer be a whole?

No.

Then the one, as appears, will have beginning, middle, and end.

It will.

But, again, the middle will be equidistant from the extremes; or it would not be in the middle?

Yes.

Then the one will partake of figure, either rectilinear or round, or a union of the two?

True.

And if this is the case, it will be both in itself and in another too.

How?

Every part is in the whole, and none is outside the whole.

True.

And all the parts are contained by the whole?

Yes.

And the one is all its parts, and neither more nor less than all?

No.

And the one is the whole?

Of course.

But if all the parts are in the whole, and the one is all of them and the whole, and they are all contained by the whole, the one will be contained by the one; and thus the one will be in itself.

That is true.

But then, again, the whole is not in the parts—neither in all the parts, nor in some one of them. For if it is in all, it must be in one; for if there were any one in which it was not, it could not be in all the parts; for the part in which it is wanting is one of all, and if the whole is not in this, how can it be in them all?

It cannot.

Nor can the whole be in some of the parts; for if the whole were in some of the parts, the greater would be in the less, which is impossible.

Yes, impossible.

But if the whole is neither in one, nor in more than one, nor in all of the parts, it must be in something else, or cease to be anywhere at all?

Certainly.

If it were nowhere, it would be nothing; but being a whole, and not being in itself, it must be in another.

Very true.

The one then, regarded as a whole, is in another, but regarded as being all its parts, is in itself; and therefore the one must be itself in itself and also in another.

Certainly.

The one then, being of this nature, is of necessity both at rest and in motion?

How?

The one is at rest since it is in itself, for being in one, and not passing out of this, it is in the same, which is itself.

True.

And that which is ever in the same, must be ever at rest?

Certainly.

Well, and must not that, on the contrary, which is ever in other, never be in the same; and if never in the same, never at rest, and if not at rest, in motion?

True.

Then the one being always itself in itself and other, must always be both at rest and in motion?

Clearly.

And must be the same with itself, and other than itself; and also the same with the others, and other than the others; this follows from its previous affections.

How so?

Everything in relation to every other thing, is either the same or other; or if neither the same nor other, then in the relation of a part to a whole, or of a whole to a part.

Clearly.

And is the one a part of itself?

Certainly not.

Since it is not a part in relation to itself it cannot be related to itself as whole to part?

It cannot.

But is the one other than one?

No.

And therefore not other than itself?

Certainly not.

If then it be neither other, nor a whole, nor a part in relation to itself, must it not be the same with itself?

Certainly.

But then, again, a thing which is in another place from 'itself,' if this 'itself' remains in the same place with itself, must be other than 'itself,' for it will be in another place?

True.

Then the one has been shown to be at once in itself and in another?

Yes.

Thus, then, as appears, the one will be other than itself?

True.

Well, then, if anything be other than anything, will it not be other than that which is other?

Certainly.

And will not all things that are not one, be other than the one, and the one other than the not-one?

Of course.

Then the one will be other than the others?

True.

But, consider:—Are not the absolute same, and the absolute other, opposites to one another?

Of course.

Then will the same ever be in the other, or the other in the same?

They will not.

If then the other is never in the same, there is nothing in which the other is during any space of time; for during that space of time, however small, the other would be in the same. Is not that true?

Yes.

And since the other is never in the same, it can never be in anything that is.

True.

Then the other will never be either in the not-one, or in the one?

Certainly not.

Then not by reason of otherness is the one other than the not-one, or the not-one other than the one.

No.

Nor by reason of themselves will they be other than one another, if not partaking of the other.

How can they be?

But if they are not other, either by reason of themselves or of the other, will they not altogether escape being other than one another?

They will.

Again, the not-one cannot partake of the one; otherwise it would not have been not-one, but would have been in some way one.

True.

Nor can the not-one be number; for having number, it would not have been not-one at all.

It would not.

Again, is the not-one part of the one; or rather, would it not in that case partake of the one?

It would.

If then, in every point of view, the one and the not-one are distinct, then neither is the one part or whole of the not-one, nor is the not-one part or whole of the one?

No.

But we said that things which are neither parts nor wholes of one another, nor other than one another, will be the same with one another:—so we said?

Yes.

Then shall we say that the one, being in this relation to the not-one, is the same with it?

Let us say so.

Then it is the same with itself and the others, and also other than itself and the others.

That appears to be the inference.

And it will also be like and unlike itself and the others?

Perhaps.

Since the one was shown to be other than the others, the others will also be other than the one.

Yes.

And the one is other than the others in the same degree that the others are other than it, and neither more nor less?

True.

And if neither more nor less, then in a like degree?

Yes.

In virtue of the affection by which the one is other than others and others in like manner other than it, the one will be affected like the others and the others like the one.

How do you mean?

I may take as an illustration the case of names: You give a name to a thing?

Yes.

And you may say the name once or oftener?

Yes.

And when you say it once, you mention that of which it is the name? and when more than once, is it something else which you mention? or must it always be the same thing of which you speak, whether you utter the name once or more than once?

Of course it is the same.

And is not 'other' a name given to a thing?

Certainly.

Whenever, then, you use the word 'other,' whether once or oftener, you name that of which it is the name, and to no other do you give the name?

True.

Then when we say that the others are other than the one, and the one other than the others, in repeating the word 'other' we speak of that nature to which the name is applied, and of no other?

Quite true.

Then the one which is other than others, and the other which is other than the one, in that the word 'other' is applied to both, will be in the same condition; and that which is in the same condition is like?

Yes.

Then in virtue of the affection by which the one is other than the others, every thing will be like every thing, for every thing is other than every thing.

True.

Again, the like is opposed to the unlike?

Yes.

And the other to the same?

True again.

And the one was also shown to be the same with the others?

Yes.

And to be the same with the others is the opposite of being other than the others?

Certainly.

And in that it was other it was shown to be like?

Yes.

But in that it was the same it will be unlike by virtue of the opposite affection to that which made it like; and this was the affection of otherness.

Yes.

The same then will make it unlike; otherwise it will not be the opposite of the other.

True.

Then the one will be both like and unlike the others; like in so far as it is other, and unlike in so far as it is the same.

Yes, that argument may be used.

And there is another argument.

What?

In so far as it is affected in the same way it is not affected otherwise, and not being affected otherwise is not unlike, and not being unlike, is like; but in so far as it is affected by other it is otherwise, and being otherwise affected is unlike.

True.

Then because the one is the same with the others and other than the others, on either of these two grounds, or on both of them, it will be both like and unlike the others?

Certainly.

And in the same way as being other than itself and the same with itself, on either of these two grounds and on both of them, it will be like and unlike itself?

Of course.

Again, how far can the one touch or not touch itself and others?—consider.

I am considering.

The one was shown to be in itself which was a whole?

True.

And also in other things?

Yes.

In so far as it is in other things it would touch other things, but in so far as it is in itself it would be debarred from touching them, and would touch itself only.

Clearly.

Then the inference is that it would touch both?

It would.

But what do you say to a new point of view? Must not that which is to touch another be next to that which it is to touch, and occupy the place nearest to that in which what it touches is situated?

True.

Then the one, if it is to touch itself, ought to be situated next to itself, and occupy the place next to that in which itself is?

It ought.

And that would require that the one should be two, and be in two places at once, and this, while it is one, will never happen.

No.

Then the one cannot touch itself any more than it can be two?

It cannot.

Neither can it touch others.

Why not?

The reason is, that whatever is to touch another must be in separation from, and next to, that which it is to touch, and no third thing can be between them.

True.

Two things, then, at the least are necessary to make contact possible?

They are.

And if to the two a third be added in due order, the number of terms will be three, and the contacts two?

Yes.

And every additional term makes one additional contact, whence it follows that the contacts are one less in number than the terms; the first two terms exceeded the number of contacts by one, and the whole number of terms exceeds the whole number of contacts by one in like manner; and for every one which is afterwards added to the number of terms, one contact is added to the contacts.

True.

Whatever is the whole number of things, the contacts will be always one less.

True.

But if there be only one, and not two, there will be no contact?

How can there be?

And do we not say that the others being other than the one are not one and have no part in the one?

True.

Then they have no number, if they have no one in them?

Of course not.

Then the others are neither one nor two, nor are they called by the name of any number?

No.

One, then, alone is one, and two do not exist?

Clearly not.

And if there are not two, there is no contact?

There is not.

Then neither does the one touch the others, nor the others the one, if there is no contact?

Certainly not.

For all which reasons the one touches and does not touch itself and the others?

True.

Further—is the one equal and unequal to itself and others?

How do you mean?

If the one were greater or less than the others, or the others greater or less than the one, they would not be greater or less than each other in virtue of their being the one and the others; but, if in addition to their being what they are they had equality, they would be equal to one another, or if the one had smallness and the others greatness, or the one had greatness and the others smallness—whichever kind had greatness would be greater, and whichever had smallness would be smaller?

Certainly.

Then there are two such ideas as greatness and smallness; for if they were not they could not be opposed to each other and be present in that which is.

How could they?

If, then, smallness is present in the one it will be present either in the whole or in a part of the whole?

Certainly.

Suppose the first; it will be either co-equal and co-extensive with the whole one, or will contain the one?

Clearly.

If it be co-extensive with the one it will be co-equal with the one, or if containing the one it will be greater than the one?

Of course.

But can smallness be equal to anything or greater than anything, and have the functions of greatness and equality and not its own functions?

Impossible.

Then smallness cannot be in the whole of one, but, if at all, in a part only?

Yes.

And surely not in all of a part, for then the difficulty of the whole will recur; it will be equal to or greater than any part in which it is.

Certainly.

Then smallness will not be in anything, whether in a whole or in a part; nor will there be anything small but actual smallness.

True.

Neither will greatness be in the one, for if greatness be in anything there will be something greater other and besides greatness itself, namely, that in which greatness is; and this too when the small itself is not there, which the one, if it is great, must exceed; this, however, is impossible, seeing that smallness is wholly absent.

True.

But absolute greatness is only greater than absolute smallness, and smallness is only smaller than absolute greatness.

Very true.

Then other things not greater or less than the one, if they have neither greatness nor smallness; nor have greatness or smallness any power of exceeding or being exceeded in relation to the one, but only in relation to one another; nor will the one be greater or less than them or others, if it has neither greatness nor smallness.

Clearly not.

Then if the one is neither greater nor less than the others, it cannot either exceed or be exceeded by them?

Certainly not.

And that which neither exceeds nor is exceeded, must be on an equality; and being on an equality, must be equal.

Of course.

And this will be true also of the relation of the one to itself; having neither greatness nor smallness in itself, it will neither exceed nor be exceeded by itself, but will be on an equality with and equal to itself.

Certainly.

Then the one will be equal both to itself and the others?

Clearly so.

And yet the one, being itself in itself, will also surround and be without itself; and, as containing itself, will be greater than itself; and, as contained in itself, will be less; and will thus be greater and less than itself.

It will.

Now there cannot possibly be anything which is not included in the one and the others?

Of course not.

But, surely, that which is must always be somewhere?

Yes.

But that which is in anything will be less, and that in which it is will be greater; in no other way can one thing be in another.

True.

And since there is nothing other or besides the one and the others, and they must be in something, must they not be in one another, the one in the others and the others in the one, if they are to be anywhere?

That is clear.

But inasmuch as the one is in the others, the others will be greater than the one, because they contain the one, which will be less than the others, because it is contained in them; and inasmuch as the others are in the one, the one on the same principle will be greater than the others, and the others less than the one.

True.

The one, then, will be equal to and greater and less than itself and the others?

Clearly.

And if it be greater and less and equal, it will be of equal and more and less measures or divisions than itself and the others, and if of measures, also of parts?

Of course.

And if of equal and more and less measures or divisions, it will be in number more or less than itself and the others, and likewise equal in number to itself and to the others?

How is that?

It will be of more measures than those things which it exceeds, and of as many parts as measures; and so with that to which it is equal, and that than which it is less.

True.

And being greater and less than itself, and equal to itself, it will be of equal measures with itself and of more and fewer measures than itself; and if of measures then also of parts?

It will.

And being of equal parts with itself, it will be numerically equal to itself; and being of more parts, more, and being of less, less than itself?

Certainly.

And the same will hold of its relation to other things; inasmuch as it is greater than them, it will be more in number than them; and inasmuch as it is smaller, it will be less in number; and inasmuch as it is equal in size to other things, it will be equal to them in number.

Certainly.

Once more, then, as would appear, the one will be in number both equal to and more and less than both itself and all other things.

It will.

Does the one also partake of time? And is it and does it become older and younger than itself and others, and again, neither younger nor older than itself and others, by virtue of participation in time?

How do you mean?

If one is, being must be predicated of it?

Yes.

But to be (einai) is only participation of being in present time, and to have been is the participation of being at a past time, and to be about to be is the participation of being at a future time?

Very true.

Then the one, since it partakes of being, partakes of time?

Certainly.

And is not time always moving forward?

Yes.

Then the one is always becoming older than itself, since it moves forward in time?

Certainly.

And do you remember that the older becomes older than that which becomes younger?

I remember.

Then since the one becomes older than itself, it becomes younger at the same time?

Certainly.

Thus, then, the one becomes older as well as younger than itself?

Yes.

And it is older (is it not?) when in becoming, it gets to the point of time between 'was' and 'will be,' which is 'now': for surely in going from the past to the future, it cannot skip the present?

No.

And when it arrives at the present it stops from becoming older, and no longer becomes, but is older, for if it went on it would never be reached by the present, for it is the nature of that which goes on, to touch both the present and the future, letting go the present and seizing the future, while in process of becoming between them.

True.

But that which is becoming cannot skip the present; when it reaches the present it ceases to become, and is then whatever it may happen to be becoming.

Clearly.

And so the one, when in becoming older it reaches the present, ceases to become, and is then older.

Certainly.

And it is older than that than which it was becoming older, and it was becoming older than itself.

Yes.

And that which is older is older than that which is younger?

True.

Then the one is younger than itself, when in becoming older it reaches the present?

Certainly.

But the present is always present with the one during all its being; for whenever it is it is always now.

Certainly.

Then the one always both is and becomes older and younger than itself?

Truly.

And is it or does it become a longer time than itself or an equal time with itself?

An equal time.

But if it becomes or is for an equal time with itself, it is of the same age with itself?

Of course.

And that which is of the same age, is neither older nor younger?

No.

The one, then, becoming and being the same time with itself, neither is nor becomes older or younger than itself?

I should say not.

And what are its relations to other things? Is it or does it become older or younger than they?

I cannot tell you.

You can at least tell me that others than the one are more than the one—other would have been one, but the others have multitude, and are more than one?

They will have multitude.

And a multitude implies a number larger than one?

Of course.

And shall we say that the lesser or the greater is the first to come or to have come into existence?

The lesser.

Then the least is the first? And that is the one?

Yes.

Then the one of all things that have number is the first to come into being; but all other things have also number, being plural and not singular.

They have.

And since it came into being first it must be supposed to have come into being prior to the others, and the others later; and the things which came into being later, are younger than that which preceded them? And so the other things will be younger than the one, and the one older than other things?

True.

What would you say of another question? Can the one have come into being contrary to its own nature, or is that impossible?

Impossible.

And yet, surely, the one was shown to have parts; and if parts, then a beginning, middle and end?

Yes.

And a beginning, both of the one itself and of all other things, comes into being first of all; and after the beginning, the others follow, until you reach the end?

Certainly.

And all these others we shall affirm to be parts of the whole and of the one, which, as soon as the end is reached, has become whole and one?

Yes; that is what we shall say.

But the end comes last, and the one is of such a nature as to come into being with the last; and, since the one cannot come into being except in accordance with its own nature, its nature will require that it should come into being after the others, simultaneously with the end.

Clearly.

Then the one is younger than the others and the others older than the one.

That also is clear in my judgment.

Well, and must not a beginning or any other part of the one or of anything, if it be a part and not parts, being a part, be also of necessity one?

Certainly.

And will not the one come into being together with each part—together with the first part when that comes into being, and together with the second part and with all the rest, and will not be wanting to any part, which is added to any other part until it has reached the last and become one whole; it will be wanting neither to the middle, nor to the first, nor to the last, nor to any of them, while the process of becoming is going on?

True.

Then the one is of the same age with all the others, so that if the one itself does not contradict its own nature, it will be neither prior nor posterior to the others, but simultaneous; and according to this argument the one will be neither older nor younger than the others, nor the others than the one, but according to the previous argument the one will be older and younger than the others and the others than the one.

Certainly.

After this manner then the one is and has become. But as to its becoming older and younger than the others, and the others than the one, and neither older nor younger, what shall we say? Shall we say as of being so also of becoming, or otherwise?

I cannot answer.

But I can venture to say, that even if one thing were older or younger than another, it could not become older or younger in a greater degree than it was at first; for equals added to unequals, whether to periods of time or to anything else, leave the difference between them the same as at first.

Of course.

Then that which is, cannot become older or younger than that which is, since the difference of age is always the same; the one is and has become older and the other younger; but they are no longer becoming so.

True.

And the one which is does not therefore become either older or younger than the others which are.

No.

But consider whether they may not become older and younger in another way.

In what way?

Just as the one was proven to be older than the others and the others than the one.

And what of that?

If the one is older than the others, has come into being a longer time than the others.

Yes.

But consider again; if we add equal time to a greater and a less time, will the greater differ from the less time by an equal or by a smaller portion than before?

By a smaller portion.

Then the difference between the age of the one and the age of the others will not be afterwards so great as at first, but if an equal time be added to both of them they will differ less and less in age?

Yes.

And that which differs in age from some other less than formerly, from being older will become younger in relation to that other than which it was older?

Yes, younger.

And if the one becomes younger the others aforesaid will become older than they were before, in relation to the one.

Certainly.

Then that which had become younger becomes older relatively to that which previously had become and was older; it never really is older, but is always becoming, for the one is always growing on the side of youth and the other on the side of age. And in like manner the older is always in process of becoming younger than the younger; for as they are always going in opposite directions they become in ways the opposite to one another, the younger older than the older, and the older younger than the younger. They cannot, however, have become; for if they had already become they would be and not merely become. But that is impossible; for they are always becoming both older and younger than one another: the one becomes younger than the others because it was seen to be older and prior, and the others become older than the one because they came into being later; and in the same way the others are in the same relation to the one, because they were seen to be older, and prior to the one.

That is clear.

Inasmuch then, one thing does not become older or younger than another, in that they always differ from each other by an equal number, the one cannot become older or younger than the others, nor the others than the one; but inasmuch as that which came into being earlier and that which came into being later must continually differ from each other by a different portion—in this point of view the others must become older and younger than the one, and the one than the others.

Certainly.

For all these reasons, then, the one is and becomes older and younger than itself and the others, and neither is nor becomes older or younger than itself or the others.

Certainly.

But since the one partakes of time, and partakes of becoming older and younger, must it not also partake of the past, the present, and the future?

Of course it must.

Then the one was and is and will be, and was becoming and is becoming and will become?

Certainly.

And there is and was and will be something which is in relation to it and belongs to it?

True.

And since we have at this moment opinion and knowledge and perception of the one, there is opinion and knowledge and perception of it?

Quite right.

Then there is name and expression for it, and it is named and expressed, and everything of this kind which appertains to other things appertains to the one.

Certainly, that is true.

Yet once more and for the third time, let us consider: If the one is both one and many, as we have described, and is neither one nor many, and participates in time, must it not, in as far as it is one, at times partake of being, and in as far as it is not one, at times not partake of being?

Certainly.

But can it partake of being when not partaking of being, or not partake of being when partaking of being?

Impossible.

Then the one partakes and does not partake of being at different times, for that is the only way in which it can partake and not partake of the same.

True.

And is there not also a time at which it assumes being and relinquishes being—for how can it have and not have the same thing unless it receives and also gives it up at some time?

Impossible.

And the assuming of being is what you would call becoming?

I should.

And the relinquishing of being you would call destruction?

I should.

The one then, as would appear, becomes and is destroyed by taking and giving up being.

Certainly.

And being one and many and in process of becoming and being destroyed, when it becomes one it ceases to be many, and when many, it ceases to be one?

Certainly.

And as it becomes one and many, must it not inevitably experience separation and aggregation?

Inevitably.

And whenever it becomes like and unlike it must be assimilated and dissimilated?

Yes.

And when it becomes greater or less or equal it must grow or diminish or be equalized?

True.

And when being in motion it rests, and when being at rest it changes to motion, it can surely be in no time at all?

How can it?

But that a thing which is previously at rest should be afterwards in motion, or previously in motion and afterwards at rest, without experiencing change, is impossible.

Impossible.

And surely there cannot be a time in which a thing can be at once neither in motion nor at rest?

There cannot.

But neither can it change without changing.

True.

When then does it change; for it cannot change either when at rest, or when in motion, or when in time?

It cannot.

And does this strange thing in which it is at the time of changing really exist?

What thing?

The moment. For the moment seems to imply a something out of which change takes place into either of two states; for the change is not from the state of rest as such, nor from the state of motion as such; but there is this curious nature which we call the moment lying between rest and motion, not being in any time; and into this and out of this what is in motion changes into rest, and what is at rest into motion.

So it appears.

And the one then, since it is at rest and also in motion, will change to either, for only in this way can it be in both. And in changing it changes in a moment, and when it is changing it will be in no time, and will not then be either in motion or at rest.

It will not.

And it will be in the same case in relation to the other changes, when it passes from being into cessation of being, or from not-being into becoming—then it passes between certain states of motion and rest, and neither is nor is not, nor becomes nor is destroyed.

Very true.

And on the same principle, in the passage from one to many and from many to one, the one is neither one nor many, neither separated nor aggregated; and in the passage from like to unlike, and from unlike to like, it is neither like nor unlike, neither in a state of assimilation nor of dissimilation; and in the passage from small to great and equal and back again, it will be neither small nor great, nor equal, nor in a state of increase, or diminution, or equalization.

True.

All these, then, are the affections of the one, if the one has being.

Of course.

1.aa. But if one is, what will happen to the others—is not that also to be considered?

Yes.

Let us show then, if one is, what will be the affections of the others than the one.

Let us do so.

Inasmuch as there are things other than the one, the others are not the one; for if they were they could not be other than the one.

Very true.

Nor are the others altogether without the one, but in a certain way they participate in the one.

In what way?

Because the others are other than the one inasmuch as they have parts; for if they had no parts they would be simply one.

Right.

And parts, as we affirm, have relation to a whole?

So we say.

And a whole must necessarily be one made up of many; and the parts will be parts of the one, for each of the parts is not a part of many, but of a whole.

How do you mean?

If anything were a part of many, being itself one of them, it will surely be a part of itself, which is impossible, and it will be a part of each one of the other parts, if of all; for if not a part of some one, it will be a part of all the others but this one, and thus will not be a part of each one; and if not a part of each, one it will not be a part of any one of the many; and not being a part of any one, it cannot be a part or anything else of all those things of none of which it is anything.

Clearly not.

Then the part is not a part of the many, nor of all, but is of a certain single form, which we call a whole, being one perfect unity framed out of all—of this the part will be a part.

Certainly.

If, then, the others have parts, they will participate in the whole and in the one.

True.

Then the others than the one must be one perfect whole, having parts.

Certainly.

And the same argument holds of each part, for the part must participate in the one; for if each of the parts is a part, this means, I suppose, that it is one separate from the rest and self-related; otherwise it is not each.

True.

But when we speak of the part participating in the one, it must clearly be other than one; for if not, it would not merely have participated, but would have been one; whereas only the itself can be one.

Very true.

Both the whole and the part must participate in the one; for the whole will be one whole, of which the parts will be parts; and each part will be one part of the whole which is the whole of the part.

True.

And will not the things which participate in the one, be other than it?

Of course.

And the things which are other than the one will be many; for if the things which are other than the one were neither one nor more than one, they would be nothing.

True.

But, seeing that the things which participate in the one as a part, and in the one as a whole, are more than one, must not those very things which participate in the one be infinite in number?

How so?

Let us look at the matter thus:—Is it not a fact that in partaking of the one they are not one, and do not partake of the one at the very time when they are partaking of it?

Clearly.

They do so then as multitudes in which the one is not present?

Very true.

And if we were to abstract from them in idea the very smallest fraction, must not that least fraction, if it does not partake of the one, be a multitude and not one?

It must.

And if we continue to look at the other side of their nature, regarded simply, and in itself, will not they, as far as we see them, be unlimited in number?

Certainly.

And yet, when each several part becomes a part, then the parts have a limit in relation to the whole and to each other, and the whole in relation to the parts.

Just so.

The result to the others than the one is that the union of themselves and the one appears to create a new element in them which gives to them limitation in relation to one another; whereas in their own nature they have no limit.

That is clear.

Then the others than the one, both as whole and parts, are infinite, and also partake of limit.

Certainly.

Then they are both like and unlike one another and themselves.

How is that?

Inasmuch as they are unlimited in their own nature, they are all affected in the same way.

True.

And inasmuch as they all partake of limit, they are all affected in the same way.

Of course.

But inasmuch as their state is both limited and unlimited, they are affected in opposite ways.

Yes.

And opposites are the most unlike of things.

Certainly.

Considered, then, in regard to either one of their affections, they will be like themselves and one another; considered in reference to both of them together, most opposed and most unlike.

That appears to be true.

Then the others are both like and unlike themselves and one another?

True.

And they are the same and also different from one another, and in motion and at rest, and experience every sort of opposite affection, as may be proved without difficulty of them, since they have been shown to have experienced the affections aforesaid?

True.

1.bb. Suppose, now, that we leave the further discussion of these matters as evident, and consider again upon the hypothesis that the one is, whether opposite of all this is or is not equally true of the others.

By all means.

Then let us begin again, and ask, If one is, what must be the affections of the others?

Let us ask that question.

Must not the one be distinct from the others, and the others from the one?

Why so?

Why, because there is nothing else beside them which is distinct from both of them; for the expression 'one and the others' includes all things.

Yes, all things.

Then we cannot suppose that there is anything different from them in which both the one and the others might exist?

There is nothing.

Then the one and the others are never in the same?

True.

Then they are separated from each other?

Yes.

And we surely cannot say that what is truly one has parts?

Impossible.

Then the one will not be in the others as a whole, nor as part, if it be separated from the others, and has no parts?

Impossible.

Then there is no way in which the others can partake of the one, if they do not partake either in whole or in part?

It would seem not.

Then there is no way in which the others are one, or have in themselves any unity?

There is not.

Nor are the others many; for if they were many, each part of them would be a part of the whole; but now the others, not partaking in any way of the one, are neither one nor many, nor whole, nor part.

True.

Then the others neither are nor contain two or three, if entirely deprived of the one?

True.

Then the others are neither like nor unlike the one, nor is likeness and unlikeness in them; for if they were like and unlike, or had in them likeness and unlikeness, they would have two natures in them opposite to one another.

That is clear.

But for that which partakes of nothing to partake of two things was held by us to be impossible?

Impossible.

Then the others are neither like nor unlike nor both, for if they were like or unlike they would partake of one of those two natures, which would be one thing, and if they were both they would partake of opposites which would be two things, and this has been shown to be impossible.

True.

Therefore they are neither the same, nor other, nor in motion, nor at rest, nor in a state of becoming, nor of being destroyed, nor greater, nor less, nor equal, nor have they experienced anything else of the sort; for, if they are capable of experiencing any such affection, they will participate in one and two and three, and odd and even, and in these, as has been proved, they do not participate, seeing that they are altogether and in every way devoid of the one.

Very true.

Therefore if one is, the one is all things, and also nothing, both in relation to itself and to other things.

Certainly.

2.a. Well, and ought we not to consider next what will be the consequence if the one is not?

Yes; we ought.

What is the meaning of the hypothesis—If the one is not; is there any difference between this and the hypothesis—If the not one is not?

There is a difference, certainly.

Is there a difference only, or rather are not the two expressions—if the one is not, and if the not one is not, entirely opposed?

They are entirely opposed.

And suppose a person to say:—If greatness is not, if smallness is not, or anything of that sort, does he not mean, whenever he uses such an expression, that 'what is not' is other than other things?

To be sure.

And so when he says 'If one is not' he clearly means, that what 'is not' is other than all others; we know what he means—do we not?

Yes, we do.

When he says 'one,' he says something which is known; and secondly something which is other than all other things; it makes no difference whether he predicate of one being or not-being, for that which is said 'not to be' is known to be something all the same, and is distinguished from other things.

Certainly.

Then I will begin again, and ask: If one is not, what are the consequences? In the first place, as would appear, there is a knowledge of it, or the very meaning of the words, 'if one is not,' would not be known.

True.

Secondly, the others differ from it, or it could not be described as different from the others?

Certainly.

Difference, then, belongs to it as well as knowledge; for in speaking of the one as different from the others, we do not speak of a difference in the others, but in the one.

Clearly so.

Moreover, the one that is not is something and partakes of relation to 'that,' and 'this,' and 'these,' and the like, and is an attribute of 'this'; for the one, or the others than the one, could not have been spoken of, nor could any attribute or relative of the one that is not have been or been spoken of, nor could it have been said to be anything, if it did not partake of 'some,' or of the other relations just now mentioned.

True.

Being, then, cannot be ascribed to the one, since it is not; but the one that is not may or rather must participate in many things, if it and nothing else is not; if, however, neither the one nor the one that is not is supposed not to be, and we are speaking of something of a different nature, we can predicate nothing of it. But supposing that the one that is not and nothing else is not, then it must participate in the predicate 'that,' and in many others.

Certainly.

And it will have unlikeness in relation to the others, for the others being different from the one will be of a different kind.

Certainly.

And are not things of a different kind also other in kind?

Of course.

And are not things other in kind unlike?

They are unlike.

And if they are unlike the one, that which they are unlike will clearly be unlike them?

Clearly so.

Then the one will have unlikeness in respect of which the others are unlike it?

That would seem to be true.

And if unlikeness to other things is attributed to it, it must have likeness to itself.

How so?

If the one have unlikeness to one, something else must be meant; nor will the hypothesis relate to one; but it will relate to something other than one?

Quite so.

But that cannot be.

No.

Then the one must have likeness to itself?

It must.

Again, it is not equal to the others; for if it were equal, then it would at once be and be like them in virtue of the equality; but if one has no being, then it can neither be nor be like?

It cannot.

But since it is not equal to the others, neither can the others be equal to it?

Certainly not.

And things that are not equal are unequal?

True.

And they are unequal to an unequal?

Of course.

Then the one partakes of inequality, and in respect of this the others are unequal to it?

Very true.

And inequality implies greatness and smallness?

Yes.

Then the one, if of such a nature, has greatness and smallness?

That appears to be true.

And greatness and smallness always stand apart?

True.

Then there is always something between them?

There is.

And can you think of anything else which is between them other than equality?

No, it is equality which lies between them.

Then that which has greatness and smallness also has equality, which lies between them?

That is clear.

Then the one, which is not, partakes, as would appear, of greatness and smallness and equality?

Clearly.

Further, it must surely in a sort partake of being?

How so?

It must be so, for if not, then we should not speak the truth in saying that the one is not. But if we speak the truth, clearly we must say what is. Am I not right?

Yes.

And since we affirm that we speak truly, we must also affirm that we say what is?

Certainly.

Then, as would appear, the one, when it is not, is; for if it were not to be when it is not, but (Or, 'to remit something of existence in relation to not-being.') were to relinquish something of being, so as to become not-being, it would at once be.

Quite true.

Then the one which is not, if it is to maintain itself, must have the being of not-being as the bond of not-being, just as being must have as a bond the not-being of not-being in order to perfect its own being; for the truest assertion of the being of being and of the not-being of not-being is when being partakes of the being of being, and not of the being of not-being—that is, the perfection of being; and when not-being does not partake of the not-being of not-being but of the being of not-being—that is the perfection of not-being.

Most true.

Since then what is partakes of not-being, and what is not of being, must not the one also partake of being in order not to be?

Certainly.

Then the one, if it is not, clearly has being?

Clearly.

And has not-being also, if it is not?

Of course.

But can anything which is in a certain state not be in that state without changing?

Impossible.

Then everything which is and is not in a certain state, implies change?

Certainly.

And change is motion—we may say that?

Yes, motion.

And the one has been proved both to be and not to be?

Yes.

And therefore is and is not in the same state?

Yes.

Thus the one that is not has been shown to have motion also, because it changes from being to not-being?

That appears to be true.

But surely if it is nowhere among what is, as is the fact, since it is not, it cannot change from one place to another?

Impossible.

Then it cannot move by changing place?

No.

Nor can it turn on the same spot, for it nowhere touches the same, for the same is, and that which is not cannot be reckoned among things that are?

It cannot.

Then the one, if it is not, cannot turn in that in which it is not?

No.

Neither can the one, whether it is or is not, be altered into other than itself, for if it altered and became different from itself, then we could not be still speaking of the one, but of something else?

True.

But if the one neither suffers alteration, nor turns round in the same place, nor changes place, can it still be capable of motion?

Impossible.

Now that which is unmoved must surely be at rest, and that which is at rest must stand still?

Certainly.

Then the one that is not, stands still, and is also in motion?

That seems to be true.

But if it be in motion it must necessarily undergo alteration, for anything which is moved, in so far as it is moved, is no longer in the same state, but in another?

Yes.

Then the one, being moved, is altered?

Yes.

And, further, if not moved in any way, it will not be altered in any way?

No.

Then, in so far as the one that is not is moved, it is altered, but in so far as it is not moved, it is not altered?

Right.

Then the one that is not is altered and is not altered?

That is clear.

And must not that which is altered become other than it previously was, and lose its former state and be destroyed; but that which is not altered can neither come into being nor be destroyed?

Very true.

And the one that is not, being altered, becomes and is destroyed; and not being altered, neither becomes nor is destroyed; and so the one that is not becomes and is destroyed, and neither becomes nor is destroyed?

True.

2.b. And now, let us go back once more to the beginning, and see whether these or some other consequences will follow.

Let us do as you say.

If one is not, we ask what will happen in respect of one? That is the question.

Yes.

Do not the words 'is not' signify absence of being in that to which we apply them?

Just so.

And when we say that a thing is not, do we mean that it is not in one way but is in another? or do we mean, absolutely, that what is not has in no sort or way or kind participation of being?

Quite absolutely.

Then, that which is not cannot be, or in any way participate in being?

It cannot.

And did we not mean by becoming, and being destroyed, the assumption of being and the loss of being?

Nothing else.

And can that which has no participation in being, either assume or lose being?

Impossible.

The one then, since it in no way is, cannot have or lose or assume being in any way?

True.

Then the one that is not, since it in no way partakes of being, neither perishes nor becomes?

No.

Then it is not altered at all; for if it were it would become and be destroyed?

True.

But if it be not altered it cannot be moved?

Certainly not.

Nor can we say that it stands, if it is nowhere; for that which stands must always be in one and the same spot?

Of course.

Then we must say that the one which is not never stands still and never moves?

Neither.

Nor is there any existing thing which can be attributed to it; for if there had been, it would partake of being?

That is clear.

And therefore neither smallness, nor greatness, nor equality, can be attributed to it?

No.

Nor yet likeness nor difference, either in relation to itself or to others?

Clearly not.

Well, and if nothing should be attributed to it, can other things be attributed to it?

Certainly not.

And therefore other things can neither be like or unlike, the same, or different in relation to it?

They cannot.

Nor can what is not, be anything, or be this thing, or be related to or the attribute of this or that or other, or be past, present, or future. Nor can knowledge, or opinion, or perception, or expression, or name, or any other thing that is, have any concern with it?

No.

Then the one that is not has no condition of any kind?

Such appears to be the conclusion.

2.aa. Yet once more; if one is not, what becomes of the others? Let us determine that.

Yes; let us determine that.

The others must surely be; for if they, like the one, were not, we could not be now speaking of them.

True.

But to speak of the others implies difference—the terms 'other' and 'different' are synonymous?

True.

Other means other than other, and different, different from the different?

Yes.

Then, if there are to be others, there is something than which they will be other?

Certainly.

And what can that be?—for if the one is not, they will not be other than the one.

They will not.

Then they will be other than each other; for the only remaining alternative is that they are other than nothing.

True.

And they are each other than one another, as being plural and not singular; for if one is not, they cannot be singular, but every particle of them is infinite in number; and even if a person takes that which appears to be the smallest fraction, this, which seemed one, in a moment evanesces into many, as in a dream, and from being the smallest becomes very great, in comparison with the fractions into which it is split up?

Very true.

And in such particles the others will be other than one another, if others are, and the one is not?

Exactly.

And will there not be many particles, each appearing to be one, but not being one, if one is not?

True.

And it would seem that number can be predicated of them if each of them appears to be one, though it is really many?

It can.

And there will seem to be odd and even among them, which will also have no reality, if one is not?

Yes.

And there will appear to be a least among them; and even this will seem large and manifold in comparison with the many small fractions which are contained in it?

Certainly.

And each particle will be imagined to be equal to the many and little; for it could not have appeared to pass from the greater to the less without having appeared to arrive at the middle; and thus would arise the appearance of equality.

Yes.

And having neither beginning, middle, nor end, each separate particle yet appears to have a limit in relation to itself and other.

How so?

Because, when a person conceives of any one of these as such, prior to the beginning another beginning appears, and there is another end, remaining after the end, and in the middle truer middles within but smaller, because no unity can be conceived of any of them, since the one is not.

Very true.

And so all being, whatever we think of, must be broken up into fractions, for a particle will have to be conceived of without unity?

Certainly.

And such being when seen indistinctly and at a distance, appears to be one; but when seen near and with keen intellect, every single thing appears to be infinite, since it is deprived of the one, which is not?

Nothing more certain.

Then each of the others must appear to be infinite and finite, and one and many, if others than the one exist and not the one.

They must.

Then will they not appear to be like and unlike?

In what way?

Just as in a picture things appear to be all one to a person standing at a distance, and to be in the same state and alike?

True.

But when you approach them, they appear to be many and different; and because of the appearance of the difference, different in kind from, and unlike, themselves?

True.

And so must the particles appear to be like and unlike themselves and each other.

Certainly.

And must they not be the same and yet different from one another, and in contact with themselves, although they are separated, and having every sort of motion, and every sort of rest, and becoming and being destroyed, and in neither state, and the like, all which things may be easily enumerated, if the one is not and the many are?

Most true.

2.bb. Once more, let us go back to the beginning, and ask if the one is not, and the others of the one are, what will follow.

Let us ask that question.

In the first place, the others will not be one?

Impossible.

Nor will they be many; for if they were many one would be contained in them. But if no one of them is one, all of them are nought, and therefore they will not be many.

True.

If there be no one in the others, the others are neither many nor one.

They are not.

Nor do they appear either as one or many.

Why not?

Because the others have no sort or manner or way of communion with any sort of not-being, nor can anything which is not, be connected with any of the others; for that which is not has no parts.

True.

Nor is there an opinion or any appearance of not-being in connexion with the others, nor is not-being ever in any way attributed to the others.

No.

Then if one is not, there is no conception of any of the others either as one or many; for you cannot conceive the many without the one.

You cannot.

Then if one is not, the others neither are, nor can be conceived to be either one or many?

It would seem not.

Nor as like or unlike?

No.

Nor as the same or different, nor in contact or separation, nor in any of those states which we enumerated as appearing to be;—the others neither are nor appear to be any of these, if one is not?

True.

Then may we not sum up the argument in a word and say truly: If one is not, then nothing is?

Certainly.

Let thus much be said; and further let us affirm what seems to be the truth, that, whether one is or is not, one and the others in relation to themselves and one another, all of them, in every way, are and are not, and appear to be and appear not to be.

Most true.

Printed in the USA
CPSIA information can be obtained
at www.ICGtesting.com
LVHW090804220224
772419LV00021B/230/J

9 781605 125008